Role of Symmetry, Groups and Matrices in Chemistry

R.S. Thakur

ATLANTIC

PUBLISHERS & DISTRIBUTORS (P) LTD

Published by
ATLANTIC
PUBLISHERS & DISTRIBUTORS (P) LTD
7/22, Ansari Road, Darya Ganj, New Delhi-110002
Phones : +91-11-40775252, 40775214, 23273880, 23275880
Fax: +91-11-23285873
Web: www.atlanticbooks.com
E-mail: orders@atlanticbooks.com

Printed & bound in India by Atlantic Print Services

In the Memory of my Reverend Mother whose
Mortal remains Alive to the Author

Dedicated to

Two Distinguished
Scholars in this field

Professor L.D. Dave (Gujarat)
Professor K.R. Chatterjee (Bihar)

FOREWORD

Publication of *Role of Symmetry, Groups and Matrices in Chemistry* under the authorship of Prof. R.S. Thakur is a pleasant news. Prof. Thakur has long been experimenting on teaching 'Symmetry and Group Theory' to students of Chemistry. Prof. Thakur, as I know, is a teacher by passion, well-read in the subject and highly aware of difficulties and pitfalls of students in learning the subject and grasping its spirit. His rich experience while rigorously presenting the essence of the subject with all its elegance has, I hope, been duly reflected in the write-up of the book. Due care has been taken while planning the contents of the book of difficulties and misconceptions the students generally have and accordingly been presented in the form of as many as twelve chapters. Owing to its distinctive features of the book I hope, would be of choice for students and instructors alike.

S.K. SENGUPTA
Head
Department of Chemistry
B.H.U., Varanasi

PREFACE

In 1923 a physical theory came into existence on combined application of group theory and matrix, the two elegant parts of mathematics. It has opened a new horizon with a rapid explosion of knowledge. An attempt was made to attack the unresolved problems of chemistry involving some new ideas. Symmetry is one of them providing a physical model to abstract groups. It originates from axioms of geometry coupled with matrix representation. Properties of groups are acceptable to multiplication table in both ways—geometrically through symmetry operations as well as through transformation matrices.

The readers of postgraduate courses in chemistry may find the book *Role of Symmetry, Groups and Matrices in Chemistry* extremely useful as it covers the syllabus widely prescribed in Indian Universities. Both symmetry and matrix are revolving around the group in chemistry. These three organs are introduced in the beginning. They are presented suitably in separate chapters. It has been soon realized that elements of group theory can cope with hidden mystery of bonding and spectra. It has remarkable capability to simplify big secular determinant by method of symmetry factorization. A rigorous attempt was made on theory of molecular vibrations by the inclusion of symmetry co-ordinates. These matters have been provided at the end. You may come across this in a number of books of Indian and foreign origins available in the market in this field. It is our endeavour to fulfil the shortcomings of all these books. A good deal of efforts have been made to provide wide applications of derivation of character table applying various approaches and also a thorough discussion of transformation matrices. Both qualitative and quantitative methods for hybridizational schemes have been elucidated in detail. Cases of multicentred bonding is described via molecular orbital description in NO^-_2 and B_2H_6. Not only this, the derivation of sine formula has been provided with full detail and a number of examples have been shown for splitting of atomic orbitals and terms in octahedral and tetrahedral crystal fields. The case of non-cubic symmetry such as D_{4h} and transformation properties of s, p and d-orbitals have been discussed on symmetry arguments. The band assignments for d^9, d^8 and d^7 systems in D_{4h} symmetry have been described by symmetry arguments and splitting diagrams for orbitals and spectroscopic states. Break-down of selection rules, vibrionic transitions, besides cases of vibrionic polarization as well as electronic polarization are suitably emphasised in exclusive chapter on Chemical Environment (Chapter-9). The book also incorporates eigen value problem, starting with cases of matrices, eigen value and eigen vector in a separate chapter. That may be considered as importance of matrices in matrix mechanics. Study of molecular vibrations have been taken up in two well distinct units, viz. Chapters 11 and 12. In the former the Group Theory and Molecular Vibrations have been described in a few cases showing IR and Raman activity, conditions of overtones and combination bands have also been discussed in such cases. While the latter, the last chapter, includes a description of the theory of molecular vibrations from classical mechanical point of view by the special applications of normal co-ordinates and normal vibrations besides the use of Wilson F and G matrices and solving secular equation $|FG-\lambda E| = 0$ with the application of normal co-ordinate analysis for cases of water and ammonia dealing with symmetry factorization and orthogonal transformation. Certain solved examples have been described and a good number of exercises have also been given.

I owe a heavy debt to Professor L.D. Dave, former Head of the Department of Chemistry, Bhavnagar University, Gujarat, and Professor K.R. Chatterjee, former Head of the Department of Physics, BRABU, Muzaffarpur as their discourses in 1984 and 1998, respectively, at the Department of Chemistry are source of inspiration to me. I am specially thankful to Dr. A.K. Shrivastava of the Department for extending his full cooperation in teaching programme. I am also thankful to my other colleagues for their co-operation and help. I am equally thankful to my well-wishers. Lastly, I give credit to my students who have done a yeomen job in bringing the final form of manuscript. I am thankful to them. Responsibility shall lie on my part of certain oversight. I would appreciate if such mistakes are brought to my notice. Any suggestion will be gratefully acknowledged.

R.S. THAKUR

CONTENTS

INTRODUCTION TO SYMMETRY, GROUP AND MATRIX IN CHEMISTRY

1

"Symmetry is the most familiar theme, group theory is the organiser and matrix is a vehicle," so comments one of the authors.

By 1930, there has been explosive expansion of knowledge in our physical world. There were certain events to propose new theories. In view of giving key concepts in our understanding of certain phenomena the subject matter of current discussion is broken into three components— symmetry, group theory and matrix. We deal with one by one.

1.1 SYMMETRY

The term symmetry is derived from the Greek word 'synmetron' meaning mutual relation of parts of something or proportion or harmony of parts. A more erudite example occurs in the poetry of William Blake.

"Tiger Tiger burning bright
In the forest of the night
what immortal hand or eye
Dare fram thy fearful symmetry"

Now it is in wide use by painters, designers and singers. A few more quotations are cited rating the word symmetry.

"A thing of beauty is joy for ever."

So writes Keats in *Endymion* in the "Ode on a Gracian Urn." The poet also wrote, "beauty is truth and truth is beauty."

Del Tolstoy gave his feeling about symmetry while drawing some figures on a board with chalk, it was suddenly struck by the idea why symmetry is pleasing to the eye. What is symmetry? It is innate feeling. But what is it based on? There is an old parable about Burdian ass. The ass starved to death because he could not decide on which heap of food to start with. Another burning example is to visualise a balanced pan with two side arms. Both the left and right pans are so identical that neither can be given preference.

Professor Herman Weyl gave a definition of symmetry. After some operations of a thing has exactly the same configuration then it is said to be symmetrical. A thing is symmetrical when it is subjected to some operation and after such operation it produces exactly the same structure. Now we go into its scientific meaning of symmetry. There is underlying mathematics in group theory and matrices. Historical development of mathematics in making use of symmetry in chemistry is made in two ways—geometrically and algebraically.

Symmetry occurs in everyday life and we consider its role in chemistry. It plays a part in certain classical topics like optical activity, dipole-moment, stereo-chemistry besides determination of structure of molecules, crystal structure, IR, Raman and U.V. Spectra. There are three geometrical entities such as line (axis of symmetry) point (centre of symmetry) and plane (plane of symmetry) about which the object is symmetrical. Atoms in molecules are equivalent. If they are in like positions. There are two sets of like atoms in benzene

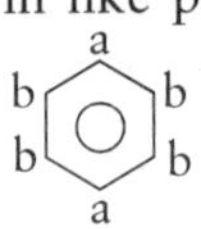

and naphthalene

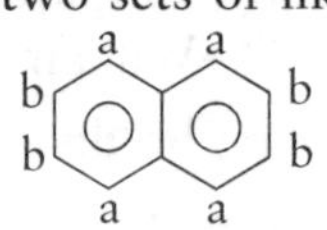

There are three sets of equivalent hydrogens in anthracene and pyrene.

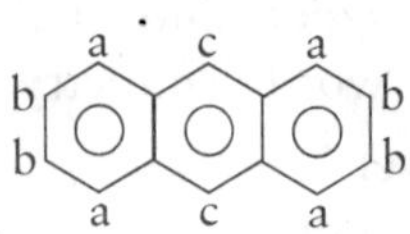

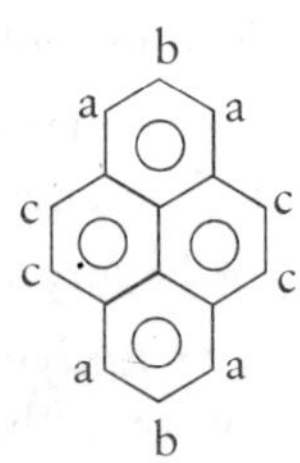

Three such derivatives have been isolated in pyrene.

We consider two geometrical figures a square and equilateral triangle.

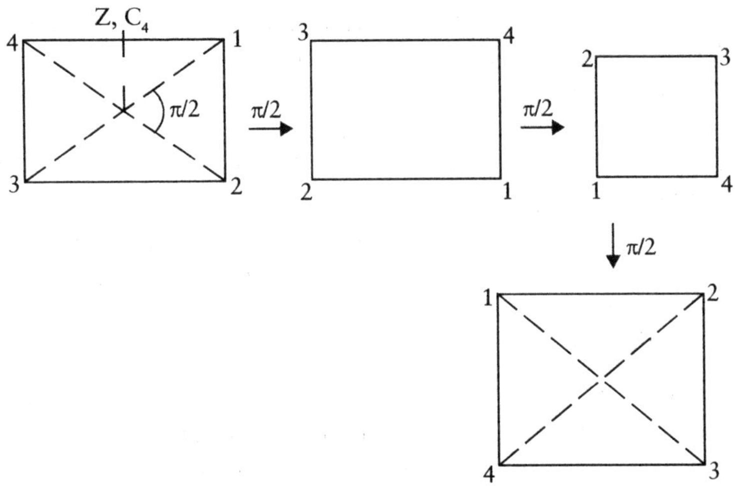

The square constitutes xy plane with x and y axes along the two diagonals and z-axis perpendicular to the plane passing through the centre.

A rotation about z-axis through π/2 leaves the equivalent positions successively till finally the structure becomes identical.

Let us take up the case of equilateral triangle.

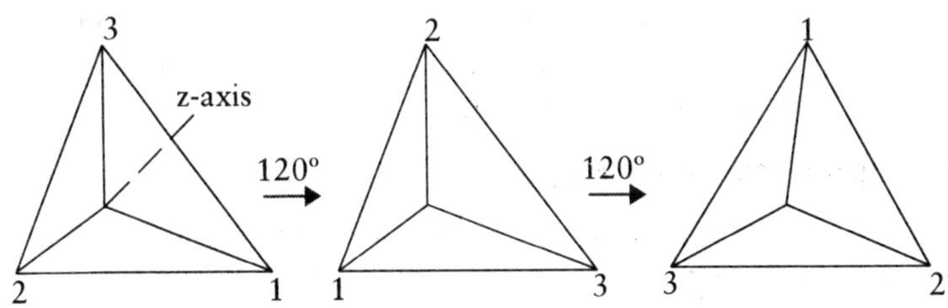

The three medians will meet at a point called centroid. A rotation about z-axis passing through 120° leaves equivalent structures till cycle is over.

This is a case of geometrical transformation clock wise in both the cases. There exists another possibility anti-clockwise rotation through 90° and 120° respectively and we get equivalent configurations.

According to H. Weyl, "Symmetry is our ideas in which the man through the edges has tried and create order, beauty and perfection". It applies to science, arts and human conduct.

If we perform certain operations geometrically to our human body the left half of the body produces the right half and human being possesses certain symmetry.

Further it was realized that invariance was a key concept in understanding a new phenomenon in physics and chemistry the mathematical tool of treating invariants and symmetry is group theory.

1.2 GROUP

Group theory is a branch of pure mathematics and is treated as an aspect of higher algebra. It is a beautiful and fascinating formalism to describe symmetry of physical systems. It is an abstract group having no physical model. There may be groups by addition, multiplication, transformation or a cyclic group. It is a set of abstract number 1, 2, 3 . . . etc. or alphabets a, b, c . . . which may be rational number, real number, integers, matrix A, B, C, D . . . or symmetry operations.

In chemistry, members of a group are symmetry operations about a point inside the molecule. For such operations there stand different matrices and there can be a physical model out of point group. Certain axioms are stated hereunder which may be satisfied by each group.

1.3 PROPERTIES OF A GROUP

A group is a collection of elements and such elements are its members. The product or combination of elements is governed by certain rules:

1.3.1 Property of Closure

The elements A, B, C, D, ... K form a group, their combination is defined as a product. The product of any two elements is also be member of the group. We define their combination.

A B = K Where K is the element of the group.

The multiplication is closed.

The square of the element is also within the group:

$$A^2 = F$$

$$B^2 = G$$

1.3.2 Commutative Law

The combination of elements A and B may be shown as product form A B or B A. Where A is right multiplied by B, and B is left multiplied by A. When A and B commute AB = BA. Such a group is called abelian group.

A case in which A and B do not commute:

$$AB \neq BA$$

Commutative law in general does not hold but in algebra commutative law always holds:

$$a + b = b + a$$

1.3.3 Presence of Unique Element

Every group has a unique element. This element commutes with all other elements and leaves them unchanged. We introduce an identity (E) here:

E.A = A.E = A etc. for all A.

E implies doing nothing.

1.3.4 Existence of Inverse

Within every set of number (group) there must have its inverse.

Let A be an element. It is associated with the inverse (reciprocal) A^{-1}, such that $AA^{-1} = E$.

But E is itself its own reciprocal.

1.4 EXAMPLES OF A GROUP

1. Let us consider a set of integers 0, ± 1, ± 2, ± 3, ... ∞ with order ∞. There are elements of group with order infinite.

There are two binary operations to satisfy the axioms, such as addition and multiplication. The additive identity is zero (0) where as multiplicative identity is 1 (unity).

1. Property of closure:

$$1 + 3 = +4 \text{ is also an element.}$$

2. Commutative law:

$$1 + 2 = 2 + 1$$

3. Associative law:

$$1 + (2 + 3) = (1 + 2) + 3$$

4. Distributive law:

$$1\ (2 + 3) = 1 \times 2 + 1 \times 3$$

5. Identity:

additive identity is 0.

$$1 + 0 = 0 + 1 = 1$$

$$-5 + 0 = 0 - 5 = -5$$

This leaves the element unchanged. Multiplicative identity is 1:

$$z.1 = 1.z = z \text{ for all z in the group.}$$

$$(+1)\ .1 = 1.\ (+1)$$

$$(-1)\ .1 = 1\ (-1)$$

$$(\pm 2)\ .1 = 1.\ (\pm 2) \text{ etc.}$$

6. Existence of inverse.

There can be an additive inverse.

$$\{z + (-z)\} = 0$$

For each z there is an element z^{-1}:

$$+1 - 1 = 0$$

$$+2 - 2 = 0$$

$$+3 - 3 = 0$$

$$+4 - 4 = 0$$

Multiplicative inverse.

There is a multiplicative inverse.

For each non-zero z denoted by z^{-1},

for which $zz^{-1} = 1$ or E.

2. Consider a group comprising an odd numbers:

$$0, \pm 1, \pm 3, \pm 5, \pm 7, ...$$

It does not form group that can be satisfied on the following considerations:

$1 + 3 = 3 + 1 = 4$ an even number that does not belong to the group.

So it does not possess property of closure.

This is enough as test for not forming a group.

3. Consider a case with even number forming a group:

$$0, \pm 2, \pm 4, \pm 6, - - - -$$

1. $2 + 0 = 0+2 = 2$

   Identity leaves the element unchanged.

2. Property of closure:

   $(\pm 2) + (\pm 4) = (\pm 6)$ property of closure.

3. Associative:

   $(+ 2) + (+4 + 6) = (2 + 4) + 6 = 12$

4. Existence of inverse:

   $+2 - 2 = 0$

5. Commutative law:

   $2 + 0 = 0+2 = +2$

A group containing even numbers as elements exists but it does not in odd number case. Groups usually appear as a set of operations that leave the system unchanged, invariant. This is an expression of symmetry.

Indeed, a symmetry is defined as the invariance of the Hamiltonian of a system under a group of transformations.

1.5 WHAT IS MATRIX AND MATRIX ALGEBRA GOVERNING IT

In quantum mechanics most of the time we handle problems that involved algebraic and geometrical processes, we undertake simplification procedure for reduction of big and lengthy equations. We do it by mathematical constructs through symbolic methods—matrices, vector and group theory.

A matrix is an ordered array of elements with some rules of operation. The elements are arranged in rows and columns. Elements may be real or complex.

A mxn matrix with m rows and n columns are written as:

$$(A)_{ij} \text{ or } a_{ij} = \begin{bmatrix} a_{11} & a_{12} & \cdots & a_{1n} \\ a_{21} & a_{22} & \cdots & a_{2n} \\ a_{m1} & a_{m2} & \cdots & a_{mn} \end{bmatrix}$$

Indexing by i and j is done for row matrix and column matrix respectively:

(i) If A = B

$a_{ij} = b_{ij}$ for all i and j.

(ii) When every element a_{ij} of A is zero. Then A is a null matrix, the symbol for which is 0:

$$A = 0$$

If $a_{ij} = 0$ for all i and j.

(iii) Unit matrix, 1.

If A = 1, and $a_{ij} = \delta_{ij}$ Kronecker delta.

It has the elements 1 whenever i = j (diagonal elements).

(iv) $(A + B)_{ij} = (A)_{ij} + (B)_{ij} = (C)_{ij}$

or $a_{ij} + b_{ij} = c_{ij}$

(v) Difference between ordinary algebra and matrix is shown in multiplication product AB = C, BA = D.

Let C_{ij} be the product element. This is obtained on multiplying a_{ik} of A by b_{kj} of B and summing all such products overall values of k.

This may be expressed as:

$$a_{ij} = \sum_k a_{ik}\, b_{kj}$$

A meaningful multiplied is said to be conformable.

Multiplication of a matrix A by a constant λ. This implies that every element of A is multiplied by λ namely:

$(\lambda A)_{ij} = \lambda\, a_{ij}$ for all i and j.

Show that (i) $[103]\begin{bmatrix}2\\1\\4\end{bmatrix}=[14]$

$$\text{LHS}=[103]\begin{bmatrix}2\\1\\4\end{bmatrix}=[1\times2+0\times1+3\times4]=[2+12]=[14]$$

(ii) $\begin{bmatrix}2\\1\\4\end{bmatrix}[103]=\begin{bmatrix}2&0&6\\1&0&3\\4&0&12\end{bmatrix}$

$$\text{L.H.S.}=\begin{bmatrix}2\\1\\4\end{bmatrix}[103]$$

$$=\begin{bmatrix}2\times1&2\times0&2\times3\\1\times1&1\times0&1\times3\\4\times1&4\times0&4\times3\end{bmatrix}$$

$$=\begin{bmatrix}2&0&6\\1&0&3\\4&0&12\end{bmatrix}$$

1.6 TRANSFORMATION OF A GROUP

U (n) represents nxn square matrices.

If matrices are non-singular and there exist inverse matrices. There can be a proof that it constitutes a group when their combination is defined:

1. AB = C and AC = B etc.
2. Associative law is applied:
   A (BC) = (AB) C = (ABC)
3. There exists unit matrix E or I:

$$E=\begin{bmatrix}1&0&0\\0&1&0\\0&0&1\end{bmatrix}$$

Such that AE = A commute.

$$\text{Let } A = \begin{bmatrix} t_{11} & t_{12} & t_{13} \\ t_{21} & t_{22} & t_{23} \\ t_{31} & t_{32} & t_{33} \end{bmatrix}$$

be square matrix of dimension 3.

Then,

$$AE = \begin{bmatrix} t_{11} & t_{12} & t_{13} \\ t_{21} & t_{22} & t_{23} \\ t_{31} & t_{32} & t_{33} \end{bmatrix} \begin{bmatrix} 1 & & 0 \\ & 1 & \\ 0 & & 1 \end{bmatrix}$$

$$= \begin{bmatrix} t_{11}+0+0 & t_{12}+0+0 & t_{13}+0+0 \\ t_{21}+0+0 & t_{22}+0+0 & t_{23}+0+0 \\ t_{31}+0+0 & t_{32}+0+0 & t_{33}+0+0 \end{bmatrix}$$

$$= \begin{bmatrix} t_{11} & t_{12} & t_{13} \\ t_{21} & t_{22} & t_{23} \\ t_{31} & t_{32} & t_{33} \end{bmatrix}$$

4. It has a reciprocal element A^{-1}, B^{-1}.

Sometimes we handle complex numbers. The complex numbers are involved in constituting the groups. Let ψ be a complex number then $|\psi|^2$ will be a real number:

(i) Consider z = a + ib where a and b are real.

Such that, $z^* = a - ib$

$$\begin{aligned} |z|^2 &= |zz^*| \\ &= (a + ib)(a - ib) \\ &= a^2 - i^2b^2 \\ &= a^2 + b^2 = \text{a real number.} \end{aligned}$$

(ii) Let us take a complex function of the form ψ' which is written as product of function ψ and an arbitrary phase factor $e^{i\theta}$:

$$\psi' = \psi e^{i\theta} \text{ so that we define}$$

$$\psi' \psi'^{*} = \psi e^{i\theta} . \psi e^{-i\theta}$$

$$= |\psi|^2 e^{i\theta - i\theta} = |\psi|^2 . e^0 = |\psi|^2 = 1$$

$[\psi]^2$ is more important. A real number is generated out of ψ' by multiplication it with complex conjugate.

1.7 USEFULNESS OF SYMMETRY

We consider an eigen value equation containing a linear operator. If the equation is eigen value type the eigen function may be classified with respect to the symmetry properties of the operator:

$$H = T + V = \frac{1}{2} \sum_{i=1}^{n} m_i \dot{r}_i^2 + V(r_1, \ldots r_n)$$

T = kinetic energy = $\frac{1}{2} m\dot{r}^2$

T is a function of velocity $\dot{r} = \frac{dr}{dt}$

V = potential energy

$V(x) = \frac{1}{2} kx^2$

In quantum mechanics we intend to solve the eigen value equation:

$$H \psi = E \psi.$$

For any system of atoms or molecules there can be a set of wave functions of energy levels. This can be generalized by the equation of the form:

$$H\psi_i = E_i \psi_i$$

It represents eigen value equation for non-degenerate case. When the system contains symmetry we include it in H.

R is a symmetry operator. Each R commutes with H.

$$RT = R \frac{1}{2} \sum_{i=1}^{n} m_i \dot{r}_i^2 = \frac{1}{2} \sum_{i=1}^{n} m_i \dot{r}_i^2$$

Because, $R \dot{r}_i^2 = \dot{r}_i^2$

$$RV(r) = V(r)$$

Since, $V(x) = \frac{1}{2} kx^2$

For symmetric operation $x \rightarrow -x$.

$V = \frac{1}{2} kx^2$ is symmetric with respect to reflection across the y-axis.

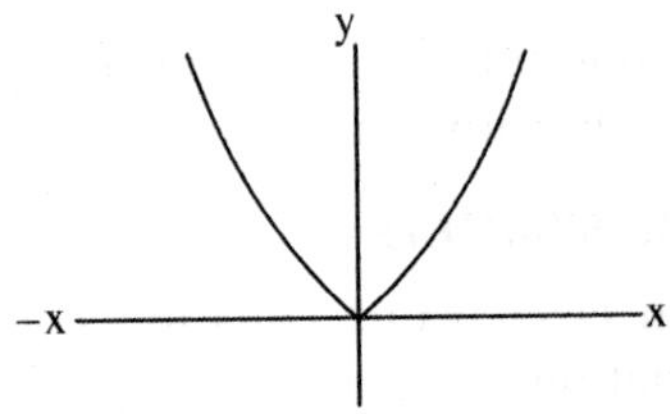

If we deal with symmetric operation there is no change in H. So H is invariant under transformation R.

i.e. $x \rightarrow -x$

Since E_i is numerical constant:

$$RH\,\psi_i = RE_i\,\psi_i.$$

$$\text{Or } H\,(R\psi_i) = E_i\,(R\psi_i) \qquad \text{...(I)}$$

The eigen function of H will be the eigen function of R. In equation (I) $R\psi_i$ is also an eigen function of H belonging to the eigen value E_i:

$R\psi_i = c\psi_i$ showing non-degeneracy.

Since, $R^2 = 1 = R.R$

$$R.R\,\psi_i = Rc\,\psi_i$$
$$= c(R\psi_i)$$
$$= c(c\psi_i) = c^2\psi_i$$

or, $R^2\,\psi_i = c^2\,\psi_i = \psi_i$

or, $\psi_i = c^2\,\psi_i$

So, R^2 is regarded as parity operator.

For non-degenerate case $c^2 = 1$

and, $c = \pm 1$

Hence, $R\,\psi_i = (\pm 1)\,\psi_i$

Therefore, the wave function ψ_i must be even or odd.

For $x = -x$, and it is invariant under this transformation, then ψ_i will be an even function of x:

$$R\,\psi_i = +\,\psi_i$$

Also when ψ_i will be odd in that case:

$$\psi_i = -\psi_i$$

The growing idea of point symmetry and group theory has a wonderful role in physical theory which span into stereochemistry, electronic spectra and molecular vibrations.

Different kinds of symmetry operations:

1. Translation in space.
2. Translation in time.
3. Rotation through a fixed angle.
4. Reflection of space.
5. Interchange of identical atoms or particles.

1.8 SYMMETRY AND CHEMISTRY

It has been pointed out earlier that symmetry stands for harmonious arrangement as well as repetition of parts producing equivalent or similar structures. This property has been used in chemistry now a days to classify molecules using point group notations. We deal with like atoms in molecule which can interchange their positions through symmetry operations by an axis of symmetry, reflection in a mirror plane or a point within the molecule (inversion centre) and by doing nothing incase of identity. There are two similar H-atoms in H_2S. We can exchange them on applying rotation through 180° and reflection in an imaginary plane. There are three like F-atoms in NF_3 which can be exchanged by rotation of 120° or reflection in plane containing the principal axis and the respective N-F bond. PCl_5 contains two sets of Cl-atoms in the TBP structure—two axial and three equatorial Cl atoms making angles of 180° and 120° respectively. Only equatorial atoms are alike which can be interchanged to obtain equivalent configurations along axial chlorine atoms on z (C_3) axis.

BrF_5 has square pyramidal structure. Only four of them present on square base and they are equivalent. They are exchangeable and the fifth one lies on z (C_4) axis perpendicular to the square base.

ClF_3 with TBP arrangement has two F-atoms on axial positions. The third fluorine atom lies on equatorial position.

The z-axis passes through the equatorial F-atom and the two F-atoms being on axial positions are interchanged.

A large number of informations is collected through symmetry and they are related to chemical properties such as dipole-moment, stereochemistry predicting transitions in UV-visible, IR and Raman spectra.

You may use symmetry for formation of SALCS to obtain group orbitals, hybrid orbitals, molecular orbitals from atomic orbitals. Apart from these we do splitting of atomic orbitals in a crystal field and solving a big secular equation. We use symmetry with Hamiltonian operator in schrödinger wave equation. Symmetry is inseparable from chemistry.

Solved Examples

1. Comment on:

(a) ***Symmetry is a familiar theme***

We apply symmetry in chemistry on certain topics. Such as dipole moment, optical activity. We now apply it for classification of molecules into point group. We consider IR and Raman activities of fundamental, overtone and combination bands on the basis of symmetry derived considerations. The idea of symmetry is applied on electronic transitions in UV-Vis. Spectroscopy through transition moment integrals. Through the method of invariance it enters in quantum mechanics and solve the lengthy secular equations. This can also be applied both in weak crystal field and strong crystal field methods to obtain split energy components. Importance of symmetry is well recognised as a most familiar theme.

(b) ***Group theory is an organiser***

A collection of numbers or letters or matrices constitute a group. Such numbers are elements or members of a group. There are four main criteria of an abstract group:

(i) Property of closure.

(ii) Existence of inverse (reciprocal).

(iii) Presence of identity, and

(iv) Associativity.

When all these properties are simultaneously fulfilled a group is said to be formed. In point symmetry such rules are widely obeyed by symmetry operations. Well distinct operations are placed into classes. The total number of all such operations turnout to be the order of the group. Thus on the basis of symmetry about a point one can deduce a mathematical group. Consequently a group is formed so the group is an organiser.

(c) ***Matrix is a vehicle***

An equation in algebra may be written in matrix form as:

$$AX = Y.$$

Where A is a square matrix which is used to bring transformation of a column vector X to another column vector. Let A be a three dimensional square matrix of the form:

$$A = \begin{bmatrix} A_{11} & A_{12} & A_{13} \\ A_{21} & A_{22} & A_{23} \\ A_{31} & A_{32} & A_{33} \\ & 3\times 3 & \end{bmatrix}$$

Both X and Y are also of the same order as A.

Viz.

$$X = \begin{bmatrix} x_1 \\ x_2 \\ x_3 \end{bmatrix} \qquad Y = \begin{bmatrix} y_1 \\ y_2 \\ y_3 \end{bmatrix}$$

The transformation is associated with algebraic process:

$$\begin{bmatrix} A_{11} & A_{12} & A_{13} \\ A_{21} & A_{22} & A_{23} \\ A_{31} & A_{32} & A_{33} \end{bmatrix} \begin{bmatrix} x_1 \\ x_2 \\ x_3 \end{bmatrix} = \begin{bmatrix} y_1 \\ y_2 \\ y_3 \end{bmatrix}$$

Symmetry processes which were carried out geometrically can also be written in the form of matrix equation. In this context matrix is used as vehicle to bring out the transformation which were previously performed geometrically.

2. Justify that a group is formed by 1, i, –1, –i.

It is a group of four members, a finite group with both real and imaginary numbers.

One can elucidate the following properties:

(i) Property of closure:

The product of any two elements is also a member of the group:

$$1.i = i$$
$$1.-i = -i$$
$$-1.-1 = 1$$
$$-1.-i = i$$

Their squares are also members of the group:

$$(1)^2 = 1$$
$$(i)^2 = -1$$
$$(-1)^2 = 1$$
$$(-i)^2 = -1$$

(ii) There is unique element like identity. Here 1 is taken to be identity.

This on multiplication leaves the elements unchanged:

$$1.1 = 1$$
$$1.-1 = -1$$
$$1.i = i$$
$$1.-i = -i$$

(iii) Existence of inverse (additive)

$$1 + (-1) = 0$$
$$i + (-i) = 0$$

There is additive identity (0).

(iv) A triple product is also member of the group:

$$(1) . (i), (-1) = -i$$
$$(1) (-i) (i) = -i^2 = 1$$
$$(1) (-i) (-1) = + i = i$$

So associativity follows.

3. Show that, E C_3 C_3^2 constitute a group. What is its order?

(i) Property of closure.

$$E\ C_3 = C_3$$
$$E\ C_3^2 = C_3^2$$
$$C_3\ C_3^2 = C_3^3 = E$$

(ii) It has identity as one of the members, E.

(iii) Existence of inverse:

E is inverse by itself.

C_3 has its inverse $C_3^{-1} = C_3^2$

C_3^2 has its inverse $C_3^{-2} = C_3$

Product of an element with its inverse gives identity:

$$C_3.C_3^{-1} = C_3 . C_3^2 = C_3^3 = E$$

$$C_3^2. C_3^{-2} = C_3^2. C_3 = C_3^3 = E$$

(iv) Consider the triplet product:

$$E\ C_3\ C_3^2 = E\ C_3^3 = E.E = E$$

Hence they form a mathematical group of order 3.

4. Construct a matrix equation out of linear equations:

$$a_{11}\ x_1 + a_{12}\ x_2 + a_{13}\ x_3 = b_1$$

$$a_{21}\ x_1 + a_{22}\ x_2 + a_{23}\ x_3 = b_2$$

$$a_{31}\ x_1 + a_{32}\ x_2 + a_{33}\ x_3 = b_3$$

Coefficients of x_1, x_2 and x_3 have been arranged in the form of array of quantities:

$$\begin{bmatrix} a_{11} & a_{12} & a_{13} \\ a_{21} & a_{22} & a_{23} \\ a_{31} & a_{32} & a_{33} \end{bmatrix} \text{ giving a } 3 \times 3 \text{ matrix,}$$

and $\begin{bmatrix} a_{11} & a_{12} & a_{13} \\ a_{21} & a_{22} & a_{23} \\ a_{31} & a_{32} & a_{33} \end{bmatrix} \begin{bmatrix} x_1 \\ x_2 \\ x_3 \end{bmatrix} = \begin{bmatrix} b_1 \\ b_2 \\ b_3 \end{bmatrix}$ is the required equation.

5. What is condition for an abelian group?

Show that D_{3h} is a non-abelian group.

If two operations P and Q commute:

$$P \times Q = Q \times P$$

The group is said to be abelian. If pairs of operation do not commute the group is non-abelian.

D_{3h} is a point group notation. Its order is h = 12 and so many members, viz.

$$E, C_3, C_3^2, 3C_2, \sigma_h, 3\sigma_v, 2S_3$$

As C_3 and σ_v do not commute so it is a non-abelian group.

6. Give a list of abelian groups:

   C_n, C_{nh}, C_{2v}, D_2 and D_{2h} all are abelian groups.

   Remaining groups are non-abelian.

7. Show that C_{2v} with E, C_2, σ_{xz}, σ_{yz}

   Constitute a mathematical group:

   1. Closure

   $$C_2 \times \sigma_{xz} = \sigma_{yz}$$

   2. Associativity $C_2 \times (\sigma_{yz} \times \sigma_{xz})$

   $$= (C_2 \times \sigma_{yz})\ \sigma_{xz}$$

   3. It consists of identity E as member, which leaves the other members unchanged:

   $$E \times C_2 = C_2 \times E = C_2$$
   $$E \times \sigma_{xz} = \sigma_{xz} \times E = \sigma_{xz}$$
   $$E \times \sigma_{yz} = \sigma_{yz} \times E = \sigma_{yz}$$

   4. Every element has its own inverse.

   $$C_2 \cdot C_2^{-1} = C_2 \cdot C_2 = E$$
   $$\sigma_{xz} \cdot \sigma_{xz}^{-1} = \sigma_{xz} \cdot \sigma_{xz} = E$$
   $$\sigma_{yz} \cdot \sigma_{yz}^{-1} = \sigma_{yz} \cdot \sigma_{yz} = E$$

8. Show that C_3 and C_3^2 are members of same class.

   Two members P and Q belong to the same class of the group when there is another element, R such that

   $$P = R^{-1} QR$$

   For C_{3v}, $\sigma_v^{-1}\, C_3^2\, \sigma_v = \sigma_v\, C_3^2\, \sigma_v = C_3$

   So C_3 and C_3^2 belong to the same class.

9. Justify the following:

   (a) A group formed by 1, i, –1, –i is only a mathematical group but it does not have a point group.

(b) Show that a group formed by 1, i, –1, –i is abelian group.

(c) Bring the resemblance of the above group with C_4 point group.

(a) It has all the properties:

(i) Closure.

(ii) Presence of unique element.

(iii) Existence of inverse.

(iv) Associativity.

Hence, they constitute a mathematical group.

These members are not associated with symmetry operations in a molecule. They do not form any point group.

(b) The combination of any two elements is also an element. Their product irrespective of their order of combination are all equal and an element in the group.

$$1 \times 1 = 1$$

$$1 \times i = i = i \times 1$$

$$1 \times -i = -i = -i \times 1$$

$$-1 \times 1 = -1 = 1 \times -1$$

The multiplications are commutative. Hence, it is an abelian group.

(c) The Cyclic group C_4 has their members:

$$C_4, C_4^2, C_4^3, C_4^4 \equiv E$$

i.e. it has E, C_4, $C_4^2 \equiv C_2$, C_4^3 with h = 4

The members 1, i, –1, –i h = 4, both have similar multiplication table retaining the order of the groups. one can co-correlate each member with each group.

QUESTIONS

1. Explain: (i) Symmetry is a familiar theme.
   (ii) Matrix is a vehicle.
   (iii) Group is an organiser of our-notion.
2. (a) How do the following transform in C_{2h} point group x, y and z co-ordinates as basis.
   (b) Give the three dimensional matrices for all symmetry operations in C_{2h}.
   (c) Perform matrix multiplication to show
   $$i \times \sigma_h = C_2$$
   (d) Complete matrix multiplication Table for C_{2h} point group.
3. (a) What are different types of symmetry operations in ammonia. Give three dimensional representation in each symmetry operation with (x, y, z) as basis set.
   (b) Workout group multiplication Table for ammonia and determine its classes.
4. Generate four dimensional representation in C_{3v} (ammonia) with atomic orbitals s, p_x, p_y and p_z.
5. Justify usefulness of symmetry.
6. (a) What are properties of a group? How do you apply conformability test between two matrices?
   (b) Comment on symmetry and chemistry.
   (c) Give the Weyl definition of symmetry.

MOLECULAR SYMMETRY 2

2.1 SYMMETRY

Symmetry plays a vital role in chemistry. It is applied as a powerful tool on classical topics like optical activity, dipole moment and conformational analysis. Such consideration is widely applied on certain modern topics in teachings of qualitative and quantitative aspects of hybridization involving σ and π bonds, group orbitals, molecular orbitals, selection rules in general in molecular spectroscopy, identification of infrared and Raman active fundamentals as well as structural inorganic chemistry. It is most popular among chemists who are engaged on molecular orbital theory. We are confined to molecules.

Molecules are now classified under symmetry elements that they possess and symmetry operations which are carried out in those cases.

TABLE 2.1

Molecules	*Symmetry Classification*	*Symmetry Operation*
1. H_2O, 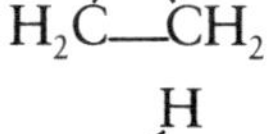	C_{2v}	E, C_2, σ_{xz}, σ_{yz}
2. 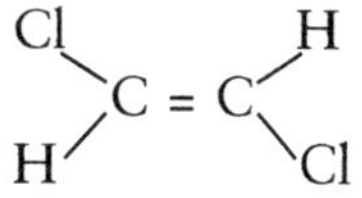 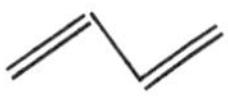 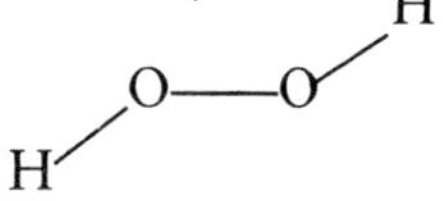	C_{2h}	E, C_2, σ_h, i

Molecules	*Symmetry Classification*	*Symmetry Operation*
3. H_3C-Cl, $CHCl_3$, NH_3	C_{3v}	$E, C_3, C_3^2, \sigma_v, \sigma'_v, \sigma''_v$
4. BF_3, BCl_3, PF_5	D_{3h}	E, $2C_3$, $3C_2$, σ_h, $3\sigma_v$, $2S_3$
5. $P_tCl_4^{2-}$, $NiCl_4^{2-}$ Trans $[Co(NH_3)_4\ Cl_2]^+$	D_{4h}	E, $2C_4$, $2C'_2$, $2C''_2$, C_2, i, σ_h, $2\sigma_v$, $2\sigma_d$, $2S_4$. etc.

We deduce the molecular structure on the basis of atomic or molecular wave-functions of electrons. These wave functions are related to symmetric restrictions. As such one can deduce molecular structure.

2.2 SYMMETRY ELEMENTS

A symmetry element is geometrical entity such as line, plane or point about which we perform symmetry operations. Both symmetry elements and symmetry operations are interlinked. There is no separate existence of either of the two. If there is a presence of symmetry element it means a set of symmetry operations will arise, alternatively, whenever there exists any symmetry operation it implies the presence of a symmetry element of a particular kind. A line is defined by a symmetry element referred to as line of symmetry (or axis of symmetry), a point by a centre of symmetry and a plane by plane of symmetry.

Summary of symmetry elements, symmetry operations and their common symbols are given in Table 2.2.

TABLE 2.2

Symmetry Elements	*Symbol*	*Symmetry Operations*
1. Plane	σ	Reflection in the plane.
2. Centre of symmetry or inversion Centre	i	Inversion of all atoms through the centre.

	Symmetry Elements	Symbol	Symmetry Operations
3.	Proper axis	C_n	One or more rotations about the axis.
4.	Improper axis	S_n	Rotation followed by reflection in a plane perpendicular to the rotation axis.
5.	Identity	E	Doing nothing.

Two kinds of symbols are in frequent applications.

Chemists symbol σ i Sn C_{2h} Cn (molecular symmetry).

International symbol m i Sn 2/m n (Crystallography).

In a point group translational elements of symmetry are not considered. When it is taken care of this becomes space groups. In crystallography translational symmetry is considered.

Comparison of molecular symmetry with crystallographic symmetry.

TABLE 2.3

	Molecules	Crystals
1.	Cn axis of order n n = 1, 2, 3, . . . ∝ is present.	Cn axis of order n (n = 1, 2, 3, 4, 6) is present.
2.	Total number of point group is not limited.	The number of point group is limited to 32 (There are 230 space groups).
3.	Rotation reflection axis is present.	Rotation inversion axis is present.
4.	Translational elements of symmetry are absent.	Translational elements of symmetry such as glide plane and screw axis are present.
5.	Schoenflies notation is used.	Herman-Mauguin notation is more commonly applied.

2.3 UNDERSTANDING OF SYMMETRY DERIVED CONSIDERATIONS

To begin with we take up a few examples:

(a) PF_5 molecule

It has TBP arrangement where all the five F atoms are non-equivalent. They belong to two sets three of them lie in a triangular plane and thus they are equivalent. The P-F equatorial bonds are also equidistant and they have same bond strength.

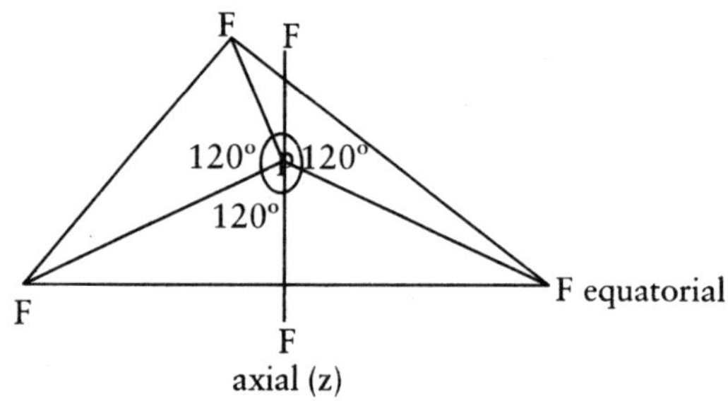

On the other hand we find two axial F-atoms. The three equatorial F-atoms can be interchanged without making any destruction. Similarly two axial F-atoms are indistinguishable. But we cannot permit interchange of F (axial) with F (equatorial). The z-axis passes through P-atom and is normal to the triangular base. Thus F-P-F axis is also C_3 axis.

(b) H_2O molecule

It has C_{2v} symmetry. The symbol implies the following:

(i) H_2O is a non-planar molecule.

(ii) $H — \hat{O} — H$ is non-linear.

(iii) The two H-atoms are equivalent.

(iv) The two O — H bonds are also equivalent.

(c) BF_3 molecule

It has D_{3h} symmetry like PF_5. We get following informations:

(i) BF_3 is a planar molecule.

(ii) $F - \hat{B} - F$ bond angle is 120°.

(iii) There are three equivalent F atoms.

(iv) Three B-F bonds are similar in strength.

Symmetry characteristics reveal three distinct types of molecules that of very high symmetry, a less symmetrical molecule or a molecule with no symmetry at all. The subject matter for the study under present context can be taken up on priority basis non-planar to planar and then the case of linear at the end.

2.4 SYMMETRY OPERATIONS

To make systematic study of symmetry we need to have certain formal tools. Such tools are nothing but symmetry operations. Various symmetry operations are discussed in two ways— (i) in purely geometric terms; and (ii) algebraically by representative matrices acting on basis vectors. The five symmetry operations and symmetry elements required for specifying molecular symmetry are as given below:

$$E, C_n, \sigma, i, S_n$$

The molecules are looking exactly similar or equivalent after and before operations. Certain operations are performed about geometrical entity which may be a point, line or plane. Thus, every molecule has certain elements of symmetry and we can associate with each certain symmetry operations. These operations (symmetry operations) have property that after the operation is over the molecule is in a position completely equivalent to the original configuration. There are two or more distinct configurations which do not have mirror image relationship but are equivalent and the process is repeated till a configuration is obtained which is identical with the original structure. We can be more specific taking example of water molecule. There are two like hydrogen atoms:

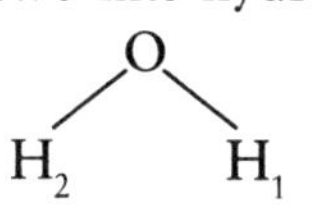

We label them putting numerals 1 & 2. Since there are two similar atoms present in water molecule we can allow them to interchange. Such a exchange is permitted in which the molecule retains its original structure by certain operations. The molecule has same appearance as it had before the operation was carried out. Let us rotate the molecule by 180° about z-axis passing through O-atom. This leads to a new configuration:

There are three like atoms in BF_3. The fluorine atoms can be distinguished on labeling them by 1, 2, 3. In fact this distinction is achieved for the sake of convenience only. The three indistinguished arrangements are :

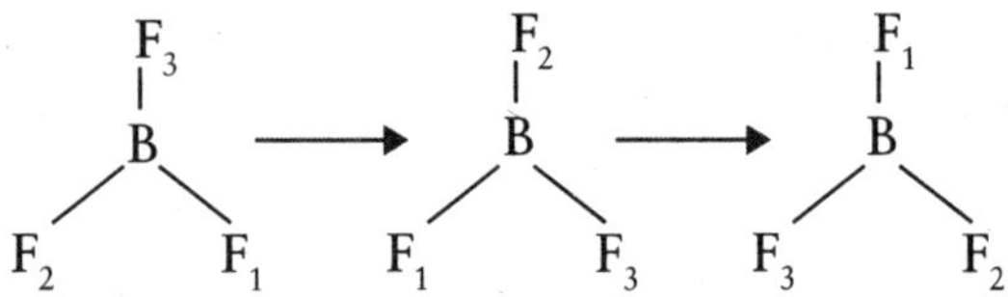

We find that such arrangements are obtained by a rotation of 120° about z-axis passing through B-atom perpendicular to the molecular plane Thus, symmetry operations signify the ways of interchanging atoms at equivalent positions. We notice two things while dealing with symmetry operations counting of like atoms for possible exchange and secondly there will be no stereo-chemical change. Like H_2O, H_2S contains two H-atoms which are equivalent. We can interchange these atoms but on turning to HSD, no such exchange is possible between H & D atoms as they are not equivalent nor S-H and S-D bonds are similar:

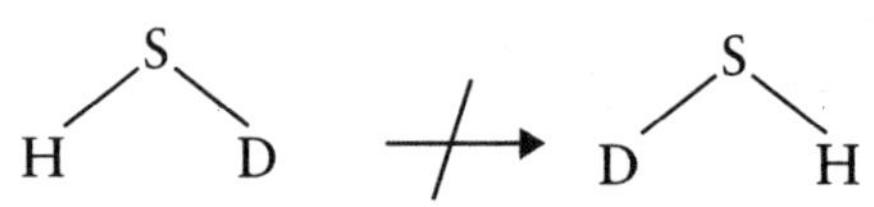

Thus, HSD does not have any symmetry.

2.5 C_n (PROPER ROTATION)

C stands for cyclic meaning rotation with n is order of rotation.

Rotation about an axis passing through molecule by an angle $2\pi/n$. If the operation is repeated n times result is to bring back to the original orientation.

n = Order of the axis or number of equivalent configurations.

n is defined as $2\pi/\alpha$, α = angle of rotation.

A rotation of $\frac{360^\circ}{2} = 180^\circ$ gives two fold axis of symmetry.

$n = \frac{2\pi}{\alpha} = \frac{2\pi}{180^\circ} = 2$, i.e. two fold axis of symmetry

A rotation of $\frac{360^\circ}{3} = 120^\circ$ gives three fold axis of symmetry.

A rotation of $\frac{360^\circ}{4} = 90^\circ$ gives four fold axis of symmetry.

A rotation of $\frac{360^\circ}{5} = 72^\circ$ gives five fold axis of symmetry.

A rotation of $\frac{360^\circ}{6} = 60^\circ$ gives six fold axis of symmetry.

The rotation is performed either clockwise or anti-clockwise (counter clockwise):

	Angle	Order
C_2 axis	180°	2
C_3 axis	120°	3
C_4 axis	90°	4
C_5 axis	72°	5
C_6 axis	60°	6

C_2 can be performed twice. This means first 180° rotation about an axis brings another equivalent configuration of the molecule:

$$A_1 - A_2 \xrightarrow{\pi} A_2 - A_1$$

The atoms occupy their original positions if we repeat the process. Another 180° rotation about the same axis produces:

$$A_2 - A_1 \xrightarrow{\pi} A_1 - A_2$$

When a 180° rotation is performed it is abbreviated as C_2, for the next 180° rotation we have another C_2 operation. When the process occurs twice the cycle is complete i.e. A 180° rotation is C_2 another 180° rotation is also C_2. Thus, rotation of 360° = two times 180° = $C_2 . C_2$ or C_2^2. This is nothing but identity E because we arrive at the same configuration as the original one.

It is immaterial whether you rotate the molecule clockwise or counter clockwise. C_2' and C_2'' (prime or inverse is used for anti-clockwise rotation).

$$C_2^{-1}, C_2^{-2}$$

C_2 axis: Let us take for example water molecule.

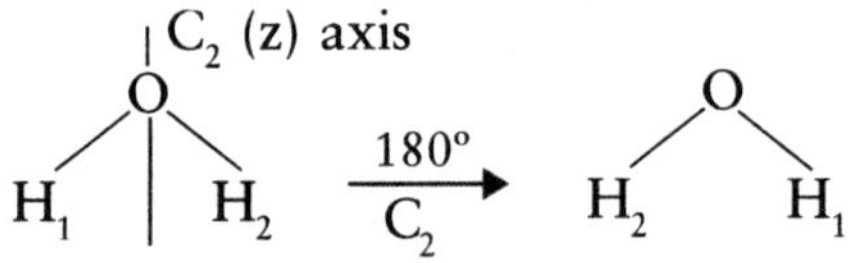

The two H-atoms which are identical can be interchanged by a rotation about z-axis through an angle of 180°. Thus it possesses C_2 axis.

C_3 axis: This represents a rotation by 120° about z-axis. Consider a triangle, the three corners are identical we number them on 1, 2, & 3 and join them from the centroid.

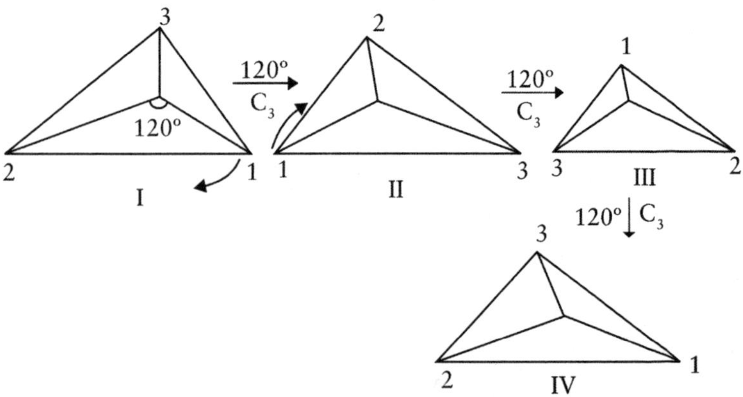

We can have three successive operation of this kind: (i) the first C_3 operation gives configuration II. (ii) the second C_3 operation brings configuration III.

When operation (i) & (ii) are performed collectively it can be counted also as 120°. 120° or a rotation of 240° in straight way. Thus, a C_3 operation on repeating it twice gives $C_3 . C_3 = C_3^2$ operation. This is nothing but a rotation of configuration I by 240° directly.

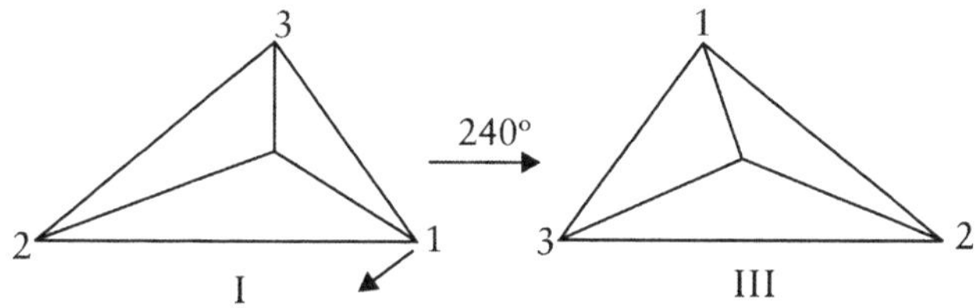

In this respect C_3 & C_3^2 are distinct operations.

(iii) When C_3 operation is repeated thrice we come back to original configuration as in figure IV. Both figures I & IV are identical. This completes a cycle (i.e. a rotation of 360°).

This is a case of identity (E):

$$120°.\ 120°.\ 120° = C_3 .\ C_3 .\ C_3 = C_3^3 = E$$
$$\text{or } 360°$$

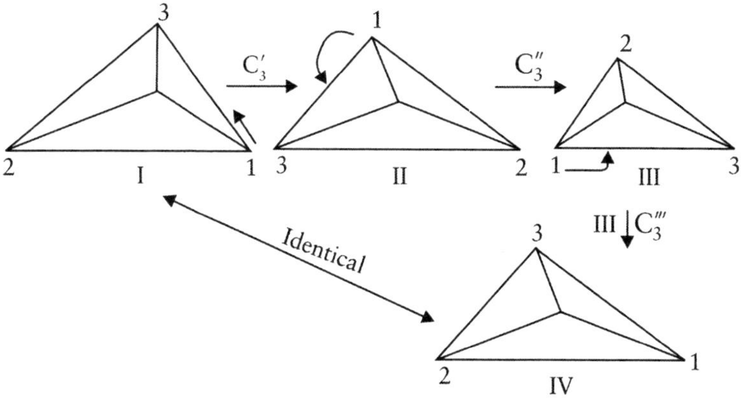

In case of rotations beyond C_2, viz. C_3, C_4 etc. onwards both clockwise and anti-clockwise rotations are counted which may lead to different but equivalent orientations of molecule.

C_3', C_3'', & C_3''', are counter clockwise operations. $C_3''' \equiv E$ again C_3' & C_3'' are distinct configurations. However, the two results are compared which brings the position:

$$C_3 \equiv C_3''$$

$$C_3^2 \equiv C_3'$$

In this way both of them are counted.

Case of 2-fold axis

Consider another plannar molecule trans - 1, 2 - dichloro ethylene.

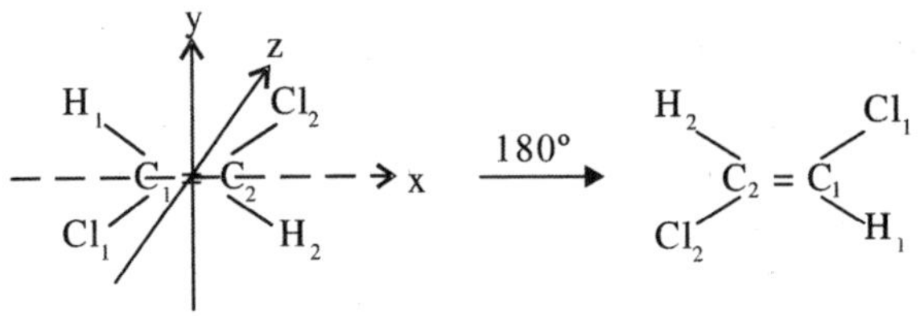

There are three sets of like atoms, a pair of H-atoms, a pair of Cl-atoms and a pair of carbon atoms. The individual atoms of each set of two cannot be distinguished and hence 180° rotation transforms each like atom into indistinguishable partner. Thus, during 360° rotation around z-axis, the molecule repeats itself twice, i.e. it has 360°/2 = C_2 axis (2-fold axis). Possibility that exists here is C_2, C_2^2 = E.

Case of 4-fold axis

Consider a planar molecule $PtCl_4^{2-}$. There are four like atoms disposed at the vertices of square:

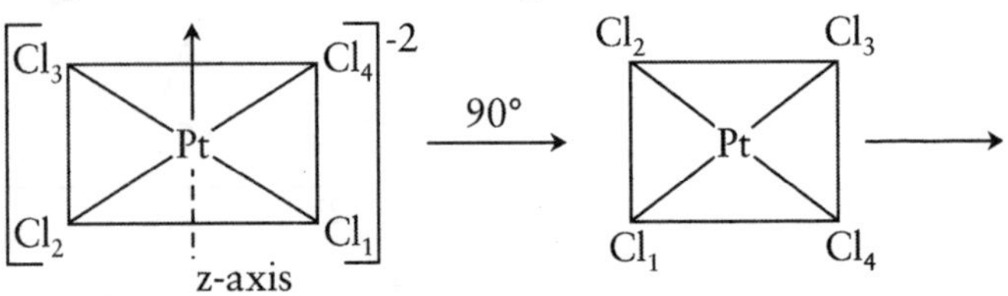

Here z-axis is the principal axis lying perpendicular to the molecular plane (XY), passing through Pt-centre. Rotations around 90°, 180° or 270° give new orientations.

A rotation of 90° brings equivalent configuration. Thus it has $\frac{360^o}{90^o} = C_4$ axis. The molecule repeats itself four times and hence z-axis is C_4 axis (4-fold axis).

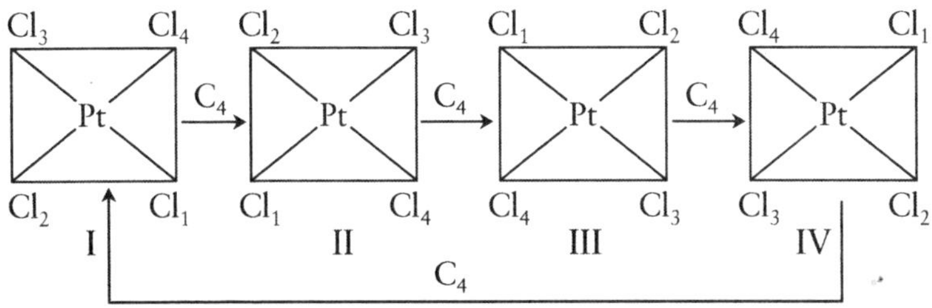

A rotation of 90° on I gives II. This is called C_4. A second rotation of 90° on II brings the structure III. This is equivalent to two successive rotations each of 90° on original configuration of $PtCl_4^{2-}$ ion. It can be shown as $C_4.C_4 = C_4^2$.

A C_4^2 rotation can also be treated as:

$$C_4 \,.\, C_4 = 2C_4 = 2 \times 90° = 180° = C_2.$$

Thus, C_4^2 is same as C_2.

Three successive operations each of 90°. On structure I results the structure IV. This is not identical with I. This means $C_4.C_4.C_4 = C_4^3$ a rotation of 270°. A four fold rotation repeating four times leads to original structure. This can be stated as $C_4.C_4.C_4.C_4 = C_4^4 (\equiv E)$. There can be three distinguished operations C_4, C_4^2, C_4^3, C_4^4 ($\equiv$ E) One can visualise counter clockwise rotations C_4', C_4'', C_4''', C_4^{IV}. The last one represents a complete revolution. Therefore, $C_4^{IV} \equiv E$.

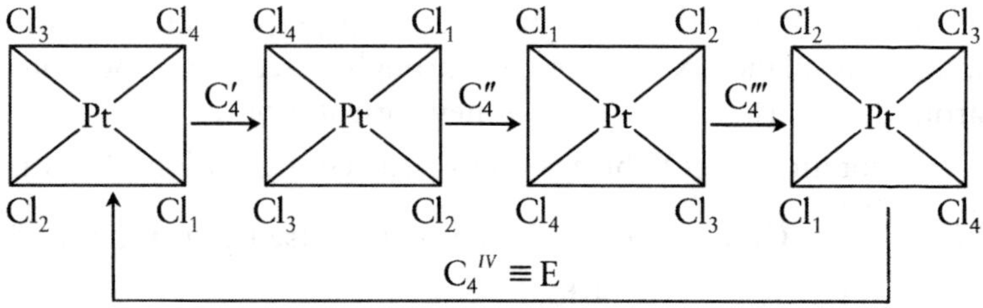

From the picture it is clear that

C_4 is same as C_4'''

C_4^2 is same as C_4''

C_4^3 is same as C_4'

Consider presence of proper rotation axes other than C_4 axis in $PtCl_4^{2-}$. There is a lack of C_3 axis. There is C_2 axis collinear with C_4 (z)-axis.

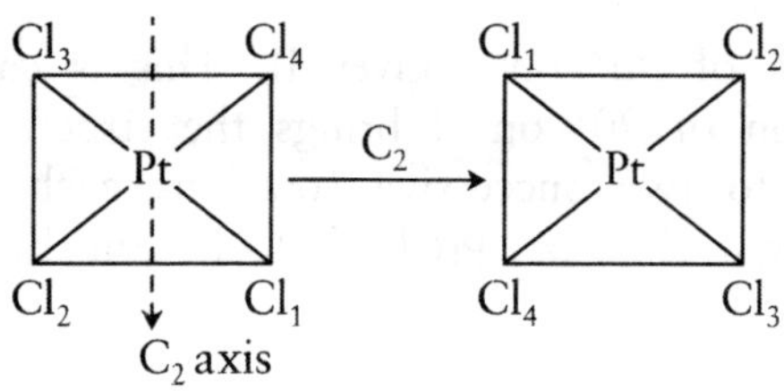

Besides this C_2 axis there are two other sets of C_2 axes. A pair of C_2 axes bisecting the XY plane through edges, i.e. bisecting Cl–Pt–Cl angle. These are C_2''.

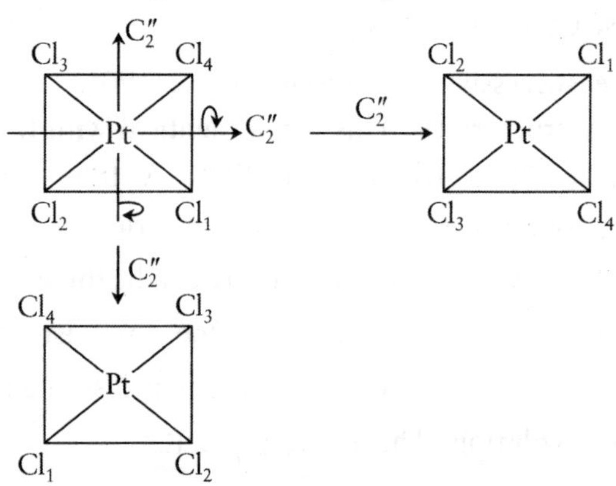

There are two more C_2 axes abbreviated C_2' passing through the corner but bisecting again the XY plane, i.e. passing through Cl–Pt–Cl line.

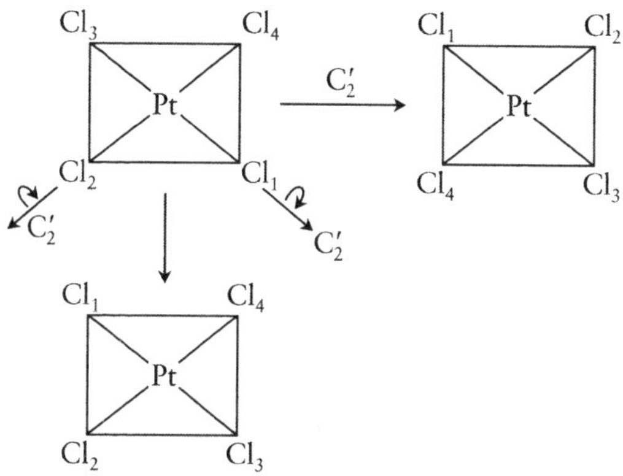

We can summarise the results as follows:

(i) It has C_4 as principal axis.

The associated operations are:

$$C_4, C_4^2 \equiv C_2.C_4^3.$$

(ii) A C_2 axis collinear with C_4.

(iii) Two C_2' and two C_2'' axes.

Altogether there are five C_2 axes belonging to three sets $C_2 \equiv C_4^2, 2C_2', 2C_2''$.

Case of 5-fold axis

Consider π-cyclepentadenyl anion ($C_5H_5^-$) as shown in the figure:

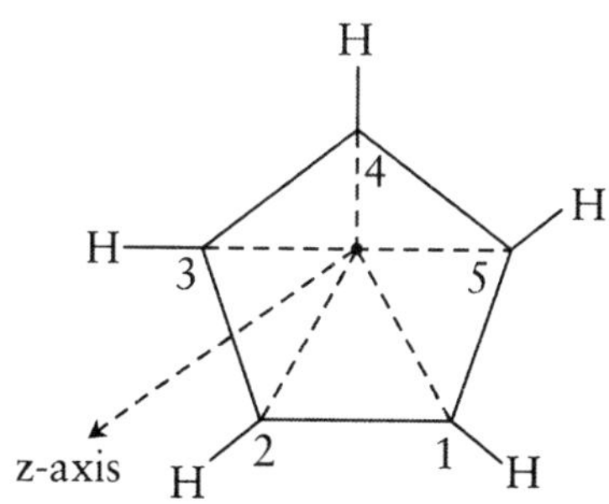

Therefore five carbon atoms in the ring 1, 2, 3, 4 & 5. The z-axis is $\perp^r$ to the molecular plane. The division of 360° by 5 brings rotations of 72°. So it has $\frac{C_{360^\circ}}{72^\circ} = C_5$ rotations. It has C_5 axis as z-axis (principal axis). A rotation of 72° about z-axis is performed and if we repeat it five times the original structure is obtained.

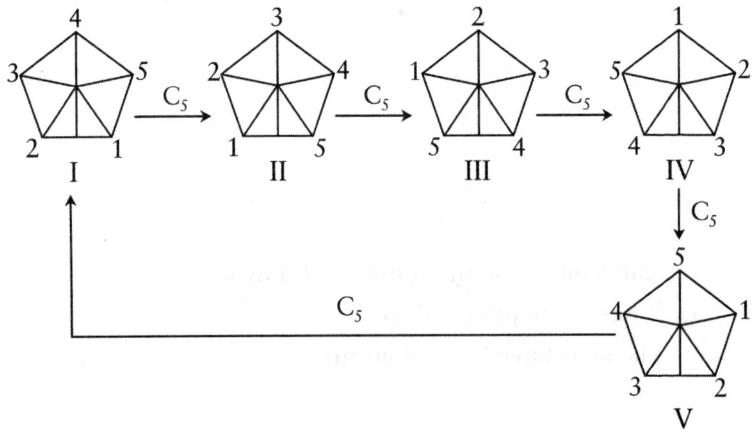

A rotation of 72° gives structure II from I. It corresponds to the operation C_5. A second rotation of 72° gives structure III which is C_5^2. A rotation of 216° changes structures I to IV gives the operation C_5^3. A 288° rotation gives the structure V, which is represented by C_5^4. The cycle is complete by a rotation of 360° that can be considered here as $C_5^5 \equiv E$.

Thus, it has C_5 axis with associated operations C_5, C_5^2, C_5^3, C_5^4 & $C_5^5 \equiv E$.

We can examine the possibility of other proper rotation axis. In fact there are five C_2 axes in the molecular plane, each coincides with C-H bond and bisects the C-C bond opposite to it.

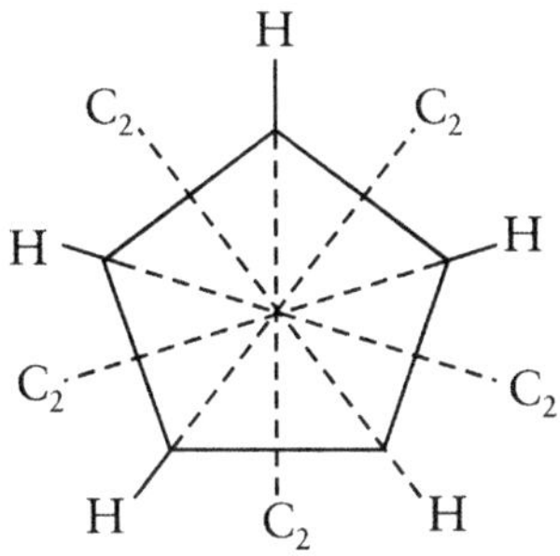

Case of 6-fold axis

We take up again a planar molecule such as benzene. The z-axis is perpendicular to the plane. There are six identical C-atoms in the benzene ring. Rotation of $\frac{360^\circ}{6} = 60^\circ$ repeats the molecule six times and it has six fold axis as the principal axis.

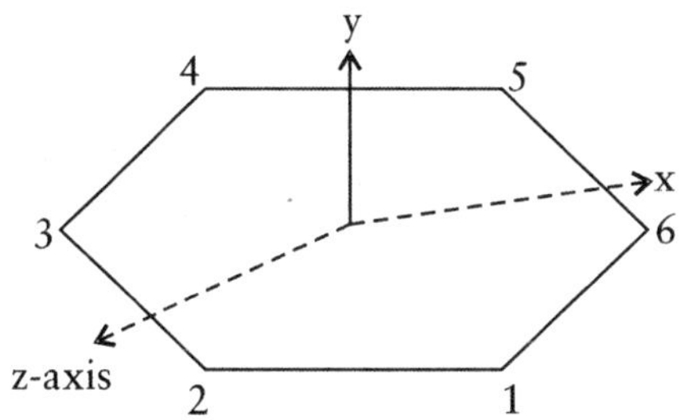

A rotation of 60° to structure I gives II (C_6).

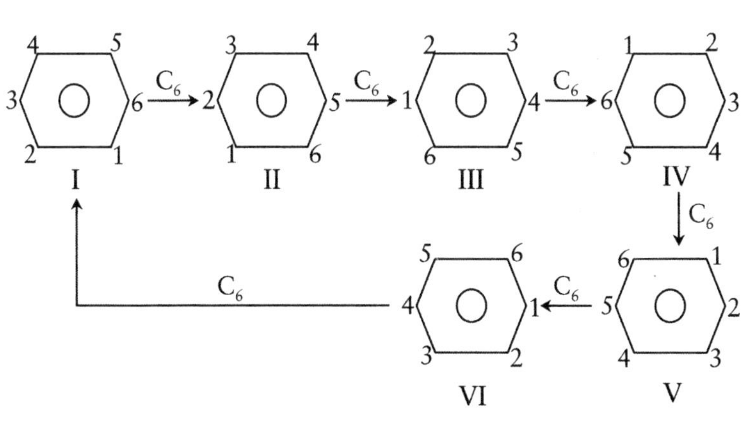

In addition to this there exists possibility of 120° $\left(C_6^2\right)$, 180° $\left(C_6^3\right)$, 240° $\left(C_6^4\right)$ and 300° $\left(C_6^5\right)$ rotations each of them will give equivalent structure. The process C_6^6 gives original configuration and it is identity (E). The 6-fold axis generates six operations:

$$C_6, C_6^2, C_6^3, C_6^4, C_6^5 \text{ and } C_6^6 \equiv E.$$

It also generates anti-clockwise rotations which have been identified with clockwise rotations. This brings some additional informations as well:

$$C_6^2 = C_6.C_6 = 2C_6 = 2 \times 60^\circ = 120^\circ = C_3$$
$$C_6^3 = C_6.C_6.C_6 = 3C_6 = 3 \times 60^\circ = 180^\circ = C_2$$
$$C_6^4 = C_6.C_6.C_6.C_6 = 4C_6 = 4 \times 60^\circ = 240^\circ$$
$$= 2 \times 120^\circ = 2C_3$$
$$= C_3^2$$

$$\begin{array}{cccccc} C_6, & C_6^2, & C_6^3, & C_6^4, & C_6^5, & C_6^6 \equiv E. \\ & ||| & ||| & ||| & & \\ & C_3 & C_2 & C_3^2 & & \end{array}$$

The z-axis is also C_3 & C_2 axes.

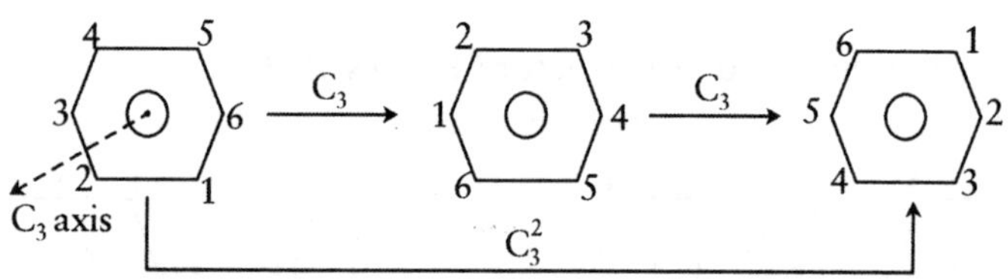

It generates, C_3, C_3^2 and E $\left(\equiv C_3^3\right)$.

A rotation of 180° about z-axis also gives equivalent structure:

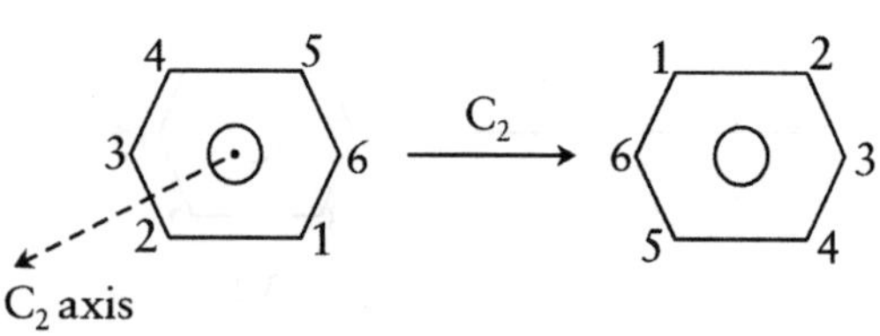

We now conclude it as follows:

C_6 axis is perpendicular to the molecular plane which is coincident with C_3 and C_2 axes.

There are six more C_2 axes, three of them pass through the C-C bond and rest three diagonally opposed carbon atoms.

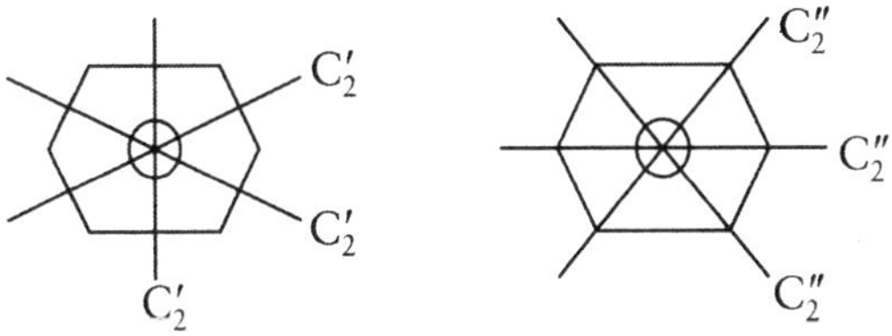

Let us practice with few more examples of common interest. Consider ethylene C_2H_4. The structure may be shown as:

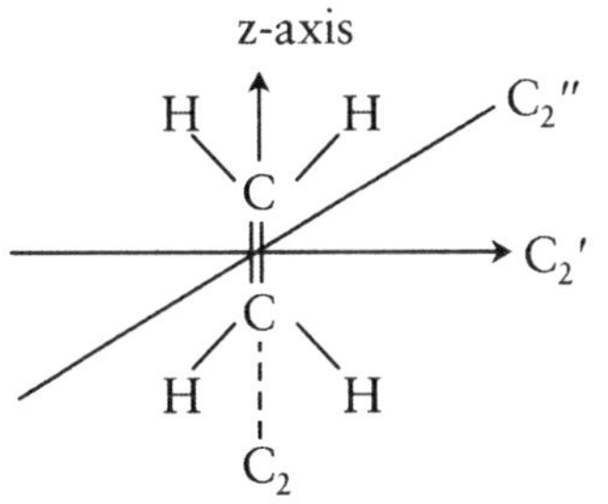

The line passing through C-atoms of CH_2 fragments is defined as z-axis. This is first C_2 axis. There are two more C_2 axis. A second C_2 axis (C_2') perpendicular to the molecular plane and bisects the C-C line. A third C_2 axis is perpendicular to C_2 and C_2' and intersects both at the middle point of the C-C line. This is C_2''.

Both allene and naphthalene have three C_2 axes. Allene resembles C_2H_4.

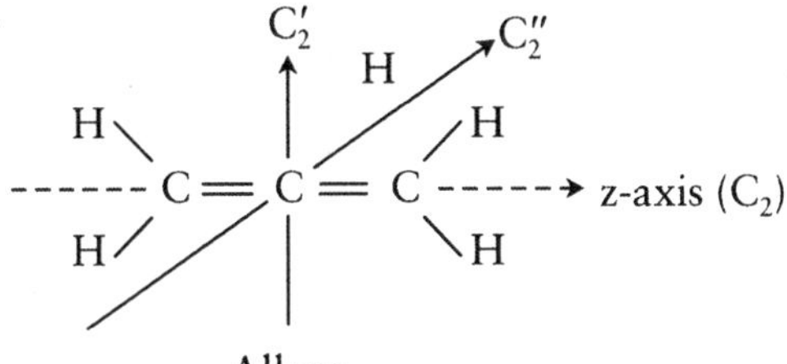

Allene

Naphthalene is a planar molecule its molecular plane is xy. Both x and y axes serve as C_2 axis. Moreover, z-axis is perpendicular to the xy plane and it is a third C_2 axis.

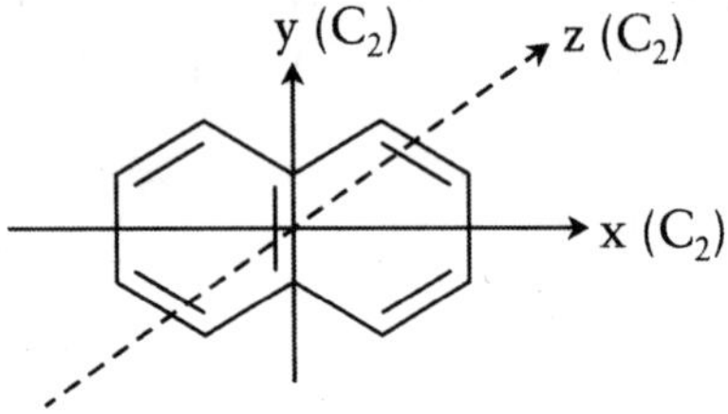

Thus, we have three C_2 axes in it.

Consider case of non-planar molecules.

For example, water is a non-planar molecule.

The three axes are defined as:

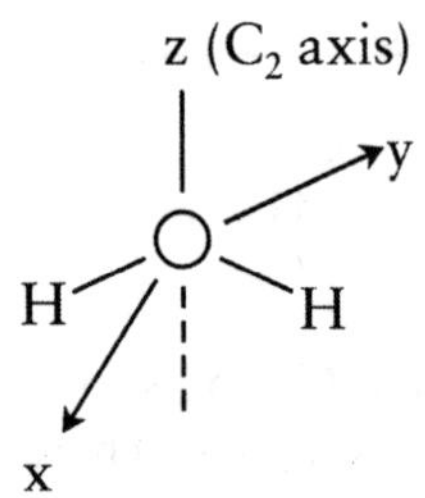

The principal axis is C_2 axis which is coincident with z-axis. The z-axis passes through the central O-atom which bisects the H—Ô—H angle.

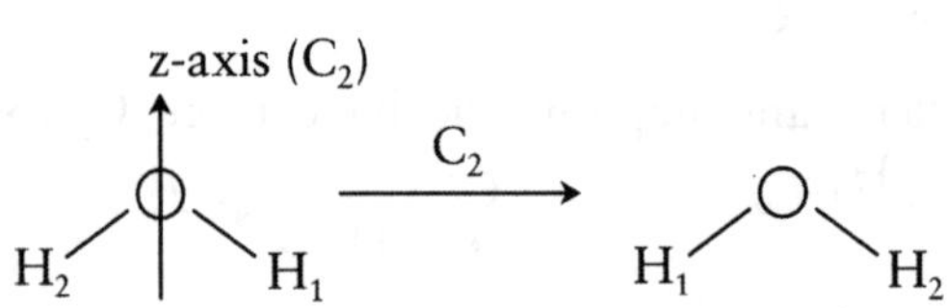

Ammonia is another non-planar molecule. The z-axis is passing through the nitrogen atom and the centre of the triangular base formed by three H-atoms.

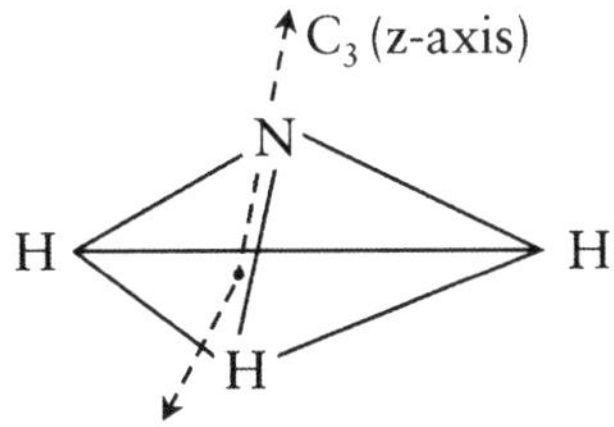

A rotation of $\frac{360^\circ}{3} = 120^\circ$ brings the equivalent structure. During 360° rotation the molecule repeats itself thrice. Indistinguishable structure is also obtained by a rotation of 240°.

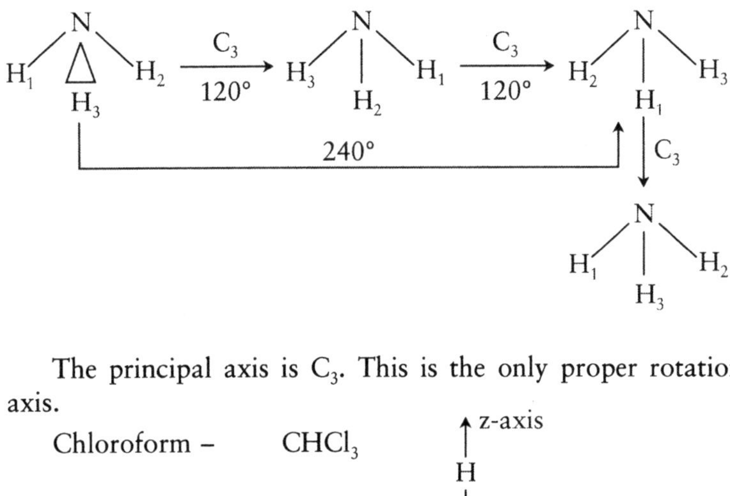

The principal axis is C_3. This is the only proper rotation axis.

Chloroform – $CHCl_3$

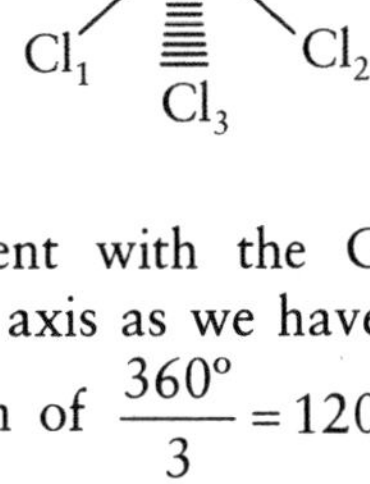

We define z-axis coincident with the C-H bond. The clockwise rotation requires C_3 axis as we have three identical Cl-atoms. Therefore a rotation of $\frac{360^\circ}{3} = 120^\circ$ is performed thrice giving 360°.

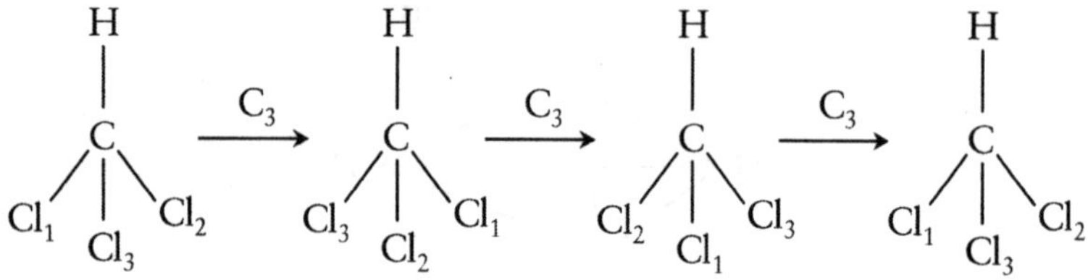

Thus, we have C_3^2 or 240° rotation other than C_3 (120°) and C_3^3 (≡ E).

Methyl Chloride CH_3Cl.

Here C – Cl axis is defined as z-axis.

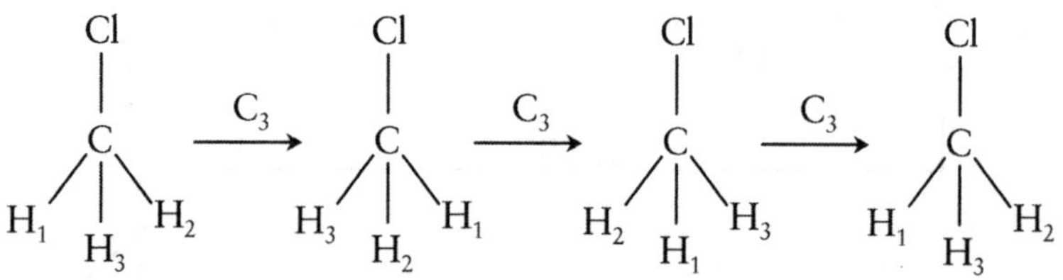

There are three equivalent H-atoms giving rotation of $\frac{360^\circ}{3} = 120^\circ$. It has a C_3 axis. The molecule is regenerated by the process C_3^3.

Choice of z-axis

z-axis is defined as follows:

(a) If there is only one rotational axis, viz. H – Cl → z-axis, C – O → z-axis. H – H → z-axis the molecular axis is considered as z-axis.

(b) If there are two or more Cn axis one of the highest order is taken as z-axis.

(c) If there are many rotational axis of highest order, the axis passing through the minimum number of atoms present is the z-axis.

In CH_3Cl, there are three H-atoms. One C and one Cl atoms. Thus, the z-axis must pass through the minimum number of atoms present in the molecule, i.e. C & Cl both.

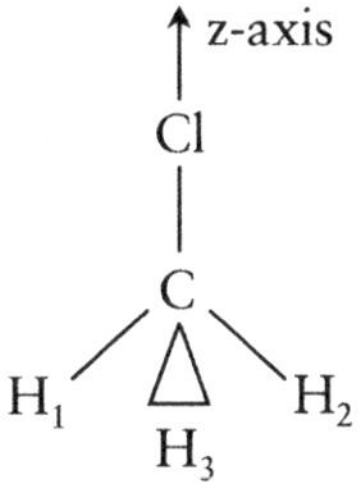

Linear molecules:

In such case molecular axis is defined as bond axis. We encounter two types of linear molecules. H_2, CO_2, H–C ≡ C–H with identical ends. CO, HCl with no like atoms.

In C – O → z-axis rotation by any angle about z-axis will bring equivalent structures. Thus, there can be C_∞ axis coincident with z-axis. However, in case of H_2, CO_2 or acetylene there can be exchange of like atoms.

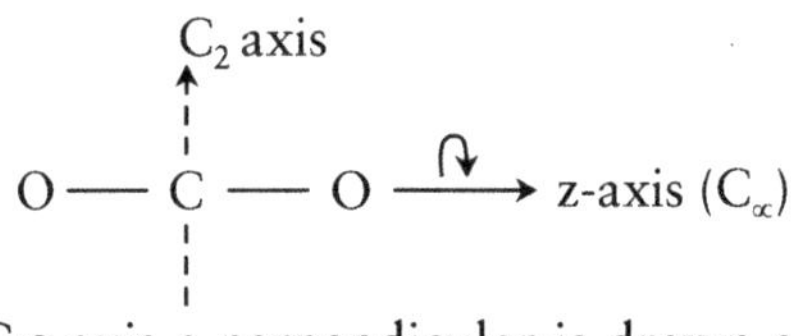

For each C∝ axis a perpendicular is drawn on it and everytime we get a C_2 axis. There are ∝ C_2 axis.

Illustration

Find proper rotation axis in B_2H_6, $CO(NH_2)_2$ C_2H_6 (staggered), C_2H_6 (eclipse), Ferrocene, Mn_2 $(CO)_{10}$.

B_2H_6: There are two BH_2 fragments which are joined together through B — H — B bridges one below and the other above the B – B –axis.

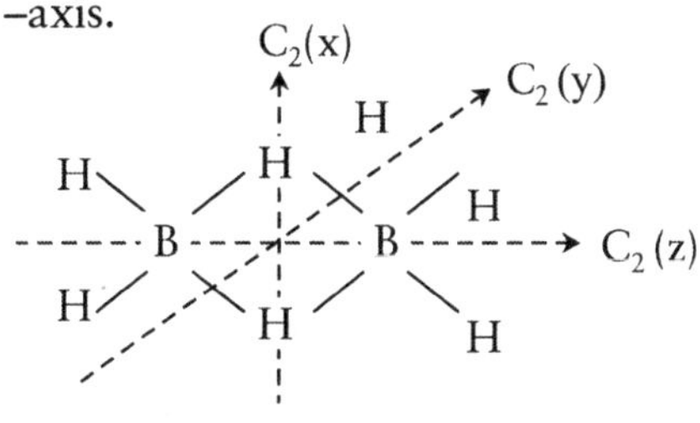

For each BH_2 unit there is C_2 axis bisecting the terminal $H - \hat{B} - H$ angles. The two such units are joined together in B_2H_6. There are three C_2 axes being mutually perpendicular which represent cartesian co-ordinate axes x, y, z. We prefer the line that passes through B-B atoms to be z-axis.

Urea:

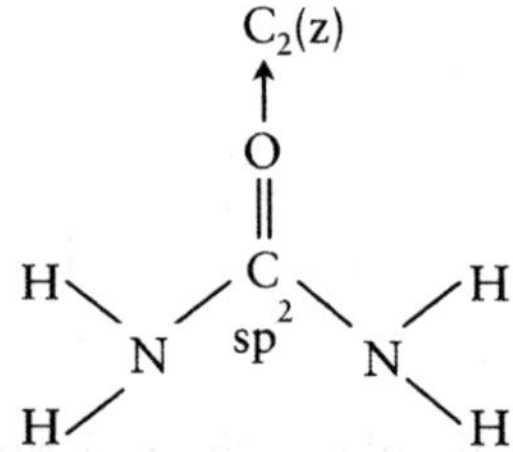

Carbon atom is planar (sp^2). The C—O line bisects $N - \hat{C} - N$ angle and hence there is a presence of C_2 (z) axis like water and ethylene oxide.

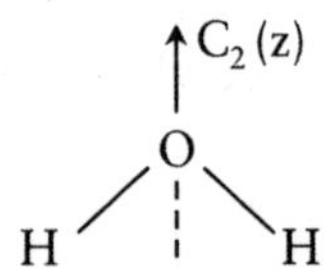

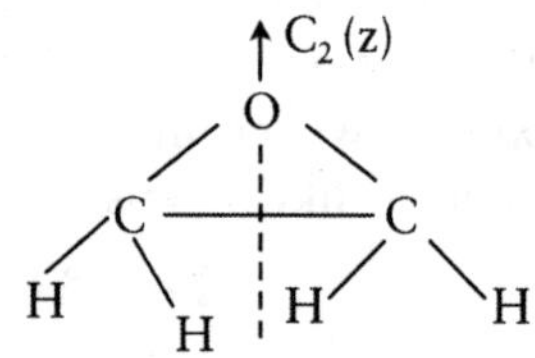

Ethane (Staggered):

We can visualise it as:

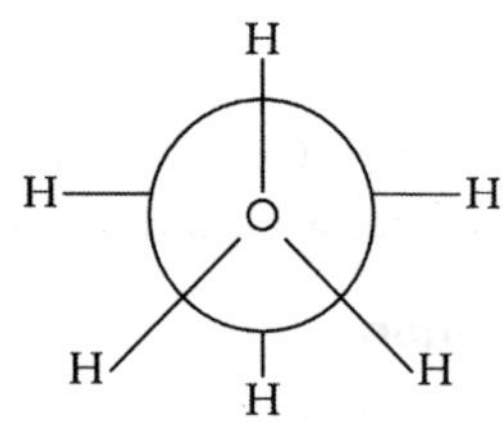

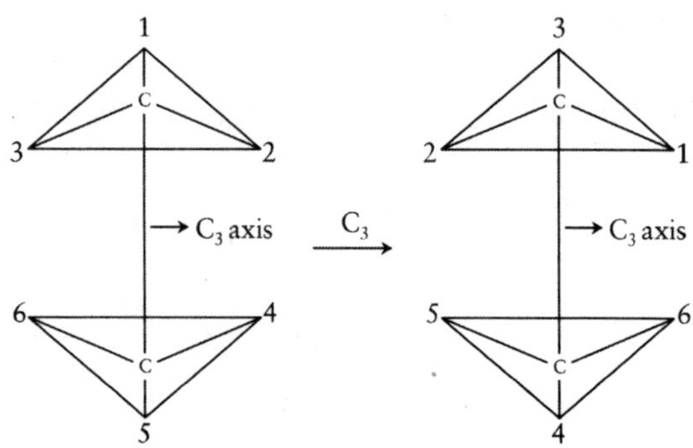

The C—C line is a C_3 axis and it is not C_6. This represents the principal axis. There are three C_2 axes along x, y and z axes and perpendicular to C_3 axis that pass through the mid point of the C-C bond.

Ethane (eclipse):

It has been shown as,

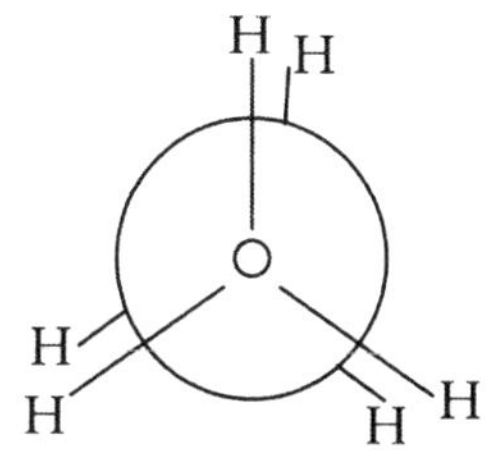

The C – C line is considered to be the C_3 axis. It does not have C_6. There are three C_2 axes.

Ferrocene: There are two conformers.

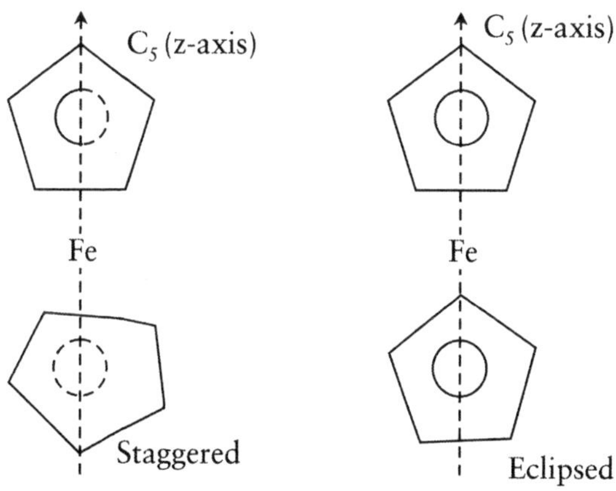

For each C_5H_5 unit we have $2\pi/5=72°$ rotation in either case. So the line passing through the centre of $C_5H_5^-$ ring and iron is C_5 axis. This is perpendicular to the ring also. The principal axis is C_5 and not C_{10}. There are five C_2 axes each of them passes through Fe atom and diagonally opposed C-atoms of the two rings. All the five C_2 axes lie perpendicular to C_5 axis.

$Mn_2\ (CO)_{10}$:

Its structure may be shown as:

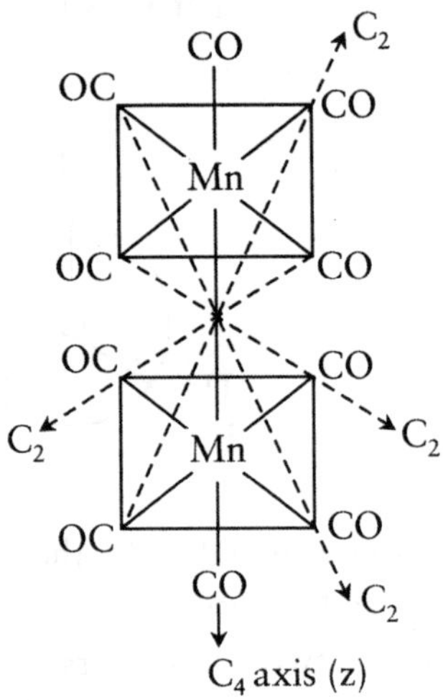

There are two Mn $(CO_5)^-$ moieties with 4CO groups at the corners of square, the fifth one at the top of the square pyramid. Thus only four of them can be interchanged. As such there is a presence of C_4 axis passing through the Mn centres perpendicular to the square base in each moiety. This C_4 axis represents Mn-Mn axis.

There are four C_2 axes which represent lines by joining CO groups from the two Mn $(CO)^-_5$ moiety. These lines pass through the centre of gravity on Mn-Mn axis.

2.6 REFLECTION (σ)

Reflection of all atoms through a plane passing through the molecule. The imaginary plane is treated as a mirror giving image behind it. The plane of symmetry (abbreviated σ) bisects the molecule into two equivalent parts one part being mirror image of the other. There can be three different sets of planes — vertical, horizontal and dihedral. σv-represents vertical plane, one containing the principal axis (z-axis) and perpendicular to xy plane. σ_h - represents a horizontal plane perpendicular to the principal axis. σ_d - represents a dihedral plane, one which bisects two adjacent 2-fold axes.

We begin with water molecule, an example of non-planar molecule so no σ_h.

There can be a vertical plane bisecting H-$\hat{O}$-H angle and includes only O-atom. This is the xz plane. This leaves the O atom fixed and allows to exchange the H-atoms. This is perpendicular to the molecular plane.

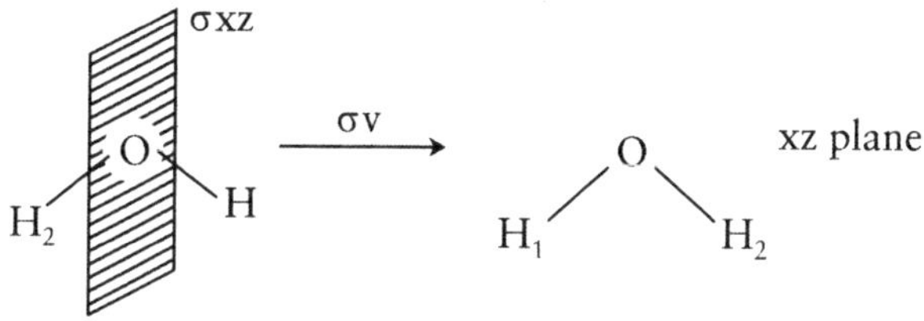

There is another plane in which both the two H-atoms and O-atom lie. This is regarded as yz plane.

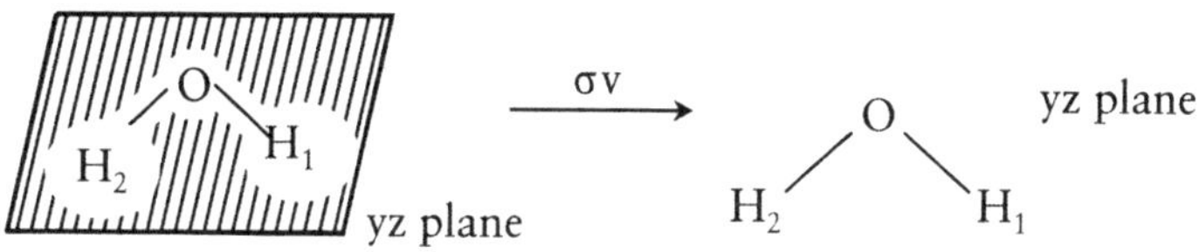

Reflection through σ_{yz} (molecular plane) leaves all the atoms unaffected. As both the planes are vertical to C_2 axis, σ_{XZ} and σ_{yz} are vertical planes σ_V and σ_V':

Methyl Chloride, CH_3Cl

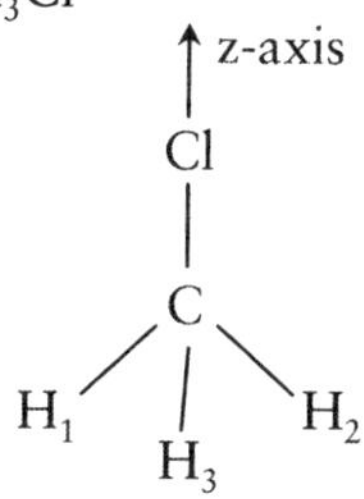

It has three σ's, one defined by each of the sets of points H-C-Cl.

$$\left.\begin{array}{l} \sigma_1 : H_1 - C - Cl \\ \sigma_2 : H_2 - C - Cl \\ \sigma_3 : H_3 - C - Cl \end{array}\right\} 3\sigma\text{'s}$$

As each of them is containing principal axis of rotation, we refer them as σ_v's $(\sigma_v, \sigma'_v, \sigma''_v)$ or $(\sigma_1, \sigma_2, \sigma_3)$

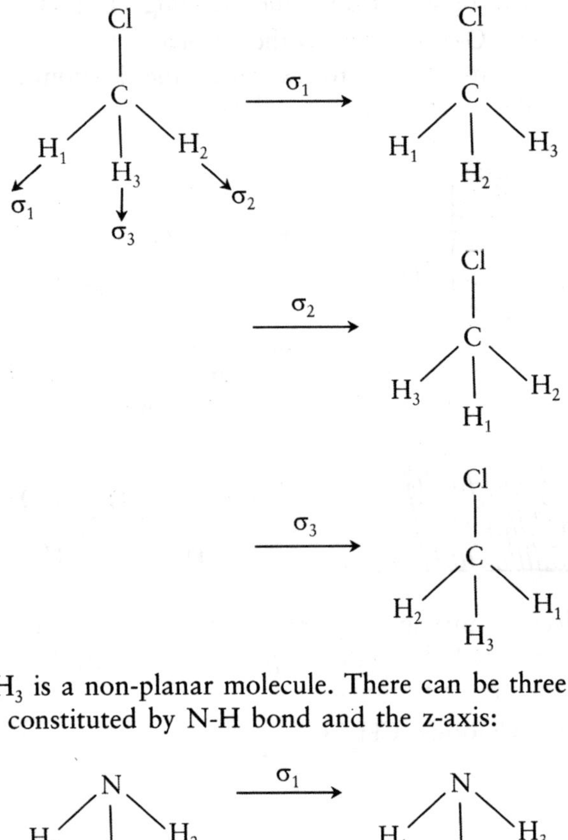

NH_3 is a non-planar molecule. There can be three vertical planes constituted by N-H bond and the z-axis:

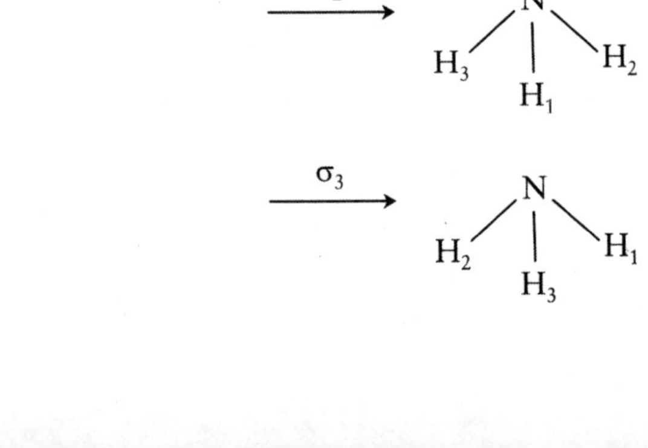

BF_3 is a planar molecule. It has a molecular plane perpendicular to C_3 axis. This is σ_h.

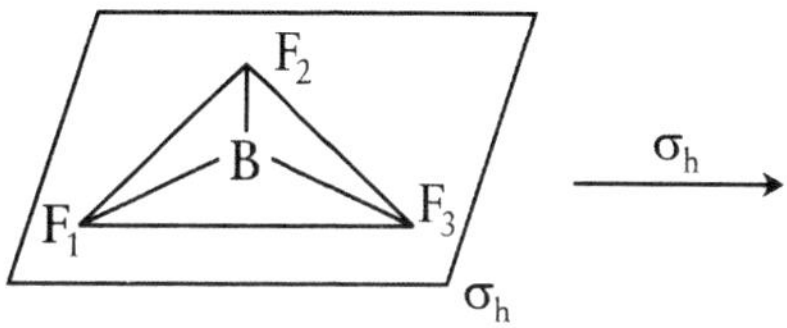

There are three vertical planes containing B-F bond and C_3 axis:

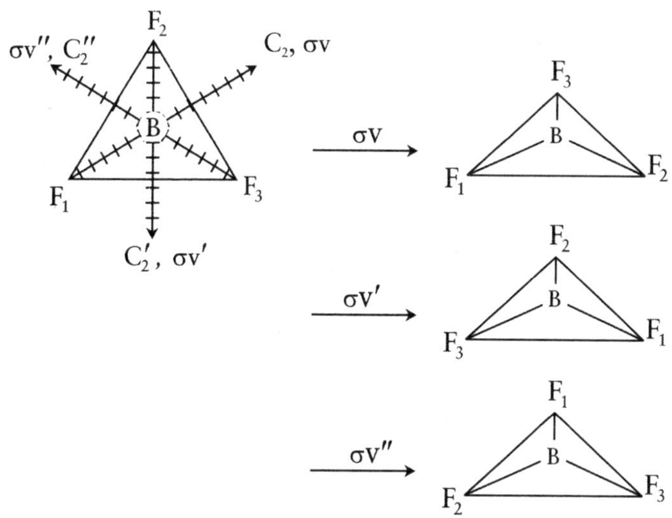

C_2H_4. It has a molecular plane σ_h.

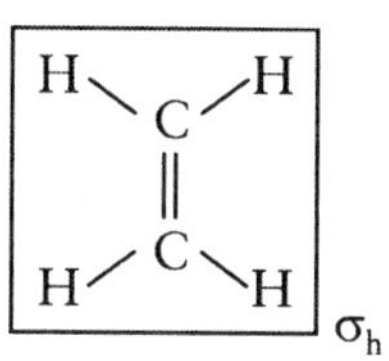

There is only σ_h in trans 1, 2 - dichloro ethylene.

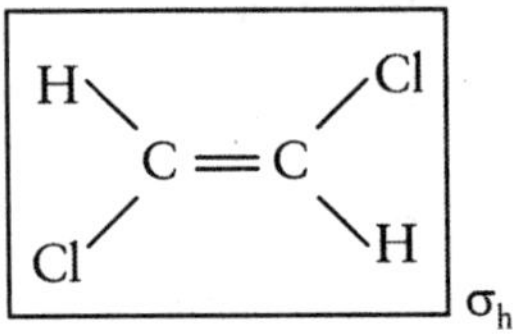

Allene: There are three C_2 axes. The line that passes through C = C = C represents z-axis.

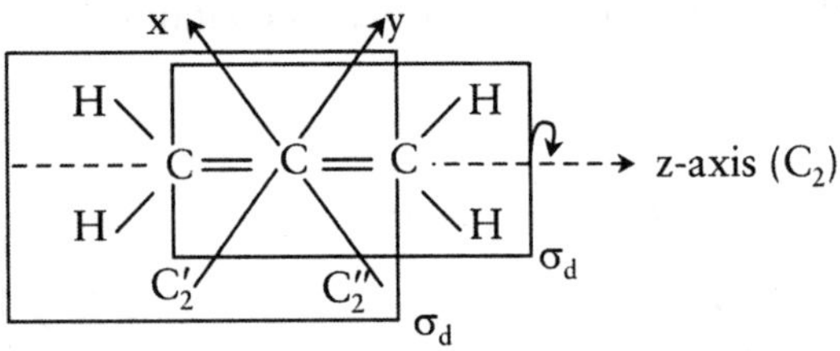

There are two dihedral planes (σ_d). Each σ_d contains two H-atoms at one carbon centre and the principal axis. C_2' & C_2'' are at 45° to the dihedral planes.

$PtCl_4^{2-}$ - ion

It is a planar system. It has molecular plane σ_h $\perp^v$ to C_4 axis.

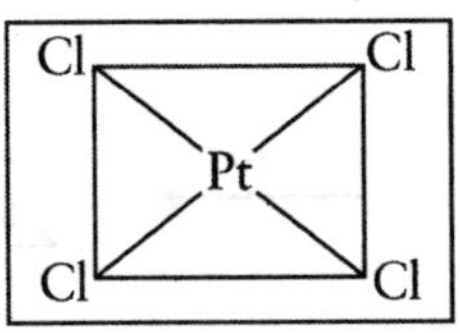

There exist four vertical planes corresponding to four C_2 axis two of them are dihedral planes which bisect C_2 axis.

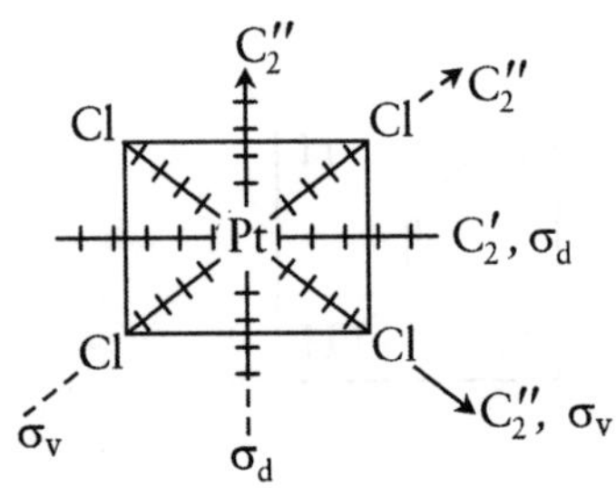

This is an example having σ_h, two σ_v and two σ_d planes.

Benzene

The molecule lies in the xy plane which is the molecular plane (σ_h).

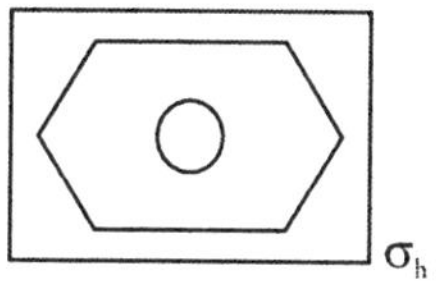

There are six vertical planes (σ_v) containing C_6 axis.

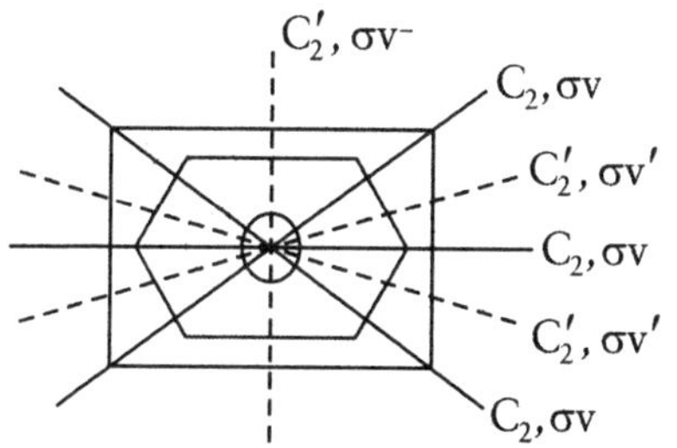

B_2H_6

There are three mutually perpendicular planes σ_{XY}, σ_{XZ}, and σ_{YZ}. The plane perpendicular to z-axis is σ_h plane (σ_{xy}), the remaining two planes namely σ_{XZ} and σ_{YZ} are vertical planes σ_v and $\sigma_{v'}$.

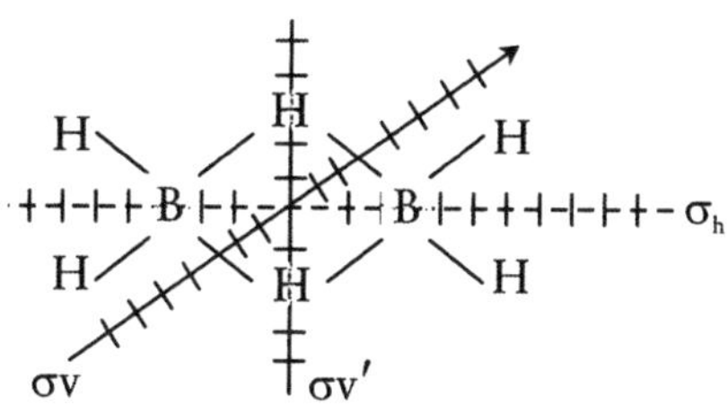

Ethane (staggered).

It does not have a plane perpendicular to C_3 aixs. Thus there is no molecular plane like σ_h. But there are three vertical mirror planes each containing two trans C-H bonds. All of them are dihedral planes as there are three C_2 axes. A pair of C_2 axes can be bisected by each such plane.

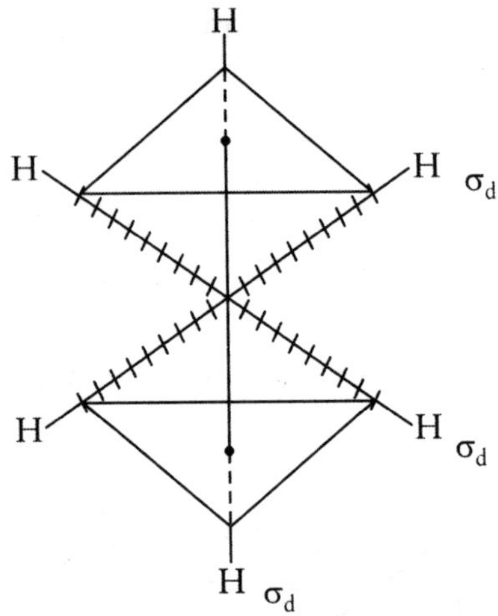

Ethane (eclipsed).

There exists a molecular plane $\perp^{v}$ to the C_3 axis, i.e. σ_h. Besides σ_h we have three σ_v's.

Consider $SOCl_2$ and SOF_2.

We can show their structure as follows:

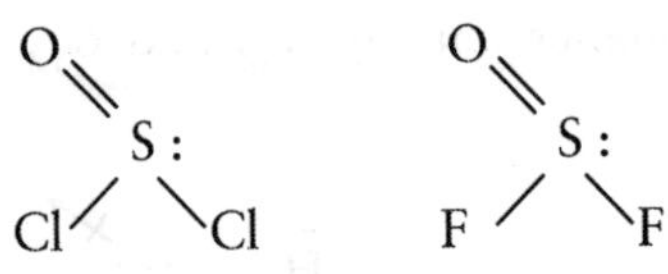

There is no proper axis of rotation. Thus it does not have C_2. There is only σ. This symmetry plane passes through S and O-atoms and is perpendicular to a plane comprising Cl, Cl, O or F, F, O respectively.

Boric acid,

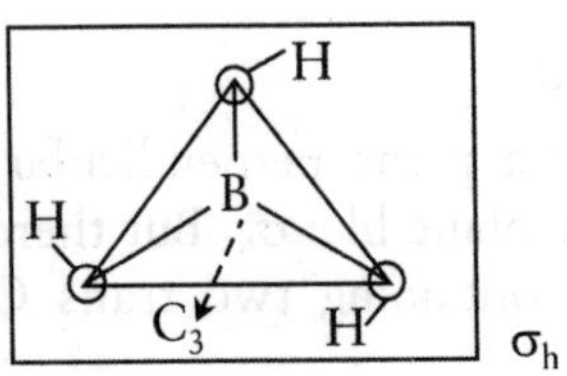

It has z-axis as C_3 axis passing throgh B-atom. The plane σ_h is perpendicular to C_3. It lacks three C_2 axes as in BO_3^{-3} and there is no σ_v as such present in the molecule.

2.7 IMPROPER ROTATION (S_n)

Improper rotation comprises proper rotation plus reflection. First part is proper rotation about some axis and its second part is reflection in a plane perpendicular to that axis. Thus, first C_n is applied followed by σ_h. Since C_n is perpendicular to σ_h so it is horizontal plane that is considered here and not σ_v $C_n\sigma_h = S_n$. The S_1 element has $S_1=C_1\sigma_h = \sigma_h$ simply.

For S_2 we have both C_2 & σ_h etc.

For improper axis there should be a proper axis (C_n) and a plane perpendicular to C_n that exists, then S_n must be there.

In trans-1, 2 dichloroethylene the line joining two carbon centres is regarded as x-axis. Although exchange of H and Cl atoms at each C centre is not permitted in symmetry consideration but for the sake of convenience we can imagine it as C_2 axis (It may be remembered that there is only one C_2 axis $\perp^r$ to x-axis which is also z-axis, this is permitted to exchange two H-atoms as well as two Cl atoms. Rotate the molecule about C_2 (x) axis. This gives a new orientation.

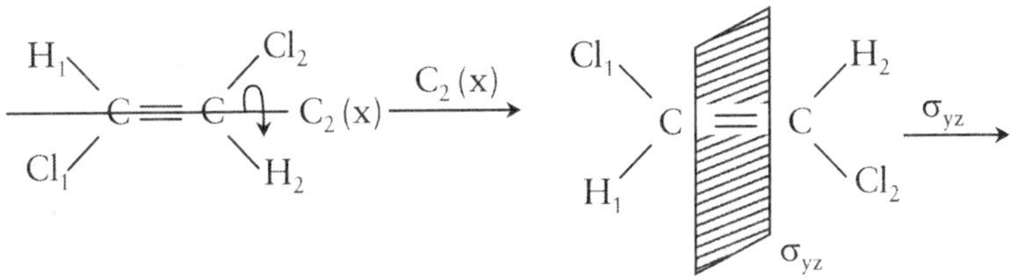

We then apply reflection in σ_{yz} that lies at right angle to x-axis. This places the chlorine atoms as follows:

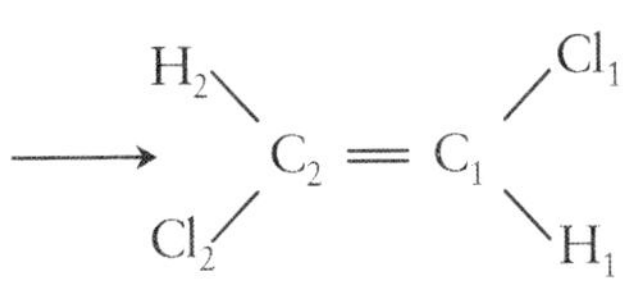

The same result is described by improper rotation S_2. $C_2\sigma = S_2$.

We find that if i is applied we get same result.

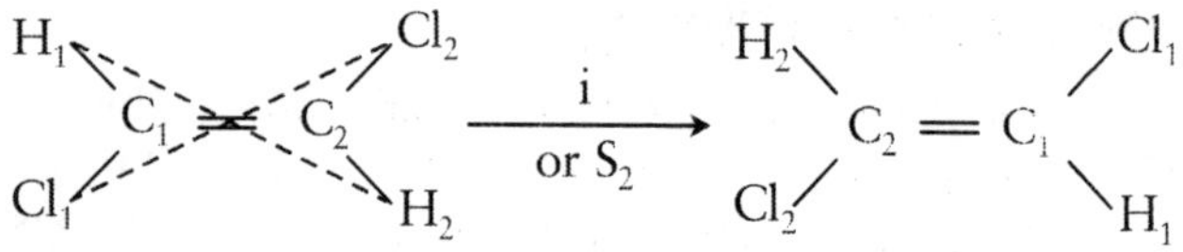

Naturally $S_2 = i$. There exists S_2 axis collinear with C_2.

The number of configurations generated in case of improper rotation is not fixed. This is given by S_n^k where k = 2n when n is odd and k = n for even value of n. The presence of S_3 axis implies k = 2 × 3 = 6 operations.

For the process $C_3\sigma_h = S_3$. Six generating operations are:

$$S_3, S_3^2, S_3^3, S_3^4, S_3^5, S_3^6.$$

$$S_3^2 = C_3^2.\sigma_h^2 = C_3^2.E = C_3^2$$

$$S_3^3 = C_3^3.\sigma_h^3 = E.(\sigma_h)^2.\sigma_h = E.E.\sigma_h = \sigma_h$$

$$S_3^4 = C_3^4.\left(\sigma_h^2\right)^2 = C_3^3 . C_3 . (E)^2 = E . C_3 = C_3$$

Since, $\sigma^2 = \sigma.\sigma = E$

$$S_3^6 = C_3^6.\left(\sigma_h^2\right)^3 = \left(C_3^3\right)^2\left(\sigma_h^2\right)^3 = (E)^2\,(E)^3 = E$$

There can be six operations for S_6 ($S_6 = C_6\,\sigma_h$). These are:

$$S_6$$

$$S_6^2 = C_6^2.(\sigma_h)^2 = C_3$$

$$S_6^3 = C_6^3 . (\sigma_h)^3 = C_2 . \sigma_h . E = C_2\,\sigma_h = S_2 = i$$

$$S_6^4 = C_6^4.\left(\sigma_h^2\right)^2 = C_3.C_3\,(E)^2 = C_3^2$$

$$S_6^5 = C_6^5\,(\sigma_h)^5$$

$$S_6^6 = C_6^6\,(\sigma_h)^6 = E . E = E$$

Improper rotation in BF_3 and $PtCl_4^{2-}$ ion.

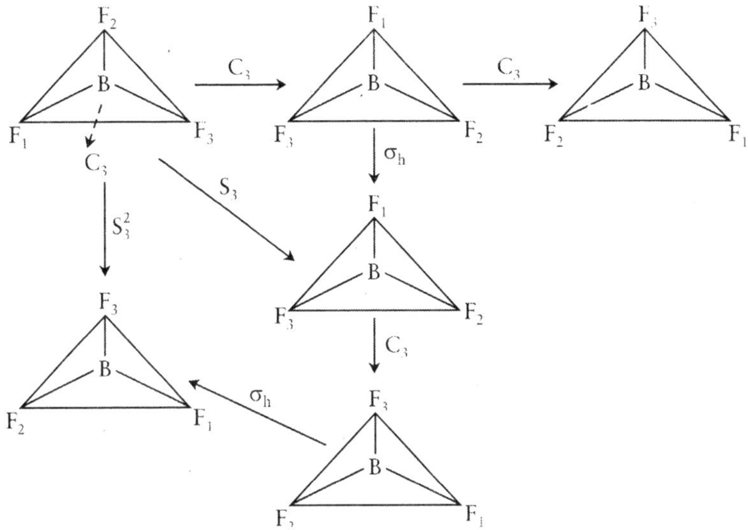

Obviously, $S_3^2 = C_3^2$.

$PtCl_4^{2-}$ contains C_4 as proper rotation axis. It has a plane perpendicular to the principal axis. This is σ_h plane. Hence S_4 must be there.

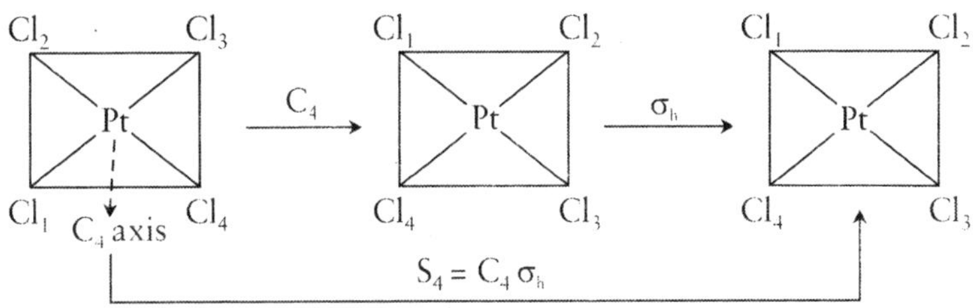

The S_4 axis is collinear with C_4 and generates only two such operations, namely S_4 and S_4^3 equivalent to $2S_4$.,

Staggered and eclipsed conformations of ethane possess improper rotation. The former does not have σ_h or C_6 by itself symmetry operation but combination of both is S_6 that exists.

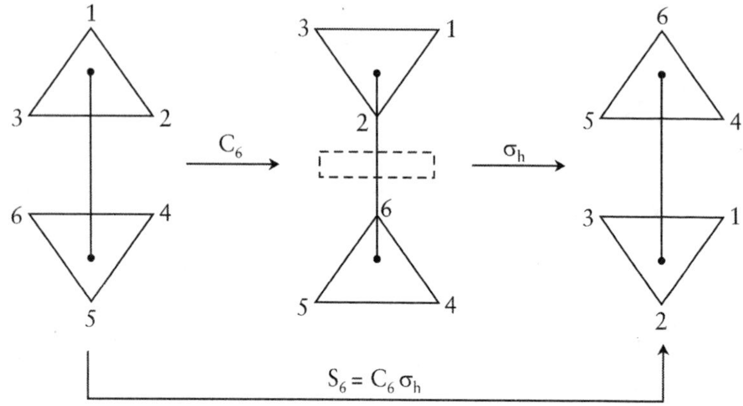

S_6 axis is collinear with the C_3 axis. Both C_3 and σ_h are present in eclipsed ethane. It has $S_3 = C_3\ \sigma_h$ collinear with C_3 axis generating $2S_3$ operations.

Allene does not have C_4 and σ_h yet it contains S_4 axis giving two such operations.

$$C_4\ \sigma_h = S_4.$$

Such as $2S_4$. The S_4 axis is collinear with C_2 (z)

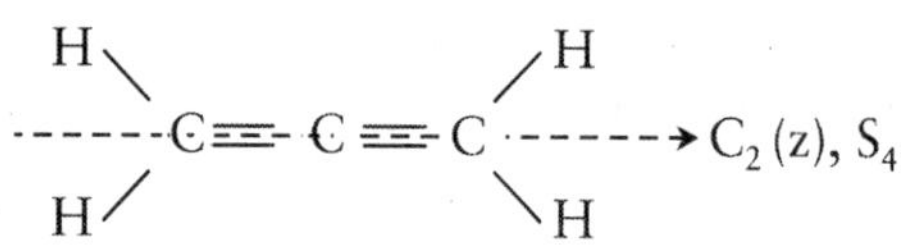

Ferrocene (Staggered).

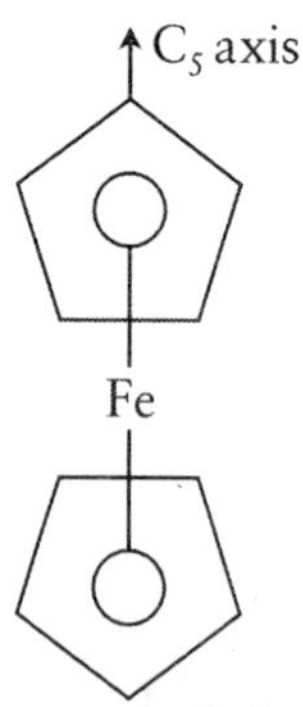

It has no σ_h and there would be no S_5 axis. We can imagine a combined effect of $C_{10}\sigma_h = S_{10}$. A rotation of 36°

followed by reflection in so-called σ_h can give the result which is equal to S_{10}.

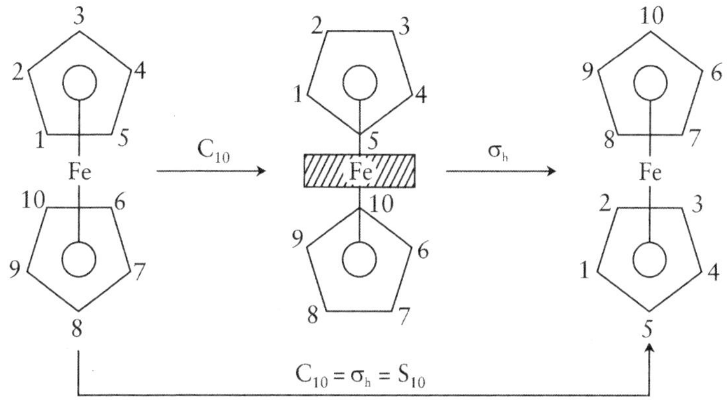

It has S_{10} axis collinear with C_5.

S_{10} generates $S_{10}, S_{10}^2 = C_5, S_{10}^3, S_{10}^4 = C_5^2,$

$S_{10}^5 = E, S_{10}^3 = C_5^3, S_{10}^7, S_{10}^8 = C_5^4, S_{10}^9, S_{10}^{10} = E$

$= 2S_{10}$ & $2S_{10}^3$.

2.8 INVERSION (i)

The inversion centre is given the symbol i. It represents reflection of all atoms through a point in the molecule. If a straight line is drawn through the centre and it encounters similar atoms which are equidistant from the centre, then the operation is called inversion. Consider a point P (x, y, z) lying in first quadrangle. It generates P″ (–x, –y, –z) after the process of inversion is applied.

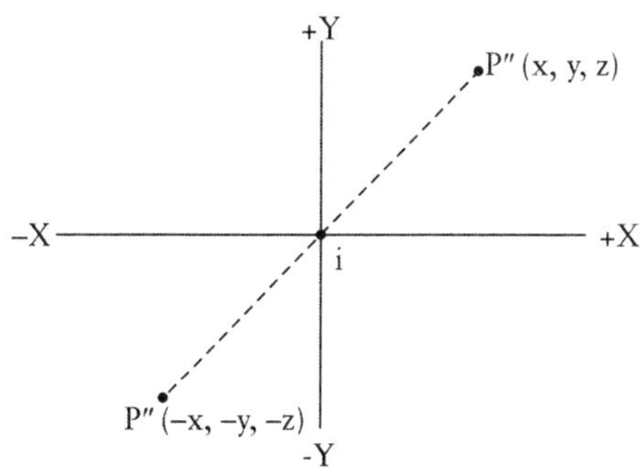

Consider C of CO_2 molecule lying at origin with two O atoms in first and third quadrangles respectively.

Consider a point P (x, y, z)

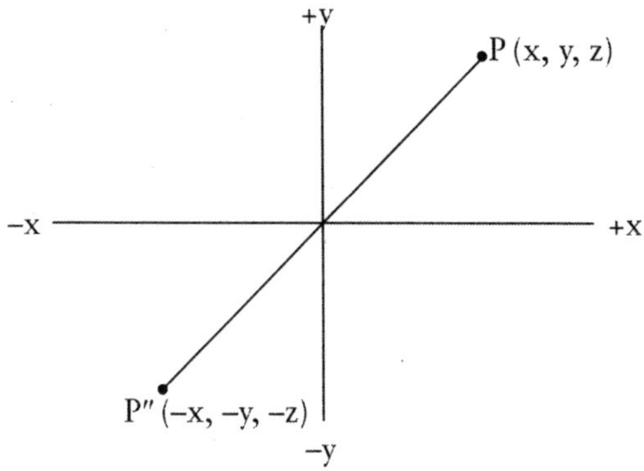

Inversion operation (i) generates only P″ (–x, –y, –z) from P (x, y, z). There must be even member of atoms for the presence of i. For instance take the case of CO_2. It is linear O=C=O, oxygen atoms occur in pair, which lie on the straight line passing through centre of gravity of the molecule that is C-atom. We notice that one half of the molecule is generated by the other half.

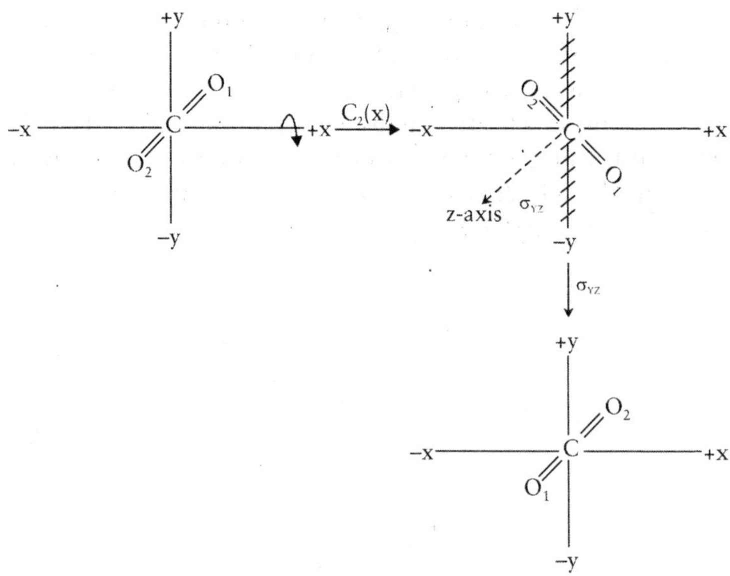

z-axis is perpendicular to the xy plane and passes through C-atom. We perform C_2 operation about x-axis followed by reflection in 6_{YZ}. This brings inversion in the orientation of the molecule.

Thus, $C_2\sigma = i$. But $C_2\sigma = S_2$.

Hence, $C_2\sigma = S_2 = i$.

We do not bother for i if odd member of atoms are present around the centre.

When n is even $i^n = E$ $i^2 = E$

When n is odd $i^n = i$

Ethylene, trans -1, 2-diclloro ethylene, benzene, Pt Cl_4^{-2}

W $(CO)_6$, Re_2 Cl_8^{-2}, ethane (Staggered), B_2 H_6 contain i.

Ethylene contains centre of symmetry. This is nothing but centre of gravity of the molecule. It so happens in B_2 H_6.

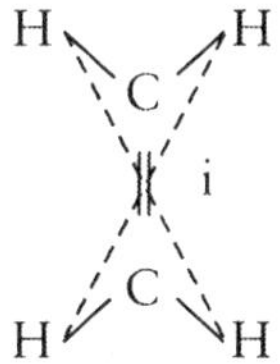

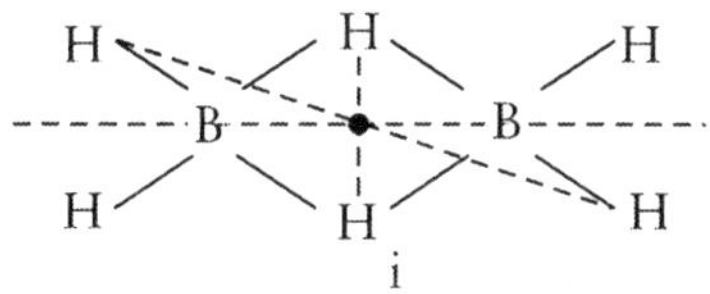

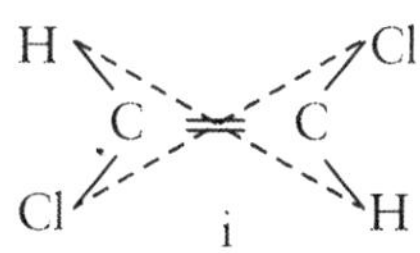

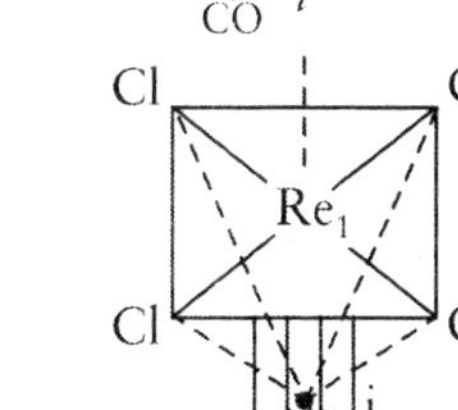

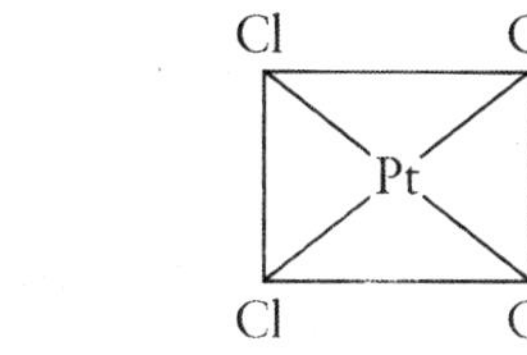

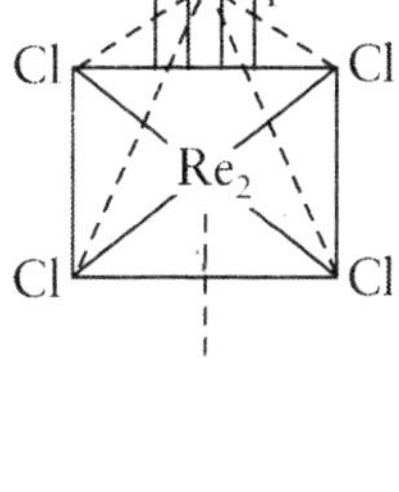

Both $C_5H_5^-$ and AB_4 (Td) do not have i. CCl_4 is Td and it does not possess inversion centre. HCCl = CHBr (cis & trans) does not have i.

Which of the following will have inversion centre hyponitrite ion, 1, 4- dioxane, Ni $(CN)_4^{-2}$ and trans dichloro tetramine Co(II)?

It has i.

$Ni(CN)_4^{-2}$ is diamagnetic with square planar geometry having i.

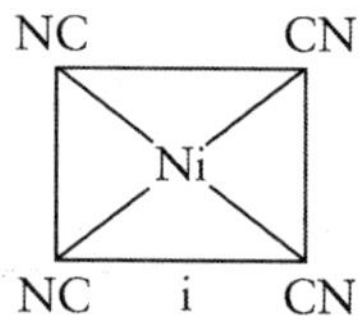

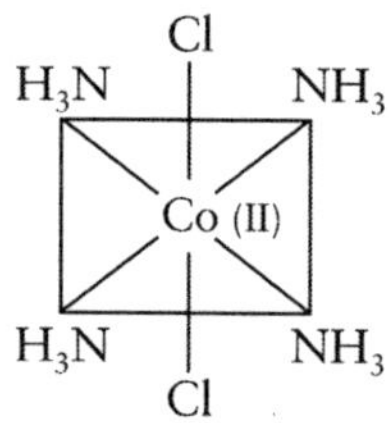

It has i.

2.9 IDENTITY (E)

By exchanging like atoms the process will continue till the original configuration is obtained. We have the case of identity (E). It means nothing is to be done or we can say that the process of getting identical structure is also a symmetry operation. The square of E is also E.

$$E^2 = E$$

$$\sigma^2 = E$$

$$i^2 = E$$

$$C_n^n = E$$

It is one of five symmetry operations. Out of five symmetry operations we associate three such operations in NH_3. It does not have i nor it has Sn as σ_h is absent (being non-planar structure).

1. It has C_3 as proper axis of symmetry.
2. It possesses σ_1, σ_2 and σ_3, i.e. plane of symmetry. These are the vertical planes containing C_3 axis.
3. There is no i.
4. It does not contain Sn.
5. It has identity (E).

In benzene all the five symmetry elements are present

(i) proper axis C_6, C_3, C_2, C_2', C_2''.
(ii) plane of symmetry σ_h & σv's.
(iii) centre of symmetry (i).
(iv) improper axis S_6.
(v) identity (E).

Summary of the Results:—

Consider Pt Cl_4^{-2} ion.

1. It is a planar molecule.
2. Its principal axis is C_4 (z). This serves as C_2 axis as well.
3. There are four more C_2 axes. These are $2C_2'$ and $2C_2''$.
4. There is σ_h $\perp^v$ to C_4 axis.
5. There is S_4 axis which is collinear with C_4 axis.
   $C_4\ \sigma_h = S_4$
6. There are four σ_v coinciding with C_2' & C_2''.
7. It has i.

Benzene is a planar molecule with six membered ring:

1. It has C_6 axis as the principal axis.
2. There are C_3 & C_2 axes collinear with C_6 axis.
3. There are six more C_2 axes, $3C_2'$ & $3C_2''$.
4. It has σ_h $\perp^v$ to C_6 axis.

5. There are six vertical planes along C_2' & C_2''.
6. The presence of σ_h implies $C_6\ \sigma_h = S_6$. Hence it has S_6 axis collinear with C_6 axis.
7. It has i.

Ammonia

It is a non-planar molecule.

1. It has C_3 axis as the principal axis.
2. There are three σ_v's.
3. It does not have S_n.
4. It has no σ_h.
5. The molecule lacks i.
6. It has E.

Water

It is a non-planar molecule.

1. It has C_2 axis as the principal axis.
2. There are two vertical planes σv & σv′.
3. It has E.

The two symmetry elements present here are axis of symmetry and plane of symmetry.

Trans — H_2O_2 (planar)

1. It has C_2 axis.
2. It has σ_h $\perp^v$ to C_2.
3. The presence of C_2 & σ_h gives $C_2\ \sigma_h = S_2 = i$.

Thus it has S_2 which is contained in i.

4. It has identity.

Cis — $H_2\ O_2$

1. It has C_2 axis.
2. There is no σ_h.
3. There are two σv's.
4. It has E.

Symmetry operations in $PtCl_4^{-2}$ ion.

1. C_4 axis gives $C_4, C_4^2, C_4^3, C_4^4 = E$

$$C_4^2 = C_2$$

   Thus there are $2C_4$ axis.

2. A C_2 axis collinear with C_4. There are another set of C_2 axes. These are $2C_2'$ and $2C_2''$.
3. It has σ_h, two σv and $2\sigma_d$.
4. It has i.
5. It has improper axis $S_4 = C_4\ \sigma_h$.

The presence of S_4 implies.

$$S_4,\ S_4^2,\ S_4^3,\ S_4^4 = E$$

$$S_4^2 = C_4^2\ \sigma^2 = C_2$$

It generates $2S_4$, i.e. S_4 and S_4^3 as distinct operations.

Altogether we have

E, $2C_4$, C_2, $2C_2'$, $2C_2''$, σ_h, i, $2\sigma v$, $2\sigma d$, $2S_4$, h = 16.

Symmetry operations in BCl_3.

1. It is a planar molecule with C_3 as its principal axis. It generates C_3 & $C_3^2 = 2C_3$.
2. There are three C_2 axis, $3C_2$.
3. It has $\sigma_h \perp^v$ to C_3.
4. There are three vertical planes $3\sigma v$.
5. The presence of C_3 & σ_h leads to another operation S_3 which generates the following operations:

S_3, S_3^2, S_3^3, S_3^4, S_3^5 and S_3^6

$$S_3^2 = C_3^2\sigma^2 = C_3^2$$

$$S_3^3 = C_3^3\sigma^3 = \sigma$$

$$S_3^4 = C_3^4.(\sigma^2)^2 = C_3$$

$$S_3^6 = C_3^6\ (\sigma^2)^3 = \left(C_3^3\right)^2 \left(\sigma^2\right)^3 = E$$

Hence distinct operations are $2S_3$.

This leaves with the molecule the following operations:

E, $2C_3$, $3C_2$, σ_h, $3\sigma v$, $2S_3$, h = 12.

Benzene

1. It has C_6 axis generating C_6, C_6^2, C_6^3, C_6^4, C_6^5 & $C_6^6 = E$

   $C_6^2 = C_3$, $C_6^3 = C_2$, $C_6^4 = C_3 . C_3 = C_3^2$

   Hence we have C_6 & C_6^5 i.e. $2C_6$ operations associated with C_6 axis.
2. It has C_3 & C_2 collinear with C_6.
3. There are six C_3 axes such as $3C_2'$ and $3C_2''$.
4. It has σ_h and there are six σ_vs.
5. There is i.
6. It has S_6 as improper axis generating S_6 and S_6^5 as distinct operations.

Thus we have,

E, $2C_6$, $2C_3$, C_2, $3C_2'$, $3C_2''$, σ_h, i, $3\sigma v'$, $3\sigma v''$ and $2S_6$, $2S_3$, h = 24.

Also $C_3 \sigma_h = S_3$ giving $2S_3$.

↑ C_2 axis

Acetylene:— – – H — C ≡ C — H – – – z-axis ($C_\propto$)

1. It is a linear molecule. It has $C_\propto$ axis as the z-axis.
2. For every $C_\propto$ axis there corresponds a C_2 axis. In fact there are $\propto C_2$ axes.
3. We can imagine a plane containing the principal axis ($C\propto$). We can have infinite number of such planes ($\propto\sigma_v$).

Illustration

1. Find out the distinct operations out of improper rotation (Sn)?

For the process repeating m times, then $S_n^m = \sigma_h C_n^1$ ...... $\sigma_n C_n^1$ m-times.

$S_n^m = \sigma_n^m C_n^m$ This is because $\sigma_n C_n^1 = C_n^1 \sigma_h$.

When Cn intersects σ_h vertically in that situation the operation S_n occurs when:

(i) m is odd, $\sigma_h^m = \sigma_h$

and $\sigma_h . \sigma_h = \sigma_h^2 = E$

$S_n^m = \sigma_h^m C_n^m = \sigma_h . C_n^m$

(ii) If m is even

$S_n^m = C_n^m , \sigma_h^m = E$

(iii) When n is even $S_n^n = \sigma_h^n C_n^n = E\,E = E$

if n is odd, $S_n^n = \sigma_h^h C_n^n = \sigma_h E = \sigma_h$

when n is odd further we have

$S_n^{n-1} = \sigma_h^{n+} C_n^{n-1} = F . C_n^{n-1} = C_n^{n-1}$

$S_n^{n+1} = \sigma_h^{n+1} C_n^{n+1}$

$= E . C_n^{n+1}$

$= C_n^{n+1}$

Note that n + p

$C_n^{n+p} = C_n^n . C_n^p = E . C_n^p = C_n^p$

2. Symmerty in Buck Minister Fullerenes, C_{60}.

In cabon-60 each carbon atom is going to be sp^2 hybridized having finite C_{11} cages with 12 pentagonal rings supplemented by 20 hexagonal rings. The molecule has been assigned I_h point group.

3. Determine the point group in following cases:
   (i) meridional ML_3abc
   (ii) face ML_3abc
   (iii) trans ML_2abcd
   (iv) cis ML_2abcd
   (v) closo $[B_6\ H_6]^{2-}$ ion
   (vi) closo 1, 2-carborane $B_4C_2H_6$
   (vii) ketene
   (viii) diazomethane

   (i) Mer ML_3abc bears the structure of the form:

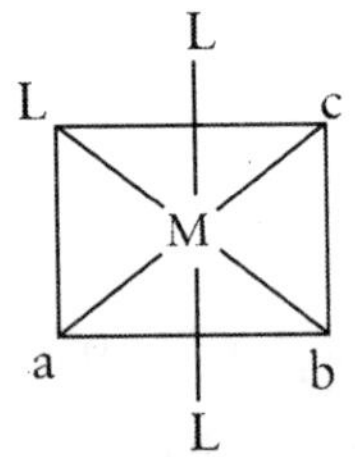

Obviously it has C_{2v} point group with ML_2 unit closer than other one.

   (ii) Fac-ML_3 abc bears the structure as given below:

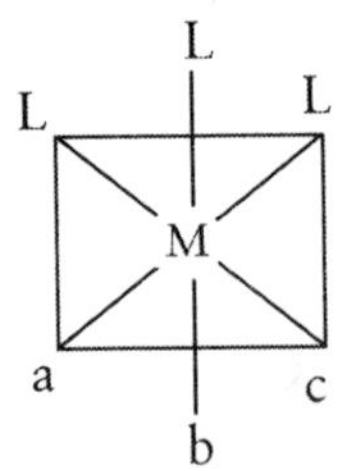

It is analogous to NH_3 with three like atoms such as H in ammonia. Consequently there are three L groups in one part that are exchangeable at 120° rotation. Hence it behaves as anmonia with C_{3v} point group.

(iii) trans ML_2abcd. It has the configuration:

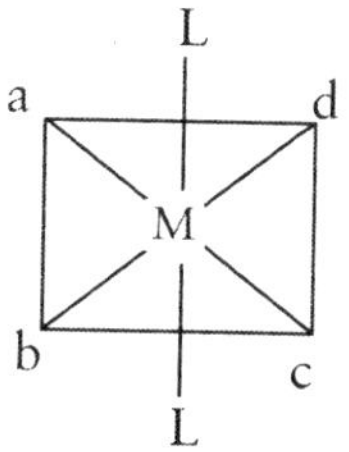

The two ligands on opposite sides along z-axis of an octahedron. The other four atoms abcd are alike giving rise to planar configuration. As such they lead to D_{4h} point group.

(iv) cis ML_2abcd. As two similar ligands are on the same part leading to angular moiety giving rise to C_{2v} point group.

(v) closo-Boron polyhedra such as closo-$B_6H_6^{2-}$ ion. It is just like to O_h system as shown below:

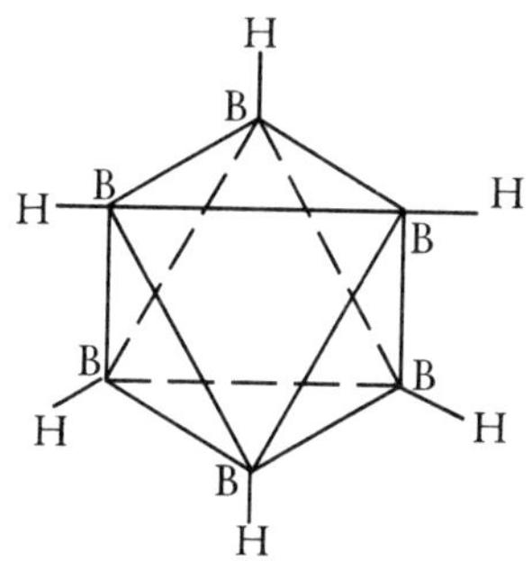

It is perfectly a regular octahedron. As such it has O_h point group.

(vi) It has 1, 2 $B_4C_2H_6$ consisting of 1, 2 carbon atoms on adjacent positions. There is a single C_2 axis passing through the mid point of octahedral edges spanned by two C-atoms with opposite edge of B-atoms. Moreover, it has two σv's first of which is made up of H_2BCH_2 square plane, the second vertical plane is bisecting the octahedron through the two carbon atoms. The line of intersection of these planes results in C_2 axis already counted. Hence the point group symbol is assigned to be C_{2v}.

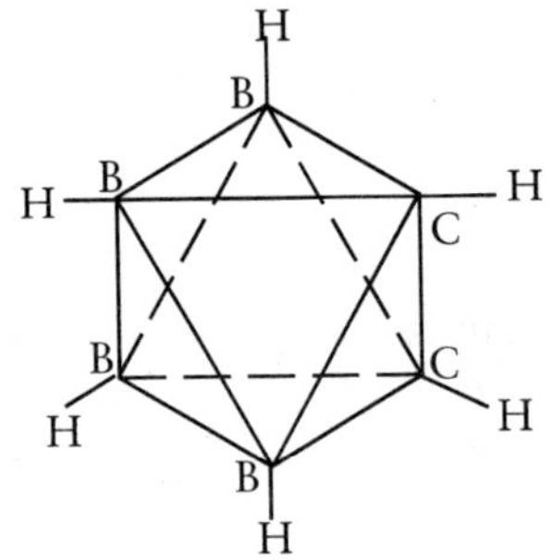

(vii) and (viii) are of C_{2v} point group with the following structures:

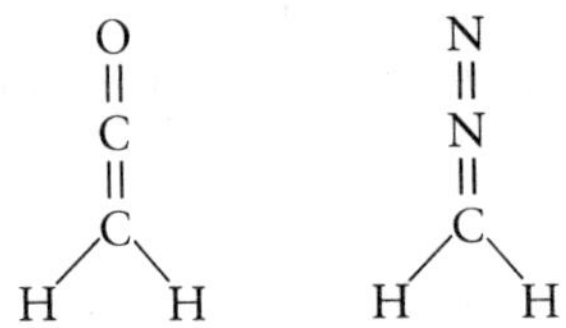

ketene C_{2v} diazomethane with C_{2v} point group

QUESTIONS

1. (a) What are symmetry operations? Give their notations and illustrate with one example in each case.
   (b) Assign symmetry elements present in each case of the following:
   ammonia, $HCCl_3$, C_2H_4, Fe (C_5H_5) $(CO)_3$
2. What is inversion centre? Find the inversion centre in the following:

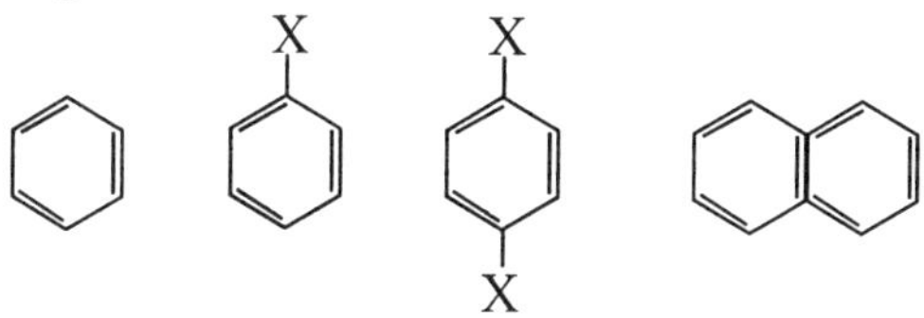

$AuCl^-_4$, CO_2

3. What are proper rotation axes associated with the symmetry operations in H—C≡C—H, H_3BO_3, H—C≡N, $Cr(CO)_6$, Pt Cl_4^{-2}.
4. Answer as indicated:
   (a) Indicate the planes containing allene.
   (b) Presence of inversion centre in $[Co(NO_2)_6]^{-3}$ and $[Co\ (NO_2)_5Cl]^{-3}$.
   (c) Sketch the different types of planes in benzene.
   (d) Number of distinct improper rotations in BF_3 and CH_4.
5. Explain the terms:
   (i) Molecular symmetry. (ii) symmetry elements.
   (iii) Symmetry operations. (iv) dihedralplane. (v) inversion centre. (vi) improper rotation.
6. What do the symbols mean?
   (a) σ_h (b) σ_v (c) σ_d (d) S_4 (e) C_n
7. Find distinct symmetry operations in $Fe(CO)_5$, $(CH_3)_2$ PF_3, Ni $(CN)_4^{2-}$, Co $(en)_3^{3+}$,

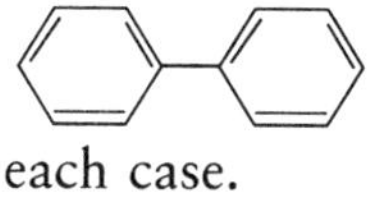

Identify principal axis in each case.

8. Comment on the following:
   (a) Staggered ethane does not have C_6 axis but it has S_6.
   (b) C_{10} axis is not possible in ferrocene (staggered) but it possesses S_{10} axis.
   (c) C_4 is not permitted in $Ni(CO)_4$ but it has S_4 axis.
9. A number of choices are given in each case. Insert the correct answer in each of then:
   (a) A molecule having inversion centre is .... (HCN, PCl_5, ClF_3, CH_4, H_2).
   (b) A molecule with C_5 axis is .... [$Fe(CO)_5$, PF_5, BrF_5 staggered ferrocene].
   (c) Water is an example containing......plane only. (horizontal, dihedral, vertical.
   (d) Benzene has .... improper axis of symmetry (C_6, S_6, S_4).

MULTIPLE OPERATIONS AND SYMMETRY GROUPS

3

3.1 MULTIPLE OPERATION

We have considered so far simple operations of the kind: E, Cn, σ, i and Sn. There can be a combination of these operations. The product operations may commute in some cases. The different multiple operations will give the result which can be put in a Tabular form that is known as group multiplication table. There are four parts in it. It comprises point group notation at the left hand corner. Over and above one finds a left hand factor and right hand factor. The result of multiple operation of LHF and RHF are given in the central part. There are h rows and h column where h is the order of the group.

3.2 MULTIPLE OPERATION GENERATED BY A POINT

All such elements in a row or column must be different. Each of the original elements appears only once. Consider a point O in xy plane. First of all we take up effect of reflection in planes perpendicular to the σ_{xy} plane (viz. σ_{xz} and σ_{yz}). The z-axis is perpendicular to x and y axis.

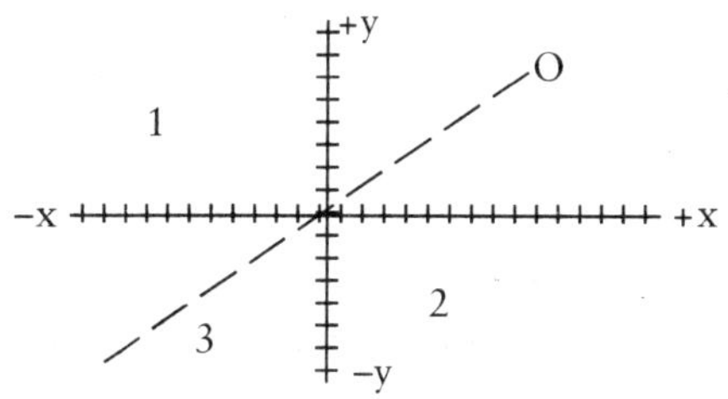

Take up point 3. This point is obtained by $C_2(z)$ from O. It can also be obtained on reflecting point O first in σ_{yz} and then in σ_{xz} and vice-versa.

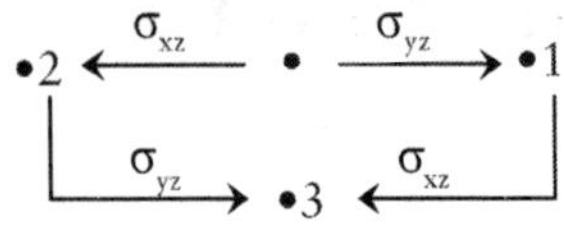

Mathematically $\sigma_{xz}.\sigma_{yz} = \sigma_{yz}.\sigma_{xz} = C_2$

The operations commute.

Also $\underset{1}{\sigma_{xz}\ \sigma_{yz}} = \underset{2}{C_2} = \underset{3}{\sigma_{yz}\ \sigma_{xz}}$

Take up point 2. Reflection in σ_{xy} gives point 2. This point 2 is also obtained when we perform C_2 on O followed by σ_{yz} on it.

$$\text{Pt} \bullet \xrightarrow{C_2} \text{Pt.3} \xrightarrow{\sigma_{yz}} \text{Pt.2}$$

Hence $\sigma_{yz}.C_2 = \sigma_{xz}$

We get it also when we reflect point • in yz plane and rotate the point 1 by 180° (C_2)

i.e. $C_2\sigma_{yz} = \sigma_{xz}$

Hence,

$$\underset{4}{\sigma_{yz}.C_2} = \underset{5}{\sigma_{xz}} = \underset{6}{C_2\sigma_{yz}}$$

Take up point 1.

$$\text{Pt.} \bullet \xrightarrow{\sigma_{yz}} \text{Pt.1}$$

Also $\text{Pt.} \bullet \xrightarrow{\sigma_{yz}} \text{Pt. 2} \xrightarrow{C_2} \text{Pt.1}$

i.e. $C_2.\sigma_{xz} = \sigma_{yz}$

When we have clockwise rotation by C_2 on Pt. •. It gives Pt. 3 and then perform σ_{xz} we get Pt. 1 again.

Hence $\underset{7}{\sigma_{yz}} = \underset{8}{C_2\sigma_{xz}} = \underset{9}{\sigma_{xz}\ C_2}$

Thus we get nine product operations. Now consider repetition of same operation. This may give us:

$\sigma_{xz}.\sigma_{xz} = E$ 10

$\sigma_{yz}.\sigma_{yz} = E$ 11

$C_2.C_2 = E$ 12

Taking E as one of the combinations in multiple operations there can be seven operations.

Four product operations are:

$E.E = E$ 13

$\sigma_{xz}.E = \sigma_{xz}$ 14

$\sigma_{yz}.E = \sigma_{yz}$ 15

$C_2.E = C_2$ 16

This makes sixteen operations in all.

TABLE 3.1

	E	C_2	σ_{xz}	σ_{yz}
E	E	C_2	σ_{xz}	σ_{yz}
C_2	C_2	E	σ_{yz}	σ_{xz}
σ_{xz}	σ_{xz}	σ_{yz}	E	C_2
σ_{yz}	σ_{yz}	σ_{xz}	C_2	E

This is applicable in case of water also.

3.3 MULTIPLICATION TABLE FOR H_2O

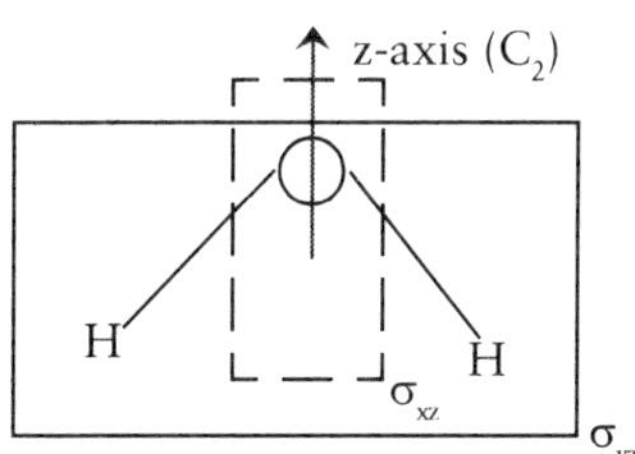

The four symmetry operations are E, $C_2(z)$, σ_{xz} (σv) and σ_{yz} ($\sigma v'$). When we consider product operations there are sixteen such operations in all, seven of them involve E and remaining nine operations are obtained out of C_2, σ_{xz} and σ_{yz}.

First seven operations are:

(i) $C_2E = C_2$ 1

(ii) $\sigma_{xz}.E = \sigma_{xz}$ 2

(iii) $\sigma_{yz}.E = \sigma_{yz}$ 3

(iv) $E.E = E$ 4

(v) $\sigma_{xz}.\ \sigma_{xz} = E$ 5

(vi) $\sigma_{yz}.\sigma_{yz} = E$ 6

(vii) $C_2.C_2 = E$ 7

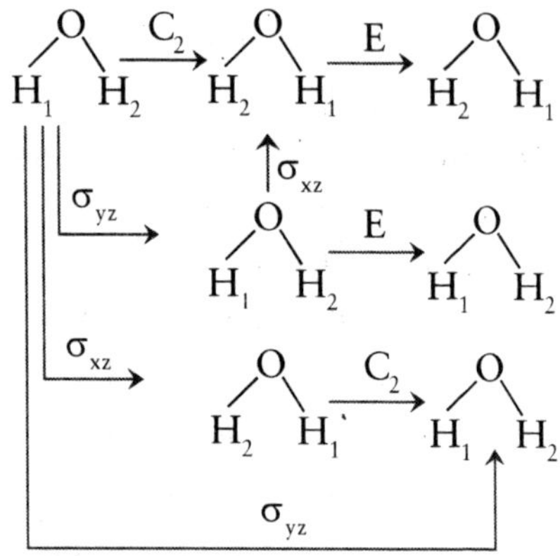

The other set of multiple operations are:

$$\underset{8}{\sigma_{xz}.\ \sigma_{yz}} = \underset{9}{\sigma_{yz}.\sigma_{xz}} = \underset{10}{C_2}$$

$$\underset{11}{\sigma_{yz}.\ C_2} = \underset{12}{C_2\ \sigma_{yz}} = \underset{13}{\sigma_{xz}}$$

$$\underset{14}{\sigma_{xz}.C_2} = \underset{15}{C_2.\sigma_{xz}} = \underset{16}{\sigma_{yz}}$$

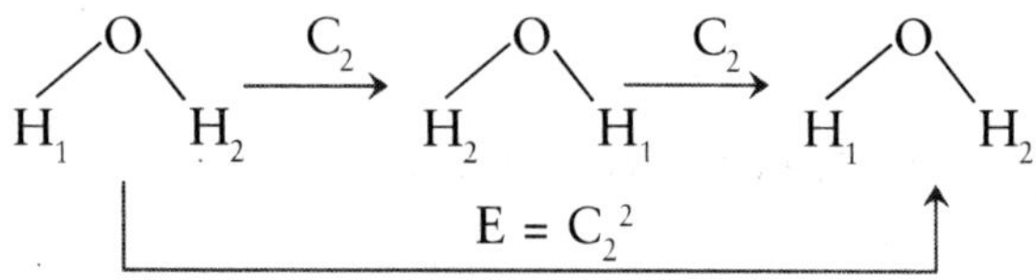

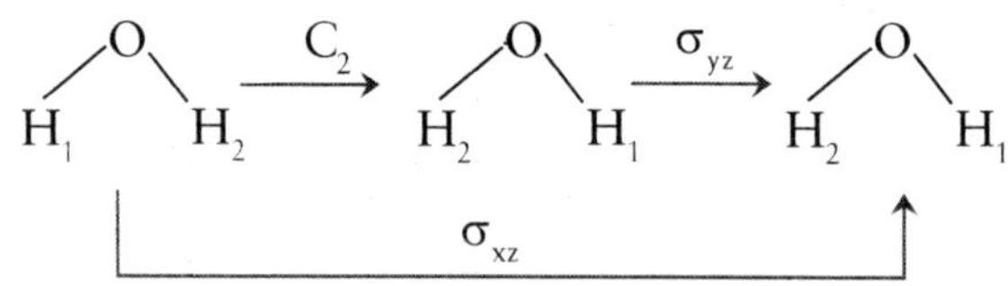

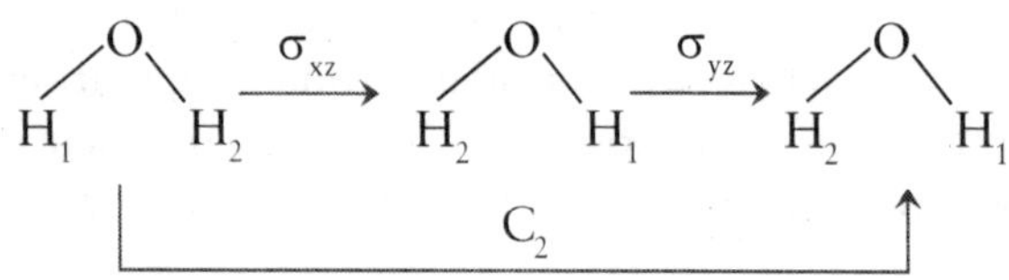

The result is summarized in a tabular form indicating point group for water (C_{2v}) on left hand corner (shown in the Table which is similar to Table 3.1).

C_{2v}	E	C_2	σ_{xz}	σ_{yz}
E	E	C_2	σ_{xz}	σ_{yz}
C_2	C_2	E	σ_{yz}	σ_{xz}
σ_{xz}	σ_{xz}	σ_{yz}	E	C_2
σ_{yz}	σ_{yz}	σ_{xz}	C_2	E

3.4 MULTIPLICATION TABLE FOR NH_3

First of all we intend to know about the simple operations. It is a non-planar molecule with following operations:

$$E,\ C_3,\ C_3^2,\ \sigma_1,\ \sigma_2 \text{ and } \sigma_3.$$

There are six elements in this group and we expect 36 product operations. Consider the geometry of the molecule:

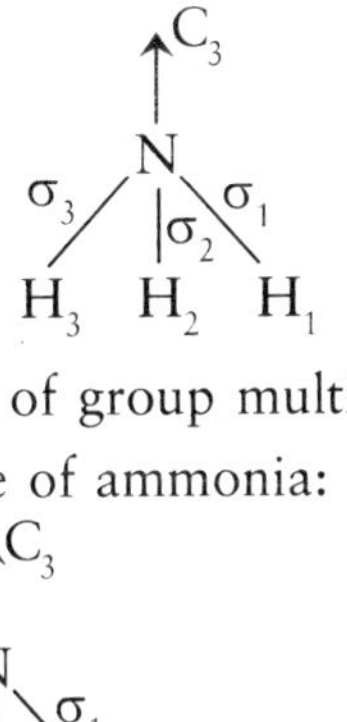

Construction of group multiplication table for C_{3v}.

Take the case of ammonia:

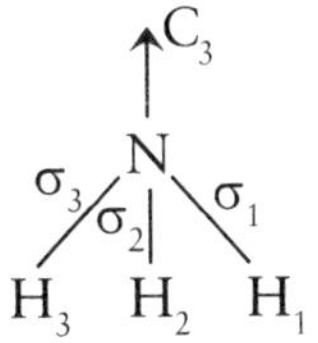

$C_3 - N - H_1 \quad \sigma_1$

$C_3 - N - H_2 \quad \sigma_2$

$C_3 - N - H_3 \quad \sigma_3$

Combination leading to identity (E):

$$E^{(1)}.E = E$$

$$\sigma_1^{(2)}.\sigma_1 = E$$

$$\sigma_2^{(3)}.\sigma_2 = E$$

$$\sigma_3^{(4)}.\sigma_3 = E$$

$$\sigma_3^{(5)}.C_3^2 = {}^{(6)}C_3^2\ .\sigma_3 = E$$

Combination with identity

$$C_3^{(7)}.E = E^{(8)}C_3 = C_3$$

$$C_3^{2(9)}.E = E^{(10)}C_3^2 = C_3^2$$

$$\sigma_1^{(11)}.E = E^{(12)}\sigma_1 = \sigma_1$$

$$\sigma_2^{(13)}.E = E^{(14)}\sigma_2 = \sigma_2$$

$$\sigma_2^{(15)}.E = E^{(16)}\sigma_3 = \sigma_3$$

C_3 with itself

$$C_3.^{(17)}C_3 = C_3^2$$

C_3^2 with itself

$$C_3^2.^{(18)}C_3^2 = C_3^3.C_3 = E.C_3 = C_3$$

Combination of σ_vs:

$$\sigma_1.^{(19)}\sigma_2 = C_3$$

$$\sigma_2.^{(20)}\sigma_1 = \sigma_2.\sigma_1 = C_3^2$$

$$\sigma_1.^{(21)}\sigma_3 = C_3^2$$

$$\sigma_3.^{(22)}\sigma_1 = C_3$$

$$\sigma_2.^{(23)}\sigma_3 = C_3$$

$$\sigma_3.^{(24)}\sigma_2 = C_3^2$$

Combination of C_3 with σ_vs:

$$C_3.^{(25)}\sigma_1 = \sigma_3$$

$$\sigma_1.^{(26)}C_3 = \sigma_3$$

$$C_3.^{(27)}\sigma_2 = \sigma_1 = \sigma_2.^{(28)}C_3$$

$$\sigma_3.^{(29)}C_3 = \sigma_2 = C_3.^{(30)}\sigma_3$$

Combination of C_3^2 and σ_vs.

$$\sigma_1 .^{(31)} C_3^2 = C_3^2 .^{(32)} \sigma_1 = \sigma_2$$

$$\sigma_2 .^{(33)} C_3^2 = C_3^2 .^{(34)} \sigma_2 = \sigma_3$$

$$\sigma_3 .^{(35)} C_3^2 = C_3^2 .^{(36)} \sigma_3 = \sigma_1$$

The result is summarized in the Table 3.2

TABLE 3.2

C_{3v}	E	C_3	C_3^2	σ_1	σ_2	σ_3
E	E	C_3	C_3^2	σ_1	σ_2	σ_3
C_3	C_3	C_3^2	E	σ_2	σ_3	σ_1
C_3^2	C_3^2	E	C_3	σ_3	σ_1	σ_2
σ_1	σ_1	σ_2	σ_2	E	C_3^2	C_3
σ_2	σ_2	σ_3	σ_1	C_3	E	C_3^2
σ_3	σ_3	σ_1	σ_2	C_3^2	C_3	E

3.5 CHARACTERISTICS OF A GROUP IN AMMONIA

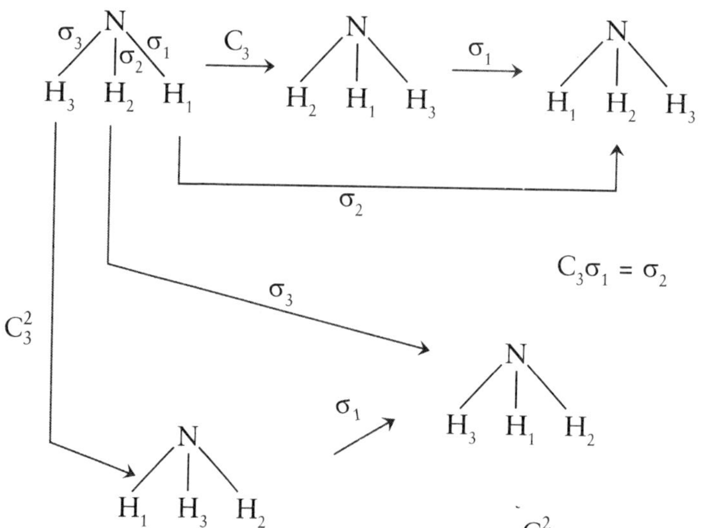

$C_3\sigma_1 = \sigma_2$

$C_3^2\,\sigma_1 = \sigma_3$

It has property of closure:

$$C_3\sigma_1 = \sigma_2$$

$$C_3^2\ \sigma_1 = \sigma_3$$

Commutative law:

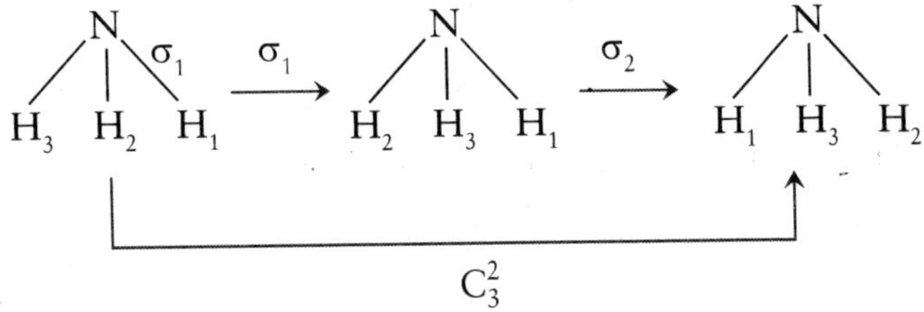

$$\sigma_1\sigma_2 = C_3^2$$

It is a non-abelian group.

Associative law:

$$E\left(C_3C_3^2\right) = C_3\left(EC_3^2\right) = \left(C_3C_3^2\right)E = E$$

3.6 HOW TO DECIDE THE POINT GROUP OF A MOLECULE

The point group to a molecule may be assigned in six steps. These steps include:

Step 1: Decide whether it is a special group?

Yes ⟶ Linear groups $C_{\alpha v}$, $D_{\alpha h}$ or other types Oh, Td, I_h

No ↓

Go to step 2

Step 2: Look at the highest rotation axis:

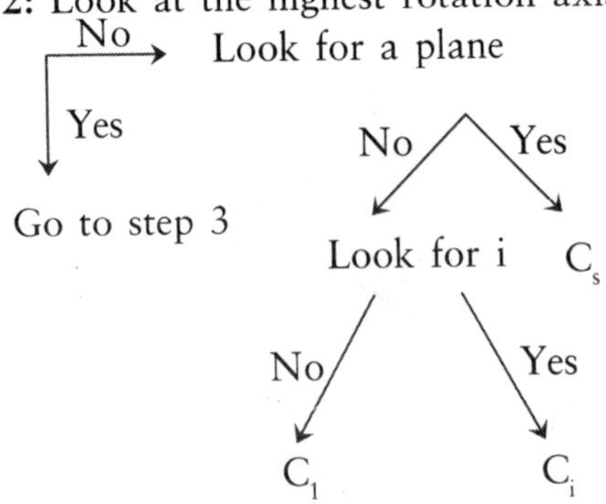

Step 3: From step 2

Select the highest order —n=2→ only $3C_2$ axis axist
↓ $n \geq 3$
Go to step 4

only $3C_2$ axis axist
↓ yes
Find anyone geometrically Unique
↓ Yes
Lok for an S_{2n} — No → Go to step 4
↓ Yes
But no other symmetry elements
↓
pt gr Sn

Lok for an S_{2n} — Yes →
If other symmetry elements exist
↓
Go to step 4

Step 4: From step 3

↓

Look for a set of nC_2 axis perpendicular to C_n

—Yes→ Dn, Dnd, Dnh
↓ Go to step 5

↓ No
Go to step 6
Cn, Cnv, Cnh

Step 5: From step 4

Dn, Dnd, Dnh

↓

Look for σ_h —No→ Look for a set of σ_d's

Look for σ_h
↓ yes
Dnh

Look for a set of σ_d's
No ↙ ↘ yes
Dn Dnd

Step 6: From step 4

Cn, Cnv, Cnh

→ Look for a σh

Yes ↙ ↘ No

Yes: Cnh

No: Look for a set of vertical planes n-vertical

yes ↙ ↘ No

yes: Cnv

No: Cn

3.7 SYMMETRY GROUPS

Like mathematical groups various symmetry operations performed about the symmetry elements constitute members of a group called symmetry groups. The different symmetry operations are known as its members. We consider a few collections:

(i) E, C_2, σ_{xz}, σ_{yz} (Water molecule).

(ii) E, C_3, C_3^2 σ_1, σ_2, σ_3 (Ammonia molecule).

(iii) E, σ (Acetaldehyde).

(iv) E, i CHClF - CHClF (Staggered):

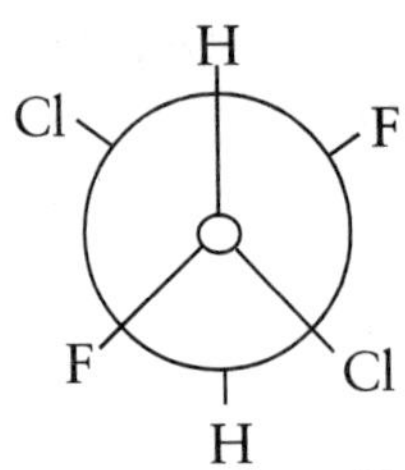

$S_2 = C_2\sigma = i$

(v) E, C_2, σ_v, $\sigma_{v'}$

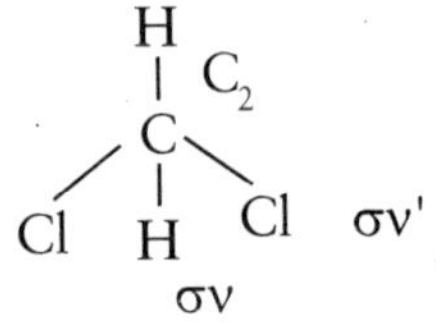

(vi) E, C_2, i, σ_h

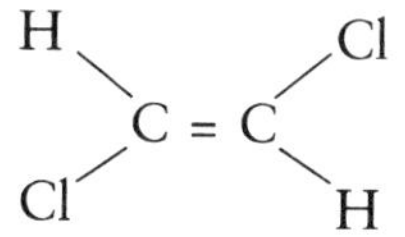

(vii) E, C_2, $2C_2'$, σ_h, $2\sigma_v$, i

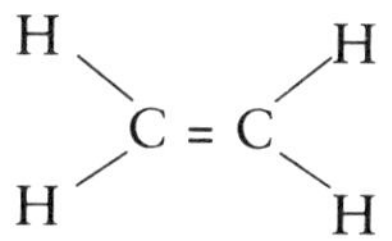

We locate a point inside the molecule that remains fixed and about this point all symmetry operations are carried out. A group is constituted about this point known as point group. There is a point group notation in every case. The symbol is written in bold face type. It is based upon the principal elements of symmetry of that point group.

It is possible to classify molecules into one of the point groups (Schoenflies symbol).

3.7.1 Only One Symmetry Element (Axis)

There can be Cn or Sn present in such cases. They are non-trivial groups. Since all molecules must have identity (E), the operations may comprise.

Rotation (Cn) + E, Reflection + E, Inversion + E. There is one operation in addition to E. The additional operation is one that is its own inverse:

$$C_1 = C_1^{-1} \text{ meaningless,}$$
$$C_2 = C_2^{-1}$$
$$\sigma = \sigma^{-1}$$
$$i = i^{-1}$$

Therefore the groups are:

E, C_2	C_2 (h=2)
E, σ	Cs ”
E, i	Ci ”

C_2: Non-planar $H_2\,O_2$

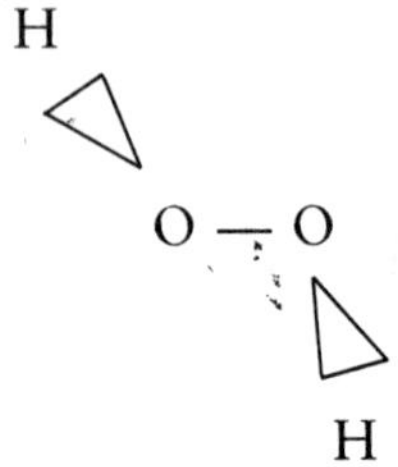

E, C_2

Cs $H_3\,C - \underset{|}{C} = O$, $H - \underset{|}{O}$ 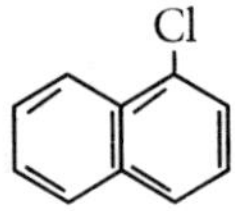 , E, σ

H Cl,

Ci 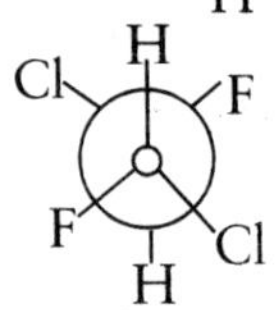

E, C_2, σ, i

$C_2.\sigma = s_2 = i$

Hence members are E and i.

3.7.2 Rotation Plus Symmetry Plane

In addition to Cn-axis there is a set of vertical planes. Its order is 2n. The group is Cnv (There are n-vertical planes):

Cnv = Cn + nσv.

Water with operations E, C_2, σv, σv'

has order 2n = 2 × 2 = 4

It belongs to C_{2V} point group.

Ammonia: There Can be E, C_3, C_3^2, σ_1, σ_2 and σ_3.

Its order 2n = 2 × 3 = 6.

Thus its point group notation is C_{3V}.

Sometimes horizontal planes σh occurs besides Cn.

The group is again of order 2n

$$Cn + \sigma h = Cnh.$$

To this category of molecules we have trans-1, 2- dichloroethylene with C_{2h} point group.

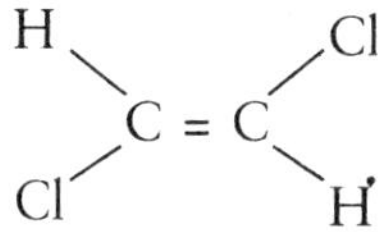

and trans butadiene

and N_2 O_2

E, C_2, σh and i

C_2 σh = S_2 = i

order = 2n = 2 × 2 = 4

C_{3h}

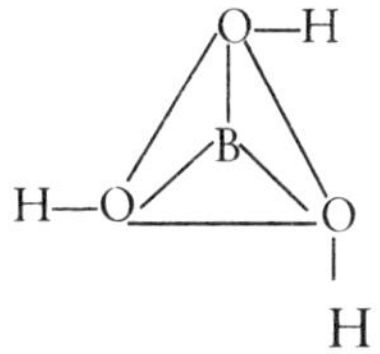

Order = 2n = 2 × 3 = 6

E, C_3, C_3^2, σh, S_3, S_3^5

= E, $2C_3$, σh, $2S_3$

3.7.3 Dihedral Groups (D)

Basic requirement is Cn + nC_2 perpendicular to Cn for D

A D_n point symmetry has more symmetry operations than Cn.

(a) Cn +nC_2 → Dn

For example Cr $(OX)_3^{-3}$ ion is of octahedral geometry but not of O_h symmetry:

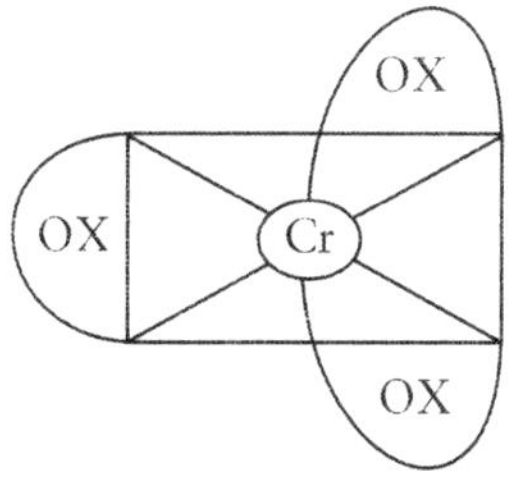

Three equivalent sets of oxalate ions occupy adjacent positions. This makes angle of rotations $\alpha = \frac{360^o}{3} = 120^o$. It has C_3-axis generating two operations C_3 and C_3^2 besides E.

There are three C_2 axes passing through Cr Centre and midway between each $C_2O_4^{-2}$ ions:

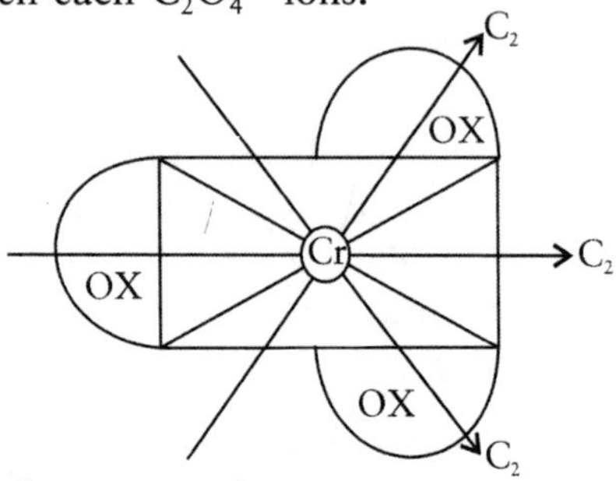

It does not have σ_h or i.

The members are E, $2C_3$, $3C_2$.

Its point group notation is D_3. (C_3 + $3C_2$).

(b) Dnh.

The preconditions for the presence of this dihedral group are:

(a) Cn.

(b) nσv (or nC_2) at an angle of $\frac{360°}{n}$ to one another and

(c) σ_h.

Ethylene, biphenyl and naphthalene molecules contain $3C_2$ axes:

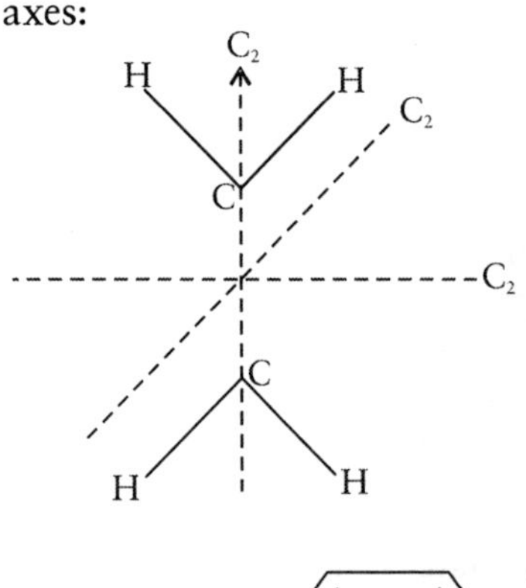

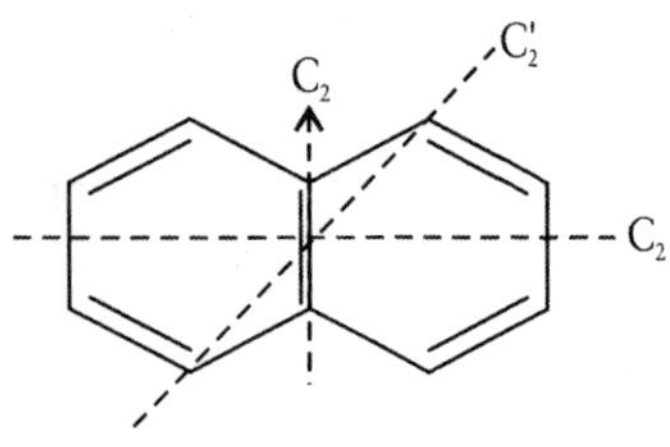

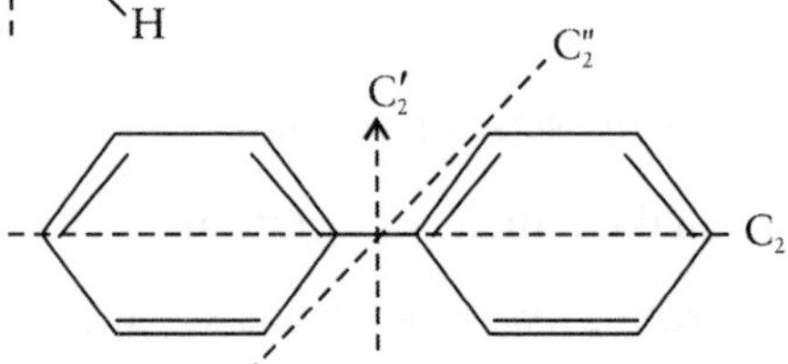

Each of them are mutually perpendicular. These molecules fulfilled the conditions for dihedral group C_2 + $2C_2$ → D_2. There are two σv's along C_2', and C_2''. It has σ_h plane. Thus D_2 + σh → D_{2h} point group. BF_3 has C_3 axis. There are:

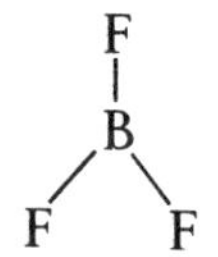

$3C_2$ axes at an angle of 120°. There are three σv's also. Molecule possesses σ_h perpendicular to C_3.

$$C_3 \perp 3C_2 \rightarrow D_3$$

$$D_3 + \sigma_h \rightarrow D_{3h}$$

It belongs to D_{3h} point group.

Cyclopentadiene radical:

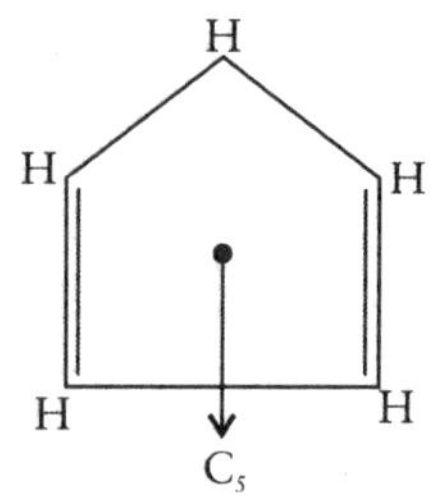

It generates C_5 and C_5^2. There are five C_2 axes each representing vertical plane also. Thus there can be five σv's. It has $C_5 - \sigma h = S_5$ generating $2S_5$ operations. It contains σ_h. We assign it to the point group $C_5 + 5C_2 = D_5$

$$D_5 + \sigma_h = D_{5h}$$

$AuCl_4^-$ ion:

1. It has C_4 axis
2. There is a C_2 axis collinear with C_4
3. $4C_2$ axes
4. σ_h
5. 4σv's which can be placed into 2σv and $2\sigma_d$ at an angle of 90°
6. i
7. $S_4 = C_4$ σh.

Its point group notation is D_{4h}.

Benzene

It is a planar molecule with the following symmetry elements:

1. A C_6 axis generating C_6 and C_6^5 operations.
2. Molecular plane σ_h.
3. Six σv at an angle of $\frac{360^o}{6} = 60^o$.
4. Seven C_2 axis, C_2, $3C_2'$, and $3C_2''$.
5. A C_3 axis giving C_3 and C_3^2.
6. i.
7. S_6 axis giving $2S_6$.

$C_6 + 6C_2 \perp^r$ to $C_6 \rightarrow D_6$

$D_6 + \sigma_h \rightarrow D_{6h}$.

B_2H_6

1. There are three C_2-axes, mutually perpendicular.
2. It has three mirror planes corresponding to C_2 axis. These are σ_{xy}, σ_{xz} and σ_{yz}. The σ_{xy} plane is known as σh whereas σ_{xz} and σ_{yz} planes are vertical planes 2σv's.

The three C_2 axes are $C_2(x)$, $C_2(y)$ and $C_2(z)$. It possesses inversion centre (i).

All the eight operations are:

E, $C_2(x)$, $C_2(y)$, $C_2(z)$, i, σh, 2σv.

Its short hand label is

$C_2 + \perp^r 2C_2 \rightarrow D_2$

$D_2 + \sigma_h \rightarrow D_{2h}$

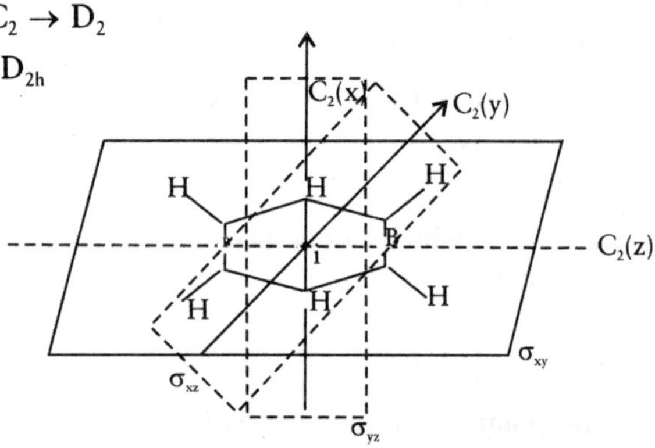

(c) Dnd

(i) Cn axis

(ii) n number of C_2 axis $\perp^r$ to Cn.

(iii) It has no σh.

(iv) n vertical planes of σ_d type.

Allene

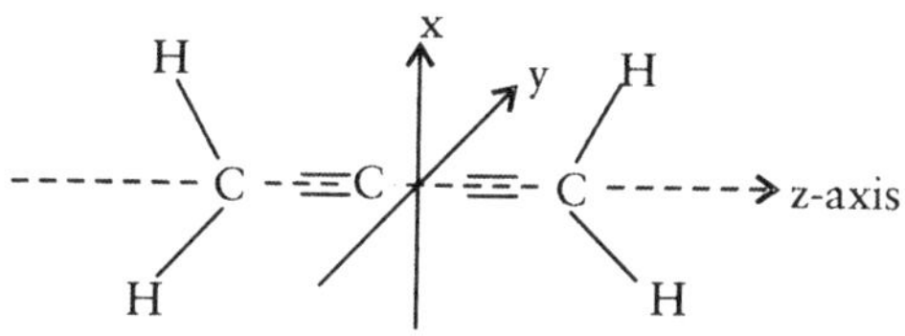

(i) E (ii) $S_2 = C_2\sigma = i$

(iii) $2\sigma_d$ (iv) $3C_2$

(v) i (vi) $C_4.\sigma = S_4$.

$C_2 + 2C_2\ (\perp^r) \rightarrow D_2$

$D_2 + 2\sigma_d \rightarrow D_{2d}$. Members are E, C_2, $2C_2'$, $2\sigma_d$, $2S_4$.

h = 8.

Ethane (staggered)

(i) Principal axis along C-C bond is C_3 giving $2C_3$

(ii) S_6 axis collinear with C_3 giving $2S_6$.

(iii) It has i.

(iv) Three C_2 axes $\perp^r$ to C_3 passing through mid point of C-C bond.

(v) There are three vertical mirror planes σv, each containing trans C-H bonds.

$C_3 + 3C_2 \rightarrow D_3$

$D_3 + 3\sigma_d$ or v $\rightarrow D_{3d}$

We assign it the point group symbol D_{3d}.

E, $2C_3$, $3C_2$ i, $2S_6$, $3\sigma_d$, h = 12

Ethane (eclipsed)

(i) C_3 axis

(ii) $3C_2$ axes $\perp^r$ to C_3.

(iii) $C_3 + \sigma_h \rightarrow S_3$ collinear with C_3.

(iv) It has σ_h.

(v) Three σv's

$$C_3 + 3C_2 \rightarrow D_3$$

$$D_3 + \sigma_h \rightarrow D_{3h}$$

Its point group is D_{3h}.

E, $2C_3$, $3C_2$, σ_h, $2S_3$, 3σv.

Ferrocene (staggered)

1. For each five membered ring we have C_5-rotation axis. Thus the line passing through the centre of the C_5H_5 rings and iron atom is C_5 axis.

   It is perpendicular to the ring. C_5 generates $2C_5$ operations.
2. There are five C_2 axis perpendicular to C_5.
3. It has no σ_h perpendicular to C_5.
4. There are five vertical planes we call them as σ_d containing C-H bond and bisecting the opposite C-C mid point in each plane. Its point group notation would be,

   $C_5 + 5C_2\ (I^r) \rightarrow D_5$.

   $D_5 + \sigma_d \rightarrow D_{5d}$
5. It has no σ_h so there is no S_5 but we can imagine a combined effect of $C_{10}\sigma_h = S_{10}$.

   It has S_{10} and $2S_{10}^3$ operations. E, $2C_5$, $2C_5^2$, $5C_2$, i, $2S_{10}^3$, $2S_{10}$, $5\sigma_d$.

Special groups

There can be axial groups $C_{\infty v}$ and $D_{\infty h}$ and cubic groups.

H — Cl → C_∞ axis:

(i) It has C_∞ axis.

(ii) It has infinite number of vertical planes σ_v.

(iii) It does not have other symmetry elements.

Hence we assign it to $C_\infty + \propto \sigma v \rightarrow C_{\infty v}$.

CO_2

1. It has C_∞ axis.
2. There are infinite C_2 axis perpendicular to C_∞.
3. It has i.
4. It has σ_h.
5. It can have $\infty\sigma v$.

Hence, point group notation for the molecule is:

$$O = C = O \qquad C_\infty + \infty C_2 \rightarrow D_\infty$$

$$D_\infty + \sigma_h \rightarrow D_{\infty h}$$

We place cubic groups to this category.

O stands for $3C_4$ + $4C_3$ +$6C_2$ only.

O_h stands for O + 9 planes. (σv + σ_d + σ_h) . +i + C_4 +S_4

SF_6 belongs to O_h symmetry.

T stands for $4C_3$ + $3C_2$ only.

Td stands for T + $6.\sigma_d$.

T_h stands for T + i

CH_4 belongs to Td.

Illustrations

1. Assign the point group to the following:

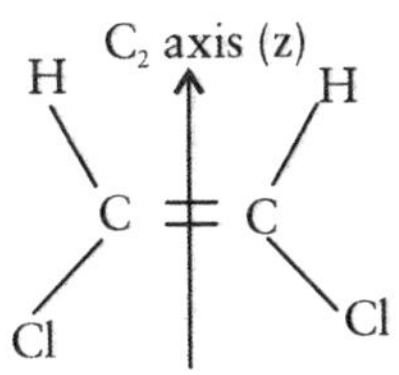

cis-1, 2 dicholoroethelene

E, C_2 (z), σ_{xz}, σ_{yz}

Hence C_{2v}

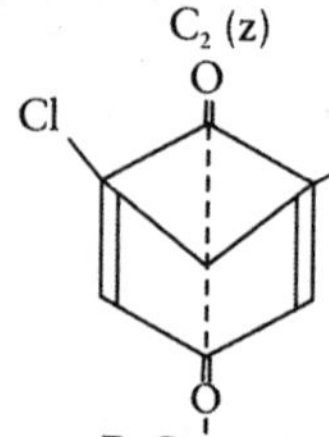

E, C_2, σ_{xz}, σ_{yz}

z-axis passing through the O-atoms bisecting the molecule as a whole.

It is C_2 axis with respect to two Cl-atoms. There is σ_{xz} plane bisecting the molecule and σ_{yz} plane is one containing all atoms.

Both are vertical planes containing the principal axis.

Its point group notation is C_{2v}.

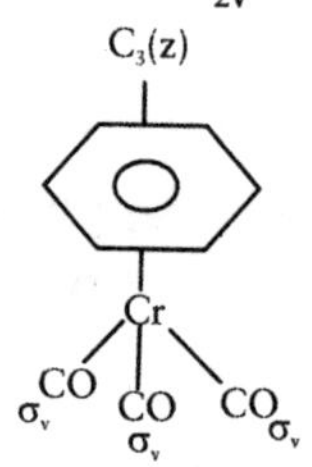

C_3 axis passing through centroid of the triangle formed for the three CO groups and Cr-atom. It passes through the centre of the benzene ring. There are three σv's.

E, $2C_3$, 3σv.

C_{3v}

Ethylene oxide

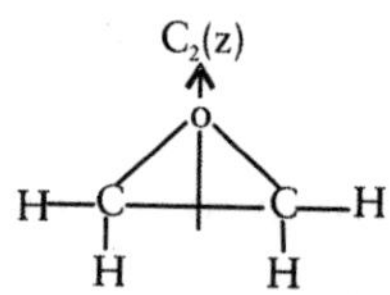

E, C_2(z), σ_{xz}, σ_{yz}

Hence, C_{2v} point group notation.

BrF_5

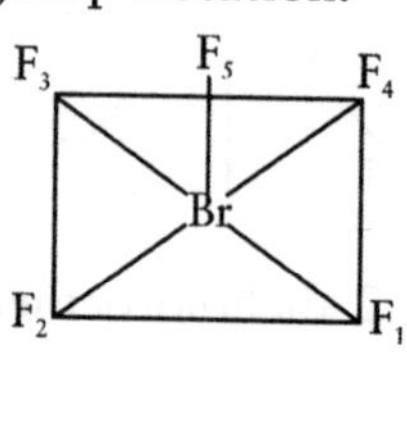

We can view it along Br -F (axial) four other F-atoms lie at the corners of a square. Br-F axial represents C_4 axis.

$$\text{This gives } C_4,\ \underset{\substack{\| \\ C_2}}{C_4^2},\ C_4^3,\ C_4^4 = E$$

There are two C_4 operations C_4 and C_4^3 = $2C_4$.

It has a C_2 axis collinear with C_4.

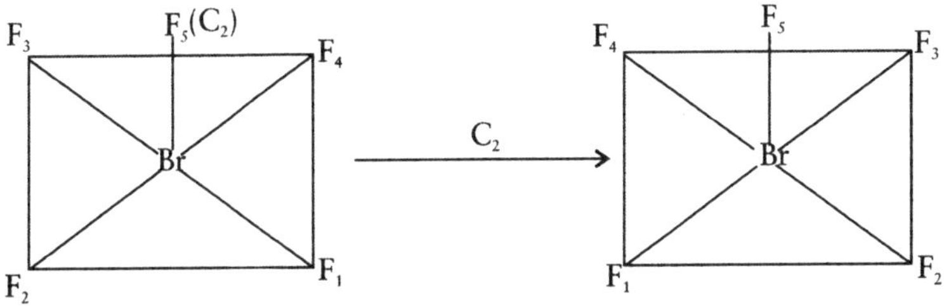

There are four mirror planes. Two planes contain Br and three F-atoms.

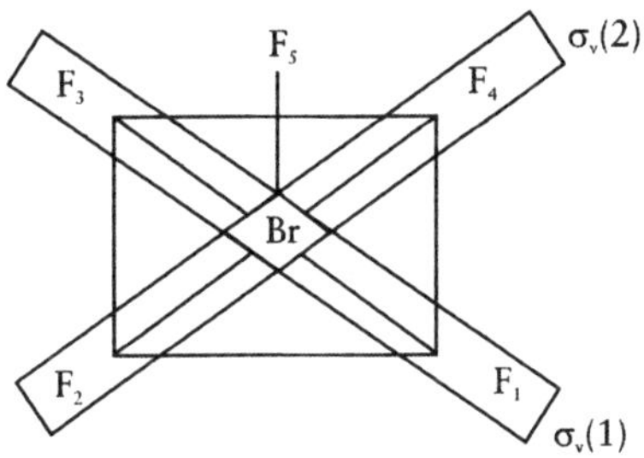

σv(1) stands for F_1 — Br — F_3 and F (axial)
σv(2) stands for F_2 — Br — F_4 and F (axial)
In each of which lie Br and 3F atoms.

There are two more planes containing Br and F (axial) as shown below:

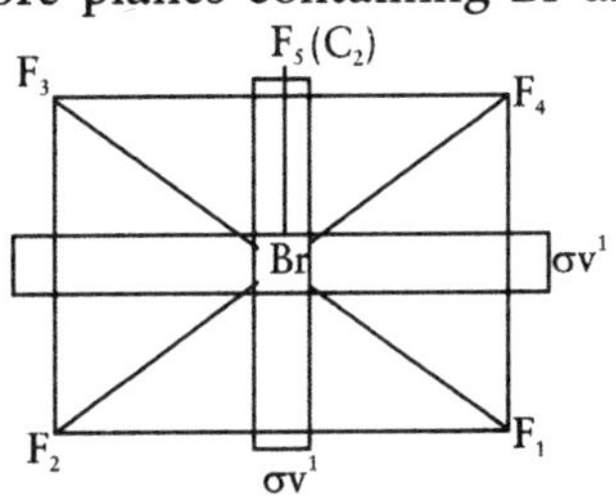

They contain C_4 axis and so they are σv's. The last two σv's are dihedral planes σ_d's

i.e. $2\sigma_d$. C_4 and no C_2 ($\perp^r$ C_4). Hence it has C_4 only.

$C_4 + \sigma_v \rightarrow C_{4v}$

The symmetry operations are E, $2C_4$, C_2 $(=C_2^{\,4})$, $2\sigma_v$, $2\sigma_d$, h = 8

2. Write down the point group notation of the following :

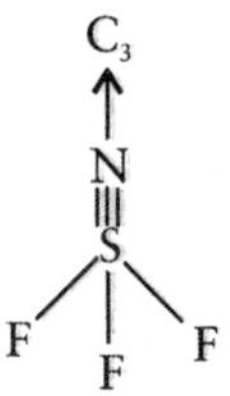

C_{3v}

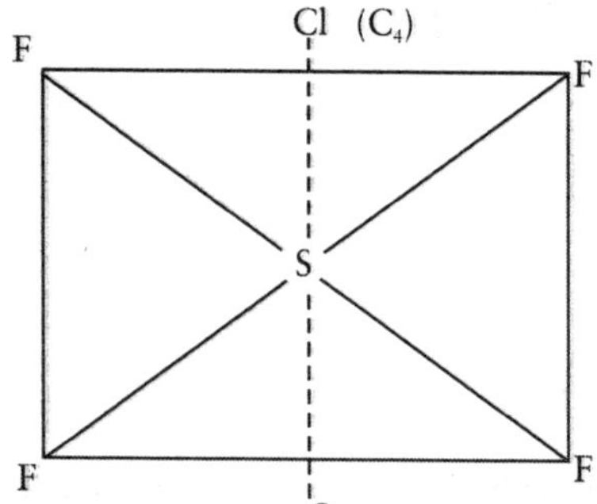

C_{4v}

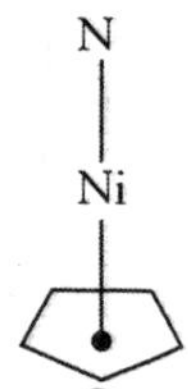

C_{5v}

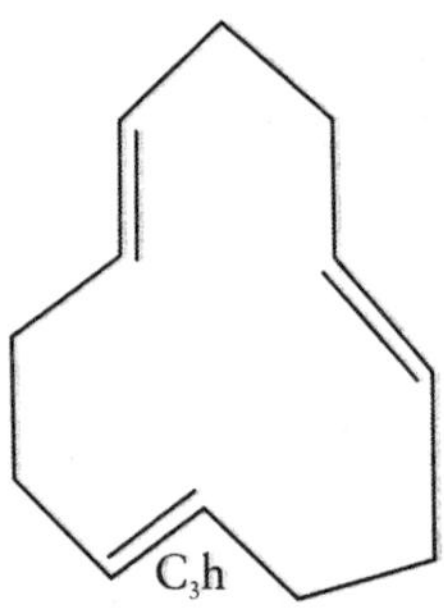

C_3h

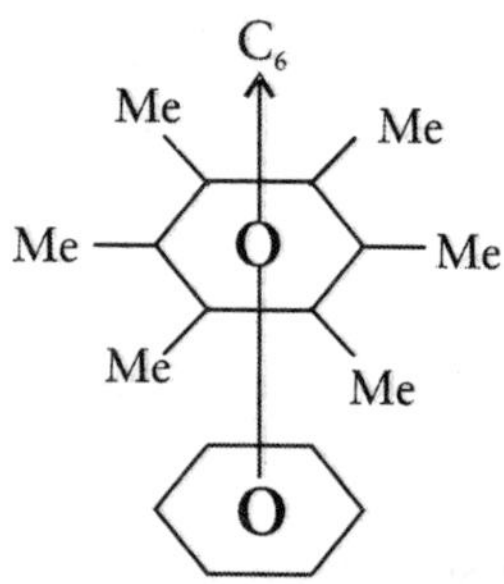

C_{6v}

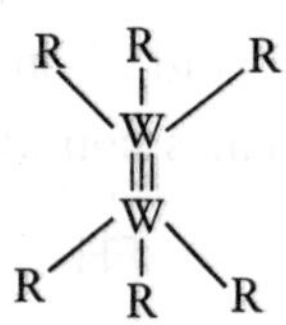

D_{3d}

$C_3 + 3C_2 \rightarrow D_3$

$D_3 + \sigma_d \rightarrow D_{3d}$

no σ_h

3. Determine the symmetry operations in $Re_2Cl_8^{2-}$ ion and assign the point group symbol to it.

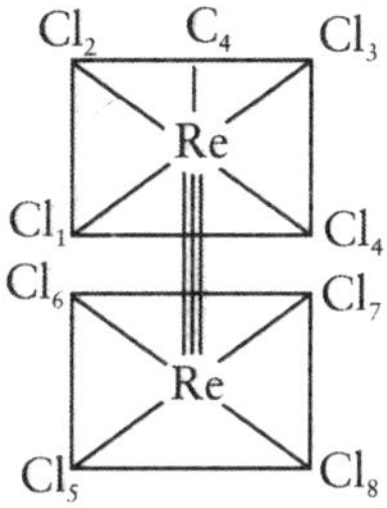

1. It has C_4 axis Re_1 — Re_2 line giving $2C_4$.
2. There is a C_2 axis collinear with C_4.
3. There are two other types of C_2 axes that exist independently.
4. It has right square prism structure.

   The two C_2 viz. C_2 and C_2' pass through the centre of opposite vertical edges of the prism.

   Another two C_2 viz. C_2'' that pass through the centres of opposite vertical faces of the prism.

   i.e. $2C_2'$ and $2C_2''$.
5. There are three type of planes:
   (a) that bisects Re_1-Re_2 bond, σh,
   (b) two type of vertical planes 2σv, $2\sigma_d$.
6. It has improper rotation axis $S_4 = C_4\sigma_h$ giving $2S_4$.
7. It has inversion centre.

   The symmetry operations are:

   E, $2C_4$, C_2, $2C_2'$, $2C_2''$, σh, i, 2σv 2σd, $2S_4$ h = 16

   Hence it is D_{4h}.

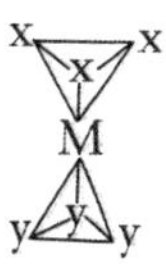

It has only C_3 axis. It belongs to C_3 point group.

4. Ascertain the point group in case of the following:-

   Cis-$Pt(NH_3)_2Br_2$ trans-$Pt(NH_3)_2Br_2$

   trans-$[Co\ (NO_2)_4Cl_2]^+$, Cis-$[Co(NO_2)_4Cl_2]^+$

   Cis- and trans-$[Co(en)_2\ Cl_2]^+$

   ClF_3, B_2Cl_4

Cis-$Pt(NH_3)_2Br_2$

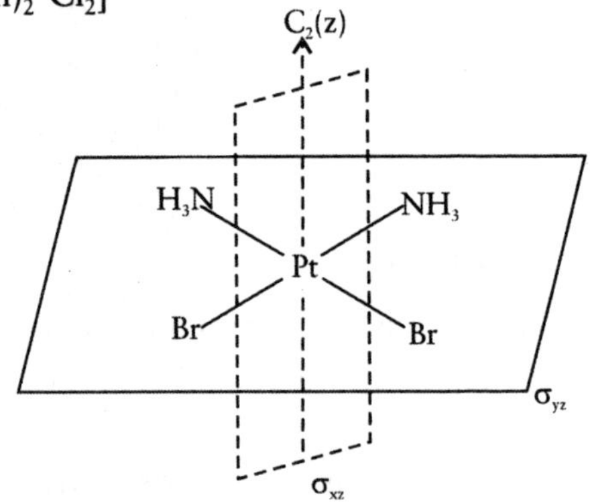

The molecule is square planar but it suffers a net loss in its symmetry. The symmetry is no longer D_{4h}.

The C_2 z-axis is bisecting, Pt/N N or Pt/Br Br angle. There is no σ_h.

The two planes σ_{xz} and σ_{yz} contain the $C_2(z)$ axis which represent vertical planes. The symmetry operations are E, C_2, σ_{xz} σ_{yz} giving C_{2v} notation.

Trans-Pt $(NH_3)_2Br_2$

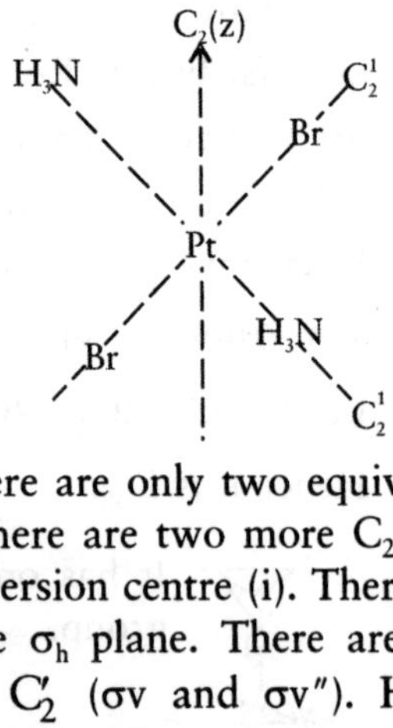

Its principal axis is $C_2(z)$ as there are only two equivalent groups (C_2 and no C_4 axis). There are two more C_2 axes across the diagonals. It has inversion centre (i). There is a plane to the principal axis the σ_h plane. There are two vertical planes collinear with C_2' (σv and $\sigma v''$). Hence symmetry operations are, E, $C_2(z)$, $2C_2'$, i, σh, $2\sigma v$, h = 8.

We deduce the point group notation out of these elements as:

$$C_2 + 2C_2\left(\perp^r\right) \rightarrow D_2$$

$$D_2 + \sigma_h \rightarrow D_{2h}$$

Trans - $[Co(NO_2)_4Cl_2]^+$

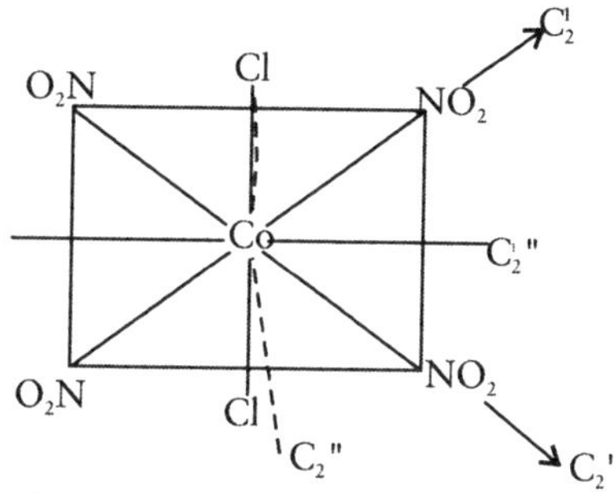

The z-axis passing through Co-atom and $\perp^r$ to the molecular plane (σ_h). It contains two Cl-atoms at trans positions and acts as C_4 axis.

C_4 generates C_4, $C_4^2 = C_2$, C_4^3 and E.

Thus z-axis acts as C_2 axis.

It has i.

It has σ_h $\perp^r$ to C_4.

There are four more C_2 axes $2C_2'$ and $2C_2''$. There are two σv^s and two σ_d^s.

The C_4 axis also acts as $S_4 = C_4\sigma_h$ axis.

It has $C_4 + 4C_2 + 4\sigma v + \sigma h$. at an angle of $\frac{360}{4} = 90^O$

Its point group would be D_{4h}.

Cis-$[Co(NO_2)_4Cl_2]^+$

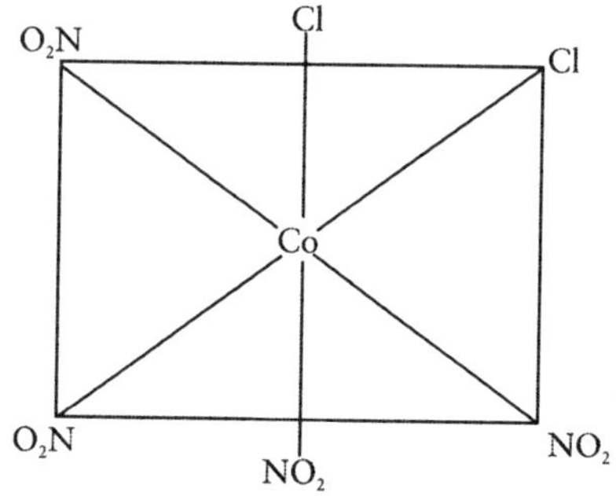

There is a loss of symmetry:

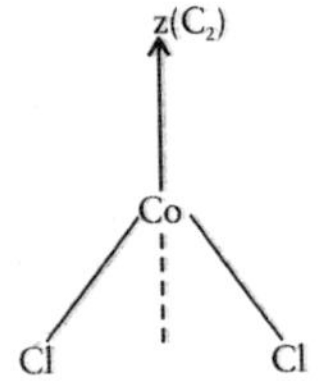

1. It has C_2 axis.
2. There are two vertical planes σ_v & $\sigma_{v'}$.
3. It has E.
4. It does not have i.

   Its point group notation would be C_{2v}.

Cis-[Co(en)$_2$ Cl$_2$]$^+$

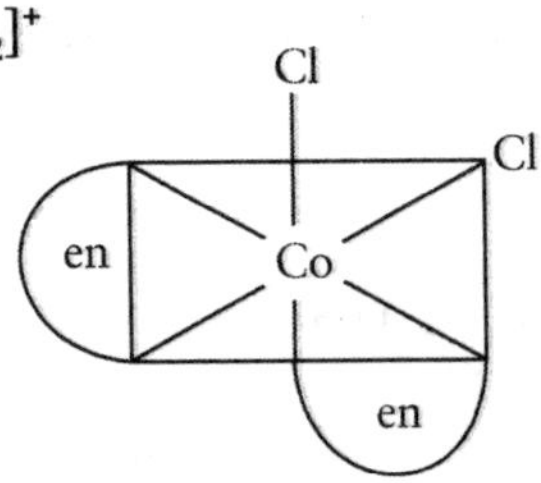

There are two like groups which are exchanged. Thus it has a C_2 (z) axis. It contains:

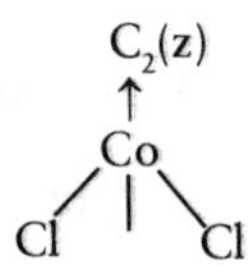

There are two vertical planes σv & σv′. Hence we assign it to C_{2v} point group.

Trans-[Co(en)$_2$ Cl$_2$)$^+$

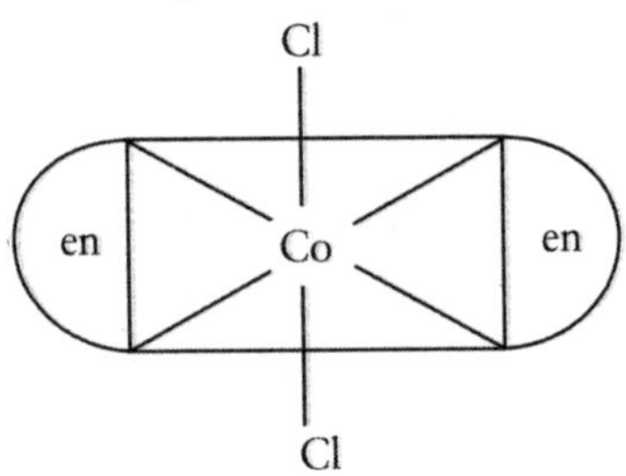

It has C_4 (z) axis passing through Cl-Co-Cl axis. Four corners of a square are occupied by like atoms and we can exchange them four times.

There are five C_2 axes, C_2, $2C_2'$ and $2C_2''$.

It has σ_h, $2\sigma v$ and $2\sigma_d$.

It has i and S_4.

Its point group notation is D_{4h}.

ClF_3

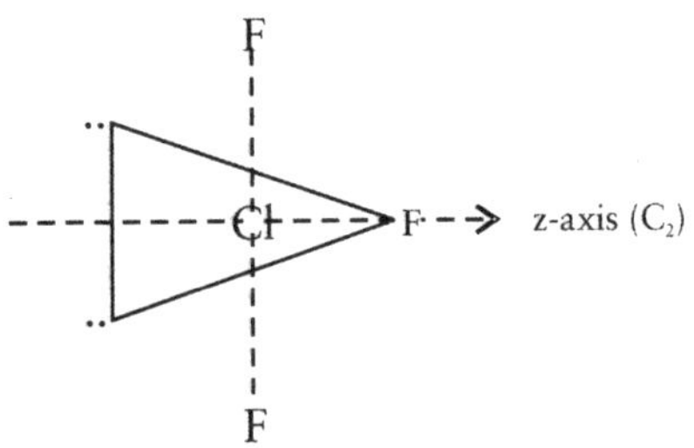

The z-axis is passing through Cl-F line. This bisects F-Cl-F angle by 45°. The z-axis is C_2 because axial fluorine atoms are equivalent (two F-atoms). There are two vertical planes σ_{xz} and σ_{yz}.

Hence its point group is C_{2v}.

B_2Cl_4

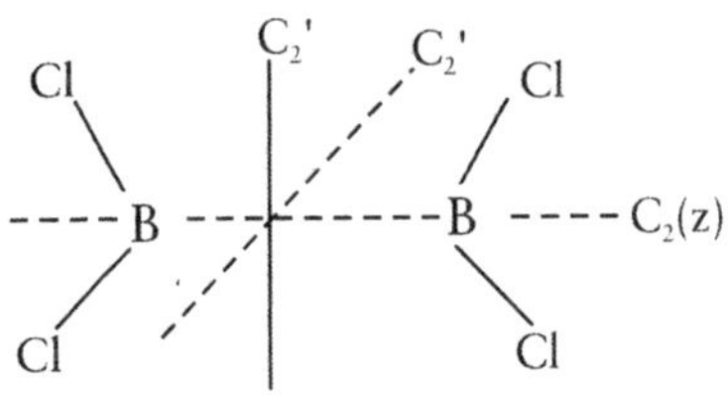

E, C_2, $2C_2'$, i, σ_h

Point group notation is $C_2 + \sigma_h \rightarrow D_{2h}$

$D_2 + \sigma_h \rightarrow D_{2h}$

5. Find the point group notation for Fe $(CO)_5$ and Fe_2 $(CO)_9$.

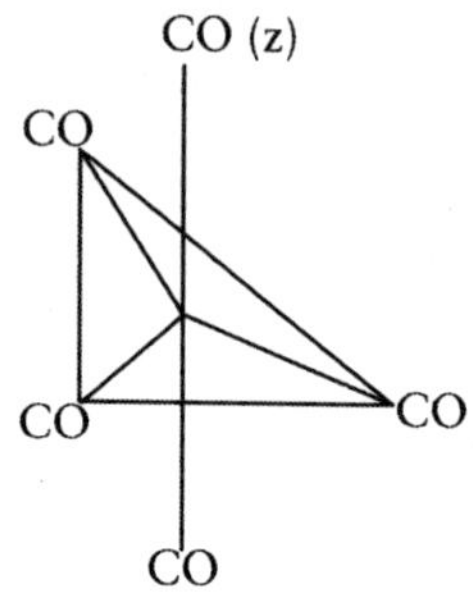

(i) E

(ii) C_3 passing through two CO groups along z-axis and perpendicular to trigonal plane (i). There are three C_2 axes.

(iii) A C_3 generates C_3 & C_3^2 operations.

(iv) It has σh ad 3σv.

Thus it has $C_3 + 3C_2 \perp^r .\text{to } C_3 \rightarrow D_3$

$$D_3 + \sigma_h \rightarrow D_{3h}$$

In $Fe_2(CO)_9$ which has three carbonyl bridges. It has the structure.

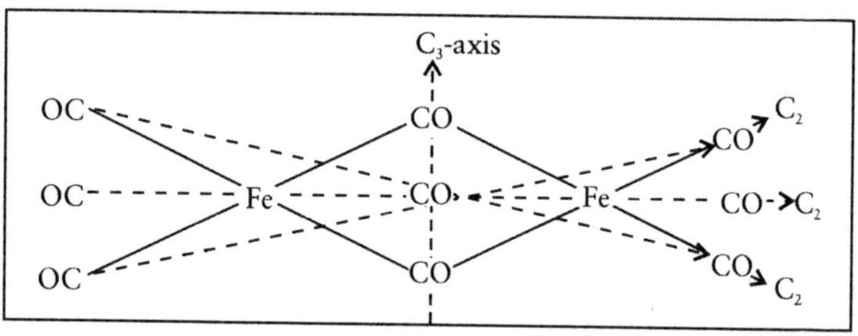

It has C_3 axis passing through bridging CO groups. The three C_2 axes each passes through terminal Fe-bridging CO in middle and another terminal CO on the opposite side.

$$C_3 + 3C_2 \rightarrow D_3$$

It has σ_h and $3\sigma_v$.

$$D_3 + \sigma_h \rightarrow D_{3h} \text{ point group.}$$

QUESTIONS

1. What is meant by multiple operations? Draw geometrically the group multiplication Tables of water and ammonia.
2. Outline the procedure of determining point group notations.
3. Assign the point group in case of the following:

   (i) X_eF_4

   (ii) $H—C\equiv C—H$

   (iii) 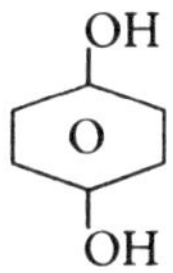

   (iv) $H—C\equiv N$ (v) CO

   (vi) $Re_2\,Cl_8$
4. Comment on: (i) Axial group.
   (ii) Dihedral group.
   (iii) Td and O_h groups.
5. Draw the multiplications Table for: (i) C_{2v} or (ii) C_{3v} point group geometrically.

MATRICES

4

4.1 ARITHMETIC, MATRIX AND DETERMINANT

In arithmetic, we deal with a single number. There are rules of addition, subtraction, multiplication and division, which give a single number. Ordinary numbers can be added and multiplied and result of such operations does not depend upon the order in which the process is applied.

Addition of quantities like 3 and 5 gives 8 irrespective of the order:

$$3 + 5 = 5 + 3 = 8.$$

Their multiplication will give 15 irrespective of the order:

$$3 \times 5 = 5 \times 3 = 15.$$

In mathematics not only we handle simple numbers but more complex quantities such as negative number, complex number as well as matrices.

Collection of numbers or functions are used in determinant and matrices. We use Table of quantities or array of numbers called elements. Array means collection of quantities that are presented among rows and columns and individual members of array are its elements in matrices and determinants. They follow certain rules for addition and multiplication. Matrices can be rectangular or square viz.:

$$2 \times 2 \text{ matrix } \begin{bmatrix} 0 & 1 \\ -1 & 0 \end{bmatrix}, \begin{bmatrix} 1 & 2 \\ 4 & 3 \end{bmatrix}$$

$$2 \times 3 \text{ matrix } \begin{bmatrix} 2 & 1 & 0 \\ 0 & 2 & 1 \end{bmatrix}, \begin{bmatrix} a_{11} & a_{12} & a_{13} \\ a_{21} & a_{22} & a_{23} \end{bmatrix}$$

$$3 \times 3 \text{ matrix} \begin{bmatrix} 2 & 1 & 0 \\ 0 & 2 & 1 \\ 0 & 1 & 0 \end{bmatrix}, \quad \begin{bmatrix} a_{11} & a_{12} & a_{13} \\ a_{21} & a_{22} & a_{23} \\ a_{31} & a_{32} & a_{33} \end{bmatrix}$$

$$4 \times 4 \text{ matrix} \begin{bmatrix} a & b & c & d \\ e & f & g & h \\ i & j & k & l \\ m & n & o & p \end{bmatrix}$$

The members are indicated by enclosing array inside bars in determinants | | or in brackets for matrices:

[ ]	( )	‖ ‖
Square bracket	semi circle	double vertical line

4.2 MATRIX AND DETERMINANT

We denote matrix by capital letters A, B, C, D, ... etc. or by elements. a_{ij} which contain indices i and j.

The former refers to row and the column the latter.

Determinant and matrix are not same thing. A determinant is a single number. Interchange of elements of row into column and vice versa does not alter its value:

$$\Delta = \begin{vmatrix} 1 & 2 & 3 \\ 2 & 3 & 1 \\ 3 & 2 & 1 \end{vmatrix} = 1\begin{vmatrix} 3 & 1 \\ 2 & 1 \end{vmatrix} - 2\begin{vmatrix} 2 & 1 \\ 3 & 1 \end{vmatrix} + 3\begin{vmatrix} 2 & 3 \\ 3 & 2 \end{vmatrix}$$

$= 1\ (3-2) - 2\ (2-3) + 3\ (4-9)$

$= 1\quad (1)\qquad -2(-1) + 3\ (-5)$

$= 1 + 2 - 15 = -12$

$$\Delta^{|} = \begin{vmatrix} 1 & 2 & 3 \\ 2 & 3 & 2 \\ 3 & 1 & 1 \end{vmatrix}$$

$$= 1\begin{vmatrix} 3 & 2 \\ 1 & 1 \end{vmatrix} - 2\begin{vmatrix} 2 & 2 \\ 3 & 1 \end{vmatrix} + 3\begin{vmatrix} 2 & 3 \\ 3 & 1 \end{vmatrix}$$

$= 1\ (3–2)\ –2\ (2–6) + 3\ (2–9)$

$= 1\times1\ –2\times\ (–4) + 3\ (–7)$

$= 1 + 8 – 21$

$= 9 – 21 = –12$

Thus Δ and Δ' are identical.

The matrices,

$$\begin{vmatrix} 1 & 2 & 3 \\ 2 & 3 & 1 \\ 3 & 2 & 1 \end{vmatrix} \text{ and } \begin{vmatrix} 1 & 2 & 3 \\ 2 & 3 & 2 \\ 3 & 1 & 1 \end{vmatrix}$$

in which rows and columns are interchanged are different.

Most familiar type of array in the determinant in which rows and columns are equal $n \times n$:

$$\Delta \text{ or } |A| = \begin{vmatrix} a_{11} & a_{12} & \cdots & a_{1n} \\ a_{21} & a_{22} & \cdots & a_{2n} \\ \cdots & \cdots & \cdots & \cdots \\ \cdots & \cdots & \cdots & \cdots \\ a_{n1} & a_{n2} & \cdots & a_{nn} \end{vmatrix}$$

But matrices can be square (quadratic) or rectangular:

$$[A] = [a_{ij}] = \begin{bmatrix} a_{11} & a_{12} & \cdots & a_{1n} \\ a_{21} & a_{22} & \cdots & a_{2n} \\ \cdots & \cdots & \cdots & \cdots \\ \cdots & \cdots & \cdots & \cdots \\ a_{m1} & a_{m2} & \cdots & a_{mn} \end{bmatrix}$$

Order of matrix = $m \times n$.

A matrix in which $m = n$, is called square matrix. then $i = j$.

Therefore a_{11}, a_{22}, a_{33}, ... a_{nn} are the diagonal elements. When the matrix contains only one row or column it is called vector as it offers the way of representing the vectors:

$$[X] = \begin{pmatrix} x_1 \\ x_2 \\ \vdots \\ xn \end{pmatrix}$$

$$[Y] = [y_1 \ y_2 \ \cdots \ y_n].$$

4.3 COMBINATION OF MATRICES

Matrices are combined to produce new matrices:

1. Two matrices are equal only if they are identical. Let [A] be one matrix and [B] another matrix. [A] and [B] are equal.

   Then [A] = [B]

   Also $[a_{ij}] = [b_{ij}]$

   or $a_{ij} = b_{ij}$ for all i and j.

2. Sum of matrices (addition and subtraction).

   Let $[A] = [a_{ij}]$ and, $[B] = [b_{ij}]$

   matrices can be added and subtracted like ordinary numbers.

   We define their sum [A] + [B] = [C]

   such that $[C] = [C_{ij}]$

   and $c_{ij} = a_{ij} + b_{ij}$

   Also, we define, [A] – [B] = [C]

   and $a_{ij} - b_{ij} = c_{ij}$.

3. Associativity:

   $$\{[A] + [B]\} + [C] = [A] + \{[B] + [C]\}$$

   Hence,

   $$[A] + [B] = [a_{ij} + b_{ij}]$$

   $$[B] + [C] = [b_{ij} + c_{ij}]$$

   $$\{[A] + [B]\} + [C] = \{[a_{ij} + b_{ij}\} + [c_{ij}]\}$$

$$[A]\ \{[B] + [C]\} = [a_{ij}] + [b_{ij} + c_{ij}]$$

$$\text{or } (a_{ij} + b_{ij}) + c_{ij} = a_{ij} + (b_{ij} + c_{ij})$$

Since a_{ij}, b_{ij} and c_{ij} are numbers.

4. Existence of inverse:

[B] is said to be negative of [A] and is denoted by $[A]^{-}$

5. Multiplication:

We can multiply two matrices A and B if number of rows of A is same as the number of columns in B.

$$A = \begin{bmatrix} a_{11} & a_{12} \\ a_{21} & a_{22} \\ a_{31} & a_{32} \end{bmatrix}, \qquad B = \begin{bmatrix} b_{11} & b_{12} & b_{13} & b_{14} \\ b_{21} & b_{22} & b_{23} & b_{24} \end{bmatrix}$$

3 × 2 matrix 2 × 4 matrix

Product AB is 3 × 4 matrix.

If the row of A is equal to column of B then A and B are conformable and their multiplication is defined as:

$$\underset{3 \times 2 \text{ matrix}}{A} \times \underset{2 \times 4 \text{ matrix}}{B} = \underset{3 \times 4 \text{ matrix.}}{C}$$

In the product AB, the matrix A is pre-factor and B is post factor.

In general the element c_{ij} will be the sum of the products of the elements of ith row in A with jth column in B:

$$[a_{ij}\ a_{i2}\ a_{i3}\ \ldots\ a_{in}], \begin{bmatrix} b_{1j} \\ b_{2j} \\ b_{3j} \\ | \\ b_{nj} \end{bmatrix}$$

Thus, for multiplication number of rows in A is equal to number of columns of B:

$$A = \begin{bmatrix} a_{11} & a_{12} \\ a_{21} & a_{22} \\ a_{31} & a_{32} \end{bmatrix} \quad 3 \times 2 \text{ matrix}$$

$$B = \begin{bmatrix} b_{11} & b_{12} & b_{13} & b_{14} \\ b_{21} & b_{22} & b_{23} & b_{24} \end{bmatrix} \; 2 \times 4 \text{ matrix}.$$

$$AB = \begin{bmatrix} a_{11}b_{11} + a_{12}b_{21} & a_{11}b_{12} + a_{12}b_{22} & a_{11}b_{13} + a_{12}b_{23} & a_{11}b_{14} + a_{12}b_{24} \\ a_{21}b_{11} + a_{22}b_{21} & a_{21}b_{12} + a_{22}b_{22} & a_{21}b_{13} + a_{22}b_{23} & a_{21}b_{14} + a_{22}b_{24} \\ a_{31}b_{11} + a_{32}b_{21} & a_{31}b_{12} + a_{32}b_{21} & a_{31}b_{13} + a_{32}b_{23} & a_{31}b_{14} + a_{32}b_{24} \\ & 3 \times 4 \text{ matrix.} & & \end{bmatrix}$$

Illustration 1

$$A = \begin{bmatrix} 2 & 3 & 4 \\ 1 & 2 & 3 \\ -1 & 1 & 2 \end{bmatrix}, \quad B = \begin{bmatrix} 1 & 3 & 0 \\ -1 & 2 & 1 \\ 0 & 0 & 2 \end{bmatrix}$$

$$3 \times 3 \qquad\qquad 3 \times 3$$

Column of A is equal to row of B. Hence conformable AB = C (3 × 3).

$$C = A.B = \begin{bmatrix} 2\times1+3(-1)+4\times0 & 2\times3+3\times2+4\times0 & 2\times0+3\times1+4\times2 \\ 1\times1+2(-1)+3\times0 & 1\times3+2\times2+3\times0 & 1\times0+2\times1+3\times2 \\ -1\times1+1(-1)+2\times0 & -1\times3+1\times2+2\times0 & -1\times0+1\times1+2\times2 \end{bmatrix}$$

$$= \begin{bmatrix} 2-3 & 6+6 & 3+8 \\ 1-2 & 3+4 & 2+6 \\ -1-1 & -3+2 & 1+4 \end{bmatrix}$$

$$= \begin{bmatrix} -1 & 12 & 11 \\ -1 & 7 & 8 \\ -2 & -1 & 5 \end{bmatrix}$$

Illustration 2

$$A = \begin{bmatrix} 1 & 2 & 3 & 4 & 5 \\ 6 & 7 & 8 & 0 & 3 \\ 6 & -3 & 4 & -2 & 1 \end{bmatrix}, \quad B = \begin{bmatrix} 1 & 2 \\ 3 & 4 \\ 5 & 6 \\ 6 & 5 \\ 7 & 0 \end{bmatrix}$$

$$3 \times 5 \qquad\qquad 5 \times 2$$

Row of B is equal to column of A. Hence conformable. AB will be 3 × 2

$$AB = \begin{bmatrix} 1\times1+2\times3+3\times5+4\times6+5\times7 & 1\times2+2\times4+3\times6+4\times5+5\times0 \\ 6\times1+7\times3+8\times5+0+3\times7 & 6\times2+7\times4+8\times6+0+0 \\ 6\times1+(-3)\times3+4\times5+(-2)6+1\times7 & 6\times2+(-3)4+4\times6+(-2)\times5+1\times0 \end{bmatrix}$$

$$= \begin{bmatrix} 1+6+15+24+35 & 2+8+18+20+0 \\ 6+21+40+0+21 & 12+28+48+0+0 \\ 6-9+20-12+7 & 12-12+24-10+0 \end{bmatrix}$$

$$= \begin{bmatrix} 79 & 48 \\ 88 & 88 \\ 12 & 14 \end{bmatrix}.$$

The matrix multiplication is not in general commutative A and B are conformable in the sense A.B. They need not be conformable in the sense B.A. But the product of two matrices depends on the order in which they are multiplied.

Let,

$$A = \begin{bmatrix} 1 & 0 \\ 0 & -1 \end{bmatrix} \text{ and } B = \begin{bmatrix} 0 & 1 \\ 1 & 0 \end{bmatrix}$$

$$AB = \begin{bmatrix} 1 & 0 \\ 0 & -1 \end{bmatrix} \begin{bmatrix} 0 & 1 \\ 1 & 0 \end{bmatrix} = \begin{bmatrix} 0 & 1 \\ -1 & 0 \end{bmatrix}$$

$$BA = \begin{bmatrix} 0 & 1 \\ 1 & 0 \end{bmatrix} \begin{bmatrix} 1 & 0 \\ 0 & -1 \end{bmatrix} = \begin{bmatrix} 0 & -1 \\ 1 & 0 \end{bmatrix}$$

The results are different which shows difference between matrix and other quantities.

A and B are non commuting matrices:

$$AB \neq BA$$

If A and B are square and are of same order 2 × 2, 3 × 3 or 4 × 4. They can be conformable in both ways AB = BA

A	B
2 × 2	2 × 2
3 × 3	3 × 3
4 × 4	4 × 4

Even when the conformability requirement is satisfied, commutation is not in general possible.

4.4 A SYSTEM OF m LINEAR EQUATIONS WITH n UNKNOWNS

$$a_{11}x_1 + a_{12}\,x_2 + \ldots + a_{1n}x_n = b_i$$

$$- \quad - \quad - \quad - \quad -$$

$$- \quad - \quad - \quad - \quad -$$

$$a_{m1}x_1 \quad a_{m2}x_2 + \ldots + a_{mn}x_n = b_n$$

We can write matrix:

$$A = \begin{bmatrix} a_{11} & a_{12} \ldots a_{1n} \\ a_{21} & a_{22} \ldots a_{2n} \\ \cdot \; \cdot & \cdot \; \cdot \; \cdot \; \cdot \\ \cdot \; \cdot & \cdot \; \cdot \; \cdot \; \cdot \\ a_{m_1} & a_{m_2} \; a_{mn} \end{bmatrix}$$

$$B = \begin{bmatrix} b_1 \\ b_2 \\ \vdots \\ b_n \end{bmatrix} \text{ and } X = \begin{bmatrix} x_1 \\ x_2 \\ \vdots \\ x_n \end{bmatrix} \quad \text{then } AX = B.$$

$$\text{or} \begin{bmatrix} a_{11} & a_{12} \ldots a_{1n} \\ a_{21} & a_{22} \ldots a_{2n} \\ = & = \; = \; = \\ a_{m1} & a_{m2} \ldots a_{mn} \end{bmatrix} \begin{bmatrix} x_1 \\ x_2 \\ \vdots \\ \vdots \\ x_n \end{bmatrix} = \begin{bmatrix} b_1 \\ b_2 \\ \vdots \\ \vdots \\ b_n \end{bmatrix}$$

4.5 DIAGONAL MATRIX

Let A = $[a_{ij}]$ be a square matrix. A square matrix is said to be a diagonal matrix if $a_{ij} = 0$. Whenever, $i \neq j$. If square matrix A is a diagonal matrix of order n then elements

$$a_{11} = d_1$$
$$a_{22} = d_2$$
$$a_{33} = d_3$$
$$a_{nn} = d_n$$ are called diagonal elements

and the matrix A is denoted by

$$\text{diag } [d_1\ d_2 - - - d_n\}$$

i.e the square matrix $\begin{bmatrix} 2 & 0 & 0 \\ 0 & 4 & 0 \\ 0 & 0 & 5 \end{bmatrix}$ is a diagonal matrix, and 2, 4 and 5 are its diagonal elements.

4.6 SCALAR MATRIX

A diagonal matrix in which all diagonal elements are equal is called a scalar matrix. The matrix $\begin{bmatrix} 2 & 0 & 0 \\ 0 & 2 & 0 \\ 0 & 0 & 2 \end{bmatrix}$ is called a scalar matrix.

4.7 UNIT MATRIX

A scalar matrix is called a unit matrix if each of its diagonal element is unity. The matrix $\begin{bmatrix} 1 & 0 \\ 0 & 1 \end{bmatrix}$ is a unit matrix of order 2.

$\begin{bmatrix} 1 & 0 & 0 \\ 0 & 1 & 0 \\ 0 & 0 & 1 \end{bmatrix}$ is a unit matrix of order 3, etc.

4.8 SINGULAR AND NON-SINGULAR MATRIX

A square matrix A is said to be singular matrix or non-singular matrix according to the determinant:

$$|A| = 0 \text{ singular}$$

$$\neq 0 \text{ non-singular}$$

Let: $A = \begin{bmatrix} 1 & 2 \\ 3 & 4 \end{bmatrix}$

Then, $\Delta = |A| = \begin{vmatrix} 1 & 2 \\ 3 & 4 \end{vmatrix} = 1 \times 4 - 2 \times 3 = 4 - 6 = -2 \neq 0$.

Hence, A is a non-singular matrix.

Suppose, $A = \begin{vmatrix} 1 & 2 \\ 3 & 6 \end{vmatrix}$

$$\Delta = |A| = \begin{vmatrix} 1 & 2 \\ 3 & 6 \end{vmatrix} = 1 \times 6 - 2 \times 3 = 6 - 6 = 0$$

Its determinant vanishes.

Hence A is a singular matrix. Only non-singular matrix have inverse.

4.9 TRANSPOSE MATRIX

It is shown by tilde A, i.e. $\tilde{A}$ or A'(prime)

The transpose matrix to A is $\tilde{A}$.$\tilde{A}$ is formed from A by interchanging rows and columns:

$$A = [a_{ij}]$$

then, $\tilde{A} = [a_{ji}]$

suppose,

$$A = \begin{bmatrix} a_{11} & a_{12} & a_{13} \\ a_{21} & a_{22} & a_{23} \\ a_{31} & a_{32} & a_{33} \end{bmatrix}$$

$$\tilde{A} = \begin{bmatrix} a_{11} & a_{21} & a_{31} \\ a_{12} & a_{22} & a_{32} \\ a_{13} & a_{23} & a_{33} \end{bmatrix}$$

4.10 ADJOINT MATRIX: (Adj A) OR Â

Let A = $[a_{ij}]$ be a square matrix and let A_{ij} be the co-factor of a_{ij} in |A|. Then transpose of the matrix $[A_{ij}]$ is called the adjugable or adjoint matrix of A and is written as A_{dj} A or Â.

Thus, Adj A = $[A'_{ij}]$ when $A'_{ij} = A_{ji}$ of A= $[a'_{ij}]$ is a non-singular matrix $\left[\frac{A_{ji}}{|A|}\right]$ or $\left[\frac{A_{dj}A}{|A|}\right]$ is called reciprocal matrix of A.

Let A be a square matrix (3 × 3).

$$A = \begin{bmatrix} a_{11} & a_{12} & a_{13} \\ a_{21} & a_{22} & a_{23} \\ a_{31} & a_{32} & a_{33} \end{bmatrix}$$

its determinant is,

$$|A| = \begin{vmatrix} a_{11} & a_{12} & a_{13} \\ a_{21} & a_{22} & a_{23} \\ a_{31} & a_{32} & a_{33} \end{vmatrix}$$

$$= a_{11}\begin{vmatrix} a_{22} & a_{23} \\ a_{32} & a_{33} \end{vmatrix} - a_{12}\begin{vmatrix} a_{21} & a_{23} \\ a_{31} & a_{33} \end{vmatrix} + a_{13}\begin{vmatrix} a_{21} & a_{22} \\ a_{31} & a_{32} \end{vmatrix}$$

The minor of a_{11} is the determinant obtained on striking out the first row and first column. If we give suitable sign with minor it is called cofactor:

$$A_{11} = +\begin{vmatrix} a_{22} & a_{23} \\ a_{32} & a_{33} \end{vmatrix}.$$

Similarly cofactor of,

$$A_{12} = -\begin{vmatrix} a_{21} & a_{23} \\ a_{31} & a_{33} \end{vmatrix}$$

$$A_{13} = \begin{vmatrix} a_{21} & a_{22} \\ a_{31} & a_{32} \end{vmatrix}$$

We can resolve the |A| along elements of II and III rows also and we can get their cofactors as well:

$$|A| = \begin{vmatrix} a_{11} & a_{12} & a_{13} \\ a_{21} & a_{22} & a_{23} \\ a_{31} & a_{32} & a_{33} \end{vmatrix} = a_{11}\begin{vmatrix} a_{22} & a_{23} \\ a_{32} & a_{33} \end{vmatrix} - a_{12}\begin{vmatrix} a_{21} & a_{23} \\ a_{31} & a_{33} \end{vmatrix}$$

$$+a_{13}\begin{vmatrix} a_{21} & -a_{22} \\ a_{31} & a_{32} \end{vmatrix} = -a_{21}\begin{vmatrix} a_{12} & a_{13} \\ a_{32} & a_{33} \end{vmatrix} + a_{22}\begin{vmatrix} a_{11} & a_{13} \\ a_{31} & a_{33} \end{vmatrix} - a_{23}\begin{vmatrix} a_{11} & a_{12} \\ a_{31} & a_{32} \end{vmatrix}$$

$$= +a_{31}\begin{vmatrix} a_{12} & a_{13} \\ a_{22} & a_{23} \end{vmatrix} - a_{32}\begin{vmatrix} a_{11} & a_{13} \\ a_{21} & a_{23} \end{vmatrix} + a_{33}\begin{vmatrix} a_{11} & a_{12} \\ a_{21} & a_{22} \end{vmatrix}$$

$$\therefore\ A_{21} = -\begin{vmatrix} a_{12} & a_{13} \\ a_{32} & a_{33} \end{vmatrix}$$

$$A_{22} = +\begin{vmatrix} a_{11} & a_{13} \\ a_{31} & a_{33} \end{vmatrix}$$

$$A_{23} = -\begin{vmatrix} a_{11} & a_{12} \\ a_{31} & a_{32} \end{vmatrix}$$

$$A_{31} = \begin{vmatrix} a_{12} & a_{13} \\ a_{22} & a_{23} \end{vmatrix}$$

$$A_{32} = -\begin{vmatrix} a_{11} & a_{13} \\ a_{21} & a_{23} \end{vmatrix}$$

$$A_{33} = \begin{vmatrix} a_{11} & a_{12} \\ a_{21} & a_{22} \end{vmatrix}.$$

A determinant from cofactors is also constituted, viz.:

$$\begin{vmatrix} A_{11} & A_{12} & A_{13} \\ A_{21} & A_{22} & A_{23} \\ A_{31} & A_{32} & A_{33} \end{vmatrix}$$

And the corresponding matrix is:

$$\left[A_{ij}\right] = \begin{vmatrix} A_{11} & A_{12} & A_{13} \\ A_{21} & A_{22} & A_{23} \\ A_{31} & A_{32} & A_{33} \end{vmatrix}$$

on transposing the matrix $[A_{ij}]$ we get another matrix $[A_{ji}]$ = $[A'_{ij}]$. This is called A_{dj} A.

In case of mxn determinant sign of cofactor is given by $(-1)^{m+n}$

When m = n = 1 sign = $(-1)^{1+1} = (-1)^2 = 1$

m = 1, n = 2 sign = $(-1)^{1+2} = (-1)^3 = 1$

m = 1, n = 3 sign = $(-1)^{1+3} = (-1)^4 = +1$

m –2, n = 1 sign = $(-1)^{2+1} = (-1)^3 = -1$

etc.

Solved examples 1

Find the Adjoint and inverse of:

$$A = \begin{bmatrix} 1 & 2 & 3 \\ 4 & 5 & 6 \\ 6 & 7 & 9 \end{bmatrix}$$

$$|A| = \begin{vmatrix} 1 & 2 & 3 \\ 4 & 5 & 6 \\ 6 & 7 & 9 \end{vmatrix}$$

$$= 1\begin{vmatrix} 5 & 6 \\ 7 & 9 \end{vmatrix} - 2\begin{vmatrix} 4 & 6 \\ 6 & 9 \end{vmatrix} + 3\begin{vmatrix} 4 & 5 \\ 6 & 7 \end{vmatrix}$$

$= 1\ (45 - 42) -2\ (36 - 36) + 3\ (28 - 30)$

$= 3 - 2 \times 0 + 3\ (-2)$

$= 3 - 6 = -3$

Hence, A is a non-singular matrix.

Thus, A^{-1} exists.

$$\text{Now, } A^{-1} = \frac{1}{A} = \frac{A_{adj}\ A}{|A|}$$

$$A_{11} = \begin{vmatrix} 5 & 6 \\ 7 & 9 \end{vmatrix}, \quad A_{12} = -\begin{vmatrix} 4 & 6 \\ 6 & 9 \end{vmatrix}, \quad A_{13}\begin{vmatrix} 4 & 5 \\ 6 & 7 \end{vmatrix}$$

$$= 45-42 = 3 \quad = -(36-36) = 0 \quad = 28-30 = -2$$

$$A_{21} = -\begin{vmatrix} 2 & 3 \\ 7 & 9 \end{vmatrix}, \quad A_{22} = \begin{vmatrix} 1 & 3 \\ 6 & 9 \end{vmatrix}, \quad A_{23} = -\begin{vmatrix} 1 & 2 \\ 6 & 7 \end{vmatrix}$$

$$= -(18-21)=3 \quad = (9-18) = -9 \quad = -(7-12) = 5$$

$$A_{31} = \begin{vmatrix} 2 & 3 \\ 5 & 6 \end{vmatrix}, \quad A_{32} = -\begin{vmatrix} 1 & 3 \\ 4 & 6 \end{vmatrix}, \quad A_{33} = \begin{vmatrix} 1 & 2 \\ 4 & 5 \end{vmatrix}$$

$$= (12-15) = -3 \quad = -(6-12) = 6 \quad = (5-8) = -3$$

$$\left[A'_{ij}\right] = \left[A_{ji}\right] = \begin{bmatrix} A_{11} & A_{21} & A_{31} \\ A_{12} & A_{22} & A_{32} \\ A_{13} & A_{23} & A_{33} \end{bmatrix} = \text{Adj } A$$

2. Suppose A is a 3 × 3 matrix:

$$A = \begin{bmatrix} 1 & 1 & 3 \\ 0 & 1 & -1 \\ 2 & 0 & -4 \end{bmatrix}$$

$$\Delta = |A| \begin{vmatrix} 1 & 1 & 3 \\ 0 & 1 & -1 \\ 2 & 0 & -4 \end{vmatrix}$$

$$= 1\begin{vmatrix} 1 & -1 \\ 0 & -4 \end{vmatrix} - 1\begin{vmatrix} 0 & -1 \\ 2 & -4 \end{vmatrix} + 3\begin{vmatrix} 0 & 1 \\ 2 & 0 \end{vmatrix}$$ When we resolve along first row.

$$= 0\begin{vmatrix} 1 & 3 \\ 0 & -4 \end{vmatrix} + 1\begin{vmatrix} 1 & 3 \\ 2 & -4 \end{vmatrix} - (-)\begin{vmatrix} 1 & 1 \\ 2 & 0 \end{vmatrix}$$ Second row.

$$= +2\begin{vmatrix} 1 & 3 \\ 0 & -1 \end{vmatrix} - 0\begin{vmatrix} 1 & 3 \\ 0 & -1 \end{vmatrix} + (-4)\begin{vmatrix} 1 & 1 \\ 0 & 1 \end{vmatrix}$$ Third row.

Cofactors are:

$$A_{11} = \begin{vmatrix} 1 & -1 \\ 0 & -4 \end{vmatrix} = -4$$

$$A_{12} = -\begin{vmatrix} 0 & -1 \\ 2 & -4 \end{vmatrix} = -|0+2| = -2$$

$$A_{13} = \begin{vmatrix} 0 & 1 \\ 2 & 0 \end{vmatrix} = 0-2 = -2$$

$$A_{21} = -\begin{vmatrix} 1 & 3 \\ 0 & -4 \end{vmatrix} = -(-4-0) = 4$$

$$A_{22} = \begin{vmatrix} 1 & 3 \\ 2 & -4 \end{vmatrix} = -4-6 = -10$$

$$A_{23} = -\begin{vmatrix} 1 & 1 \\ 2 & 0 \end{vmatrix} = -(0-2) = 2$$

$$A_{31} = \begin{vmatrix} 1 & 3 \\ 1 & -1 \end{vmatrix} = -1-3 = -4$$

$$A_{32} = -\begin{vmatrix} 1 & 3 \\ 0 & -1 \end{vmatrix} = -(-1-0) = 1$$

$$A_{33} = \begin{vmatrix} 1 & 1 \\ 0 & 1 \end{vmatrix} = (1-0) = 1.$$

Thus matrix (instituted by its cofactors) is:

$$\begin{vmatrix} -4 & -2 & -4 \\ 4 & -10 & 2 \\ -4 & 1 & 1 \end{vmatrix}$$

On transposing the resultant matrix

we get,

$$\begin{vmatrix} -4 & 4 & -4 \\ -2 & -10 & 1 \\ -2 & 2 & 1 \end{vmatrix}$$

$$\therefore A_{dj} \ A = \begin{vmatrix} -4 & 4 & -4 \\ -2 & -10 & 1 \\ -2 & 2 & 1 \end{vmatrix}$$

If $A = [a_{ij}]$ is a non-singular matrix the matrix $\left[\frac{A_{ji}}{|A|}\right]$ or $\frac{A_{ji}}{|A|}$ is called A^{-1} = Reciprocal matrix (Inverse matrix) of A.

Reciprocal of $A = \frac{A_{dj} \ A}{|A|}$

$$= \begin{bmatrix} A_{11} & A_{21} & A_{31} \\ A_{12} & A_{22} & A_{32} \\ A_{13} & A_{23} & A_{33} \end{bmatrix} \Big/ |A|$$

$$= \begin{bmatrix} \frac{A_{11}}{|A|} & \frac{A_{21}}{|A|} & \frac{A_{31}}{|A|} \\ \frac{A_{12}}{|A|} & \frac{A_{22}}{|A|} & \frac{A_{32}}{|A|} \\ \frac{A_{13}}{|A|} & \frac{A_{23}}{|A|} & \frac{A_{33}}{|A|} \end{bmatrix}$$

On multiplying with A on both sides

$$A^{-1} = \frac{A_{adj} A}{|A|}$$

and $AA^{-1} = \dfrac{A_{adj}A.A}{|A|} = \dfrac{\hat{A}\ A}{|A|}$

or, $\hat{A}.A = |A|\ AA^{-1}$

$= |A|\ E$ where, $AA^{-1} = E$ (identity).

If the matrices A and B are such that:

$$AB = BA = E$$

Then B is called the inverse of A and is written as A^{-1}. If a matrix A has inverse it is a square matrix. The ratio A/B is regarded as the product AB^{-1}.

Illustration 1. Given $AA^{-1} = A^{-1}A = 1$. Evaluate A^{-1} for

$$A = \begin{bmatrix} a_{11} & a_{12} \\ a_{21} & a_{22} \end{bmatrix}$$

$$|A| = \begin{vmatrix} a_{11} & a_{12} \\ a_{21} & a_{22} \end{vmatrix} = |a_{11}\ a_{22} - a_{12}\ a_{21}|.$$

Hence, $|A|$ is a non-singular matrix. As such A^{-1} exists:

$$A^{-1} = \frac{1}{A} = \frac{A_{adj}.A}{|A|}$$

$$A_{11} = |a_{11}|,\ A_{21} = |a_{21}| \qquad A^{-1} = \frac{\begin{vmatrix} A_{11} & A_{12} \\ A_{21} & A_{22} \end{vmatrix}}{|a_{11}\ a_{22} - a_{12}\ a_{21}|}$$

$$A_{12} = |a_{12}|,\ A_{21} = |a_{22}|$$

4.11 ORTHOGONAL MATRIX

A^1 = Transpose matrix.

The square matrix A is said to be orthogonal if $A^1A = E$.

Every orthogonal matrix is non-singular and $|A| = \pm 1$.

Unit matrix E is also on orthogonal matrix $EE^1 = E^1E = E$

The product of two orthogonal matrices is orthogonal.

Let A and B be the two orthogonal matrices.

Then $A^1A = E$, $B^1B = E$

$$\text{Or } (AB)'(AB) = (B^1A^1)(AB)$$
$$= B^1(A^1A)B$$
$$= B^1EB$$
$$= B^1B = E$$

Hence, A and B are orthogonal matrices.

The transpose A^1 of an orthogonal matrix

A is orthogonal and $A^1 = A^{-1}$

Let A be an orthogonal matrix.

Then A is non-singular and so A has an inverse B.

Thus, $AB = E$

Now $A^1A = E$

$$\text{Also } A^1 = A^1E = A^1(AB)$$
$$= (A^1A)B$$
$$= EB$$
$$= B$$

$AB = AA^1 = E$

Hence $(AA^1)^1 = E^1 = E.$

Or $(A^1)'A^1 = E.$

Hence A is orthogonal and $A^1 = B = A^{-1}$.

4.12 PROPERTIES OF ORTHOGONAL MATRIX

Let A be an orthogonal matrix. Its inverse is equal to the transpose. A has its inverse A^{-1} and is equal to its transpose A^1. Then $A^{-1} = A^1$. It plays important role. Every orthogonal matrix must be square otherwise there will be no inverse.

Consider a 3 × 3 orthogonal matrix:

$$[A] = \begin{bmatrix} A_{11} & A_{12} & A_{13} \\ A_{21} & A_{22} & A_{23} \\ A_{31} & A_{32} & A_{33} \end{bmatrix}$$

$$\text{Its transpose, } A^1 = \begin{bmatrix} A_{11} & A_{21} & A_{31} \\ A_{12} & A_{22} & A_{32} \\ A_{13} & A_{23} & A_{33} \end{bmatrix}$$

Since A is orthogonal matrix its inverse A^{-1} is identical to its transpose A^1.

$$\therefore \quad AA^{-1} = E$$

$$AA^1 = E$$

Placing these matrices in the proper form:

$$\begin{bmatrix} A_{11} & A_{12} & A_{13} \\ A_{21} & A_{22} & A_{23} \\ A_{31} & A_{32} & A_{33} \end{bmatrix} \times \begin{bmatrix} A_{11} & A_{21} & A_{31} \\ A_{12} & A_{22} & A_{32} \\ A_{13} & A_{23} & A_{33} \end{bmatrix} =$$

$$\begin{bmatrix} A_{11}^2 + A_{12}^2 + A_{13}^2 & A_{11}A_{21} + A_{12}A_{22} + A_{13}A_{23} & A_{11}A_{31} + A_{12}A_{33} + A_{13}A_{33} \\ A_{21}A_{11} + A_{22}A_{12} + A_{23}A_{13} & A_{21}^2 + A_{22}^2 + A_{23}^2 & A_{21}A_{31} + A_{22}A_{32} + A_{23}A_{33} \\ A_{31}A_{11} + A_{32}A_{12} + A_{33}A_{13} & A_{31}A_{21} + A_{32}A_{22} + A_{3}A_{23} & A_{31}^2 + A_{32}^2 + A_{33}^2 \end{bmatrix}$$

$$= E = \begin{bmatrix} 1 & 0 & 0 \\ 0 & 1 & 0 \\ 0 & 0 & 1 \end{bmatrix}$$

We can resolve to obtain:

$$A_{11}^2 + A_{12}^2 + A_{13}^2 = 1$$

$$A_{21}^2 + A_{22}^2 + A_{23}^2 = 1$$

$$A_{31}^2 + A_{32}^2 + A_{33}^2 = 1$$

and, $A_{11}A_{21} + A_{12}A_{22} + A_{13}A_{23} = 0$

$$A_{11}A_{31}+A_{12}A_{32}+A_{13}A_{33} = 0 \text{ etc.}$$

Thus, in general an orthogonal matrix must obey the following relations:

(i) Sum of the square of the elements of any row is unity.

(ii) For any two row the sum of the products of the corresponding elements must be equal to zero.

(iii) A third property is also emerged as follows:

A is orthogonal matrix that brings the transformation of a column matrix:

$$X = \begin{bmatrix} x_1 \\ x_2 \\ \vdots \\ x_n \end{bmatrix}$$ into a set of new quantities.

$x_1^1, x_2^1, ... x_x^1$ the single column matrix $X^1 = \begin{bmatrix} x_1^1 \\ x_2^1 \\ \vdots \\ x_n^1 \end{bmatrix}$

Then $X^1 = AX^1$ It is pre-multiplied from both sides by A^{-1} we have,

$$A^{-1}X^1 = A^{-1}AX$$
$$= (A^{-1}A)\ X = X.$$

Its transpose is $(A^{-1}\ X^1)^1 = X^1$

or $\quad (X)^1 = (X^1)^1\ (A^{-1})^1$

$$= (X^1)^1\ (A^1)^1$$
$$= (X^1)^1\ A$$

The product:

$$= (X)^1X$$
$$= (X^1)^1\ AX$$
$$= (X^1)^1X^1$$

Since X^1 is a single column matrix so its transpose will be $(X^1)^1$ a single row matrix.

The transpose of X, i.e. $(X)^1$ should be a row matrix as X is column matrix itself:

$$= [x_1,\ x_2,\ x_3.....]$$

$$\therefore (X)^1\ X = \begin{bmatrix} x_1 x_2 x_3 \end{bmatrix} \begin{bmatrix} x_1 \\ x_2 \\ x_3 \end{bmatrix} = x_1^2 + x_2^2 + x_3^2 = \Sigma x_i^2$$

Similarly RHS $(x^1)^1$ will take the form. X^1 is a single column matrix $= \begin{bmatrix} x_1^1 \\ x_2^1 \\ x_3^1 \end{bmatrix}$.

Its transpose $(X^1)^1$ = A single row matrix

$$\therefore (X^1)^1 X^1 = \begin{bmatrix} x_1^1 & x_2^1 & x_3^1 \end{bmatrix} \begin{bmatrix} x_1^1 \\ x_2^1 \\ x_3^1 \end{bmatrix}$$

$$= x_1^{1^2} + x_2^{1^2} + x_3^{1^2}$$

$$= \Sigma x_i^{1^2}$$

Consequently $= \Sigma x_i^{1^2} = \Sigma x_i^2$

This leaves the transformation affected by the orthogonal matrix unchanged. The sum of the squares of the elements are unchanged. This type of transformation is known as orthogonal transformation.

4.13 BLOCK DIAGONALIZATION OF MATRICES

Representative matrices can be of any dimension. For n-atomic molecules each atom is specified by three coordinates. This will give a representation consisting of 3n × 3n matrices. For instance we take the case of benzene the matrices will be of 3 × 12 × 3 × 12 = 36 × 36. In order to handle and analyse such matrices it is essential to reduce them to a much smaller size to those of fundamental representations. Such fundamental representations are 1 × 1, 2 × 2 or 3 × 3. These matrices entered on the principal diagonal and zero everywhere else.

Consider an square matrix A of dimension 3.

$$A = \begin{bmatrix} a_{11} & a_{12} & a_{13} \\ a_{21} & a_{22} & a_{23} \\ a_{31} & a_{32} & a_{33} \end{bmatrix}_{3 \times 3}$$

The matrix A is to be transformed into B. The matrix retains its dimension during transformation. $A \rightarrow B$. This can be accomplished by similarity transformation.

$Q^{-1}AQ = B$ represents similarity transformation. The process is repeated so that a point in reached when similarity transformation does not further reduce the dimensions.

The matrix will be rearranged so that the zero elements are symmetrically distributed about the diagonal. The non zero elements are distributed into blocks along the diagonal.

$$Q^{-1}AQ = Q^{-1}\begin{bmatrix} a_{11} & a_{12} & a_{13} \\ a_{21} & a_{22} & a_{23} \\ a_{31} & a_{32} & a_{33} \end{bmatrix} Q \rightarrow$$

$$= \left[\begin{array}{cc|c} b_{11} & b_{12} & 0 \\ b_{21} & b_{22} & 0 \\ \hline 0 & 0 & b_{33} \end{array}\right] = B.$$

The matrix B is regarded as built up from two smaller matrices B_1 and B_2. Here we get a 2×2 block and a 1×1 block such that

$$B_1 = \underset{2 \times 2}{\begin{bmatrix} b_{11} & b_{12} \\ b_{21} & b_{22} \end{bmatrix}}$$

$$B_2 = \underset{1 \times 1}{\begin{bmatrix} b_{33} \end{bmatrix}}$$

Both B_1 and B_2 form representation separately to the point group. We have now converted the three dimensions representation A to another three dimensional representations of smaller diamentions B_1 and B_2. Thus we have affected the reduction of the original representation.

4.14 SIMILARITY TRANSFORMATION

Consider two sets of coordinate system such as $(x_1, x_2, x_3 \ldots x_n)$ and $\left(x_1^1, x_2^1, x_3^1 \ldots x_n^1\right)$ are taken to be as column vectors.

Like $X = \begin{bmatrix} x_1 \\ x_2 \\ x_3 \\ ' \\ : \\ x_n \end{bmatrix}$ and $X' = \begin{bmatrix} x_1' \\ x_2' \\ x_3' \\ ' \\ : \\ x_n' \end{bmatrix}$. These two column vectors are interrelated through $X = QX^1$ with Q as n dimensioned transformation matrix.

$$\begin{bmatrix} x_1 \\ x_2 \\ x_3 \\ ' \\ : \\ x_n' \end{bmatrix} = Q \begin{bmatrix} x_1' \\ x_2' \\ x_3' \\ ' \\ : \\ x_n' \end{bmatrix}$$

. A new kind of transformation is achieved by matrix A such that $AX = Y$, where $Y = QY^1$. Both X and Y belong to the same system of coordinates. An additional transformation is given by $A^1X^1 = Y^1$. An established relationship may exist, between A and A^1. As $X = QX^1$ $Y = QY^1$ and $Q^{-1}AQX^1 = Y^1$. Also $A^1X^1 = Y^1$. Since Q is a non-singular matrix hence multiply by Q^{-1} such that $Q^{-1}AQ\,X^1 = Q^{-1}\,QY^1 = Y^1$. This transformation is regarded as similarity transformation. The two matrices A and A^1 are similar.

$Q^{-1}AQ = X_A$

$Q^{-1}BQ = X_B$

X_A and X_B are numbers which commute so that

$Q^{-1}X_BQ = Q^{-1}Q\,X_B = X_B$

$Q^{-1}X_AQ = Q^{-1}Q\,X_A = X_A$

QUESTIONS

1. (i) (a) Differentiate between arithmatics determinant and matrix.
   (b) Give the matrix for a vector.
   (ii) Comment on "matrices be rectangular or square but determinant can only be square".
2. (i) Comment on:
   (a) unit matrix,
   (b) square matrix,
   (c) singular and non-singular matrices.
   (ii) What do you understand from a transpose matrix and adjoint matrix.
3. (i) Explain orthogonal matrix.
   (ii) What are the characteristics of an orthogonal matrix. Illustrate each of them.
   (iii) What do you understand from block diagonization of matrices. What role the similarity transformation plays in such a procedure.
4. Give an account of similarity transformation. What do you understand from two matrices are similar?

THEORY OF MOLECULAR GROUPS (Properties of Groups, Matrix Representations of Symmetry Operations, Multiplication Table)

5

5.1 SUB-GROUP

We introduce a sub-group of small order inside a main group. Elements of a group forming group of smaller order is referred to a sub-group.

Let g be the order of a sub-group, the ratio h/g = integer.

The ratio of the order of a group to that of sub-group turns out to be a whole number. For instance, C_2 is a sub-group of C_4.

C_2	C_4
E . C_2	E, C_4, $C_4^2 = C_2$, C_4^3
g = 2	h = 4

Similarly C_3 is a sub-group of C_{3v}.

C_3	C_{3v}
E, C_3, C_3^2	E, C_3, C_3^2, σ_1 σ_2 σ_3
g = 3	h = 6

E is omnipresent. It is a member of sub-group with g = 1.

Similarly a bigger group is divided into 2, 3, 4, 5, etc. A Cyclic group of order 6 may have sub-groups of order 1, 2, 3.

Sub-groups are factors of main group.

ML_6 belongs to O_h group, but ML_4 L''_2 (D_{4h}) and ML_4 (D_{4h}).

As such D_{4h} is a sub-group of O_h because there is loss of symmetry in O_h to obtain D_{4h} with h = 16. Further D_4 with E, C_4, $C_4^2 = C_2$, C_4^3, $4C_2$ having g = 8 is a sub-group of h = 48, D_{2h} with operations E, C_2, C_2', C_2'', i, σ_h, σ_v σ_v', h = 8 has a sub-group D_2 with g = 4, E, C_2, C_2', C_2''.

5.2 SYMMETRY OPERATIONS IN A CLASS

Order of a class may be integral factor of a main group. If the elements are conjugate to each other they are members of the same class.

Let A and B be two matrices of same dimensions. X is also in the same group of A and B, then the combination X^{-1} AX is defined as B.

Such that $X^{-1} A X = B$.

A and B are called conjugate elements, A and B are related by similarity transformation. Consider the case of C_{3v}.

E is a class by itself.

$E^{-1} E E = E E E = E$

$C_3^{-1} E C_3 = \left(C_3^2 C_3\right)E = C_3^3 E = EE = E$

$\sigma_a^{-1} E \sigma_a = \sigma_a (E \sigma_a) = \sigma_a (\sigma_a E) = (\sigma_a \sigma_a) E = E.E = E$

$\sigma_b^{-1} E \sigma_b = \sigma_b (E\sigma_b) = \sigma_b (\sigma_b E) = (\sigma_b.\sigma_b)E = E.E = E$

$\sigma_c^{-1} E \sigma_c = \sigma_c (E \sigma_c) = (\sigma_c.\sigma_c).E = E.E = E.$

Hence, E is a class by itself. Consider the cases of C_3 and C_3^2.

$$\sigma_a C_3 \sigma_a = C_3^2$$

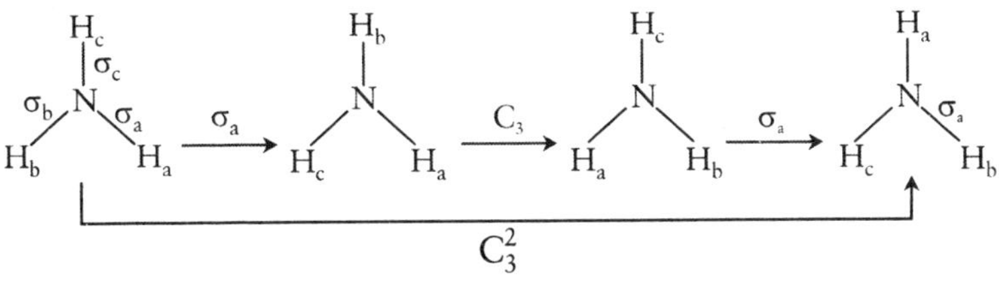

Similarly

$$\sigma_b\ C_3\ \sigma_b = C_3^2$$

$$\sigma_C\ C_3\ \sigma_C = C_3^2$$

$$E\ C_3\ E = C_3$$

$$E\ C_3^2\ E = C_3^2$$

$$C_3^{-1}\ C_3\ C_3 = (C_3^2 . C_3) . C_3 = C_3^3 . C_3 = E\ C_3 = C_3$$

$$C_3^{-2}\ C_3\ C_3^2 = C_3^{-1}\ C_3^{-1}\ (C_3 C_3^2)$$

$$= C_3^{-1}\ C_3^{-1}\ C_3^3 = C_3^2 . C_3^2 . E = C_3^3 . C_3 . E$$

$$= E.E.C_3 = C_3$$

$$C_3^{-1}\ C_3^2\ C_3 = C_3^2 \left(C_3^2 . C_3\right)$$

$$= C_3^2 . E = C_3^2$$

$$C_3^{-2}\ C_3^2\ C_3^2 = \left(C_3 . C_3^2\right) C_3^2 = \left(C_3^3\right) C_3^2 = E\ C_3^2 = C_3^2$$

$$\sigma_a\ C_3^2\ \sigma_a = C_3$$

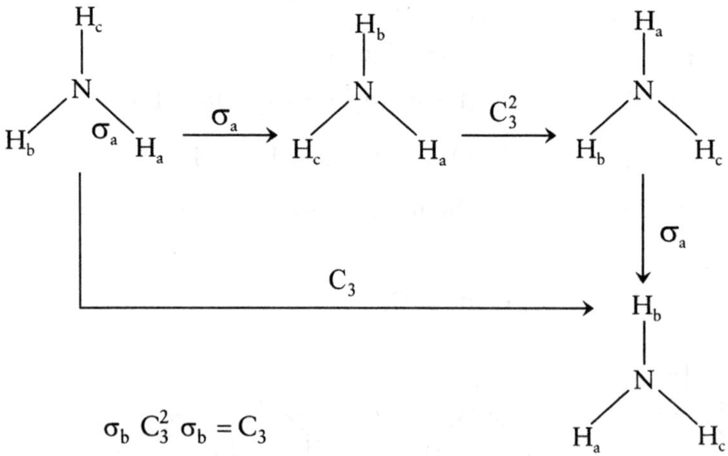

$$\sigma_b\ C_3^2\ \sigma_b = C_3$$

$$\sigma_c\ C_3^2\ \sigma_c = C_3$$

Thus, C_3 and C_3^2 constitute a class.

Cases of $\sigma_a\ \sigma_b\ \sigma_c$

$$E\ \sigma_a\ E = \sigma_a$$

$$C_3^{-1}\ \sigma_a C_3 = C_3^2\ \sigma_a\ C_3 = \sigma_c$$

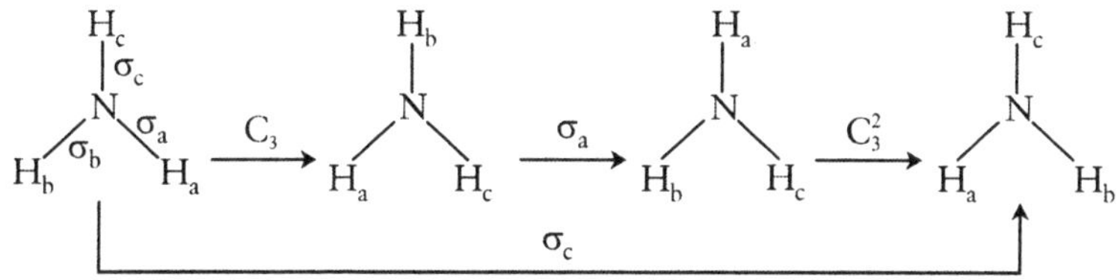

$$C_3^{-2}\ \sigma_a\ C_3^2 = C_3.\sigma_a.C_3^2 = \sigma_b$$

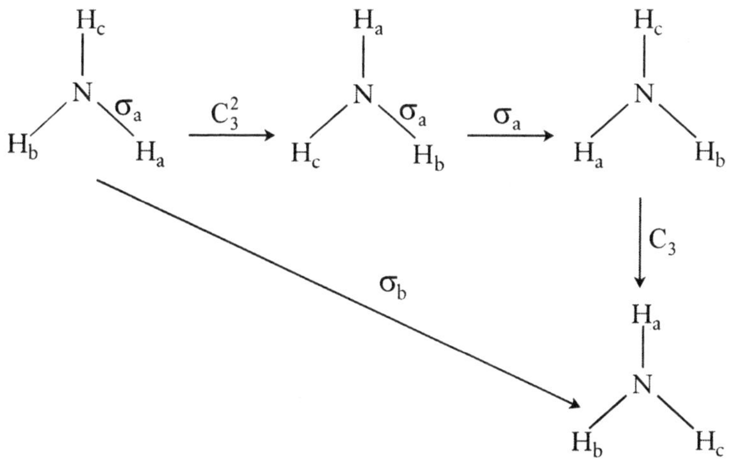

$$\sigma_a\quad \sigma_a\quad \sigma_a = \sigma_a$$

$$\sigma_b\quad \sigma_a\quad \sigma_b = \sigma_c$$

$$\sigma_c\quad \sigma_a\quad \sigma_c = \sigma_b$$

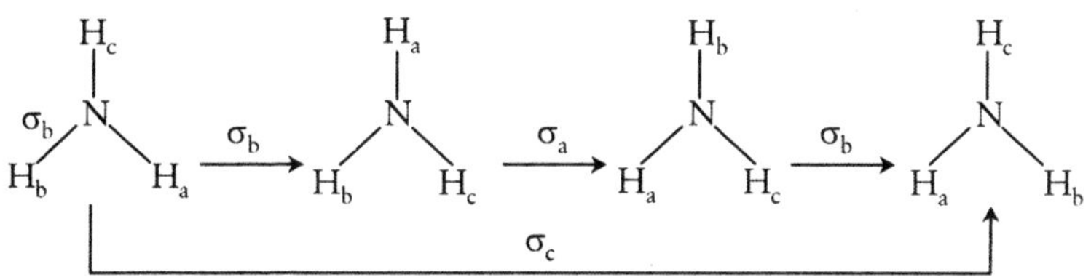

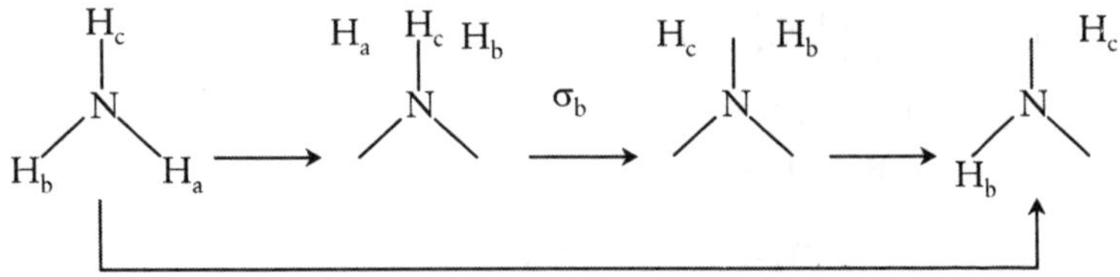

5.3 CONJUGATE ELEMENTS AS A MEMBER OF CLASS

Let there be P, Q and R as members of a group. Since Q is a member. Its reciprocal is defined Q^{-1} an another element of the group.

Alternatively, combination leads to another element through the process Q^{-1} PQ of the group. Such a combination gives the element. R, thus Q^{-1} PQ = R. So P is transformed by Q^{-1} and Q to a new element R.

Both P and R are said to be conjugate elements. An equally good relation is also established as:

$$P = Q\,R\,Q^{-1}$$

Either of two relations will be used for determining conjugate elements of a group. If P is conjugate to Q and Q is conjugate to R. It can easily be shown that P and R are conjugate elements.

Let $P = X^{-1}\,QX$

and $Q = Y^{-1}\,RY$.

Substitution of Q in the first equation gives,

$$P = X^{-1}\,Q\,X \text{ and } Q = Y^{-1}\,RY.$$

Substituting Q in the first equation.

$$P = X^{-1}\,(Y^{-1}\,RY)X$$

$$= X^{-1}\,Y^{-1}\,RYX$$

$$=(XY)^{-1}\,R\,(YX)$$

Since YX must be an element of the group say it to be Z then,

$$Z^{-1}\,RZ = P$$

It demonstrates that P and R are conjugate to one another.

5.4 RULES FOR CLASSES OF SYMMETRY OPERATIONS

We, may set for the following rules for finding a straight forward discussions of symmetry elements into classes. There are altogether seven rules for symmetry operations for assignment of classes:

1. The identity is always a class by itself.
2. The inversion operation is always in a class by itself, because it commutes with other symmetry operations.
3. The rotational element proper axis Cn and its inverse C_n^{-k} (C_n^{n-k}) will belong to the same class under two conditions:
   (a) There are n vertical mirror planes (σ_v or σ_d) present.
   (b) There are n two fold axis perpendicular to the rotation axis where neither the vertical mirror plane nor two fold axis are present, C_n^k and C_n^{-k} are not separate classes by themselves.
4. Rule 3 holds for improper rotations.
5. Two representations will belong to the same class when there exists in the group an operation which interchanges all the points on the corresponding mirror planes.

   Hence in C_{nv} groups all the σ_v operations belong to the same class because C_n^k operations interchange the mirror but in D_{nh} groups the σ_v and σ_d reflections belong to separate group likewise reflection across a horizontal mirror plane σ_h is always in a class by itself.
6. As in rule 5 two rotations C_n^k and $C_{n'}^{k'}$ about two different rotation axis are in the same class when there exists in the group an operation which interchanges all the points on the two axes. Hence in D_{nh} group all the axes $\perp^r$ to the principal axis are in the same class but not so in D_{nh} group.
7. Rule 6 holds for improper axis.

5.5 ABELIAN AND NON-ABELIAN GROUP

C_{2v} is an abelian group because all members commute with one another.

Viz. $C_2\,\sigma_{xz} = \sigma_{yz}$

$C_2 . \sigma_{yz} = \sigma_{xz}$

$\sigma_{xz} . \sigma_{yz} = C_2$

$\sigma_{yz} . \sigma_{xz} = C_2$

So, $C_2\,\sigma_{xz} = \sigma_{xz}\,C_2 = \sigma_{yz}$

$C_2\,\sigma_{yz} = \sigma_{yz}\,C_2 = \sigma_{xz}$

$\sigma_{yz} . \sigma_{xz} = \sigma_{xz} . \sigma_{yz} = C_2$

C_{3v} is a non-abelian group. Its members do not commute such as:

$\sigma_1 \times \sigma_2 = C_3$, $\quad \sigma_2 \times \sigma_1 = C_3^2$

Similarly $\sigma_3 \times \sigma_1 = C_3$, $\quad \sigma_1 \times \sigma_3 = C_3^2$

$\sigma_2 \times \sigma_3 = C_3$, $\quad \sigma_3 \times \sigma_2 = C_3^2$.

All other members E, C_3 and C_3^2 commute. But σ's are non-commuting. Hence it is a non-abelian group.

5.6 CYCLIC GROUP

A group represented by C_n is cyclic. The same member is repeating in a cycle till its power becomes equal to the order of the group. h is the order of cyclic group.

C_2 is a cyclic group of order 2.

Its members are E and C_2.

Other cyclic groups of order 2 are,

C_i, E, i and C_s E σ.

h = 3, E, C_3, C_3^2 is of order 3.

h = 4, E, C_4, $C_4^2 = C_2$, C_4^3 with order 4.

h = 5, E, C_5, C_5^2, C_5^3, C_5^4 with order 5.

h = 6, E, C_6, $C_6^2 = C_3$, $C_6^3 = C_2$, C_6^4 (C_3^2), C_6^5, with order = 6.

5.7 ISOMORPHIC GROUP

There are two or more groups whose multiplication tables are identical with equal orders, such groups are isomorphic. They have same algebraic structure of multiplication tables. Groups of order two are isomorphic such as C_2, C_s, C_i and a group containing 1,–1 as members

TABLE 5.1

(a)			(b)			(c)			(d)		
	E	C_2		E	σ		E	i		1	–1
E	E	C_2	E	E	σ	E	E	i	1	1	–1
C_2	C_2	E	σ	σ	E	i	i	E	–1	–1	1

There is only one way of giving their multiplication Table with order 2.

Multiplication Table for order 4 can be drawn with the members 1 i –1 –i

TABLE 5.2

	1	i	–1	–i
1	1	i	–1	–i
i	i	–1	–i	1
–1	–1	–i	1	i
–i	–i	1	i	–1

C_4 group with order 4 is isomorphic with the group described above:

TABLE 5.3

C_4	E	C_4	C_4^2	C_4^3
E	E	C_4	C_4^2	C_4^3
C_4	C_4	C_4^2	C_4^3	E
C_4^2	C_4^2	C_4^3	E	C_4
C_4^3	C_4^3	E	C_4	C_4^2

The multiplication table of the group with 1, i, –1, –i has the same algebraic structure with a group E A A^2 A^3 of order 4. They can be related to the elements.

$$1 \leftrightarrow E$$
$$i \leftrightarrow A$$
$$-1 \leftrightarrow A^2$$
$$-i \leftrightarrow A^3$$

Also the four elements of the C_4 group are generated from powers of i.

C	C_4^2	C_4^3	$C_4^4 = E$
i	i^2	i^3	i^4
i	–1	–i	1

They have same set of irreducible representations and same set of characters.

Groups C_{3v} and D_3 are isomorphic and they have same equivalent character tables.

C_{3v}: $E\ C_3\ C_3^2\ \sigma_1\ \sigma_2\ \sigma_3$

D_3: $E\ 2C_3\ 3C_2$

Their C.T are:

TABLE 5.4

(a)

C_{3v}	E	$2C_3$	$3\sigma_v$
A_1	1	1	1
A_2	1	1	–1
E	2	–1	0

(b)

D_3	E	$2C_3$	$3C_2$
A_1	1	1	1
A_2	1	1	–1
E	2	–1	0

5.8. CHARACTER

In chemistry people are using the word 'character' in physics it is 'trace' and in mathematics they are using 'spur.' These three words character, trace and spur are synonymous. Character is defined as the sum of diagonal elements in a square matrix.

$$A = \begin{bmatrix} a_{11} & a_{12} & a_{13}\ldots a_{1n} \\ a_{21} & a_{22} & a_{23}\ldots a_{2n} \\ \ldots & \ldots & \ldots \quad \ldots \\ a_{n1} & a_{n2} & a_{n3}\ldots a_{nn} \end{bmatrix}$$

The sum of the diagonal elements:

$$X = \sum_{i=1}^{n} a_{ii}$$

$$= a_{11} + a_{22} + a_{33} \ldots + a_{nn}$$

It is an important property of a matrix.

Character is a scalar quantity. The difficulty that we encounter in writing out the representative matrices is overcome through a quantity like character.

5.8.1 Properties of Characters

Let there be two square matrices A and B of same dimensions one can combine in the order AB or in reverse order BA.

All informations gathered from matrices for symmetry operations are contained in their characters.

Let AB = C

BA = D

Where A, B, C and D are square matrices of same dimensions.

Then, χ (C) = χ (D)

Proof: $\chi\ (C) = \sum_i C_{ii} = \sum_k \sum_j a_{jk}\, b_{kj}$

$$\chi(D) = \sum_j d_{jj} = \sum_k \sum_j b_{kj}\, a_{jk}$$

$$= \sum_j \sum_k a_{jk}\, b_{kj} = \sum_j d_{jj}$$

So $\chi(C) = \chi(D)$

Character remains unchanged by the order in which the matrices are multiplied.

Illustration 1

$$[A] = \begin{bmatrix} 1 & 2 \\ 0 & 3 \end{bmatrix}, \quad [B] = \begin{bmatrix} 1 & 1 \\ 2 & 0 \end{bmatrix}$$

$$[A]\,[B] = \begin{bmatrix} 1 & 2 \\ 0 & 3 \end{bmatrix} . \begin{bmatrix} 1 & 1 \\ 2 & 0 \end{bmatrix}$$

$$= \begin{bmatrix} 1\times1+2\times2 & 1\times1+2\times0 \\ 0\times1+3\times2 & 0\times1+3\times0 \end{bmatrix} = \begin{bmatrix} 1+4 & 1+0 \\ 0+6 & 0+0 \end{bmatrix}$$

$$= \begin{bmatrix} 5 & 1 \\ 6 & 0 \end{bmatrix}$$

$$\chi = 5 + 0 = 5$$

$$[B]\,[A] = \begin{bmatrix} 1 & 1 \\ 2 & 0 \end{bmatrix} . \begin{bmatrix} 1 & 2 \\ 0 & 3 \end{bmatrix}$$

$$= \begin{bmatrix} 1\times1+1\times0 & 1\times2+1\times3 \\ 2\times1+0\times0 & 2\times2+0\times3 \end{bmatrix} = \begin{bmatrix} 1+0 & 2+3 \\ 2+0 & 4+0 \end{bmatrix}$$

$$= \begin{bmatrix} 1 & 5 \\ 2 & 4 \end{bmatrix}$$

$$\chi = 1 + 4 = 5$$

5.8.2 Character Remains Unchanged by Similarity Transformation

Let there be two square matrices A and B of same dimensions. Q be another element in the same group. Its reciprocal also exists Q^{-1}. Now we pre-multiply it by Q^{-1} and post-multiply by Q to A.

$$Q^{-1} AQ = B$$

$$\text{or } B = Q^{-1} AQ$$

$$\chi\,(B) = \chi\,(Q^{-1} AQ)$$

Multiplication holds associative law, so that:

$$Q^{-1} A = AQ^{-1}$$

$$\begin{aligned}\text{Now, } \chi\,(B) &= \chi\,(Q^{-1} AQ)\\ &= \chi\,(AQ^{-1})\,Q\\ &= \chi\,\{A\,(Q^{-1}Q)\}\\ &= \chi\,(A.E)\\ &= \chi\,(A)\end{aligned}$$

5.8.3 Members of Same Class will have the Same Character

$$E \qquad C_3 \qquad C_3^2$$

$$\begin{bmatrix}1 & 0 & 0\\ 0 & 1 & 0\\ 0 & 0 & 1\end{bmatrix} \quad \begin{bmatrix}-1/2 & \frac{\sqrt{3}}{2} & 0\\ -\frac{\sqrt{3}}{2} & -1/2 & 0\\ 0 & 0 & 1\end{bmatrix} \quad \begin{bmatrix}-1/2 & -\frac{\sqrt{3}}{2} & 0\\ \frac{\sqrt{3}}{2} & -1/2 & 0\\ 0 & 0 & 1\end{bmatrix}$$

$\chi = 3$

$\chi = -\frac{1}{2} - \frac{1}{2} + 1 = -1 + 1 = 0$

$\chi = -\frac{1}{2} - \frac{1}{2} + 1 = -1 + 1 = 0$

$$\sigma_1 \qquad \sigma_2 \qquad \sigma_3$$

$$\begin{bmatrix}-1 & 0 & 0\\ 0 & 1 & 0\\ 0 & 0 & 1\end{bmatrix} \quad \begin{bmatrix}+1/2 & -\frac{\sqrt{3}}{2} & 0\\ -\frac{\sqrt{3}}{2} & -1/2 & 0\\ 0 & 0 & 1\end{bmatrix} \quad \begin{bmatrix}1/2 & -\frac{\sqrt{3}}{2} & 0\\ -\frac{\sqrt{3}}{2} & -1/2 & 0\\ 0 & 0 & 1\end{bmatrix}$$

$\chi = -1+1+1 = 1$

$\chi = +\frac{1}{2} - \frac{1}{2} + 1 = 1$

$\chi = \frac{1}{2} - \frac{1}{2} + 1 = 1$

Matrices which belong to the same class of operation have the same character.

In other words, conjugate matrices have the same character.

Thus, C^3 and C_3^2 belong to the same class.

Similarly σ_1, σ_2 and σ_3 have the same character and are members of same class. The character of operations of same class are identical in a given irreducible representation. It is not necessary to write out the characters for all the symmetry operations inside a class. Only of one typical member is shown in a character Table togather with the number of operations.

5.9 LINEAR TRANSFORMATION

We know matrices. The results of symmetry operations are summarized in multiplication Table for different point groups. The product operations were considered purely in geometric terms. We can get identical result by the application of matrices. All the five symmetry operations E, C_a, σ, i and S_n are replaced by matrices which constitute their representation. Matrices obey the same set of rules and laws that we followed in group operations. Symmetry operations such as rotation and reflection are conveniently described mathematically by making use of matrix language. In matrix method we use a basis function. Whatever we select for representation is called a basis function.

We can obtain representation for axis (X, Y, Z) co-ordinate for a point (X, Y, Z), orbitals (p_x, p_y, p_z) combination of orbitals (½ p + 3/2d, etc.), translational vectors. (T_x, T_y, T_z) rotational vectors (R_x, R_y R_z).

A linear transformation is represented by a matrix equation AX = B and we review matrices at this stage.

Consider two dimensional matrices for the present.

Then,

$$A = \begin{bmatrix} a_{11} & a_{12} \\ a_{21} & a_{22} \end{bmatrix} = \begin{bmatrix} a_{ij} \end{bmatrix}$$

i represents row and j column.

$$X = \begin{bmatrix} x_1 \\ x_2 \end{bmatrix}$$ a matrix with only column is called column matrix or vector.

and, $$B = \begin{bmatrix} b_1 \\ b_2 \end{bmatrix}$$ is another column matrix.

Now a system of linear equation are.

$$a_{11}\, x_1 + a_{12}\, x_2 = b_1$$

$$a_{21}\, x_1 + a_{22}\, x_2 = b_2.$$

Also, AX = B

$$\begin{bmatrix} a_{11} & a_{12} \\ a_{21} & a_{22} \end{bmatrix} \begin{bmatrix} x_1 \\ x_2 \end{bmatrix} = \begin{bmatrix} b_1 \\ b_2 \end{bmatrix}$$

Square Matrix Column Column
Vector Vector

The result of multiplying a matrix with a column vector is always a column vector. Similarly the product of a matrix and a row vector yields a row vector.

Let us consider another case where,

$$A = \begin{bmatrix} a_{11} & a_{12} \\ a_{21} & a_{22} \end{bmatrix} \qquad B = \begin{bmatrix} b_{11} & b_{12} \\ b_{21} & b_{22} \end{bmatrix}.$$

Now A.B is defined as a new matrix C such that,

$$C = A.B = \underset{2 \times 2}{\begin{bmatrix} a_{11} & a_{12} \\ a_{21} & a_{22} \end{bmatrix}} \underset{2 \times 2}{\begin{bmatrix} b_{11} & b_{12} \\ b_{21} & b_{22} \end{bmatrix}}.$$

Multiplying first row and first column and so on,

$$= \begin{bmatrix} a_{11}\, b_{11} + a_{12}\, b_{21} & a_{11}\, b_{12} + a_{12}\, b_{22} \\ a_{21}\, b_{11} + a_{22}\, b_{21} & a_{21}\, b_{12} + a_{22}\, b_{22} \end{bmatrix}$$

Also we have, $A = \begin{bmatrix} a_{11} & a_{12} \\ a_{21} & a_{22} \end{bmatrix}$, $B = \begin{bmatrix} b_{11} \\ b_{21} \end{bmatrix}$, a column vector.

Then, $$AB = \begin{bmatrix} a_{11} & a_{12} \\ a_{21} & a_{22} \end{bmatrix} \begin{bmatrix} b_{11} \\ b_{21} \end{bmatrix}$$

$$= \begin{bmatrix} a_{11}\, b_{11} + a_{12}\, b_{21} \\ a_{21}\, b_{11} + a_{22}\, b_{21} \end{bmatrix} \text{ Column vector.}$$

If $B = \begin{bmatrix} b_{11} & b_{12} \end{bmatrix}$ a row vector, then,

$$AB = \begin{bmatrix} a_{11} & a_{12} \\ a_{21} & a_{22} \end{bmatrix} \begin{bmatrix} b_{11} & b_{12} \end{bmatrix}$$

$$= \begin{bmatrix} a_{11}\, b_{11} + a_{21}\, b_{12} & a_{12}\, b_{11} + a_{22}\, b_{12} \end{bmatrix}$$

row vector.

5.10 MATRIX REPRESENTATION FOR SYMMETRY OPERATIONS

First of all we build two dimensional representations and then the case of three dimensional one. We want to see the effect of such operations on a single vector. It is represented by a point A (x, y) in a plane, called xy plane. We consider here the Cartesian co-ordinates x and y as basis function with origin (0, 0).

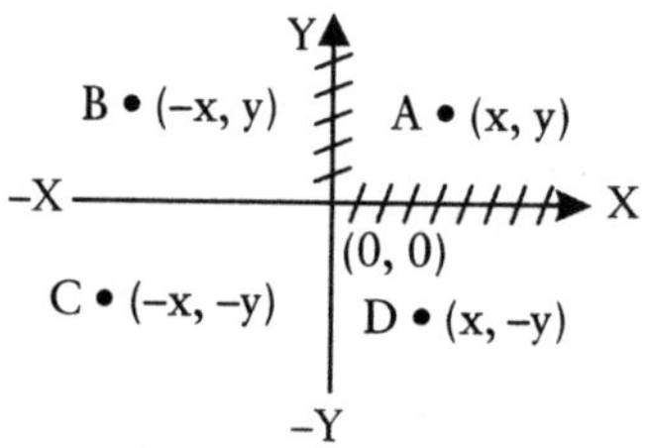

Now, consider reflection on point A. This leaves the co-ordinate unchanged whose axis defines the plane but there is an effect of changing the sign of the co-ordinate measured perpendicular to the plane.

For example, we perform reflection in σ_{yz} a new point B (x′, y′) is obtained. Here only x changes its sign to –x.

i.e. $x \to -x$

$y \to y$

but no change in y.

$$A\,(x, y) \xrightarrow{\sigma_{yz}} B\,(-x, y).$$

Since the point B has co-ordinates (x′, y′) then x′ = –x and y′ = +y or in the form of a linear equation.

$$x' = (-1)x + (0)\,y$$
$$y' = (0)x + (+1)\,y$$

Now the operation σ_{yz} on the point (x, y) is given as:

$$\sigma_{yz}\begin{pmatrix} x \\ y \end{pmatrix} = \begin{pmatrix} x' \\ y' \end{pmatrix} = \begin{pmatrix} -1 & 0 \\ 0 & 1 \end{pmatrix}\begin{pmatrix} x \\ y \end{pmatrix}$$

Similarly reflection of point A in σ_{xz} gives another point D wherein only y changes to –y while x remains unaffected.

$$A\ (x, y) \xrightarrow{\sigma_{xz}} D\ (x, -y)$$

This transformation may be shown as:

$$x \rightarrow +x,\ y \rightarrow -y$$

or $x' = (+1)\,x + (0)\,y$

$y' = (0)\,x + (-1)\,y$

or

$$\begin{pmatrix} x' \\ y' \end{pmatrix} = \begin{pmatrix} 1 & 0 \\ 0 & -1 \end{pmatrix}\begin{pmatrix} x \\ y \end{pmatrix}.$$

Now we extend this procedure to three dimension. A point is called a single vector. The three Cartesian co-ordinates x, y, z are basis function with (0, 0, 0) as its origin.

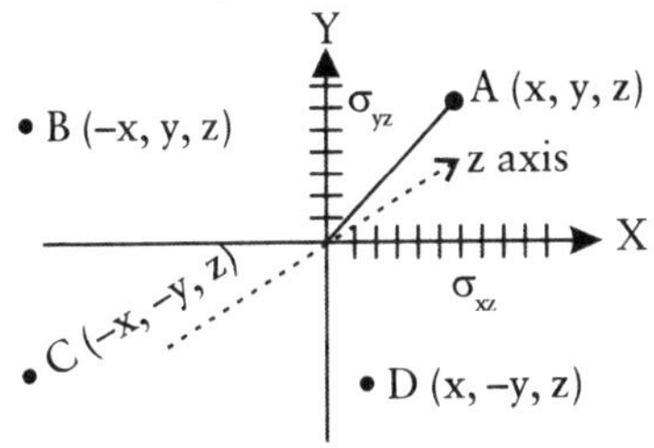

The point (x, y, z) is first reflected in yz plane, this leaves a new point B (–x, y, z). Here x changes its sign only and so $x' = -x$

or $x' = (-1)\,x + (0)y + (0)z,$

$y' = (+1)\,y$

or $y' = (0)x + (+1)\,y + (0)z,$

$z' = (+1)\,z$

or $z' = (0)x + (0)y + (+1)z.$

The matrix represenatation for the three equations is:

$$\begin{pmatrix} x' \\ y' \\ z' \end{pmatrix} = \begin{pmatrix} -1 & 0 & 0 \\ 0 & 1 & 0 \\ 0 & 0 & 1 \end{pmatrix}\begin{pmatrix} x \\ y \\ z \end{pmatrix} = \sigma_{yz}\begin{pmatrix} x \\ y \\ z \end{pmatrix}$$

Similarly reflection in xz plane gives,

$$x = (+1)\ x,\ y \rightarrow (-1)y,\ z \rightarrow (+1)z$$

Both x and z remain unaffected only y changes its sign.

$$x' = (+1)x + (0)y + (0)z$$
$$y' = (0)x + (-1)y + (0)z$$
$$z' = (0)x + (0)y + (+1)z$$

In matrix form these notations may be given as:

$$\begin{pmatrix} x' \\ y' \\ z' \end{pmatrix} = \begin{pmatrix} 1 & 0 & 0 \\ 0 & -1 & 0 \\ 0 & 0 & 1 \end{pmatrix} \begin{pmatrix} x \\ y \\ z \end{pmatrix} = \sigma_{xz} \begin{pmatrix} x \\ y \\ z \end{pmatrix}$$

This is the three dimensional representation. If we perform σ_{xy}, the reflection in xy plane itself, only z changes here neither x nor y changes its sign:

i.e. $x \rightarrow (+1)x,\ y \rightarrow (+1)y,\ z \rightarrow (-1)z,$

or $x' = (+1)x + (0)y + (0)z$

$$y' = (0)x + (+1)y + (0)z$$
$$z' = (0)x + (0)y + (-1)z,$$

or $$\sigma_{xy} \begin{pmatrix} x \\ y \\ z \end{pmatrix} = \begin{bmatrix} 1 & 0 & 0 \\ 0 & 1 & 0 \\ 0 & 0 & -1 \end{bmatrix} \begin{bmatrix} x \\ y \\ z \end{bmatrix} = \begin{bmatrix} x' \\ y' \\ z' \end{bmatrix}$$

3 × 3 matrix A   column vector B   column vector C

A is a representative matrix acting on basis function or vector (x, y, z). There have been three transformation matrices for reflection:

$$\sigma_{xz} : \begin{pmatrix} 1 & 0 & 0 \\ 0 & -1 & 0 \\ 0 & 0 & 1 \end{pmatrix}, \quad \sigma_{yz} : \begin{pmatrix} -1 & 0 & 0 \\ 0 & 1 & 0 \\ 0 & 0 & 1 \end{pmatrix}, \quad \sigma_{xy} : \begin{pmatrix} 1 & 0 & 0 \\ 0 & 1 & 0 \\ 0 & 0 & -1 \end{pmatrix}$$

Consider representative matrix for C_2 (z) operation. The result of this symmetry operation on point A (x, y, z) gives point C (–x, –y, z), so that there is no change in the sign of the co-ordinate z as we perform it about z axis:

$$x \rightarrow (-1)\,x,\ y \rightarrow (-1)y,\ z \rightarrow (+1)z$$

Thus,

$$x' = (-1)x, + (0)y + (0)z$$
$$y' = (0)\,x + (-1)y + (0)\,z$$
$$z' = (0)x + (0)y + (+1)z$$

In matrix language we have,

$$\begin{pmatrix} x' \\ y' \\ z' \end{pmatrix} = \begin{pmatrix} -1 & 0 & 0 \\ 0 & -1 & 0 \\ 0 & 0 & 1 \end{pmatrix} \begin{pmatrix} x \\ y \\ z \end{pmatrix} = C_2 \begin{pmatrix} x \\ y \\ z \end{pmatrix}$$

Thus the transformation matrix for C_2 is:

$$\begin{pmatrix} -1 & 0 & 0 \\ 0 & -1 & 0 \\ 0 & 0 & 1 \end{pmatrix}$$

Identity (E)

Consider the case of identity, E. There is no effect of E on the three co-ordinates of point A, i.e. there is no change in sign of x, y or z.

$$A\ (x, y, z) \xrightarrow{E} A\ (x, y, z)$$

i.e. $x \rightarrow (+1)x,\ y \rightarrow (+1),\ z \rightarrow (+1)z,$

or $x' = (+1)x + (0)y + (0)z$

$$y' = (0)x + (+1)y + (0)z$$
$$z' = (0)x + (0)y + (+1)z,$$

or
$$\begin{pmatrix} x' \\ y' \\ z' \end{pmatrix} = \begin{pmatrix} 1 & 0 & 0 \\ 0 & 1 & 0 \\ 0 & 0 & 1 \end{pmatrix} \begin{pmatrix} x \\ y \\ z \end{pmatrix}$$

or $$E\begin{pmatrix} x \\ y \\ z \end{pmatrix} = \begin{pmatrix} 1 & 0 & 0 \\ 0 & 1 & 0 \\ 0 & 0 & 1 \end{pmatrix}\begin{pmatrix} x \\ y \\ z \end{pmatrix}$$

The transformation matrix for E operation is:

$$\begin{pmatrix} 1 & 0 & 0 \\ 0 & 1 & 0 \\ 0 & 0 & 1 \end{pmatrix}$$

Inversion Centre (i)

All the three co-ordinates change their signs:

$$\text{Pt}\ (x, y, z) \xrightarrow{\ i\ } \text{Pt}\ (-x, -y, -z)$$

$$\underset{(-x,\,-y,\,-z)}{O_2} - C - \underset{(x,\,y,\,z)}{O_1} \xrightarrow{\ i\ } \underset{(-x,\,-y,\,-z)}{O_1} - C - \underset{(x,\,y,\,z)}{O_2}$$

$$x \rightarrow -x,\ y \rightarrow -y,\ z \rightarrow -z$$

$$x' = (-1)x + (0)y + (0)z$$

$$y' = (0)x + (-1)y + (0)z$$

$$z' = (0)x + (0)y + (-1)z,$$

or $$i\begin{pmatrix} x \\ y \\ z \end{pmatrix} = \begin{pmatrix} x' \\ y' \\ z' \end{pmatrix} = \begin{pmatrix} -1 & 0 & 0 \\ 0 & -1 & 0 \\ 0 & 0 & -1 \end{pmatrix}\begin{pmatrix} x \\ y \\ z \end{pmatrix}$$

Hence representative matrix for i is:

$$i: \begin{pmatrix} -1 & 0 & 0 \\ 0 & -1 & 0 \\ 0 & 0 & -1 \end{pmatrix}$$

5.11 LINEAR TRANSFORMATION OF CO-ORDINATES

Consider a two dimensional vector r on point (x, y) which is rotated in a plane that makes an angle α with the x direction to a new position described by (x′, y′). We can see the effect of clockwise and anti-clockwise rotation of this vector by an angle α. The vector reaches to a new point (x′, y′) as a result of clockwise rotation. It was originally placed at an angle θ.

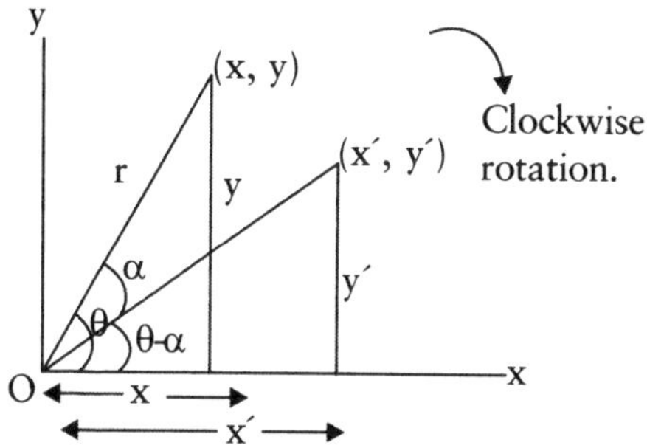

So, $\cos(\theta-\alpha) = x'/r$ Also, $\cos\theta = x/r$

$\sin(\theta-\alpha) = y'/r$, $\sin\theta = y/r$

$$\sin(\theta-\alpha) = \sin\theta.\cos\alpha - \cos\theta.\sin\alpha$$

$$\frac{y'}{r} = \frac{y}{r}\cos\alpha - \frac{x}{r}\sin\alpha$$

or $$y' = y\cos\alpha - x\sin\alpha$$
$$= (-\sin\alpha)\,x + (\cos\alpha)\,y$$

$$\cos(\theta-\alpha) = \cos\theta\cos\alpha + \sin\theta.\sin\alpha$$

$$\frac{x'}{r} = \frac{x}{r}\cos\alpha + \frac{y}{r}\sin\alpha$$

or $$x' = x(\cos\alpha) + y(\sin\alpha)$$

Two equations are $x' = (\cos\alpha)\,x + (\sin\alpha)y$

$$y' = (-\sin\alpha)\,x + (\cos\alpha)y$$

They can be written in the matrix form:

$$\frac{C_{360°}}{\alpha}\begin{pmatrix} x \\ y \end{pmatrix} = \begin{pmatrix} x' \\ y' \end{pmatrix} = \begin{pmatrix} \cos\alpha & \sin\alpha \\ -\sin\alpha & \cos\alpha \end{pmatrix}\begin{pmatrix} x \\ y \end{pmatrix}$$

$$2 \times 2$$

This matrix defines the linear transformation of the co-ordinate (x, y) to (x′, y′). We can convert it in 3 dimensional matrix on adding 0, 0, 1.

$$\text{Cn (clockwise):} \quad \underset{3 \times 3}{\begin{pmatrix} \cos\alpha & \sin\alpha & 0 \\ -\sin\alpha & \cos\alpha & 0 \\ 0 & 0 & 1 \end{pmatrix}}$$

For which the third equation is $z' = (0)\,x + (0)y + (+1)z$.

Let us consider transformation matrix for anticlockwise rotation by an angle α.

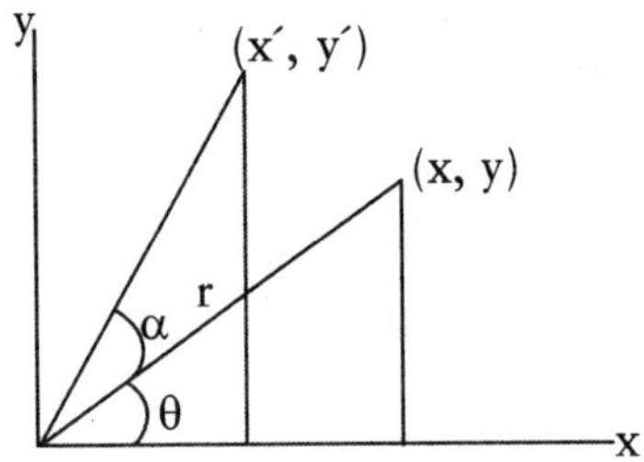

$$\cos(\theta+\alpha) = \frac{x'}{r} \qquad \cos\theta = \frac{x}{r}$$

$$\sin(\theta+\alpha) = \frac{y'}{r} \qquad \sin\theta = \frac{y}{r}$$

$$\cos(\theta+\alpha) = \cos\theta.\cos\alpha - \sin\theta.\sin\alpha$$

$$\frac{x'}{r} = \frac{x}{r}.\cos\alpha - \frac{y}{r}.\sin\alpha$$

$$x' = x(\cos\alpha) + y(-\sin\alpha)$$

Similarly, $\sin(\theta+\alpha) = \sin\theta.\cos\alpha + \cos\theta.\sin\alpha$

$$\frac{y'}{r} = \frac{y}{r}\cos\alpha + \frac{x}{r}\sin\alpha$$

$$y' = (\cos\alpha)\,y + (\sin\alpha)\,x$$

Two equations are:

$$x' = (\cos\alpha)\,x + (-\sin\alpha)y$$

$$y' = (\sin\alpha)\,x + (\cos\alpha)y$$

or,
$$\begin{pmatrix} x' \\ y' \end{pmatrix} = \begin{pmatrix} \cos\alpha & -\sin\alpha \\ \sin\alpha & \cos\alpha \end{pmatrix} \begin{pmatrix} x \\ y \end{pmatrix} = \frac{C_{360^\circ}}{\alpha} \uparrow$$

$$\therefore\ C_n^{-1} : \begin{pmatrix} \cos\alpha & -\sin\alpha \\ \sin\alpha & \cos\alpha \end{pmatrix}$$

In three dimension,

$$C_n^{-1} : \begin{pmatrix} \cos\alpha & -\sin\alpha & 0 \\ \sin\alpha & \cos\alpha & 0 \\ 0 & 0 & 1 \end{pmatrix}.$$

5.12 TRANSPOSE MATRIX

Let A be a matrix. Its transpose is denoted as A^1 or A^-. The inverse of A is its transpose. Transpose matrix is determined by interchanging rows and columns of A.

$$A^- = A^1 = \begin{bmatrix} \cos\alpha & \sin\alpha & 0 \\ -\sin\alpha & \cos\alpha & 0 \\ 0 & 0 & 1 \end{bmatrix}$$

$$\text{where } A = \begin{bmatrix} \cos\alpha & -\sin\alpha & 0 \\ \sin\alpha & \cos\alpha & 0 \\ 0 & 0 & 1 \end{bmatrix}.$$

The inverse of matrix A, denoted by A^{-1} is defined by $A\,A^{-1} = A^{-1}\,A = E$.

By definition matrices and their inverse commute. For orthogonal matrix its inverse and transpose are identical.

$$A^{-1} = \text{inverse of matrix A.}$$

$$A^1 = \text{transpose matrix of A.}$$

$$A\,A^1 = A^1\,A = E.$$

Show that the product of $\frac{C_{360^\circ}}{\alpha}\swarrow$ & $\frac{C_{360^\circ}}{\alpha}\nwarrow$ is unitary matrix, E:

$$\frac{C_{360^\circ}}{\alpha}\swarrow = \begin{bmatrix} \cos\alpha & \sin\alpha \\ -\sin\alpha & \cos\alpha \end{bmatrix}$$

on interchanging the column into row we get:

$$\frac{C'_{360^\circ}}{\alpha} = \begin{bmatrix} \cos\alpha & -\sin\alpha \\ \sin\alpha & \cos\alpha \end{bmatrix} \quad C'_3 \text{ refers to anti-clockwise}$$

For product $\frac{C_{360^\circ}}{\alpha}.\frac{C'_{360^\circ}}{\alpha}$

$$= \begin{bmatrix} \cos\alpha & \sin\alpha \\ -\sin\alpha & \cos\alpha \end{bmatrix} \begin{bmatrix} \cos\alpha & -\sin\alpha \\ \sin\alpha & \cos\alpha \end{bmatrix}$$

$$= \begin{bmatrix} \cos^2\alpha + \sin^2\alpha & -\cos\alpha.\sin\alpha + \sin\alpha.\cos\alpha \\ -\sin\alpha.\cos\alpha + \cos\alpha.\sin\alpha & \sin^2\alpha + \cos^2\alpha \end{bmatrix}$$

$$= \begin{bmatrix} \cos^2\alpha + \sin^2\alpha & 0 \\ 0 & \sin^2\alpha + \cos^2\alpha \end{bmatrix}$$

$$= \begin{bmatrix} 1 & 0 \\ 0 & 1 \end{bmatrix} = E$$

Hence C_n and C_n^{-1} are inverse to each other.

5.13 REPRESENTATIVE MATRIX FOR IMPROPER ROTATION

S_n is a two step process, a proper rotation followed by reflection. We have transformation matrices for C_n and σ_{xy} and from which the transformation matrix for S_n can be constructed :

$$S_n = \sigma_{xy}.C_n$$

For a point (x, y, z) lying in xy plane the transformation matrix will be given as:

$$\sigma_{xy}\begin{pmatrix} x \\ y \\ x \end{pmatrix} = \begin{pmatrix} 1 & 0 & 0 \\ 0 & 1 & 0 \\ 0 & 0 & -1 \end{pmatrix}\begin{pmatrix} x \\ y \\ z \end{pmatrix}$$

For proper rotation of order n (C_n) clockwise:

$$C_n\begin{pmatrix} x \\ y \\ z \end{pmatrix} = \begin{pmatrix} \cos\alpha & \sin\alpha & 0 \\ -\sin\alpha & \cos\alpha & 0 \\ 0 & 0 & 1 \end{pmatrix}\begin{pmatrix} x \\ y \\ z \end{pmatrix}$$

$$\text{Hence, } C_n : \begin{pmatrix} \cos\alpha & \sin\alpha & 0 \\ -\sin\alpha & \cos\alpha & 0 \\ 0 & 0 & 1 \end{pmatrix}, \quad \sigma_{xy} : \begin{pmatrix} 1 & 0 & 0 \\ 0 & 1 & 0 \\ 0 & 0 & -1 \end{pmatrix}$$

$$\sigma_{xy}.C_n \begin{pmatrix} x \\ y \\ z \end{pmatrix} = \begin{pmatrix} 1 & 0 & 0 \\ 0 & 1 & 0 \\ 0 & 0 & -1 \end{pmatrix} \begin{pmatrix} \cos\alpha & \sin\alpha & 0 \\ -\sin\alpha & \cos\alpha & 0 \\ 0 & 0 & 1 \end{pmatrix} \begin{pmatrix} x \\ y \\ z \end{pmatrix}.$$

This on multiplication results:

$$\begin{pmatrix} \cos\alpha + 0 + 0 & \sin\alpha + 0 + 0 & 0 + 0 + 0 \\ -\sin\alpha + 0 + 0 & \cos\alpha + 0 + 0 & 0 + 0 + 0 \\ 0 & 0 & -1 \end{pmatrix} \begin{pmatrix} x \\ y \\ z \end{pmatrix}$$

$$= \begin{pmatrix} \cos\alpha & \sin\alpha & 0 \\ -\sin\alpha & \cos\alpha & 0 \\ 0 & 0 & -1 \end{pmatrix} \begin{pmatrix} x \\ y \\ z \end{pmatrix} = S_n \begin{pmatrix} x \\ y \\ z \end{pmatrix}.$$

Hence the transformation matrix for S_n is:

$$S_n : \begin{pmatrix} \cos\alpha & \sin\alpha & 0 \\ -\sin\alpha & \cos\alpha & 0 \\ 0 & 0 & -1 \end{pmatrix}.$$

The transformation matrix for S_n^{-1} is obtained on interchanging row into column for the transformation matrix of S_n

$$\text{viz. } S_n^{-1} : \begin{pmatrix} \cos\alpha & -\sin\alpha & 0 \\ \sin\alpha & \cos\alpha & 0 \\ 0 & 0 & -1 \end{pmatrix}.$$

5.14 RESULT OF PERFORMING GROUP OPERATIONS UPON UNIT VECTORS e_1, e_2 AND e_3 IN CASE OF NH_3

There are unit vectors e_1, e_2 and e_3. At each point in space (x_1, x_2, x_3) the position vector is given by $p = e_1 x_1 + e_2 x_2 + e_3 x_3$

e_1, e_2 and e_3 are orthogonal base vectors. They are mutually perpendicular unit vectors.

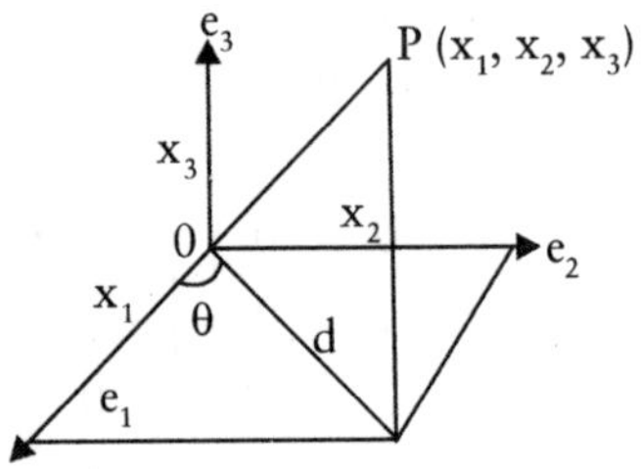

x_1, x_2, x_3 are components of the position vector. Now we see the effect of symmetry operations upon a point or position vector. A clockwise rotation by $\alpha = 2\pi/n$ about the direction e_3 is C_n.

If d is the projection of OP on plane which contains e_1 & e_2 and θ the angle that makes with e_1 then following relations hold between the component OP of initial vector P (x_1, x_2, x_3) and those final vector $P'(x_1', x_2', x_3')$:

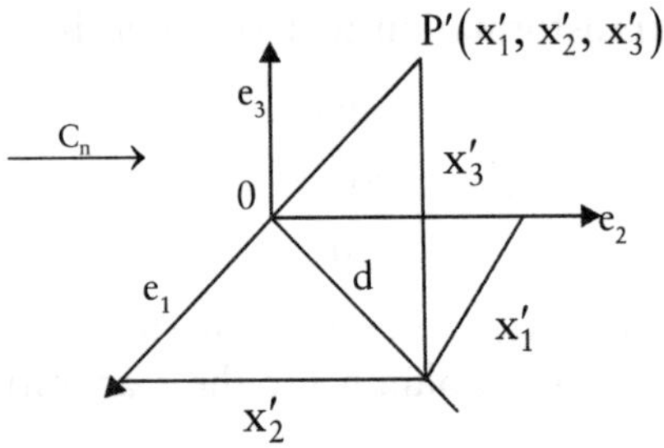

effect of C_n on P

$$
\begin{aligned}
x_1' &= d \cos(\theta - \alpha) \\
&= d [\cos\theta.\cos\alpha + \sin\theta.\sin\alpha] \\
&= d\cos\theta.\cos\alpha + d\sin\theta.\sin\alpha
\end{aligned}
$$

$$\cos\theta = \frac{x_1}{d}, \sin\theta = \frac{x_2}{d}$$

$$
\begin{aligned}
&= d.\frac{x_1}{d}.\cos\alpha + d.\frac{x_2}{d}.\sin\alpha \\
&= x_1 \cos\alpha + x_2 \sin\alpha
\end{aligned}
$$

$$
\begin{aligned}
x_2' &= d \sin(\theta - \alpha) \\
&= d\,[\sin\theta.\cos\alpha - \cos\theta.\sin\alpha] \\
&= d.\frac{x_2}{d}\cos\alpha - d.\frac{x_1}{d}\sin\alpha \\
&= -x_1 \sin\alpha + x_2 \cos\alpha \\
x_3' &= x_3
\end{aligned}
$$

We can express set of equations (linear) in the form of a matrix equation out of:

$$
\begin{aligned}
x_1' &= x_1 \cos\alpha + x_2 \sin\alpha + 0.x_3 \\
x_2' &= -x_1 \sin\alpha + x_2 \cos\alpha + 0.x_3 \\
x_3' &= (o)\, x_1 + (o)\, x_2 + (1)\, x_3
\end{aligned}
$$

$$
\begin{bmatrix} \cos\alpha & \sin\alpha & 0 \\ -\sin\alpha & \cos\alpha & 0 \\ 0 & 0 & 1 \end{bmatrix}
\begin{bmatrix} x_1 \\ x_2 \\ x_3 \end{bmatrix}
=
\begin{bmatrix} x_1' \\ x_2' \\ x_3' \end{bmatrix}
$$

We define a matrix $D(C_n)$ which corresponds to the C_n operation.

$$
\begin{bmatrix} x_1' \\ x_2' \\ x_3' \end{bmatrix}
= D(C_n)
\begin{bmatrix} x_1 \\ x_2 \\ x_3 \end{bmatrix}
$$

$$
\text{and } D\,(C_n) = \begin{bmatrix} \cos\alpha & \sin\alpha & 0 \\ -\sin\alpha & \cos\alpha & 0 \\ 0 & 0 & 1 \end{bmatrix}
$$

Its inverse is found to be:

$$
D(C_n)^{-1} = \begin{bmatrix} \cos\alpha & -\sin\alpha & 0 \\ \sin\alpha & \cos\alpha & 0 \\ 0 & 0 & 1 \end{bmatrix}
$$

The effect on P of a reflection in the plane containing e_2 and e_3 viz. σ_{23} is shown as:

$$x_1' = -x_1,\ x_2' = x_2,\ x_3' = x_3$$

$$\begin{bmatrix} x_1' \\ x_2' \\ x_3' \end{bmatrix} = D(\sigma_{23}) \begin{bmatrix} x_1 \\ x_2 \\ x_3 \end{bmatrix} = \begin{bmatrix} -1 & 0 & 0 \\ 0 & 1 & 0 \\ 0 & 0 & 1 \end{bmatrix} \begin{bmatrix} x_1 \\ x_2 \\ x_3 \end{bmatrix}$$

$$D(\sigma_{23}) = \begin{bmatrix} -1 & 0 & 0 \\ 0 & 1 & 0 \\ 0 & 0 & 1 \end{bmatrix}$$

Similarly we can also obtain D (σ_{12}) and D (σ_{13})

$$D(\sigma_{12}) = \begin{bmatrix} 1 & 0 & 0 \\ 0 & 1 & 0 \\ 0 & 0 & -1 \end{bmatrix}, \quad D(\sigma_{13}) = \begin{bmatrix} 1 & 0 & 0 \\ 0 & -1 & 0 \\ 0 & 0 & 1 \end{bmatrix}$$

σ_{12} is a plane containing e_1 and e_2 and σ_{13}a plane having e_1 and e_3

The effect of inversion on a vector will be to invert it. Consequently we have:

$$x_1' = -x_1,\ x_2' = -x_2,\ x_3' = -x_3 \text{ and}$$

$$D(i) = \begin{bmatrix} -1 & 0 & 0 \\ 0 & -1 & 0 \\ 0 & 0 & -1 \end{bmatrix}$$

Consider a rotation by α about the e_3 base vector followed by reflection in the σ_{12} plane. Components of point P will be first transformed by the rotation (C_n) and thereafter the new components will be transformed by reflection:

$$D(S_n) = \begin{bmatrix} 1 & 0 & 0 \\ 0 & 1 & 0 \\ 0 & 0 & -1 \end{bmatrix} \begin{bmatrix} \cos\alpha & \sin\alpha & 0 \\ -\sin\alpha & \cos\alpha & 0 \\ 0 & 0 & 1 \end{bmatrix}$$

$$= \begin{bmatrix} \cos\alpha & \sin\alpha & 0 \\ -\sin\alpha & \cos\alpha & 0 \\ 0 & 0 & -1 \end{bmatrix}$$

Identity: It has to do nothing in operation

$$x_1' = x_1,\ x_2' = x_2,\ x_3' = x_3$$

$$D(E) = \begin{bmatrix} 1 & 0 & 0 \\ 0 & 1 & 0 \\ 0 & 0 & 1 \end{bmatrix}$$

Since all matrices are orthogonal

$$RP = R\ (x_1\ e_1 + x_2\, e_2 + x_3\ e_3)$$

$$= x_1'\ e_1 + x_2' e_2 + x_3' e_3$$

$$\text{or}\quad D(R)\begin{bmatrix} x_1 \\ x_2 \\ x_3 \end{bmatrix} = \begin{bmatrix} x_1' \\ x_2' \\ x_3' \end{bmatrix}$$

5.15 CASE OF AMMONIA MOLECULE

Consider the case of ammonia molecule, which has C_{3v} point group. There are six symmetry operations in NH_3 namely E, C_3, C_3^2, σ_v', σ_v'', σ_v'''. All such operations obey group multiplication Table.

TABLE 5.5

C_3V	$D(E)$	$D(C_3)$	$D(C_3^2)$	$D(\sigma_v')$	$D(\sigma_v'')$	$D(\sigma_v''')$
$D(E)$	$D(E)$	$D(C_3)$	$D(C_3^2)$	$D(\sigma_v')$	$D(\sigma_v'')$	$D(\sigma_v''')$
$D(C_3)$	$D(C_3)$	$D(C_3^2)$	$D(E)$	$D(\sigma_v''')$	$D(\sigma_v')$	$D(\sigma_v'')$
$D(C_3^2)$	$D(C_3^2)$	(DE)	$D(C_3)$	$D(\sigma_v'')$	—	—
$D(\sigma_v')$	$D(\sigma_v')$	—	—	—	—	—
$D(\sigma_v'')$	$D(\sigma_v'')$	—	—	—	—	—
$D(\sigma_v''')$	$D(\sigma_v''')$	—	—	—	—	—

The six matrices, D(E), $D(C_3)$, $D(C_3^2)$, $D(\sigma_v')$, $D(\sigma_v'')$, and $D(\sigma_v''')$ form a group for which the combining rule is maltiplication. This is identical with the multiplication Table for symmetry operation. Hence, six matrices constitute representation for C_{3v}.

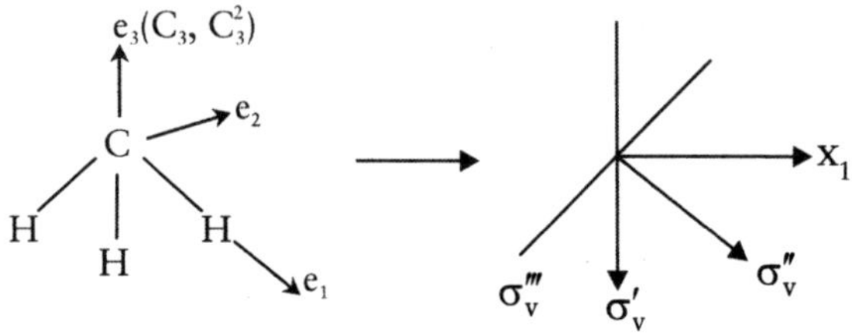

Centre of mass represents origin of e_1, e_2 and e_3 and σ_v', σ_v'' and σ_v''' are perpendicular to the page. C_3 denotes rotation about e_3 with angle $\alpha = \frac{2\pi}{3}$ and C_3^2 (roration about e_3) with $\alpha = \frac{4\pi}{3}$. σ_v' is reflection in a plane containing e_2 and e_3.

Case of D(E),

$$x_1' = \cos 0^\circ.x_1 + \sin 0^\circ.x_2 + 0.x_3$$

$$x_2' = -\sin 0^\circ.x_1 + \cos 0^\circ.x_2 + 0.x_3$$

$$x_3' = 0.x_1 + 0.x_2 + \cos 0.x_3$$

$$x_1' = 1.x_1 + 0.x_2 + 0.x_3$$

$$x_2' = 0.x_1 + 1.x_2 + 0.x_3$$

$$x_3' = 0.x_1 + 0.x_2 + 1.x_3$$

$$\begin{bmatrix} x_1' \\ x_2' \\ x_3' \end{bmatrix} = \begin{bmatrix} 1 & 0 & 0 \\ 0 & 1 & 0 \\ 0 & 0 & 1 \end{bmatrix} \begin{bmatrix} x_1 \\ x_2 \\ x_3 \end{bmatrix}$$

$$D(E) = \begin{bmatrix} 1 & 0 & 0 \\ 0 & 1 & 0 \\ 0 & 0 & 1 \end{bmatrix}$$

$D(\sigma'_v)$

$$x'_1 = (-1)x_1 + (0)x_2 + (0)x_3$$
$$x'_2 = (0)x_1 + (1)x_2 + (0)x_3$$
$$x'_3 = (0)x_1 + (0)x_2 + (1)x_3$$

$$\begin{bmatrix} x'_1 \\ x'_2 \\ x'_3 \end{bmatrix} = \begin{bmatrix} -1 & 0 & 0 \\ 0 & 1 & 0 \\ 0 & 0 & 1 \end{bmatrix} \begin{bmatrix} x_1 \\ x_2 \\ x_3 \end{bmatrix}$$

$$D(\sigma_v{}') = \begin{bmatrix} -1 & 0 & 0 \\ 0 & 1 & 0 \\ 0 & 0 & 1 \end{bmatrix}$$

$D(C_3)$

$$x'_1 = -\cos 60^\circ\ x_1 + \sin 60^\circ x_2 + (0)x_3$$
$$x'_2 = -\sin 60^\circ + (-\cos 60^\circ)x_2 + (0)x_3$$
$$x'_3 = (0)x_1 + (0)x_2 + (1)x_3$$

or
$$x'_1 = -1/2x_1 + \frac{\sqrt{3}}{2}x_2 + 0.x_3$$
$$x'_2 = -\frac{\sqrt{3}}{2}x_1 - 1/2x_2 + 0.x_3$$
$$x'_3 = 0.x_1 + 0.x_2 + 1.x_3$$

$$D(C_3) = \begin{bmatrix} -1/2 & \frac{\sqrt{3}}{2} & 0 \\ -\frac{\sqrt{3}}{2} & -1/2 & 0 \\ 0 & 0 & 1 \end{bmatrix}$$

$$D(C_3^2) = \begin{bmatrix} -1/2 & -\frac{\sqrt{3}}{2} & 0 \\ \frac{\sqrt{3}}{2} & -1/2 & 0 \\ 0 & 0 & 1 \end{bmatrix}$$

We can also obtain matrices for $D(\sigma_v'')$ and $D(\sigma_v''')$

$$D(\sigma_v'') = D(C_3^2).D(\sigma_v')$$

$$D(\sigma_v'') = \begin{bmatrix} -1/2 & -\frac{\sqrt{3}}{2} & 0 \\ \frac{\sqrt{3}}{2} & -1/2 & 0 \\ 0 & 0 & 1 \end{bmatrix} \begin{bmatrix} -1 & 0 & 0 \\ 0 & 1 & 0 \\ 0 & 0 & 1 \end{bmatrix}$$

$$= \begin{bmatrix} 1/2 & -\frac{\sqrt{3}}{2} & 0 \\ -\frac{\sqrt{3}}{2} & -1/2 & 0 \\ 0 & 0 & 1 \end{bmatrix}$$

$$D(\sigma_v''') = D(C_3) \, . \, D(\sigma_v')$$

$$= \begin{bmatrix} -1/2 & +\frac{\sqrt{3}}{2} & 0 \\ -\frac{\sqrt{3}}{2} & -1/2 & 0 \\ 0 & 0 & 1 \end{bmatrix} \begin{bmatrix} -1 & 0 & 0 \\ 0 & 1 & 0 \\ 0 & 0 & 1 \end{bmatrix}$$

$$= \begin{bmatrix} 1/2 & \frac{\sqrt{3}}{2} & 0 \\ \frac{\sqrt{3}}{2} & -1/2 & 0 \\ 0 & 0 & 1 \end{bmatrix}$$

5.16 ALTERNATIVE WAY FOR REPRESENATIVE MATRICES OF C_{3v} POINT GROUP

Consider the case fo NH_3, the three H nuclei are in the form of a triangle labelled a, b, c.

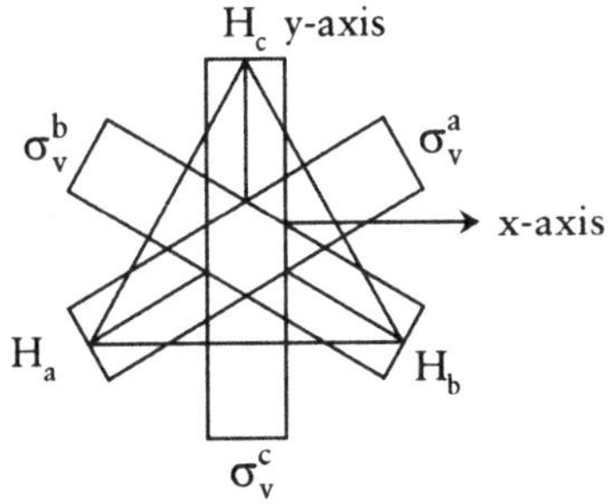

We consider here a two dimensional representation taking co-ordinates (x, y) of one the nuclei a, b or c. There are E, C_3, C_3^2, σ_v^a, σ_v^b and σ_v^c as symmetry operations. The transformation matrix for clockwise rotation C_n is:

$$\begin{pmatrix} \cos\alpha & \sin\alpha \\ -\sin\alpha & \cos\alpha \end{pmatrix}$$

For E, $\alpha = 0°$

$$\therefore\ E : \begin{pmatrix} \cos 0 & \sin 0 \\ -\sin 0 & \cos 0 \end{pmatrix} = \begin{pmatrix} 1 & 0 \\ 0 & 1 \end{pmatrix}$$

or

$$E\begin{pmatrix} x \\ y \end{pmatrix} = \begin{pmatrix} x' \\ y' \end{pmatrix} = \begin{pmatrix} \cos 0 & \sin 0 \\ -\sin 0 & \cos 0 \end{pmatrix}\begin{pmatrix} x \\ y \end{pmatrix}$$

$$= \begin{pmatrix} 1 & 0 \\ 0 & 1 \end{pmatrix}\begin{pmatrix} x \\ y \end{pmatrix}$$

C_3 operation represents a clockwise rotation by 120°.

Hence,

$$C_3\begin{pmatrix} x \\ y \end{pmatrix} = \begin{pmatrix} \cos 120° & \sin 120° \\ -\sin 120° & \cos 120° \end{pmatrix}\begin{pmatrix} x \\ y \end{pmatrix} = \begin{pmatrix} x' \\ y' \end{pmatrix}$$

$$= \begin{pmatrix} -1/2 & \frac{\sqrt{3}}{2} \\ -\frac{\sqrt{3}}{2} & -1/2 \end{pmatrix} \begin{pmatrix} x \\ y \end{pmatrix}$$

$$\therefore \quad C_3 \; : \; \begin{pmatrix} -1/2 & \frac{\sqrt{3}}{2} \\ -\frac{\sqrt{3}}{2} & -1/2 \end{pmatrix}$$

Consider C_3^2 operation. The result is same as C_3' or C_3^{-1} i.e. it is anticlock wise rotation by an angle of 120°.

$$C_3^2 \begin{pmatrix} x \\ y \end{pmatrix} = \begin{pmatrix} x' \\ y' \end{pmatrix} = \begin{pmatrix} \cos\alpha & -\sin\alpha \\ \sin\alpha & \cos\alpha \end{pmatrix} \begin{pmatrix} x \\ y \end{pmatrix}$$

$$= \begin{pmatrix} \cos 120° & -\sin 120° \\ \sin 120° & \cos 120° \end{pmatrix} \begin{pmatrix} x \\ y \end{pmatrix}$$

$$= \begin{pmatrix} -1/2 & -\frac{\sqrt{3}}{2} \\ \frac{\sqrt{3}}{2} & -1/2 \end{pmatrix} \begin{pmatrix} x \\ y \end{pmatrix}$$

$$\therefore \; C_3^2 \; : \; \begin{pmatrix} -1/2 & -\frac{\sqrt{3}}{2} \\ \frac{\sqrt{3}}{2} & -1/2 \end{pmatrix}$$

We define x and y-axis such that y-axis passes through the atom c and x-axis as shown in the figure. Let us consider reflection of the co-ordinate (x, y) in σ_v^c plane. This gives a new co-ordinate system such that a is replaced by b and vice-versa.

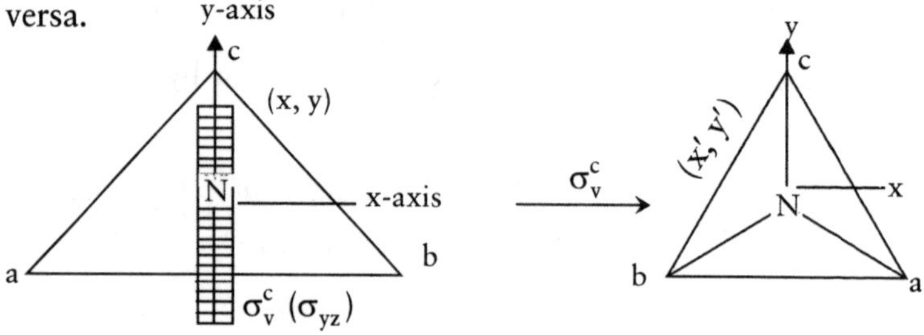

Since σ_v^c is nothing but a yz plane thus only x changes its sign whereas y remains unchanged.

i.e. $x \rightarrow (-1)\,x,\; y \rightarrow (+1)\,y$

This operation gives,

$$x' = (-1)\,x + (0)\,y$$

$$y' = (0)x + (+1)\,y$$

$$\therefore\ \sigma_v^c \begin{pmatrix} x \\ y \end{pmatrix} = \begin{pmatrix} x' \\ y' \end{pmatrix} = \begin{pmatrix} -1 & 0 \\ 0 & 1 \end{pmatrix} \begin{pmatrix} x \\ y \end{pmatrix}$$

$$\therefore\ \sigma_v^a = \begin{pmatrix} 1/2 & \frac{\sqrt{3}}{2} \\ \frac{\sqrt{3}}{2} & -1/2 \end{pmatrix}$$

This can be achieved using the relation:

$$C_v^a = C_3.\sigma_v^c$$

$$\sigma_v^b \begin{pmatrix} x \\ y \end{pmatrix} = C_3^{-1}\ \sigma_v^c \begin{pmatrix} x \\ y \end{pmatrix}$$

$$= \begin{pmatrix} -1/2 & -\frac{\sqrt{3}}{2} \\ \frac{\sqrt{3}}{2} & -1/2 \end{pmatrix} \begin{pmatrix} -1 & 0 \\ 0 & 1 \end{pmatrix} \begin{pmatrix} x \\ y \end{pmatrix}$$

$$= \begin{pmatrix} +1/2+0 & 0-\frac{\sqrt{3}}{2} \\ -\frac{\sqrt{3}}{2}+0 & 0-1/2 \end{pmatrix} \begin{pmatrix} x \\ y \end{pmatrix}$$

$$= \begin{pmatrix} 1/2 & -\frac{\sqrt{3}}{2} \\ -\frac{\sqrt{3}}{2} & -1/2 \end{pmatrix} \begin{pmatrix} x \\ y \end{pmatrix}$$

$$\sigma_v^b \quad : \quad \begin{pmatrix} 1/2 & -\frac{\sqrt{3}}{2} \\ -\frac{\sqrt{3}}{2} & -1/2 \end{pmatrix}$$

The three dimensional representation can be constructed also adding $\begin{array}{ccc|} & & 0 \\ & & 0 \\ 0 & 0 & 1 \end{array}$

2. To prove that C_3 and C_3^2 are inverse matrices:

$$C_3^2 = C_3'$$

$$C_3 : \begin{pmatrix} -1/2 & \frac{\sqrt{3}}{2} \\ -\frac{\sqrt{3}}{2} & -1/2 \end{pmatrix}, \; C_3' = \begin{pmatrix} -1/2 & -\frac{\sqrt{3}}{2} \\ \frac{\sqrt{3}}{2} & -1/2 \end{pmatrix}$$

Thier product is defined as $C_3\, C_3'$:

$$= \begin{pmatrix} -1/2 & \frac{\sqrt{3}}{2} \\ -\frac{\sqrt{3}}{2} & -1/2 \end{pmatrix} \begin{pmatrix} -1/2 & -\frac{\sqrt{3}}{2} \\ \frac{\sqrt{3}}{2} & -1/2 \end{pmatrix}$$

$$= \begin{pmatrix} -1/2 \times -1/2 + \frac{\sqrt{3}}{2} \times \frac{\sqrt{3}}{2} & -1/2 \times -\frac{\sqrt{3}}{2} + \frac{\sqrt{3}}{2} - 1/2 \\ -\frac{\sqrt{3}}{2} \times -1/2 + \frac{\sqrt{3}}{2} \times -1/2 & \frac{\sqrt{3}}{2} \times -\frac{\sqrt{3}}{2} + (-1/2) \times (-1/2) \end{pmatrix}$$

$$= \begin{pmatrix} \frac{1}{4} + \frac{3}{4} & \frac{\sqrt{3}}{4} - \frac{\sqrt{3}}{4} \\ \frac{\sqrt{3}}{4} - \frac{\sqrt{3}}{4} & \frac{3}{4} + \frac{1}{4} \end{pmatrix} = \begin{pmatrix} 1 & 0 \\ 0 & 1 \end{pmatrix} = E$$

Hence, C_3' is C_3^{-1}.

5.17 GROUP MULTIPLICATION TABLE

Consider the case of water. The four symmetry operations present here are E, C_2, σ_{xz} and σ_{yz}. From the representative matrices we can generate product operations in case of water.

$$E:\begin{pmatrix}1 & 0 & 0\\ 0 & 1 & 0\\ 0 & 0 & 1\end{pmatrix},\quad C_2(z):\begin{pmatrix}-1 & 0 & 0\\ 0 & -1 & 0\\ 0 & 0 & 1\end{pmatrix}$$

$$\sigma_{xz}:\begin{pmatrix}1 & 0 & 0\\ 0 & -1 & 0\\ 0 & 0 & 1\end{pmatrix},\quad \sigma_{yz}:\begin{pmatrix}-1 & 0 & 0\\ 0 & 1 & 0\\ 0 & 0 & 1\end{pmatrix}$$

The multiple symmetry operations follow the rule of commutation:

$$\text{(i)}\ E\,C_2=\begin{pmatrix}1 & 0 & 0\\ 0 & 1 & 0\\ 0 & 0 & 1\end{pmatrix}\begin{pmatrix}-1 & 0 & 0\\ 0 & -1 & 0\\ 0 & 0 & 1\end{pmatrix}=\begin{pmatrix}-1 & 0 & 0\\ 0 & -1 & 0\\ 0 & 0 & 1\end{pmatrix}=C_2$$

Also $C_2 . E = C_2$

$$\text{(ii)}\ \sigma_{xz}.C_2=\begin{pmatrix}1 & 0 & 0\\ 0 & -1 & 0\\ 0 & 0 & 1\end{pmatrix}\begin{pmatrix}-1 & 0 & 0\\ 0 & -1 & 0\\ 0 & 0 & 1\end{pmatrix}=\begin{pmatrix}-1 & 0 & 0\\ 0 & 1 & 0\\ 0 & 0 & 1\end{pmatrix}=\sigma_{yz}$$

Also $C_2.\sigma_{xz} = \sigma_{yz}$

$$\text{(iii)}\ \sigma_{yz}.C_2=\begin{pmatrix}-1 & 0 & 0\\ 0 & 1 & 0\\ 0 & 0 & 1\end{pmatrix}.\begin{pmatrix}-1 & 0 & 0\\ 0 & -1 & 0\\ 0 & 0 & 1\end{pmatrix}$$

$$=\begin{pmatrix}1 & 0 & 0\\ 0 & -1 & 0\\ 0 & 0 & 1\end{pmatrix}=\sigma_{xz}=C_2\sigma_{yz}$$

$$\text{(iv) } \sigma_{xz}.\sigma_{yz} = \begin{pmatrix} 1 & 0 & 0 \\ 0 & -1 & 0 \\ 0 & 0 & 1 \end{pmatrix} . \begin{pmatrix} -1 & 0 & 0 \\ 0 & 1 & 0 \\ 0 & 0 & 1 \end{pmatrix}$$

$$= \begin{pmatrix} -1 & 0 & 0 \\ 0 & -1 & 0 \\ 0 & 0 & 1 \end{pmatrix} = C_2 = \sigma_{yz}.\sigma_{xz}$$

Similarly, $E\ \sigma_{xz} = \sigma_{xz}\ E = \sigma_{xz}$

$E\ \sigma_{yz} = \sigma_{yz}\ E = \sigma_{yz}$

$C_2 \cdot C_2 = E,\ \sigma_{xz}\ \sigma_{xz} = E,\ \sigma_{yz} \cdot \sigma_{yz} = E,$

$E.E. = E$

Now, the representative matrices form the elements of a group which has exactly the same multiplication Table as the group of symmetry operations from which they derive. The group multiplication Table is as follows:

TABLE 5.6

C_{2v}	E	C_2	σ_{xz}	σ_{yz}
E	E	C_2	σ_{xz}	σ_{yz}
C_2	C_2	E	σ_{yz}	σ_{xz}
σ_{xz}	σ_{xz}	σ_{yz}	E	C_2
σ_{yz}	σ_{yz}	σ_{xz}	C_2	E

We have verified that the transformation matrices for C_{2v} give a multiplication Table of exactly the same form as the multiplication Table obtained by symmetry operations. The representative matrices given are acting on basis vectors. The basis vectors may be defined interms of any set of co-ordinates and therefore, transformation matrices are not unique but dependent on the basis. It is, therefore, necessary to find a property of the representative that does not depend on the axes chosen. This property turns out to be the trace (spur) or character of the representative. The character of a matrix is sum of diagonal elements. Also look at 5.8 for details.

5.18 MULTIPLICATION TABLE FOR C_{2h}

Symmetry operations are E, C_2, σ_h and i. Consider a vector (x, y, z) lying in xy plane. A new position (x′, y′, z′) is assumed by this vector through symmetry operations. Then,

$$E : \begin{pmatrix} 1 & 0 & 0 \\ 0 & 1 & 0 \\ 0 & 0 & 1 \end{pmatrix}, \quad C_2 : \begin{pmatrix} -1 & 0 & 0 \\ 0 & -1 & 0 \\ 0 & 0 & 1 \end{pmatrix}$$

$$\sigma_h : \begin{pmatrix} 1 & 0 & 0 \\ 0 & 1 & 0 \\ 0 & 0 & -1 \end{pmatrix}, \quad i : \begin{pmatrix} -1 & 0 & 0 \\ 0 & -1 & 0 \\ 0 & 0 & -1 \end{pmatrix}$$

$$i \begin{pmatrix} x \\ y \\ z \end{pmatrix} = \begin{pmatrix} -x \\ -y \\ -z \end{pmatrix}$$

Multiple Operations are:

$$\therefore\ i\,.\,i \begin{pmatrix} x \\ y \\ z \end{pmatrix} = i \begin{pmatrix} -x \\ -y \\ -z \end{pmatrix} = \begin{pmatrix} x \\ y \\ z \end{pmatrix} = E$$

or

$$i\,.\,i \begin{pmatrix} x \\ y \\ z \end{pmatrix} = \begin{pmatrix} -1 & 0 & 0 \\ 0 & -1 & 0 \\ 0 & 0 & -1 \end{pmatrix} \begin{pmatrix} -1 & 0 & 0 \\ 0 & -1 & 0 \\ 0 & 0 & -1 \end{pmatrix} \begin{pmatrix} x \\ y \\ z \end{pmatrix}$$

$$= \begin{pmatrix} +1 & 0 & 0 \\ 0 & +1 & 0 \\ 0 & 0 & +1 \end{pmatrix} \begin{pmatrix} x \\ y \\ z \end{pmatrix} = E \begin{pmatrix} x \\ y \\ z \end{pmatrix}$$

$$\therefore \qquad i^2 = i\,.\,i = E$$

$$C_2\ i \begin{pmatrix} x \\ y \\ z \end{pmatrix} = \begin{pmatrix} -1 & 0 & 0 \\ 0 & -1 & 0 \\ 0 & 0 & 1 \end{pmatrix} \begin{pmatrix} -1 & 0 & 0 \\ 0 & -1 & 0 \\ 0 & 0 & -1 \end{pmatrix} \begin{pmatrix} x \\ y \\ z \end{pmatrix}$$

$$= \begin{pmatrix} 1 & 0 & 0 \\ 0 & 1 & 0 \\ 0 & 0 & -1 \end{pmatrix} \begin{pmatrix} x \\ y \\ z \end{pmatrix} = \sigma_h \begin{pmatrix} x \\ y \\ z \end{pmatrix}$$

$$\therefore \quad C_2 \,.\, i = \sigma_h$$

Also,
$$i\,\sigma_h = \begin{pmatrix} -1 & 0 & 0 \\ 0 & -1 & 0 \\ 0 & 0 & -1 \end{pmatrix} \begin{pmatrix} 1 & 0 & 0 \\ 0 & 1 & 0 \\ 0 & 0 & -1 \end{pmatrix}$$

$$= \begin{pmatrix} -1 & 0 & 0 \\ 0 & -1 & 0 \\ 0 & 0 & 1 \end{pmatrix} = C_2 \text{ etc.}$$

A multiplication Table is now formed:

TABLE 5.7

C_{2h}	E	C_2	i	σ_h
E	E	C_2	i	σ_h
C_2	C_2	E	σ_h	i
i	i	σ_h	E	C_2
σ_h	σ_h	i	C_2	E

3. Through matrices deduce the group multiplication table for D_2 which is abelian.

Take a point P(x, y, z) in xy plane z-axis is up, out of the plane of paper. Rotation by $C_2(z)$ brings the point in –x, –y plane with co-ordinates (–x, –y, z). The same point of rotation

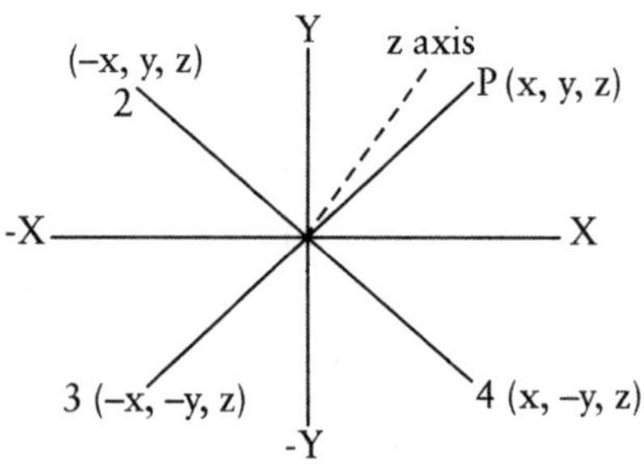

through C_2 (y) gives the position 2. (–x, y, z). When we perform $C_2(x)$ operation it reaches to the point 4 (x, –y, z).

$$\text{so, } C_2(z) = \begin{bmatrix} -1 & 0 & 0 \\ 0 & -1 & 0 \\ 0 & 0 & 1 \end{bmatrix}, \quad C_2(x) = \begin{bmatrix} 1 & 0 & 0 \\ 0 & -1 & 0 \\ 0 & 0 & 1 \end{bmatrix}$$

$$C_2(y) = \begin{bmatrix} -1 & 0 & 0 \\ 0 & 1 & 0 \\ 0 & 0 & 1 \end{bmatrix}$$

$C_2(x)\ C_2(z) = C_2(z)\ C_2(x)$

$$\begin{bmatrix} 1 & 0 & 0 \\ 0 & -1 & 0 \\ 0 & 0 & 1 \end{bmatrix}\begin{bmatrix} -1 & 0 & 0 \\ 0 & -1 & 0 \\ 0 & 0 & 1 \end{bmatrix} = \begin{bmatrix} -1 & 0 & 0 \\ 0 & 1 & 0 \\ 0 & 0 & 1 \end{bmatrix} = C_2(y)$$

Similarly, $C_2(y)\ \ C_2(x) = C_2(x)\ C_2(y) = C_2(z)$

$C_2(y)\ \ C_2(z) = C_2(z)\ C_2(y) = C_2(x)$

$C_2(x)\ \ C_2(y) = C_2(y).C_2(x)$

$$= \begin{bmatrix} 1 & 0 & 0 \\ 0 & -1 & 0 \\ 0 & 0 & 1 \end{bmatrix}\begin{bmatrix} -1 & 0 & 0 \\ 0 & 1 & 0 \\ 0 & 0 & 1 \end{bmatrix} = \begin{bmatrix} -1 & 0 & 0 \\ 0 & -1 & 0 \\ 0 & 0 & 1 \end{bmatrix} = C_2(z)$$

On the basis of combination of two matrices, we deduce the group multiplication Table for point group D_2.

TABLE 5.8

D_2	E	$C_2(z)$	$C_2(y)$	$C_2(x)$
E	E	$C_2(z)$	$C_2(y)$	$C_2(x)$
$C_2(z)$	$C_2(z)$	E	$C_2(x$	$C_2(y)$
$C_2(y)$	$C_2(y)$	$C_2(x)$	E	$C_2(z)$
$C_2(x)$	$C_2(x)$	$C_2(y)$	$C_2(z)$	E

4. What you understand from improper rotation. Show that $S_2 = \sigma_h.C_2 = i$, $S_n = \sigma_h.C_n$ rotation through C_n followed by reflection in σ_h:

$$S_2\begin{pmatrix} x \\ y \end{pmatrix} = \sigma_h C_2 \begin{pmatrix} x \\ y \\ z \end{pmatrix} = \sigma_h \begin{pmatrix} -x \\ -y \\ z \end{pmatrix}$$

$$= \begin{pmatrix} -x \\ -y \\ -z \end{pmatrix} = i$$

This shows $S_2 = \sigma_h C_2 = i$.

The second operation is obtained on following the first operation with another 180° rotation and reflection:

$$S_2^2 \begin{pmatrix} x \\ y \\ z \end{pmatrix} = S_2.S_2 \begin{pmatrix} x \\ y \\ z \end{pmatrix} = S_2 \begin{pmatrix} -x \\ -y \\ -z \end{pmatrix}$$

$$= \begin{pmatrix} +x \\ +y \\ +z \end{pmatrix} = E.$$

So even under improper axis $S_n^n = E$ In general, these are number of rotation it will generate n/2 improper rotation.

n/2–1 proper rotation and the identity (E)

So n = n/2 + (n/2–1) + 1

= n/2 + n/2 = n.

Odd order improper axis has 2n operation.

5. Construct matrix equation out of homogeneous equation,

$x + y = 2$

$3x - 4y = 5$

In the matrix form we have,

$$\begin{bmatrix} 1 & 1 \\ 3 & -4 \end{bmatrix} \begin{bmatrix} x \\ y \end{bmatrix} = \begin{bmatrix} 2 \\ 5 \end{bmatrix}$$

6. Find AB and BA the product matrics where,

$$A = \begin{bmatrix} -3 & 0 & 1 \\ 1 & 4 & 0 \\ 1 & 1 & 1 \end{bmatrix}, B = \begin{bmatrix} 1 & 2 & 1 \\ 3 & 0 & -1 \\ -1 & -1 & 2 \end{bmatrix}$$

$$BA = \begin{bmatrix} 1 & 2 & 1 \\ 3 & 0 & -1 \\ -1 & -1 & 2 \end{bmatrix} \begin{bmatrix} -3 & 0 & 1 \\ 1 & 4 & 0 \\ 1 & 1 & 1 \end{bmatrix}$$

$$= \begin{bmatrix} -3\times1+2\times1+1\times1 & 1\times0+2\times4+1\times1 & 1\times1+2\times0+1\times1 \\ 3\times-3+0\times1+(-1)\times1 & 3\times0+0\times4+(-1)\times1 & 3\times1+0\times0+(-1)\times1 \\ -1\times(-3)+(-1)\times1+2\times1 & -1\times0+(-1)\times4+2\times1 & -1\times1+(-1)\times0+2\times1 \end{bmatrix}$$

$$= \begin{bmatrix} -3+2+1 & 0+8+1 & 1+0+1 \\ -9+0-1 & 0+0-1 & 3+0-1 \\ 3-1+2 & 0-4+2 & -1+0+2 \end{bmatrix}$$

$$= \begin{bmatrix} 0 & 9 & 2 \\ -10 & -1 & 2 \\ 4 & -2 & 1 \end{bmatrix}$$

$$AB = \begin{bmatrix} -3 & 0 & -1 \\ 1 & 4 & 0 \\ 1 & 1 & 1 \end{bmatrix} \begin{bmatrix} 1 & 2 & 1 \\ 3 & 0 & -1 \\ -1 & -1 & 2 \end{bmatrix}$$

$$= \begin{bmatrix} -3\times1+0\times3+1(-1) & -3\times2+0\times0+(-1) & (-1)-3\times1+0\times(-1)+(-1)\times2 \\ 1\times1+4\times3+0\times1 & 1\times2+4\times0+0\times(-1) & 1\times1+4(-1)+0\times2 \\ 1\times1+1\times3+1\times(-1) & 1\times2+1\times0+1\times(-1) & 1\times1+1\times(-1)+1\times2 \end{bmatrix}$$

$$= \begin{bmatrix} -3-1 & -6+1 & -3-2 \\ 1+12 & 2 & 1-4 \\ 1+3-1 & 2-1 & 1-1+2 \end{bmatrix}$$

$$= \begin{bmatrix} -4 & -5 & -5 \\ 13 & 2 & -3 \\ 3 & 1 & 2 \end{bmatrix}$$

$AB \neq BA$ they are non-commuting matrics.

QUESTIONS

1. A vector r is lying in xy plane. Deduce the transformation matrix for clockwise and counter clockwise rotation through an angle α.
2. (i) Explain basis function and representative matrices.
   (ii) Generate representative matrices for σ_{xy}, σ_{xz}, and σ_{yz} using co-ordinates as bases.
   (iii) How will you obtain transformation matrix for S_n?
3. Prove that S_n and S_n^{-1} are inverse matrices.
4. (a) How will you obtain representation of a molecular point group.
   (b) Find the representative matrices for C_{2v}.
   (c) What do you mean by transpose matrix? Under what condition a transpose matrix A is equal to its inverse?
   (d) With the help of transformation matrices show that all operations commute in C_{2v}.
5. Write out multiplication Table for H_2O from representative matrices.
6. Comment on: (i) Cyclic group.
   (ii) Isomorphic group.
   (iii) Abelian and non-abelian groups.
   (iv) Character of a matrix.
7. (a) Explain Properties of Character.
   (b) Deduce the matrices for all symmetry operations in D_2 point group. On the basis of such matrices deduce the group multiplication Table for it.
8. Deduce the multiplication Table for C_{2h} on the basis of representative matrices for it.
9. Show that: (i) C_2 has its own inverse.
   (ii) C_3 and C_3^2 are inverse to each other.
   (iii) σ_h its own inverse.
   (iv) D_{2h} is abelian group whereas D_{3h} is non-abelian group.

10. If $AA^{-1} = A^{-1}A$ Find A^{-1} where A is given by $\begin{bmatrix} a_{11} & a_{12} \\ a_{21} & a_{22} \end{bmatrix}$.

11. Demonstrate that C_{2v} is abelian and C_{3v} as non-abelian group.

12. Prove that : (i) $A = \begin{bmatrix} 0 & 1 \\ 1 & 0 \end{bmatrix}, B = \begin{bmatrix} 1 & 0 \\ 0 & -1 \end{bmatrix}$

(ii) $A = \begin{bmatrix} 2 & 1 \\ 0 & 1 \end{bmatrix}, B = \begin{bmatrix} 1 & 1 \\ 0 & 1 \end{bmatrix}$

do not commute.

13. Some simultaneous equations are given. Put them in matrix form:

(a) $x + y + z = 3$
$3x - 4y + 2z = 4$
$3x + 2y - 5z = 6$

(b) $x - y = 5$
$2x + 3y = 4$

(c) $a_1x + b_1y + c_1z = d_1$
$a_2x + b_2y + c_2z = d_2$
$a_3x + b_3y + c_3z = d_3$
$a_4x + b_4y + c_4z = d_4$

14. Tell whether the matrices are commuting or non-commuting. Verify them:

(i) $A = \begin{bmatrix} 1 & 2 \\ 2 & 1 \end{bmatrix}, B = \begin{bmatrix} 1 & 1 \\ 1 & 1 \end{bmatrix}$

(ii) $A = \begin{bmatrix} 2 & 3 \\ 2 & 2 \end{bmatrix}, B = \begin{bmatrix} 2 & 2 \\ 1 & 1 \end{bmatrix}$

(iii) $A = \begin{bmatrix} 3 & 4 \\ 4 & 3 \end{bmatrix}, B = \begin{bmatrix} 2 & 4 \\ 4 & 2 \end{bmatrix}$

6 IRREDUCIBLE REPRESENTATIONS, ORTHOGONALITY THEOREM, CHARACTER TABLE AND REPRESENTATION OF GROUPS

A collection of matrices that represent symmetry operations for a given point group and obey the laws of multiplication Table is known as Representation of the Group. It is denoted by the symbol G (Capital gama). We know character of a matrix. It is fundamental property. Character serves as representation for each symmetry operation in a point group. A number of possible representations have been encountered.

6.1 REDUCIBLE AND IRREDUCIBLE REPRESENTATIONS

Representation is of two types based on character of a matrix—reducible and irreducible. A matrix of bigger dimension which is reducible can be broken down to sub-matrices of smaller dimensions in a block diagonalization of matrices. Fortunately they fall into 1-, 2- and 3-dimensions. Such matrices fall across the leading diagonals. We find their characters, which are of fundamental in nature. They do not split further hence irreducible. They can never beyond three dimension.

Any reducible representation (Γ_R) is a linear combination of irreducible representation (Γ_{1R}):

$$\Gamma_R = a_1 \Gamma_{1\ (1R)} + a_2 \Gamma_{2\ (1R)} + a_3 \Gamma_{3\ (1R)} \ldots\ldots + a_n \Gamma_{n\ (1R)}.$$

They are numbered in increasing order of their dimensions. The a_n are 1, 2, 3...etc. or zero.

If l_i denotes dimension of the ith irreducible representation there can be $l_i = 1$, one-dimensional and we have either A or B representation.

$l_i = 2$, two dimensional representation, E.

$l_i = 3$, three dimensional representation, T.

Properties of Irreducible Representations

They have properties listed here under:

1. Sum of the squares of dimensions of IR of a group is h (order)

$$\Sigma l_i^2 = h$$

For the case of C_{2v}, h = 4

$$\Sigma li^2 = h$$

or, $l_1^2 + l_2^2 + l_3^2 + l_4^2 = 4$

It has a single solution, $l_1 = l_2 = l_3 = l_4$

i.e $\quad (+1)^2 + (+1)^2 + (+1)^2 + (+1)^2 = 4$

$= 1+1+1+1 = 4$

Since, l is the dimension of representation, we have four one-dimensional irreducible representations or 1×1 sub-matrices.

2. Sum of the squares of the characters of IRs of identity operation is equal to order of the group.

$$\Sigma \chi_i^2(E) = h$$

C_{2v} case $= \chi_1^2 + \chi_2^2 + \chi_3^2 + \chi_4^2$

$= 1^2 + 1^2 + 1^2 + 1^2$

$= 1 + 1 + 1 + 1 = 4 = h$

C_{3v} case $= \chi_1^2 + \chi_2^2 + \chi_3^2$

$= 1^2 + 1^2 + 2^2$

$= 1 + 1 + 4$

$= 6 = h$

3. Number of irreducible representations equals the number of class.

   Thus, for C_{2v}, Γ_1, Γ_2, Γ_3 and Γ_4 are irreducible representations.

C_{2v}	E	C_2	σ_v	σ'_v
Γ_1				
Γ_2				
Γ_3				
Γ_4				

In C_{3v} case we have E, $2C_3$, $3\sigma_v$ and, so there are three irreducible representation Γ_1, Γ_2, and Γ_3.

C_{3v}	E	$2C_3$	$3\sigma_v$
Γ_1			
Γ_2			
Γ_3			

$\chi_1^2 + \chi_2^2 + \chi_3^2 = h$. Its order h = 6.

It has three solutions:

$$l_1^2 + l_2^2 + l_3^2 = 6$$

or $\quad l_1 = 1,\ l_2 = 1,\ l_3 = 2.$

There are two one-dimensional representations and one two dimensional representation.

Sum of the squares of characters taken over all symmetry operations for an IR is h.

i.e. $\quad \Sigma\chi_j^2\,(\text{IR}) = h$

C_{2v} case

		E	C_2	σ_v	σ'_v
(i)	Γ_1	1	1	1	1
(ii)	Γ_2	1	1	–1	–1
(iii)	Γ_3	1	–1	1	–1
(iv)	Γ_4	1	–1	–1	1

For, Γ_1, $\chi_1^2 + \chi_2^2 + \chi_3^2 + \chi_4^2$

$= 1^2 + 1^2 + 1^2 + 1^2 = 4 = h$

Γ_2, $\chi_1^2 + \chi_2^2 + \chi_3^2 + \chi_4^2$

$= (1)^2 + (1)^2 + (-1)^2 + (-1)^2$

$= 1 + 1 + 1 + 1 = 4$

Γ_3, $\chi_1^2 + \chi_2^2 + \chi_3^2 + \chi_4^2$

$= (1)^2 + (-1)^2 + (1)^2 + (-1)^2$

$= 1 + 1 + 1 + 1 = 4$

Γ_4, $\chi_1^2 + \chi_2^2 + \chi_3^2 + \chi_4^2$

$= (1)^2 + (-1)^2 + (-1)^2 + (1)^2$

$= 1 + 1 + 1 + 1 = 4.$

For,

C_{3v}	E	$2C_3$	$3\sigma_v$
Γ_1	1	1	1
Γ_2	1	1	–1
Γ_3	2	–1	0

Γ_1 case, $(\chi_1^2) + \chi_2^2 + \chi_3^2$

$= (1)^2 + 2(1)^2 + 3(1)^2$

$= 1 + 2 + 3 = 6 = h$

Γ_2 case, $\chi_1^2 + \chi_2^2 + \chi_3^2$

$= (1)^2 + 2(1)^2 + 3(-1)^2$

$= 1 + 2 + 3 = 6$

Γ_3 case, $\chi_1^2 + \chi_2^2 + \chi_3^2$

$= (2)^2 + 2(-1)^2 + 3(0)^2$

$= 4 + 2 = 6.$

5. The irreducible representations are orthogonal:

$$\sum_j \chi_i\,(IR)\,\chi_j\,(IR) = h\,\delta_{ij}$$

When i = j it is h

$i \neq j$ it is 0

Consider the case of orthogonality for C_{3v} point group.

C_{3v}	E	$2C_3$	$3\sigma v$
Γ_1	1	1	1
Γ_2	1	1	–1
Γ_3	2	–1	0

Any two of them are orthogonal:

$$\begin{aligned}\Gamma_1 \times \Gamma_2 &= 1 \times 1 \times 1 + 2 \times 1 \times 1 + 3 \times 1 \times (-1) \\ &= 1 + 2 - 3 \\ &= 0.\end{aligned}$$

Hence, Γ_1 and Γ_2 are orthogonal.

$$\begin{aligned}\Gamma_1 \times \Gamma_3 &= 1 \times 1 \times 1 + 2 \times 1 \times (-1) + 3 \times 1 \times 0 \\ &= +2 - 2 + 0 \\ &= 2 - 2 = 0.\end{aligned}$$

Hence, Γ_1 and Γ_3 are orthogonal.

$$\begin{aligned}\Gamma_2 \times \Gamma_3 &= 1 \times 1 \times 2 + 2 \times 1 \times -1 + 3 \times 1\ (-1) \times 0 \\ &= +2 - 2 + 0 \\ &= 2 - 2 = 0.\end{aligned}$$

Hence, Γ_2 and Γ_3 are orthogonal.

Reduction of a reducible representation.

Let, Γ_R = reducible representation

h = order of the group

χ_R = character of reducible representation

χ_{IR} = character of irreducible representation

n = number of operations belonging of the same class.

Then the number of times an IR occurs in a reducible representation is given by a_j (for the ith IR).

$$a_j = \frac{1}{h} \Sigma\, \chi\,(\text{IR})\ \chi_i(\text{R})$$

Consider $\Gamma(R)$ for C_{3v} as 5 2–1

$$a_1 = \frac{1}{6}[1 \times 5 \times 1 + 2 \times 2 \times 1 + 3 \times (-1) \times 1]$$

$$= \frac{1}{6}[5 + 4 - 3] = \frac{6}{6} = 1$$

$$a_2 = \frac{1}{6}[1 \times 5 \times 1 + 2 \times 2 \times 1 + 3 \times (-1) \times (-1)]$$

$$= \frac{1}{6}[5 + 4 + 3] = \frac{12}{6} = 2$$

$$a_3 = \frac{1}{6}[1 \times 5 \times 1 + 2 \times 2 \times (-1) + 3 \times (-1) \times 0]$$

$$= \frac{1}{6}[10 - 4 + 0] = \frac{6}{6} = 1$$

$$\Gamma_R = \Gamma_1 + 2\Gamma_2 + \Gamma_3$$

$$= A_1 + 2A_2 + E.$$

6.2 SYMMETRY OPERATION AND CHARACTER OF MATRIX

Identity	$\chi = 3$
Rotation	$2 \cos \theta + 1$
Inversion	-3
Inproper rotation	$+2 \cos \theta - 1$
Reflection	1

Where θ refers to angle of rotation about the axis.

6.3 REPRESENTATION

We will examine the difference between reducible and irreducible representation. $\Gamma^{(R)}$ is a representation of group G, sometimes specific matrix for element R.

Reduced form: Consider a matrix representation $\Gamma^{(R)}$ that is a collection of matrices of dimension n, if by n similarity transformations we get $\Gamma^{(R)} = S^{-1}\,\Gamma^{(R)}\,S$. For all $R \in G(1)$. All the matrices of $\Gamma^{(R)}$ can simultaneously be put into the form.

$$\Gamma'^{(R)} = \left(\begin{array}{c|c} \Gamma_1^{(R)} & G^{(R)} \\ \hline O & \Gamma_2^{(R)} \end{array}\right) \quad \text{(i)}$$

The representation $\Gamma^{(R)}$ is said to be reducible, and $\Gamma'^{(R)}$ is said to be the reduced form of $\Gamma^{(R)}$.

Note that, $\left.\begin{array}{l}\Gamma_1^{(R)} \text{ is an } n_1 \times n_1 \text{ matrix} \\ \Gamma_2^{(R)} \text{ is an } n_2 \times n_2 \text{ matrix}\end{array}\right\} n_1 + n_1 = n$

$Q^{(R)}$ is an $n_1 \times n_2$ matrix.

$\Gamma^{(R)} \rightarrow n \times n$ matrix. They are in blocked form.

If all the matrices of a representation cannot simultaneously be put into a reduced form, the representation is said to be completely reduced. That is, $\Gamma_1^{(R)}$ and $\Gamma_2^{(R)}$ may or may not be reducible, then $\Gamma^{1(R)}$ is completely reduced.

Ir $\Gamma^{1(R)}$ is unitary then $Q^{(R)} = 0$

$$\left(\Gamma^{1(R)}\right)^{-1} = \Gamma^{1(R)\dagger} = \text{transpose matrix.}$$

$$\Gamma^{1(R)}\dagger = \left(\begin{array}{c|c}\Gamma_1^{(R)}\dagger & 0 \\ \hline Q^{(R)}\dagger & \Gamma_2^{(R)}\dagger\end{array}\right)$$

can be obtained on interchanging row into column. But $R^{-1} \in G$ and $(\Gamma^{(R)})^{-1} \in \Gamma^{(R)}$ of G. Therefore $\Gamma^{1(R)+}$ must also be in reduced form.

But,

$$\Gamma^{l(R)}\dagger = \left(\begin{array}{c|c}\Gamma_1^{(R)}\dagger & 0 \\ \hline Q^{(R)}\dagger & \Gamma_2^{(R)}\dagger\end{array}\right)$$

$$= \left(\begin{array}{c|c}\Gamma_1^{(R)} & Q^{(R)} \\ \hline 0 & \Gamma_2^{(R)}\end{array}\right)$$

So that, $Q^{(R)}\dagger = 0$, when $\Gamma^{l(R)}$ is unitary. Thus, for a reduced unitary representation:

$$\Gamma^{l(R)} = \left(\begin{array}{c|c}\Gamma_1^{(R)} & 0 \\ \hline 0 & \Gamma_2^{(R)}\end{array}\right)$$

which is often written as the direct sum:

$$\Gamma^{l(R)} = \Gamma_1^{(R)} \oplus \Gamma_2^{(R)}$$

$\Gamma_1^{(R)}$ and $\Gamma_2^{(R)}$ are both representations of the group G.

Example:

$$\begin{pmatrix} a_{11} & a_{12} & a_{13} \\ a_{21} & a_{22} & a_{23} \\ a_{31} & a_{32} & a_{33} \end{pmatrix} \rightarrow \left(\begin{array}{cc|c} b_{11} & b_{12} & 0 \\ b_{21} & b_{22} & 0 \\ \hline \multicolumn{2}{c|}{0} & b_{33} \end{array}\right)$$

6.4 ORTHOGONALITY THEOREM

We consider two irreducible representations i and j in a point group with l_i and l_j dimensions respectively of order h. R denotes symmetry operation.

Now, further consider an element in a matrix with m^{th} row and n^{th} column of ith irreducible representation $\{\Gamma_i(R)_{mn}\}$ and another element in the jth irreducible representation in the m'^{th} and n'^{th} column $\{\Gamma_j(R)\}$ m′n′.

The two irreducible representations are related through orthogonality theorem by the relation:

$$\{\Gamma_i(R)\}_{mn}\ \{\Gamma_j(R)\}_{m'n'} = \frac{h}{\sqrt{l_i l_j}}.\delta_{ij}\quad \delta mm^1\ .\ \delta nn^1$$

We consider a case when m = n and m' = n'. There is a situation in which we have two square matrices for i^{th} and j^{th} irreducible representations:

$$\sum_R \{\Gamma_i(R)\}_{mm}\ \{\Gamma_j(R)\}_{m'm'} = \sum_R \frac{h}{l_i}\ \delta_{ij}.\delta_{mm}\ ,$$

On further taking the sum over l_i and l_j we obtain,

$$\sum_m^{li}\ \sum_{m'}^{l_j} \left\{\sum_R [\Gamma_i(R)]\right\}_{mm}\ \{\Gamma_j\ (R)\}_{m'm'}$$

$$= \frac{h}{l_i}\ \delta_{ij} \sum_m^{l_i} \sum_{m'}^{l_j} \delta mm'$$

Then summation part on R.H.S is the dimension of the reprsentation = l_i

$$= \frac{h}{l_i}\ \delta_{ij}.l_i$$

$$= h\ \delta_{ij}$$

$$\text{L.H.S.} = \sum_{R} \left\{ \sum_{m}^{li} \left[\Gamma_i (R)_{mm} \right] \sum_{m^1}^{lj} \left[\Gamma_j (R) m'm' \right] \right\}$$

Square matrix Its sum of the diagonal element is χ_i (R)	Another square matrix. Its sum of the diagonal element is χ_j (R)

$$\sum_{R} \chi_i(R)\, \chi_j\, (R)$$

such that, $\sum_{R} \chi_i(R)\, \chi_j\, (R) = h.\delta_{ij}$

(I) Put $i \neq j$, $\delta_{ij} = 0$

$\Sigma\chi_i$ (R) χj (R) = 0 orthogonality.

(II) Put i = j, $\sum_{R} \chi_i\, (R) \chi_i\, (R) = h,$

or $\sum_{R} \{\chi_i(R)\}^2 = h$.

Reduction formula: Consider character of a reducible representation. Its character in irreducible representation occurs which is given by the coefficient a_i.

$$\chi_R = \sum_{i} a_i \chi_i(R)$$

It will decompose different square matrices with their characters shown by $\chi_j(R)$ so we take sum over R.

$$\sum_{R} \chi(R)\, \chi_j(R)$$

$$= \sum_{R} \sum_{i} a_i\, \chi_i\, (R) \chi_j\, (R)$$

$$= \sum_{i} a_j \sum_{r} \chi_j\, (R) \chi_j\, (R)$$

This part is already obtained as $h.\sigma_{ij}$.

$$= \sum_{i} a_j\, .\, h\, .\, \delta_{ij}$$

$$= a_i\; h.\delta_{ij}$$

When i = j, $= a_j \cdot h \cdot 1 = a_j.h$

Thus, $\sum_R \chi(R)\chi_j(R) = a_j h$

or $a_j = \frac{1}{h}\sum_R \chi(R)\,\chi_j(R)$

Reduction formula

In general it is given by,

$$a_j = \frac{1}{h}\sum_R g_j\,\chi(R)\chi_j(R)$$

g_j is the order of the class.

6.5 CHARACTER TABLE

Characters also constitute representations. In character Table, characters of symmetry operations of each-class in a point group are written down for each symmetry species (IR). There are all together six parts like A, B, C, D, F and G in character Table.

A	B	C	D
F	G		

Part A–refers to the point group such as D_{4h}, T_d, O_h etc.

Part B–represents distinct symmetry operations arrange into respective classes.

Part C–one of the following three will be present in this part:

(a) Translational vectors — T_x, T_y, T_z

(b) Coordinates — x, y, z

(c) Orbitals — p_x, p_y, p_z

(d) Rotational vectors — R_x, R_y, R_z

They are placed together.

Part D–represents product functions.

(a) s – orbital is shown by $x^2 + y^2$ in a planar molecule, and as $x^2 + y^2 + z^2$ in three dimension.

(b) d – orbitals such as $x^2 - y^2$, z^2, xy xz and yz.

(c) Polarizability α_{xx}, α_{yy}, α_{zz}, α_{xy} etc. which are included in Raman spectra.

Let us take the case of D_{4h} which stands for tetragonal or square planar arrangement.

It has C_4 axis as the principal axis. The clockwise rotations are C_4, C_4^2, C_4^3, C_4^4. Anti-clockwise rotations are C_4^{-1}, C_4^{-2}, C_4^{-3}, C_4^{-4}. It can be shown as $C_4^{-1} = C_4^3$ so it goes out:

$$C_4^{-2} = C_4^2$$

$$C_4^{-3} = C_4$$

Thus inverse rotations are eliminated. There is a C_2 axis collinear with C_4. They are produced together. The C_4 operations will be $2C_4$ only. They belong to same class as $2C_4$.

(i) Apart from this there will be $C_2 \equiv C_4^2$:

(ii) There are two sets of C_2–axis, two C_2' and two C_2'', C_2' passes through corners of square. C_2'' passes through the edge of square:

$2C_2'$

$2C_2''$

Let us see the effect of C_2' and C_2'' on $dx^2–y^2$.

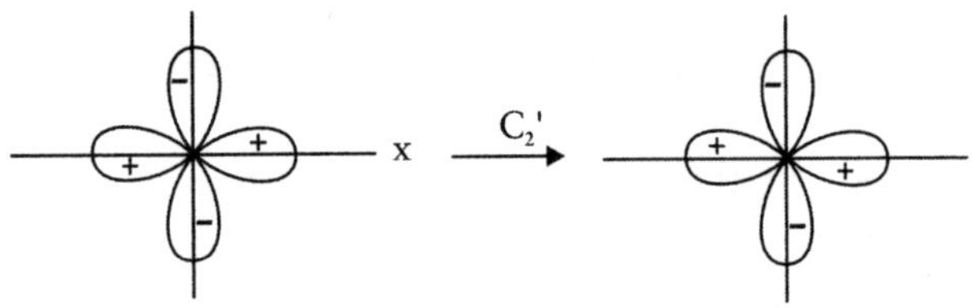

$C_2'\ (x^2 - y^2) \qquad = (+1)\,(x^2 - y^2)$ symmetric

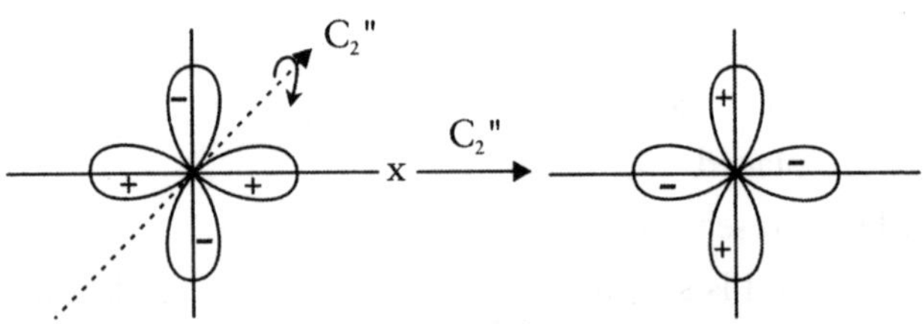

$C_2''\ (x^2 - y^2) \qquad = (-1)\,(x^2 - y^2)$ anti-symmetric

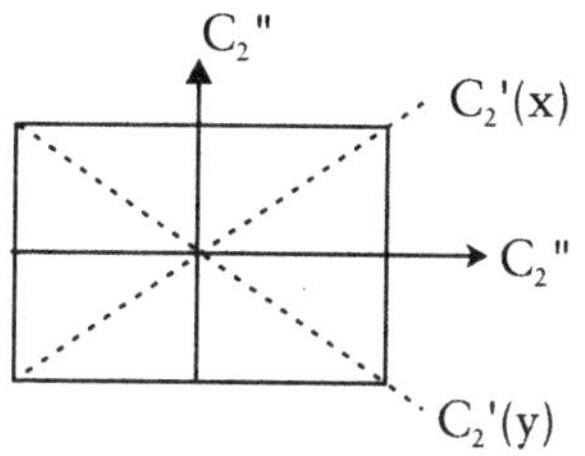

Thus, both C_2' and C_2'' are placed separately in C.T.

Inversion center, i is present.

Improper rotation axis S_4 exists. It generates:

$S_4, S_4^2, S_4^3, S_4^4 = E$

$S_4^{-1}, S_4^{-2}, S_4^{-3}, S_4^{-4} = E$

$S_4^{-1} = S_4^3, S_4^{-2} = S_4^2, S_4^{-3} = S_4$

Thus S_4^{-1}, S_4^{-2} and S_4^{-3} are redundant.

It has one σ_h, $2\sigma_v$ and $2\sigma_d$.

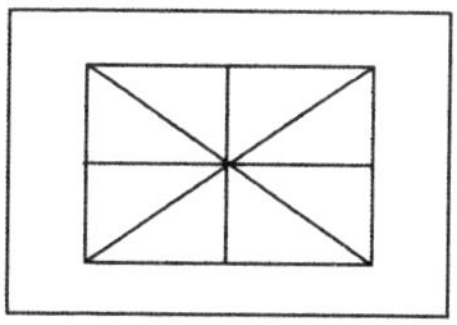

Thus, B part includes, E, $2C_4$, $C_2 \equiv C_4^2$, $2C_2'$, $2C_2''$, $i = S_2$ $2S_4$ σ_h $2\sigma_v$ $2\sigma_d$.

In C part orbital like p_x, p_y etc. are placed.

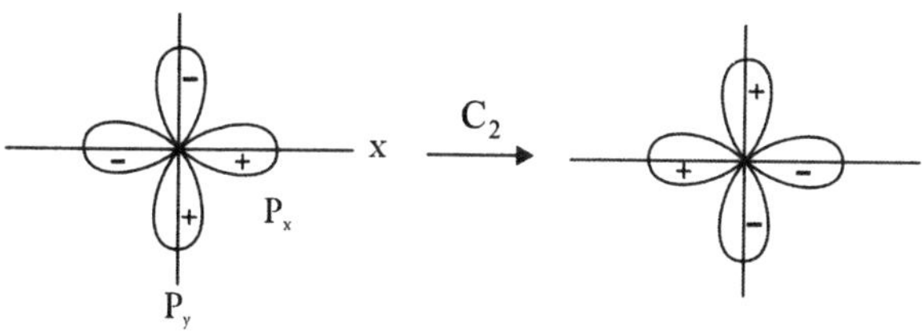

$C_2(x) = (-1)\ x$

$C_2(y) = (-1)\ y$

They are separate.

But, C_4 (x) = (+) y

C_4 (y) = (+1) x

They are placed together as E (x, y).

D_{4h}	E	$2C_4$	$C_2 = C_4^2$	$2C_1^{|}$	$2C_1^{||}$	$i=S_2$	$2S_4$	σ_h	$2\sigma_v$	$2\sigma_d$
A	1		A_1A_2	A_{1g}, A_{2g}		g or u				
B	1		B_1B_2	A_{1g}, A_{2g}				A_{1u}, A_{2u}		
E	2		E	B_{1g}, B_{2g}				B_{1u}, B_{2u}		
T_1	3			E_g				E_u		
T_2	3									

χ(E) dimension 1 A or B, dimension 2–E.

$\chi(C_4)$. A or B . . ., C_2 χ + 1 A_1 –1 A_2 B_1, B_2

χ (i), +1 g, –1u A_{1g} A_{2g} A_{1u} A_{2u} B_{1g} B_{2g} B_{1u} B_{2u} Eg Eu.

F part contains irreducible representation. Number of irreducible representation is equal to the number of class. We assign Mulliken notation or species:

A and B are non-degenerate.

A, χ = +1 for principal axis.

B, χ = –1 for principal axis.

In D_{4h} the principal axis is C_4.

s – orbital remains unaffected under C_4.

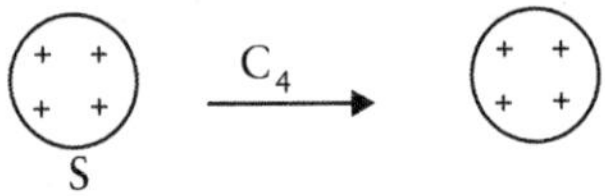

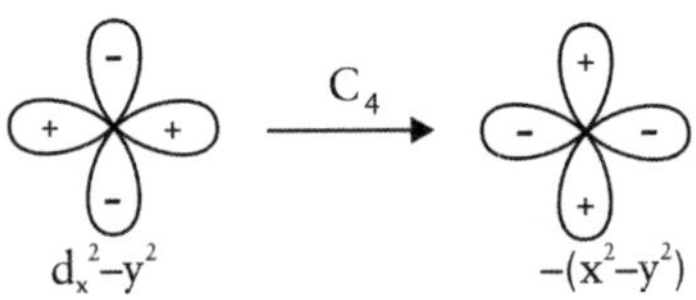

It changes sign. Hence B.

A_1 A C_2 axis perpendicular to C_4 +1, A_1 or B_1

A_2 –1, A_2 B_2

B_1

B_2

If C_2 is absent character of σ_v or σ_d will be negative for A_2 and B_2, positive for A_1 and B_1.

A and B are non-degenerate.

E – means doubly degenerate, character for identity is 2.

T – means triply degenerate T_1 and T_2.

When we have σ_h there will be dash.

If i is present we have g and u.

G – part of C.T. consists of characters obtained from the sum of the diagonal elements in the transformation matrices.

6.6 CHARACTER TABLE FOR C_{2v} POINT GROUP

It requires in the beginning two things:

(a) the list of symmetry operations, and

(b) the choice of basis functions for constituting representations for them. Three kinds of basis are generally employed for constructing character Tables:

   (i) Atomic orbital s, p_x, p_y, p_z, d_{xy}, d_{xz}, d_{yz} etc.

   (ii) Translational vectors, T_x, T_y, T_z

   (iii) Rotational vectors, R_x, R_y, R_z

A four dimensional representation is obtained using s, p_x, p_y and d_{xy} orbitals as basis functions. Both s and p_z have same transformation property and either of the two is taken in C_{2v}.

The four symmetry operations are, E, C_2, σ_{xz}, σ_{yz}.

A four dimensional representation for identity (E) is built in the following way:

$$\tilde{E}(s) = (+1)\ s,\ \tilde{E}(p_x) = (+1)\ p_x,\ \tilde{E}(p_y) = (+1)\ p_y$$
$$\tilde{E}(d_{xy}) = (+1)\ d_{xy}.$$

or,
$$s' = (+1)\, s + [0]\, p_x + [0]\, p_y + [0] d_{xy}$$

$$p_x = [0] s + [+1]\, p_x + [0]\, p_y + [0] d_{xy}$$

$$p_y = [0]\, s + [0]\, p_x + [+1]\, p_y + [0] d_{xy}$$

$$d_{xy} = [0] s + [0]\, p_x + [0]\, p_y + (+1)\, d_{xy}$$

$$\therefore\ E\begin{pmatrix} s \\ p_x \\ p_y \\ d_{xy} \end{pmatrix} = \begin{pmatrix} s' \\ p_x' \\ p_y' \\ dxy' \end{pmatrix} = \begin{pmatrix} 1 & 0 & 0 & 0 \\ 0 & 1 & 0 & 0 \\ 0 & 0 & 1 & 0 \\ 0 & 0 & 0 & 1 \end{pmatrix}\begin{pmatrix} s \\ p_x \\ p_y \\ dxy \end{pmatrix}$$

$$E = \begin{pmatrix} \Gamma_1 & 0 & 0 & 0 \\ 0 & \Gamma_2 & 0 & 0 \\ 0 & 0 & \Gamma_3 & 0 \\ 0 & 0 & 0 & \Gamma_4 \end{pmatrix}$$

This can be blocked out into four 1 × 1 sub-matrices:

$\Gamma_1(1)$	$\Gamma_2(1)$	$\Gamma_3(1)$	$\Gamma_4(1)$
$\chi_1=1$	$\chi_2=1$	$\chi_3=1$	$\chi_4=1$

All one-dimensional representations.

Now consider C_2 symmetry operation.

The matrices for it can be obtained:

$\tilde{C}_2(s) = (1)s$

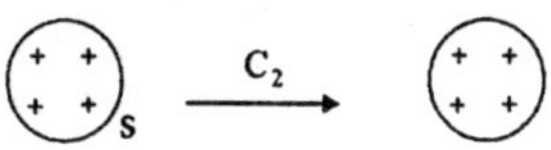

$\tilde{C}_2(p_x) = (-1)p_x$

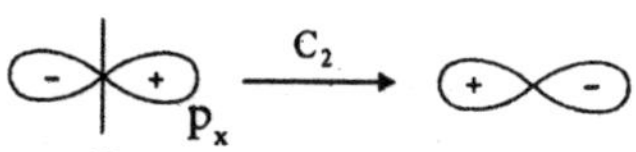

$\tilde{C}_2(p_y) = (-1)p_y$

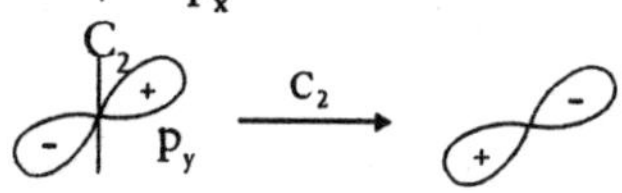

$\tilde{C}_2(dxy) = (+1)\ dxy$

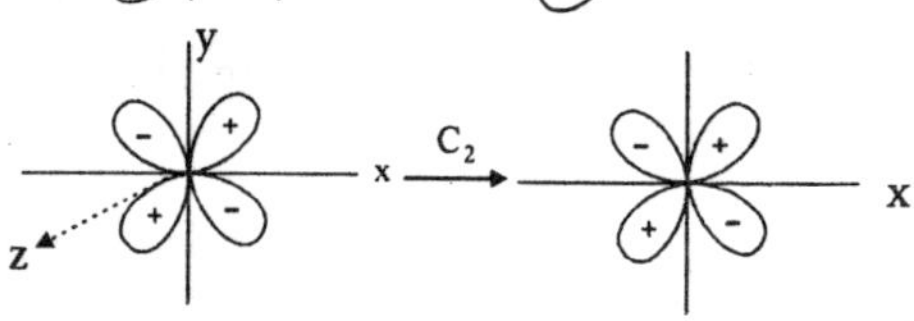

No change in sign of the lobes.

$$\therefore\qquad s' = (+1)\ s + (0)\ p_x + (0) p_y\ (0)\ dxy$$

$$p_x' = (0)\ s + (-1)\ p_x + (0)\ p_y + (0)\ dxy$$

$$p_y' = (0)\ s + (0)\ p_x + (-1)\ p_y + (0)\ dxy$$

$$d_{xy}' = (0)s + (0)\ p_x + (0)\ p_y + (+1)\ dxy$$

$$\tilde{C}_2\begin{pmatrix} s \\ p_x \\ p_y \\ d_{xy} \end{pmatrix} = \begin{pmatrix} s' \\ p'_x \\ p'_y \\ d'xy \end{pmatrix} = \begin{pmatrix} 1 & 0 & 0 & 0 \\ 0 & -1 & 0 & 0 \\ 0 & 0 & -1 & 0 \\ 0 & 0 & 0 & 1 \end{pmatrix}\begin{pmatrix} s \\ p_x \\ p_y \\ dxy \end{pmatrix}$$

$$\therefore \ C_2 \ : \ \underset{4\times 4}{\begin{pmatrix} 1 & 0 & 0 & 0 \\ 0 & -1 & 0 & 0 \\ 0 & 0 & -1 & 0 \\ 0 & 0 & 0 & 1 \end{pmatrix}}$$

This representation for C_2 in C_{2v} point group can be blocked out into four 1×1 matrices:

Γ_1: (1) $\chi_1 = 1$

Γ_2: (–1) $\chi_2 = -1$

Γ_3: (–1) $\chi_3 = -1$

Γ_4: (1) $\chi_4 = 1$

Consider representative matrices for σ_{xz}.

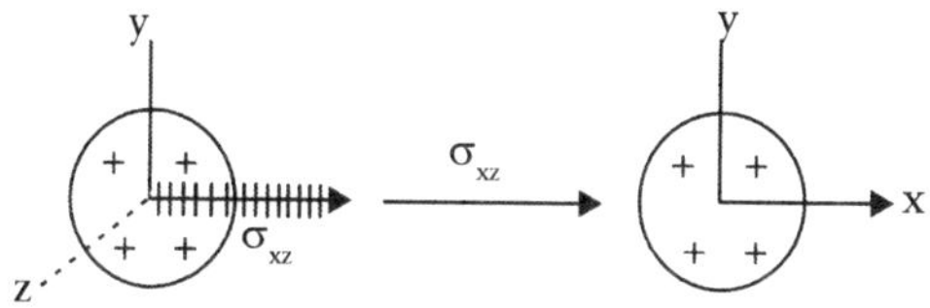

$$\tilde{\sigma}_{xz}(s) \to (+1)s$$

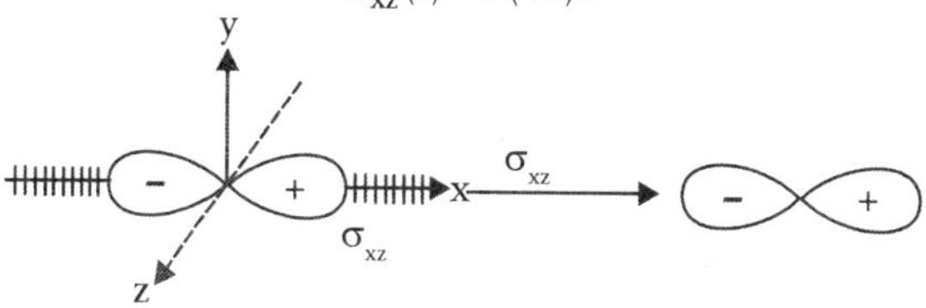

$$\tilde{\sigma}_{xz}(p_x) = (+1)\,p_x$$

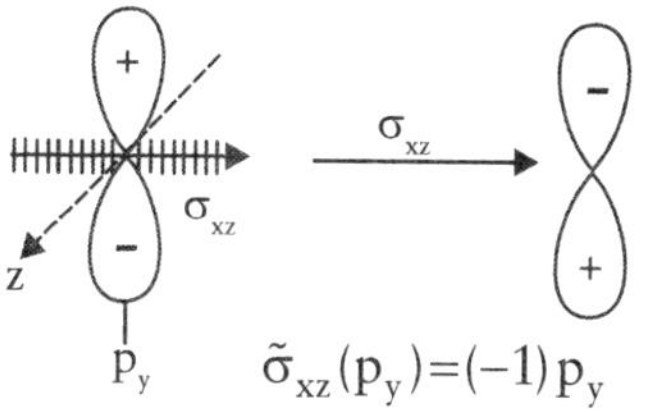

$$\tilde{\sigma}_{xz}(p_y) = (-1)\,p_y$$

$$s' = (+1)s + (0)p_x + (0)p_y + (0)\,dxy$$

$$p_x' = (0)s + (+1)\,p_x + (0)\,p_y + (0)\,dxy$$

$$p_y' = (0)s + (+0)\,p_x + (-1)\,p_y + (0)\,dxy$$

$$d_{xy}' = (0)s + (0)\,p_x + (0)\,p_y + (-1)\,dxy$$

$$\sigma_{xz}\begin{pmatrix} s \\ p_x \\ p_y \\ d_{xy} \end{pmatrix} = \begin{pmatrix} 1 & 0 & 0 & 0 \\ 0 & 1 & 0 & 0 \\ 0 & 0 & -1 & 0 \\ 0 & 0 & 0 & -1 \end{pmatrix}\begin{pmatrix} s \\ p_x \\ p_y \\ d_{xy} \end{pmatrix}$$

$$\therefore\ \sigma_{xz}\ :\ \begin{pmatrix} 1 & 0 & 0 & 0 \\ 0 & 1 & 0 & 0 \\ 0 & 0 & -1 & 0 \\ 0 & 0 & 0 & -1 \end{pmatrix}$$

The four 1 × 1 sub-matrices give characters for,

$\Gamma_1, \Gamma_2, \Gamma_3$ and Γ_4

Γ_1: (1) $\quad 1 \times 1$, $\chi_1 = 1$

Γ_2: (1) $\quad 1 \times 1$, $\chi_2 = 1$

Γ_3: (–1) $\quad -1 \times 1$, $\chi_3 = 1$

Γ_4: (–1) $\quad -1 \times 1$, $\chi_4 = 1$

Consider σ_{yz} operation:

$$\tilde{\sigma}_{yz}\,(s) = (+1)\,s$$

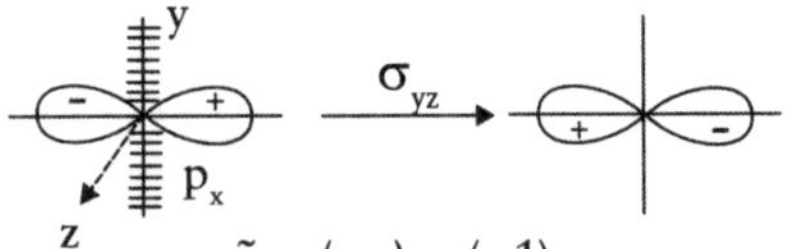

$$\tilde{\sigma}_{yz}\,(p_x) = (-1)\,p_x$$

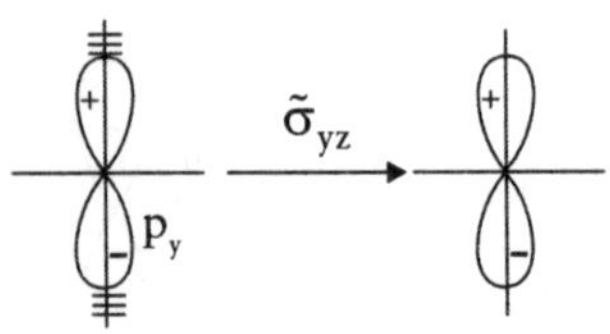

$$\tilde{\sigma}_{yz}\,(p_y) = (+1)\,p_y$$

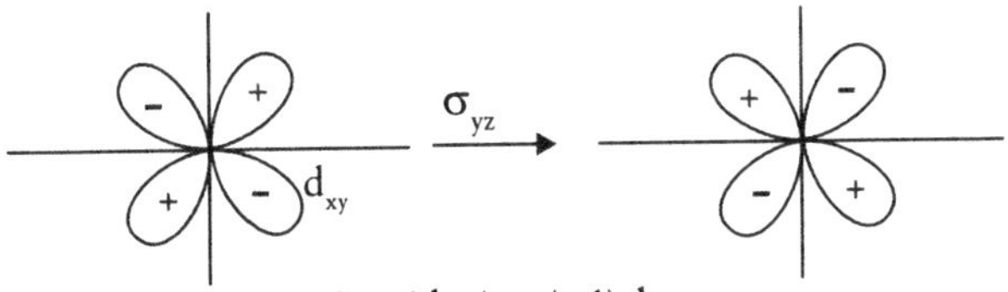

$$\tilde{\sigma}_{yz}\,(d_{xy}) = (-1)\,d_{xy}$$

Γ_1, $\chi_1 = +1$, A

Γ_2, $\chi_2 = +1$, A

Γ_3, $\chi_3(C_2) = -1$ anti-symmetric, $\chi(\sigma_{xz}) = -1$ anti-symmetric $= B_2$

Γ_4, $\chi_4(C_2) = +1$, symmetric,
$\chi(\sigma_{xz}) = -1$, anti-symmetric A_2.

Now we can arrange it as:

C_{2v}	E	C_2	σ_{xz}	σ_{yz}
A_1	1	1	1	1
A_2	1	1	–1	–1
B_1	1	–1	1	–1
B_2	1	–1	–1	1

6.7 CHARACTER TABLE FOR C_{2h}

The symmetry operations are E, C_2, σ_h and i. Consider four dimensional representations with s, p_x, p_z and d_{xz} as bases. The representative matrices for C_{2h} in trans –N_2O_2, trans –H_2O_2 or trans-butadiene can be written as:

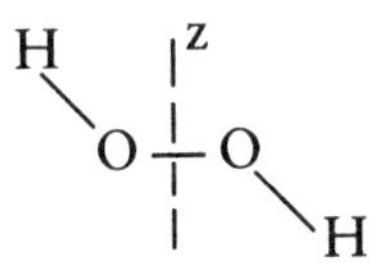

$$\tilde{E}(s) = (+1)\,s$$

$$\tilde{E}(p_x) = (+1)\,p_x$$

$$\tilde{E}(p_z) = (+1)\,p_z$$

$$\tilde{E}(d_{xz}) = (+1)\,d_{xz}$$

$$\therefore\; s' = (+1)s + (0)\,p_x + (0)\,p_z + (0)\,d_{xz}$$

$$p_x' = (0)s + (+1)\,p_x + (0)\,p_z + (0)\,d_{xz}$$

$$p_z' = (0)s + (0)\,p_x + (1)\,p_z + (0)\,d_{xz}$$
$$d_{xz}' = (0)s + (0)\,p_x + (0)\,p_z + (+1)\,d_{xz}$$

$$\tilde{E}\begin{pmatrix} s \\ p_x \\ p_z \\ d_{xz} \end{pmatrix} = \begin{pmatrix} s' \\ p_x' \\ p_z' \\ d_{xz}' \end{pmatrix} = \begin{pmatrix} 1 & 0 & 0 & 0 \\ 0 & 1 & 0 & 0 \\ 0 & 0 & 1 & 0 \\ 0 & 0 & 0 & 1 \end{pmatrix}\begin{pmatrix} s \\ p_x \\ p_z \\ d_{xz} \end{pmatrix}$$

$$\therefore\ E : \begin{pmatrix} 1 & 0 & 0 & 0 \\ 0 & 1 & 0 & 0 \\ 0 & 0 & 1 & 0 \\ 0 & 0 & 0 & 1 \end{pmatrix}$$

Since p_x and p_z cannot be mixed. Thus the representative matrix of order 4 will be block-diagonalized into four 1×1 sub-matrices.

$$\begin{pmatrix} 1 & 0 & 0 & 0 \\ 0 & 1 & 0 & 0 \\ 0 & 0 & 1 & 0 \\ 0 & 0 & 0 & 1 \end{pmatrix}$$

Γ_1: (1) $\quad 1 \times 1, \quad \chi_1 = 1$

Γ_2: (1) $\quad 1 \times 1, \quad \chi_2 = 1$

Γ_3: (1) $\quad 1 \times 1, \quad \chi_3 = 1$

Γ_4: (1) $\quad 1 \times 1, \quad \chi_4 = 1$

All are one dimensional representations. Transformation matrix for C_2:

$$\tilde{C}_2(s) = (+1)\,s$$

$$\tilde{C}_2(p_x) = (-1)\,p_x$$

$$\tilde{C}_2(p_z) = (+1)\,p_z$$

$$\tilde{C}_2(d_{xz}) = (-1)\,d_{xz}$$

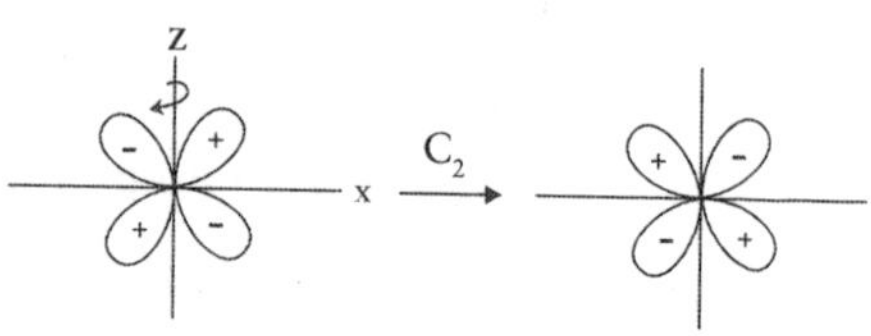

$$s' = (+1)s + (0)\,p_x + (0)\,p_z + (0)\,d_{xz}$$

$$p_x' = (0)s + (+1)\,p_x + (0)\,p_z + (0)\,d_{xz}$$

$$p_z' = (0)s + (0)\,p_x + ()1)\,p_z + (0)\,d_{xz}$$

$$d_{xz}' = (0)s + (0)\,p_x + (0)\,p_z + (-1)\,d_{xz}$$

$$\text{or, } C_2 \begin{pmatrix} s \\ p_x \\ p_z \\ d_{xz} \end{pmatrix} = \begin{pmatrix} s' \\ p_x' \\ p_z' \\ d_{xz}' \end{pmatrix} = \begin{pmatrix} 1 & 0 & 0 & 0 \\ 0 & -1 & 0 & 0 \\ 0 & 0 & 1 & 0 \\ 0 & 0 & 0 & -1 \end{pmatrix} \begin{pmatrix} s \\ p_x \\ p_z \\ d_{xz} \end{pmatrix}$$

$$C_2 : \begin{pmatrix} 1 & 0 & 0 & 0 \\ 0 & -1 & 0 & 0 \\ 0 & 0 & 1 & 0 \\ 0 & 0 & 0 & -1 \end{pmatrix}$$

$$4 \times 4$$

After blocking it out we get four 1 × 1 sub-matrices.

Γ_1: (1) 1 × 1, $\chi_1 = +1$

Γ_2: (−1) 1 × 1, $\chi_2 = -1$

Γ_3: (1) 1 × 1, $\chi_3 = 1$

Γ_4: (−1) 1 × 1, $\chi_4 = -1$

Now consider,

$\tilde{i}\,(s) = (+1)\,s$

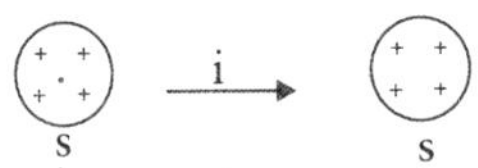

$\tilde{i}\,(p_x) = (-1)\,p_x$

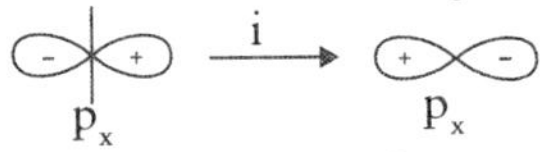

$\tilde{i}\,(p_z) = (-1)\,p_z$

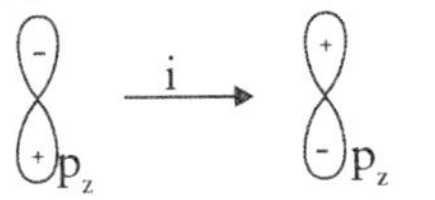

$\tilde{i}\,(d_{xz}) = (+1)\,d_{xz}$

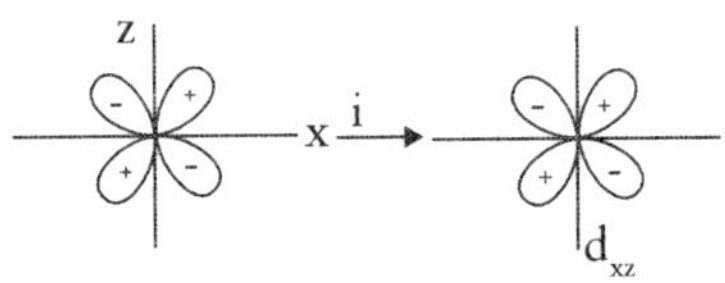

$$\therefore\ i \begin{pmatrix} s \\ p_x \\ p_z \\ d_{xz} \end{pmatrix} = \begin{pmatrix} s' \\ p_x' \\ p_z' \\ d_{xz}' \end{pmatrix} \begin{pmatrix} 1 & 0 & 0 & 0 \\ 0 & -1 & 0 & 0 \\ 0 & 0 & -1 & 0 \\ 0 & 0 & 0 & 1 \end{pmatrix} \begin{pmatrix} s \\ p_x \\ p_z \\ d_{xz} \end{pmatrix}$$

$$i : \begin{pmatrix} 1 & 0 & 0 & 0 \\ 0 & -1 & 0 & 0 \\ 0 & 0 & -1 & 0 \\ 0 & 0 & 0 & 1 \end{pmatrix}$$

The four sub matrices are 1×1 and their characters are:

Γ_1: (1) 1×1, $\chi_1 = 1$

Γ_2: (1) 1×2, $\chi_2 = 1$

Γ_3: (–1) 1×1, $\chi_3 = -1$

Γ_4: (–1) 1×2, $\chi_4 = -1$

Consider σ_h (or σ_{xy}) operation

$$\tilde{\sigma}_h\ (s) = (+1)\ s$$

$$\tilde{\sigma}_h\ (p_x) = (+1)\ p_x$$

$$\tilde{\sigma}_h\ (p_z) = (-1)\ p_z$$

$$\tilde{\sigma}_h\ (d_{xz}) = (-1)\ d_{xz}$$

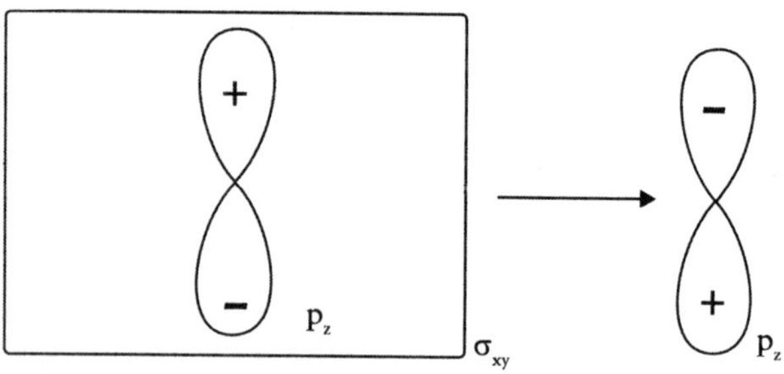

Reflection is done in xy plane. So z-co-ordinate of d_{xy}, changes from +z to –z. as a result it reverses sign.

It has neither C_2 ⊥r to C_n nor any σ_v but it has inversion centre.

Γ_1 (A)	x (i) = +1 sym g	Ag
Γ_2 (B)	−1 anti u	Bu
Γ_3 (A)	−1 anti u	Au
Γ_4 (B)	+1 sym g	Bg

These representations can be shown as:

C_{2h}	E	C_2	i	σ_h
Ag	1	1	1	1
Bg	1	−1	1	−1
Au	1	1	−1	−1
Bu	1	−1	−1	1

6.8 CHARACTER TABLE FOR C_{3V} POINT GROUP

There are so many ways of deriving the character Tables. One of them is by the use of transformation matrix followed by block diagonalization for various symmetry operations. There is also a method to follow the consequences of orthogonality theorem with the help of simple algebra.

Let us consider the case of point group C_{3v}. The symmetry operations belong to three classes.

E is a class by itself.

C_3, C_3^2 are placed together known as $2C_3$ in a separate class.

σ_1, σ_2, σ_3 the three vertical planes are placed together as $3\sigma_v$.

Number of class–three – E, $2C_3$, $3\sigma_v$ and, we expect three irreducible representations Γ_1, Γ_2 and Γ_3.

Now, sum of the squares of character for various symmetry–operations for a given irreducible representation multiplied by the order of the classes is equal to the order of the group.

Thus, $g_1\{\chi(E)\}^2 + g_2\{\chi(C_2)\}^2 + g_3\{\chi(\sigma_v)\}^2 = 6$.

It has characters for operations of three classes simply unity.

$$1 \times 1^2 + 2 \times 1^2 + 3 \times 1^2 = 6.$$

The first row is totally symmetrical now apply other rule. The sum of the squares of the characters of identity operation in all the irreducible representations is equal to the order h.

$$\left\{\chi_1^{A_1}(E)\right\}^2 + \left\{\chi_2^{A_2}(E)\right\}^2 + \left\{\chi_3^{E}(E)\right\}^2 = 6.$$

The position values are $\chi_1(E)$, $\chi_2(E)$ and $\chi_3(E)$, 1, 1 and 2 respectively:

$$1^2 + 1^2 + 2^2$$

$$= 1 + 1 + 4 = 6$$

Representation:	$\chi(E)$	$\chi(C_3)$	$\chi(\sigma_v)$
Γ_1	1	1	1
Γ_2	1	a	b
Γ_3	2	c	d

Let a, b, c and d be the remaining characters. We apply orthogonality condition. On applying the equation:

$$\sum_{p=1}^{k} g_p\, \chi_i(R_p)\, \chi_j(R_p) = 0$$

$$\text{or,} \quad \sum_{p=1}^{3} g_p\, \chi_i(R_p)\, \chi_j(R_p) = 0.$$

For Γ_1 and Γ_2 $\sum_{p=1}^{3} g_p\, \chi_i(R_p)\, \chi_2(R_p) = 0$

$$= g_1\, \chi_1(E)\, \chi_2(E) + g_2\, \chi_1(C_3) \cdot \chi_2(C_3)$$

$$+ g_3\, \chi_1(\sigma_v)\, \chi_2(\sigma_v) = 0$$

here $g_1 = 1$, $g_2 = 2$, $g_3 = 3$

$$1 + 2a + 3b = 0$$

when the equation $\sum_{0=1}^{k} g_p \left\{\chi_i\left(R_p\right)\right\}^2 = h = 6$

is applied to the representation Γ_2 we get

$$1^2 + 2a^2 + 3b^2 = 6.$$

but we have 2a + 3b = −1

$$\text{or,}\quad 2a = -(3b + 1)$$

$$a = -\frac{1}{2}(3b+1)$$

$$2a^2 + 3b^2 = 5$$

$$\not{2} \times \frac{1}{\not{4}_2}(3b+1)^2 + 3b^2 = 5$$

or, $(3b + 1)^2 + 6b^2 = 10$

or, $9b^2 + 6b + 1 + 6b^2 = 10$

or, $15b^2 + 6b - 9 = 0$

or, $5b^2 + 2b - 3 = 0$

or, $$b = \frac{-2 \pm \sqrt{4 - 4 \times 5x\,(-3)}}{2 \times 5}$$

$$= \frac{-2 \pm \sqrt{4+60}}{10}$$

$$= \frac{-2 \pm \sqrt{64}}{10}$$

$$= \frac{-2 \pm 8}{10}$$

Here, b is $= \frac{-10}{10}$ or $\frac{6}{10} = \frac{3}{5}$

$= -1$ or $3/5$

We cannot accept a fraction of 3/5.

Hence, $b = -1$

$$a = -\frac{(3b+1)}{2} = \frac{-(-3+1)}{2} = \frac{-(-2)}{2} = 1$$

Similar calculation is performed to calculate c and d in the representation Γ_3.

The equations are:

$$2 + 2c + 3d = 0$$

and, $$4 + 2c^2 + 3d^2 = 6$$

$$2C + 3d = -2$$

$$2C = -2 - 3d$$

or, $$C = \frac{-(3d+2)}{2}$$

$$\not{2}.\frac{(3d+2)^2}{\not{4}_2} + 3d^2 = 6 - 4 = 2$$

or, $$(3d + 2)^2 + 6d^2 = 4$$

or, $$9d^2 + 12d + 4 + 6d^2 = 4$$

or, $$15d^2 + 12d = 0$$

or, $$5d^2 + 4d = 0$$

or $$d(5d + 4) = 0$$

$d = 0$ or $\frac{-4}{5}$ a fraction which cannot be accepted.

Hence, $$d = 0$$

$$2C = -(3d + 2)$$

$$2C = 0 - 2$$

$$C = \frac{-\not{2}}{\not{2}} = -1$$

We get the following character Table:

TABLE 6.1

C_{3v}	E	$2C_3$	$3\sigma_v$
Γ_1	1	1	1
Γ_2	1	1	–1
Γ_3	2	–1	0

True or Faithful Representations

Consider the C_{2v} point group. Its C.T. is:

C_{2v}	E	C_2	σ_v	$\sigma_{v'}$
A_1	1	1	1	1
A_2	1	1	–1	–1
B_1	1	–1	1	–1
B_2	1	–1	–1	1

We take product operations:

	$C_2 \times C_2 = E$	$C_2 \times E = C_2$	$C_2 \times \sigma_{xz} = \sigma_{yz}$
A_1	$1 \times 1 = 1$	$1 \times 1 = 1$	$1 \times 1 = 1$
A_2	$1 \times 1 = 1$	$1 \times 1 = 1$	$1 \times 1 = -1$
B_1	$-1 \times -1 = 1$	$-1 \times 1 = -1$	$-1 \times 1 = -1$
B_2	$-1 \times -1 = 1$	$-1 \times 1 = -1$	$-1 \times -1 = 1$

So they are faithful or true representations.

6.9 CONSIDER CHARACTER TABLE FOR C_{4V} POINT GROUP

There are five classes in this group:

$$E, 2C_4, C_2, 2\sigma_V, 2\sigma_d.$$

So the number of irreducible representations is 5. Its order is 8, so the dimensions of the 1 Rs. are determined by:

$$l_1^2 + l_2^2 + l_3^2 + l_4^2 + l_5^2 = 8$$

$$l_1 = l_2 = l_3 = l_4 = 1, l_5 = 2.$$

There will be five number where squares add upto 8 are:

$$1^2 + 1^2 + 1^2 + 1^2 + 2^2 = 8 \cdot$$

There must be one totally symmetric representation (Γ_1):

	E	$2C_4$	C_2	$2\sigma_v$	$2\sigma_d$
Γ_1	1	1	1	1	1
Γ_2	1	1	1	–1	–1
Γ_3	1	–1	1	1	–1
Γ_4	1	–1	1	–1	1
Γ_5	2	a	b	c	d

Representations for Γ_2, Γ_3 and Γ_4 can easily be worked out from orthogonality with Γ_1 and sum of the squares is the order 8:

$$\begin{aligned} \Gamma_1\Gamma_2 &= 1\times1\times1+2\times1\times1+1\times1\times1+2\times1\times-1+2\times1\times-1 \\ &= \cancel{1} + \cancel{2} + \cancel{1} - \cancel{2} - \cancel{2} = 0 \\ \Gamma_1\Gamma_3 &= 1\times1\times1+2\times(-1)\times1+1\times1\times1+2\times1\times1+2\times1\times(-1) \\ &= \cancel{1} - \cancel{2} + \cancel{1} + \cancel{2} - \cancel{2} = 0 \end{aligned}$$

$$\Gamma_1\Gamma_4 = 1\times1\times1+2\times(-1)\times1+1\times1\times1+2\times(-1)\times1+2\times1\times1$$

$$= 1 - 2 + 1 + 2 - 2 = 0$$

and $$2^2 + 2a^2 + b^2 + 2c^2 + 2d^2 = 8$$

$$\Gamma_1\times\Gamma_5 \quad 2 + 2a + b + 2c + 2d = 0$$

$$\Gamma_2\times\Gamma_5 \quad 2 + 2a + b - 2c - 2d = 0$$

$$\Gamma_3\times\Gamma_5 \quad 2 - 2a + b + 2c - 2d = 0$$

$$\Gamma_4\times\Gamma_5 \quad 2 - 2a + b - 2c + 2d = 0$$

Addition of first two one gets:

$$2 + 2a + b + 2c + 2d = 0$$

$$2 + 2a + b - 2c - 2d = 0$$

$$4 + 4a + 2b = 0$$

$$2 + 2a + b = 0$$

$$2a + b = -2$$

$$2a = -2 - b$$

$$a = \frac{-(2+b)}{2} \qquad 2a = -b - 2$$

$$b = -2a - 2$$

$$= -2\ (a + 1)$$

Subtraction of third and fourth one has:

$$2 - 2a + b + 2c - 2d = 0$$

$$2 - 2a + b - 2c + 2d = 0$$

$$\underline{-\quad+\quad-\quad+\quad\quad-}$$

$$4c - 4d = 0$$

$$c - d = 0$$

$$c = d$$

Now from:

$$4 + 2a^2 + b^2 + 2c^2 + 2d^2 = 8$$

$$2a^2 + b^2 + 4c^2 = 4$$

Also,

$$2 + 2a + b + 2c + 2d = 0$$

$$\underset{-}{2} \underset{+}{-} 2a \underset{-}{+} \underset{+}{b} - 2\underset{-}{c} + 2d = 0$$

$$4a + 4c = 0$$

$$a + c = 0$$

$$a = -c = -d$$

$$2a^2 + b^2 + 4c^2 = 4$$

$$2c^2 + b^2 + 4c^2 = 4$$

$$b^2 + 6c^2 = 4$$

There is also a rule that sum of the products of the χ for any two different classes taken over all the representations is zero.

$$\sum_{i=1}^{n} \chi_i (\mu) \chi_j (\upsilon) = 0 \qquad \text{if } \mu = \upsilon$$

Where as μ and υ are two different classes of C_{4v} group.

$$\chi(E) \times \chi(C_4)$$

Γ_1 $\quad 1 \times 1$

$+$

Γ_2 $\quad 1 \times 1$

$+$

Γ_3 $\quad 1 \times -1$

$+$

Γ_4 $\quad 1 \times -1$

$+$

Γ_5 $\quad \dfrac{2 \times a}{0}$

Its sum is

$$1 + 1 - 1 - 1 + 2a = 0$$

$$2a = 0$$

$$a = 0$$

χ (E) × χ (C_2)

Γ_1 1 × 1

Γ_2 1 × 1

Γ_3 1 × 1

Γ_4 1 × 1

Γ_5 $\frac{2 \times b}{0}$

Sum is:

1+1+1+1+2b=0

4+2b=0

b+2=0

b=–2

χ (E) × χ (σ_u)

Γ_1 1 × 1

Γ_2 1 × –1

Γ_3 1 × 1

Γ_4 1 × –1

Γ_5 $\frac{2 \times c}{0}$

Sum is:

1–1+1–1+2c=0

2c=0

c=0

χ (E) × χ (σ_d)

1 × 1

1 × –1

1 × –1

1 × 1

$\frac{2 \times d}{0}$

Its sum is 1 –1 –1 +1 + 2d = 0

2d = 0

d = 0

Character Table for C_{4v}.

C_{4v}	E	$2C_4$	C_2	$2\sigma_v$	$2\sigma_d$
A_1	1	1	1	1	1
A_2	1	1	1	–1	–1
B_1	1	–1	1	1	–1
B_2	1	–1	1	–1	1
E	2	0	–2	0	0

D_5 Point Group

$C_5 + 5C_2 \rightarrow D_5$

C_5, C_5^2, C_5^3, C_5^4

E, $2C_5$, $2C_5^2$ $5C_2$

The order of the group is 10 and symmetry operations belong to four classes. Hence there are four irreducible representations.

Two of them are non-degenerate and other two are doubly degenerate:

$$l_1^2 + l_2^2 + l_3^2 + l_4^2 = 10$$

$$1^2 + 1^2 + 2^2 + 2^2$$

$$= 1 + 1 + 4 + 4 = 10$$

	E	$2C_5$	$2C_5^2$	$5C_2$	
Γ_1	1	1	1	1	Totally symmetric.
Γ_2	1	1	1	–1	
Γ_3	2	a	b	c	
Γ_4	2	d	e	f	

$\Gamma_1 \times \Gamma_3$ $1 \times 2 + 2 \times 1 \times a + 2 \times 1 \times b + 5 \times 1 \times c = 0$

$$2 + 2a + 2b + 5c = 0$$

$\Gamma_2 \times \Gamma_3$

$$1 \times 2 + 2 \times 1 \times a + 2 \times 1 \times b + 5 \times (-1) \times c = 0$$

or, $2 + 2a + 2b - 5c = 0$

Subtraction leads to:

$$2 + 2a + 2b + 5c = 0$$
$$2 + 2a + 2b - 5c = 0$$
$$- \quad - \quad - \quad +$$

$$10c = 0$$

$$c = 0$$

While on addition:

$$4 + 4a + 4b = 0$$

$\Gamma_1 \times \Gamma_4$

$$1 \times 2 + 2 \times 1 \times d + 2 \times 1 \times e + 5 \times 1 \times f = 0$$

$$2 + 2d + 2e + 5f = 0$$

$\Gamma_2 \times \Gamma_4$

$$1 \times 2 + 2 \times 1 \times d + 2 \times 1 \times e + 5 \times (-1) \times f = 0$$

On subtraction:

$$\begin{array}{r} 2 + 2d + 2e + 5f = 0 \\ 2 + 2d + 2e - 5f = 0 \\ - \quad - \qquad - \quad + \qquad \\ \hline 10f = 0. \text{ Hence } f = 0 \end{array}$$

Their addition gives: $4 + 4d + 4e = 0$

on addition of these equations.

$$4 + 4a + 4b = 0 \quad \text{or} \quad a + b = -1$$
$$4 + 4d + 4e = 0 \quad \text{or} \quad d + e = -1$$

Also

$$2^2 + 2a^2 + 2b^2 + 5c^2 = 10$$
$$2^2 + 2d^2 + 2e^2 + 5f^2 = 1$$

or, $2a^2 + 2b^2 = 10 - 4 \quad (\because c = 0)$

$$2(a^2 + b^2) = 6$$
$$a^2 + b^2 = 3.$$

Also $a + b = -1$

$$(a + b)^2 = 1$$
$$a^2 + 2ab + b^2 = 1$$
$$3 + 2ab = 1$$
$$2ab = -2$$
$$ab = -1$$

$$(a - b)^2 = (a+b)^2 - 4ab$$
$$= (-1)^2 - 4 \times (-1)$$
$$= 1 + 4 = 5$$

or $a - b = \sqrt{5}$

$$\begin{array}{l} a + b = -1 \\ a - b = \sqrt{5} \\ \hline 2a = -1 + \sqrt{5} \end{array}$$

$$a = \frac{-1 + \sqrt{5}}{2}$$

$$2b = -1 - \sqrt{5}$$

$$b = \frac{-1-\sqrt{5}}{2}$$

$a = 2 \cos 72°$ or $2 \cos \theta$ $\quad b = 2 \cos 144°$

$= 2 \cos 2\theta$ where $\theta = 72°$

Likewise $d = 2 \cos 2\theta$, $e = 2 \cos \theta$

TABLE 6.2

D_5	E	$2C_5$	$2C_5^2$	$5C_2$
Γ_1	1	1	1	1
Γ_2	1	1	1	–1
Γ_3	2	$2 \cos \theta$	$2 \cos 2\theta$	0
Γ_4	2	$2 \cos 2\theta$	$2 \cos \theta$	0

6.10 CHARACTER TABLE OF CYCLIC GROUPS

Members of a cyclic group are complex:

$$C_n^n = E$$

so $\quad \chi (C_n)^n = 1 = \chi (E)$

so $\quad \chi (C_n)$ must all consist of the number +1 or –1 for the character of such numbers in general are complex of the form:

$$\chi (c_n)^n = (e^{i\theta})^n = 1 = e^{iz\pi m}$$

where $m = 0, 1, 2, 3, ...$

and $\theta = 2\pi m/n$

Leading to the character of rotation:

$$\chi (C_n) = e^{i2\pi m/n}$$

For one dimensional representation with the symmetry classes:

$$E \quad Cn \quad C_n^2 \quad C_n^3 \quad .... \quad C_n^{n-1}$$

$$e^0 \quad e^{2\pi i/n} \quad e^{2.2\pi i/n} \quad e^{3.2\pi i/n} ....e^{(n-1)\frac{2\pi i}{n}}$$

We denote one of the irreducible representations by ϵ^m where:

$$\epsilon = e^{2\pi i/n}$$

with m = 0, 1, 2 .... n-1.

A set of exponential e^{2m} is an irreducible representation.

For C_3 group the irreducible representations are obtained for setting rotations C_n^k with K = 1, 2, ... (n-1).

K represents classes for cyclic group it gives the irreducible representations m = 0, 1, 2.....

Character Table for C_3 group is given below:

TABLE 6.3

C_3	$C_3^3 = E$	C_3	C_3^2
Γ_1	1	1	1
Γ_2	1	ϵ	ϵ
Γ_3	1	ϵ	ϵ

For first member Γ_1 put m = 0, in the expression.

$$= e^{2\pi i/n} \qquad n = 3$$

$$= e^{2\pi i/3}$$

we take $\dfrac{2\pi imk}{3}$ with m = 0 case k = 1, 2, 3

$$\chi(C_3) = e^0 = 1 \qquad \chi(C_3^2) = e^0 = 1$$

$$\chi(C_3^3) = e^0 = 1$$

Γ_1, 1, 1, 1 This corresponds to m = 0.

For Γ_2 we put m = 1

k = 1, 2, 3

$$\chi(C_3) = e^{2\pi i/3} = \epsilon$$

$$\chi\left(C_3^2\right) = e^{2.2\pi i/3} = e^{4\pi i/3}$$

$$\chi\left(C_3^3\right) = e^{3.2\pi i/3} = e^{6\pi i/3}$$

Let, $\xi = e^{2\pi i/3}$

$= \cos 2\pi/3 + i \ \sin 2\pi/3$

$e^{4\pi i/3} = \cos\left(2\pi - 2\pi/3\right) + i \sin\left(2\pi - 2\pi/3\right)$

$= \cos 2\pi/3 - i \sin 2\pi/3 = \xi^*$

$e^{6\pi i/3} = e^{2\pi i} = \cos 2\pi + i \sin 2\pi$

$= \cos (2\pi - 0) + i \sin (2\pi - 0)$

$= \cos 0 - i \ \sin 0$

$= 1 - i \times 0 = 1$

$\therefore \quad \Gamma_2 \ . \ 1 \ \xi \ \xi^*$

For Γ_3, we put m = 2.

Such that ξ (C_3)

K = 1, 2, 3

Such that, ξ (C_3), m = 2, k = 1

$$\chi(C_3) = e^{2\pi i} \frac{\times 2 \times 1}{3} = e^{4\pi i/3}$$

$$= \cos\left(2\pi - \frac{2\pi}{3}\right) + i \sin\left(2\pi - \frac{2\pi}{3}\right)$$

$$= \cos\frac{2\pi}{3} - i \sin\frac{2\pi}{3}$$

$$= \xi^*$$

$$\begin{matrix} m = 2 \\ k = 2 \end{matrix} \quad \chi\left(C_3^2\right) = \frac{e^{2\pi i \times 2 \times 2}}{3}$$

$$= e^{8\pi i/3} = \cos\left(2\pi + \frac{2\pi}{3}\right) + i \sin\left(2\pi + \frac{2\pi}{3}\right)$$

$$= \cos^{2\pi/3} + i \sin^{2\pi/3} = \xi$$

$$\begin{matrix} m = 2 \\ k = 3 \end{matrix} \quad \chi\left(C_3^3\right) = e^{2\pi i} \times 2 \times \frac{3}{3}$$

$$= e^{12\pi i/3}$$

$$= e^{4\pi i}$$

$$\cos(2\pi + 2\pi) + i \sin(2\pi + 2\pi)$$
$$= \cos 2\pi + i \sin 2\pi$$
$$= \cos(2\pi - 0) + i \sin(2\pi - 0)$$
$$= \cos 0 + i \sin 0$$
$$= 1 + i \times 0 = 1$$

Γ_3 1 ξ^* ξ

Γ_2 and Γ_3 are complex conjugate. They combine to give:

1	ξ	ξ^*	
1	ξ^*	ξ	
2	$2\cos\theta$	$2\cos\theta$	with $\theta = 2\pi/3$

C_4 Point Group

The members are $C_4^4 = E, C_4, C_4^2, C_4^3$

$$\chi(C_n) = e^{2\pi i\, mk/4}$$

There are four classes for which:

we put Γ_1, Γ_2, Γ_3, Γ_4

with k = 1, 2, 3, 4

and m = 0, 1, 2, 3 respectively.

m = 0 case Γ_1. Characters are:

$e^0 \quad e^0 \quad e^0 \quad e^0$

The first representation is obtained on putting m = 0.

where, Γ_1	1	1	1	1
	$E = C_4^4$	C_4	C_4^2	C_4^3
	4	k=1	2	3

For, m = 1 (case Γ_2) we have

$$e^{2\pi i/4}, \quad e^{2.2\pi i/4}, \quad e^{3.2\pi i/4}, \quad e^{4.2\pi i/4}$$

$$= e^{\pi i/2}, \quad e^{\pi i}, \quad e^{\frac{3\pi}{2}i}, \quad e^{2\pi i}$$

$$e^{\frac{\pi i}{2}} = \cos \pi/2 + i \sin \pi/2$$

$$= \cos(\pi/2 = 0) + i \sin(\pi/2 - 0)$$

$$= \sin 0° + i \cos 0°$$

$$= 0 + i.1 = i$$

$$e^{\pi i} = \cos \pi + i \sin \pi$$

$$= \cos(\pi - 0) + i \sin(\pi - 0)$$

$$= -\cos 0 + i \sin 0$$

$$= -1 + i \times 0 = -1$$

$$e^{\frac{3\pi i}{2}} = \cos 3\pi/2 + i \sin 3\pi/2$$

$$= \cos(2\pi - \pi/2) + i \sin\left(2\pi - \frac{\pi}{2}\right)$$

$$= \cos \pi/2 - i \sin \pi/2$$

$$= 0 - i \times \cos 0°$$

$$= -i$$

$$e^{2\pi i} = \cos(2\pi) + i \sin 2\pi$$

$$= \cos 0° - i \sin 0°$$

$$= 1 - i \times 0 = 1$$

$$\Gamma_2 = 1, i, -1, -i$$

Consider m = 2 case

	K = 1	K = 2	K = 3	K = 4
m = 2	$e^{2.2\pi i/4}$	$e^{2.2\pi i \times 2/4}$	$e^{2 \times 2\pi i \times 3/4}$	$e^{2.2\pi i \times 4/4}$
	$= e^{4\pi i/4}$	$e^{\frac{8\pi i}{4}}$	$e^{\frac{12\pi i}{4}}$	$e^{\frac{16\pi i}{4}}$
				$= e^{4\pi i}$
	$= e^{\pi i}$,	$e^{2\pi i}$,	$e^{3\pi i}$,	$e^{4\pi i}$

$$
\begin{aligned}
e^{\pi i} &= \cos\pi + i\sin\pi \\
&= -\cos 0° + i\sin 0 \\
&= -1 + i\times 0 \\
&= -1 \\
e^{2\pi i} &= \cos 2\pi + i\sin 2\pi \\
&= \cos 0° + i\sin 0° \\
&= 1 + i\times 0 = 1 \\
e^{3\pi i} &= \cos(2\pi+\pi)\ i\sin(2\pi+\pi) \\
&= \cos\pi + i\sin\pi \\
&= -\cos 0° + i\sin 0° \\
&= -1 + i\times 0 \\
&= -1 \\
e^{4\pi i} &= \cos 4\pi + i\sin 4\pi \\
&= \cos(2\pi+2\pi) + i\sin(2\pi+2\pi) \\
&= \cos 2\pi + i\sin 2\pi \\
&= \cos 0° + i\sin 0° \\
&= 1 + i\times 0 \\
&= 1
\end{aligned}
$$

$$\Gamma_3 = 1, -1, 1, -1$$

m = 3 case we have,

$$e^{3.2\pi i/4} \qquad e^{\frac{3.2\pi i\times 2}{4}} \qquad e^{\frac{3.2\pi i\times 3}{4}} \qquad e^{\frac{3.2\pi i\times 4}{4}}$$

$$= e^{\frac{3\pi i}{2}} \qquad e^{3\pi i} \qquad e^{\frac{9\pi i}{2}} \qquad e^{6\pi i}$$

$$
\begin{aligned}
e^{3\pi i/2} &= \cos 3\pi/2 + i\sin 3\pi/2 \\
&= \cos(2\pi - \pi/2) + i\sin(2\pi - \pi/2) \\
&= \cos\pi/2 - i\sin\pi/2 \\
&= \sin 0° - i\cos 0° \\
&= 0 - i\times 1 = -i
\end{aligned}
$$

$$e^{3\pi i} = \cos(2\pi+\pi) + i\sin(2\pi+\pi)$$
$$= \cos\pi + i\sin\pi$$
$$= -\cos 0° + i\sin 0°$$
$$= -1 + i\times 0 = -1$$
$$e^{9\pi i/2} = \cos(4\pi+\pi/2) + i\sin(4\pi+\pi/2)$$
$$= \cos(2.2\pi+\pi/2) + i\sin(2.2\pi-\pi/2)$$
$$= \cos\pi/2 - i\sin\pi/2$$
$$= \sin 0° + i\cos 0°$$
$$= 0 + i\times 1 = i$$
$$e^{6\pi i} = \cos(2.2\pi+2\pi) + i\sin(2.2\pi+2\pi)$$
$$= \cos 2\pi - i\sin 2\pi$$
$$= \cos 0° + i\sin 0°$$
$$= 1 + i\times 0 = 1$$

Γ_4 1, −i, −1, i

TABLE 6.4

C_4	$E \equiv C_4^4$	C_4	C_4^2	C_4^3
Γ_1	1	1	1	1
Γ_2	1	i	−1	−i
Γ_3	1	−1	1	−1
Γ_4	1	−i	−1	i

6.11 CHARACTER TABLE ON TAKING DIRECT PRODUCT OF SMALLER GROUPS

Let us take up the case of D_3 and C_s groups. In D_3 point group the six operations are:

E, $2C_3$, $3C_2$ and there are two symmetry operations E and σ in C_s. The symmetry operations which result from their product are:

$$(E, 2C_3, 3C_2) \times (E, \sigma)$$
$$= E, 2C_3, 3C_2, \sigma_h, 2S_3, 3\sigma_v$$

There are 12 operations in $D_3 + \sigma_h \rightarrow D_{3h}$ which are obtained by taking the direct product $D_3 \times C_s$.

D_3	E	$2C_3$	$3C_2$		C_s	E	σ
A_1	1	1	1	X	A′	1	1
A_2	1	1	–1		A″	1	–1
E	2	–1	0				

We multiply their characters of matrices of D_3 and C_s and their direct product result in formation of C. T for D_{3h} point group.

TABLE 6.5

D_{3h}	E	$2C_3$	$3C_2$	σ_h	$2S_3$	$3\sigma_v$
A_1'	1	1	1	1	1	1
A_2'	1	1	–1	1	1	–1
E′	2	–1	0	2	–1	0
A_1''	1	1	1	–1	–1	–1
A_2''	1	1	–1	–1	–1	1
E″	2	–1	0	–2	1	0

We can also obtain character Table taking the direct product of two sub-groups for illustration. We construct a C_{2h} point group using the sub-groups C_2 and $C_i = C_s$.

C_2	E	C_2		C_s	E	i
A	1	1	X	Ag	1	1
B	1	–1		Au	1	–1

$C_2 \times C_s = C_{2h}$

C_{2h}	E	C_2	i	σ_h
Ag	1	1	1	1
Bg	1	–1	1	–1
Au	1	1	–1	–1
Bu	1	–1	–1	1

In general we get the character Tables of point groups.

n = odd	n = even
$C_n \times C_s = C_{nh}$	$C_n \times C_i = C_{nh}$
$D_n \times C_s = D_{nh}$	$D_n \times C_i = D_{nh}$
$D_n \times C_i = D_{nd}$	
$O \times C_i = O_h$	

6.12 REPRESENTATION OF GROUPS

We shall see here the effect of symmetry operations on (a) coordinates, and (b) vectors. A vector is a line of given length and direction:

(a) Consider representation for x, y, z coordinates under C_{2v} point symmetry. We use the coordinate system and symmetry operations for SO_2 (C_{2v}).

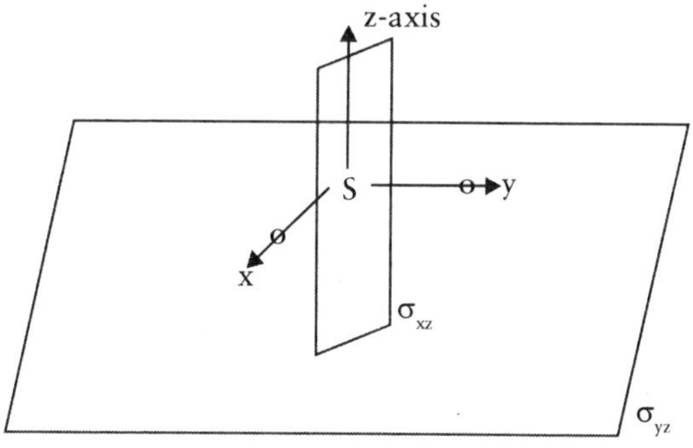

Their coordinates are used as bases. They are transformed into themselves with either positive or negative sign.

Transformation properties of x

$$\tilde{E}\,(x) = (+1)\,x$$

$$\tilde{C}_z\,(x) = (-1)\,x$$

$$\tilde{\sigma}_{xz}\,(x) = (+1)\,x$$

$$\tilde{\sigma}_{yz}\,(x) = (-1)\,x$$

Transformation properties of y

$$\tilde{E}\,(y) = (+1)\,y$$
$$\tilde{C}_z\,(y) = (-1)\,y$$
$$\tilde{\sigma}_{xz}\,(y) = (-1)\,y$$
$$\tilde{\sigma}_{yz}\,(y) = (+1)\,y$$

Transformation properties of z

$$\tilde{E}\,(z) = (+1)\,z$$
$$\tilde{C}_z\,(z) = (+1)\,z$$
$$\tilde{\sigma}_{xz}\,(z) = (+1)\,z$$
$$\tilde{\sigma}_{yz}\,(z) = (+1)\,z$$

The resulting representations are summarized below:

C_{2v}	E	$C_2(z)$	σ_{xz}	σ_{yz}
x	1	–1	1	–1
y	1	–1	–1	1
z	1	1	1	1

All the three are one dimensional representations since X(E) = 1, in each case. The Mulliken notation are B, B and A respectively:

x transforms as B_1

y transforms as B_2

z transforms as A_1

(b) Consider representation generated by p_x, p_y and p_z orbitals under C_{2v} point group.:

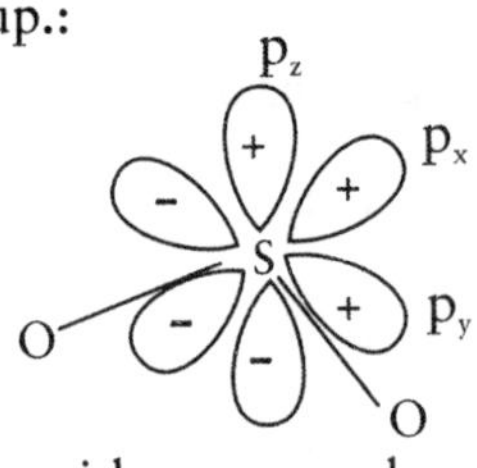

We use SO_2-molecule with p_x, p_y and p_z orbital of S-atom in it.

The effect of E_1, C_2, σ_{xz} and σ_{yz} is considered.

Transformation properties of p_x

$$\tilde{E}\ (p_x) = (+1)\, p_x$$

$$\hat{C}_2\ (p_x) = (-1)\, p_x$$

$$\tilde{\sigma}_{xz}\ (p_x) = (+1)\, p_x$$

$$\tilde{\sigma}_{yz}\ (p_x) = (-1)\, p_x$$

Transformation properties of p_y

$$\tilde{E}\ (p_y) = (+1)\, p_y$$

$$\hat{C}_2\ (p_y) = (-1)\, p_y$$

$$\tilde{\sigma}_{xz}\ (p_y) = (-1)\, p_y$$

$$\tilde{\sigma}_{yz}\ (p_y) = (+1)\, p_y$$

Transformation Properties of p_z

$$\tilde{E}\ (p_z) = (+1)\, p_z$$

$$\hat{C}_2\ (p_z) = (+1)\, p_z$$

$$\sigma_{xz}\ (p_z) = (+1)\, p_z$$

$$\sigma_{yz}\ (p_z) = (+1)\, p_z$$

The result can be given in a tabular form:

C_{2v}	E	C_2	σ_{xz}	σ_{yz}	Mulliken notation
p_x	1	–1	1	–1	B_1
p_y	1	–1	–1	1	B_2
p_z	1	1	1	1	A_1

(c) Translational vectors as basis function. Vectors can be used to generate representation. consider C_{2v} case, e.g. SO_2.

Now a set of Cartesian coordinates is placed on S and two O atoms.

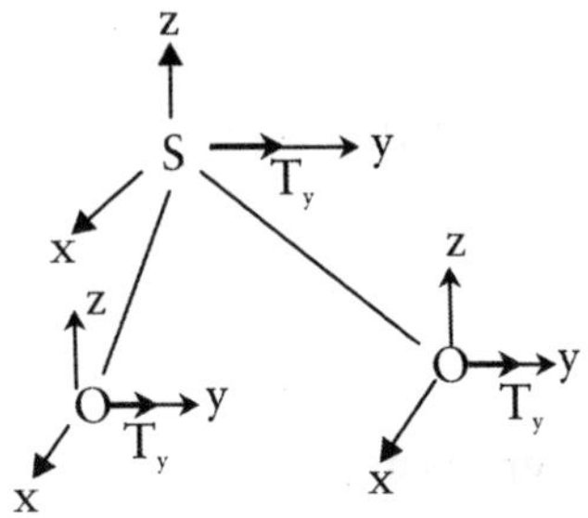

Then we draw a vector from each atom along its own y-axis. (All of the vectors being of the same length). We can have a set of vectors for translational motion of the molecule in y-direction and two other such vectors about x and z-axes. These are Ty, Tx and Tz vectors attached to the molecule.

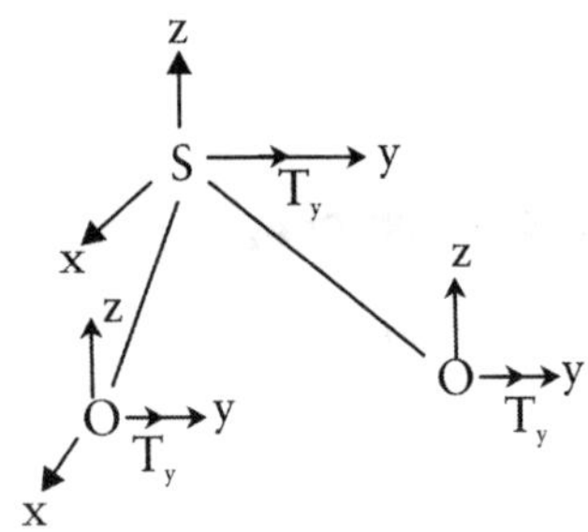

The bold lines indicate the translational vector T_y (small arrows) at each center by T_x and T_z vectors are shown at each centre by small bold arrows along x and z-axis. The effect of E, C_2, σ_{xz} and σ_{yz} on T_y leaves the vector completely unaffected or reverses its direction.

Take at first C_2 operation. This represents rotation about z-axis by 180°.

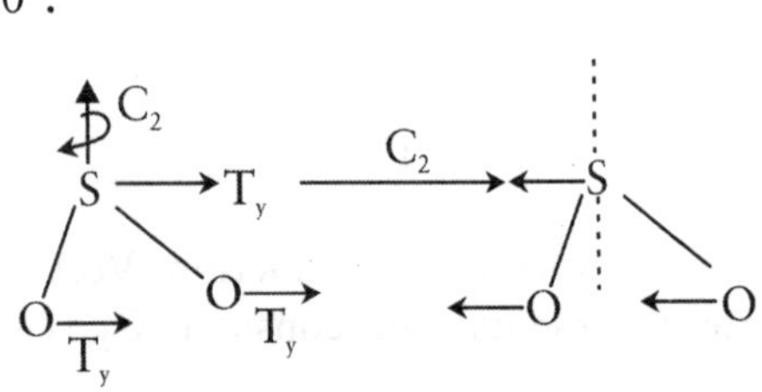

We assign (+1) if the vector remains unchanged and (–1) when the direction is reversed. It appears from the figure that $\tilde{C}_2\ (T_y) = (-1)\ T_y$.

For E operation:

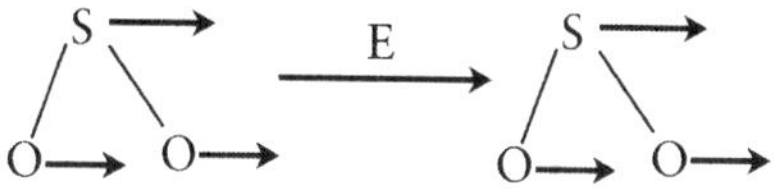

The vector remains unaffected.

Thus, $\tilde{E}\ (T_y) = (+1)\ T_y$

Consider reflection in σ_{xz} plane:

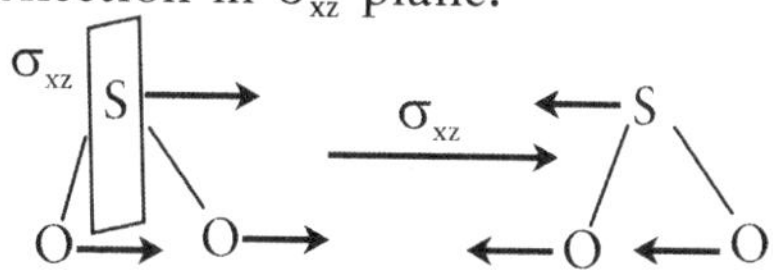

$$\tilde{\sigma}_{xz}(T_y) = (-1)\ T_y$$

The vector remains unchanged in case of reflection in σ_{yz} plane:

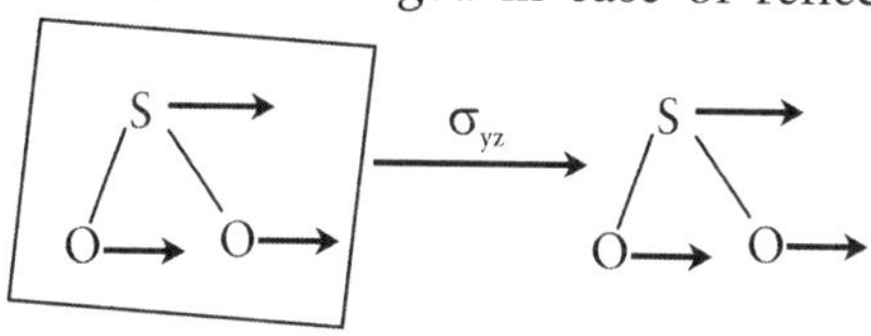

$$\therefore\ \tilde{\sigma}_{yz}(T_y) = (+1)\ T_y$$

We can summarize the result as follows:

C_{2v}	E	C_2	σ_{xz}	σ_{yz}
T_y	1	–1	–1	1

And it belongs to B_2 representation.

Case of T_x vector under C_{2v}. we generate the representation in the following way:

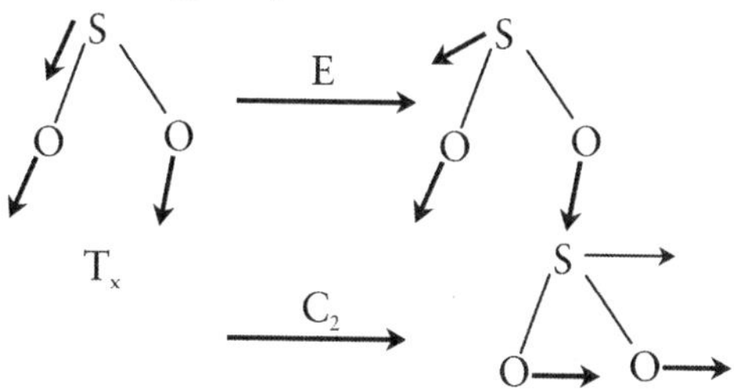

$$\tilde{E}(T_x) = (+1) T_x$$

This changes the directions accompanied by inversion in sign:

$$\tilde{C}_z\,(T_x) = (-1)\,T_x$$

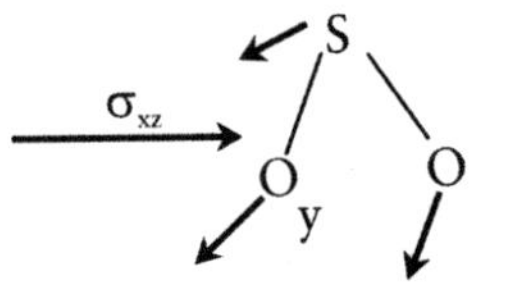

No change.

$$\tilde{\sigma}_{xz}\,(T_x) = (+1)\,T_x$$

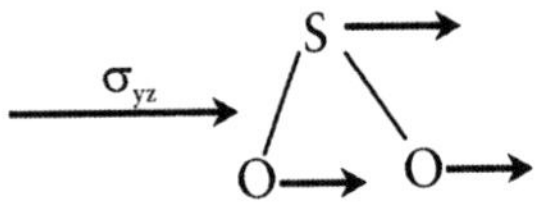

This reverses sign:

$$\tilde{\sigma}_{yz}\,(T_x) = (-1)\,T_x$$

Similarly one gets the representation for T_z vector:

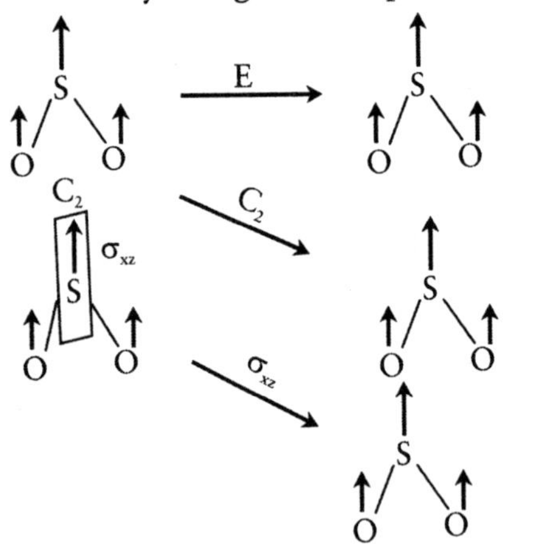

, $\tilde{E}\,(T_z) = (+1)\,T_z$

, $\tilde{C}\,(T_z) = (+1)\,T_z$

, $\tilde{\sigma}_{xz}\,(T_z) = (+1)\,T_z$

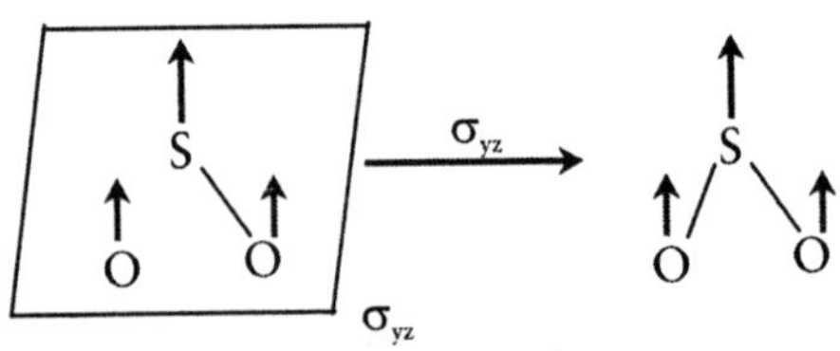

, $\tilde{\sigma}_{yz}\,(T_z) = (+1)\,T_z$

Thus, we have the following change: 1 1 1 1 A_1 (T_z)

(d) Use of rotational vectors R_x, R_y and R_z. Consider a set of vectors which correspond to molecular rotation about the x, y, z-axes. These vectors are R_x, R_y and R_z about x, y and z-axes respectively. Let us take the vector R_y for the rotation about y-axis. Since rotation about the y-axis has three vectors:

(i) Two of them along x-axis at O-atoms and (ii) the third one about –x and at S-atom.

Thus, it involves x coordinates.

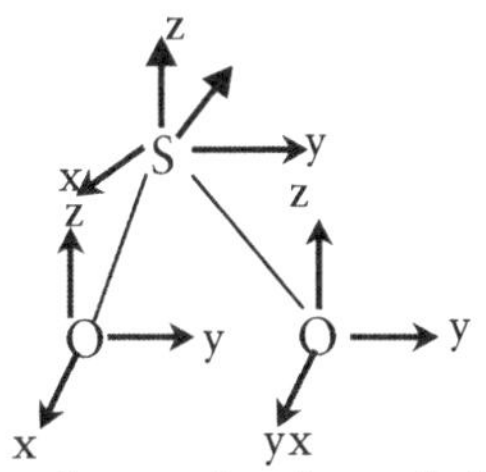

(R_y)

This leaves no change in sign of the rotational vector in xz plane but it reverses sign in yz plane.

$$\tilde{E}(R_y) = (+1)\ R_y$$
$$\tilde{C}_z(R_y) = (-1)\ R_y$$

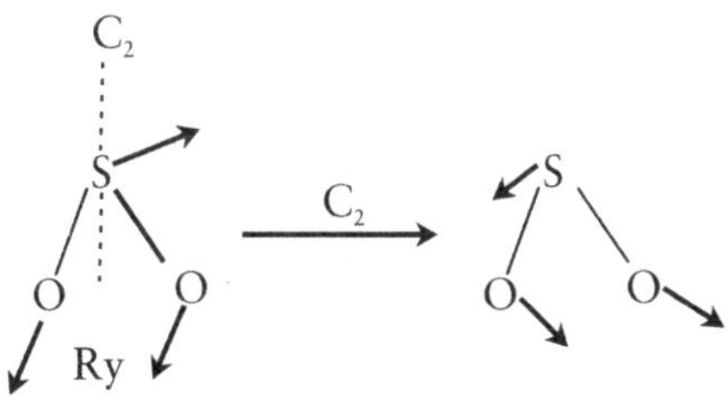

reverses sign.

$$\tilde{\sigma}_{xz}(R_y) = (+1)\ R_y$$
$$\tilde{\sigma}_{yz}(R_y) = (-1)\ R_y$$

C_{2v}	E	C_2	σ_{xz}	σ_{yz}	
R_y	1	–1	1	–1	(B_1)

Effect on R_x vector of SO_2. This vector at the three points lies along y-direction as shown in the figure.

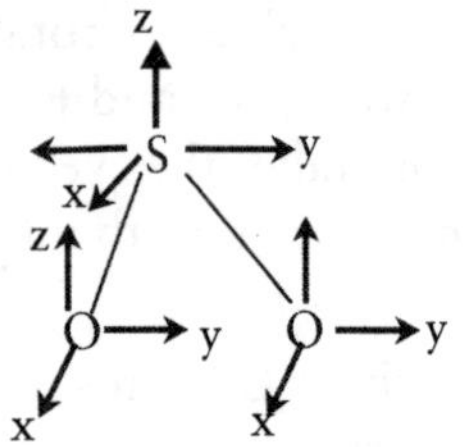

(R_x)

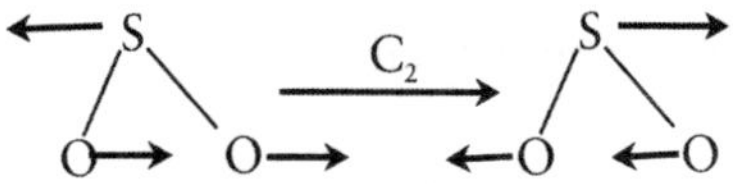

$$\tilde{C}_2(R_x) = (-1)R_x$$

Also, $\tilde{\sigma}_{xz}(R_x) = (-1)\,R_x$

$$\tilde{\sigma}_{yz}(R_x) = (+1)\,R_x$$

C_{2v}	E	C_2	σ_{xz}	σ_{yz}	
R_x	1	−1	−1	1	(B_2)

For R_z vector we have the following effects:

$$\tilde{E}(R_z) = (+1)\,R_z$$

$$\tilde{C}_z(R_z) = (+1)\,R_z$$

$$\tilde{\sigma}_{xz}(R_z) = (-1)\,R_z$$

$$\tilde{\sigma}_{yz}(R_z) = (-1)\,R_z$$

C_{2v}	E	C_2	σ_{xz}	σ_{yz}	
R_x	1	−1	−1	1	(B_2)
R_y	1	−1	1	−1	(B_1)
R_z	1	1	−1	−1	(A_2)

Transformation Properties of Translational and Rotational Vectors under C_{3v}

In C_{3v} case T_x and T_y are transformed into a pair of vectors which are mixtures of the original ones. They cannot be discussed separately as in C_{2v} point group. We ignore H-atoms in NH_3 and the coordinates of the N-atom are taken as bases only. The effect of symmetry are much less easy to visualize although identical to the effects on the N-vectors.

Translational vectors T_x and T_y are shown in the diagram along x and y-axes:

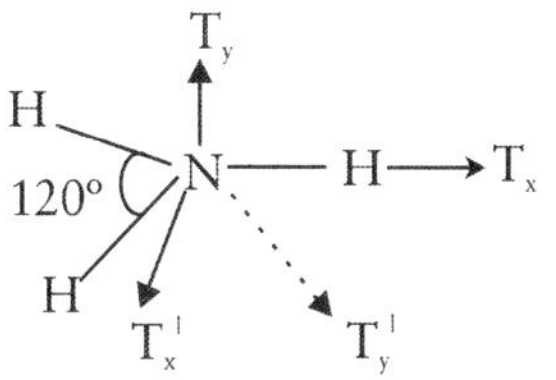

Consider the effect of C_3 rotation on T_x and T_y vectors of NH_3. T_x is transformed as T_x' and T_y as T_y' .

Transformation matrices can be obtained geometrically as it is related to 120° rotation. Let us consider clockwise rotation:

$$\begin{Bmatrix} x' = x \cos\alpha + y \sin\alpha \\ y' = -x \sin\alpha + y \cos\alpha \end{Bmatrix}$$

Similarly,

$$T_x' = T_x \cos 120° + T_y \sin 120°$$
$$T_y' = -T_x \sin 120° + T_y \cos 120°$$

or,

$$T_x' = T_x\left(-\frac{1}{2}\right) + T_y\left(\frac{\sqrt{3}}{2}\right)$$

$$T_y' = -T_x\left(\frac{\sqrt{3}}{2}\right) + T_y\left(-\frac{1}{2}\right)$$

or,

$$T_x' = -\frac{1}{2}T_x + \frac{\sqrt{3}}{2}T_y$$

$$T_y' = -\frac{\sqrt{3}}{2}T_x - \frac{1}{2}T_y$$

Therefore, the transformation matrix for T_x and T_y is:

$$C_3 : \begin{pmatrix} -1/2 & \dfrac{\sqrt{3}}{2} \\ -\dfrac{\sqrt{3}}{2} & -1/2 \end{pmatrix}$$

Similarly, $$E\begin{pmatrix} T_x \\ T_y \end{pmatrix} = \begin{pmatrix} T'_x \\ T'_y \end{pmatrix} = \begin{pmatrix} 1 & 0 \\ 0 & 1 \end{pmatrix} \begin{pmatrix} T_y \\ T_y \end{pmatrix}$$

$$E : \begin{pmatrix} 1 & 0 \\ 0 & 1 \end{pmatrix}$$

For C_3^2 case: Since C_3 and C_3^2 are inverse matrices C_3 and C_3^{-1}, we get the transformation matrix for C_3^{-1} transposing members of row into columns:

$$C_3^{-1} = C_3^2 : \begin{pmatrix} -1/2 & -\dfrac{\sqrt{3}}{2} \\ \dfrac{\sqrt{3}}{2} & -1/2 \end{pmatrix}$$

For three vertical planes we have:

$$\begin{pmatrix} 1 & 0 \\ 0 & -1 \end{pmatrix}, \begin{pmatrix} -1/2 & \dfrac{\sqrt{3}}{2} \\ \dfrac{\sqrt{3}}{2} & 1/2 \end{pmatrix}, \begin{pmatrix} -1/2 & -\dfrac{\sqrt{3}}{2} \\ -\dfrac{\sqrt{3}}{2} & \dfrac{-1}{2} \end{pmatrix}$$

Vectors R_x and R_y are not easily visualized as the T_x and T_y vectors. They are found to behave in exactly the same way as the pair T_x and T_y. The T_z and R_z vectors, on the other hand, are like the vectors of the C_{2v} system:

$$\tilde{E}\ (T_z) = (+1)\ T_z$$
$$\tilde{C}_3\ (T_z) = (+1)\ T_z$$
$$\tilde{C}_3^2\ (T_z) = (+1)\ T_z$$
$$\tilde{\sigma}_v\ (T_z) = (+1)\ T_z$$

whereas:

$$\tilde{E}\ (R_z) = (+1)\ R_z$$
$$\tilde{C}_3\ (R_z) = (+1)\ R_z$$
$$\tilde{C}_3^2\ (R_z) = (+1)\ R_z$$
$$\sigma_v\ (R_z) = (-1)\ R_z$$

C_{3v}	E	C_3	C_3^2	σ_v	σ_v'	σ_v''
T_z	1	1	1	1	1	1
R_z	1	1	1	–1	–1	–1
T_x, T_y	1					
	1					

Illustration

1. Verify that $\chi(C_{3h}) = \chi(C_s) \times \chi\,(C_3)$ character tables for the two cyclic groups C_2 and C_3 are as follows:

C_s	E	σ_h
	1	1
	1	–1

C_3	E	C_3	C_3^2
	1	1	1
	1	ε	ε^*
	1	ε^*	ε

We take their direct product of characters:

$$\overset{C_s}{\begin{bmatrix} E_2 & \sigma_h \\ 1 & 1 \\ 1 & -1 \end{bmatrix}} \times \overset{C_3}{\begin{bmatrix} E & C_3 & C_3^2 \\ 1 & 1 & 1 \\ 1 & \varepsilon & \varepsilon^* \\ 1 & \varepsilon^* & \varepsilon \end{bmatrix}}$$

$$= \begin{bmatrix} E & C_3 & C_3^2 & \sigma_h & S_3 & S_3^3 \\ 1\times1 & 1\times1 & 1\times1 & 1\times1 & 1\times1 & 1\times1 \\ 1\times1 & 1\times\varepsilon & 1\times\varepsilon^* & 1\times1 & 1\times\varepsilon & 1\times\varepsilon^* \\ 1\times1 & 1\times\varepsilon^* & 1\times\varepsilon & 1\times1 & 1\times\varepsilon^* & 1\times\varepsilon \\ 1\times1 & 1\times1 & 1\times1 & -1\times1 & -1\times1 & -1\times1 \\ 1\times1 & 1\times\varepsilon & 1\times\varepsilon^* & -1\times1 & -1\times\varepsilon & -1\times\varepsilon^* \\ 1\times1 & 1\times\varepsilon^* & 1\times\varepsilon & -1\times1 & -1\times\varepsilon^* & -1\times\varepsilon \end{bmatrix}$$

$$
= \begin{bmatrix}
 & C_{3h} & & & & \\
E & C_3 & C_3^2 & \sigma_h & S_3 & S_3^5 \\
1 & 1 & 1 & 1 & 1 & 1 \\
1 & \varepsilon & \varepsilon^* & 1 & \varepsilon & \varepsilon^* \\
1 & \varepsilon^* & \varepsilon & 1 & \varepsilon^* & \varepsilon \\
1 & 1 & 1 & -1 & -1 & -1 \\
1 & \varepsilon & \varepsilon^* & -1 & -\varepsilon & -\varepsilon^* \\
1 & \varepsilon^* & \varepsilon & -1 & -\varepsilon^* & -\varepsilon
\end{bmatrix}
$$

2. Taking the direct product $D_3 \times C_s$ workout C.T. for D_{3h} point group.

Let us take up the case of D_3 having six symmetry operations E, $2C_3$, $3C_2$ and there are two symmetry operations in case of C_s namely E and σ. Their direct product leads to (E, $2C_3$, $3C_2$) $\times$ (E, σ) = E $2C_3$ $3C_2$ σ_h $2S_3$ $3\sigma_4$. Their direct product is obtained using C.T.

D_3	E	$2C_3$	$3\sigma_2$
A_1	1	1	1
A_2	1	1	–1
E	2	–1	0

C_s	E	σ
A_1'	1	1
A_1''	1	–1

Multiplication of their characters result in formation of character Table for D_{3h} point group.

D_{3h}	E	$2C_3$	$3C_2$	σ_h	$2S_3$	$3\sigma_4$
A_1'	1	1	1	1	1	1
A_2'	1	1	–1	1	1	–1
E′	2	–1	0	2	–1	0
A_1''	1	1	1	–1	–1	–1
A_2''	1	1	–1	–1	–1	1
E″	2	–1	0	–2	1	0

QUESTIONS

1. Explain:
   (a) Representation.
   (b) Reducible representation
   (c) Irreducible representation, How are the two related?
   (d) Dimension of representation.
2. (a) What are properties of irreducible representatons?
   (b) Give the Mulliken symbol for such representation.
   (c) Show that (i) A_1 and A_2 and A_1 & E are orthogonal under C_{3v} point group.
3. Explain orthogonality theorem. On this basis how do you obtain reducton formula and orthogonality conditions?

   Illustrate the different properties of irreducible representation taking the use of character Table of C_{2v} point group.
4. There are four irreducible representations in case of C_{2v} point group. Comment on it. For the same decompose the character in case of C_{3v} given as 5, 2, –1.
5. (a) Define class of symmetry operation.
   (b) Give the rules governing classes.
   (c) Explain character Table and its parts.
6. (a) Give the effect of C_2', C_2'' on (i) $dx^2 - y^2$ in D_{4h} point group.
   (b) Show that x and y coordinates transform as E (doubly degenerate) representation in D_{4h}.
7. Construct 4 × 4 transformation matrices for symmetry operations in water and deduce the character Table for the same adopting block diagonalisation into 1 × 1 sub-matrices (use s, p_x, p_y and d_{xy} as basis).
8. Deduce the character Table for C_{2h} as in case of trans-H_2O_2 making use of s, p_x, p_z and dxz orbitals as basis vectors on obtaining 4 × 4 matrices.
9. (a) Deduce the C.T. for C_{3v} point group on the basis of orthogronality theorem.

(b) How do following transform in C_{3v} point group z, xz, yz?

10. What do you mean by true representaton. Show it with the various operations in C_{2v} & C_{3v} point groups.

11. Construct characterables for:

(i) C_{4v} (ii) D_5

12. (a) Deduce the CT for a cyclic group having complex number as in C_3 or C_4.

(b) Having known C.T. for C_2 and C_s

C_2	E	C_2
A	1	1
B	1	–1

C_i	E	i
Ag	1	1
Au	1	–1

Obtain character Table for C_{2h} takinig their direct product.

13. (a) How do the following transform:

(i) x, y, z coordinates; and

(ii) p_x, p_y and p_z orbitals in C_{2v}.

(b) Obtain the representation for translational and rotational vectors for SO_2 molecule.

14. (a) Show that translational component T_x and T_y give the doubly degenerate representation in C_{3v} and T_z transform as A_1.

(b) Obtain character Table for C_{3h} using character Table for cyclic groups C_s and C_3.

15. Make a distinction between reducible and irreducible representations. What are the property of irreducible representations? Enlist them and ilustrate them with specific examples.

16. Find the components of irreduable representation for the given reducible representation for C_{3v} point group 5, 2 –1

17. Explain character Table and its parts. State clearly its importance.

18. What do you mean by dimension of representation? Explain E and T representations.

19. Using basis functions s, px, py, dxy for C_{2v} deduce its character Table.
20. (a) Deduce the C-T for C_{2h} point group using s p_x p_z and d_{xz} orbitals as basis functions.
    (b) Deduce the character Table for C_{3v} point group on the basis of orthogonality theorem.
21. What do you understand from faithful or true representations. Verify whether the character Table for C_{2v} and C_{2h} contain such representation.

QUALITATIVE AND QUANTITATIVE ASPECTS OF HYBRID ORBITALS

7

There are two basic sub-divisions of hybridization a qualitative approach based on character Table and a quantitative approach through formation of SALCS. In the latter case both symmetry operator and projection operator methods are underwide applications. In both ways contributions of combining atomic orbitals have been determined through formation of SALCS (symmetry adapted linear combinations), cases of σ and π bonding involve hybridization and are covered adequately.

7.1 USE OF CHARACTER TABLE IN DERIVING HYBRID σ-ORBITALS (A QUALITATIVE APPROACH)

(a) Sp^2 hybridization

Consider BCl_3 belonging to D_{3h} point group. It is a planar molecule. The various symmetry operations are:

(i) E (identity).

(ii) C_3 axis, this passes through B-atom and acting perpendicular to the molecular plane.

Two distinct operations are C_3 and C_3^2 constituting a class $2C_3$.

(iii) There are three C_2 axes pointed along B-Cl bonds. They form another class $3C_2$.

(iv) It has a molecular plane containing all the four atoms σ_h.

(v) There are three vertical planes along the directions of C_2 axis. They constitute a class $3\sigma_v$.

(vi) There exists a rotation reflection axis $C_3\sigma_h = S_3$. As n is odd there are 2n operations for S_3 axis.

$$
\begin{array}{cccccc}
S_3, & S_3^2, & S_3^3, & S_3^4, & S_3^5, & S_3^6 \\
 & \| & \| & \| & & \| \\
 & C_3^2 & \sigma_h & C_3 & & E
\end{array}
$$

Giving $2S_3$ as a separate class.

The members of the group are:

$$E,\ 2C_3,\ 3C_2,\ \sigma_h,\ 2S_3,\ 3\sigma_v.$$

with order h = 12

Since number of class in a point group is equal to the number of irreducible representation. Thus, there are six irreducible representations:

$$A_1',\ A_2'',\ E',\ A_1'',\ A_2'',\ E''.$$

Three B-Cl axes represent vectors r_1, r_2 and r_3 which are used here as bases. Now transformation matrices for operations of each class are constructed we get character of reducible representation.

There are 3σ bonds in BCl_3.

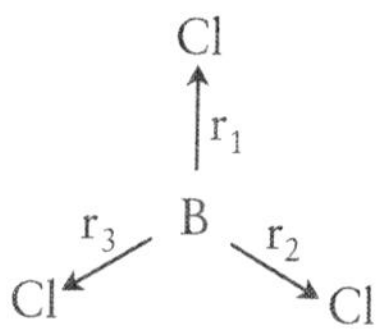

1. All the three are unchanged in identity. Hence,

   $E(r_1) = +1(r_1)$, $E(r_2) = (+1)r_2$, $E(r_3) = (+1)r_3$.

   We get three equations such as:

   $$r_1' = (+)r_1 + (0)\ r_2 + (0)r_3$$

   $$r_2' = (0)r_1 + (+1)r_2 + (0)r_3$$

   $$r_3' = (0)r_1 + (0)r_2 + (+1)r_3$$

   This can be shown in the matrix notation, viz.

   $$E\begin{pmatrix} r_1 \\ r_2 \\ r_3 \end{pmatrix} = \begin{pmatrix} r_1' \\ r_2' \\ r_3' \end{pmatrix} = \begin{pmatrix} 1 & 0 & 0 \\ 0 & 1 & 0 \\ 0 & 0 & 1 \end{pmatrix}\begin{pmatrix} r_1 \\ r_2 \\ r_3 \end{pmatrix}$$

   Hence its character will be, 1 + 1 + 1 = 3

2. Let us apply C_3 operation. Here r_1 goes to r_2, r_2 to r_3 and r_3 to r_1.

i.e.
$$C_3\,(r_1) = (+1)r_2 = r_1'$$
$$C_3\,(r_2) = (+1)r_3 = r_2'$$
$$C_3\,(r_3) = (+1)r_1 = r_3'$$

Three linear equations can be made out of these:

$$r_1' = (0)r_1 + (+1)r_2 + (0)r_3$$
$$r_2' = (0)r_1 + (0)r_2 + (+1)r_3$$
$$r_3' = (+1)\ r_1 + (0)r_2 + (0)r_3$$

$$\therefore C_3\begin{pmatrix} r_1 \\ r_2 \\ r_3 \end{pmatrix} = \begin{pmatrix} r_1' \\ r_2' \\ r_3' \end{pmatrix} = \begin{pmatrix} 0 & 1 & 0 \\ 0 & 0 & 1 \\ 1 & 0 & 0 \end{pmatrix}\begin{pmatrix} r_1 \\ r_2 \\ r_3 \end{pmatrix}$$

$$\chi\ (C_3) = 0 + 0 + 0 = 0$$

3. We generate transformation matrix for C_2 in the following way:

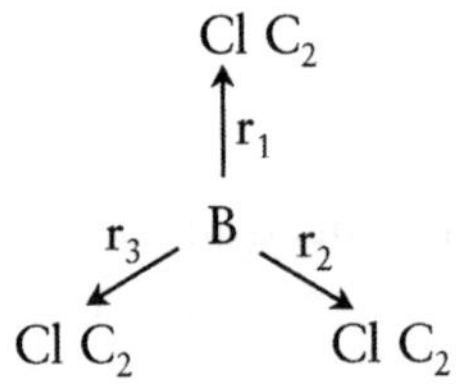

Consider anyone of the C_2 axis (as character of members of a class is same). Suppose it points along r_1 direction. The effect of rotation by 180° about r_1 is to cause a shift in positions of r_2 and r_3. Thus,

$$r_1' = (+1)r_1,\ r_2' = (+1)r_3,\ r_3' = (+1)r_2$$

$$\text{Now, } C_2\begin{pmatrix} r_1 \\ r_2 \\ r_3 \end{pmatrix} = \begin{pmatrix} r_1' \\ r_2' \\ r_3' \end{pmatrix} = \begin{pmatrix} 1 & 0 & 0 \\ 0 & 0 & 1 \\ 0 & 1 & 0 \end{pmatrix}\begin{pmatrix} r_1 \\ r_2 \\ r_3 \end{pmatrix}$$

$$\therefore\ \chi\,(C_2) = 1 + 0 + 0 = 1.$$

4. In σ_h all the vectors are un-shifted as they lie in this plane:

i.e., $r_1' \rightarrow (+1)r_1,\ r_2' = (+1)r_2,\ r_3' = (+1)r_3$

$$\therefore \sigma_h \begin{pmatrix} r_1 \\ r_2 \\ r_3 \end{pmatrix} = \begin{pmatrix} r_1' \\ r_2' \\ r_3' \end{pmatrix} = \begin{pmatrix} 1 & 0 & 0 \\ 0 & 1 & 0 \\ 0 & 0 & 1 \end{pmatrix} \begin{pmatrix} r_1 \\ r_2 \\ r_3 \end{pmatrix}$$

$$\chi(\sigma_h) = 1 + 1 + 1 = 3$$

5. In $S_3 = C_3\ \sigma_h$

$$= \begin{pmatrix} 0 & 1 & 0 \\ 0 & 0 & 1 \\ 1 & 0 & 0 \end{pmatrix} \begin{pmatrix} 1 & 0 & 0 \\ 0 & 1 & 0 \\ 0 & 0 & 1 \end{pmatrix}$$

$$= \begin{pmatrix} 0 & 1 & 0 \\ 0 & 0 & 1 \\ 1 & 0 & 0 \end{pmatrix}$$

$$\therefore \chi(S_3) = 0$$

6. In each σ_v (if we apply method of un-shifted vectors). One vector remains un-shifted.

$$\therefore \chi(\sigma_v) = 1$$

We thus have Γ_R under D_{3h} point group:

D_{3h}	E	$2C_3$	$3C_2$	σ_h	$2S_3$	$3\sigma_v$
Γ_R	3	0	1	3	0	1

We reduce Γ_R into fundamental representations by formula:

$$a_i = \frac{1}{h}\left[g_i\ \chi_R\ \chi_{IR}\right]$$

$$^{a}A_1' = \frac{1}{12}\left[1\times3\times1+0+3\times1\times1+3\times1\times1+0+3\times1\times1\right]$$

$$= \frac{1}{12}\left[3+3+3+3\right] = \frac{12}{12} = 1$$

$$^{a}E' = \frac{1}{12}\left[6+0+0+6+0+0\right] = 1.$$

All others are zero.

$$\therefore \Gamma_R = \Gamma_{A_1'} + \Gamma_{E'}$$
$$(1) \quad (2)$$

Dimensions of A_1' & E' give character of identity, i.e. 3. Each bond in BCl_3 contains a contribution from A_1' and E'.

C.T. for D_{3h} reveals.

A_1' has s, dz^2

E' has $dx^2-y^2.dxy$

E' px. py

A_1'	E'
s	px.py
dz^2	$dx^2-y^2.dxy$

Out of these four combinations would be

(i) $s + p_x + p_y$
(ii) $s + dx^2-y^2 + d_{xy}$
(iii) $dz^2 + px + py$
(iv) $dz^2 + dx^2-y^2 + dxy$.

First case is energetically favoured.

(b) Tetrahedral Arrangement

Consider a tetrahedron. There are four faces (shown as equilateral triangles) four vertices and six edges.

Symmetry elements and associated operations:

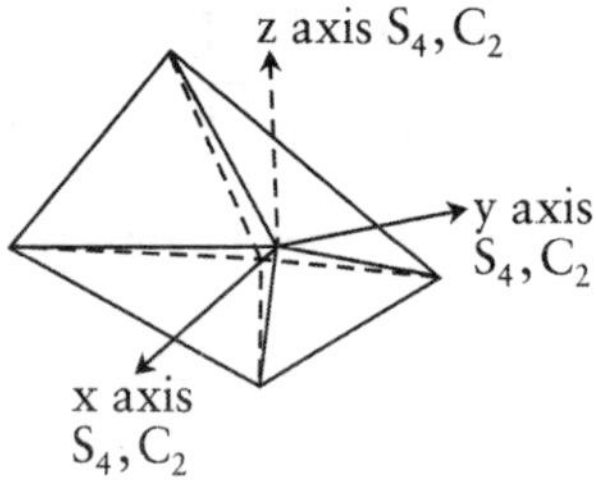

1. Three S_4 axis coinciding with x, y, z axis.

   Each S_4 axis generates:

$$S_4, \quad S_4^2, \quad S_4^3, \quad S_4^4 = E$$
$$S_4^2 = C_2$$

Two distinct operations = $2S_4$.

As there are three such axes each generating $2S_4$. We have $3 \times 2 = 6S_4$ operations belonging to same class.

2. Three C_2 axes coinciding with x, y, z axes each of which generates a single C_2 operation. Thus, we have $3C_2$ operations in all. These C_2 operations have also been generated by S_4^2.
3. There are four C_3 axes each of which passes through one apex and the centre of the opposite face.

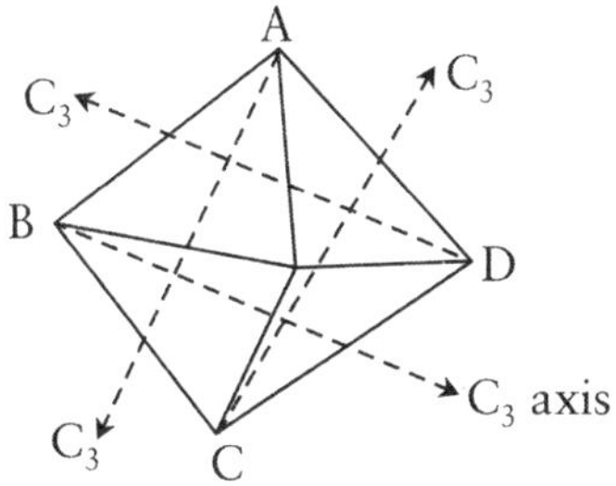

Each C–H bond in methane represents C_3 axis. Each C_3 axis generates two operations C_3, C_3^2. Thus four C_3 can generate $4 \times 2 = 8C_3$ operations.

4. There are six symmetry planes. All of them are dihedral planes (σ_d) defined as H_1–C–H_2, H_1–C–H_3, H_1–C–H_4, H_2–C–H_3, H_2–C–H_4 and H_3–C–H_4. Members of the T_d group are:

$$E,\ 8C_3,\ 3C_2,\ 6S_4,\ 6\sigma_d,\ h = 24.$$

Case of Methane

The molecule belongs to T_d point group. We should know the atomic orbitals of C which form four σ-orbitals at that centre. These σ-orbitals have their lobes directed to H-atoms lying at four vertices of a tetrahedron.

We represent four σ-hybrid orbitals by the vectors r_1, r_2, r_3 and r_4 respectively. We use these vectors as bases:

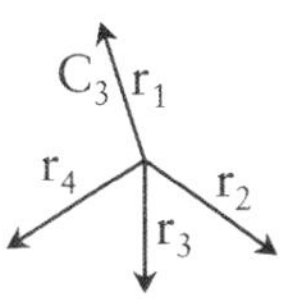

We deduce the characters of the representations using r_1, r_2, r_3 and r_4 as basis functions. We count the number of un-shifted vectors.

There are E, C_3, C_2, S_4 and σ_d operations.

Take identity (E).

All the four r's remain un-shifted,

or $\quad r_1' = r_1,\ r_2' = r_2$, etc.

$$r_1' = (+1)r_1 + (0)r_2 + (0)r_3 + (0)r_4$$

$$r_2' = (0)r_1 + (+1)r_2 + (0)r_3 + (0)r_4$$

$$r_3' = (0)r_1 + (0)r_2 + (+1)r_3 + (0)r_4.$$

$$r_4' = (0)r_1 + (0)r_2 + (0)r_3 + (+1)r_4.$$

$$\therefore \begin{pmatrix} r_1' \\ r_2' \\ r_3' \\ r_4' \end{pmatrix} = \begin{pmatrix} 1 & 0 & 0 & 0 \\ 0 & 1 & 0 & 0 \\ 0 & 0 & 1 & 0 \\ 0 & 0 & 0 & 1 \end{pmatrix} \begin{pmatrix} r_1 \\ r_2 \\ r_3 \\ r_4 \end{pmatrix}$$

$$\therefore E : \begin{pmatrix} 1 & 0 & 0 & 0 \\ 0 & 1 & 0 & 0 \\ 0 & 0 & 1 & 0 \\ 0 & 0 & 0 & 1 \end{pmatrix}$$

$$\chi\ (E) = 4$$

If we treat it by method of un-shifted vectors. All of them are un-shifted each contributing (+1) towards character.

$$\therefore \chi\ (E) = 4 \times (1) = 4$$

Consider one of the C_3 axis coincident with the vector r_1. Then rotate these vectors about this axis by 120°. This results in:

$$r_1' = r_1$$

$$r_2' = r_3$$

$$r_3' = r_4$$

$$r_4' = r_2$$

$$\therefore\ r_1' = (+1)\, r_1 + (0)\, r_2 + (0)\, r_3 + (0)\, r_4$$

$$r_2' = (0)\, r_1 + (0)\, r_2 + (+1)\, r_3 + (0)\, r_4$$

$$r_3' = (0)\, r_1 + (0)\, r_2 + (0)\, r_3 + (+1)\, r_4$$

$$r_4' = (0)\, r_1 + (+1)\, r_2 + (0)\, r_3 + (0)\, r_4$$

$$\therefore \begin{pmatrix} r_1' \\ r_2' \\ r_3' \\ r_4' \end{pmatrix} = \begin{pmatrix} 1 & 0 & 0 & 0 \\ 0 & 0 & 1 & 0 \\ 0 & 0 & 0 & 1 \\ 0 & 1 & 0 & 0 \end{pmatrix} \begin{pmatrix} r_1 \\ r_2 \\ r_3 \\ r_4 \end{pmatrix} = C_3 \begin{pmatrix} r_1 \\ r_2 \\ r_3 \\ r_4 \end{pmatrix}$$

$$\therefore\ \chi\ (C_3) = 1 + 0 + 0 + 0 = 1\,.$$

In C_3, r_1 remains unshifted. Hence $\chi(C_3) = 1 \times (+1) = 1$ Consider C_2 axis that lies along z, x or y axis. All the vectors are shifted.

$$\chi\ (C_2) = 0 \times (+1) = 0$$

Similarly for S_4 coincident with C_2 all the four vectors are shifted.

$$\therefore\ \chi\ (S_4) = 0$$

In σ_d plane two of the vectors will lie and rest two are reflected. Thus, those lying within the plane remain ushifted while others are shifted.

Hence, $\chi\ (\sigma_d) = 2\ .\ (+1) = 2$

T_d	E	$8C_3$	$3C_2$	$6S_4$	$6\sigma_d$
Γ_R	4	1	0	0	2
A_1	1	1	1	1	1
A_2	1	1	1	–1	–1
E	2	–1	2	0	0
T_1	3	0	–1	1	–1
T_2	3	0	–1	–1	1

$$a_{A_1} = \frac{1}{24}\left[1 \times 4 \times 1 + 8 \times 1 \times 1 + 0 + = +6 \times 2 \times 1\right] = \frac{1}{24}\left[4 + 8 + 12\right] = 1.$$

$$a_{A_2} = \frac{1}{24}[4+8+0+0+6\,(2)\,(-1)] = 0$$

A_2 is rejected.

a_E = 0, Hence E does not occur.

$$a_{T_1} = \frac{1}{24}[12+0+0+0-12] = 0$$

$$a_{T_2} = \frac{1}{24}[12+0+0+0+6\times 2\times 1] = 1$$

$\therefore\ \Gamma_R = A_1 + T_2.$

We select one atomic orbital from A_1 and three atomic orbitals from T_2 representations. Atomic orbitals of carbon belonging to A_1 type is s:

T_2 type – (p_x, p_y, p_z) (d_{xy}, d_{xz}, d_{yz})

We may have two sets of hybrid orbitals:

(i) $s + p_x + p_y + p_z \rightarrow sp^3$

(ii) $s + d_{xy} + d_{xz} + d_{yz} \rightarrow sd^3$.

Both sp^3 and sd^3 have the same symmetry. In case of carbon, sp^3 is energetically favoured and not sd^3 as the 3d orbitals in C lie at 230 Kcl. mol^{-1} higher in energy than 2p.

(c) Hybridization Scheme for Square Planar Case

It has D_{4h} point symmetry. Let the four vectors be r_1, r_2, r_3 and r_4. The character is equal to the number of un-shifted vectors representing hybrid orbitals by the symmetry operatons:

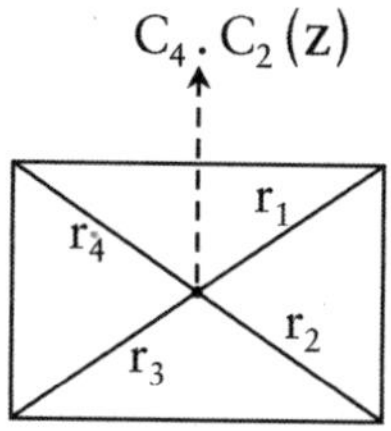

Now we find the character for various representations using principle of un-shifted vectors. The members of the group are:

E, $2C_4$, C_2, $2C_2'$, $2C_2''$, i, $2S_4$, σ_h, $2\sigma_v$, $2\sigma_d$.

In identity all the four are unshifted each contributing (+1) towards character:

$$\chi\,(E) = 4\,(+1) = 4.$$

In C_4 operation all the four are shifted.

Hence, $\chi\,(C_4) = 0$

In C_2 operation all the four are shifted.

Hence, $\chi\,(C_2) = 0$ (It is collinear with C_4)

In C_2' operation r_1 and r_3 remain un-shifted while rest two are shifted. Thus the number of un-shifted atoms = 2:

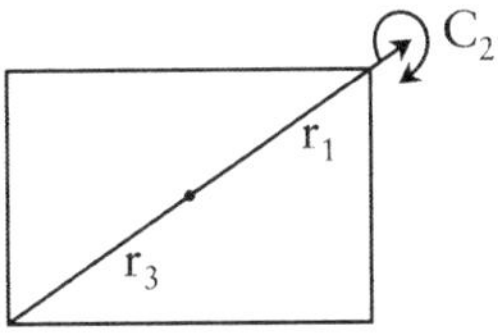

$$\therefore\ \chi\,(C_2') = 2 \times 1 = 2.$$

In C_2'' operation all of them are shifted. Hence number of un-shifted atoms = 0

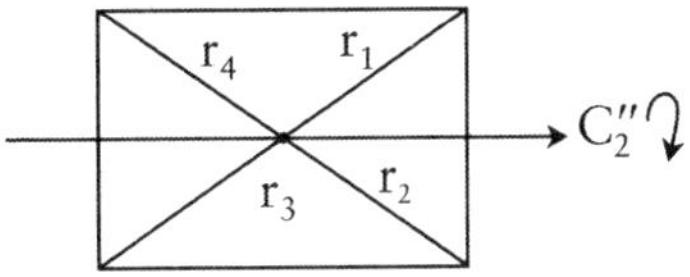

$$\chi\left(C_2''\right) = 0\,.$$

In σ_h all unshifted giving $\chi\,(\sigma_h) = 4$.

In S_4 all are shifted leading to $\chi\,(S_4) = 0$.

In σ_v like C_2' two of them are un-shifted giving $\chi\,(\sigma_v) = 2$.

All the four vectors are shifted in σ_d plane (as in case of C_2''). Hence,

$$\chi\,(\sigma_d) = 0.$$

In inversion all are shifted thus χ (i) = 0.

Thus characters for Γ_R in D_{4h} symmetry are:

D_{4h}	E	$2C_4$	C_2	$2C_2'$	$2C_2''$	i	$2S_4$	σ_h	$2\sigma_v$	$2\sigma_d$
Γ_R	4	0	0	2	0	0	0	4	2	0

$$a_{A_{1g}} = \frac{1}{16}[4+2\times2\times1+4\times1\times1+2\times2\times1] = \frac{16}{16} = 1$$

$$a_{A_{2g}} = \frac{1}{16}[4\times1\times1+2\times2\times(-1)+1\times4\times1+2\times2\times(-1)]$$

$$= \frac{1}{16}[4-4+4-4] = 0$$

$$a_{B_{1g}} = \frac{1}{16}[4+2\times2\times1+4\times1\times1+2\times2\times1]$$

$$= \frac{1}{16}[4+4+4+4] = \frac{16}{16} = 1$$

$$a_{E_g} = \frac{1}{16}[4\times2\times1+2\times2\times0+4\times1\times(-2)+2\times2\times0]$$

$$= \frac{1}{16}[8+0-8+0] = 0$$

$$a_{A_{1u}} = \frac{1}{16}[4+4-4-4] = 0$$

$$a_{A_{2u}} = \frac{1}{16}[4-4+(-4)+4] = 0$$

$$a_{B_{1u}} = \frac{1}{16}[4+4-4-4] = 0$$

$$a_{B_{2u}} = \frac{1}{16}[4-4-4+4] = 0$$

$$a_{E_u} = \frac{1}{16}[4\times2\times1+0+4\times2\times1+0] = \frac{16}{16} = 1.$$

Hence, $\Gamma_R = A_{1g} + B_{1g} + E_{2u}$.

Representation	*Orbitals*
A_{1g}	s, dz^2
B_{1g}	$dx^2 - y^2$
E_{2u}	p_x, p_y

Possible combinations are:

(i) s + $dx^2 - y^2 + p_x + p_y \rightarrow sdp^2$ or dsp^2

(ii) $dz^2 + dx^2 - y^2 + p_x + p_y \rightarrow d^2p^2$

Usually dz^2 will be absent in bonding and so d^2p^2 hybridisation is rejected.

(d) ML_5 system can have two possible arrangements TBP as in PCl_5 and square pyramidal in case of BrF_5.

(d) TBP Structure

We wish to find what atomic orbitals situated at P centre are used for σ bond formation with five fluorine atoms. The five bonds are represented by the vectors r_1, r_2, r_3, r_4 and r_5. which constitute basis functions:

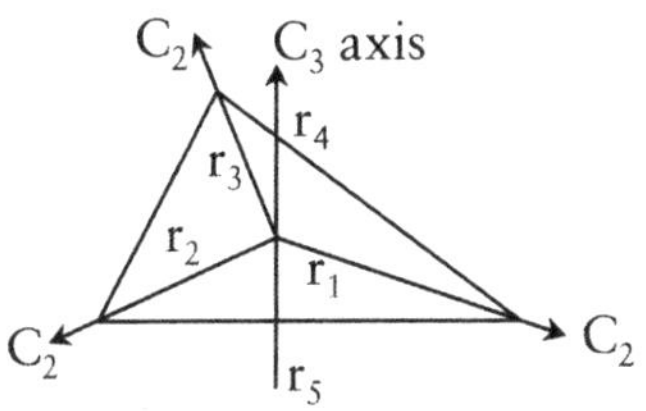

It belongs to D_{3h} point group because it has $C_3 + 3C_2$ ($\perp^r$ to C_3) + σ_h plane.

Symmetry operations are:

$$E,\ 2C_3,\ 3C_2,\ \sigma_h,\ 2S_3,\ 3\sigma_v \text{ with } h = 12.$$

We generate representations using five vectors as bases.

Character of E

All the five vectors are un-shifted in identity operation.

Hence $\chi(E) = 5$.

Character of C_3

In $C_3(z)$ operation only three vectors present in the equatorial plane are shifted, the other two along z-axis (C_3) are absent. Thus the member of un-shifted vectors is 2.

$$\chi(C_3) = 2$$

Character of C_2

All of them are shifted except one that lies along C_2 axis. This makes the member of un-shifted vectors 1:

$$\chi(C_2) = 1$$

Character of σ_h

Only three of them lies in σ_h which do not shift; those lying along z-axis interchange their positions. In this way two of them are shifted. Thus, the member of un-shifted vectors is 3:

$$\chi(\sigma_h) = 3.$$

Character of S_3

$$S_3 = C_3\ \sigma_h$$

In C_3 the vectors lying along C_3 are un-shifted while in σ_h these two vectors exchange their positions. Thus, all five have been shifted in rotation-reflection operation.

This makes $\chi(S_3) = 0$.

Character of σ_v

C_2 axis represents σ_v. Hence in σ_v some of the vectors are shifted except those in the σ_v containing z-axis. There are two vectors along z-axis and one along C_2, which do not shift. Thus, three of them remain un-shifted:

$$\chi(\sigma_v) = 3.$$

D_{3h}	E	$2C_3$	$3C_2$	σ_h	$2S_3$	$3\sigma_v$
Γ_R	5	2	1	3	0	3

Decomposition leads to the following IR[s]:

$$\Gamma_R = 2A_1' + A_2'' + E'$$

Representation	Orbitals
$2A_1'$	s, dz^2
A_2''	p_z
E'	$(dx^2{-}y^2, dxy)$, (p_x, p_y)

The possible combinations are:

(i) s + dz^2 + p_x + p_y + p_z → sdp^3 or sp^3d.

(ii) s + dz^2 + p_z + $dx^2{-}y^2$ + d_{xy} → spd^3 or sd^3p.

Some other possible combinations which are energetically not favourable are:

(iii) ns + (n + 1) s + p_z + p_x + p_y (s^2p^3).

(iv) $ns + (n + 1)\ s + p_z + dx^2 - y^2 + d_{xy}$ (s^3pd^2).

(v) $ndz^2 + (n + 1)\ dz^2 + p_z + p_x + p_y$ (d^2p^3).

(vi) $ndz^2 + (n + 1)\ dz^2 + px + dx^2 - y^2 + d_{xy}$ (pd^4).

Square Pyramidal Arrangement

It has C_{4v} point symmetry

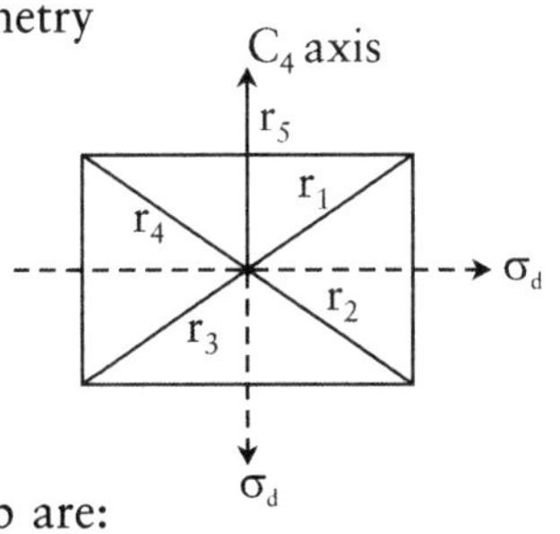

Members of the group are:

$$E,\ 2C_4,\ C_2\ (\equiv C_4^2),\ 2\sigma_v,\ 2\sigma_d.$$

Character of E

All five unshifted, $\chi(E) = 5$.

Character of C_4

Only one unshifted, $\chi(C_4) = 1$.

Character of C_2

It is collinear with C_4. Only one is unshifted $\chi(C_2) = 1$.

Character of σ_v

All the four vectors that lie in xy plane are shifted but this plane also comprises the principal axis. Hence, r_5 does not shift:

$$\chi\ (\sigma_d) = 1$$

C_{4v}	E	$2C_4$	$C_2\ (\equiv C_4^2)$	$2\sigma_v$	$2\sigma_d$
Γ_R	5	1	1	3	1

It appears from the character Table that:

$$\Gamma_R = 2\ A_1 + B_1 + E$$

Possible combinations are:

$2A_1$	s	dz^2	pz
B_1		$dx^2{-}y^2$	
E		dxz, dyz	px, py

(i) $s + dz^2 + dx^2 - y^2 + p_x + p_y \rightarrow sd^2p^2$.

(ii) $s + dz^2 + dx^2 - y^2 + dxz + dyz \rightarrow sd^4$.

(iii) $s + pz + dx^2 - y^2 + p_x + p_y \rightarrow sdp^3 = dsp^3$.

The last one is more favoured.

(e) ML_6 case with O_h symmetry

A octahedron has the following symmetry elements and operations:

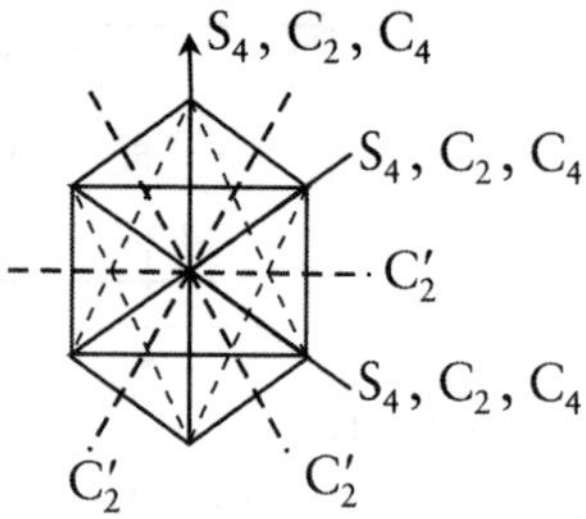

1. Three S_4 axes each passing through a pair of opposite apices.

   Each S_4 generates S_4 and S_4^3 operations.

   Thus there are $3 \times 2 = 6$ operations, i.e. $6S_4$.
2. Three C_2 axes collinear with S_4. They give $3C_2$.
3. Three C_4 axes collinear with C_2 and S_4.

   Each C_4 contains C_4 & $C_4^3 = 2C_4$ operations.

   As such there can be $2 \times 3 = 6$ such operations, i.e. $6C_4$.
4. There are $6C_2'$ axes which bisect opposite edges.
5. There are 8 triangular faces. A S_6 axis passes through the centres of opposite triangular faces. So there are four S_6 axes:

$$
\begin{array}{cccccc}
S_6, & S_6^2, & S_6^3, & S_6^4, & S_6^5, & E \\
 & \| & \| & \| & & \\
 & C_3 & C_2\sigma_h & C_3^2 & & \\
 & & \| & & & \\
 & & S_2 = i. & & &
\end{array}
$$

Hence, we have S_6, C_3, i, C_3^2 and S_6^5 for every S_6. As we have four S_6 axes giving $4 \times 2S_6 = 8S_6$ operations.

6. Four C_3 axes collinear with S_6. Each C_3 generates C_3 & C_3^2. Hence, $4 \times 2C_3 = 8C_3$.
7. It has an inversion centre, i.
8. There are three σ_h which pass through four of the six apices, i.e., $3\sigma_h$.
9. There are six σ_d which pass through two apices and bisect two opposite edges, $6\sigma_d$.

O_h	E	$8C_3$	$6C_4$	$6C_2$	$3C_2$	i	$6S_4$	$8S_6$	$3\sigma_h$	$6\sigma_d$
Γ_R	6	0	2	0	2	0	0	0	4	2

Let us have six vectors r_1, r_2, ... r_6. All of them are un-shifted in identity operation. $\chi(E) = 6$. In C_3 operation all the vectors are shifted, $\chi(C_3) = 0$.

In C_4 two vectors are un-shifted $\chi(C_4) = 2$.

There are $6C_2$. For C_2 collinear with S_4 and C_4. Two vectors are un-shifted so that $\chi(C_2) = 2$.

In C_2'

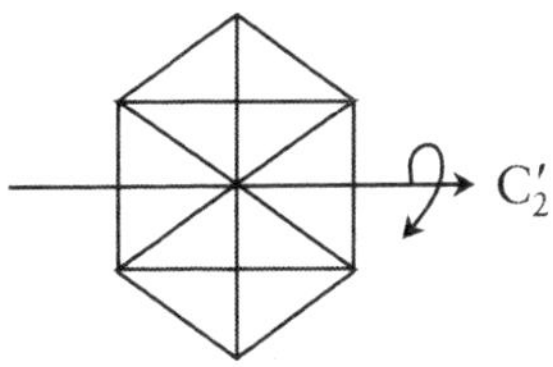

all the vectors are shifted giving $\chi(C_2') = 0$.

In i all the vectors are shifted, so χ (i) = 0.

For $S_4 = C_4\,\sigma_h$ four of them are shifted in C_4 and rest two in σ_h. Atogether all of them have been shifted. Thus its χ $(S_4) = 0$:

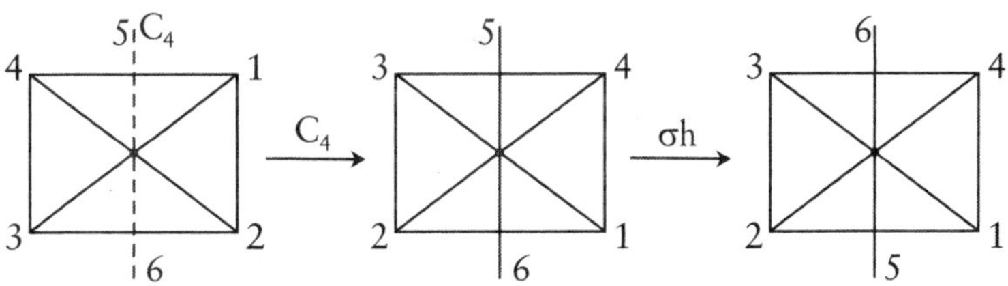

Like S_4 all vectors are shifted in S_6.

Its χ $(S_6) = 0$.

In σ_h four vectors remain un-shifted. Thus we have $\chi(\sigma_h) = 4$. As they lie in σ_h plane:

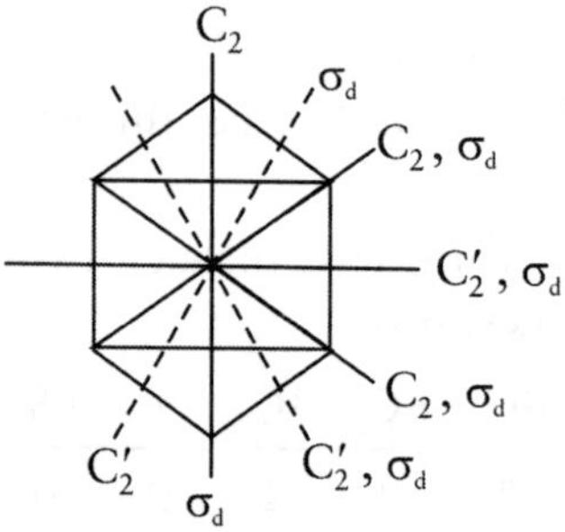

Reflections in σ_d plane leaves those lying in that plane un-shifted, i.e. two of them are un-shifted:

$$\chi(\sigma_d) = 2.$$

$$a_{A_{1g}} = \frac{1}{48}[6 \times 1 \times 1 + 0 + 6 \times 2 \times 1 + 3 \times 2 \times 1 + 0 + 0 + 0 + 3 \times 4 \times 1 \quad 6 \times 2 \times 1]$$

$$= \frac{1}{48}[6 + 12 + 6 + 12 + 12] = \frac{48}{48} = 1$$

$$a_{A_{2g}} = \frac{1}{48}[6 \times 1 \times 1 + 0 + 6 \times 2 \times (-1) + 3 \times 2 \times 1 + 0 + 0 + 0 + 0 \quad 3 \times 4 \times 2 + 6 \times 2 \times (-1)]$$

$$= \frac{1}{48}[6 - 12 + 6 + 12 - 12] = 0$$

$$a_{Eg} = \frac{1}{48}[6 \times 1 \times 2 + 0 + 3 \times 2 \times 2 + 3 \times 4 \times 2 + 0] = 1$$

$$a_{T_{2g}} = \frac{1}{48}[6 \times 1 \times 3 + 0 + 6 \times 2\,(-1) + 3 \times 2 \times (-1) + 3 \times 4 \times (-1) \quad 3 \times 4 \times 1 + 6 \times 2 \times 1]$$

$$= \frac{1}{48}[18 - 12 - 6 - 12 + 12] = 0$$

$$a_{T_{1u}} = \frac{1}{48}[6 \times 1 \times 3 + 6 \times 2 \times 1 + 3 \times 2 \times (-1) + 3 \times 4 \times 1 + 6 \times 2 \times 1]$$

$$= \frac{1}{48}[18 + 12 - 6 + 12 + 12] = 1$$

$\Gamma_R = A_{1g} + Eg + T_{1u}$

A_{1g} s

Eg dz^2, $dx^2 - y^2$

T_{1u} p_x, p_y, p_z

There is only one combination of the type.

$s + p_x + p_y + p_z + dx^2{-}y^2 + dz^2$. This is abbreviated as $d^2\,sp^3$.

7.2 QUANTITATIVE DESCRIPTION OF HYBRID ORBITALS

We construct hybrid orbitals on the central atom. A with the required set of pendant atoms B. The next problem is how to write the explicit form of hybrid orbitals so that we must know the contribution of the amount of atomic orbitals to the hybrid orbitals.

For instance let us take up the case of AB_3 system which is planar. It has D_{3h} point group (BCl_3 etc.). It has three hybrid orbitals, ϕ_1, ϕ_2 and ϕ_3 at A-atom. There are three equivalent orbitals σ_1, σ_2, σ_3 at pendant atoms B.

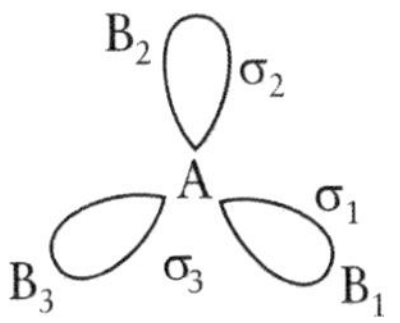

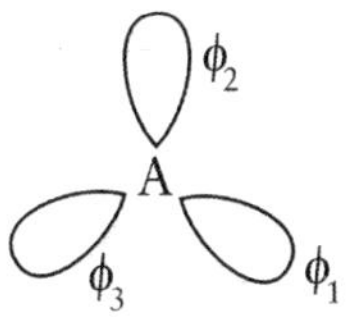

The coefficients of three hybrid orbitals are to be ascertained as matrix M with basis function of pure atomic orbitals. We determine the type of atomic orbitals used in such combination from the method of un-shifted vectors as follows:

In E all equivalent orbitals σ_1, σ_2, σ_3 are un-shifted:

$$\chi = \underset{\substack{\downarrow \\ \text{No. of} \\ \text{vectors}}}{3} \times \underset{\substack{\downarrow \\ \text{Contribution of} \\ \text{character per} \\ \text{un-shifted atom.}}}{1} = 3$$

In C_3 all shifted $\chi = 0$.

In C_2 one is un-shifted $\chi = 1 \times 1 = 1$.

In σ_h all are un-shifted $\chi = 3 \times 1 = 3$.

In σ_v only one is un-shifted $\chi = 1 \times 1 = 1$.

In $S_3 = C_3\ \sigma_h$ all are shifted $\chi = 0$.

D_{3h}	E	$2C_3$	$3C_2$	σ_h	$3\sigma_v$	$2S_3$
$\Gamma\sigma$	3	0	1	3	1	0

$$a'_{A_1} = \frac{1}{12}[3\times1\times1+0+3\times1\times1+3\times1\times1+3\times1\times1]$$

$$= \frac{1}{12}[3+3+3+3] = \frac{1}{12} = 1$$

$$a_{E'} = \frac{1}{12}\left[2\times3\times1+0+3\times1\times0+1\times3\times2+2\times(-1)\times0+3\times1\times0\right]$$

$$= \frac{1}{12}[6+6] = 1$$

Others are zero, $\Gamma\sigma = A'_1 + E'$

A suitable set of atomic orbitals will be from C.T.

$A'_1 - s$

$E' - p_x, p_y$

$$\begin{bmatrix} s \\ p_x \\ p_y \end{bmatrix} = \begin{bmatrix} l_{11} & l_{12} & l_{13} \\ l_{21} & l_{22} & l_{23} \\ l_{31} & l_{32} & l_{33} \end{bmatrix} \begin{bmatrix} \phi_1 \\ \phi_2 \\ \phi_3 \end{bmatrix}$$

It is an L matrix. There can be inverse transformation of L, i.e. L^{-1} which can be given as matrix M:

$$\begin{bmatrix} \phi_1 \\ \phi_2 \\ \phi_3 \end{bmatrix} = \underset{M}{\begin{bmatrix} m_{11} & m_{12} & m_{13} \\ m_{21} & m_{22} & m_{23} \\ m_{31} & m_{32} & m_{33} \end{bmatrix}} \begin{bmatrix} s \\ p_x \\ p_y \end{bmatrix}$$

L & M matrices of same dimensions are inverse to each other.

Let L & M be orthogonal matrices so the inverse is its transpose, one way is to determine the matrix L and then on taking its inverse as transpose matrix we may ascertain matrix M easily.

For convenience instead of D_{3h}. We take up a pure rotational group C_3 with its members E, C_3, C_3^2.

C_3	E	C_3	C_3^2	
A	1	1	1	
E	$\left.\begin{matrix}1\\1\end{matrix}\right\}$	$\begin{matrix}\xi\\\xi^*\end{matrix}$	$\begin{matrix}\xi^*\\\xi\end{matrix}$	$\xi = e^{i2\pi/n} = e^{i2\pi/3}$

Applying projection operator technique on σ_1 using A & E symmetry species we have:

$$\tilde{P}^{A}_{\sigma_1} = \frac{1}{3}\left[1\times\tilde{E}\sigma_1 + 1\times\tilde{C}_3\sigma_1 + 1\times\tilde{C}_3^2\sigma_1\right]$$

$$\simeq \sigma_1 + \sigma_3 + \sigma_2$$

$$= \sigma_1 + \sigma_2 + \sigma_3$$

$$N = \frac{1}{\sqrt{3}}$$

$$\Psi_A = \frac{1}{\sqrt{3}}(\sigma_1 + \sigma_2 + \sigma_3)$$

$$\tilde{P}^{Ea'}_{\sigma 1} \simeq 1\times\tilde{E}\sigma_1 + \xi\times C_3\sigma_1 + \xi^*\times C_3^2\sigma_1$$

$$Ea' = \sigma_1 + \xi\sigma_3 + \xi^*\sigma_2$$

$$\tilde{P}^{Eb'}_{\sigma 1} = 1\times\tilde{E}\sigma_1 + \xi^*\times C_3\sigma_1 + \xi\times C_3^2\sigma_1$$

$$Eb' = \sigma_1 + \xi^*\sigma_3 + \xi\sigma_2$$

There can be two linear combinations:

$$Ea' + Eb' = 2\sigma_1 + (\xi+\xi^*)\,\sigma_3 + (\xi^*+\xi)\,\sigma_2$$

$$\xi+\xi^* = \cos 2\pi/3 + i\,\sin 2\pi/3 + \cos 2\pi/3 - i\,\sin 2\pi/3$$

$$= 2\cos 2\pi/3 = 2\cos 120° = 2\,(-1/2) = -1$$

$$Ea' + Eb' = 2\sigma_1 + (-1)\,\sigma_3 + (-1)\,\sigma_2$$

$$= 2\sigma_1 - \sigma_2 - \sigma_3$$

$$\therefore \Psi_{Ea} = \frac{1}{\sqrt{6}}\left(2\sigma_1 - \sigma_2 - \sigma_3\right)$$

$$\frac{Ea' - Eb'}{-i} = \frac{(\epsilon - \epsilon^*)\sigma_3 + (\epsilon^* - \epsilon)\sigma_2}{-i}$$

$$\epsilon - \epsilon^* = \cancel{\cos}\ \frac{2\pi}{3} + i\sin\frac{2\pi}{3} - \cancel{\cos}\ \frac{2\pi}{3} + i\sin\frac{2\pi}{3}$$

$$\frac{\epsilon - \epsilon^*}{-i} = \frac{2\cancel{i}}{-\cancel{i}}\sin 2\pi/3 = -2\sin 2\pi/3 = -\cancel{2} \times \sqrt{3}/\cancel{2} = -\sqrt{3}$$

$$\epsilon^* - \epsilon = \cos\frac{\cancel{2\pi}}{3} - i\sin 2\pi/3 - \cancel{\cos}\ 2\pi/3 - i\sin 2\pi/3$$

$$\frac{\epsilon^* - \epsilon}{-i} = \frac{-2\cancel{i}}{-\cancel{i}}\sin 2\pi/3 = 2\sin 2\pi/3 = \cancel{2} \times \sqrt{3}/\cancel{2} = \sqrt{3}$$

$$\Psi_{Eb} = \sqrt{3}\left(\sigma_2 - \sigma_3\right) \simeq \sigma_2 - \sigma_3$$

$$N = \frac{1}{\sqrt{2}}, = \frac{1}{\sqrt{2}}\left(\sigma_2 - \sigma_3\right)$$

The expressions are:

$$\Psi_A = \frac{1}{\sqrt{3}}\sigma_1 + \frac{1}{\sqrt{3}}\sigma_2 + \frac{1}{\sqrt{3}}\sigma_3$$

$$\Psi_{Ea} = \frac{1}{\sqrt{6}}\sigma_1 - \frac{1}{\sqrt{6}}\sigma_2 - \frac{1}{\sqrt{6}}\sigma_3$$

$$\Psi_{Eb} = \frac{1}{\sqrt{2}}\sigma_2 - \frac{1}{\sqrt{2}}\sigma_3$$

σ's are equivalent orbitals. Matrix of the coefficient is given as:

$$\begin{bmatrix} 1/\sqrt{3} & 1/\sqrt{3} & 1/\sqrt{3} \\ 2/\sqrt{6} & -1/\sqrt{6} & -1/\sqrt{6} \\ 0 & 1/\sqrt{2} & -1/\sqrt{2} \end{bmatrix}$$

Its inverse is taken which is transpose of the matrix.

The transpose of which is:

$$\begin{bmatrix} 1/\sqrt{3} & 2/\sqrt{6} & 0 \\ 1/\sqrt{3} & -1/\sqrt{6} & 1/\sqrt{2} \\ 1/\sqrt{3} & -1/\sqrt{6} & -1/\sqrt{2} \end{bmatrix}$$

This matrix is applied to a column vector of atomic orbitals to generate hybrid orbitals.

$$\begin{bmatrix} 1/\sqrt{3} & 2/\sqrt{6} & 0 \\ 1/\sqrt{3} & -1/\sqrt{6} & 1/\sqrt{2} \\ 1/\sqrt{3} & -1/\sqrt{6} & -1/\sqrt{2} \end{bmatrix} \begin{bmatrix} s \\ p_x \\ p_y \end{bmatrix} = \begin{bmatrix} 1/\sqrt{3}\, s + 2/\sqrt{6}\, p_x + 0.p_y \\ 1/\sqrt{3}\, s - 1/\sqrt{6}\, p_x + 1/\sqrt{2}\, p_y \\ 1/\sqrt{3}\, s - 1/\sqrt{6}\, p_x - 1/\sqrt{2}\, p_y \end{bmatrix}$$

$$= \begin{bmatrix} \phi_1 \\ \phi_2 \\ \phi_3 \end{bmatrix}$$

As such, $\phi_1 = \frac{1}{\sqrt{3}} s + \frac{2}{\sqrt{6}} p_x$

$$\phi_2 = \frac{1}{\sqrt{3}} s - \frac{1}{\sqrt{6}} p_x + \frac{1}{\sqrt{2}} p_y$$

$$\phi_3 = \frac{1}{\sqrt{3}} s - \frac{1}{\sqrt{6}} p_x - \frac{1}{\sqrt{2}} p_y$$

7.3 HYBRIDIZATION IN SQUARE PLANAR SYSTEM OF AB_4 TYPE MOLECULE

There are four equivalent σ orbitals at the pendant (B) atoms. It has D_{4h} symmetry. The equivalent orbitals are σ_1, σ_2, σ_3, & σ_4.

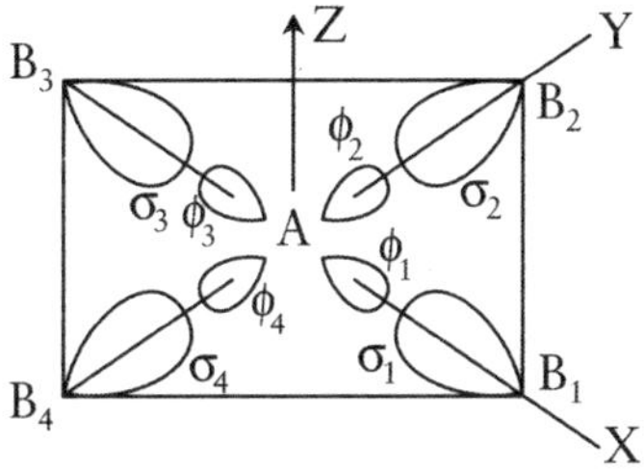

Consider symmetry species of the σ-bond hybrids. We follow method of un-shifted atom/vector. A vector which remains un-shifted contributes 1 towards character per σ vector. If all are shifted from their initial position there is nothing contribution in all.

In case of identity all four σ's are unshifted. $\chi = 4 \times 1 = 4$.

In C_4 all are shifted $\chi = 0$.

In $C_2 = C_4^2$ all are shifted $\chi = 0$.

In C_2' (along the diagonals) two of them are un-affected while other two are shifted. $\chi = 2 \times 1 = 2$.

In C_2'' (dividing the square base) all the four are shifted $\chi = 0$.

In i all are affected $\chi = 0$.

In $S_4 = C_4\, \sigma_h$ all are shifted $\chi = 0$.

In σ_v two of them are un-shifted along the leading diagonal. So $\chi = 2 \times 1 = 2$.

In σ_d all are shifted $\chi = 0$

In σ_h all are un-shifted $\chi(\sigma_h) = 4 \times 1 = 4$

D_{4h}	E	$2C_4$	$C_2 \equiv C_4^2$	$2C_2'$	$2C_2''$	i	$2S_4$	σ_h	$2\sigma_v$	$2\sigma_d$
Γσ	4	0	0	2	0	0	0	4	2	0

Through the decomposition formula we obtain.

$$\Gamma\sigma = A_{1g} + B_{1g} + E_g$$

The hybrid orbitals belong to the representations A_{1g}. B_{1g}, E_g. There correspond the following set of atomic orbitals of atom A from D_{4h}:

$A_{1g} - s$

$B_{ig} - d_{x^2-y^2}$

$E_g - p_x, p_y$

A suitable linear combination of atomic orbitals will take place in the following steps.

We constitute SALC's with the C_4 cyclic group instead of D_{4h}.

C_4	E	C_4	$C_4^2 \equiv C_2$	C_4^3	
A	1	1	1	1	$x^2 + y^2 + z^2$
B	1	–1	1	–1	$x^2 - y^2$, xy
E	1	i	–1	–i	
	1	–i	–1	i	(x, y)

$$\tilde{P}_{\sigma_1}^{A} \cong 1\times\tilde{E}\sigma_1 + 1\times C_4\sigma_1 + 1\times C_2\times\sigma_1 + 1\times C_4^3\sigma_1$$

$$= \sigma_1 + \sigma_4 + \sigma_3 + \sigma_2$$

$$N = \frac{1}{\sqrt{4}} = \frac{1}{2}$$

$$\Psi_A = \frac{1}{2}\left(\sigma_1 + \sigma_2 + \sigma_3 + \sigma_4\right)$$

$$\tilde{P}_{\sigma_1}^{B} \cong 1\times\tilde{E}\sigma_1 + (-1)\,\tilde{C}_4\sigma_1 + 1\times C_2\sigma_1 + (-)\,\tilde{C}_4^3\,\sigma_1$$

$$= \sigma_1 - \sigma_4 + \sigma_3 - \sigma_2$$

$$= \sigma_1 - \sigma_2 + \sigma_3 - \sigma_4$$

$$N = \frac{1}{2},$$

$$\Psi_B = \frac{1}{2}\left(\sigma_1 - \sigma_2 + \sigma_3 - \sigma_4\right)$$

$$\tilde{P}_{\sigma_1}^{Ea'} = 1\times\tilde{E}\sigma_1 + i\times C_4\,\sigma_1 - 1\times C_2\sigma_1 - i\times\tilde{C}_4^3\sigma_1$$

$$= \sigma_1 + i\sigma_4 - \sigma_3 - i\sigma_2$$

$$\tilde{P}_{\sigma_1}^{Eb'} = 1\times\tilde{E}\sigma_1 - i\,\tilde{C}_4\sigma_1 - 1\times\tilde{C}_2\sigma_1 + i\times\tilde{C}_4^3\sigma_1$$

$$= \sigma_1 - i\sigma_4 - \sigma_3 + i\sigma_2$$

$$Ea' + Eb' = \sigma_1 + i\not{\sigma}_4 - \sigma_3 - i\not{\sigma}_2$$

$$\frac{\sigma_1 - i\not{\sigma}_4 - \sigma_3 + i\not{\sigma}_2}{2\sigma_1 - 2\sigma_3 = 2\left(\sigma_1 - \sigma_3\right)}$$

$$\simeq \sigma_1 - \sigma_3$$

$$\Psi_{Ea} = \frac{1}{\sqrt{2}}(\sigma_1 - \sigma_3)$$

$$\frac{Ea' - Eb'}{-i} = \sigma_1 + i\sigma_4 - \sigma_3 - i\sigma_2$$

$$\frac{-\sigma_1 + i\sigma_4 + \sigma_3 - i\sigma_2}{\qquad}$$

$$\frac{-i(\sigma_2 - \sigma_4)}{-i} = \sigma_2 - \sigma_4$$

$$\Psi_{E_b} = \frac{1}{\sqrt{2}}(\sigma_2 - \sigma_4)$$

We constitute the matrix as:

$$\begin{bmatrix} s \\ dx^2 - y^2 \\ p_x \\ p_y \end{bmatrix} = \begin{bmatrix} 1/2 & 1/2 & 1/2 & 1/2 \\ 1/2 & -1/2 & 1/2 & -1/2 \\ 1/\sqrt{2} & 0 & -1/\sqrt{2} & 0 \\ 0 & 1/\sqrt{2} & 0 & -1/\sqrt{2} \end{bmatrix} \begin{bmatrix} \sigma_1 \\ \sigma_2 \\ \sigma_3 \\ \sigma_4 \end{bmatrix}$$

Its transpose matrix will be of the type:

$$\begin{bmatrix} \frac{1}{2} & \frac{1}{2} & \frac{1}{\sqrt{2}} & 0 \\ \frac{1}{2} & -\frac{1}{2} & 0 & \frac{1}{\sqrt{2}} \\ \frac{1}{2} & \frac{1}{2} & -\frac{1}{\sqrt{2}} & 0 \\ \frac{1}{2} & -\frac{1}{2} & 0 & -\frac{1}{\sqrt{2}} \end{bmatrix}$$

Applying the inverse matrix to the column vectors of atomic orbitals s, $dx^2–y^2$, p_x, p_y.

We have,

$$\begin{bmatrix} \frac{1}{2} & \frac{1}{2} & \frac{1}{\sqrt{2}} & 0 \\ \frac{1}{2} & -\frac{1}{2} & 0 & \frac{1}{\sqrt{2}} \\ \frac{1}{2} & \frac{1}{2} & -\frac{1}{\sqrt{2}} & 0 \\ \frac{1}{2} & -\frac{1}{2} & 0 & -\frac{1}{\sqrt{2}} \end{bmatrix} \begin{bmatrix} s \\ dx^2 - y^2 \\ p_x \\ p_y \end{bmatrix} = \begin{bmatrix} \phi_1 \\ \phi_2 \\ \phi_3 \\ \phi_4 \end{bmatrix}$$

The four hybrid orbitals ϕ_1, ϕ_2, ... ϕ_4, are obtained as:

$$\phi_1 = \frac{1}{2}s + \frac{1}{2}dx^2 - y^2 + \frac{1}{\sqrt{2}}p_x$$

$$\phi_2 = \frac{1}{2}s - \frac{1}{2}dx^2 - y^2 + \frac{1}{\sqrt{2}}p_y$$

$$\phi_3 = \frac{1}{2}s + \frac{1}{2}dx^2 - y^2 - \frac{1}{\sqrt{2}}p_x$$

$$\phi_4 = \frac{1}{2}s - \frac{1}{2}dx^2 - y^2 - \frac{1}{\sqrt{2}}p_y$$

7.4 HYBRIDIZATION IN TETRAHEDRAL ENVIRONMENT

In tetrahedron there are four faces shown by four equilateral triangles:

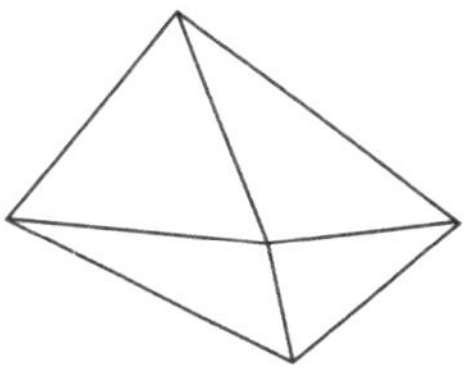

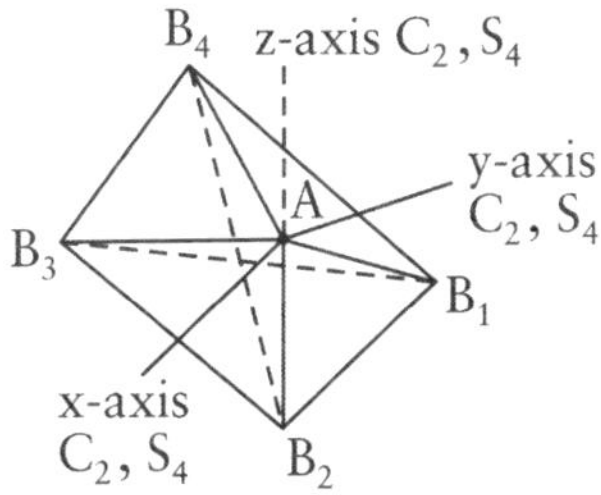

There are four vertices and six edges. The symmetry elements and associated symmetry operations are as follows:

1. It has three S_4 axes coinciding with the x, y, and z-axes and each S_4 produces:

$$S_4, \quad S_4^2, \quad S_4^3, \quad S_4^4 \equiv E$$

$$S_4^2 = C_4^2(\sigma_h)^2 = C_4^2 = C_2$$

It has two distinct operations $2S_4$. As we have three S_4 axes which may lead to $3 \times 2S_4 = 6S_4$ operations.

2. There are three C_2 axes coinciding with x, y & z-axes and we have three $3C_2$ operations.
3. There are four C_3 axes each of them passes through one point and the centre of the opposite face.

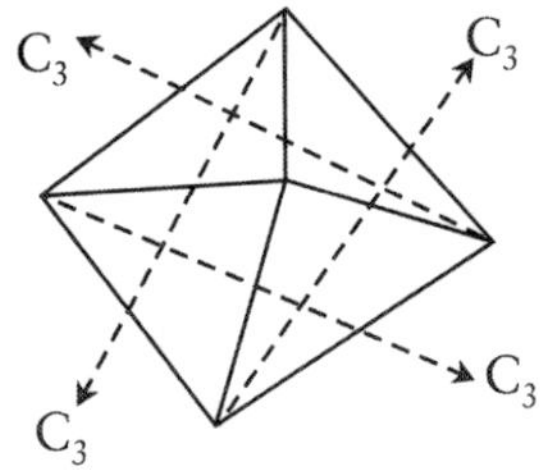

Each C-H bond in methane represents a C_3 axis. There are two operations in case of each C_3 axis.

$$C_3,\ C_3^2 = 2C_3 \text{ giving } 4 \times 2C_3 = 8C_3 \text{ operations.}$$

4. There are six symmetry planes. They all are dihedral planes (σ_d) defined as H_1–C–H_2, H_1–C–H_3, H_1–C–H_4, H_2–C–H_4, H_2–C–H_3 and H_3–C–H_4.

So we have $6\sigma_d$.

$$E,\ 8C_3,\ 3C_2,\ 6S_4\ 6\sigma_d \quad h = 24$$

In case of AB_4, there are four pendant atoms (B) and four equivalent orbitals at B are σ_1, σ_2, σ_3 and σ_4.

In identity all are unshifted $\chi = 4 \times 1 = 4$.

Let us consider a vector σ_1 along C_3 axis. So σ_1 does not change its position while others are:

$$C_3(\chi) = 1 \times 1 = 1.$$

In C_2 which lies along x, y or z axis in which the equivalent orbitals are shifted $C_2(\chi) = 0$.

S_4 is coincident with C_2 all vectors are shifted $S_4(\chi) = 0$

In σ_d two of the equivalent orbitals may lie while remaining two will be reflected so that two of them are un-shifted $\chi = 2 \times 1 = 2$

Td	E	$8C_3$	$3C_2$	$6S_4$	$6\sigma_d$
$\Gamma(\sigma)$	4	1	0	0	2

$$a_{A_1} = \frac{1}{24}\left[1 \times 4 \times 1 + 8 \times 1 \times 1 + 0 + 0 + 6 \times 2 \times 1\right]$$

$$= \frac{1}{24}\left[4 + 8 + 12\right] = \frac{24}{24} = 1$$

$$a_{A_2} = \frac{1}{24}\left[4 \times 8 + 0 + 6 \times 2\ (-1)\right]$$

$$= \frac{12 - 12}{24} = \frac{0}{24} = 0.$$

a_E does not occur.

$$a_{T_1} = \frac{1}{24}\left[4 \times 3 \times 1 + 0 + 0 + 0 - 12\right] = \frac{0}{24} = 0$$

$$a_{T_2} = \frac{1}{24}\left[1 \times 3 \times 1 + 0 + 1 + 0 \times 6 \times 2 \times 1\right]$$

$$= \frac{12 + 12}{24} = \frac{24}{24} = 1$$

$$\Gamma_{(\sigma)} = A_1 + T_2 \qquad \begin{matrix} A_1 & s \\ T_2 & p_x,\ p_y,\ p_z;\ d_{xy},\ d_{xz},\ d_{yz} \end{matrix}$$

There can be a combination of s and p_x, p_y and p_z or s + d_{xy} + d_{xz} + d_{yz}.

In terms of unknown coefficients the four hybrid orbitals are as ϕ_1, ϕ_2, ϕ_3 and ϕ_4.

$$\phi_1 = C_{11}s + C_{12}\,p_x + C_{13}\,p_y + C_{14}\,p_z$$

$$\phi_2 = C_{21}s + C_{22}\,p_x + C_{23}\,p_y + C_{24}\,p_z$$

$$\phi_3 = C_{31}s + C_{32}\,p_x + C_{33}\,p_y + C_{34}\,p_z$$

$$\phi_4 = C_{41}s + C_{42}\,p_x + C_{43}\,p_y + C_{44}\,p_z$$

In the matrix form we have:

$$\begin{bmatrix} \phi_1 \\ \phi_2 \\ \phi_3 \\ \phi_4 \end{bmatrix} = \begin{bmatrix} C_{11} & C_{12} & C_{13} & C_{14} \\ C_{21} & C_{22} & C_{23} & C_{24} \\ C_{31} & C_{32} & C_{33} & C_{34} \\ C_{41} & C_{42} & C_{43} & C_{44} \end{bmatrix} \begin{bmatrix} s \\ p_x \\ p_y \\ p_z \end{bmatrix}$$

We establish some relationships among coefficients. Consider C_2 axis along z-direction. It relates ϕ_1, ϕ_2, ϕ_3, ϕ_4. Let us consider ϕ_1.

$$C_2^z\ \phi_1 = \phi_2$$

$$C_2^{(z)}\ (C_{11}\,s + C_{12}\,p_x + C_{13}\,p_y + C_{14}\,p_z) = C_{21}s + C_{22}\,p_x + C_{23}\,p_y + C_{24}p_z.$$

The Cij are coefficients, constant quantities they commute with the symmetry operators. The equation may also be written as:

$$C_{11}\left[C_2^z\,s\right]+C_{12}\left[C_2^z\ p_x\right]+C_{13}\left[C_2^z\,p_y\right]+C_{14}\left(C_2^z\ p_z\right)$$

$$= C_{21}\,s + C_{22}\,p_x + C_{23}\,p_y + C_{24}\,p_z$$

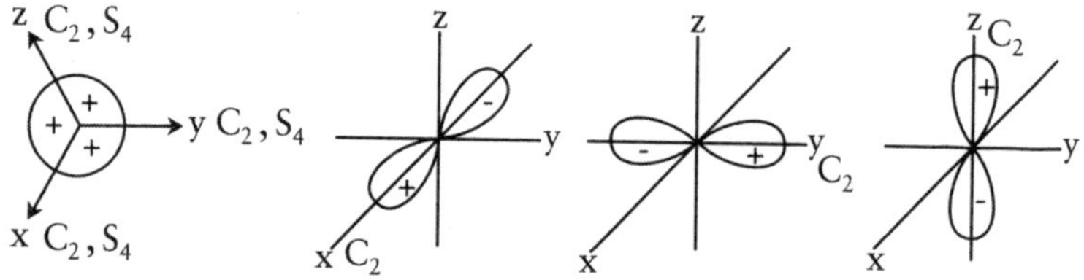

From which we determine the relations:

$$C_2s = s,\ C_2\,p_x = -p_x\ C_2p_y = -p_y$$

$$C_2p_z = p_z$$

Hence, $C_{11}s - C_{12}\,p_x - C_{13}p_y + C_{13}\,p_z$

$$=C_{21}s + C_{22}\,p_x + C_{23}\,p_y + C_{24}\,p_z.$$

In order that ϕ_1 and ϕ_2 are equivalent under symmetry operations of T_d the coefficients of each atomic orbital equal on bothsides.

Hence, $C_{11} = C_{21}$, $-C_{12} = C_{22}$, $-C_{13} = C_{23}$, $C_{14} = C_{24}$.

As hybrid orbitals are equivalent so the contribution of s to them must be equal.

Hence, $C_{11} = C_{21} = C_{31} = C_{41}$.

By analogy we can have a similar relationships for ϕ_3 and ϕ_4 in respect of C_2.

$$\begin{aligned} C_{31} &= C_{41} \\ -C_{32} &= C_{42} \\ -C_{33} &= C_{43} \\ C_{34} &= C_{44} \end{aligned}$$

Let us consider S_4^2 in the same figure and we can have:

$$S_4^2\ s = s \qquad S_4^2\ p_x = -p_y = S_4^2\ p_y = p_x$$

$$S_4^2\ p_z = -p_z$$

and $S_4^2\ \phi_1 = \phi_3$

$$S_4^2\left[C_{11}\, s + C_{12} p_x + C_{13} p_y + C_{14}\, p_z\right] = C_{31}\, s + C_{32}\, p_x + C_{33}\ p_y + C_{34}\, p_z$$

or, $\qquad C_{11}\, s + C_{12}(-p_y) + C_{13}(p_z) + C_{14}(-p_z)$

$$= C_{31}\, s + C_{32}\ p_x + C_{33}$$

or, $\qquad C_{11}\, s - C_{12}\, p_y + C_{13}\, p_x = C_{14}\ p_z$

$$C_{31}\ s + C_{32}\ p_x + C_{33}\ p_y + C_{34}\ p_z$$

By setting coefficients of identical atomic orbitals:

$$C_{11} = C_{31} = C_{12} = C_{33},\ C_{13} = C_{32}, = C_{12} = C_{34}$$

This leaves us with four unknown coefficients:

$$\begin{aligned} \phi_1 &= C_{11}\, s + C_{12}\ p_x + C_{13}\ p_y + C_{14}\, p_z \\ \phi_2 &= C_{11}\, s - C_{12}\ p_x + -C_{13}\ p_y + C_{14}\, p_z \\ \phi_3 &= C_{11}\, s + C_{13}\ p_x + -C_{12}\ p_y + C_{14}\, p_z \\ \phi_4 &= C_{11}\, s - C_{13}\ p_x - C_{12}\ p_y - C_{14}\, p_z \end{aligned}$$

Now we apply one more symmetry operation σ_d relative to p_x and p_y atomic orbitals.

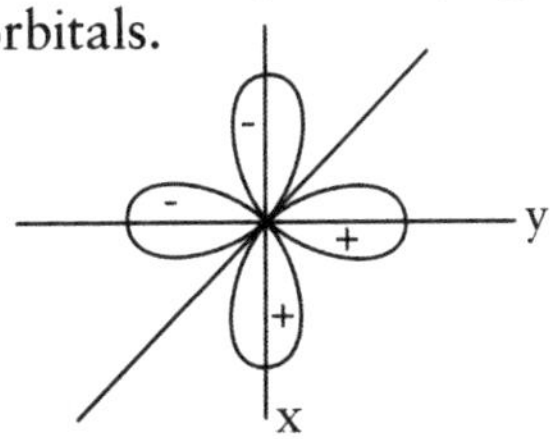

$$\sigma_d \ \phi_1 = \phi_2$$

$$\sigma_d (C_{11}s + C12 \ p_x + C_{13} \ p_y + C_{14} \ p_z) = C_{11} \ s - C_{12} \ p_x - C_{13} \ p_y + C_{14}p_z$$

There can be, $\sigma_d \ s = s, \ \sigma_d \ p_x = -p_y$

$$\sigma_d \ p_y = -p_x, \ \sigma_d \ p_z = p_z$$

$$C_{11} \ s + C_{12} \ (-p_y) + C_{13} \ (-p_x) + C_{14} \ p_2 = C_{11}s - C_{12} \ p_x - C_{13} \ p_y + C_{14}p_z.$$

$$C_{11}s - C_{12} \ p_y - C_{13} \ p_x + C_{14} \ p_z = C_{11} \ s - C_{12}p_x - C_{13} \ p_y + C_{14} \ p_z \text{ and } C_{12} = C_{13}.$$

Now there are only three unknown coefficients.

Hence,

$$\phi_1 = C_{11} \, s + C_{12} \ p_x - C_{12} \ p_y - C_{14} \, p_z$$

$$\phi_2 = C_{11} \, s - C_{12} \ p_x - C_{12} \ p_y - C_{14} \, p_z$$

$$\phi_3 = C_{11} \, s + C_{12} \ p_x - C_{12} \ p_y - C_{14} \, p_z$$

$$\phi_4 = C_{11} \, s - C_{12} \ p_x - C_{12} \ p_y - C_{14} \, p_z$$

$$\int \phi_1^2 \, dz = 1, \ \int \phi_1 \, \phi_2 \, dz = 0, \ \int \phi_1 \, \phi_3 \ dz = 0$$

From which we establish three equations:

$$C_{11}^2 + C_{12}^2 + C_{13}^2 + C_{14}^3 = 1$$

$$C_{11}^2 - C_{12}^2 - C_{12}^2 + C_{14}^2 = 0$$

$$C_{11}^2 + C_{12}^2 - C_{12}^2 - C_{14}^2 = 0$$

or, $C_{11}^2 = C_{12}^2$

$C_{11} = \pm C_{14}$

&

$$\begin{array}{l} C_{11}^2 + C_{12}^2 + C_{12}^2 + C_{14}^2 = 1 \\ \underset{-}{C_{11}^2} \underset{+}{-} C_{12}^2 \underset{+}{-} C_{12}^2 \underset{-}{+} C_{14}^2 = 0 \\ \hline 4C_{12}^2 = 1 \end{array}$$

$$C_{12}^2 = 1/4$$

$$C_{12} = \pm \frac{1}{2}$$

Now from $\quad C_{11}^2 + C_{12}^2 + C_{12}^2 + C_{14}^2 = 1$

or $\quad C_{11}^2 + 2C_{12}^2 + C_{14}^2 = 1$

or $\quad C_{11}^2 + 2 \times \frac{1}{4} + C_{14}^2 = 1$

$$C_{11}^2 + C_{14}^2 = 1 - \frac{1}{2} = \frac{1}{2}$$

But $\quad C_{11} = C_{14},\ zC_{11}^1 = \frac{1}{2}$

$$C_{11}^2 = 1/4$$

$$C_{11} = \pm 1/2$$

We assign only positive values in all cases:

$$C_{11} = C_{14} = C_{12} = \frac{1}{2}$$

and we have hybrid wave functions:

$$\therefore \ \phi_1 = \frac{1}{2}(s + p_x + p_y + p_z)$$

$$\phi_2 = \frac{1}{2}(s - p_x - p_y + p_z)$$

$$\phi_3 = \frac{1}{2}(s + p_x - p_y - p_z)$$

$$\phi_4 = \frac{1}{2}(s - p_x + p_y - p_z)$$

7.5 HYBRIDIZATION INVOLVING π-BONDING

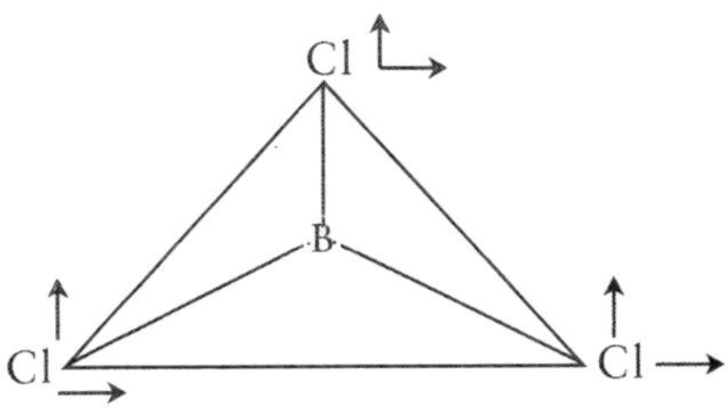

BCl_3 is a case involving both σ and π-bonds. The case of σ-hybridization has already been discussed. Let us take up π-hybridization in this example. At each Cl-atom there are two vectors one set is parallel (in the plane) and another set is perpendicular (out of the plane). So there are six vectors in all three of them are || and rest three $\perp^r$. We consider them as follows:

D_{3h}	E	$2C_3$,	$3C_2$	σ_h	$2S_3$	$3\sigma_v$
$\Gamma\perp^r$	3	0	–1	–3	0	1
$\Gamma_{\|\|}$	3	0	–1	3	0	–1

$$\Gamma\perp^r = A_2'' + E''$$

$$\Gamma_{11} = A_2' + E'$$

In order to form hybrid orbitals with π-bonds in chlorine atoms and the B-atom, the B-atom must supply orbitals with the following transformation properties:

$\|\| A_2' + E$ $\qquad\qquad$ $\perp^r\ A_2'' + E''$

(none) (p_x, p_y) $\qquad\qquad$ (p_z) (d_{xz}, d_{yz})

$(dx^2–y^2, dxy)$

Vectors perpendicular to the plane are ($\perp^r$) and those vectors being in the plane are (||). The (p_x, p_y) set is engaged in the σ-bonding and they are not further available for bonding. If p_z and d_{xz} and d_{yz} are not used in σ-bonding they may combine to form π–orbitals. A vector which is shifted does not contribute anything to the character which does not shift but changes direction in the reverse order. Its character contribution is-1.

The π–bond is formed from the contribution of orbitals which are perpendicular to the molecular plane. They are used here as:

$A_2'' + E''$, A_2'' giving rise to (one) and E'' (two) with the formation of $p_z + d_{xz} + d_{yz}$.

(one) (two)

(p_z) (d_{xz}, d_{yz})

In case of || hybrid there is none in A_2'. So it follows that there can be two π–bonds (||) equally shared with three chlorine atoms.

QUESTIONS

1. Discuss principles of group theory in qualitative aspects of hybridization involving σ–bonds:
   (i) in BCl_3 . sp^2
   (ii) in CH_4 . sp^3
2. Applying method of un-shifted atoms calculate the characters for symmetry operations in D_{3h} point group in case of BCl_3 and decompose from the standard formula to give irreducible components out of it and examine with the help of C.T. the possibility of hybridization schemes.
3. (a) Arrange the symmetry operations in T_d point group into classes.
   (b) Calculate the characters for four C-H bonds in methane forming 4 × 4 matrices in all symmetry operations.

   Decompose the characters for T_d into symmetry species and examine the possible hybridization with the use of character Table.
4. Applying group theory in a qualitative approach deduce the character through the formation of 4 × 4 matrices in all cases of square planar system such as $PtCl_4^{2-}$ ion and establish the hybridizational scheme possible.
5. An AB_5 system can have two schemes of hybridization for TBP and square pyramidal structures with the use of group theory in a qualitative sense. Establish the scheme in any one case the possible system of hybridization in the molecule.
6. Layout the qualitative scheme of hybridization in an octahedral system with the help of group theory and establish the final conclusion.
7. (a) Find out all the symmetry operations in an octahedral system and arrange them into classes. Find its order.
   (b) Applying method of un-shifted atoms calculate the characters for reducible representation for it.
   (c) Use the reduction formula and determine the symmetry species.

8. Discuss the quantitative scheme of hybridization adopting projection operator method and deduce the expression for hybrid orbitals in BCl_3.
9. (a) Explain SALCS.
   (b) The characters for equivalent orbitals in BCl_3 are determined to be:

D_{3h}	E	$2C_3$	$3C_2$	σ_h	$3\sigma_v$	$2S_3$
Γ_R	3	0	1	3	1	0

   obtain symmetry species out of Γ_R.

   (c) Using charactor Table for cyclic group C_3 use the projection operator to form explicit expression of three molecular wave functions.

SALCS AND MOLECULAR ORBITALS

8

8.1 SALCS

Simple molecules such as water, ammonia, formaldehyde, NO_2^- ion and B_2H_6 are considered for formation of group orbitals leading to the formation of molecular orbitals on the basis of symmetry arguments. Hybridization schemes based on formation of SALCS through symmetry operators or the method of projection operator has already been considered to obtain different forms of hybrid atomic orbitals. SALCS is an abbreviation that can be read as symmetry adapted linear combination.

This takes place in two ways. The method is abbreviated as SALCS. One can obtain SALCS either through the effect of symmetry operations on the linear combination for the formation of group orbitals and determine the characters for such transformation belonging to a given irreducible representation in a point group.

In case of water molecule there are two group orbitals on linear combinations of atomic orbitals of H-atoms, viz. $ISH_A + ISH_B$ and $ISH_A - ISH_B$. The normalizing factor will be $\frac{1}{\sqrt{2}}$. As water has C_{2v} point group, it has E, C_2, σ_{xz} and σ_{yz} operations. We can visualize the effect of all the four symmetry operations on these two linear combinations and find out the characters for transformation which determine the symmetry species in the point group.

$$\tilde{E}\left[ISH_A + ISH_B\right] = 1\left[ISH_A + ISH_B\right]$$

$$\tilde{C}_2\left[ISH_A + ISH_B\right] = 1\left[ISH_B + ISH_A\right]$$
$$= 1\left[ISH_A + ISH_B\right]$$
$$\tilde{\sigma}_{xz}\left[ISH_A + ISH_B\right] = 1\left[ISH_B + ISH_A\right]$$
$$= 1\left[ISH_A + ISH_B\right]$$
$$\tilde{\sigma}_{yz}\left[ISH_A + ISH_B\right] = 1\left[ISH_A + ISH_B\right]$$

So the linear combination or group orbital transformation is shown as:

E	C_2	σ_{xz}	σ_{yz}	
1	1	1	1	$= A_1$

This gives A_1 representations in C_{2v} point group. Let us consider the other linear combination $\frac{1}{\sqrt{2}}\left[ISH_A - ISH_B\right]$ and determine its symmetry species.

$$\tilde{E}\left[ISH_A - ISH_B\right] = 1\left[ISH_A - ISH_B\right]$$
$$\tilde{C}_2\left[ISH_A - ISH_B\right] = (1)\left[ISH_B - ISH_A\right]$$
$$= (-1)\left[ISH_A - ISH_B\right]$$
$$\tilde{\sigma}_{xz}\left[ISH_A - ISH_B\right] = (1)\left[ISH_B - ISH_A\right]$$
$$= (-1)\left[ISH_A - ISH_B\right]$$
$$\tilde{\sigma}_{yz}\left[ISH_A - ISH_B\right] = (1)\left[ISH_A - ISH_B\right]$$

As such it transforms as B_2 symmetry species in C_{2v} point group:

E	C_2	σ_{xz}	σ_{yz}
1	–1	–1	1

Now molecular orbitals are made known on considering matching symmetry of valence orbitals of oxygen atom from the character Table for C_{2v}.

8.2 PROJECTION OPERATOR METHOD

We can have a similar result that had from symmetry operator adopting an alternative procedure known as projection operator. A symmetry operator is $\tilde{R}$ and projection operator is $\tilde{p}$. In symmetry operation we need to have a basis function to obtain SALC. It is the character that has been applied in case of various irreducible representations along with the symmetry operators. So a projection operator acts through character χ_i.

$$\tilde{P}_{\phi}^{\Gamma_i} = \frac{li}{h}\sum_{R}\chi_R^{\Gamma i}\,.\,\tilde{R}\phi \cong \sum_{R}\chi_R^{\Gamma i}\,.\,\tilde{R}\phi$$

ϕ is the basis function. Consider C_{2v} point group having $\tilde{E}$, $\tilde{C}_2$, $\tilde{\sigma}_{xz}$ and $\tilde{\sigma}_{yz}$ operators and A_1, A_2, B_1, B_2 irreducible representations. So projection operator is applied in all the four cases as follows:

$$\tilde{P}_{\phi}^{A_1} \cong \chi_E^{A_1}.\tilde{E}\phi + \chi_{C_2}^{A_1}.\tilde{C}_2\phi + \chi_{\sigma_{xz}}^{A_1}.\tilde{\sigma}_{xz}\phi + \chi_{\sigma_{yz}}^{A_1}.\tilde{\sigma}_{yz}\phi$$

$$= 1\times\tilde{E}\phi + 1\tilde{C}_2\phi + 1.\tilde{\sigma}_{xz}\phi + 1\times\tilde{\sigma}_{yz}\phi$$

$$= \tilde{E}\phi + \hat{C}_2\phi + \tilde{\sigma}_{xz}\phi + \tilde{\sigma}_{yz}\phi$$

$$\tilde{P}_{\phi}^{A_2} \cong \chi_E^{A_2}\,\tilde{E}\phi + \chi_{C_2}^{A_2}.\tilde{C}\phi + \chi_{xz}^{A_z}\,\tilde{\sigma}_{xz}\phi + \chi_{\sigma_{yz}}^{A_z}.\tilde{\sigma}_{yz}\phi$$

$$= 1\times\tilde{E}\phi + 1\times\tilde{C}_2\phi - 1\times\tilde{\sigma}_{xz}\phi - 1\times\tilde{\sigma}_{yz}\phi$$

$$= \tilde{E}\phi + \tilde{C}_2\phi - \tilde{\sigma}_{xz}\phi - \tilde{\sigma}_{yz}\phi$$

$$\tilde{P}_{\phi}^{B_1} \cong \chi_E^{B_1}\,\tilde{E}\phi + \chi^{B_1}.\tilde{C}_2\phi + \chi_{\sigma_{xz}}^{B_1}\,\tilde{\sigma}_{xz}\phi + \chi_{\sigma_{yz}}^{B_1}.\tilde{\sigma}_{yz}\phi$$

$$= 1\times\tilde{E}\phi - 1\times\tilde{C}_2\phi + 1\times\tilde{\sigma}_{xz}\phi - 1\times\tilde{\sigma}_{yz}\phi$$

$$= \tilde{E}\phi - \tilde{C}_2\phi + \tilde{\sigma}_{xz}\phi - \tilde{\sigma}_{yz}\phi$$

$$\tilde{P}_{\phi}^{B_2} \cong \chi_E^{B_2}.\tilde{E}\phi + \chi_{C_2}^{B_2}.\tilde{C}_2\phi + \chi_{\sigma xz}^{B_z}\,\tilde{\sigma}_{xz}\phi + \chi_{\sigma_{yz}}^{B_z}.\tilde{\sigma}_{yz}\phi$$

$$= 1\times\tilde{E}\phi + 1\,(-1)\times\tilde{C}_2\phi + (-1)\times\tilde{\sigma}_{xz}\phi + (1)\times\tilde{\sigma}_{yz}\phi$$

$$= \tilde{E}\phi - \tilde{C}_2\phi - \tilde{\sigma}_{xz}\phi + \tilde{\sigma}_{yz}\phi$$

$$= \tilde{E}\phi - \tilde{C}_2\phi - \tilde{\sigma}_{xz}\phi + \tilde{\sigma}_{yz}\phi$$

8.3 DIATOMIC SYSTEM

It is advantageous to use symmetry elements in dealing with molecular orbitals for the case of diatomic molecule AB (homo-nuclear case):

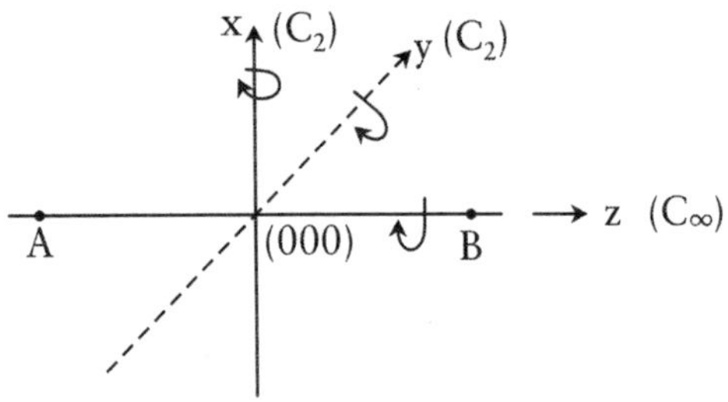

The origin of the co-ordinate system is half way in between A and B. Let us see the effect of rotation first. When we rotate the molecule around x or y-axis through 180° (C_2). A will go into B and B into A. We can also allow to rotate the molecule about z-axis by any angle (C∝). We can a reflect it in the molecular plane σ_h containing AB. It will bring no change. Inversion of AB through centre of connecting line takes A into B and B into A. There are $\propto\sigma_v$ taking the principal axis (z-axis). Symmetry aspects of bonding and anti-bonding molecular orbitals in H_2^+ ion.

$$\Psi_+ = \frac{1}{\sqrt{2(1+s)}}(\Psi_A + \Psi_B)$$

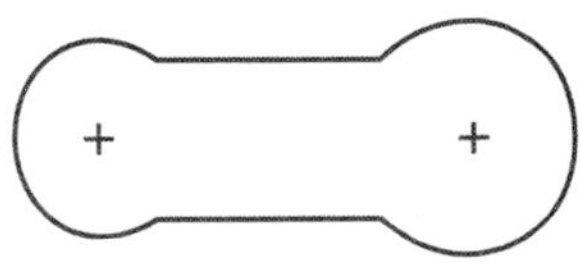

σ_b

$$\Psi_- = \frac{1}{\sqrt{2(1-s)}}(\Psi_A - \Psi_B)$$

σ_a

Let us examine how do Ψ_+ and Ψ_- behave symmetry operations such as E, σ_v, Cϕ (rotation by an angle ϕ) i and C_2.

(a) There is no change in identity:

$$\tilde{E}\Psi_+ = (+1)\Psi_+, \left(\Psi_A + \Psi_B\right) = (+1)\,\Psi_+$$

(b) $\tilde{\sigma}_v\ \Psi_+ = \Psi_A + \Psi_B = (+1)\ \Psi_+$

$\tilde{\sigma}_v\ \Psi_- = \Psi_A - \Psi_B = (+1)\ \Psi_-$

(c) $\tilde{C}_\phi\ \Psi_+ = \Psi_A + \Psi_B = (+1)\ \Psi_+$

$\tilde{C}_\phi\ \Psi_- = \Psi_A - \Psi_B = (+1)\ \Psi_-$

(d) $\tilde{i}\ \Psi_+ = \left(\Psi_A + \Psi_B\right) = (+1)\ \Psi_+$

$\Psi_- = \left(-\Psi_A + \Psi_B\right) = (-1)\left(\Psi_A - \Psi_B\right) = (-1)\ \Psi_-$

(e) $\tilde{C}_2$ (about x or y axis)

$$\tilde{C}_2\Psi_+ = \tilde{C}_2\left(\Psi_A + \Psi_B\right) = \Psi_B + \Psi_A$$

$$= \Psi_A + \Psi_B = (+1)\ \Psi_+$$

$$\tilde{C}_2\Psi_- = \tilde{C}_2\left(\Psi_A - \Psi_B\right) = \left(-\Psi_A + \Psi_B\right)$$

$$= (-1)\left[\Psi_A - \Psi_B\right] = (-1)\ \Psi_-$$

Both Ψ_+ and Ψ_- change phase during symmetry operations :

$$\tilde{R}\Psi = \lambda\Psi\cdot$$

Where λ is the eigen value which turns out to be ± 1.

8.4 BONDING IN WATER

If H–O–H angle is 180° the bonding will be linear and s and p_z will contribute to the σ-bonds and p_x and p_y orbitals to π–bonds. In H_2O the bond angle is 104.5° instead of 90°. As such the combination is less clear. We resort to group theory to identify the symmetry species in C_{2v} point group. The effect of symmetry operation in p_x orbital leads to the following changes:

	E	C_2	σ_{xz}	σ_{yz}	
p_x	1	–1	1	–1	B_1

The effect of symmetry operations on p_y orbital may bring the transformation as:

E	C_2	σ_{xz}	σ_{yz}	
1	–1	–1	1	B_2

$$\tilde{E}(p_y) = (+1)p_y,\ \tilde{C}_2(p_y) = (-1)\ p_y$$

$$\tilde{\sigma}_{xz}(p_y) = (-1)p_y,\ \tilde{\sigma}_{yz}\ p_y = (+1)\ p_y$$

$$\tilde{E}(\tilde{p}_x) = (+1)p_x,\ \tilde{C}_2(p_x) = (-1)\ p_x$$

$$\tilde{\sigma}_{xz}(p_x) = (+1)p_x,\ \tilde{\sigma}_{yz}(p_x) = (-1)\ p_x$$

		E	C_2	σ_{xz}	σ_{yz}	
So	p_x	1	–1	1	–1	B_1

Symmetry species	*Group orbital*	*Atomic oxygen orbital of*
A_1	$\frac{1}{\sqrt{2}}(ISH_A + ISH_B)$	2s, $2p_z$
B_1	none	$2p_x$
B_2	$\frac{1}{\sqrt{2}}(ISH_A - ISH_B)$	$2p_y$

Consider the method of un-shifted vector to find the reducible representations for group orbitals for water:

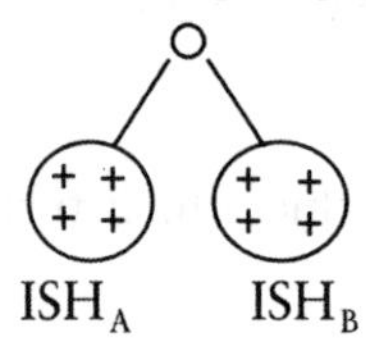

In identity both 1s atomic orbitals are un-shifted:

$$\chi(E) = 2 \times 1 = 2$$

In C_2 both are exchanged their positions:

$$\chi(C_2) = 2 \times 0 = 0$$

In σ_{xz} both are shifted:

$$\chi(\sigma_{xz}) = 2 \times 0 = 0$$

In σ_{yz} both are un-shifted:

$$\chi(\sigma_{yz}) = 2 \times 1 = 2.$$

	E	C_z	σ_{xz}	σ_{yz}
$\Gamma(R)$	2	0	0	2

This reduces to,

$$a_1 = \frac{1}{4}[2\times1\times1+0+0+2\times1\times1]$$

$$= \frac{1}{4}[2+2] = \frac{4}{4} = 1$$

$$a_2 = \frac{1}{4}[2\times1\times1+0+0+2\times(-1)\times1]$$

$$= \frac{1}{4}[2-2] = 0$$

$$b_1 = \frac{1}{4}[2\times1\times1+0+0+2\times(-1)\ 1]$$

$$= \frac{1}{4}[2-2] = 0$$

$$b_2 = \frac{1}{4}[2\times1\times1+0+0+2\times1\times1]$$

$$= \frac{4}{4} = 1$$

$$\Gamma_{(\sigma)} = A_1 + B_2$$

Applying projection operator we have:

$$\tilde{p}^{A_1}\phi_1 \cong 1\times\tilde{E}\ \phi_1 + 1\times\tilde{C}_2\phi_1 + 1\times\tilde{\sigma}_{xz}\phi_1 + 1\times\tilde{\sigma}_{yz}\phi_1$$

$$= \phi_1 + \phi_2 + \phi_2 + \phi_1$$

$$= 2\phi_1 + 2\phi_2$$

$$= 2(\phi_1 + \phi_2)$$

$$\simeq \phi_1 + \phi_2$$

$$N = \frac{1}{\sqrt{2}},\ \frac{1}{\sqrt{2}}(\phi_1 + \phi_2)$$

Group orbital $\Psi_{A_1} = \frac{1}{\sqrt{2}}[\phi_1 + \phi_2]$

The other linear combination based on symmetry operation is given by:

$$\tilde{P}^{B_2}\,\phi_1 \cong 1\times\tilde{E}\,\phi_1 + (-1)\,\tilde{C}_2\,\phi_1 + (-1)\,\tilde{\sigma}_{xz}\,\phi_1 + (1)\,\tilde{\sigma}_{yz}\,\phi_1$$

$$= 1\times\phi_1 - \phi_2 - \phi_2 + \phi_1$$

$$= 2\,(\phi_1 - \phi_2)$$

$$\cong \phi_1 - \phi_2$$

$$N = \frac{1}{\sqrt{2}}, \frac{1}{\sqrt{2}}\,(\phi_1 - \phi_2).$$

Consider combination with A_1 symmetry. There are two such combinations bonding molecular orbital ψ_1 and anti-bonding molecular orbital ψ_6.

$$\psi_1 = a_1 = \lambda_1\,(2s) + \lambda_2\,(2p_z) + \lambda_3\,(ISH_A + ISH_B)$$

$$\psi_6 = a_1^* = \lambda_{10}\,(2s) + \lambda_{11}\,(2p_z) + \lambda_{12}\,(ISH_A + ISH_B)$$

In case of B_2 symmetry species two molecular orbitals are formed as ψ_2 and ψ_5.

$$\psi_2 = b_2 = \lambda_4\,(2p_y) + \lambda_5\,(ISH_A - ISH_B)$$

$$\psi_5 = b_2^* = \lambda_8\,(2p_y) + \lambda_9\,(ISH_A - ISH_B)$$

The case of B_1 symmetry species will lead to non-bonding molecular orbital ψ_3.

$$\Psi_3 = b_1\,(n) = 2\,p_x$$

There is an additional non-bonding molecular orbital at O formed by, $2p_z$ and 2s. This is ψ_4.

$$\Psi_4 = a_1\,(n) = \lambda_6\,(2s) + \lambda_7\,(2p_z)$$

a_1 and b_2 are bonding molecular orbitals corresponding to two O-H bonds, b_1 is non-bonding molecular orbital. All eight electrons are arranged as:

$$(a_1)^2\ (b_2)^2\ [b_1(n)]^2\ [a_1(n)]^2$$

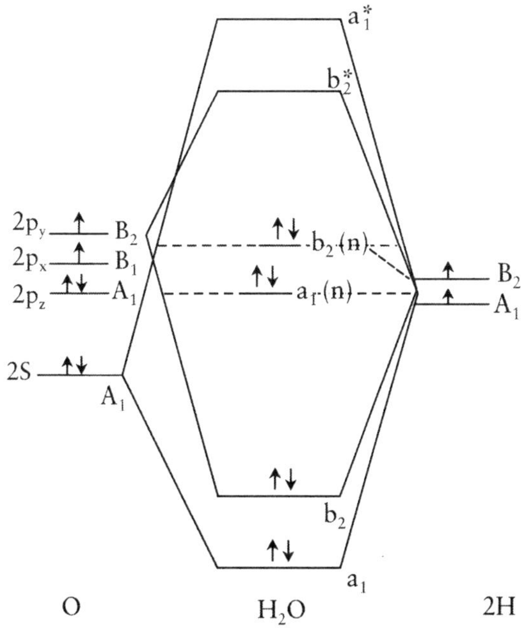

1. Illustration for projection operator:

$$\tilde{P}^{\Gamma_i}\,\phi = \chi_E^{\Gamma_i}\ \tilde{E}\phi + \chi_{c_2}^{\Gamma_i}.\tilde{C}_2\,\phi + \chi_{\sigma xz}^{\Gamma_i}\ \tilde{\sigma}_{xz}\,\phi + \chi_{\sigma yz}^{\Gamma_i}\ \tilde{\sigma}_{yz}\,\phi$$

We neglect the numerical factor $\frac{l^{\Gamma i}}{h}$. When projection operator is applied on a function it projects out the same function or it vanishes. For water, we consider C_{2v} point group.

C_{2v}	E	C_2	σ_{xz}	σ_{yz}	
A_1	1	1	1	1	p_z, $x^2 + y^2$
A_2	1	1	–1	–1	
B_1	1	–1	1	–1	p_x
B_2	1	–1	–1	1	p_y

p_z orbital in oxygen atom belongs to A_1 representation. We can apply Γ_{A_1} on it.

$$\tilde{p}^{A_1}_{\hat{p}_z} \cong \sum_R \chi_R^{A_1} \tilde{R}(p_z)$$

$$= 1\times\chi_E^{A_1}\tilde{E}(\hat{p}_z)\,1\times\chi_{C_2}^{A_1}\tilde{C}_2(\hat{p}_z)$$

$$+ 1\times\chi_{\sigma_{xz}}^{A_1}\tilde{\sigma}_{xz}(\hat{p}_2) + 1\times\chi_{\sigma_{yz}}^{A_1}\tilde{\sigma}_{yz}(p_2)$$

$$= 1\times\tilde{E}(p_z) + 1\times\tilde{C}_2(p_z)1\times\tilde{\sigma}_{xz}(p_z) + 1\times\sigma_{yz}(p_z)$$

$$= p_z + p_z + p_z + p_z$$

$$= 4p_z$$

$$\simeq p_z$$

2. Let us try to see the effect of $\tilde{p}^{A_1}$ on p_x orbital:

$$\tilde{p}^{A_1}_{p_x} \cong \chi_R^{A_1}\left(\tilde{R}_{p_x}\right)$$

$$= \chi_E^{A_1}.\tilde{E}\,p_x + \chi_{C_2}^{A_1}\,p_x +$$

$$\chi_{\sigma_{xz}}^{A_1}\tilde{\sigma}_{xz}\,p_x + \chi_{\sigma_{yz}}^{A_1}\tilde{\sigma}_{yz}\,p_x$$

$$= 1\times\tilde{E}\,p_x + 1\times\tilde{C}_2\,p_x + 1\times\tilde{\sigma}_{xz}\,p_x + 1\times\sigma_{yz}\,p_x$$

$$= \cancel{p_x} - \cancel{p_x} + \cancel{p_x} - \cancel{p_x} = 0$$

3. Let us see the effect of projection operator that corresponds to B_1 symmetry species on p_z and p_x orbitals of oxygen atom:

$$\tilde{p}^{B_1}\,p_z \cong \sum_R \chi_R^{B_1}\left(\tilde{R}\,p_z\right)$$

$$= 1\times\tilde{E}\,p_z + (-1)\,\tilde{C}_2(p_z) + 1\times\tilde{\sigma}_{xz}(p_z) + (-1)\,\tilde{\sigma}_{yz}(p_z)$$

$$= p_z - p_z + p_z - p_z = 0$$

Now, $\tilde{p}^{B_1}_{p_x} \cong \sum_R \chi_R^{B_1}\left(\tilde{R}p_x\right)$

$$= (+1)\,\tilde{E}\,p_x + (-1)\,\tilde{C}_2(p_x) + (+1)\tilde{\sigma}_{xz}(p_x) + (-1)\tilde{\sigma}_{yz}(p_x)$$

$$= p_x - \tilde{C}_2(p_x) + \tilde{\sigma}_{xz}(p_x) - \tilde{\sigma}_{yz}p_x$$

$$= p_x - (-p_x) + p_x - (-p_x)$$

$$= p_x + p_x + p_x + p_x$$

$$= 4p_x \simeq p_x$$

So $\tilde{p}^{B_1}$ projects out p_x itself out of p_x but the project set vanishes in $\tilde{p}^{A_1}$ applied on p_x. For C_{2v} the four projection operators are:

$$\tilde{p}^{A_1} = \tilde{E} + \tilde{C}_2 + \tilde{\sigma}_{xz} + \tilde{\sigma}_{yz}$$

$$\tilde{p}^{B_1} = \tilde{E} - \tilde{C}_2 + \tilde{\sigma}_{xz} - \tilde{\sigma}_{yz}$$

$$\tilde{p}^{A_2} = \tilde{E} + \tilde{C}_2 - \tilde{\sigma}_{xz} - \tilde{\sigma}_{yz}$$

$$\tilde{p}^{B_2} = \tilde{E} - \tilde{C}_2 - \tilde{\sigma}_{xz} + \tilde{\sigma}_{yz}$$

8.5 BONDING IN AMMONIA

Ammonia (C_{3v}) has three H-atoms each with IS atomic orbital. We label the three atoms as H_A, H_B and H_C.

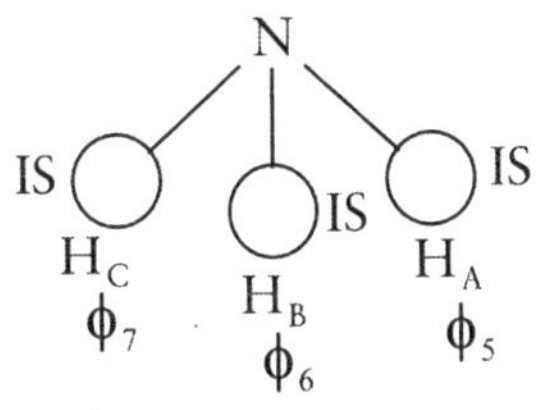

The nitrogen atom has 2s orbibtal as (ϕ_1), $2p_z$ (ϕ_2), $2p_x$ (ϕ_3) and $2p_y$ (ϕ_4) and the three atomic orbitals of H are ϕ_5, ϕ_6 and ϕ_7 respectively:

C_{3v}	E	$2C_3$	$3\sigma_v$		
A_1	1	1	1	z	$z^2, x^2 + y^2$
A_2	1	1	−1	R_z	
E	2	−1	0	x, y	$(xy, x^2 - y^2)$ (xz, yz)

Let us determine irreducible representation for 3H-atoms under C_{3v} point group.

Applying method of un-shifted atoms all three H-atoms are un-shifted in identity $\chi(E) = 3 \times 1 = 3$

All three H-atoms are shifted in C_3:

$$\chi\ (C_3) = 3 \times 0 = 0$$

In either of the σ_v one H-atom is un-shifted while other two atoms are shifted:

$$\chi\ (\sigma_v) = 1 \times 1 = 1$$

	E	$2C_3$	$3\sigma_v$
$\Gamma_R(\sigma)$	3	0	1

From decomposition formula we obtain:

$$a_{A_1} = \frac{1}{6}\left[3\times1\times1+0+3\times1\times1\right] = \frac{6}{6} = 1$$

$$a_{A_2} = \frac{1}{6}\left[3\times1\times1+0+3\times(-1)\times1\right]$$

$$= \frac{3-3}{6} = 0$$

$$A_E = \frac{1}{6}\left[3\times2\times1+0+0\right] = \frac{6}{6} = 1$$

$$\Gamma_R = A_1 + E.$$

In order to get group orbitals we apply projection operator technique. The group orbital of A_1 symmetry is given by:

$$\tilde{p}^{A_1}\,\phi_5 = \frac{1}{6}\left[1\times\tilde{E}\,\phi_5 + 1\times\tilde{C}_3\,\phi_5 + 1\times\tilde{C}_3\phi_5 + \tilde{\sigma}_1\,\phi_5 + \tilde{\sigma}_2\,\phi_5 + \tilde{\sigma}_3\,\phi_5\right]$$

$$= \left[\phi_5 + \phi_6 + \phi_7 + \phi_5 + \phi_7 + \phi_6\right]$$

$$= 2\left(\phi_5 + \phi_6 + \phi_7\right)$$

$$\cong \phi_5 + \phi_6 + \phi_7$$

From the normalization condition:

$$N = \frac{1}{\sqrt{3}}$$

$$\Psi_{A_1} = \frac{1}{\sqrt{3}}\left(\phi_5 + \phi_6 + \phi_7\right)$$

The group orbitals for E symmetry are obtained as:

$$\tilde{p}^E \phi_5 \cong \frac{1}{6}\left[2\times\tilde{E}\phi_5 + (-1)\,\tilde{C}_3\,\phi_5 + (-1)\,\tilde{C}_3\,\phi_5 + 0\times\tilde{\sigma}_1\,\phi_5 + 0\times\tilde{\sigma}_2\,\phi_5 + (0)\,\tilde{\sigma}_3\,\phi_3\right]$$

$$\cong\left[2\phi_5 - \phi_6 - \phi_7 + 0\right]$$

$$= 2\phi_5 - \phi_6 - \phi_7$$

Normalizing factor will be:

$$\left[2^2 + 1^2 + 1^2\right]^{-1/2} = \frac{1}{\sqrt{6}}$$

$$\psi_2 = \psi_E = \frac{1}{\sqrt{6}}\left(2\phi_5 - \phi_6 - \phi_7\right)$$

Consider second function of E symmetry:

$$\tilde{p}^E \phi_6 \cong \frac{1}{6}\left[2\times\phi_6 - 1\times\left(\phi_7 + \phi_5\right) + 0\right]$$

$$= 2\phi_6 - \phi_5 - \phi_7$$

$$\tilde{p}^E \phi_7 \cong \frac{1}{6}\left[2\phi_7 + (-1)\{\phi_5 + \phi_6\}\right]$$

$$= \left[2\phi_7 - \phi_5 - \phi_6\right]$$

Their linear combination on subtraction:

$$\begin{array}{l} 2\phi_6 - \phi_5 - \phi_7 \\ 2\phi_7 - \phi_5 - \phi_6 \\ - \quad\;\; + \quad\;\; + \\ \hline 3\,(\phi_6 - \phi_7) = \phi_6 - \phi_7 \end{array}$$

Normalizing factor is, $(1^2 + 1^2)^{-½} = \frac{1}{\sqrt{2}}$

$$\psi_3 = \psi_E = \frac{1}{\sqrt{2}}\left(\phi_6 - \phi_7\right)$$

Thus SALCs for 1S hydrogen atomic orbitals are:

$$\psi_1^E = \frac{1}{\sqrt{3}}(\phi_5 + \phi_6 + \phi_7)$$

$$\psi_2^E = \frac{1}{\sqrt{6}}(2\phi_5 - \phi_6 - \phi_7)$$

$$\psi_3^E = \frac{1}{\sqrt{2}}(\phi_6 - \phi_7)$$

They now interact with N orbitals of the same symmetry.

N valence shells are $2s^2 2p^3$. From C_{3v} character Table we have:

$$\phi_1 = 2s \qquad A_1$$

$$\phi_2 = 2p_z \qquad A_1$$

$$\left.\begin{array}{l}\phi_3 = 2p_x \\ \phi_4 = 2p_y\end{array}\right\} \qquad E$$

Inspection shows that ϕ_3 and ϕ_4 form a doubly degenerate basis set and they must belong to E:

Symmetry of N-atom orbital	*Group orbitals from the combination of IsH*
A_1 2s (ϕ_1)	$\frac{1}{\sqrt{3}}(\phi_5 + \phi_6 + \phi_7)$
A_1 $2p_z$ (ϕ_2)	$\frac{1}{\sqrt{6}}(2\phi_5 - \phi_6 - \phi_7)$
E $\left.\begin{array}{l}2p_x (\phi_3) \\ 2p_y (\phi_4)\end{array}\right\}$	$\frac{1}{\sqrt{2}}(\phi_6 - \phi_7)$

The A_1 set gives a_1, a_1^* and $a_1(n)$ molecular orbitals. The doubly degenerate E set gives e and e^*. There are five molecular orbitals in all.

A qualitative m.o. diagram for NH_3 is shown below:

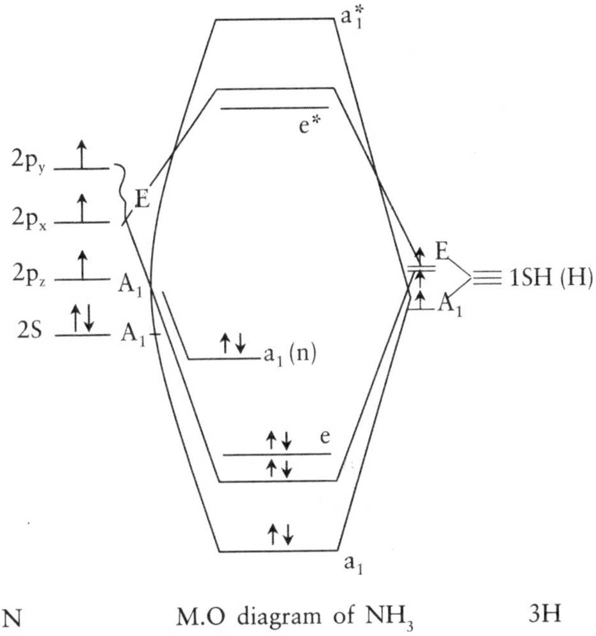

M.O diagram of NH_3

8.6 M,O. DIAGRAM AND ELECTRONIC TRANSITIONS IN FORMALDEHYDE

It has the structure as follows:

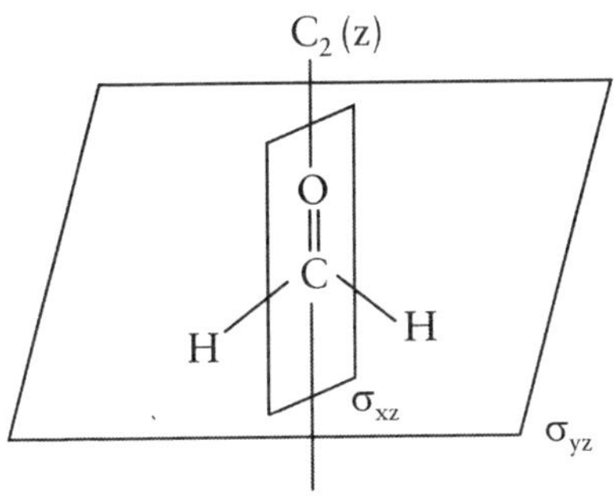

Carbon atom is sp^2 hybridized. It has π-electron in p_x orbital of carbon atom. There are three σ-bonds, two of them with two H-atoms through sp^2 – s overlap and the third σ-bond with the oxygen atom with sp^2–p_z overlap. The carbonyl carbon atom consists of a π-bond in addition to σ-bond and there are two lone pairs of electrons at oxygen atom. The π bonding results through $p_x - p_x$ overlap.

It bears the electronic configuration as:

$$(\sigma CO)^2 (\pi CO)^2 (ns)^2 (np)^2$$

The qualitative molecular orbital diagram may be shown as:

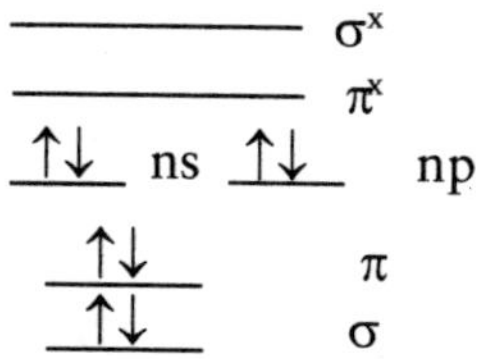

A high energy is involved in σ–σ^* transition and we ignore $(\sigma\ CO)^2$ configuration any more.

The excited state configurations are:

$$(\pi\ CO)^2\ (ns)^2\ (np)^1\ (\pi^*)^1 \qquad n \rightarrow \pi^*$$

$$(\pi\ CO)^1\ (ns)^2\ (np)^2\ (\pi^*)^1 \qquad \pi - \pi^*$$

There are E, C_2, σ_{xz} and σ_{yz} operations with C_{2v} point group for the molecule σ_{yz} plane is selected containing all the four atoms in formaldehyde. We carry out the symmetry operations E, C_2, σ_{xz}, σ_{yz} on σ σ*, π, π* and n-molecular orbitals. The effect on π-orbital on the symetry operations may be described below:

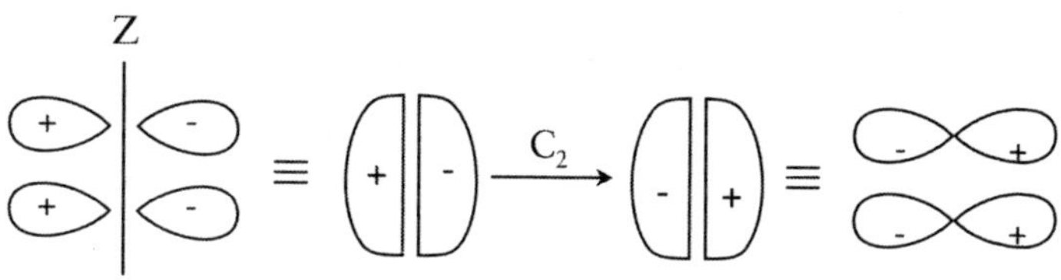

In identity the π-molecular orbital is same irrespective of effect E(π) = (+1) π whereas in C_2 operation it changes sign $C_2\ (\pi) = (-1)\pi$:

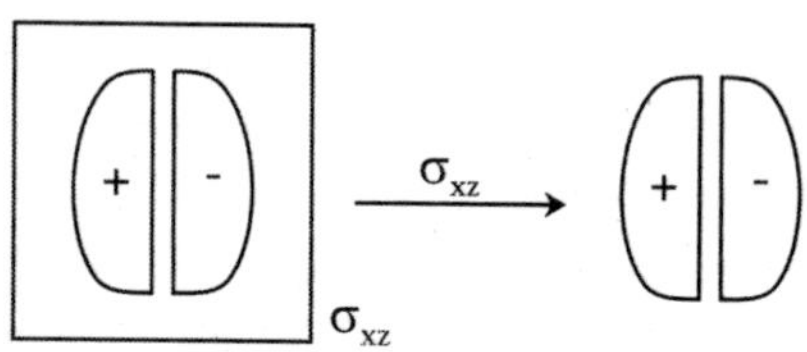

Further since p_x orbital is involved in bonding there is no change in sign on reflection in σ_{xz}:

$$\sigma_{xz}\ (\pi) = (+1)\ \pi$$

Since p_x is perpendicular to y axis so does in σ_{yz} plane. As a result there appears reversion of sign in σ_{yz} plane on π orbital:

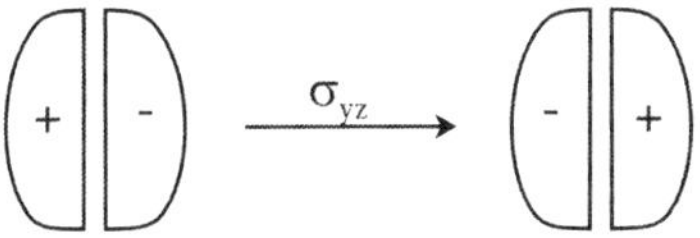

$$\sigma_{yz}\ (\pi) = (-1)\ \pi$$

The effect of symmetry on π-orbital may be shown as:

E	C_2	σ_{xz}	σ_{yz}
1	–1	1	–1

The result is identical to B_1 symmetry species.

Similarly we apply symmetry operations on π^* orbital:

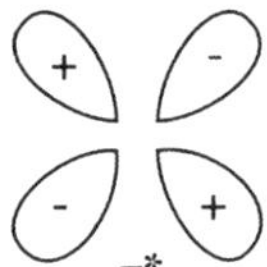

π^*

$$E\ (\pi^*) = (+1)\ \pi^*$$
$$C_2\ (\pi^*) = (-1)\ \pi^*$$
$$\sigma_{xz}\ (\pi^*) = (+1)\ \pi^*$$
$$\sigma_{yz}\ (\pi^*) = (-1)\ \pi^*$$

It has character 1 –1 1 –1 and it belongs to B_1 symmetry species again.

Now consider the effect of symmetry operations on σ and σ^*:

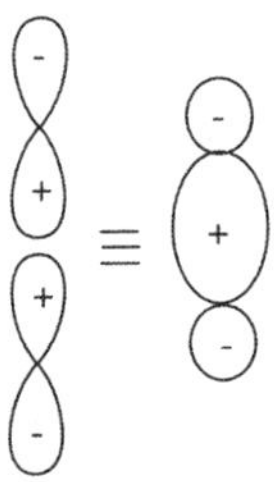

$$E\ (\sigma) = (+1)\ \sigma$$
$$C_2\ (\sigma) = (+1)\ \sigma$$
$$\sigma_{xz}\ (\sigma) = (+1)\ \sigma$$
$$\sigma_{yz}\ (\sigma) = (+1)\ \sigma$$

It has 1 1 1 1 belonging to A_1 representation.

Consider symmetry properties of σ^* molecular orbital:

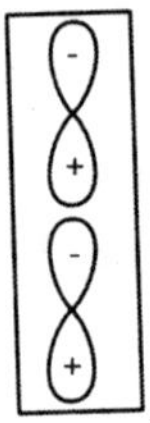

σ_{xz}

$$\sigma_{xz}\ (\sigma^*) = (+1)\ \sigma^*$$

It so happens in σ_{yz} it is also $\sigma_{yz}\ (\sigma^*) = (+1)\sigma^*$.

It belongs to A_1 symmetry species.

Now consider effect of symmetry on ns and np orbitals.

ns orbital has the following transformation:

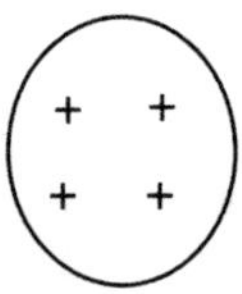

$$\tilde{E}\ (ns) = (+1) ns$$
$$\tilde{C}_2\ (ns) = (+1)\ ns$$
$$\tilde{\sigma}_{xz}\ (ns) = (+1)\ ns$$
$$\sigma_{yz}\ (ns) = (+1)\ ns$$

1, 1, 1, 1 – A_1 representation.

Now further consider the effect of symmetry operations on (np) orbital:

p_y orbital

$$\tilde{E}\ (np) = (+1)\ np$$
$$\tilde{C}_2\ (np) = (-)\ np$$
$$\tilde{\sigma}_{xz}\ (np) = (-1)\ np$$
$$\tilde{\sigma}_{yz}\ (np) = (+1)\ np$$

p_y orbital is np.

Characters are 1, –1, –1, 1 and hence transforms as B_2.

We designate the molecular orbitals in terms of symmetry species using small letters:

ns	np	π	π^*	σ	σ^*
a_1	b_2	b_1	b_1	a_1	a_1

Molecular states are designated by capital letters.

The ground state of formaldehyde is determined by:

$$(\sigma CO)^2(\pi CO)^2 \ (ns)^2 \ (np)^2$$

$$a_1 \times a_1 \quad b_1 \times b_1 \quad a_1 \times a_1 \quad b_2 \times b_2$$

The direct product is shown as:

$$= (a_1 \times a_1) \times (b_1 \times b_1) \times (a_1 \times a_1) \times (b_2 \times b_2)$$

$$= a_1 \times a_1 \times a_1 \times a_1$$

$$= a_1 \times a_1 = a_1 = A_1.$$

The ground state is A_1. Consider the case of $n \rightarrow \pi^*$ transition which takes place from np level to π^* level np is b_2 and π^* is b_1 so it is represented as $b_2 \rightarrow b_1$ transition.

Its direct prduct is given by:

$b_2 \times b_1$	E	C_2	σ_{xz}	σy_2
	1×1	-1×-1	-1×1	1×-1
	1	1	−1	−1

which belongs to A_2. It describes $A_1 \rightarrow A_2$.

The electronic configuration for $np \rightarrow \pi^*$ transition is

$$a_1^2 \ b_1^2 \ b_2^1 \ b_1^1$$

which occurs from $A_1 \rightarrow A_2$. Transition momentum integral is given by:

$$M = \int \Psi_i \cdot \mu \psi_f \, d\tau$$

$$\begin{pmatrix} M_x \\ M_y \\ M_z \end{pmatrix} = \int \psi_i \begin{pmatrix} \mu_x \\ \mu_y \\ \mu_z \end{pmatrix} \Psi_f \, d\tau$$

If any one of the three integrals is non-zero transition is said to be allowed. The direct product is obtained between

$\Psi_i \times \Psi_f$ followed by direct product with the component of dipolemoment:

$$(\Psi_i \times \psi_f) \times \mu_i$$

$$\int(\Gamma_i \times \Gamma_f) \times \Gamma_{T_x}$$

$$= \int A_1 \times A_2 \times \Gamma_{T_x} \qquad \Gamma_{T_x} = B_1 \text{ From C.T.}$$

$$= \int A_2 \times B_1$$

The direct product is finalised as:

	$A_2 \times B_1$	1×1	1×-1	-1×1	-1×-1 where
A_2	1 1 –1 –1	1	–1	–1	1 = B_2
B_1	1 –1 1 –1				

$$M_y = \int \psi_i \; \mu_y \; \Psi_f \; d\tau \qquad \mu_y \text{ or } \Gamma_y \text{ is } B_2$$

$$= \int (\Gamma_i \times \Gamma_f) \times \Gamma_y$$

$$= \int (A_1 \times A_2) \times B_2$$

$A_2 \times B_2 = B_1$ as follows:

A_2	1	1	–1	–1
B_2	1	–1	–1	1
$A_2 \times B_2$	1×1	1×-1	-1×-1	-1×1
	1	–1	1	–1 = B_1

$$M_z = \int \Psi_i \times \psi_f \times \Gamma_z \qquad T_z \text{ or } \Gamma_z = \text{is } A_1$$

$$= \int (\Gamma_i \times \Gamma_f) \times \Gamma_z$$

$$= \int A_1 \times A_2 \times A_1$$

$$= \int A_2 \times A_1$$

$$= \int A_2$$

In all three cases the transition moment components are zero because of odd symmetry and so the transition $n \rightarrow \pi^*$ is forbidden. Cases of $n \rightarrow \sigma^*$, $\pi \rightarrow \pi^*$ and $\pi - \sigma^*$ transitions.

For the case of $n \rightarrow \sigma^*$ the configuration is:

$$(ns)^2 \quad (np)^1 \quad (\pi\ CO)^2 \quad (\sigma^*)^1$$

$$(a_1)^2 \quad (b_2)^1 \quad (b_1)^2 \quad (a_1)^1$$

$$a_1 \times a_1 \times b_2 \times b_1 \times b_1 \times a_1$$

$$= a_1 \times b_2 \times \underbrace{b_1 \times b_1}_{a_1} \times a_1$$

$$= b_2 \times a_1 \times a_1$$

$$= b_2 \times a_1 = b_2$$

$$\Psi_i = A_1, \Psi_f = B_2$$

$$M_x = \int(\Gamma_i \times \Gamma_f) \times \Gamma_x$$

$$M_y = \int(\Gamma_i \times \Gamma_f) \times \Gamma_y$$

$$M_z = \int(\Gamma_i \times \Gamma_f) \times \Gamma_z$$

For, $M_x = \int(A_1 \times B_2) \times B_1$ $\qquad \Gamma_x = B_1$

$= \int B_2 \times B_1$ $\qquad \Gamma_y = B_2$

$= \int A_2$ $\qquad \Gamma_z = A_1$

forbidden

$$M_y = \int(A_1 \times B_2) \times B_2$$

$$= \int B_2 \times B_2$$

$= \int A_1$ allowed

$$M_z = \int (A_1 \times B_2) \times A_1$$

$$= \int B_2 \text{ forbidden}$$

For $\pi - \pi^*$ transition the distribution will be:

$$a_1^2\ b_1^1\ b_2^2\ b_1^1.$$

Its direct product is

$$= a_1 \times a_1 \times b_1 \times b_2 \times b_2 \times b_1$$
$$= a_1 \times b_1 \times a_1 \times b_1$$
$$= b_1 \times b_1$$
$$\equiv A_1$$

$$\Gamma_i = A_1,\ \Gamma_f = A_1,\ \Gamma_x = B_1$$

$$M_x = \int (A_1 \times A_1) \times B_2 = \int A_1 \times B_1 = \int B_1 \text{ forbidden}$$

$$M_y = \int (A_1 \times A_1) \times B_2$$

$$= \int A_1 \times B_2 = B_2 \quad \text{forbidden}$$

$$M_z = \int (A_1 \times A_1) \times A_1$$

$$= \int A_1 \quad \text{allowed.}$$

For, π — σ^* transition:

$$(a_1)^2\ (b_1)^1\ (b_2)^2\ (a_1)^2$$

$$\frac{a_1 \times a_1}{a_1} x b_1 \times \frac{b_2 \times b_2}{a_1} \times a_1$$

$$a_1 \times b_1 \times a_1 \times a_1$$
$$= b_1 \times a_1$$

$$= b_1 \equiv B_1$$

$\Psi_i = A_1 = \Gamma_i$ $\qquad\qquad$ $\mu_x = B_1$

$\Psi_f = B_1 = \Gamma_f$ $\qquad\qquad$ $\mu_y = B_2$

$\mu_z = A_1$

$$M_x = \int (A_1 \times B_1) \times B_1$$

$$= \int B_1 \times B_1 = \int A_1 \quad \text{allowed}$$

$$M_y = \int (A_1 \times B_1) \times B_2$$

$$= \int B_2 \times B_1 = \int A_2 \quad \text{forbidden}$$

$$M_z = \int (A_1 \times B_1) \times A_1$$

$$= \int B_1 \times A_1$$

$$= \int B_1 \quad \text{forbidden.}$$

8.7 σ AND π BONDING IN NO_2^- ION.

The nitrogen atom with $-2s^2\ 2p_x^1\ 2p_y^1$ and $2p_z^1$ configuration is going to have sp^2 hybridization. There are two oxygen atoms one bearing a negative charge and hence an additional electron is present at the centre:

$$-2s^2\ 2p_x^2\ 2p_y^2\ 2p_z^1\ (0^-)$$

$$-2s^2\ 2p_x^1\ 2p_y^2\ 2p_z^1\ (0)$$

The V.B. description involves one N = 0 double bond:

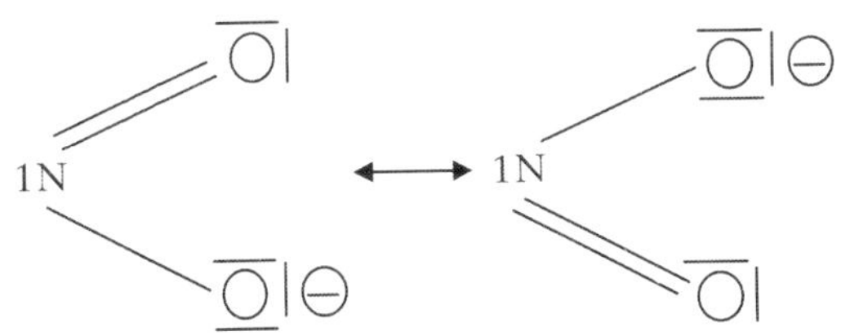

In M.O. description there are two σ-bonds through overlapping between sp^2 hybridized orbitals and p_z orbital. The NO_2^- has C_{2v} point group. There is a case of three centred–bonding in NO_2^- ion. Now p_x orbitals are available at

N and two oxygen centres which can interact to form bonding, anti-bonding and one more combination of non-bonding molecular orbital.

Group theoretical treatment of π-bonding:

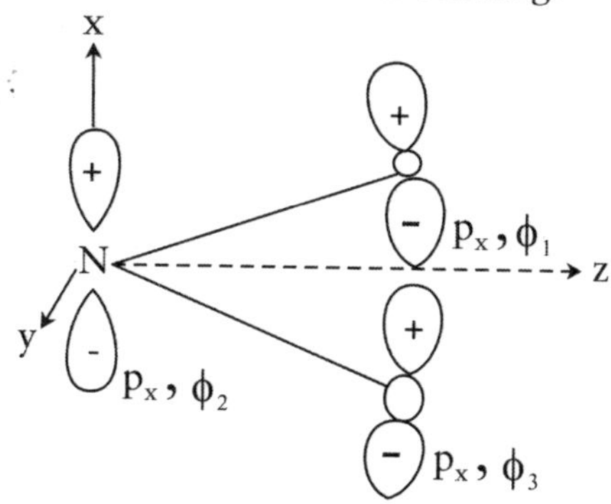

We use oxygen (pπ) orbitals ϕ_1 & ϕ_3 to generate reducible representation. In identity, both ϕ_1 & ϕ_3 are un-shifted:

$$\chi(E) = 2 \times 1 = 2$$

In C_2 both ϕ_1 and ϕ_3 are shifted.

There is no contribution $\chi\ (C_2) = 2 \times 0 = 0$.

In σ_{xz} both are shifted:

$$\chi(\sigma_{xz}) = 2 \times 0 = 0$$

In σ_{xz} both ϕ_1 and ϕ_3 are un-shifted:

$$\chi(\sigma_{yz}) = 2 \times (-1) = -2$$

but the sign of the lobe is reversed so it contributes −1 to the character:

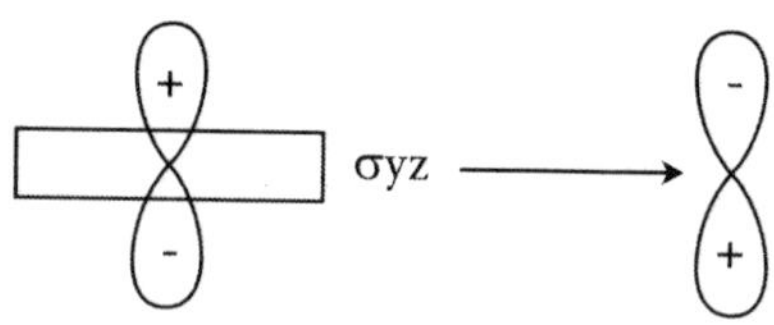

	E	C_2	σ_{xz}	σ_{yz}
Γ(π)	2	0	0	−2

$$a_1 = \frac{1}{4}[2 \times 1 \times 1 + 0 + 0 - 2 \times 1 \times 1]$$

$$= \left[\frac{2-2}{4}\right] = \frac{0}{4} = 0$$

$$a_2 = \frac{1}{4}\left[2\times1\times1+0+0-2\times1\times-1\right]$$

$$= \frac{1}{4}\left[2+2\right] = \frac{4}{4} = 1$$

$$b_1 = \frac{1}{4}\left[2\times1\times1+0+0+(-2)\,(-1)\times1\right]$$

$$= \frac{1}{4}\left[2+2\right] = \frac{4}{4} = 1$$

$$\Gamma_\pi = a_2 + b_1$$

We apply projection operator:

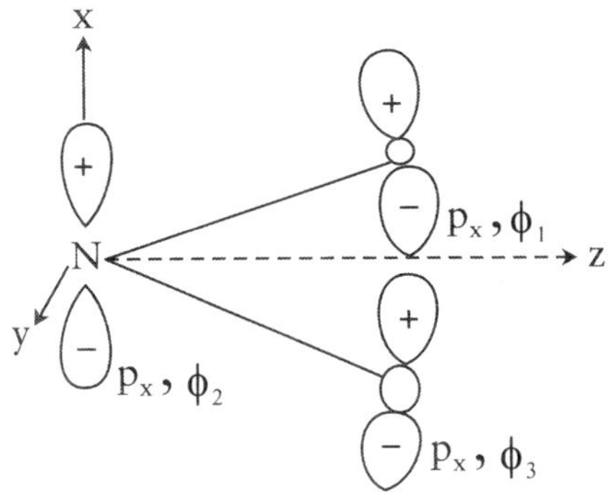

$$\tilde{p}A_2\ \phi_1 \cong 1\times\tilde{E}\phi_1 + 1\times\tilde{C}_2\,\phi_1 - 1\times\tilde{\sigma}_{xz}\,\phi_1 - 1\times\tilde{\sigma}_{yz}\phi_1$$

$$= \phi_1 + 1(-)\,\phi_3 - (+1)\,\phi_3 - (-1)\,\phi_1$$

$$= 2\phi_1 - 2\phi_3 \simeq \phi_1 - \phi_3$$

$$\Psi A_2 = \frac{1}{\sqrt{2}}\left(\phi_1 - \phi_3\right)$$

$$\tilde{p}B_2\ \phi_1 \cong 1\times\tilde{E}\phi_1 - 1\times\tilde{C}_2\,\phi_1 - 1\times\tilde{\sigma}_{xz}\,\phi_1 + 1\times\tilde{\sigma}_{yz}\phi_1$$

$$= \phi_1 - (-1)\,\phi_3 - 1\times(+1)\,\phi_3 + 1\times(-1)\,\phi_1$$

$$= \phi_1 + \phi_3 - \phi_3 - \phi_1 = 0$$

$$\tilde{p}B_1\ \phi_1 \cong 1\times\tilde{E}\phi_1 - 1\times\tilde{C}_2\,\phi_1 + 1\times\tilde{\sigma}_{xz}\,\phi_1 - 1\times\tilde{\sigma}_{yz}\phi_1$$

$$= \phi_1 - (-\phi_3) + \phi_3 - (-\phi_1)$$

$$= \phi_1 + \phi_3 + \phi_3 + \phi_1$$
$$= 2(\phi_1 + \phi_3)$$
$$= \phi_1 + \phi_3$$
$$\Psi_{B_1} = \frac{1}{\sqrt{2}}(\phi_1 + \phi_3)$$
$$\tilde{p}_{\phi_2}^{B_1} \cong 1 \times \tilde{E}\ \phi_2 - 1 \times C_2\ \phi_2 + 1 \times \tilde{\sigma}_{xz}\ \phi_2 - 1 \times \sigma_{yz}\ \phi_2$$
$$= \phi_2 - 1 \times (-1)\ \phi_2 + 1 \times \phi_2 - \times(-)\phi_2$$
$$= \phi_2 + \phi_2 + \phi_2 + \phi_2$$
$$= 4\ \phi_2 \simeq \phi_2$$

There are two B_1 combinations both bonding and non-bonding. The four electrons will be accommodated both in non-bonding and bonding molecular orbitals:

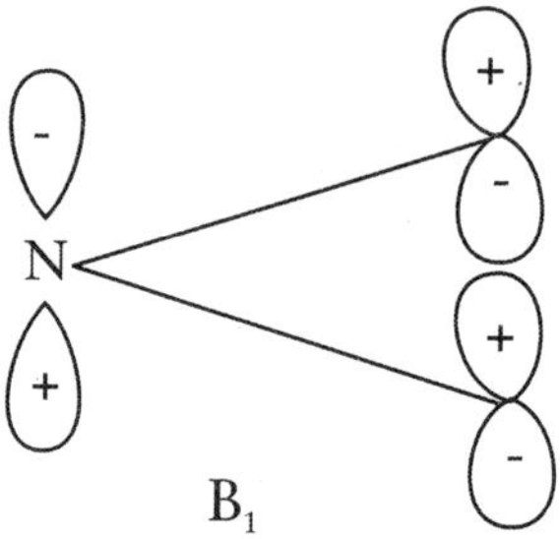

B_1

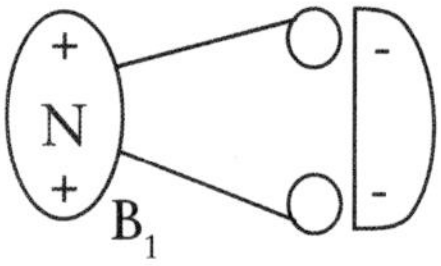

B_1

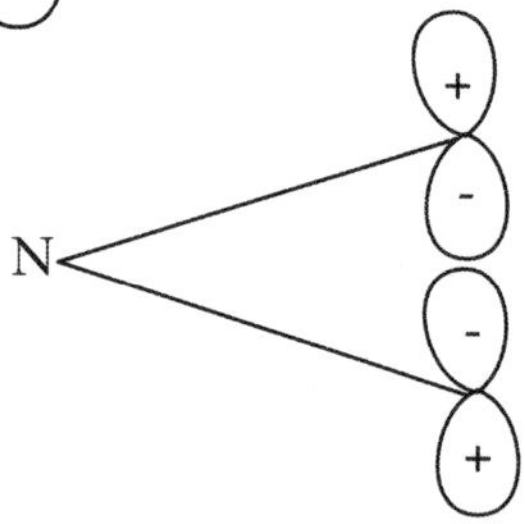

A_2 (non)

Two wave functions are obtained from B_1 symmetry species as:

$$\psi_1 = a\phi_1 + b\phi_2 + a\phi_3$$
$$\psi_2 = a'\phi_1 - b'\phi_2 + a'\phi_3$$

The following diagram is proposed for three centre π-bounding:

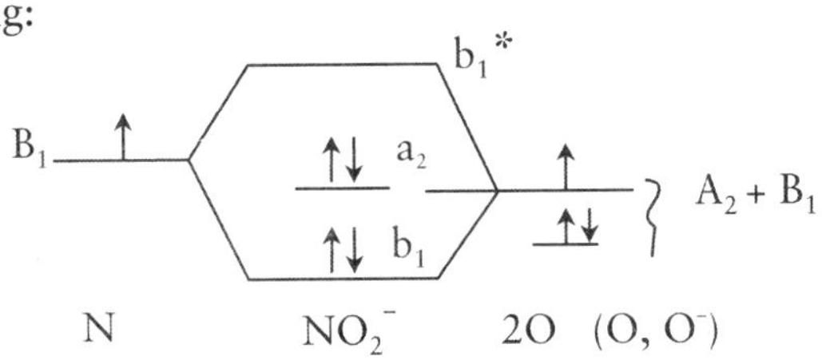

M.O. energy level diagram for NO_2^-

8.8 BONDING IN ELECTRON DEFICIENT MOLECULE, B_2H_6

It has eight atoms and we expect at least 7 bonds and it requires $7 \times 2 = 14$ electros for normal covalent bonds. Instead the molecule contains $3 \times 2 + 1 \times 6 = 6 + 6 = 12$ electrons. Hence the molecule is electron deficient. It has a planar B_2 H_4. To this plane there is additional xz plane perpendicular to it and two bridging H-atoms lie in xz plane. Eight electrons are involved in four terminal bonds so four electrons are left with the bridging bonds. y-axis is upward from the plane of the paper:

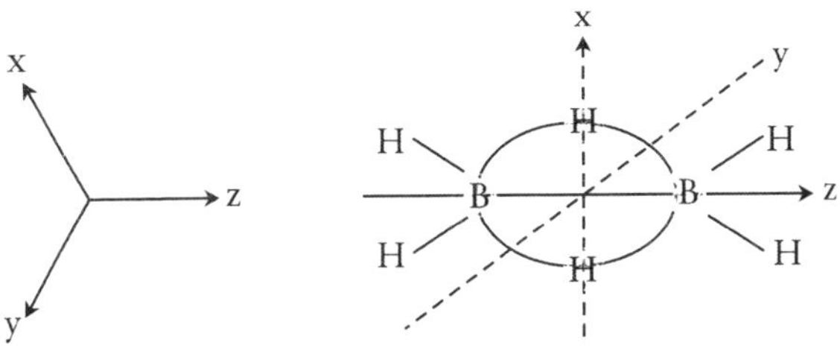

Each BH_2 unit is sp^3 hybridized two of sp^3 are used to account for terminal B-H bonds. The bridging H-atoms lie on x-axis perpendicular to yz plane. The line linking the two B centres is unique axis z-axis. There are three C_2 axes C_2 (z), C_2 (y) and C_2 (x). It has inversion centre i. It has horizontal plane σ_h, (σxy) and two vertical planes σ_{xz} and σ_{yz}. This makes the group consting of eight members:

$$E\ C_2(z)\ C_2(y)\ C_2(x)\ i\ \sigma_h\ \sigma_{yz}\ \sigma_{xz}.$$

The point group notation may be assigned as follows:

$$C_2 + 2C_2 \perp^r \text{ to the principal axis} \rightarrow D_2$$

$$D_2 + \sigma_h \rightarrow D_{2h}$$

There are two bridge bonds which involve two sp^3 hybrids from each B centre and two orbitals of H-atoms. The bridge bonds are considered in this case through the method of the un-shifted vectors:

D_{2h}	E	$C_2(z)$	$C_2(y)$	$C_2(x)$	i	σ_h	σ_{yz}	σ_{xz}
four sp^3	4	0	0	0	0	0	0	4
two IS of H-atoms	2	0	0	2	0	2	0	2

In identity all four sp^3 are un-shifted χ (E) = 1 × 4 = 4.

In C_2 operation all are shifted:

$$\chi\left(C_2^{(z)}\right) = 0, \qquad \chi\left(C_2^{(x)}\right) = 0$$

$$\chi\left(C_2^{(y)}\right) = 0$$

In inversion the vectors are shifted χ (i) = 0.

σ_{xy} is a vertical because y is perpendicular to z-axis all are shifted χ $(\sigma_{xy}) = 0$.

In σ_{yz} all are shifted:

$$\chi\,(\sigma_{yz}) = 0$$

In σ_{xz} all the four sp^3 are un-shifted because they lie in the xz plane:

$$\chi\,(\sigma_{xz}) = 1 \times 4 = 4.$$

For bridging hydrogens the 1s orbitals lie on x-axis both are un-shifted in identity:

$$\chi\,(E) = 1 \times 2 = 2.$$

Similarly, C_2 (z) = 0, C_2 (y) = 0

but in C_2 (x) both are un-shifted χ (C_2 (x)) = 1 × 2 = 2.

The 1s orbitals remain un-shifted in xy and xz planes but shifted in yz plane:

$$\chi\,(\sigma_{xy}) = 1 \times 2 = 2$$

$$\chi\,(\sigma_{xz}) = 1 \times 2 = 2$$

$$\chi\,(\sigma_{yz}) = 0$$

D_{2h}	E	$C_2(z)$	$C_2(y)$	$C_2(x)$	i	σ_{xy}	σ_{xz}	σ_{xz}
Ag	1	1	1	1	1	1	1	1
B_1g	1	1	–1	–1	1	1	–1	–1
B_2g	1	–1	1	–1	1	–1	–1	1
B_3g	1	–1	–1	1	1	–1	–1	1
A_u	1	1	1	1	–1	–1	–1	–1
B_{1u}	1	–1	1	–1	–1	1	1	1
B_{3u}	1	–1	–1	1	–1	1	–1	1

$$a_{A_g} = \frac{1}{8}\left[4\times1\times1+0+0+0+0+0+0+4\times1\times1\right]$$

$$= \frac{1}{8}\left[4+4\right] = \frac{8}{8} = 1$$

$$a_{B_{2g}} = \frac{1}{8}\left[4\times1\times1+0+0+0+0+0+0+4\times1\times1\right]$$

$$= \frac{1}{8}\left[2+2+2+2\right] = \frac{8}{8} = 1$$

$$a_{B_{1u}} = \frac{1}{8}\left[4\times1\times1+0+0+0+0+0+0+4\times1\times1\right]$$

$$= \frac{1}{8}\left[4+4\right] = \frac{8}{8} = 1$$

$$a_{B_{3u}} = \frac{1}{8}\left[4\times1\times1+0+0+0+0+0+0+4\times1\times1\right]$$

$$= \frac{1}{8}\left[4+4\right] = \frac{8}{8} = 1$$

$\Gamma_{B,\,B}$ = Ag + B_{2g} + B_{1u} + B_{3u}

For decomposition of ΓH.H. we have:

$$a_{A_g} = \frac{1}{8}\left[2\times1\times1+0+0+2\times1\times1+0+2\times1\times1+0+2\times1\times1\right]$$

$$= \frac{1}{8}\left[2+2+2+2\right] = \frac{8}{8} = 1$$

$$a_{B_{3u}} = \frac{1}{8}[2\times1\times1+0+0+2\times1\times1+0+0\times2\times1\times1+0+2\times1\times1]$$

$$= \frac{1}{8}[2+2+2+2] = \frac{8}{8} = 1$$

$\Gamma_{H,H} = Ag + B_{3u}$

We apply rotational group D_2 to obtain SALCs by projection operators:

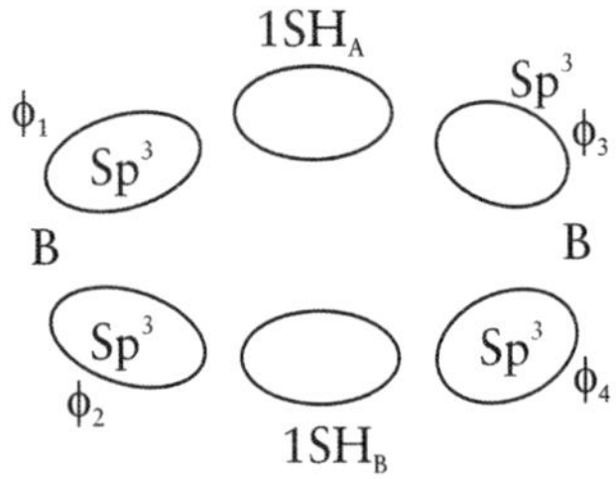

D_2	E	C_2 (z)	C_2 (y)	C_2 (x)
A	1	1	1	1
B_1	1	1	–1	–1
B_2	1	–1	1	–1
B_3	1	–1	–1	1

$$\tilde{p}^A_{\phi_1} = \chi_A \tilde{E}\phi_1 + \chi_A^{C_2}\ \tilde{C}_2\ (z)\ \phi_1 + \chi_A^{C_2}\ \tilde{C}_2\,(y)\phi_1 + \chi_A^{C_2}\ \tilde{C}_2\,(x)\phi_1$$

$$= 1\ .\ \tilde{E}\,\phi_1 + 1.\tilde{C}_2\,(z)\ \phi_1 + 1\ .\ \tilde{C}_2\,(y)\ \phi_1 + 1\ .\ \tilde{C}_2\ (x)\ \phi_1$$

$$= \phi_1 + \phi_2 + \phi_4 + \phi_3$$

$$= \phi_1 + \phi_2 + \phi_3 + \phi_4$$

$$N = \frac{1}{\sqrt{1+1+1+1}} = \frac{1}{\sqrt{4}} = \frac{1}{2}$$

$$\Psi_{Ag} = \Psi_A = \frac{1}{2}(\phi_1 + \phi_2 + \phi_3 + \phi_4)$$

$$\tilde{p}^{B_2}\ \phi_1 \cong \chi^E_{B_2}\ \tilde{E}\ \phi_1 + \chi_{B_2}^{C_2^{(z)}}\ C_2(z)\phi_1 + \chi_{B_2}^{C_2(y)}.C_2(y)\ \phi_1 + \chi_{B_2}^{C_2(x)}.\tilde{C}_2(x)\phi_1$$

$$= 1 \,.\, \tilde{E}\phi_1 + (-)\,\tilde{C}_2(z)\phi_1 + (1)\tilde{C}_2(y)\,\phi_1 + (-1)\,C_2\,(x)\,\phi_1$$

$$= \phi_1 - \phi_2 - \phi_3 + \phi_4$$

$$\psi_{B_{2g}} = \Psi_{B_2} = \frac{1}{2}\left(\phi_1 - \phi_2 - \phi_3 + \phi_4\right)$$

$$\tilde{p}^{B_3}\,\phi_1 \cong \chi^{E}_{B_3}\,\tilde{E}\phi_1 + \chi^{C_2(z)}_{B_3}\,\tilde{C}_2(z)\,\phi_1$$

$$+\chi^{C_2(y)}_{B_3}.\tilde{C}_2\,(y)\phi_1 + \chi^{C_2(x)}_{B_3}\,\tilde{C}_2(x)\phi_1$$

$$= 1.\tilde{E}\phi_1 - \tilde{C}_2(C_2)\phi_1 - \tilde{C}_2(y)\,\phi_1 + \tilde{C}_2\,(x)\,\phi_1$$

$$= \phi_1 + \phi_2 - \phi_4 - \phi_3$$

$$= \phi_1 + \phi_2 - \phi_3 - \phi_4$$

$$\psi_{B_{3u}} = \psi_{B_3} = \frac{1}{2}\left[\phi_1 - \phi_2 + \phi_3 - \phi_4\right]$$

$$\tilde{p}^{B_1}\phi_1 \cong \chi^{E}_{B_1}.\tilde{E}\phi_1 + \chi^{C_2)z)}_{B_1}\tilde{C}_2\,(z)\,\phi_1 + \chi^{C_2(y)}_{B_1}\,\tilde{C}_2(y)\phi_1 + \chi^{C_2(x)}_{B_1}C_2(x)\phi_1$$

$$= \tilde{E}\phi_1 + \tilde{C}_2\,(z)\,\phi_1 - \tilde{C}_2(y)\,\phi_1 - \tilde{C}_2\,(x)\,\phi_1$$

$$= \phi_1 + \phi_2 - \phi_4 - \phi_3$$

$$= \phi_1 + \phi_2 - \phi_3 - \phi_4$$

$$\psi_{B_{1u}} = \psi_{B_1} = \frac{1}{2}\left(\phi_1 + \phi_2 - \phi_3 - \phi_4\right)$$

Formation of SALCS for bridging 1sH orbitals:

$$\tilde{p}^{A}\,(1sH_A) = \chi^{E}_{A}\,\tilde{E}(1sH_A) + \chi^{C_2(z)}_{A}\,\tilde{C}_2(z)\,1sH_A$$

$$+\chi^{C_2(y)}_{A}\,\tilde{C}_2(y)\,1sH_A + \chi^{C_2(x)}_{A}\,\tilde{C}_2\,(x)1sH_A$$

$$= 1\times E^2\,1sH_A + 1\times\tilde{C}_2\,(z)(1sH_A) + 1\times\tilde{C}_2(y)\,(1sH_A) +$$

$$1\times\tilde{C}_2\,(x)\,(1sH_A)$$

$$1sH_A + 1sH_B + 1sH_B + 1sH_A$$

$$= 2(1sH_A + 1sH_B) \cong 1sH_A + 1sH_B$$

$$\Psi_{A_g} = \Psi_A = \frac{1}{\sqrt{2}}\left(1sH_A + 1sH_B\right)$$

$$\tilde{p}^{B_3}(1sH_A) \cong \chi_{B_3}^{E}\ \tilde{E}(1sH_A) + \chi_{B_3}^{C_2(z)}\ \tilde{C}_2(z)\ 1sH_A +$$
$$\chi_{B_3}^{C_2(y)}.\tilde{C}_2(y)\ (1sH_A) + \chi_{B_3}^{C_2(z)}\ \tilde{C}_2(x)\ (1sH_A)$$
$$= 1 \times \tilde{E}(1sH_A) - 1 \times \tilde{C}_2(z)(1sH_A) - 1 \times C_2(y)(1sH_A)$$
$$+ 1 \times C_2(x)\ (1sH_A)$$
$$= 1sH_A - 1sH_B - 1sH_B + 1sH_A$$
$$= 2\ (1sH_A - 1sH_B)$$
$$= 1sH_A - 1sH_B$$
$$\psi_{B_{3u}} = \psi_{B_3} = \frac{1}{\sqrt{2}}\left(1sH_A - 1sH_B\right)$$

Both bonding and anti-bonding orbitals are formed in case of group orbitals with matching symmetry. Both Ag and B_{3u} having suitable partners may form bonding and anti-bonding molecular orbitals while other two B_{1u} and B_{2g} do not have matching partners and remain non-bonding molecular orbitals:

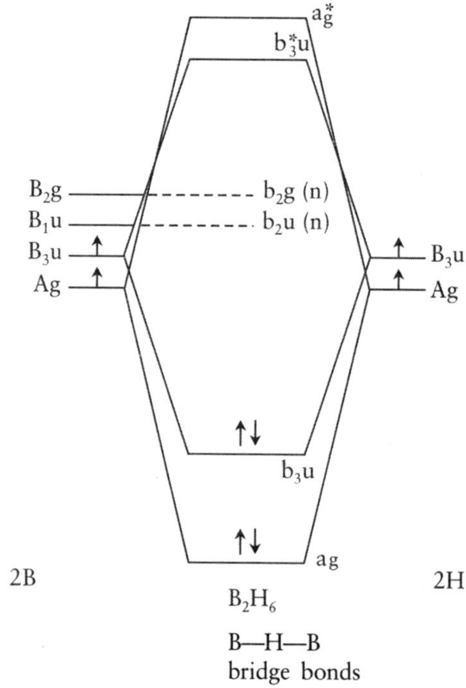

There are two bridge bonds each as two electron three centre bond.

Solved Examples

1. Show that p_x and p_y orbitals of N-atom in ammonia belong to a doubly degenerate representation (E).

   Consider C_3 operation of p_x and p_y orbitals on N-atom:

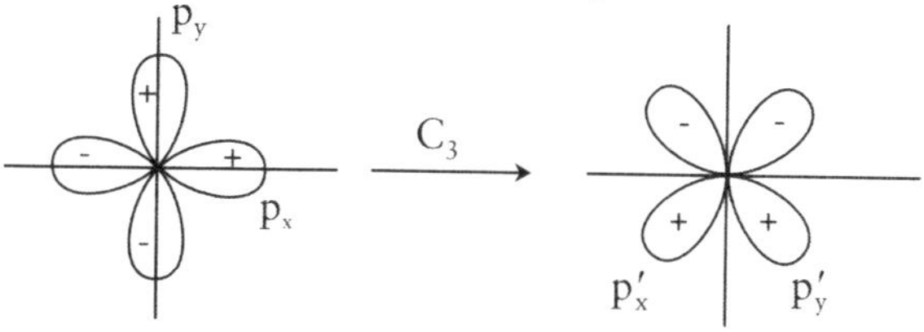

$$p'_x = C_3 p_x = \cos 120^\circ\, p_x + \sin 120^\circ\, p_y$$
$$= (-\cos 60^\circ) p_x + (\sin 60^\circ) p_y$$
$$= -\frac{1}{2} p_x + \frac{\sqrt{3}}{2} p_y$$
$$p'_y = C_3 p_y = -\sin 120^\circ\, p_x + \cos 120^\circ\, p_y$$
$$= -\sin 60^\circ\, p_x - \cos 60^\circ\, p_y$$
$$= -\frac{\sqrt{3}}{2} p_x - \frac{1}{2} p_y$$
$$C_3 \begin{pmatrix} p_x \\ p_y \end{pmatrix} = \begin{pmatrix} p'_x \\ p'_y \end{pmatrix} = \begin{bmatrix} -\frac{1}{2} & \frac{\sqrt{3}}{2} \\ -\frac{\sqrt{3}}{2} & -\frac{1}{2} \end{bmatrix} \begin{bmatrix} p_x \\ p_y \end{bmatrix}$$

Its character is $-\frac{1}{2} - \frac{1}{2} = -1$

Consider σ_3 as shown in the figure:

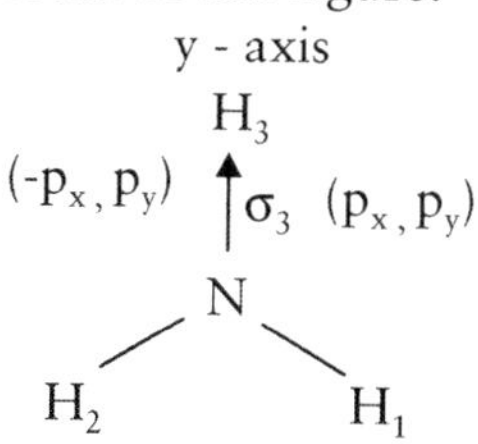

where y-axis passes through H_3:

$$\sigma_3\,(p_x) = -p_x,\ \sigma_3\,(p_y) = (+1)\ p_y$$

$$\sigma_3 \begin{bmatrix} p_x \\ p_y \end{bmatrix} = \begin{bmatrix} p'_x \\ p'_y \end{bmatrix} = \begin{bmatrix} -1 & 0 \\ 0 & 1 \end{bmatrix} \begin{bmatrix} p_x \\ p_y \end{bmatrix}$$

$$\chi\left(\sigma_3\right) = -1 + 1 = 0$$

Now, consider the case of identity operation:

$$\tilde{E}(p_x) = (+1)\,p_x,\ \tilde{E}(p_y) = (+1)\,p_y$$

$$E \begin{bmatrix} p_x \\ p_y \end{bmatrix} = \begin{bmatrix} p'_x \\ p'_y \end{bmatrix} = \begin{bmatrix} 1 & 0 \\ 0 & 1 \end{bmatrix} \begin{bmatrix} p_x \\ p_y \end{bmatrix}$$

$$\chi\,(E) = 1 + 1 = 2$$

For C_{3v} point group:

C_{3v}	E	$2C_3$	$3\sigma_v$
E	2	–1	0

2. Apply $\tilde{p}E$ on p_x as well as on p_y at N-atom in NH_3 and show that they represent doubly degenerate representations.

$$\tilde{p}E\,p_x \cong \frac{2}{6}\left[2\times 1\times \tilde{E}p_x + (-1)\tilde{C}_3\,p_x + (-1)\,\tilde{C}_3^2\,p_x + 0.\left(\tilde{\sigma}.p_x + \tilde{\sigma}_2 p_x + \tilde{\sigma}_3\,p_x\right)\right]$$

$$= \frac{1}{3}\left[2p_x - \left(-\frac{1}{2}\,p_x + \frac{\sqrt{3}}{2}\,p_y\right) - 1\tilde{C}_3^{-1}\ p_x\right]$$

$$= \frac{1}{3}\left[2p_x + \frac{1}{2}\,p_x - \frac{\sqrt{3}}{2}\,p_y + \frac{1}{2}\,P_x + \frac{\sqrt{3}}{2}\,p_y\right]$$

$$= \frac{1}{3}\times 3\,p_x = p_x$$

Similarly,

$$\tilde{p}E\ p_y = p_y\,.$$

Thus p_x and p_y are present in doubly degenerate representations. Show that: $\tilde{p}^{A_1}\,(s) = s$

$$\tilde{p}^{A_1}\,(p_z) = p_z$$

$$\tilde{p}^{A_1}(s) = \frac{1}{6}\left[1\times 1\times \tilde{E}(s) + 1\times \tilde{C}_s(s) + 1\times \tilde{C}_3(s) + 1\times \tilde{\sigma}_1(s) + 1\times \tilde{\sigma}_2(s) + 1\times \tilde{\sigma}_3(s)\right]$$

$$= \frac{1}{6}\left[s+s+s+s+s+s\right] = \frac{1}{6}.6\times s$$

$$= s$$

Hence, s belongs to A_1

$$\tilde{p}^{A_1}(p_z) \cong \frac{1}{6}\left[1\times \tilde{E}(p_z) + 1\times \tilde{C}_3\,(p_z) + 1\times \tilde{C}_3 + (p_z)\right)$$

$$\tilde{p}^{A_1}(p_z) \cong \frac{1}{6}\left[1\times \tilde{E}(p_z) + 1\times \tilde{C}_3\,(p_z) + 1\times \tilde{C}_3 + (p_z)\right)$$

$$= \frac{1}{6}\left[p_z + p_z + p_z + p_z + p_z + p_z\right]$$

$$= p_z$$

p_z belongs to A_1 symmetry species.

QUESTIONS

1. (a) Explain SALCs. Illustrate that SALCs can be formed both by symmetry operators as well as by projection operator methods, taking the case of water or ammonia.

   (b) Give qualitatively formation of molecular orbitals and draw M.O. diagram in case of water.

2. (a) Determine the point group in ammonia and find the symmetry species of SALCs for it.

   (b) Determine the SALCs for the molecule and draw M.O. diagram showing electron occupancy.

   Designate the bonding nonbonding and anti-bonding m.o.s. using symmetry labels.

3. (a) Assign point group notation for formaldehyde. Draw qualitatively M.O. diagram for $> C = \bar{O}^1$ chromophore in formaldehyde.

   (b) Discuss the effect of symmetry operations on non-bonding, bonding and anti-bonding molecular orbitals in formaldehyde and assign the symmetry species to which they belong to.

   (c) Comment on symmetry selection rules for electronic transition in this case.

4. (a) Discuss the effect of symmetry for ground and excited states for M.O. configurations of formaldehyde molecule taking the direct product for electron configuration for all possible states and obtain the symmetry species in each case.

   (b) Examine the possibility of electronic transitions such as $n \rightarrow \pi^*$, $n \rightarrow \sigma^*$, $\pi \rightarrow \pi^*$ taking the direct product representation in transition moment integrals.

5. Discuss the case of three centre π-electron bonding in NO_2^- giving the explicit forms of SALCs and draw π-electron m.o. diagram for it showing electron occupancy.

6. Give an account for B–H–B bonding in B_2H_6 through the formation of SALCs for bridge bonds and hydrogen atoms involved.

Draw the m.o. diagram for B-H-B bonds indicating electron occupancy.

7. (a) Show that in NH_3, p_x and p_y atomic orbitals of N-atom belong to doubly degenerate representation E.

   (b) Find the SALCs for their group orbitals of hydrogen atoms in ammonia.

8. Find the characters for reducible representation for π-bonding in NO_2^- ion and decompose it into irreducible components. Give the formation of SALCs for atomic orbitals with π-symmetry at three centres in NO_2^- in explicit form and draw the shape of bonding, non-bonding and anti-bonding molecular orbitals for π-electron in it and give m.o. diagram for it.

SPLITTING OF LEVELS AND TERMS IN CHEMICAL ENVIRONMENT

9

This chapter includes outlines of tetrahedral and octahedral symmetry besides derivation of sine formula, use of sine formula in a system of O or T. Symmetry of orbitals and terms and their transformation into O_h and T_d point groups, strong field configuration and their components along with a brief idea of correlation diagram in a few cases. A case of non-cubic symmetry (D_{4h}) is thorougly described.

9.1 TETRAHEDRAL AND OCTAHEDRAL SYMMETRY

Both tetrahedron and octahedron are related to a cube. While only one octahedron is inscribed in a cube but two tetrahedra may be formed inside a cube:

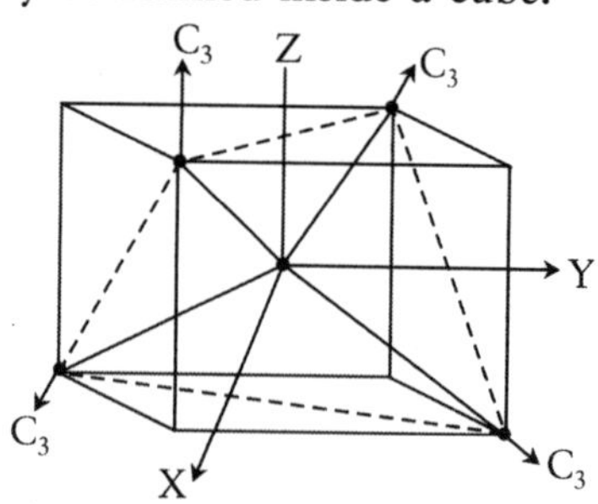

We can illustrate on taking the case of CH_4 (methane). There are four C–H bonds. The molecule is rotated about any one of the C–H bonds (say C–H_1) through an angle of 120°, the other three atoms (2, 3 and 4) will interchange their position with each other. When it completes a cycle by rotation of 360° the tetrahedron passes through equivalent structures. For a complete cycle $C_3^3 = E$. Thus it has C_3 axis along C–H bonds. There are four C_3 axis which makes $4C_3 \times 2 = 8C_3$ operations each containing C_3 and C_3^2 distinct operations.

We define x, y and z axis representing C_2 axis.

So we have $3C_2$ axis leading to tetrahedral (T) point group :

$$4\ C_3 + 3\ C_2 \rightarrow T$$

In order to have T_d symmetry there can be further addition of mirror plane. There are six mirror planes, one of them contains C and two hydrogens (1 and 2). All three atoms remain unchanged by reflection. The other two H-atoms (3 and 4) can be interchanged on reflection in this plane. There is another mirror plane containing carbon-atom with the 3 and 4 hydrogen atoms. All three atoms (C, H_3 and H_4) lie in this plane. H_2 infront of the mirror is regarded as the mirror of H_1:

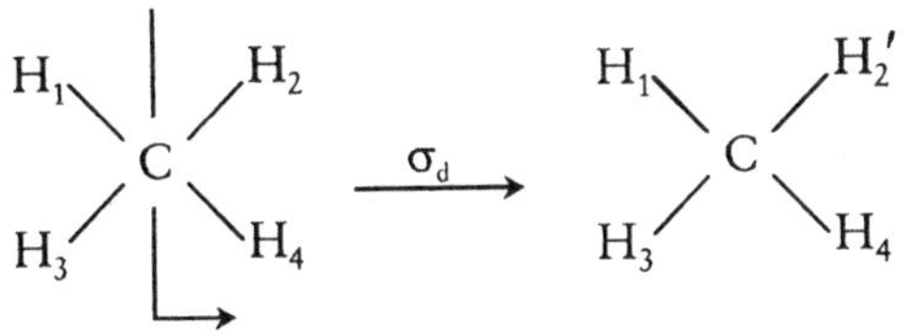

Neither it has C_4 nor i (inversion centre) but it involves a S_4 rotation and brings the position of H_2 to H_2'. This is followed by inversion through the carbon centre. So it has four fold in version centre (C_4 . i).

The S_4 axis collinear with C_2 are generated by the combination of σ_d followed by C_2 in σ_d containing C and H_3 and H_4. The reflection of H_1 will be H_2. So $\sigma(1) = \sigma(2)$.

When rotation of 120° is preformed about C-H_3 axis:

$$C_3\ (2) = (4)$$

or, $$C_3\sigma_1\ (1) = (4)$$

So, $$S_4\ (1) = (4)$$

Naturally, $$C_3\ \sigma_1 = S_4$$

A T_d has E $8C_3$, $3C_2$, $6S_4$ and $6\sigma_d$.

9.2 OCTAHEDRAL SYMMETRY

An octahedron is also related to a cube:

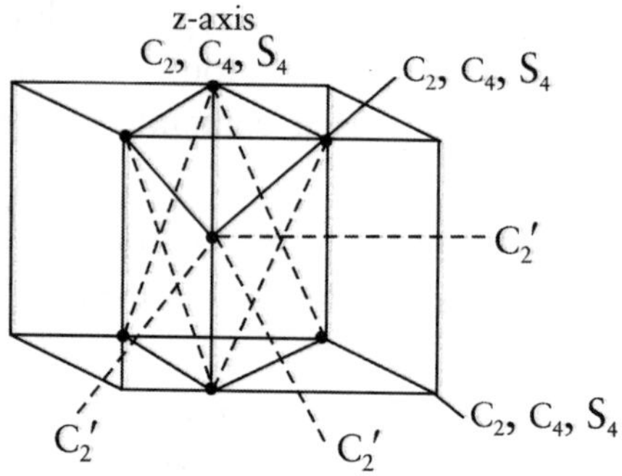

It generates the following symmetry elements and operations :

1. It has three C_2 axes collinear with C_4 and S_4.
2. For each C_4 axis there are C_4 and C_4^3 distinct operations. Hence there can be:

$$3 \times 2C_4 = 6C_4$$

3. There are six C_2' axis bisecting opposite edges ($6\,C_2'$).
4. There are three S_4 axes each passing through a pair of opposite apices. Each S_4 generates S_4 and $S_4^3 = 2S_4$ operations making altogether $3 \times 2S_4 = 6S_4$.
5. There are four S_6 axes passing through centres of opposite triangular faces.
6. It has four C_3 axes collinear with S_6 axis.

Each S_6 generates:

$$S_6, \quad S_6^2 = C_6^2.\sigma_h^2 = C_3, \quad S_6^3 = C_6^3.\sigma_h^3 = C_2.\sigma_h = S_2 = i, \quad S_6^4 = C_6^4.\sigma_h^4 = C_3^2, \quad S_6^5, \quad S_6^6 = E$$

So, $\quad 4 \times 2S_6 = 8S_6$

Each C_3 gives $2C_3$ operations C_3 and C_3^2.

$$\text{So,} \quad 4 \times 2C_3 = 8C_3.$$

7. It has i.
8. There are three σ_h which pass through four of the six apices. $3\sigma_h$
9. There are six σ_d planes passing through two apices and bisecting two opposite edges. $6\sigma_d$.

9.3 SPLITTING OF LEVELS AND TERMS IN CUBIC SYMMETRY

Consider the case of d orbitals (l=2) in O_h symmetry.

Its $\psi_{orbital}$ is expressed as:

$$\psi_{3,2,ml} = R_{32}(r) P_2^{ml} (\cos\theta) \left(\frac{1}{2\pi}\right)^{1/2} e^{iml\phi}$$

ml values range from l, (l–1) ... 0 ... –(l–1)

with ml $\leq$ l.

The radial part of wave function remains invariant.

The angular part $P_2^{ml}(\cos\theta) = \Theta_{2ml}^{(\theta)}$ is θ dependent which makes with z axis. This is the axis of rotation. So θ is invariant. This leaves only ϕ function to change in rotation about z-axis. Let it be rotated by an angle α about the z-axis so that a new angle is $\phi' = \phi + \alpha$.

$$e^{iml\phi} \xrightarrow{C_{360°/\alpha}} e^{iml\,\phi'} = e^{iml\,(\phi+\alpha)}$$

So that for	$m_l = +1$	$e^{il\,\phi} \xrightarrow{\alpha} e^{il(\phi+\alpha)}$
	$m_l = l - 1$	$e^{i(l-1)\,\phi} \rightarrow e^{i(l-1)\,(\phi+\alpha)}$
	- - - - - - - - -	- - - - - - - - - - - - - - -
	- - - - - - - - -	- - - - - - - - - - - - - - -
	0	- - - - $e^{io\,\phi} \rightarrow e^{io\,(\phi+\alpha)}$
	$m_l = -1$	$e^{-il\,\phi} \rightarrow e^{-il\,(\phi+\alpha)}$

A column vector is:

$$\begin{bmatrix} e^{il\phi} \\ e^{i(l-1)\phi} \\ \vdots \\ e^{-il\phi} \end{bmatrix} \xrightarrow[\text{rotation by } \alpha]{\alpha} \begin{bmatrix} e^{il(\phi+\alpha)} \\ e^{i(l-1)(\phi+\alpha)} \\ \vdots \\ e^{-il(\phi+\alpha)} \end{bmatrix}$$

on rotation through α new set of wave functions are obtained as:

$$\phi_l = e^{il(\phi+\alpha)} + 0.e^{i(l-1)(\phi+\alpha)} + 0 + \ldots$$
$$\phi_{(l-1)} = 0.e^{il(\phi+\alpha)} + e^{i.(l-1)(\phi+\alpha)} + 0 + \ldots$$
$$\phi_0 = 0 + 0 + \ldots\ldots\ldots + e^{i\,0\,(\phi+\alpha)} + \ldots.$$
$$\vdots$$
$$\phi_{-l} = 0 + 0 + 0\ldots\ldots + e^{-1l(\phi+\alpha)} + \ldots.$$

It can be shown in matrix from:

$$\begin{bmatrix} \phi_l \\ \phi_{l-1} \\ \vdots \\ \phi_0 \\ \vdots \\ \phi_{-l} \end{bmatrix} = \begin{bmatrix} e^{il\alpha} & 0 & 0 & 0 \\ 0 & e^{i(l-1)\alpha} & 0 & \cdots \\ \vdots & \vdots & e^{i(l-2)\alpha} & \\ \vdots & \vdots & \vdots & \\ \vdots & \vdots & \vdots & \\ 0 & 0 & 0 & e^{-il\alpha} \end{bmatrix} \begin{bmatrix} e^{il\phi} \\ e^{i(l-1)\phi} \\ e^{i(l-2)\phi} \\ e^{0} \\ \vdots \\ e^{-il\phi} \end{bmatrix}$$

$$= C_{360°/\alpha} \begin{bmatrix} e^{il\phi} \\ \vdots \\ e^{-il\phi} \end{bmatrix}$$

Its character is:

$$\chi(\alpha) = e^{il\alpha} + e^{i(l-1)\alpha} + e^{i(l-2)\alpha} + e^{0} + \ldots + e^{-il\alpha}$$

For d orbitals the five diagonal elements are:

$$\chi(\alpha) = e^{i2\alpha} + e^{il\alpha} + e^{i0\alpha} + e^{-il\alpha} + e^{-i2\alpha}$$
$$= e^{i2\alpha} + e^{-i2\alpha} + e^{i\alpha} + e^{-i\alpha} + 1$$

$$= 2\cos 2\alpha + 2\cos\alpha + 1$$

$$= 2(\cos 2\alpha + \cos\alpha) + 1$$

$$= 1 + 2\left\{2\cos\frac{2\alpha+\alpha}{2}.\cos\frac{2\alpha-\alpha}{2}\right\}$$

$$= 1 + 4\cos\frac{3\alpha}{2}.\cos\alpha/2 \times \frac{\sin\alpha/2}{\sin\alpha/2}$$

$$= 1 + \frac{2}{\sin\alpha/2}.\cos\frac{3\alpha}{2}.2\sin\alpha/2\cos\alpha/2$$

$$= 1 + \frac{2}{\sin\alpha/2}.\cos\frac{3\alpha}{2}.\sin\alpha$$

$$= 1 + \frac{1}{\sin\alpha/2}\left[2\cos\frac{3\alpha}{2}.\sin\alpha\right]$$

$$= 1 + \frac{1}{\sin\alpha/2}\left[\sin\left(\frac{3\alpha}{2}+\alpha\right) - \sin\left(\frac{3\alpha}{2}-\alpha\right)\right]$$

$$= 1 + \frac{1}{\sin\alpha/2}\left[\sin\frac{5\alpha}{2} - \sin\alpha/2\right]$$

$$= 1 + \frac{\sin\frac{5\alpha}{2}}{\sin\alpha/2} - 1 = \frac{\sin(2l+1)\alpha/2}{\sin\alpha/2} \qquad \text{sine formula}$$

It is valid for $\alpha \neq 0$.

For identity (E) $\alpha = 0$ the diagonal elements are all 1.

$$\chi(E) = 2l + 1$$

For splitting of terms in O_h field. We have,

$$\chi(E) = 2L + 1 \qquad \text{Capital L for angular momentum.}$$

$$\chi(C_4) = \frac{\sin 5\alpha/2}{\sin\alpha/2} = \frac{\sin 5\times 90^\circ/2}{\sin 90^\circ/2} = \frac{\sin 5\times 45^\circ}{\sin 45^\circ}$$

$$= \frac{\sin 225^\circ}{\sin 45^\circ} = \frac{\sin(270^\circ - 45^\circ)}{\sin 45^\circ} = \frac{-\sin 45^\circ}{\sin 45^\circ} = -1$$

$$\chi(C_2) = \frac{\sin 5/2.180^\circ}{\sin \frac{180^\circ}{2}} = \frac{\sin 450^\circ}{\sin 90^\circ} = \frac{\sin 90^\circ}{\sin 90^\circ} = 1$$

$$\chi(C_3) = \frac{\sin \frac{5}{\cancel{2}} \times \cancel{120^\circ}\,60^\circ}{\sin \frac{\cancel{120^\circ}\,60^\circ}{\cancel{2}}} = \frac{\sin 300^\circ}{\sin 60^\circ} = \frac{\sin(360^\circ - 60^\circ)}{\sin 60^\circ}$$

$$= -\frac{\sin \cancel{60^\circ}}{\cancel{\sin} 60^\circ} = -1$$

	E	$6C_4$	$3C_2$	$6C_2'$	$8C_3$
$\Gamma_{R(d)}$ =	5	−1	1	1	−1

A five dimensional representation must split:

O	E	$6C_4$	$3C_2\left(=C_4^2\right)$	$6C_2'$	$8C_3$	b = 24
A_1	1	1	1	1	1	$x^2 + y^2$
A_2	1	−1	1	−1	1	
E	2	0	2	0	−1	$x^2 - y^2, z^2$
T_1	3	1	−1	−1	0	x, y, z
T_2	3	−1	−1	1	0	xy, xz, yx
$\Gamma_{R(d)}$	5	−1	1	1	−1	

$$n_{a_1} = \frac{1}{24}(1\times 5\times 1 + 6\times 1\times -1 + 3\times 1\times 1 + 6\times 1\times 1 + 8\times 1\times -1)$$

$$= \frac{1}{24}(\cancel{5} - \cancel{6} + \cancel{3} + \cancel{6} - \cancel{8})$$

$$= \frac{1}{24}[0] = 0$$

$$n_{a_2} = \frac{1}{24}[5 + 6\times -1\times -1 + 3\times 1\times 1 + 6\times -1\times 1 + 8\times 1\times -1]$$

$$= \frac{1}{24}[\cancel{8} + \cancel{6} + \cancel{3} - \cancel{6} - \cancel{8}]$$

$$= 0$$

$$n_e = \frac{1}{24}\left[5\times 2 + 0 - 3\times 2\times 1 + 6\times 0\times 1 + 8\times(-1)\times(-1)\right]$$

$$= \frac{1}{24}\left[10 + 6 + 0 + 8\right]$$

$$= \frac{1}{24}\times 24 = 1$$

$$n_{t_1} = 0$$

$$n_{t_2} = \frac{1}{24}\left[1\times 3\times 5 + 6\times(-1)\times(-1) + 3\times(-1)\times 1 + 6\times 1\times 1 + 8\,(0)\,(-1)\right]$$

$$= \frac{1}{24}\left[15 + 6 - 3 + 6 + 0\right]$$

$$= \frac{1}{24}\left[24\right] = 1$$

$$\Gamma_{R(d)} = 1\times e + 1\times t_2 = e + t_2$$

0	0_h	C.T.
e	e_g	$dx^2 - y^2$, dz^2
t_2	t_{2g}	dxy, dxz, dyz

9.4 CONSIDER TRANSFORMATION OF s-ORBITAL

$$l = 0,\ 2\,l + 1 = 2\times 0 + = 1$$

$$\chi\,(E) = 2l + 1 = 1$$

$$\chi\,(C_4) = \frac{\sin \alpha/2}{\sin \alpha/2} = \frac{\sin 45^\circ}{\sin 45^\circ} = 1$$

$$\chi\,(C_2) = \frac{\sin \alpha/2}{\sin \alpha/2} = \frac{\sin 90^\circ}{\sin 90^\circ} = 1,\ \chi\left(C_2'\right) = 1$$

$$\chi\,(C_3) = \frac{\sin \alpha/2}{\sin \alpha/2} = \frac{\sin 60^\circ}{\sin 60^\circ} = 1$$

	E	$6C_4$	$3C_2$	$6C_2'$	$8C_3$
$\Gamma_{R(S)}$	1	1	1	1	1

It corresponds to a totally symmetric representation a_1 or A_1 which is shown as a_{1g} irreducible representation in O_h.

It does so for S term, L = 0, 2L + 1 = 1, χ (E) = 1

all other are 1 1 1 1 – A_{1g}

9.5 CASE OF p-ORBITALS

$l = 1,\ 2l + 1 = 3,\ \chi\ (E) = 3$

$$\chi(C_4) = \frac{\sin 3\alpha/2}{\sin \alpha/2} = \frac{\sin 3\times 90°/2}{\sin 90°/2} = \frac{\sin 135°}{\sin 45°} = \frac{\sin (180° - 45°)}{\sin 45°}$$

$$= \frac{\sin 45°}{\sin 45°} = 1$$

$$\chi(C_2) = \frac{\sin \frac{3}{2}\times 180°}{\sin \frac{180°}{2}} = \frac{\sin 270°}{\sin 90°} = \frac{\sin(360° - 90°)}{\sin 90°} = \frac{-\sin 90°}{\sin 90°} = -1$$

$$\chi(C_3) = \frac{\sin \frac{3}{2}\times 120°}{\sin \frac{120°}{2}} = \frac{\sin 180°}{\sin 60°} = \frac{\sin 0°}{\sin 60°} = 0$$

O	E	$6C_4$	$3C_2$	$6C_2'$	$8C_3$
$\Gamma_{R(p)}$	3	1	–1	–1	0

Similar is the case with P-term L = 1, 2L + 1 = 3

χ (E) = 3 etc.

It corresponds to t_1 representation. So it transforms as t_{1u} (porbital l = 1, odd, u-type).

It so happens for P-term which transforms as T_{1g} in O_h.

9.6 SPLITTING OF f-ORBITALS IN O_h SYMMETRY

For f-orbital, $l = 3,\ 2l + 1 = 2 \times 3 + 1 = 7$

χ (E) = 7

$$\chi\ (C_4) = \frac{\sin 7\alpha/2}{\sin \alpha/2} = \frac{\sin 7\times 45°}{\sin 45°} = \frac{\sin 315°}{\sin 45°}$$

$$= \frac{\sin (360° - 45°)}{\sin 45°} = \frac{-\sin 45°}{\sin 45°} = -1$$

$$\chi(C_3) = \frac{\sin 7\times 60^\circ}{\sin 60^\circ} = \frac{\sin 420^\circ}{\sin 45^\circ} = \frac{\sin(360^\circ+60^\circ)}{\sin 60^\circ}$$

$$= \frac{\sin 60^\circ}{\sin 60^\circ} = 1$$

$$\chi(C_2) = \frac{\sin 7\times 90^\circ}{\sin 90^\circ} = \frac{\sin 630^\circ}{\sin 90^\circ} = \frac{\sin(360^\circ+270^\circ)}{\sin 90^\circ}$$

$$= \frac{\sin 270^\circ}{\sin 90^\circ} = \frac{\sin(360^\circ-90^\circ)}{\sin 90^\circ}$$

$$= \frac{-\sin 90^\circ}{\sin 90^\circ} = -1$$

O	E	$6C_4$	$3C_2\left(=C_4^2\right)$	$6C_2'$	$8C_3$
$\Gamma_{R(f)}$	7	–1	–1	–1	1

$$na_1 = \frac{1}{24}\left[7+6(-1)(1)+3\times(-1)\times 1+6\times(-1)\times(1)+8\times 1\times 1\right]$$

$$= \frac{1}{24}[7-6-3-6+8] = \frac{0}{24} = 0$$

$$na_2 = \frac{1}{24}\left[7-6\times(-1)+3\times(-1)\times 1+6\times(-1)\times(-1)+8\times 1\times 1\right]$$

$$= \frac{1}{24}[7+6-3+6+8] = \frac{24}{24} = 1$$

$$nt_1 = \frac{1}{24}[7\times 3\times 1+6\times -1\times 1+3\times -1\times -1+6\times -1\times -1$$
$$+8\times(0)\times 1]$$

$$= \frac{1}{24}[21-6+3+6+0] = \frac{24}{24} = 1$$

$$nt_2 = \frac{1}{24}[7\times 3\times 1+6\times -1\times -1+3\times(-1)\times(-1)+6\times(-1)\times(1)$$
$$+8\times 1\times 0]$$

$$= \frac{1}{24}[21+6+3-6+0] = \frac{24}{24} = 1$$

$$\Gamma_f = 0.a_1 + 1\times a_2 + 1.t_1 + 1.t_2$$

$$= a_2 + t_1 + t_2$$

In conversion O → O_h the point group transforms having inversion centre but f orbital is u type. As such f orbitals in O_h symmetry split into three components as $a_{2u} + t_{1u} + t_{2u}$.

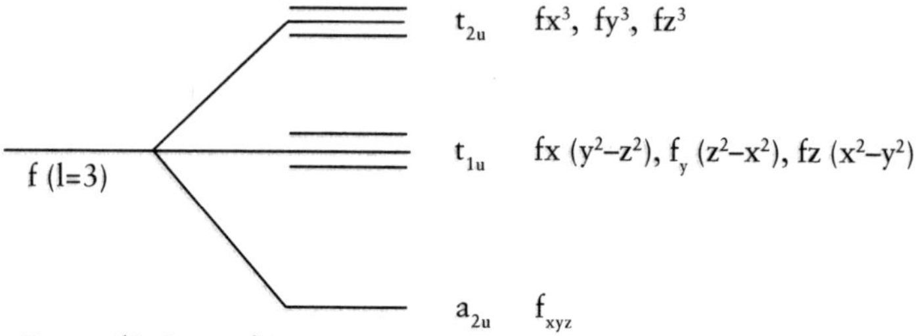

For splitting of F term in O_h.

2L + 1 = 7, χ (E) = 7 etc.

O	E	$6C_4$	$3C_2$	$6C_2'$	$8C_3$
Γ_F	7	–1	–1	–1	1

$$\Gamma_F = A_2 + T_1 + T_2$$

In O_h symmetry the components are labelled using g suffix.

$$\Gamma_F = A_{2g} + T_{1g} + T_{2g}$$

9.7 SPLITTING OF g ORBITALS IN O_h

l = 4 for g orbital 2l + 1 = 9

$$\chi\ (E) = 9$$

$$\chi(C_4) = \frac{\sin 9 \times 90°/2}{\sin 90°/2} = \frac{\sin 9 \times 45°}{\sin 45°} = \frac{\sin 405°}{\sin 45°}$$

$$= \frac{\sin (360° + 45°)}{\sin 45°} = \frac{+\sin 45°}{\sin 45°} = 1$$

$$\chi(C_2) = \frac{\sin 0 \times 90°}{\sin 90°} = \frac{\sin 810°}{\sin 0°} = \frac{\sin (360° + 360° + 90°)}{\sin 90°}$$

$$= \frac{\sin 90°}{\sin 90°} = 1$$

$$\chi(C_3) = \frac{\sin 9 \times 120°/2}{\sin 60°} = \frac{\sin 540°}{\sin 60°} = \frac{\sin (360° + 180°)}{\sin 60°}$$

$$= \frac{\sin 0°}{\sin 60°} = \frac{0}{\sqrt{3/2}} = 0$$

O	E	$6C_4$	$3C_2$	$6C_2'$	$8C_3$
$\Gamma_{R(g)}$	9	1	1	1	0

$$n_{a_1} = \frac{1}{24}[9\times1\times1+6\times1\times1+3\times1\times1+6\times1\times1+8\times0\times1]$$

$$= \frac{1}{24}[9+6+3+6+0] = \frac{24}{24} = 1$$

$$n_e = \frac{1}{24}[9\times2\times1+6\times1\times0+3\times2\times1+6\times1\times0+8\times0\times(-1)]$$

$$= \frac{1}{24}[18+6] = \frac{24}{24} = 1$$

$$n_{t_1} = \frac{1}{24}[9\times3\times1+6\times1\times1+3\times1\times(-1)+6\times1\times(-1)+8\times0\times0]$$

$$= \frac{1}{24}[27+6-3-6+0] = \frac{24}{24} = 1$$

$$n_{t_2} = \frac{1}{24}[9\times3\times1+1\times6\times(-1)+1\times3\times(-1)+1\times6\times1+0\times8\times0]$$

$$= \frac{1}{24}[27-6-3+6] = \frac{24}{24} = 1$$

$$\therefore\ \Gamma_g = a_1 + e + t_1 + t_2$$

In O_h point group with l = 4 (even). We have inversion centre and we use the suffix g here:

$$\Gamma_g = a_{1g} + e_g + t_{1g} + t_{2g}$$

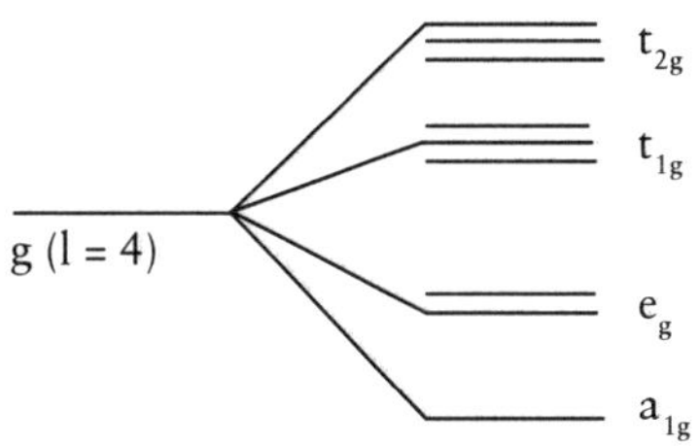

It so happens with G term:

$$2L + 1 = 9 \text{ etc.}$$

The split components are:

$$\Gamma_G = A_{1g} + E_g + T_{1g} + T_{2g}$$

The use of subscripts g and u is governed by the two rules :

(i) If the point group of environment has centre of symmetry and (i) orbital even or odd we assign g or u.

(ii) If the point group does not possess i, no subscripts are used, as they do not carry any meaning.

9.8 SPLITTING IN TETRAHEDRAL FIELD APPLYING SINE FORMULA

$T \times \sigma_h = T_h$ and $T \times \sigma_d = T_d$.

In both cases of the T_h and T_d there are plane of symmetry σ_h and σ_d and so the formula does not work.

The sine formula is effective in case of T point group as in O. as it does not have any mirror plane.

C.T. for T group is:

T	E	$4C_3$	$4C_3^2$	$3C_2$	h = 12
A	1	1	1	1	$x^2+y^2+x^2$
E	1	ε	ε^*	1	
	1	ε	ε		
T	3	0	0	–1	(x, y, z) (xy, xz, yz)

9.9 SPLITTING OF d-ORBITALS

Splitting of d-orbitals is taken up in tetrahedral field:

$$l = 2, \quad 2l + 1 = 5, \qquad \chi\,(E) = 5$$

$$\chi\left(C_3\right) = \frac{\sin 5\alpha/2}{\sin \alpha/2} = \frac{\sin 5 \times 60°}{\sin 60°} = \frac{\sin 300°}{\sin 60°}$$

$$= \frac{\sin\left(360° - 60°\right)}{\sin 60°} = \frac{-\sin 60°}{\sin 60°} = -1$$

$$\chi\left(C_3^2\right) = -1$$

$$\chi\left(C_2\right) = \frac{\sin 5 \times 90°}{\sin 90°} = \frac{\sin 450°}{\sin 90°} = \frac{\sin\,(360° + 90°)}{\sin 90°}$$

$$= \frac{\sin 90°}{\sin 90°} = 1$$

T	E	$4C_3$	$4C_3^2$	$3C_2$
$\Gamma_{R(d)}$	5	−1	−1	1

Decomposition of Γ_d into irreducible components in T symmetry is done as:

$$a_A = \frac{1}{12}\left[5\times1\times1+4\times(-1)\times1+4\times(-1)+3\times1\times1\right]$$
$$= \frac{1}{12}[5-4-4+3] = 0$$

$$^aE^a = \frac{1}{12}\ [5\times1\times1+4\times\epsilon(-1)+4\epsilon^*(-1)+3\times1\times1]$$
$$= \frac{1}{12}\ [5+3-4\ (\epsilon+\epsilon^*)]$$
$$= \frac{1}{12}[8-4\times2\cos2\pi/3] = \frac{1}{12}[8-8\cos120°]$$
$$= \frac{1}{12}\left[8-8\times\left(-\frac{1}{2}\right)\right]$$
$$= \frac{1}{12}[8+4] = \frac{12}{12} = 1$$

$$^aE^b = \frac{1}{12}\ [5\times1\times1+4\epsilon^*\ (-1)+4\epsilon(-1)+3\times1\times1]$$
$$= \frac{1}{12}\ [5+3-4\ (\epsilon+\epsilon^*)]$$
$$= \frac{1}{12}[8-4\times2\cos120°]$$
$$= \frac{1}{12}\left[8-8\times\left(-\frac{1}{2}\right)\right]$$
$$= \frac{1}{12}[8+4] = 1$$

$$a_T = \frac{1}{12}\left[5\times3\times1+4\times(-1)\times0+4\times(-)\times0+3\times(-)\times1\right]$$
$$= \frac{1}{12}\left[15+0+0-3\right] = 12/12 = 1$$

Γ_d = E + T

E comprises both: $2z^2 - x^2 - y^2$ and $x^2 - y^2 = dz^2, dx^2 - y^2$

T comprises: dxy, dxz and dyz

Now, we come to cubic group Td.

T_d	E	$8C_3$	$3C_2$	$6S_4$	$6\sigma d$	
A_1	1	1	1	1	1	$x^2+y^2+z^2$
A_2	1	1	1	–1	–1	
E	2	–1	2	0	0	$2z^2-x^2-y^2, x^2-y^2$
T_1	3	0	–1	1	–1	
T_2	3	0	–1	–1	1	xy, xz, yz

We have in C.T. both, T_1 and T_2 but T_1 does not correspond to any d-orbital, whereas the three d-orbitals belong to T_2 symmetry such as dxy, dxz, dyz

Hence, $\Gamma_d = e + t_2$

$\Gamma_D = E + T_2$

9.10 SPLITTING OF H TERM

$$L = 5,\ 2L + 1 = 11$$

$$\chi = \frac{\sin 11\,\alpha/2}{\sin \alpha/2} \quad \chi(C_3) = \frac{\sin 11 \times 120°/2}{\sin 60°} = \frac{\sin 660°}{\sin 60°}$$

$$= \frac{\sin 360° + 360° - 60°}{\sin 60°} = \frac{-\sin 60°}{\sin 60°} = -1$$

$$\chi\left(C_3^2\right) = -1$$

$$\chi\left(C_2\right) = \frac{\sin 11 \times 90°}{\sin 90°} = \frac{\sin 990°}{\sin 90°} = \frac{\sin\left(3 \times 360° - 90°\right)}{\sin 90°}$$

$$= \frac{-\sin 90°}{\sin 90°} = -1$$

T	E	$4C_3$	$4C_3^2$	$3C_2$
$\Gamma_{R(H)}$	11	–1	–1	–1

$$a_A = \frac{1}{12}\left[11 \times 1 \times 1 + 4 \times (-1) \times 1 + 4 \times (-) \times 1 + 3 \times (-1) \times 1\right]$$

$$= \frac{1}{12}\left[11 - 4 - 4 - 3\right] = \frac{0}{12} = 0$$

$$a_E' = \frac{1}{12}[11\times1\times1+4\times(-1)\times\epsilon_\phi+4\times(-)\times\epsilon_\phi^*+3\ \ (-1)\times1$$

$$= \frac{1}{12}[11-4\ \ (\epsilon_\phi+\epsilon_\phi^*)\ -3]$$

$$= \frac{1}{12}\ [8-4\ (\epsilon_\phi+\epsilon_\phi^*)]$$

$$a_E'' = \frac{1}{12}\ [11\times1\times1+4\times(-1)\times\epsilon_\phi^*+4\times(-1)\times\epsilon_\phi+3\times(-1)\times1]$$

$$= \frac{1}{12}[8-4\ \ (\epsilon_\phi^*+\epsilon_\phi)]$$

$$\epsilon_\phi = e^{i2\pi/3}$$

$$\epsilon_\phi^* = e^{-i2\pi/3}$$

$$\epsilon_\phi+\epsilon_\phi^* = \cos 2\pi/3 + i\sin 2\pi/3 + \cos 2\pi/3 - i\sin 2\pi/3$$

$$= 2\cos 2\pi/3 = 2(-)\cos 60°$$

$$= -2\times1/2 = -1$$

$$a_E' = \frac{1}{12}[8+4] = \frac{12}{12} = 1$$

$$a_E'' = \frac{1}{12}[8+4] = \frac{12}{12} = 1$$

$$E = a_E' + a_E'' = 1+1 = 2$$

$$a_T = \frac{1}{12}[11\times3\times1+4\times(-1)\times0+4\times(-)\times0+3\times(-)\times(-1)]$$

$$= \frac{1}{12}(33+0+0+3) = \frac{1}{12}\times36 = 3$$

$$\Gamma_H = 2E + 3T$$

Symmetry aspects of s, p and d orbitals in D_{4h}

The sine formula does not work in case of non-cubic symmetry. We directly apply the effect of symmetry operation on such orbitals.

For D_{4h} the members are:

E, $2C_4$, $C_2 = C_4^2$, $2C_2'$, i, σ_h, $2\sigma_v$ $2\sigma_d$ and $2S_4$ with h = 16

Its sub-groups are D_4 and C_4.

D_4	E	$2C_4$	$C_2 \equiv C_4^2$	$2C_2'.2C_2''$,	h = 8
C_4	E	C_4	C_2	C_4^3	h = 4

Let us consider D_4 for which the character Table is depicted:

D_4	E	$2C_4$	$C_2 \equiv C_4^2$	$2C_2'$	$2C_2''$
A_1	1	1	1	1	1
A_2	1	1	1	–1	–1
B_1	1	–1	1	1	–1
B_2	1	–1	1	–1	1
E	2	0	–2	0	0

Take the case of p_z orbital:

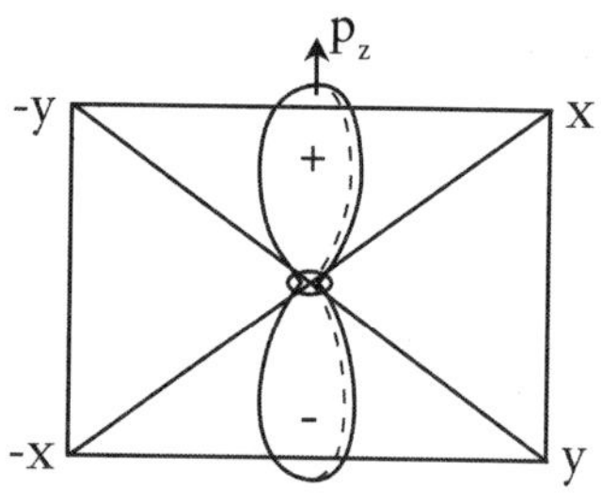

$$E\ (p_z) = (1)\ p_z$$
$$C_4\ (p_z) = (1)\ p_z$$
$$C_2\ (p_z) = (1)\ p_z$$
$$C_2'\ (p_z) = (-1)\ p_z$$
$$C_2''\ (p_z) = (-1)\ p_z$$

p_z transforms as 1, 1, 1, –1, –1 and it falls in A_2 under D_4 and consequently it is a_{2u} in D_{4h} point group as l = 1 is an odd number with u symmetry.

There are p_x and p_y orbitals which mix on the action of C_4 operation and we consider them in pair:

$$E\begin{pmatrix} p_x \\ p_y \end{pmatrix} = \begin{pmatrix} 1 & 0 \\ 0 & 1 \end{pmatrix} \begin{pmatrix} p_x \\ p_y \end{pmatrix}$$

$$\chi = 1 + 1 = 2$$

$$C_4 \ (p_x) = (+1) \ p_y$$

$$C_4 \ (p_y) = (-1) \ p_x$$

$$C_4 \begin{pmatrix} p_x \\ p_y \end{pmatrix} = \begin{pmatrix} 0 & 1 \\ -1 & 0 \end{pmatrix} \begin{pmatrix} p_x \\ p_y \end{pmatrix} \quad \chi = 0 + 0 = 0$$

$$C_2 \ (p_x) = (-1) \ p_x$$

$$C_2 \ (P_y) = (-1) \ p_y$$

$$C_2 \begin{pmatrix} p_x \\ p_y \end{pmatrix} = \begin{pmatrix} -1 & 0 \\ 0 & -1 \end{pmatrix} \begin{pmatrix} p_x \\ p_y \end{pmatrix}$$

$$\chi = -1 - 1 = -2$$

$$C_2' \ (p_x) = (+1) \ p_x$$

$$C_2' \ (p_y) = (-1) \ p_y$$

$$C_2' \begin{pmatrix} p_x \\ p_y \end{pmatrix} = \begin{pmatrix} 1 & 1 \\ 0 & -1 \end{pmatrix} \begin{pmatrix} p_x \\ p_y \end{pmatrix}$$

$$\chi = 1 - 1 = 0$$

$$C_2'' \ (p_x) = (+1) \ p_y$$

$$C_2'' \ (p_y) = (+1) \ p_x$$

$$C_2'' \begin{pmatrix} p_x \\ p_y \end{pmatrix} = \begin{pmatrix} 0 & 1 \\ 1 & 0 \end{pmatrix} \begin{pmatrix} p_x \\ p_y \end{pmatrix}$$

$$\chi = 0 + 0 = 0$$

χ (characters) are:

E	C_4	C_2	C_2'	C_2''
2	0	–1	0	0

It belongs to e symmetry which is converted into e_u representation in D_{4h} symmetry.

Let us consider the effect on s orbital and we always have no change due to symmetry operation:

$$E \quad C_4 \quad C_2 \quad C_2' \text{ and } C_2''$$

E (s) = (+1) s $\quad$ C_4 (s) = (+1) s, $\quad$ C_2 (s) = (+1) s,

C_2'(s) = (+1) s, $\quad$ C_2''(s) = (+1) s ,

All are unity, viz.

1, 1, 1, 1, 1 hence it belongs to a_1 or a_{1g}.

Now, we take up the case of five d-orbitals, such as (dz^2), ($dx^2–y^2$), (dxz, dyz) and (dxy) separately:

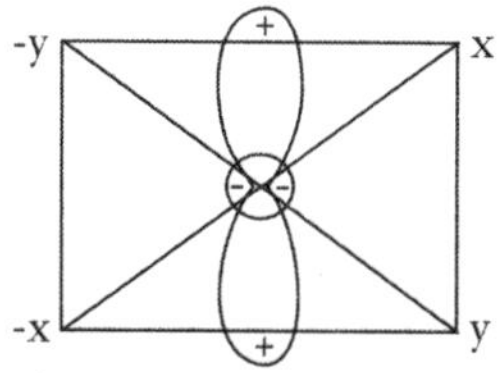

$$E\,(dz^2) = (+1)\,dz^2$$
$$C_4\,(dz^2) = (+1)\,dz^2$$
$$C_2\,(dz^2) = (+1)\,dz^2$$
$$C_2'\,(dz^2) = (+1)\,dz^2$$
$$C_2''\,(dz^2) = (+1)\,dz^2$$

It transforms as 1, 1, 1, 1, 1 and hence it has a_1 or a_{1g} symmetry species on the basis of correlation Table from $D_4 \rightarrow D_{4h}$

Now consider the case of $dx^2–y^2$:

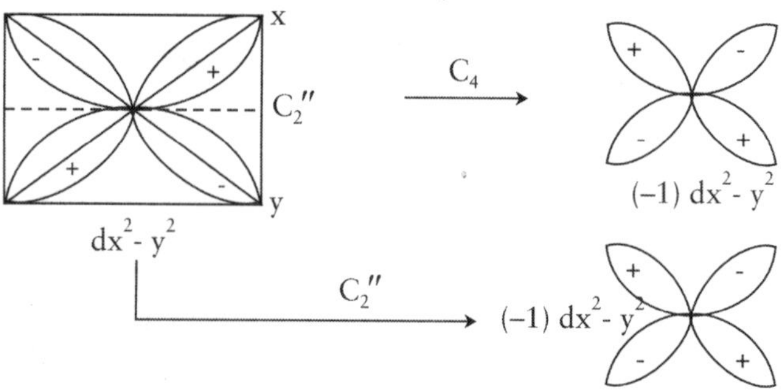

$$E\ (dx^2\!-\!y^2) = (1)\ dx^2\!-\!y^2$$
$$C_4\ (dx^2\!-\!y^2) = (-1)\ dx^2\!-\!y^2$$
$$C_2\ (dx^2\!-\!y^2) = (+1)\ dx^2\!-\!y^2$$
$$C_2'\ (dx^2\!-\!y^2) = (+1)\ dx^2\!-\!y^2$$
$$C_2''\ (dx^2\!-\!y^2) = (-1)\ dx^2\!-\!y^2$$

Γx^2-y^2 has the characters 1, –1, 1, 1, –1, which belongs to b_1 representation. Hence it has b_{1g} symmetry species in D_{4h} point group. Consider the case of d_{xz} and d_{yz} orbitals:

In E there is no effect.

But in C_4 operation mixing occurs between d_{xz} and d_{yz}.

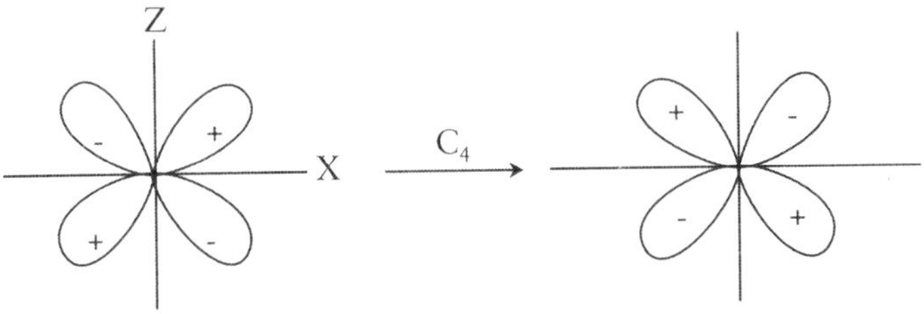

$$d_{xz}\ (C_4) = (-1)\ d_{yz}$$

and we consider this combination.

$$E\ (d_{xz}) = (+1)\ d_{xz}$$
$$E\ (d_{yz}) = (+1)\ d_{yz}$$

$$\begin{pmatrix} dxz' \\ dyz' \end{pmatrix} = E \begin{pmatrix} dxz \\ dyz \end{pmatrix} = \begin{pmatrix} 1 & 0 \\ 0 & 1 \end{pmatrix} \begin{pmatrix} dxz \\ dyz \end{pmatrix}$$

$$\chi = 1 + 1 = 2$$

$$C_4\ (dxz) = (-1)\ dyz$$
$$C_4\ (dyz) = (-1)\ dxz$$

$$\begin{pmatrix} dxz' \\ dyz' \end{pmatrix} = C_4 \begin{pmatrix} dxz \\ dyz \end{pmatrix} = \begin{pmatrix} 0 & -1 \\ -1 & 0 \end{pmatrix} \begin{pmatrix} dxz \\ dyz \end{pmatrix}$$

$$\chi = 0 + 0 = 0$$

$$\begin{pmatrix} dxz' \\ dyz' \end{pmatrix} = C_2 \begin{pmatrix} dxz \\ dyz \end{pmatrix} = \begin{pmatrix} -1 & 0 \\ 0 & -1 \end{pmatrix} \begin{pmatrix} dxz \\ dyz \end{pmatrix}$$

$$\chi = -1 - 1 = -2$$

Since,

$$C_2\ (d_{xz}) = (-1)\ d_{xz}$$

$$C_2\ (d_{yz}) = (-1)\ d_{yz}$$

Similarly $C_2'\ (d_{xz}) = (-1) d_{xz}$

$$C_2'\ (d_{yz}) = (+1) d_{yz}$$

C_2^x is perpendicular to the yz plane a rotation by 180° does not alter the sign of the lobes (as they are inter-changed simply):

$$C_2' \begin{pmatrix} d_{xz} \\ d_{yz} \end{pmatrix} = \begin{pmatrix} -1 & 0 \\ 0 & +1 \end{pmatrix} \begin{pmatrix} d_{xz} \\ d_{yz} \end{pmatrix}$$

$$\chi = -1 + 1 = 0$$

It so happens in C_2''

$$C_2''\ (d_{xz}) = (\pm 1)\ d_{yz}$$

$$C_2''\ (d_{yz}) = (\pm 1)\ d_{xz}$$

$$\begin{pmatrix} d_{xz}' \\ d_{yz}' \end{pmatrix} = C_2'' \begin{pmatrix} d_{xz} \\ d_{yz} \end{pmatrix} = \begin{pmatrix} 0 & \pm 1 \\ \pm 1 & 0 \end{pmatrix}$$

$$\chi = 0 + 0 = 0$$

Giving 2, 0, –2, 0, 0 and it has e or eg representation.

Consider the case of dxy in D_4 point group:

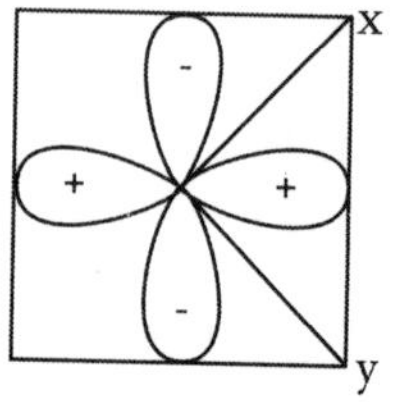

$$E\ (d_{xy}) = (+1)\ d_{xy}$$

$$C_4\ (d_{xy}) = (-1)\ d_{xy}$$

$$C_2\ (d_{xy}) = (+1)\ d_{xy}$$

$$C_2'\ (d_{xy}) = (-1)\ d_{xy}$$

$$C_2''\ (d_{xy}) = (+1)\ d_{xy}$$

1, –1, 1, –1, 1 = Belonging to b_2 in D_4 and it is converted into b_{2g} in D_{4h}.

As such five d orbitals decompose to give $a_{1g} + b_{1g} + b_{2g} +$ eg species in D_{4h}.

Co (II) d^7 O_h ground state $(t_{2g})^6\ (e_g)^1 = (e_g)^1$ leads to 2_{Eg}.

Ni (II) d^8 O_h ground state $(t_{2g})^6\ A_{1g}\ (e_g)^2 = (e_g)^2\ e_g \times e_g \rightarrow {}^3A_{2g}$

Cu (II) d^9 O_h " " $t_2g^6\ e_g^{\ 3} \rightarrow e_g^{\ 4-1} \equiv e_g^{\ 1} =$ Eg

Zn (II) d^{10} O_h " " $t_{2g}^{\ 6}\ e_g^{\ 4} = A_{1g}$

$O_h \rightarrow D_{4h}$ for d^9 with J.T. distortion.

1	$b_{1g}\ (x^2 - y^2)$
2	$a_{1g}\ (z^2)$
2	$b_{2g}\ (xy)$
4	e_g (xz, yz)
D_{4h}	

ground state configuration in D_{4h} is $(e_g)^4\ (b_{2g})^2\ (a_{1g})^2\ (b_{1g})^1$

$$eg \times eg = A_{1g}$$

$$b_{2g} \times b_{2g} = A_{1g}$$ As such ground state is ${}^2B_{1g}$.

$$a_{1g} \times a_{1g} = A_{1g}$$

$$b_{1g} - B_{1g}$$

$$\xrightarrow[\text{(i)}]{h\nu} \underset{A_{1g}}{\underset{\downarrow}{(eg)^4}}\ \underset{A_{1g}}{\underset{\downarrow}{(b_{2g})^2}}\ \underset{A_{1g}}{\underset{\downarrow}{\left(a_{1g}\right)^1}}\ \underset{A_{1g}}{\underset{\downarrow}{(b_{1g})^2}} = A_{ig}$$

excited state is ${}^2A_{1g}$

$$\xrightarrow[\text{(ii)}]{h\nu} (e_g)^4 \; (b_{2g}) \; (a_{1g})^2 \; (b_{1g})^2$$

$$\begin{array}{cccc} \downarrow & \downarrow & \downarrow & \downarrow \\ A_{1g} & B_{2g} & A_{1g} & A_{1g} \end{array}$$

the second excited state is B_{2g}

$$\xrightarrow[\text{(iii)}]{h\nu} (e_g)^3 \; (b_{2g})^2 \; (a_{ig})^2 \; (b_{1g})^2$$

$$\begin{array}{cccc} \downarrow & \downarrow & \downarrow & \downarrow \\ E_g & A_{1g} & A_{1g} & A_{1g} \\ \multicolumn{2}{c}{\underbrace{\hspace{3em}}_{E_g}} & \multicolumn{2}{c}{\underbrace{\hspace{3em}}_{A_{1g}}} \end{array}$$

the third excited state is E_g.

There are three excited state configurations:

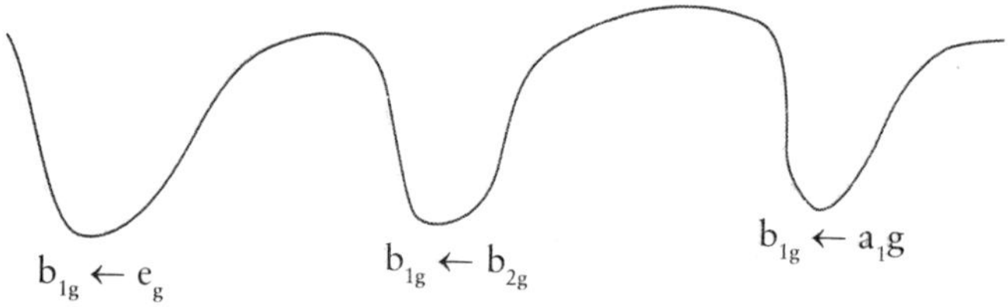

For the state the term diagram is reversed:

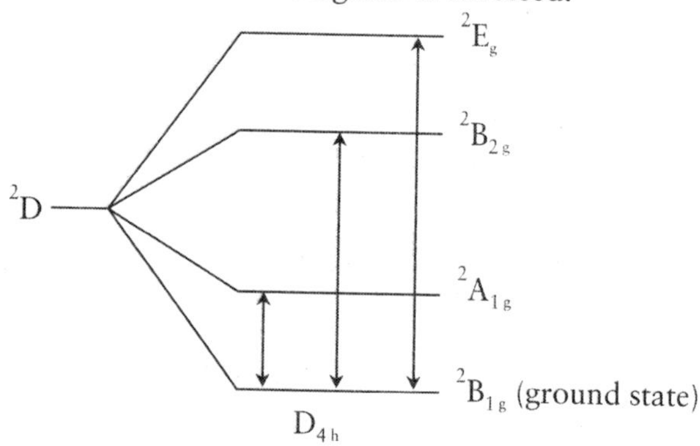

For the transition B_{1g} is the starting point. Case of Ni(II) d^8 in D_{4h} symmetry, its ground electronic configuration will be:

$$\begin{array}{ccc} (e_g)^4 & (b_{2g})^2 & (a_{1g})^2 \\ \downarrow & \downarrow & \downarrow \\ A_{1g} & A_{1g} & A_{1g} \rightarrow {}^1A_{1g} \end{array}$$

$2S + 1 = 1$
because $S = 0$

Its first excited state configuration is:

$$\begin{array}{cccc} (eg)^4 & (b_{2g})^2 & (a_{1g})^1 & (b_{1g})^1 \\ \downarrow & \downarrow & \downarrow & \downarrow \\ A_{1g} & A_{1g} & A_{1g} & B_{1g} \end{array}$$

$$A_{1g} \times B_{1g} = B_{1g}$$

$$2S + 1 = 1 \text{ or } 3$$

$$^1B_{1g} \,\&\, ^3B_{1g}$$

$3_{B_{1g}}$ is lower in energy but it denotes spin forbidden from singlet → triplet. So we ignore $^3B_{1g}$; weak.

Second excited state is obtained out of:

$$\begin{array}{cccc} (e_g)^4 & (b_{2g})^1 & (a_{1g})^2 & (b_{1g})^1 \\ \downarrow & \downarrow & \downarrow & \downarrow \\ A_{1g} & B_{2g} & A_{1g} & B_{1g} \end{array}$$

$$B_{2g} \times B_{1g} = A_{2g}$$

$b_{2g} \rightarrow b_{1g}$ is represented by $^1A_{1g} \rightarrow {^1A_{2g}}$ band.

Second band is represented by $^1A_{1g} \rightarrow {^1A_{2g}}$.

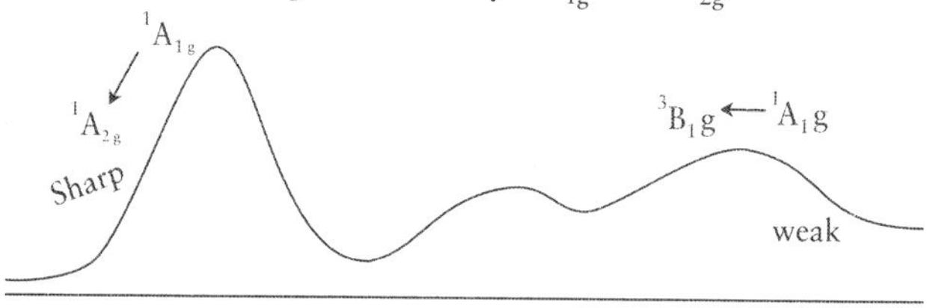

The third band corresponds to $(eg)^3\,(b_{2g})^2\,(a_{1g})^2\,(b_{1g})^1$

$$E_g \times B_{1g} = E_g$$

$$e_g \rightarrow b_{1g}$$

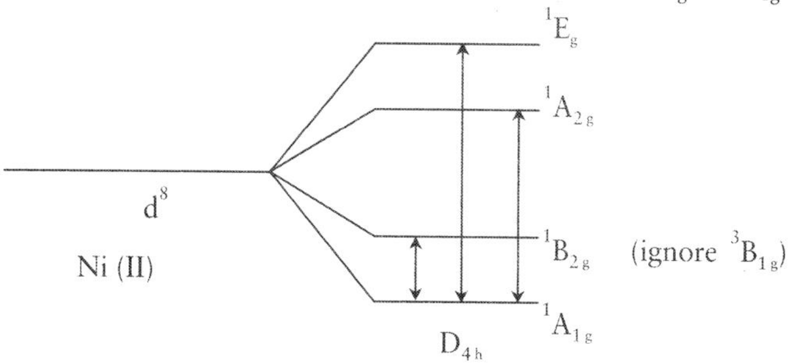

(i) $a_{1g} \rightarrow b_{1g}$ viz $^1A_{1g} \rightarrow {}^1B_{1g}$

(ii) $b_{2g} \rightarrow b_{1g}$ viz. $^1A_{1g} \rightarrow {}^1A_{2g}$

(iii) $e_g \rightarrow b_{1g}$ viz. $^1A_{1g} \rightarrow {}^1E_g$

Strong Field Approach

A d^n configuration of free ion may be subjected to a number of perturbing factors such as strong crystal field potential (V_{CF}), inter electronic repulsion $\left(\sum_i \sum_{j>i} \frac{e^2}{r_{ij}}\right)$, Spin-orbit coupling $\Sigma \xi$ (i) $l_i\, s_i$ and magnetic field (H).

It is customary to apply largest perturbation effect first and weakest at last. In strong field limit the crystal field potential is very large in comparison with others and as such d^n will be subjected to splitting (in a 10 Dq a high value) into t_{2g} and e_g levels in O_h environment leading to strong field configurations for instance a d^2 configuration may give rise to $(t_{2g})^2$ as the ground state and other two excited states are $(t_{2g})^1$ $(e_g)^1$ and $(eg)^2$. Such configurations are affected by inter electronic repulsion which causes to split them leading to several states on taking their direct product. These are known as strong field components. A second aspect of strong field method is related to spin-multiplicity. Because of 10Dq values being much larger than pairing energy. There is every chance of electron pairing. This may complicate this procedure. There can be two types of cases, first d^1, d^2, d^3, d^8 and d^9 are always with high spin whereas d^4, d^5, d^6 and d^7 systems in O_h field can form both low and high spin complexes.

Strong Field Components for d^2 System

Two electrons may be accommodated first in t_{2g} levels, because of large splitting between t_{2g} and e_g levels giving ground state configuration $(t_{2g})^2$ with its energy value of the order $2\times(-4dq) = -8D_q$.

The other excited states are with the values $(t_{2g})^1$ $(eg)^1$ -4 Dq + 6Dq = +2Dq and $(eg)^2$ with $2 \times (+1)6$Dq = 12Dq. A difference of 10Dq is always maintained in all these configurations.

It has been found that state derived from strong field method do not match with the actual field produced by the ligands. In actual practice the field will be of intermediate value. So neither inter-electronic repulsion nor $V_{C.F}$ is too high or low. To meet with this situation one can correlate with the energy levels derived from weak field as well as strong field treatments. We apply the use of character Table for taking direct products such as:

$\Gamma_{t_{2g} \times t_{2g}}$, $\Gamma_{t_{2g} \times e_g}$ and $\Gamma_{e_g \times e_g}$ in O point group instead of O_h.

O	E	$6C_4$	$3C_2 (\equiv C_4^2)$	$8C_3$	$6C_2$		O_h
A_1	1	1	1	1	1	$x^2+y^2+z^2$	
A_2	1	−1	1	1	−1		
E	2	0	2	−1	0	$z^2, x^2 - y^2$	e_g
T_1	3	1	−1	0	−1	x, y, z	
T_2	3	−1	−1	0	1	xz, yz, xy	t_{2g}

$\Gamma_{t_{2g} \times t_{2g}}$	3×3	−1×1	−1×−1	0×0	1×1
	9	1	1	0	1
$\Gamma_{t_{2g} \times e_g}$	3×2	−1×0	−1×2	0×−1	1×0
	6	0	−2	0	0
$\Gamma_{e_g \times e_g}$	2×2	0×0	2×2	−1×−1	0×0
	4	0	4	1	0

Irreducible components can be derived using decomposition formula:

$$a_{A_{1g}} = \frac{1}{24}[9 \times 1 \times 1 + 6 \times 1 \times 1 + 3 \times 1 \times 6 + 8 \times 1 \times 0 + 6 \times 1 \times 1]$$

$$= \frac{1}{24}[9 + 6 + 3 + 0 + 0 + 6] = \frac{1}{24}[24] = 1$$

$$a_{E_g} = \frac{1}{24}[9 \times 2 \times 1 + 6 \times 1 \times 0 + 3 \times 1 \times 2 + 8 \times 0 \times (-1) + 6 \times 1 \times 0]$$

$$= \frac{1}{24}[18 + 0 + 6 + 0 + 0] = \frac{24}{24} = 1$$

$$a_{T_{1g}} = \frac{1}{24}[9\times3\times1+6\times1\times1+3\times1\times-1+8\times1\times0+6\times1\times-1]$$

$$= \frac{1}{24}[27+6-3-6] = \frac{24}{24} = 1$$

$$a_{T_{2g}} = \frac{1}{24}[9\times3\times1+6\times-1\times1+3\times-1\times1+8\times0\times0+6\times1\times1]$$

$$= \frac{1}{24}[27-6-3+0+6]$$

$$= \frac{1}{24}\times24 = 1$$

$$\Gamma_{t_{2g}\times t_{2g}} = {}^{a}A_{1g} + {}^{b}E_{g} + {}^{C}T_{1g} + {}^{d}T_{2g}$$

This compensates orbital degeneracy 9.

We determine the spin degeneracy of states out of total degeneracy as given by:

$$^{2n}C_r = \frac{2n!}{2n-r!r!},$$

with n as orbital multiplicity and r the number of electrons:

$$= \frac{2\times3!}{2\times3-2!2!} = \frac{6!}{4!2!} = \frac{6\times5\times4\times3\times2\times1}{4\times3\times2\times1\times2\times1} = \frac{30}{2} = 15$$

For $(t_{2g})^2$ configuration:

$${}^{a}A_{1g} + {}^{b}Eg + {}^{c}T_{1g} + {}^{d}T_{2g} = 15$$

$$a \times 1 + b \times 2 + c \times 3 + d \times 3 = 15$$

$$a + 2b + 3c + 3d = 15$$

There are three possible solutions:

		a	b	c	d
a = b = c = 1, d = 3	I	1	1	1	3
a = b = d = 1, c = 3	II	1	1	3	1
a = b = 3, c = d = 1	III	3	3	1	1

There can be three set of components:

$${}^{1}A_{1g} + {}^{1}E_{g} + {}^{1}T_{1g} + {}^{3}T_{2g},\quad {}^{1}A_{1g} + {}^{1}E_{g} + {}^{3}T_{1g} + {}^{1}T_{2g}$$

and ${}^{3}A_{1g} + {}^{3}E_{g} + {}^{1}T_{1g} + {}^{1}T_{2g}$.

Since on the weak field side the ground state is $T_{1g}(F)$ and by this analogy we have the most suitable choice by $^1A_{1g}$ + ^1E_g + $^3T_{1g}$ + $^1T_{2g}$. The relative order is obtained from the Hund's rule having $^3T_{1g}$ as the ground state. The next excited state configuration is $(t_{2g})^1$ $(e_g)^1$ which gives the direct product:

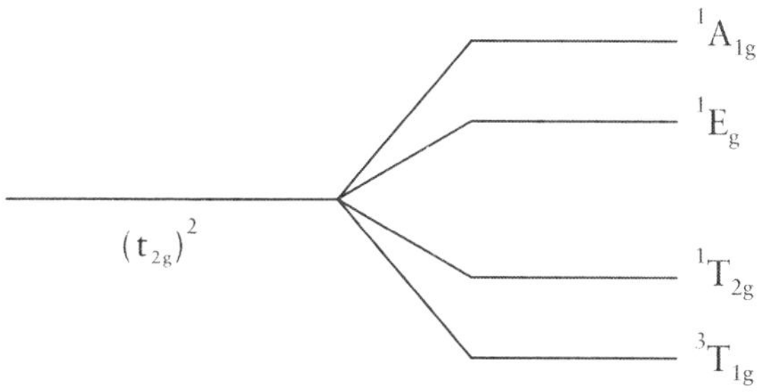

$\Gamma_{t_{2g} \times e_g}$ 6 0 −2 0 0 leading to

$$a_{T_{1g}} = \frac{1}{24}\left[6\times3\times1+3\times(-2)\times(-)+0+0\right]$$

$$= \frac{1}{24}\left[18+6\right] = \frac{24}{24} = 1$$

$$a_{T_{2g}} = \frac{1}{24}\left[6\times3\times1+0-3\times(-2)\times(-1) = 0+0\right]$$

$$= \frac{1}{24}\left[18+6\right] = \frac{24}{24} = 1$$

$\Gamma_{t_{2g} \times e_g} \rightarrow$ Γ_{1g} + T_{2g} for which the total degeneracy is given by:

$$^{2n}C_r \times ^{2n}C_r = \frac{2\times3!}{2\times3-1!\;1!} \times \frac{2\times2!}{2\times2-1!\;1!}$$

$$= \frac{6\,!}{5!} \times \frac{4!}{3!} = 6\times4 = 24$$

$$^aT_{1g} + {}^bT_{2g} = 24$$

$$a \times 3 + b \times 3 = 24$$

$$a + b = 8, \quad \text{so} \quad a = 3 \text{ or } 1$$

$$b = 3 \text{ or } 1$$

$^3T_{1g} + {}^3T_{2g} + {}^1T_{1g} + {}^1T_{2g}$ accordingly the degeneracy is 24.

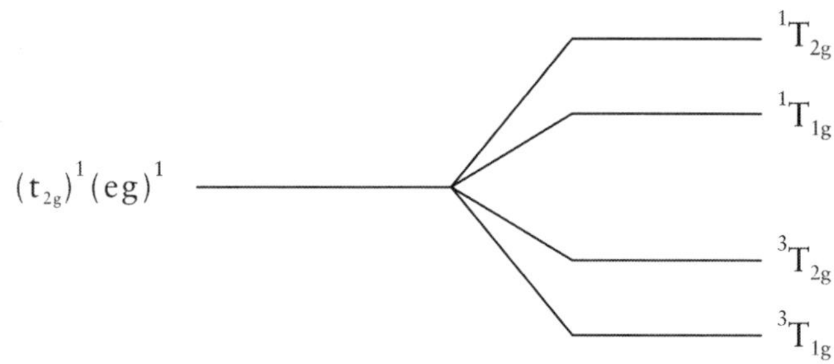

Consider the case of $(e_g)^2$ configuration Its direct product given by $\Gamma_{eg\times eg}$ is giving rise to ${}^aA_{1g} + {}^bA_{2g} + {}^cE_g$.

The total degeneracy for $(e_g)^2$ is given by:

$$^{2n}C_r = \frac{2\times 2!}{2\times 2-2!\,2!} = \frac{4!}{2!\,2!} = \frac{4\times 3\times 2}{2\times 2} = 6$$

$$1a + 1b + 2c = 6$$

	a	b	c	
I	1	3	1	${}^1A_{1g} + {}^3A_{2g} + {}^1E_g$
II	3	1	1	${}^3A_{1g} + {}^1A_{2g} + {}^1E_g$

It is well accounted in:

$$ {}^1A_{1g} \;+\; {}^3A_{2g} \;+\; {}^1E_g$$

$$1 \;+\; 3 \;+\; 2$$

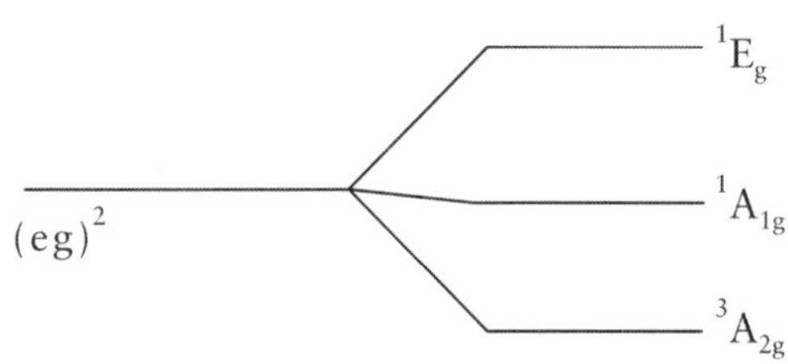

9.11 CORRELATION DIAGRAM

We consider how those states arising out of strong O_h field are related to those in the weak field case. The left hand side comprises weak field components derived from free ion terms on the right hand side we have strong field configurations and the states obtained from each of them. The diagram is drawn as a function of ligand field strength. This is based on two principles:

1. One to one correspondance occurs between states of same symmetry and spin multiplicity.

   On weak field and strong field parts a state with ${}^3T_{1g}$ weak field side correlates with ${}^3T_{1g}$ on the right hand side.

   $${}^3T_{1g}\ (F) \rightarrow {}^3T_{1g} \text{ of } (t_{2g})^2$$

   $${}^3T_{1g}\ (P) \rightarrow {}^3T_{1g} \text{ of } (t_{2g})^1\ (e_g)^1$$

2. On relative increase in the field strength states with same symmetry and multiplicity do not cross (non-crossing rule). We correlate two lower terms with the same symmetry and multiplicity which would never cross each other.

   Under O_h symmetry we obtain weak field components such as:

${}^1S$	${}^1A_{1g}$
${}^3P$	${}^3T_{1g}$ (p)
${}^1D$	${}^1T_{1g} + {}^1E_g$
${}^3F$	${}^3T_{1g} + {}^3T_{2g} + {}^3A_{2g}$
${}^1G$	${}^1T_{1g} + {}^1T_{2g} + {}^1E_g + {}^1A_{1g}$

   The order of energy is:

   $${}^3F < {}^1D < {}^3P < {}^1G < {}^1S$$

There is dominance of inter-electronic repulsion on the crystal field potential and L-S coupling scheme works well. We apply spectroscopic terms which has been subjected to crystal field and there are split components.

Correlation diagram for d^2 case in O_h point group:

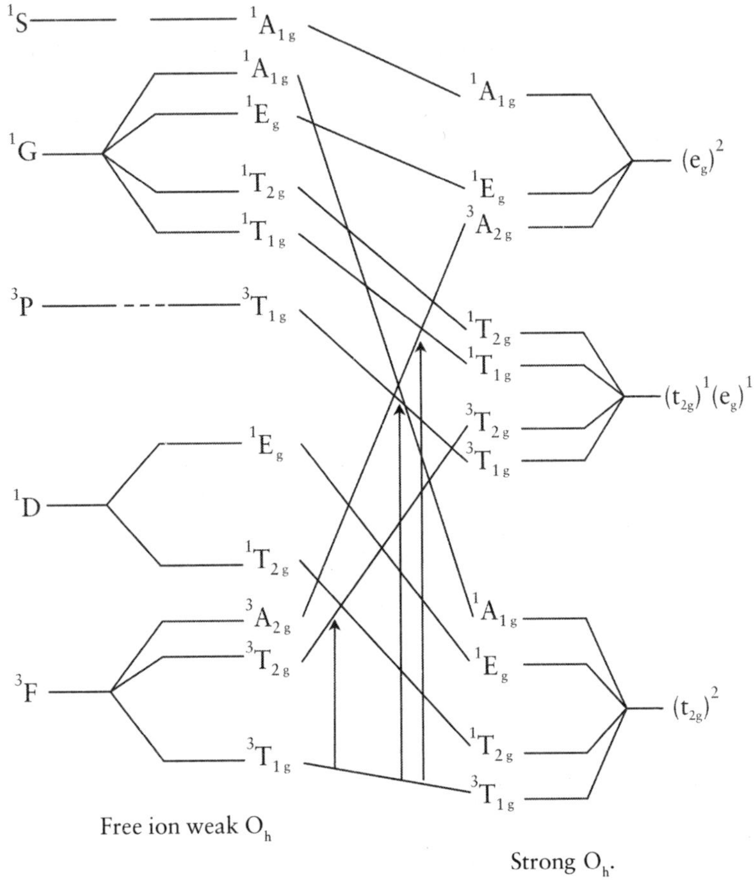

Correlation diagram for, d^2 O_h.

Diagram predicts three transitions in medium field, viz.

$$^3T_{1g}\,(F) \rightarrow {}^3T_{2g}\,(F)$$

$$^3T_{1g}\,(F) \rightarrow {}^3T_{1g}\,(P)$$

$$^3T_{1g}\,(F) \rightarrow {}^3A_{2g}\,(F)$$

9.12 d^2 CASE WITH T_d SYMMETRY

In a weak field the terms and their components are:

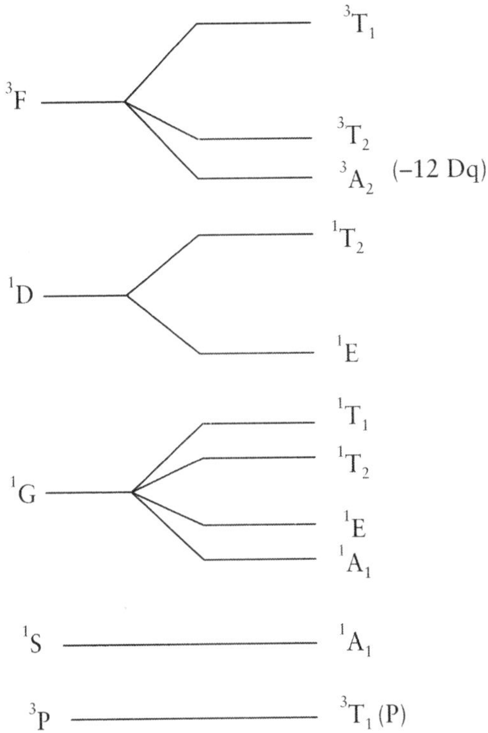

In strong field case of d^2 configuration the d-orbitals split into:

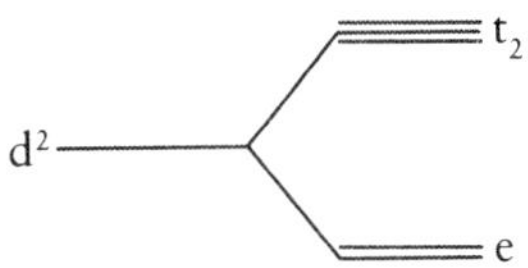

Ground state configuration is $(e)^2$ and excited states are $(e)^1\ (t_2)^1$ and $(t_2)^2$.

Energy consideration may be given as:

$(e)^2$	$E = -12$ Dq.
$(e)^1\ (t_2)^1$	$E = -6$ Dq $+ 4$ Dq $= -2$ Dq.
$(t_2)^2$	$E = +8$ Dq.

T_d	E	$8C_3$	$3C_2$	$6S_4$	$6\sigma_d$	order h=24
A_1	1	1	1	1	1	
A_2	1	1	1	–1	–1	
E	2	–1	2	0	0	
T_1	3	0	–1	1	–1	
T_2	3	0	–1	–1	1	
$e \times e$	4	1	4	0	0	
$e \times t_2$	6	0	–2	0	0	
$t_2 \times t_2$	9	0	1	1	1	

$$a_{A_1} = \frac{1}{24}[4\times1\times1+8\times1\times1+3\times4\times1+0+0]$$

$$= \frac{1}{24}\times24 = 1$$

$$a_{A_2} = \frac{1}{24}[4\times1\times1+8\times1\times1+3\times1\times4+6\times-1\times0+6\times-1\times0]$$

$$= \frac{1}{24}[4+8+12] = \frac{24}{24} = 1$$

$$a_E = \frac{1}{24}[1\times2\times4+8\times-1\times1+3\times2\times4+0+0]$$

$$= \frac{1}{24}[8-8+24] = \frac{24}{24} = 1$$

$\Gamma_R\,(e\times e) = A_1 + A_2 + E$

$(e)^1\, t_2)^1$

$$a_{A_1} = \frac{1}{24}[6\times1\times1+0+3\times-2\times1] = 0$$

$$a_{A_2} = \frac{1}{24}[6\times1\times1+0+3\times-2\times1] = 0$$

$$a_E = \frac{1}{24}[6\times2\times1+0+3\times-2\times2] = 0$$

$$a_{T_1} = \frac{1}{24}\times24 = 1$$

$$a_{T_2} = \frac{1}{24}\times24 = 1$$

$\Gamma_R\ (e \times t_2) = T_1 + T_2$

$(t_2)^2\quad \Gamma t_2 \times t_2 \qquad 9 \qquad 0 \qquad 1 \qquad 1 \qquad 1$

$$a_{A_1} = \frac{1}{24}\left[9\times1\times1+3\times1\times1+1\times1\times1+6\times1\times1\right]$$

$$= \frac{24}{24} = 1$$

$$a_{A_2} = \frac{1}{24}\left[9\times1\times1+3\times1\times1+6\times1\times-1+6\times1\times-1\right] = 0$$

$$a_E = \frac{1}{24}\left[6\times2\times1+0+3\times(-2)\times2\right]$$

$$= \frac{1}{24}\left[12+12\right] = \frac{24}{24} = 1$$

$$a_{T_1} = \frac{1}{24}\left[9\times3+-3\times1\times1+6\times4+6\times1\times-1\right] = \frac{24}{24} = 1$$

$$a_{T_2} = \frac{1}{24}\left[27-3-6+6\right] = \frac{24}{24} = 1$$

$\Gamma_R\ t_2 \times t_2 \;=\; A_1 + E + T_1 + T_2$

$3 \times 3 \qquad 1 \quad 2 \quad 3 \quad 3$

$= 9$

e^2 Case

Determination of spin multiplicity:

$$^{2n}C_r = \frac{2\times2\,!}{2\,!\,2\,!} = \frac{4\times3\times2}{2\times2} = 6$$

$\Gamma(R)\ (e \times e) = A_1 + A_2 + E$

$^aA_1 + {}^bA_2 + {}^cE$

$a \times 1 + b \times 1 + c \times 2 = 6$

or, $a + b + 2c = 6$

$a = b = 1,\ c=2$

$a = c = 1,\ b = 3$

	a	b	c
I	1	1	2
II	1	3	1

But there is no doublet in weak field side with E but $^3A_2$. Hence, solution II is acceptable:

$$\Gamma e \times e \rightarrow {}^1A_1 + {}^3A_2 + {}^1E$$

Applying Hund's rule we have:

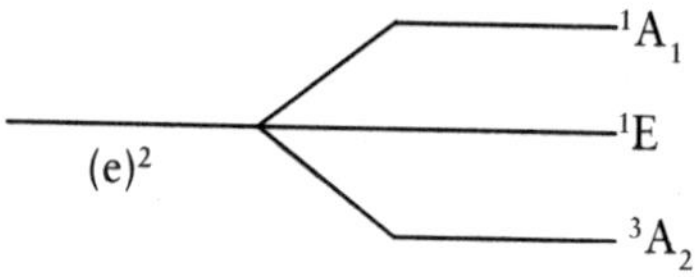

for $(e)^1 (t_2)^1$

$$\Gamma e \times t_2 \rightarrow T_1 + T_2$$

$$(e)^1 \times (t_2)^1 \rightarrow {}^aT_1 + {}^bT_2$$

$$^{2n}C_r \times {}^{2n}C_r = {}^{2\times2}C_1 \times {}^{2\times3}C_1$$

$$= \frac{4!}{3!} \times \frac{6!}{5!} = \frac{4\times3\times2}{3\times2} \times \frac{6\times5\times4\times3\times2}{5\times4\times3\times2} = 24$$

$$3a + 3b = 24$$

$$a + b = 8.$$

So, $a = b = 3$

$a = b = 1$

$$\rightarrow \; {}^1T_1 + {}^1T_2 + {}^3T_1 + {}^3T_2$$

3 3 9 9

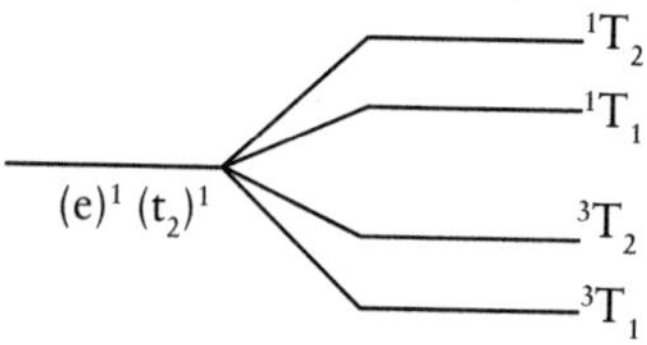

For:

$$(t_2)^2 \rightarrow {}^aA_1 + {}^bE + {}^cT_1 + {}^dT_2$$

$$^{2n}C_r = {}^{2\times3}C_2 = \frac{6!}{4!\,2!} = 15$$

$$a \times 1 + b \times 2 + 0 \times 3 + d \times 3 = 15$$

$$a + 2b + 3c + 3d = 15$$

	a	b	c	d
I	1	1	3	1
II	1	1	1	3
III	3	3	1	1

Solution I is acceptable as it gives rise to $^3T_1$ on the right hand side which also occurs on the left hand side:

$$(t_2)^2 \rightarrow {}^1A_1 + {}^1E + {}^3T_1 + {}^1T_2$$

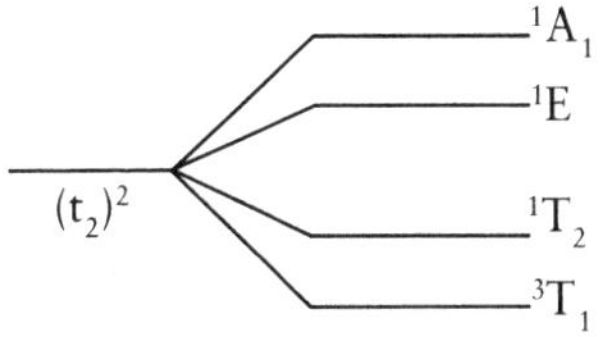

We now correlate states from the weak field with the strong field sides:

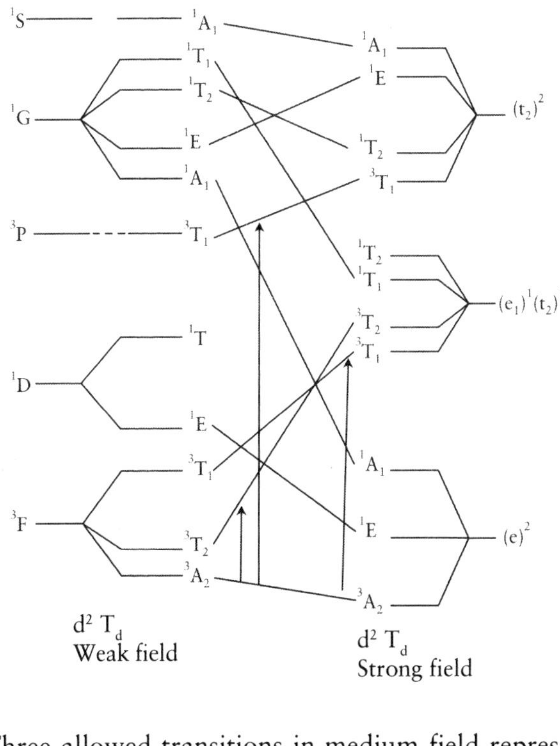

Three allowed transitions in medium field represented as,

$^3A_2 \rightarrow {}^3T_2$

$\rightarrow {}^3T_1(F)$

$\rightarrow {}^3T_1(P)$

Transition Moment Integral and Intensity of Band

There can be classification of electronic spectra on the basis of intensity and band width of spectral bands. There can be weak or high intensed bands. A highly intensed band occurs when transition is allowed, a feebly intensed band represents forbidden transition.

Experimental area of the band = $\int \in (\bar{\upsilon})\, d\bar{\upsilon}$.

Theoretically the band intensity is related to area of the band:

$$I = \int \in (\bar{\upsilon})\, d\bar{\upsilon}$$

The plot indicates that the point of maximum absorption is shown by λ_{max} in abscissa scale and $\in_{max.}$ in ordinate scale.

$\in_{max}$	high	strong band
$\in_{max}$	low	weak band

Intensity of the band is theoretically explained by the use of a quantity (of theoretical interest), oscillator strength or dipole strength D:

$$f \propto \sqrt{D} \text{ and } I \propto \sqrt{D}$$

$\sqrt{D}$ is given by the transition moment integral.

$$\sqrt{D} = \int \Psi_i\, \mu \Psi_f\, d\tau = M$$

dipole moment = $\Sigma\, e_i\, x_i = \mu$. It resolves into three parts.

The transition moment integral should be totally symmetric for its non-zero value. In other words, it must be A_1 or A_{1g} of the direct product $\Gamma_{\Psi_0} \times \Gamma_{\Psi_f} \times \Gamma_{\mu_z}$ or Γ_{μ_y} or Γ_{μ_x} should have A_1 or A_{1g} symmetry.

Symmetry Selection Rule for d-d transition

Usually d-d transitions in octahedral complexes are symmetry forbidden such transitions are taking place between wave functions of same parity g – g which gives rise to $g \times g = g$.

In order to have non-zero value of transition moment integral M:

$$\int \Psi_i \ \mu \ \Psi_f \ d\tau$$

The cross-product of symmetry of ground state electronic wave function Ψ_i and excited state wave function should differ in parity u × g = g × u = u. As the dipole moment (μ) always resembles the translational vectors, and are always u type such that triple cross-product of the wave functions and dipole moment should have non-vanishing value with overall g symmetry (even). So the transition is allowed with difference in parity.

For d-d transition the integral consists of:

$$\int \underset{g}{\Psi_i} \ \underset{u}{\mu} \ \underset{g}{\Psi_f} \ d\tau$$

$$(g \times g) \times u = g \times u = u = 0$$

The integral vanishes. As such transition is forbidden.

Relaxation in Selection Rule and Vibronic Coupling

Even in so many octahedral complexes involving d-d transition the integral vanishes, but it has been observed that in such cases the $\in_{max} \simeq 10^{-3}$ and the intensity is on a high value. A mechanism has been invoked by interaction between vibronic parts of the wave function with the electronic parts of the wave function. This is termed as vibronic coupling and the transitions are relaxed under the modified scheme.

Vibronic coupling is important as the vibrational mode is excited simultaneously with the electronic transition causing distortion of centre of symmetry of O_h system that makes the transition allowed to some extent. The transition moment integral is suitably amended involving vibrational wave functions :

$$M = \int \Psi_i \ \Psi_v^{gr} \ \mu \Psi_f \ \Psi_\upsilon^{ex} \ d\tau$$

$$= \int \Psi_i \ \mu \ \Psi_f \ d\tau \ . \int \Psi_\upsilon^{gr} \ \Psi_\upsilon^{ex} \ d\tau$$

There may be ground state wave function for vibrational level Ψ_0 or Ψ_1 to electronic state with different vibrational level (1 or 0). As a consequence of this type of coupling between $0 \rightarrow 1$ or $1 \rightarrow 0$ with the electronic transition the electronic band is a bit allowed. The involvement of $0 \rightarrow 1$ vibrational wave function which belongs to A_1 or A_{1g} symmetry under a given point group then there is only the question of vibrational wave function and its symmetry species. If the cross product of the representation of the electronic state along with the translational vector is same as that of vibrational mode, i.e.:

$$\int \left(\Gamma_{\Psi_i} \times \Gamma_{\Psi_f}\right) \times \Gamma_{T_x} = \Gamma_i$$

$$\times \Gamma_{T_y}$$

$$\times \Gamma_{T_z}$$

The Γ_i corresponds to the Γ_i representation of the vibrational mode, $\Gamma_i \times \Gamma_i = A_1$ or A_{1g} etc., a totally symmetric species. The transition is vibronically allowed.

Consider the case of vibronic coupling in $[CO(NH_3)_6]^{3+}$. It represents a strong field case with configuration $(t_{2g})^6$ with S = O 2S + 1 = 1

Its ground state is, $^1A_{1g}$. There are two excited states $^1T_{1g}$ and $^1T_{2g}$:

$$\Psi_i = {}^1A_{1g},\ \Psi_f = {}^1T_{1g} \text{ or } {}^1T_{2g}.$$

The two spin allowed but symmetry forbidden bands are:

$$^1A_{1g} \rightarrow {}^1T_{1g}$$

$$\rightarrow {}^1T_{2g}$$

The translational components transform as T_{1u} and therefore for: $^1A_{1g} \rightarrow {}^1T_{1g}$ transition the cross product is:

$$(A_{1g} \times T_{1g}) \times T_{1u} = T_{1g} \times T_{1u}$$

T_{1g}	3	0	−1	−1	1	3	0	−1	−1	1
T_{1u}	3	0	−1	−1	1	−3	0	1	1	−1
$T_{1g} \times T_{1u}$	9	0	1	1	1	−9	0	−1	−1	−1

$$= A_{1u} + Eu + T_{1u} + T_{2u}$$

For T_{2g} transition, the transition moment integral takes the form:

$$T_{2g} \times T_{1u} = A_{2u} + Eu + T_{1u} + T_{2u}$$

In both cases the components are T_{1u} and T_{2u} and looking at M-N vibrational component in O_h point group the vibrational modes are: A_{1g}, E_g, $2T_{1u}$, T_{2g}, T_{2u}.

Since, T_{1u} and T_{2u} are common in both the two cases:

$$\Gamma_i (e) \times \Gamma_i (v)$$

$$= T_{1u} \times T_{1u} = A_{1g} \text{ etc. totally symmetric species.}$$

Also, $T_{2u} \times T_{2u} = A_{1g}$ etc.

One of the components in either case is totally symmetric and hence the band is vibronically allowed.

Vibronic Polarization and Electronic Polarization of d-d Spectra

When there is further relaxation in O_h symmetry by way of descending into D_{4h} and D_3 symmetries, through tetragonal distortion in presence of un-symmetrical ligands such as in trans-dichloro bis ethylene diamine Co (III), trans $[CoCl_2(en)_2]^+$ the three components of translational vectors do not belong to same symmetry species in D_{4h} but they have different directional properties. The z component corresponds to A_{2u} while (x, y) components to Eu and there will be a case of vibronic polarization in D_{4h}. There is loss of O_h symmetry due to tetragonal distortion in a six coordinated complex. It has a non-cubic symmetry and undergoes vibronic polarization.

In cubic symmetry all the translational vectors irrespective of direction, correspond to T_{1u} symmetry species and hence there is no effect of polarization. Co (III) d^6 system gives rise to $^1A_{1g}$ state the three bands are assigned to:

$$^1A_{1g} \rightarrow {}^1A_{2g}$$
$$\rightarrow {}^1B_{2g}$$
$$\rightarrow {}^1E_g$$

z-Polarization of Transition

$$\int \Psi_i \Psi_\upsilon^{gr} \mu \Psi_f \Psi_\upsilon^{ex} d\tau$$
$$= \int \Psi_i \mu \Psi_f d\tau \times \int \Psi_\upsilon^{gr} \Psi_\upsilon^{ex} d\tau$$

In case of $^1A_{1g} \rightarrow {}^1A_{2g}$ transition.

$$\int \Psi_i \mu \Psi_f d\tau = \left(A_{1g} \times A_{2g}\right) \times A_{2u}$$
$$= A_{2g} \times A_{2u} = A_{1u}$$

A_{2u}	1	1	1	–1	–1	–1	–1	–1	1	1	
A_{2g}	1	1	1	–1	–1	1	1	1	–1	–1	
$A_{2g} \times A_{2u}$	1	1	1	1	1	–1	–1	–1	–1	–1	$= A_{1u}$

The M-N vibrational modes in $[CoCl_2\ N_4]^+$ unit in D_{4h} point group may have:

$$2A_{1g},\ B_{1g},\ B_{2g},\ E_g,\ 2A_{2u},\ B_{1u},\ 3E_u.$$

It does not have A_{1u} and hence the band is forbidden to z-polarization.

(x, y) Polarization

Now, consider (x, y) polarization; (x, y) belongs to Eu symmetry species:

$$\left(\Gamma_{\Psi_i} \times \Gamma_{\Psi_f}\right) \times E_u$$
$$= (A_{1g} \times A_{2g}) \times E_u$$
$$= A_{2g} \times E_u$$

A_{2g}	1	1	1	–1	–1	1	1	1	–1	–1	
E_u	2	0	–2	0	0	–2	0	2	0	0	
$A_{2g} \times E_u$	2	0	–2	0	0	–2	0	2	0	0	$= E_u$

Now there is vibration with Eu mode so that:

$$Eu \times Eu = 4\ 0\ 4\ 0\ 0\ 4\ 0\ 4\ 0\ 0$$

on applying reduction formula.

We obtain, $A_{1g} + A_{2g} + B_{1u} + B_{2u}$

$$^{a}A_{1g} = \frac{1}{16}(4\times1\times1+0+4\times1\times1+0+0+4\times1\times1+0$$
$$+0+4\times1\times1+0+0)$$
$$= \frac{1}{16}[4+4+4+4] = 1$$

$$^{a}A_{2g} = \frac{1}{16}(4\times1\times1+0+4\times1\times1+0+0+4\times1\times1+0+$$
$$4\times1\times1+0+0)$$
$$= \frac{1}{16}\times16 = 1$$

$$^{a}E_{g} = \frac{1}{16}(4\times2\times1+0+4\times-2\times1+0+0+4\times2\times1+0$$
$$4\times-2\times1+0+0)$$
$$= \frac{1}{16}[8-8+8-8] = 0$$

$$^{a}B_{1u} = \frac{1}{16}(4\times1\times1+0+4\times1\times1+0+0+4\times1\times1+0$$
$$4\times1\times1+0+0)$$
$$= \frac{1}{16}\times16 = 1$$

$$^{a}B_{2u} = \frac{1}{16}(4\times1\times1+0+4\times1\times1+0+0+4\times1\times1+0$$
$$4\times1\times1+0+0)$$
$$= \frac{1}{16}\times16 = 1.$$

So, $Eu \times Eu \rightarrow A_{1g} + A_{2g} + B_{1u} + B_{2u}$.

It has a totally symmetric species like A_{1g}. This renders the band allowed to (x, y) polarization.

Let us take up the case of second transition:

$$A_{1g} \rightarrow B_{2g}$$

For z–polarization can be seen as follows:

$$\int \psi_i \, \mu_z \, \Psi_f \, d\tau \times \int \psi_u^{gr} \, \psi_u^{ex} \, d\tau$$
$$=(A_{1g} \times B_{2g}) \times A_{2u}$$
$$= B_{2g} \times A_{2u}$$

We have,										
B_{2g}	1	–1	1	–1	1	1	–1	1	–1	1
A_{2u}	1	1	1	–1	–1	–1	–1	–1	1	1
$B_{2g} \times A_{2u} =$	1	–1	1	1	–1	–1	1	–1	–1	1

$$\equiv B_{1u}$$

The cross product is B_{1u}.

There is vibration with B_{1u} symmetry species. The triple product B_{1u} may combine with B_{1u} vibrational mode to give:

$$B_{1u} \times B_{1u} = A_{1g}$$

It is vibronically allowed and the band is z-polarized.

This band for (x, y) component is now considered:

$$\int \Psi_i \left(\mu_x, \mu_y\right) \Psi_f \, d\tau . \int \Psi_v \, \Psi_{v^1} \, dz$$

The triple product is given by:

$$(A_{1g} \times B_{2g}) \times E_u = B_{2g} \times E_u$$

B_{2g}	1	–1	1	–1	1	1	–1	1	–1	1
E_u	2	0	–2	0	0	–2	0	2	0	0
$B_{2g} \times E_u =$	2	0	–2	0	0	–2	0	2	0	0

$$\equiv E_u$$

Again $E_u \times E_u$ leads to $A_{1g} + A_{2g} + B_{1u} + B_{2u}$ and so the band is allowed for (x, y) polarization as it has A_{1g} symmetry sepcies.

Let us consider the third transition:

$$A_{1g} \rightarrow E_g$$

$$\int \Psi_i \; \mu_z \; \Psi_f \, d\tau . \int \Psi_v \; \Psi_v \, . \, d\tau$$

$$= (A_{1g} \times E_g) \times (A_{2u})$$

$$= E_g \times A_{2u} = E_u$$

As one of the vibrations belongs to Eu symmetry species. So

$$E_u \times E_u$$

4 0 4 0 0 4 0 4 0 0

giving $A_{1g} + A_{2g} + B_{1u} + B_{2u}$.

It has a totally symmetric species A_{1g}. And hence the transition is z–polarized.

For the case of (x, y) polarization we see the effect of cross product of: $E_g \times E_u$

Eg	2	0	–2	0	0	2	0	–2	0	0
Eu	2	0	–2	0	0	–2	0	2	0	0
giving	4	0	4	0	0	–4	0	–4	0	0

This gives $A_{1u} + A_{2u} + B_{1u} + B_{2u}$ as symmetry species which may have common A_{2u} and B_{1u} with the vibrational modes so that:

$$A_{1u} \times A_{1u} = A_{1g}$$

$$B_{1u} \times B_{1u} = A_{1g}.$$

The third transition is also (x, y) polarized. The following results have been obtained:

The first band ($A_{1g} \rightarrow A_{2g}$) is vibronically forbidden for z polarization.

The second band is due to $A_{1g} \rightarrow E_g$ which is vibronically allowed in both directions.

The third band is assigned to $A_{1g} \rightarrow B_{2g}$ transition. This band is allowed in all directions.

Electronic Polarization

For tris-oxalato chromium (III) ion it has octahedral structure, but it does not have O_h symmetry rather it belongs to D_3 point group.

From correlation Table:

O_h	D_3
A_{1g}	A_2 (Ground State)
T_{1g}	$A_2 + E$
T_{2g}	$A_1 + E$

It has A_2 ground state. The excited states are $A_2 + E$ and $A_1 + E$. on the basis of correlation Table for O_h and D_3 point groups There are three transitions as follows:

$$A_2 \rightarrow A_1,\ A_2 \rightarrow A_2 \text{ and } A_2 \rightarrow E.$$

There is polarization of these electronic transitions.

In D_3, z belongs to A_2 and (x, y) to E. Case of $A_2 \rightarrow A_1$ transition:

For z-polarization we have:

$\int \Psi_i \ \mu_z \ \Psi_f \ d\tau$

$= (A_2 \times A_1)\ A_2 = A_2 \times A_2 = A_1$

(Totally symmetric) allowed.

For (x, y) polarization:

$\int \Psi_i \ (\mu_x \cdot \mu_y)\ \Psi_f \ d\tau$

$= (A_2 \times A_1) \times E = A_2 \times E$

A_2	1	1	–1
E	2	–1	0

$A_2 \times E = 2\ {-1}\ 0 \equiv E$ (forbidden)

For $A_2 \rightarrow A_2$ transition:

Consider z polarization first:

$(A_2 \times A_2) \times A_2$

$= A_1 \times A_2 = A_2$ (forbidden)

For the case of (x, y) polarization:

$(A_2 \times A_2) \times E$

$= A_1 \times E = E$ (forbidden)

Let us consider $A_2 \rightarrow E$ transition:

$(A_2 \times E) \times A_2$ for z polarization.

$E \times A_2 = E$ (forbidden)

For (x, y) polarization:

$(A_2 \times E)$ x E

$E \times E = 4\ 1\ 0$

It decomposes to give:

$${}^{a}A_1 = \frac{1}{6}(1 \times 4 \times 1 + 2 \times 1 \times 1 + 3 \times 1 \times 0)$$

$$= \frac{1}{6} \times 6 = 1$$

$${}^{a}A_2 = \frac{1}{6}(1 \times 4 \times 1 + 2 \times 1 \times 1 + 3 \times -1 \times 0)$$

$$= \frac{1}{6} \times 6 = 1$$

$$a_E = \frac{1}{6}(1\times4\times2+2\times1\times(-1)+3\times0\times0)$$
$$= \frac{1}{6}[8-2] = \frac{6}{6} = 1$$

It consists of a totally symmetric component A_1.
Hence allowed.

Illustration

1. In $[Ni(NH_3)_6]^{2+}$ ion having O_h symmetry.
There are symmetry forbidden bands:
$$^3A_{2g} \rightarrow {}^3T_{1g},\ {}^3A_{2g} \rightarrow {}^3T_{2g}$$
It shows M-N vibrations belonging to species:
$$A_{1g} + E_g + T_{2g} + T_{1u} + T_{2u}$$
Tell which are vibonically allowed?
$[Ni(NH_3)_6]^{2+}$ ion has O_h symmetry, under weak ligand field. It has 3_F as ground term which corresponds to three components:
$^3A_{2g} + {}^3T_{1g} + {}^3T_{2g}$ with $^3A_{2g}$ as ground state.
For $^3A_{2g} \rightarrow {}^3T_{1g}$ and $^3A_{2g} \rightarrow {}^3T_{2g}$ transitions, the direct product of representation of ground electronic and excited states have:
$$^3A_{2g} \times {}^3T_{1g} = {}^3T_{2g}$$
$$^3A_{2g} \times {}^3T_{2g} = {}^3T_{1g}$$
components of dipole moments are T_{1u} in O_h symmetry.
The direct products are:
$$^3T_{2g} \times T_{1u} = {}^3A_{2u} + {}^3E_u + {}^3T_{1u} + {}^3T_{2u}$$
$$^3T_{1g} \times T_{1u} = {}^3A_{1u} + {}^3E_u + {}^3T_{1u} + {}^3T_{2u}$$
They have odd symmetry species T_{1u} and T_{2u} and the components of vibrations belong also to T_{1u} and T_{2u} symmetry.
Their direct product will be:
$$^3T_{1u} \times {}^3T_{1u} = {}^3A_{1g}{}^{+} \ldots..$$
$$^3T_{2u} \times {}^3T_{2u} = {}^3A_{1g}{}^{+} \ldots..$$
Thus the transitions are vibronically allowed.

2. What are seven f-orbitals?

   Discuss the irreducible components of f-orbitals in tetrahedral, octahedral fields using sine formula and character Table.

Ans. There are seven f-orbitals namely:

$$f_z(x_2-y_2)\ f_y(z_2-x_2)\ f_x(y_2-z_2),\ f_{xyz},\ f_x^{\,3},\ f_y^{\,3},\ f_z^{\,3}.$$

They constitute three sets of irreducible representation $a_{2u} + t_{1u} + t_{2u}$.

For f orbital l = 3, an odd number, so it is labelled 'u' type.

We can deduce the character for splitting of f orbitals in O and T fields out of which we obtain such components in O_h field. There is no suffix in T_d symmetry.

3. How does G term split in O_h symmetry?

   Give the result on the basis of sine formula.

   The sine formula is given by:

$$\sin\frac{(2L+1)\,\alpha/2}{\sin\alpha/2}$$

where L is total orbital momentum quantum number. It has:

L = 4 for G term

$$2L + 1 = 2 \times 4 + 1 = 9$$

$$C_n = \frac{\sin 9\alpha/2}{\sin\alpha/2}$$

There are C_4, C_2, C_3 symmetry operations in octahedral symmetry:

$$C_4 = \frac{\sin 9\times 45^\circ}{\sin 45^\circ} = \frac{\sin 405^\circ}{\sin 45^\circ} = \sin\frac{(360^\circ+45^\circ)}{\sin 45^\circ}$$

$$= \frac{\sin 45^\circ}{\sin 45^\circ} = 1$$

$$C_3 = \frac{\sin 9\times 60°}{\sin 60°} = \frac{\sin 540°}{\sin 60°} = \frac{\sin (360° + 180°)}{\sin 60°} = \frac{\sin 180°}{\sin 60°}$$

$$= \frac{\sin 0°}{\sin 60°} = 0$$

$$C_2 = \frac{\sin 9\times 90°}{\sin 90°} = \frac{\sin 810°}{\sin 90°} = \frac{\sin (2\times 360° + 90°)}{\sin 90°}$$

$$= \frac{\sin 90°}{\sin 90°} = 1$$

Look at the text for components of G term similar to g orbitals. They all are 'g' type.

4. Discuss conditions of effective working of sine formula:

(i) It is applicable for a cyclic group of cubic symmetry T or O, in which pure rotations are considered.

(ii) It does not apply for identity operation as $\alpha = 0$, it is always applicable in case of $\alpha \neq 0$. We obtain character for identity by the total degeneracy of orbital or term:

$$(2l + 1) \text{ or } (2L + 1)$$

(iii) It does not work in case of system with σ_h or σ_d present.

Both O_h and T_d are using σ_h and σ_d respectively. So we cannot apply directly.

It is desirable to get the characters for T or O group and with the help of correlation determine the symmetry in O_h and T_d if possible.

(iv) Suffices like u and g will be decided on the basis of odd or even value. In case of term the split components in O_h environment will be always g type and no suffix is assigned to T_d environment.

QUESTIONS

1. Discuss the symmetry operations in different classes of O_h and T_d point groups.
2. Derive sine formula for splitting of d-orbitals in octahedral field. What are its limitations?
3. Show that:
   (a) An s orbital does not split but transforms as a_{1g} symmetry species in octahedral field.
   (b) p-orbitals only transform as t_{1u} in octahedral field.
   (c) Five d-orbitals split into t_{2g} and eg sets in O_h field but e and t_2 set in T_d field.

   Your answer should be based on symmetry consideration using C.T.
4. How do the F term split in an octahedral field and also the g orbitals in the same field?
5. (a) What do you understand from strong field d^n configuration taking the case of d^2 configuration. Propose the possible strong field configurations in octahedral field.
   (b) Find the strong field components in an octahedral field giving orbital degeneracy and spin multiplicity of states.
6. (a) Applying sine formula give the splitting of d-orbitals into irreducible components in an octahedral crystal-field.
   (b) Discuss symmetry selection rule for d-d transition in O_h symmetry and its relaxation through vibronic-coupling.
7. (a) Discuss an example of vibronic coupling in O_h field in detail.
   (b) Obtain symmetry species of five d-orbitals in D_{4h} point group with suitable transformation matrices.
8. (a) Determine the symmetry species of $(t_{2g})^2$, $(t_{2g})^1$ $(eg)^1$ and $(eg)^2$ configurations in strong O_h field with the use of character Table.

(b) What are merits of sine formula? What are its disadvantages?

9. Give the different rules for drawing of correlation diagram in weak field and strong field cases.

   How do you predict the transition in a medium crystalline field out of it on the basis of d^2 system in octahedral symmetry?

10. Discuss the band assignments in d^1 and d^8 systems for D_{4h} symmetry on the basis of electronic configuration and term energy diagrams.

11. Consider the electronic polarization of d-d bands in $(Cr\ (ox)_3]^{3-}$ in D_3 symmetry and discuss the following:

    (a) The irreducible representation of translational vectors for the system.

    (b) Electronic polarization of the band based on symmetry arguments.

12. Vibronic polarization is seen in trans-dichlorobis-ethylene diamine Co (III) ion. You are required to answer the following:

    (a) Assign the point group notation.

    (b) Classify translational vectors into irreducible components.

    (c) Predict the polarized absorption spectra using the cross-product of transition moment integral and vibrational modes which are:

$$A_{1g}, B_{1g}, B_{2g}, E_g, 2A_{2u}, B_{1u}, 3E_u.$$

13. Comment on relaxation in symmetry selection rules. What do you understand from vibronic coupling.

14. Discuss cases of vibronic coupling in $[Co(NH_3)_6]^{+3}$ and $[Ni(NH_3)_6]^{+3}$ having M-N stretching mode of vibrations A_{1g}, E_g, T_{2g}, $2T_{1u}$, T_{2u} and A_{1g}, E_g, T_{2g}, T_{1u}, T_{2u} respectively.

15. Predict the transitions in Cu(II)d^9 and Ni(II)d^8 systems in D_{4h} environment on the basis of orbital splitting diagram as well as term splitting diagram and make the band assignments.

MATRICES, EIGEN VALUES AND EIGEN VECTORS

10

10.1 BASIC IDEA

We apply matrix algebra as a mathematical tool in quantum mechanical calculation on molecules. Matrices have been applied in formulating much of the theory of quantum mechanics.

A matrix is an array of numbers. The different members constituting the matrix are known as matrix elements.

A matrix may be rectangular or square. It is not equal to a single number. We define sum of two matrices:

$$A + B = C$$

$$a_{ij} + b_{ij} = C_{ij}$$

The product is defined as C = AB, A= mxn , B = n x p, then C is mxp whose elements are:

$$C_{ij} = a_{i1}b_{1j} + a_{i2}b_{2j} + \ldots\ldots\ldots\ldots\ldots$$

$$a_{in}b_{nj} = \sum_{k=1}^{n} a_{ik}b_{kj}$$

In arithmetic irrespective of the order:

$$3 \times 5 = 5 \times 3 = 15$$

product of multiplication has the same value but in matrices the product may be same or different.

To calculate C_{ij} we consider the row of matrix A, the row elements are a_{i1}, a_{i2}, a_{i3} ...... a_{in}. Now multiply each element of this row by the corresponding element of column j of B, the b_{1j}, b_{2j}, b_{3j} ...... b_{nj} and add the n product.

e.g.,

$$A = \begin{bmatrix} -1 & 3 & 1/2 \\ 0 & 4 & 1 \end{bmatrix}_{2\times 3}, \quad B = \begin{bmatrix} 1 & 0 & -2 \\ 2 & 5 & 6 \\ -8 & 3 & 10 \end{bmatrix}_{3\times 3}$$

This product C = AB is 2 × 3

$$C = \begin{bmatrix} C_{11} & C_{12} & C_{13} \\ C_{21} & C_{22} & C_{23} \end{bmatrix}_{2\times 3}$$

$$\begin{aligned} C_{11} &= a_{11}b_{11} + a_{12}b_{21} + a_{13}b_{31} \\ &= -1 \times 1 + 3 \times 2 + ½ (-8) \\ &= -1 + 6 - 4 = -5 + 6 = 1 \\ C_{12} &= a_{11}b_{12} + a_{12}\, b_{22} + a_{13}\, b_{32} \\ &= -1 \times 0 + 3 \times 5 + ½ \times 3 \\ &= 0 + 15 + 3/2 = 16½ \\ C_{13} &= a_{11}b_{13} + a_{12}b_{23} + a_{13}b_{33} \\ &= (-11)\,(-2) + 3 \times 6 + ½ \times 10 \\ &= 2 + 18 + 5 \\ &= 25 \text{ etc.} \end{aligned}$$

$$C = \begin{bmatrix} 1 & 16½ & 25 \\ 0 & 23 & 34 \end{bmatrix}$$

Matrix multiplication is not commutative. The product AB is defined but BA is not defined in the preceding case.

B is 3 × 3 and A is 2 × 3.

The column of B (3) does not tally with the row of A which is (2) so the product BA is undefined. Hence,

$$AB \neq BA$$

A matrix with equal number of row and column is a square matrix. Its order is equal to the number of row.

A diagonal matrix of order n is square matrix whose n-diagonal elements lie on its principal diagonal, a_{11}, a_{22}, ..., a_{nn} while off diagonal elements are zero.

A diagonal matrix with diagonal elements unity is a unit matrix. I represents unit matrix, e.g. 3 × 3 unit matrix is:

$$\begin{bmatrix} 1 & 0 & 0 \\ 0 & 1 & 0 \\ 0 & 0 & 1 \end{bmatrix} = I$$

B is square matrix of the same order as I. I.B = B.

Because, ijth elements of the product IB is given by $(IB)_{ij}$

$$= \sum_k (I)_{ik} (B)_{kj}$$

$$= \sum_k \delta_{ik} \, B_{kj}$$

$$= b_{ij}$$

This is valid for all i and j. We have IB = B.

10.2 MATRIX ELEMENT

Similarly, BI = B multiplication by unit matrix has no effect.

Let [f] be the basis function, the various integrals are the matrix elements for operator $\hat{A}$ which constitute elements of matrix A:

$$\begin{bmatrix} \langle f_1 | \hat{A} | f_1 \rangle & \langle f_1 | \hat{A} | f_2 \rangle & \cdots\cdots \\ \langle f_2 | \hat{A} | f_1 \rangle & \langle f_2 | \hat{A} | f_2 \rangle & \cdots\cdots \\ \cdots\cdots & \cdots\cdots & \cdots\cdots \\ \cdots\cdots & \cdots\cdots & \cdots\cdots \end{bmatrix}$$

The matrix representative of the linear operator $\hat{A}$ is:

$$A = \begin{bmatrix} A_{11} & A_{12} & A_{13} & \cdots\cdots \\ A_{21} & A_{22} & A_{23} & \cdots\cdots \\ \cdots\cdots & \cdots\cdots & \cdots\cdots & \cdots\cdots \\ \cdots\cdots & \cdots\cdots & \cdots\cdots & \cdots\cdots \end{bmatrix}$$

so that,

$$\begin{bmatrix} A_{11} & A_{12} & A_{13} & \cdots\cdots \\ A_{21} & A_{22} & A_{23} & \cdots\cdots \\ \cdots\cdots & \cdots\cdots & \cdots\cdots & \cdots\cdots \\ \cdots\cdots & \cdots\cdots & \cdots\cdots & \cdots\cdots \end{bmatrix}$$

$$= \begin{bmatrix} < f_1 | \hat{A} | f_1 > & < f_1 | \hat{A} | f_2 > & \cdots\cdots \\ < f_2 | \hat{A} | f_1 > & < f_2 | \hat{A} | f_2 > & \cdots\cdots \\ \cdots\cdots & \cdots\cdots & \cdots\cdots \\ \cdots\cdots & \cdots\cdots & \cdots\cdots \end{bmatrix}$$

10.3 MATRIX TRANSFORMATION OF LINEAR EQUATION

Matrices are introduced as short hand notation for dealing with linear simultaneous equations and for linear transformation from one set of variables to another:

$$AX = B$$

$$\begin{bmatrix} a_{11} & a_{12} & a_{13} & \cdots\cdots & a_{1n} \\ a_{21} & a_{22} & a_{23} & \cdots\cdots & a_{2n} \\ \cdots & \cdots & \cdots & \cdots\cdots & \cdots \\ a_{n1} & a_{n2} & a_{n3} & \cdots\cdots & a_{nn} \end{bmatrix} \begin{bmatrix} x_1 \\ x_2 \\ \cdots \\ \cdots \\ x_n \end{bmatrix} = \begin{bmatrix} b_1 \\ b_2 \\ \cdots \\ \cdots \\ b_n \end{bmatrix}$$

A is a coefficient matrix, X is a column matrix, B also is another column matrix.

Inverse of A is a square matrix, whose product with A is the identity matrix, I of order n:

$$AA^{-1} = A^{-1} A = I$$

A^{-1} exist if and only if $A \neq 0$.

Now $AX = B$.

Let $A \neq 0$, then A^{-1} exists. We multiply this equation on left by A^{-1} to obtain $A^{-1} (AX) = A^{-1} B$.

Since, multiplication is always associative:

$$A(BC) = (AB)C$$

Hence, $A^{-1} (AX) = (A^{-1}A) X = IX = X$

So, that $x = A^{-1} B$.

This is the solution for the unknowns in the linear equation.

10.4 METHOD OF LINEAR VARIATION

The matrix algebra gives the most efficient method to solve equations of linear variation method. The linear equations are given as:

$$
\begin{array}{lll}
H_{11}C_1 + H_{12} C_2 + & \cdots\cdots\cdots & + H_{1n} C_n = WC_1 \\
H_{21} C_1 + H_{22} C_2 + & \cdots\cdots\cdots & H_{2n} C_n = WC_2 \\
\cdots\cdots\cdots\cdots & \cdots\cdots\cdots & \cdots\cdots\cdots\cdots \\
\cdots\cdots\cdots\cdots & \cdots\cdots\cdots & \cdots\cdots\cdots\cdots \\
H_{n1}C_1 + H_{n2} C_2 + & \cdots\cdots\cdots & +H_{nn} C_n = WC_n
\end{array}
$$

$$
\begin{bmatrix} H_{11} & H_{12} & \cdots & H_{1n} \\ H_{21} & H_{22} & \cdots & H_{2n} \\ \cdots & \cdots & \cdots & \cdots \\ \cdots & \cdots & \cdots & \cdots \\ H_{n1} & H_{n2} & \cdots & H_{nn} \end{bmatrix} \begin{bmatrix} C_1 \\ C_2 \\ \vdots \\ \vdots \\ C_n \end{bmatrix} = W \begin{bmatrix} C_1 \\ C_2 \\ \vdots \\ \vdots \\ C_n \end{bmatrix}
$$

or $HC = WC$

H – square matrix

C = column vector.

Here, C and W are unknowns to be solved. If W is scalar then C is said to be an eigen vector of A and W is an eigen value of A.

It has non-trivial solution only if $\det (H_{ij} - \delta_{ij} W) = 0$.

It has n roots for W and there are so many eigen values and n independent eigen vectors:

Let us presume that C has its inverse matrix. So, we can multiply each side by C^{-1} on the left to obtain.

$$
\begin{aligned}
C^{-1} HC &= C^{-1} (WC) \\
&= C^{-1} (CW) \\
&= (C^{-1}C) W = IW = W
\end{aligned}
$$

10.5 TRANSPOSE MATRIX Ã

Transpose matrix of A is written as Ã. It is formed by interchanging rows into columns of A. So that column 1 becomes row 1 and so on. The elements $\tilde{a}_{ij}$ of Ã are related to the elements of A by $\tilde{a}_{ij} = \tilde{a}_{ji}$ for square matrix transpose is found by reflecting the elements about the principal diagonal A symmetric matrix B means its all elements satisfy $b_{ij} = b_{ji}$. The elements are symmetric about the principal diagonal, i.e. $b_{12} = b_{21}$. A symmetric matrix is equal to its transpose Ã = A.

A complex conjugate A* of A is the matrix formed by taking complex conjugate of each element of A. The conjugate transpose A^+ is formed by taking transpose of A*.

Thus,

$$A^+ = \tilde{A}^*$$

and $$A_{ij}^+ = a_{ji}^*$$

This matrix A^+ is also called adjoint of A.

10.6 ORTHOGONAL MATRIX

A matrix whose inverse is equal to its transpose $A^+ = \tilde{A}$ if A is orthogonal.

A unitary matrix is one whose inverse is equal to its conjugate transpose.

$U^{-1} = U^+$ if U is unitary.

From the definition, we have,

$$U^{-1} = U^+ \text{ If U is unitary.}$$

From the difinition, we have,

$$U^+U = 1. \text{ If U is unitary.}$$

10.7 MATRIX FORM OF AN EQUATION FOR OPERATORS A AND B

$$\int \Psi_m \hat{A} \Psi_n d\tau = \langle m \mid a \mid n \rangle = A_{mn}$$

$$\langle m \mid n \rangle = \delta_{mn}, \delta_{mn} = 0 \text{ or } 1$$

$$Ars = \langle r \mid A \mid s \rangle$$

$$Bsc = \langle s \mid B \mid c \rangle$$

product of the two is:

$$\sum_s \langle r \mid A \mid s\rangle \langle s \mid B \mid c\rangle$$

$$= \sum_s A_{rs}\ B_{sc} = (AB)_{rc}$$

$$= \langle r \mid AB \mid c\rangle \sum_s < s \mid s >= 1 \text{ under normalization}$$

$$= \langle r \mid AB \mid c\rangle$$

A single column matrix element of the product operator AB.

10.8 MATRIX FORM OF SCHRÖDINGER WAVE EQUATION

It provides idea of hamiltonian matrix, H:

$$H\Psi = E\Psi$$

Consider a set of function ϕ_1, ϕ_2 .... ϕ_n. Express Ψ as linear combination of ϕ's as:

$$\Psi = \sum_n C_n \phi_n$$

$$= \sum_n C_n \mid n >$$

Consider operation of H on Ψ:

$$H\Psi = \sum_n C_n\ H|n\rangle = E\sum_n C_n|n\rangle$$

on multiplication by bra $\langle m| = \phi_m$

$$\sum_n \langle m|C_n\ H|n\rangle = E\sum_n C_n\ \langle m|n\rangle$$

$$C_1H_{11} + C_2\ H_{22} + \ldots\ldots\ldots\ldots + C_n\ H_{mn}$$

$$= EC_1\langle 1|1\rangle + EC_2\ \langle 2|2\rangle + \ldots\ldots\ldots\ldots\ldots\ldots\ldots\ldots + C_n\langle m|n\rangle$$

$$C_1\ H_{11} + C_2\ H_{22} + \ldots\ldots + 0 = EC_1 + EC_2 + \ldots\ldots + 0$$

when $n = m$ $\langle m|n \rangle = 1$, $\langle m|n \rangle = 0$ when $m \neq n$.

Hence, $C_m H_{mm} = E\ C_m$

Since, $C_m H_{mm}$ commute so

$$H_{mm} C_m = E\, C_m$$

There will be m separate matrix equations, viz.

$$H_{11} C_1 = E_1 C_1$$

$$H_{22} C_2 = E_2 C_2$$

$$H_{33} C_3 = E_3 C_3$$

When matrix is diagonalised $H = H_{mm}$

$$= \begin{bmatrix} H_{11} & H_{12} & H_{12} & \cdots\cdots\cdots & H_{1n} \\ H_{21} & H_{22} & H_{23} & \cdots\cdots\cdots & H_{2n} \\ \cdots\cdots & \cdots\cdots & \cdots\cdots & \cdots\cdots & \cdots\cdots \\ \cdots\cdots & \cdots\cdots & \cdots\cdots & \cdots\cdots & \cdots\cdots \\ H_{m1} & H_{m2} & H_{m3} & \cdots\cdots\cdots\cdots & H_{mm} \end{bmatrix}$$

C_m is a column vector with m = 1, 2, 3 ..... m.

$$C_m = \begin{bmatrix} C_1 \\ C_2 \\ \vdots \\ \vdots \\ C_m \end{bmatrix}$$

$$H_{mm} C_m - EC_m = 0$$

$$(H_{mm} - EI)\, C_m = 0.$$

Where I is the identity matrix of the same dimension. This is the required S-equation for given H find E and C.

10.9 MATRIX FORM OF SECULAR EQUATION

For secular equation:

$$C_1 (H_{11}-ES_{11}) + C_2 (H_{12} - ES_{12}) + \ldots C_n (H_{1n} - ES_{1n}) = 0$$

$$C_1 (H_{21} - ES_{21}) + C_2 (H_{22} - ES_{12}) + \ldots C_n (H_{2n} - ES_{1n}) = 0$$

$$\vdots$$

$$\vdots$$

$$C_1 (H_{n1} - ES_{n1}) + C_2 (H_{n2} - ES_{n2}) + \ldots C_n (H_{nn} - ES_{nn}) = 0.$$

The matrix equation for this will be:

$$\begin{bmatrix} H_{11}-ES_{11} & H_{12}-ES_{12} & \cdots\cdots\cdots & H_{1n}-ES_{1n} \\ H_{21}-ES_{21} & H_{22}ES_{22} & \cdots\cdots\cdots & H_{2n}-ES_{1n} \\ \cdots\cdots\cdots & \cdots\cdots\cdots & \cdots\cdots\cdots & \cdots\cdots\cdots \\ \cdots\cdots\cdots & \cdots\cdots\cdots & \cdots\cdots\cdots & \cdots\cdots\cdots \\ H_{n1}-ES_{n1} & H_{n2}-E_{n2} & \cdots\cdots\cdots & H_{nn}-ES_{nn} \end{bmatrix} \begin{bmatrix} C_1 \\ C_2 \\ \vdots \\ \vdots \\ C_n \end{bmatrix} = 0 = \begin{bmatrix} 0 \\ 0 \\ \vdots \\ \vdots \\ 0 \end{bmatrix}$$

The first matrix on LHS is differences of two matrices:

$$\left\{ \begin{bmatrix} H_{11} & H_{12} & \cdots\cdots & H_{1n} \\ H_{21} & H_{22} & \cdots\cdots & H_{2n} \\ \cdots\cdots & \cdots\cdots & \cdots\cdots & \cdots\cdots \\ \cdots\cdots & \cdots\cdots & \cdots\cdots & \cdots\cdots \\ H_{n1} & H_{n2} & \cdots\cdots & H_{nn} \end{bmatrix} - E \begin{bmatrix} S_{11} & S_{12} & \cdots\cdots & S_{1n} \\ S_{21} & S_{22} & \cdots\cdots & S_{2n} \\ \cdots\cdots & \cdots\cdots & \cdots\cdots & \cdots\cdots \\ \cdots\cdots & \cdots\cdots & \cdots\cdots & \cdots\cdots \\ S_{n1} & S_{n2} & \cdots\cdots & S_{nn} \end{bmatrix} \right\} \begin{bmatrix} C_1 \\ C_2 \\ \vdots \\ \vdots \\ C_n \end{bmatrix} = \begin{bmatrix} 0 \\ 0 \\ \vdots \\ \vdots \\ 0 \end{bmatrix}$$

or,

$$\begin{bmatrix} H_{11} & H_{12} & \cdots\cdots & H_{1n} \\ H_{21} & H_{22} & \cdots\cdots & H_{2n} \\ \cdots\cdots & \cdots\cdots & \cdots\cdots & \cdots\cdots \\ H_{n1} & H_{n2} & \cdots\cdots & H_{nn} \end{bmatrix} \begin{bmatrix} C_1 \\ C_2 \\ \vdots \\ \vdots \\ C_n \end{bmatrix} = E \begin{bmatrix} S_{11} & S_{12} & \cdots\cdots & S_{1n} \\ S_{21} & S_{22} & \cdots\cdots & S_{2n} \\ \cdots\cdots & \cdots\cdots & \cdots\cdots & \cdots\cdots \\ \cdots\cdots & \cdots\cdots & \cdots\cdots & \cdots\cdots \\ S_{n1} & S_{n2} & \cdots\cdots & S_{nn} \end{bmatrix} \begin{bmatrix} C_1 \\ C_2 \\ \vdots \\ \vdots \\ C_n \end{bmatrix}$$

or $HCi = ESCi$

This represents n separate matrix equations. The suffix indicates that there are as many possible values of E there are so many examples of m.os as basis function.

Ci is the eigen vector which is a column vector and each element in C is multiplied by scalar Ei.

$$HC_1 = E_1S_1\, C_1$$
$$HC_2 = E_2S_2\, C_2$$
$$\vdots \qquad \vdots$$
$$HC_n = E_nS_n\, C_n$$

There are n separate matrix equations.

These matrix equations can be reduced into a single matrix equation. We do this by stacking the nC vectors together and side by side to produce a mxn matrix C. This is accomplished in the following equation:

$$\begin{bmatrix} H_{11} & H_{12} \cdots\cdots & H_{1n} \\ H_{21} & H_{22} \cdots\cdots & H_{2n} \\ \cdots & \cdots & \cdots \\ \cdots & \cdots & \cdots \\ H_{n1} & H_{n2} \;\cdots & H_{nn} \end{bmatrix} \begin{bmatrix} C_{11} & C_{12} \cdots & C_{1n} \\ C_{21} & C_{22} \cdots & C_{2n} \\ \cdots & \cdots & \cdots \\ \cdots & \cdots & \cdots \\ C_{n1} & C_{n2} \cdots\cdots & C_{nn} \end{bmatrix}$$

$$= \begin{bmatrix} S_{11} & S_{12} & \cdots & S_{1n} \\ S_{21} & S_{22} & \cdots & S_{2n} \\ \cdots & \cdots & \cdots & \cdots \\ \cdots & \cdots & \cdots & \cdots \\ S_{n1} & S_{n2} & \cdots & S_{nn} \end{bmatrix} \begin{bmatrix} C_{11} & C_{12} & \cdots & C_{1n} \\ C_{21} & C_{22} & \cdots & C_{2n} \\ \cdots & \cdots & \cdots & \cdots \\ \cdots & \cdots & \cdots & \cdots \\ C_{n1} & C_{n2} & \cdots & C_{nn} \end{bmatrix} \times \begin{bmatrix} E_1 & 0 & 0 & \cdots & 0 \\ 0 & E_2 & 0 & \cdots & 0 \\ 0 & 0 & E_3 & \cdots & 0 \\ \cdots & \cdots & \cdots & \cdots & \cdots \\ \cdots & \cdots & \cdots & \cdots & \cdots \\ 0 & 0 & 0 & \cdots & E_n \end{bmatrix}$$

This can be finally shown as:

$$HC = SCE$$

We note that:

E is diagonal matrix of orbital energies (matrix of eigen values).

C – matrix coefficient

(matrix of eigen vectors)

and each column refers to a different m.o. First column of C refers to the m.o. having energy E_1.

$$[C_{i1}\ C_{i2}\ \ldots\ C_{in}]\begin{bmatrix} C_{1i} \\ C_{2i} \\ \cdots \\ \cdots \\ C_{ni} \end{bmatrix} = I \text{ (identity) orthogonal}$$

$$C^{-1}\ HC = C^{-1}\ CE = I\ E = E$$

This gives energy expression.

10.10 CASE OF ALLYL SYSTEM

Consider allyl skeleton $C_1 — C_2 — C_3$ for which there will be secalar equations:

$$C_{11}\ (H_{11} - ES_{11}) + C_{12}\ (H_{12} - ES_{12}) + \ldots\ldots = 0 \text{ etc.}$$

The hamiltonian matrix is given as:

$$H = \begin{bmatrix} H_{11} & H_{12} & H_{13} \\ H_{21} & H_{22} & H_{23} \\ H_{31} & H_{32} & H_{33} \end{bmatrix} = \begin{bmatrix} \alpha & \beta & 0 \\ \beta & \alpha & \beta \\ 0 & \beta & \alpha \end{bmatrix}$$

HMO coefficients are:

	$C_1\ (C_{11})$	$C_2\ (C_{12})$	$C_3\ (C_{13})$
Ψ_1	$\frac{1}{2}$	$\frac{1}{\sqrt{2}}$	$\frac{1}{2}$
	C_{21}	C_{22}	C_{23}
Ψ_2	$\frac{1}{\sqrt{2}}$	0	$-\frac{1}{\sqrt{2}}$
	C_{31}	C_{32}	C_{33}
Ψ_3	$\frac{1}{2}$	$-\frac{1}{\sqrt{2}}$	$\frac{1}{2}$

$$\text{Therefore, } C = \begin{bmatrix} \frac{1}{2} & \frac{1}{\sqrt{2}} & \frac{1}{2} \\ \frac{1}{\sqrt{2}} & 0 & -\frac{1}{\sqrt{2}} \\ \frac{1}{2} & -\frac{1}{\sqrt{2}} & \frac{1}{2} \end{bmatrix}$$

and its transpose is C^1 so that,

$$CC^1 = \begin{bmatrix} \frac{1}{\sqrt{2}} & \frac{1}{\sqrt{2}} & \frac{1}{2} \\ \frac{1}{\sqrt{2}} & 0 & -\frac{1}{\sqrt{2}} \\ \frac{1}{2} & -\frac{1}{\sqrt{2}} & \frac{1}{2} \end{bmatrix} \begin{bmatrix} \frac{1}{2} & \frac{1}{\sqrt{2}} & \frac{1}{2} \\ \frac{1}{\sqrt{2}} & 0 & -\frac{1}{\sqrt{2}} \\ \frac{1}{2} & -\frac{1}{\sqrt{2}} & \frac{1}{2} \end{bmatrix}$$

$$= \begin{bmatrix} \frac{1}{4}+\frac{1}{2}+\frac{1}{4} & \frac{1}{2\sqrt{2}}+0-\frac{1}{2\sqrt{2}} & \frac{1}{4}-\frac{1}{2}+\frac{1}{4} \\ \frac{1}{2\sqrt{2}}+0-\frac{1}{2\sqrt{2}} & \frac{1}{2}+0+\frac{1}{2} & \frac{1}{2\sqrt{2}}-0-\frac{1}{2\sqrt{2}} \\ \frac{1}{4}-\frac{1}{2}+\frac{1}{4} & \frac{1}{2\sqrt{2}}+0-\frac{1}{2\sqrt{2}} & \frac{1}{4}+\frac{1}{2}+\frac{1}{4} \end{bmatrix}$$

$$= \begin{bmatrix} 1 & 0 & 0 \\ 0 & 1 & 0 \\ 0 & 0 & 1 \end{bmatrix} = I$$

$$C^1HC = \begin{bmatrix} \frac{1}{2} & \frac{1}{\sqrt{2}} & \frac{1}{2} \\ \frac{1}{\sqrt{2}} & 0 & -\frac{1}{\sqrt{2}} \\ \frac{1}{2} & -\frac{1}{\sqrt{2}} & \frac{1}{2} \end{bmatrix} H \begin{bmatrix} \frac{1}{2} & \frac{1}{\sqrt{2}} & \frac{1}{2} \\ \frac{1}{\sqrt{2}} & 0 & -\frac{1}{\sqrt{2}} \\ \frac{1}{2} & -\frac{1}{\sqrt{2}} & \frac{1}{2} \end{bmatrix}$$

$$= \begin{bmatrix} \frac{1}{2} & \frac{1}{\sqrt{2}} & \frac{1}{2} \\ \frac{1}{\sqrt{2}} & 0 & -\frac{1}{\sqrt{2}} \\ \frac{1}{2} & -\frac{1}{\sqrt{2}} & \frac{1}{2} \end{bmatrix} \begin{bmatrix} \alpha & \beta & 0 \\ \beta & \alpha & \beta \\ 0 & \beta & \alpha \end{bmatrix} \begin{bmatrix} \frac{1}{2} & \frac{1}{\sqrt{2}} & \frac{1}{2} \\ \frac{1}{\sqrt{2}} & 0 & -\frac{1}{\sqrt{2}} \\ \frac{1}{2} & -\frac{1}{\sqrt{2}} & \frac{1}{2} \end{bmatrix}$$

$$= \begin{bmatrix} \frac{1}{2} & \frac{1}{\sqrt{2}} & \frac{1}{2} \\ \frac{1}{\sqrt{2}} & 0 & -\frac{1}{\sqrt{2}} \\ \frac{1}{2} & -\frac{1}{\sqrt{2}} & \frac{1}{2} \end{bmatrix} \begin{bmatrix} \frac{1}{2}\alpha + \frac{1}{\sqrt{2}}\beta & \frac{1}{\sqrt{2}}\alpha & \frac{1}{2}\alpha - \frac{1}{\sqrt{2}}\beta \\ \frac{\beta}{2} + \frac{\alpha}{\sqrt{2}} + \frac{\beta}{2} & \frac{\beta}{\sqrt{2}} - \frac{\beta}{\sqrt{2}} & \frac{\beta}{2} - \frac{\alpha}{\sqrt{2}} + \frac{\beta}{2} \\ \frac{B}{\sqrt{2}} + \frac{\alpha}{2} & \frac{-\alpha}{\sqrt{2}} & \frac{-\beta}{\sqrt{2}} + \frac{\alpha}{2} \end{bmatrix}$$

10.11 EIGEN VALUE AND EIGEN VECTOR

If a vector X has the property with respect to a given matrix A of satisfying:

$$AX = \lambda X$$

Where λ is scalar, X is said to be an eigen vector of A with eigen value λ:

$$AX = \lambda$$

also, $\quad Y = \lambda X$

then, $\quad Y = AX = \lambda X$

Where A is a square matrix:

$$\begin{bmatrix} a_{11} & a_{12} & \cdots & a_{1n} \\ a_{21} & \cdots & \cdots & \cdots \\ \cdots & \cdots & \cdots & \cdots \\ \cdots & \cdots & \cdots & \cdots \\ a_{n1} & \cdots & \cdots & a_{nn} \end{bmatrix}$$

X is a column vector:

$$\begin{bmatrix} x_1 \\ x_2 \\ \vdots \\ \vdots \\ x_n \end{bmatrix}$$

Y is another column vector:

$$\begin{bmatrix} y_1 \\ y_2 \\ \vdots \\ \vdots \\ y_n \end{bmatrix}$$

A vector Y is described by a set of co-ordinates y = (y_1 y_2 .... y_i ... y_n)

Now, co-ordinate, y_i (i = 1 , 2 ... n) of co-ordinate y is proportional to the respective co-ordinate x_i of the vector X. We can use λ as proportionality factor λ is defined as λ (x_1, x_2, ... x_n).

and, $AX = \lambda x.$

The λ is the eigen values which have characteristic value of a matrix transformation AX = λX.

λ – scalar, X – vector, A = matrix.

$$\text{For } A = \begin{bmatrix} 2 & 0 \\ 0 & ½ \end{bmatrix} \text{ and } X = \begin{bmatrix} x_1 \\ x_2 \end{bmatrix}$$

L.H.S of the equation becomes:

$$AX = \begin{bmatrix} 2 & 0 \\ 0 & ½ \end{bmatrix} \begin{bmatrix} x_1 \\ x_2 \end{bmatrix} = \begin{bmatrix} 2x_1 + 0x_2 \\ 0x_2 + \frac{1}{2}x_2 \end{bmatrix} = \begin{bmatrix} 2x_1 \\ \frac{1}{2}x_2 \end{bmatrix}$$

and $\lambda x = \lambda\begin{bmatrix} x_1 \\ x_2 \end{bmatrix} = \begin{bmatrix} \lambda x_1 \\ \lambda x_2 \end{bmatrix}$ such that $\begin{bmatrix} 2x_1 \\ \frac{1}{2}x_2 \end{bmatrix} = \lambda\begin{bmatrix} x_1 \\ x_2 \end{bmatrix}$

There are two equations : $2x_1 = \lambda x_1$

$$\frac{1}{2}x_2 = \lambda x_2$$

Hence, $\lambda = 2$ & $\lambda = ½$.

Illustration 1

$$A = \begin{bmatrix} 2 & 0 \\ 0 & 1/2 \end{bmatrix}$$

The $AX = \lambda X$ is satisfied when,

$$x = \begin{pmatrix} 1 \\ 0 \end{pmatrix}$$

$$\text{L.H.S.} \quad = \begin{bmatrix} 2 & 0 \\ 0 & 1/2 \end{bmatrix} \begin{bmatrix} 1 \\ 0 \end{bmatrix} = \begin{bmatrix} 2\times 1 + 0\times 0 \\ 0\times 1 + \frac{1}{2}\times 0 \end{bmatrix}$$

$$= \begin{bmatrix} 2 \\ 0 \end{bmatrix}$$

$$\text{R.H.S} = \lambda x = \begin{bmatrix} \lambda\times 1 \\ \lambda\times 0 \end{bmatrix} = \begin{bmatrix} \lambda \\ 0 \end{bmatrix}$$

$$AX = \lambda X, \begin{bmatrix} 2 \\ 0 \end{bmatrix} = \begin{bmatrix} \lambda \\ 0 \end{bmatrix} \text{obviously } \lambda = 2.$$

2. The operator is, $\begin{bmatrix} 1 & 0 \\ 0 & 0 \end{bmatrix}$ it possesses eigen vector of the form:

$$x = \begin{bmatrix} x \\ 0 \end{bmatrix}$$

$$\text{L.H.S.} \begin{bmatrix} 1 & 0 \\ 0 & 1 \end{bmatrix} \begin{bmatrix} x \\ 0 \end{bmatrix} = \begin{bmatrix} 1\times x + 0\times 0 \\ 0\times x + 0\times 0 \end{bmatrix} = \begin{bmatrix} x \\ 0 \end{bmatrix}$$

$$\text{R.H.S. } \lambda x = \lambda\begin{bmatrix} x \\ 0 \end{bmatrix} = \begin{bmatrix} \lambda x \\ \lambda x0 \end{bmatrix} = \begin{bmatrix} \lambda x \\ 0 \end{bmatrix}$$

$$\therefore \begin{bmatrix} x \\ 0 \end{bmatrix} = \begin{bmatrix} \lambda x \\ 0 \end{bmatrix}$$

$$\therefore x = \lambda x$$

$$\therefore \lambda = 1.$$

The eigen value $\lambda = 1$.

3. Find the eigen values of matrix $\begin{bmatrix} 2 & 0 \\ 0 & \frac{1}{2} \end{bmatrix}$ and find the eigen vectors for each value of λ_i.

The eigen value equation is:

$$AX = \lambda X, \text{ or } AX — \lambda X = 0.$$

A linear equation is obtained taking identity matrix I of the same dimension as that of A:

$$\text{i.e. } (A - \lambda I)\, X = 0$$

For non-trivial solution det $(A - \lambda I) = 0$

or, $$\left[(A) - \lambda(I)\right] = 0$$

or, $$\left[\begin{pmatrix} 2 & 0 \\ 0 & \frac{1}{2} \end{pmatrix} - \lambda\begin{pmatrix} 1 & 0 \\ 0 & 1 \end{pmatrix}\right] = 0$$

or, $$\left[\begin{pmatrix} 2 & 0 \\ 0 & \frac{1}{2} \end{pmatrix} - \begin{pmatrix} \lambda & 0 \\ 0 & \lambda \end{pmatrix}\right] = 0$$

or, $$\begin{bmatrix} 2-\lambda & 0-0 \\ 0-0 & \frac{1}{2}-\lambda \end{bmatrix} = 0$$

or, $$(2-\lambda)\left(\frac{1}{2}-\lambda\right)=0.$$

Hence, $\lambda_1 = 2$ & $\lambda_2 = ½$.

The two eigen values of matrix $\begin{bmatrix} 2 & 0 \\ 0 & \frac{1}{2} \end{bmatrix}$ are $\lambda_1 = 2$ and $\lambda_2 = \frac{1}{2}$.

Now, we seek to find the eigen vector for each root (λ_i)

We put $\lambda = \lambda_1$ in the equation $AX = \lambda_1 x$.

The matrix equation is $(A - \lambda_1 I)\, x^{(1)} = 0$

or, $$\left[\begin{pmatrix} 2 & 0 \\ 0 & \frac{1}{2} \end{pmatrix} - 2\begin{pmatrix} 1 & 0 \\ 0 & 1 \end{pmatrix}\right]\begin{pmatrix} x_1 \\ x_2 \end{pmatrix} = \begin{pmatrix} 0 \\ 0 \end{pmatrix}$$

or, $$\left[\begin{pmatrix} 2 & 0 \\ 0 & \frac{1}{2} \end{pmatrix} - \begin{pmatrix} 2 & 0 \\ 0 & 2 \end{pmatrix}\right]\begin{pmatrix} x_1 \\ x_2 \end{pmatrix} = \begin{pmatrix} 0 \\ 0 \end{pmatrix}$$

or, $$\begin{bmatrix} 2-2 & 0-0 \\ 0-0 & \frac{1}{2}-2 \end{bmatrix}\begin{bmatrix} x_1 \\ x_2 \end{bmatrix} = \begin{bmatrix} 0 \\ 0 \end{bmatrix}$$

or, $$\begin{bmatrix} 0 & 0 \\ 0 & -3/2 \end{bmatrix}\begin{bmatrix} x_1 \\ x_2 \end{bmatrix} = \begin{bmatrix} 0 \\ 0 \end{bmatrix}$$

We have two linear equations:

$0.x_1 + 0.x_2 = 0$ Both $x_1 \neq x_2 \neq 0$

$0.x_1 - 3/2\, x_2 = 0$

Hence, $x_1 \neq 0$ $x_2 = 0$.

The normalization of eigen vector requires:

$$x_1^2 + x_2^2 = 1 = (x_1)^2$$

or, $(x_1)^2 + 0^2 = 1$

$\therefore\ x_1 = \pm 1$

$$\therefore\ x^{(1)} = \begin{bmatrix} x_1 \\ x_2 \end{bmatrix} = \begin{bmatrix} 1 \\ 0 \end{bmatrix} \text{ or } \begin{bmatrix} -1 \\ 0 \end{bmatrix}$$

for, $\lambda_2 = \dfrac{1}{2}$

$$\begin{bmatrix} 2-\lambda_2 & 0 \\ 0 & \dfrac{1}{2}-\lambda_2 \end{bmatrix} \begin{bmatrix} x_1 \\ x_2 \end{bmatrix} = \begin{bmatrix} 0 \\ 0 \end{bmatrix}$$

or, $[2-\lambda_2]\, x_1 + 0.x_2 = 0$

$$0.x_1 + \left(\frac{1}{2}-\lambda_2\right)x_2 = 0$$

or, $\left(2-\dfrac{1}{2}\right) x_1 + (0)\, x_2 = 0$

$$0.x_1 + \left(\frac{1}{2}-\frac{1}{2}\right) x_2 = 0$$

or, $\dfrac{3}{2}x_1 + 0x_2 = 0$

$0x_1 + 0x_2 = 0.$

So, $x_1 = 0$, $x_2 \neq 0$.

From normalization condition:

$$x_1^2 + x_2^2 = 1$$

$$x^{(2)} = \begin{bmatrix} x_1 \\ x_2 \end{bmatrix} = \begin{bmatrix} 0 \\ 1 \end{bmatrix} \text{ or } \begin{bmatrix} 0 \\ -1 \end{bmatrix}$$

or, $$0 + x_2^2 = 1$$

$$x_2 = \pm 1$$

4. Find the eigen values corresponding to the matrix $\begin{bmatrix} 6 & 2 \\ 2 & 3 \end{bmatrix}$

The linear equation is:

$$(A - \lambda I)\, X = 0$$

or, $$\left[\begin{pmatrix} 6 & 2 \\ 2 & 3 \end{pmatrix} - \lambda \begin{pmatrix} 1 & 0 \\ 0 & 1 \end{pmatrix}\right] \begin{bmatrix} x_1 \\ x_2 \end{bmatrix} = \begin{bmatrix} 0 \\ 0 \end{bmatrix}$$

or, $$\left[\begin{pmatrix} 6 & 2 \\ 2 & 3 \end{pmatrix} - \begin{pmatrix} \lambda & 0 \\ 0 & \lambda \end{pmatrix}\right] \begin{bmatrix} x_1 \\ x_2 \end{bmatrix} = \begin{bmatrix} 0 \\ 0 \end{bmatrix}$$

$$\begin{bmatrix} 6-\lambda & 2 \\ 2 & 3-\lambda \end{bmatrix} \begin{bmatrix} x_1 \\ x_2 \end{bmatrix} = \begin{bmatrix} 0 \\ 0 \end{bmatrix}$$

$$\det |A - \lambda I| = 0$$

or, $$\begin{vmatrix} 6-\lambda & 2 \\ 2 & 3-\lambda \end{vmatrix} = 0$$

or, $$(6 - \lambda)(3 - \lambda) - 2 \times 2 = 0$$

or, $$18 - 6\lambda - 3\lambda + \lambda^2 - 4 = 0$$

$$\lambda^2 - 9\lambda + 18 - 4 = 0$$

or, $$\lambda^2 - 9\lambda + 14 = 0$$

$$\lambda^2 - 2x - 7\lambda + 14 = 0$$

or, $$\lambda(\lambda - 7) - 2(\lambda - 7) = 0$$

or, $$\lambda_1 = 7 \text{ and } \lambda_2 = 2.$$

Eigen vector corresponding to $\lambda_1 = 7$ is $x^{(1)} = \begin{bmatrix} x_1 \\ x_2 \end{bmatrix}$

$$\begin{bmatrix} 6-\lambda_1 & 2 \\ 2 & 3-\lambda_1 \end{bmatrix} \begin{bmatrix} x_1 \\ x_2 \end{bmatrix} = 0$$

$$(6-\lambda_1)\,x_1 + 2x_2 = 0$$

$$2x_1 + (3-\lambda_1)\,x_2 = 0$$

or, $$(6-7)\,x_1 + 2x_2 = 0$$
$$2x_1 + (3-7)\,x_2 = 0$$

or, $$-x_1 + 2x_2 = 0$$
$$2x_1 - 4x_2 = 0$$

or, $$x_1 = 2x_2$$

and $$2x_1 = 4x_2$$
$$x_1 = 2x_2.$$

Also, $$x_1^2 + x_2^2 = 1$$

$$(2x_2)^2 + (x_2)^2 = 1$$

$$4x_2^2 + x_2^2 = 1$$

$$5x_2^2 = 1$$

$$x_2 = \frac{1}{\sqrt{5}}$$

$$x_1 = 2x_2 = 2 \times \frac{1}{\sqrt{5}} = \frac{2}{\sqrt{5}}$$

$$x^{(1)} = \begin{bmatrix} x_1 \\ x_2 \end{bmatrix} = \begin{bmatrix} \frac{2}{\sqrt{5}} \\ \frac{1}{\sqrt{5}} \end{bmatrix} = \frac{1}{\sqrt{5}} \begin{bmatrix} 2 \\ 1 \end{bmatrix}$$

Also, for $x^{(2)}$, $\lambda_2 = 2$

$$\begin{bmatrix} 6-\lambda_2 & 2 \\ 2 & 3-\lambda_2 \end{bmatrix} \begin{bmatrix} x_1 \\ x_2 \end{bmatrix} = 0 = \begin{bmatrix} 0 \\ 0 \end{bmatrix}$$

$$(6-\lambda_2)\,x_1 + 2x_2 = 0$$

$$2x_1 + (3-\lambda_2)\,x_2 = 0$$

or, $$(6-2)x_1 + 2x_2 = 0$$

$$2x_1 + (3-2)x_2 = 0$$

or, $4x_1 + 2x_2 = 0$

$2x_1 + x_2 = 0$

$x_2 = -2x_1$

and, $x_2^2 + x_1^2 = 1$

$x_1^2 + 4x_1^2 = 1$

$5x_1^2 = 1$

$$x_1 = \frac{1}{\sqrt{5}}$$

$$x_2 = -2x_1 = -\frac{2}{\sqrt{5}}$$

$$x^{(2)} = \begin{bmatrix} x_1 \\ x_2 \end{bmatrix} = \begin{bmatrix} \frac{1}{\sqrt{5}} \\ -\frac{2}{\sqrt{5}} \end{bmatrix} = \frac{1}{\sqrt{5}}\begin{bmatrix} 1 \\ -2 \end{bmatrix}$$

5. Find the eigen values and eigen vectors of the matrix $\begin{bmatrix} 2 & 1 \\ 1 & 2 \end{bmatrix}$

We write down the linear equation $(A - \lambda I)\, X = 0$

Det $\begin{vmatrix} 2 & 1 \\ 1 & 2 \end{vmatrix} - \begin{vmatrix} \lambda & 0 \\ 0 & \lambda \end{vmatrix} = 0$

or, $\begin{vmatrix} 2-\lambda & 1-0 \\ 1-0 & 2-\lambda \end{vmatrix} = 0$

or, $\begin{vmatrix} 2-\lambda & 1 \\ 1 & 2-\lambda \end{vmatrix} = 0$

$(2 - \lambda)^2 - 1 = 0$

or, $4 + \lambda^2 - 4\lambda - 1 = 0$

$\lambda^2 - 4\lambda + 3 = 0$

or, $\lambda^2 - 3\lambda - \lambda + 3 = 0$

$\lambda(\lambda - 3) - 1(\lambda - 3) = 0$

or, $(\lambda - 1)(\lambda - 3) = 0$

or, $\lambda = 1$ or $\lambda = 3$

$\lambda_1 = 1$ and $\lambda_2 = 3$.

These are the eigen values of matrix A. Let us seek the eigen vectors. $x^{(1)} = \begin{bmatrix} x_1 \\ x_2 \end{bmatrix}$ corresponding to the value $\lambda_1 = 1$.

The matrix equation is:

$$(A - \lambda_1 I)\, x^{(1)} = 0$$

or, $$\left[\begin{pmatrix} 2 & 1 \\ 1 & 2 \end{pmatrix} - \lambda \begin{pmatrix} 1 & 0 \\ 0 & 1 \end{pmatrix}\right] x^{(1)} = 0$$

or, $$\left[\begin{pmatrix} 2 & 1 \\ 1 & 2 \end{pmatrix} - \begin{pmatrix} \lambda & 0 \\ 0 & \lambda \end{pmatrix}\right] x^{(1)} = 0$$

or, $$\left[\begin{pmatrix} 2-\lambda 1-0 \\ 1-0 2-\lambda \end{pmatrix}\right] x^{(1)} = 0$$

or, $$\begin{bmatrix} 2-\lambda & 1 \\ 1 & 2-\lambda \end{bmatrix} \begin{bmatrix} x_1 \\ x_2 \end{bmatrix} = 0 = \begin{bmatrix} 0 \\ 0 \end{bmatrix}$$

or, $$\begin{bmatrix} 2-1 & 1 \\ 1 & 2-1 \end{bmatrix} \begin{bmatrix} x_1 \\ x_2 \end{bmatrix} = \begin{bmatrix} 0 \\ 0 \end{bmatrix}$$

$$\begin{bmatrix} 1 & 1 \\ 1 & 1 \end{bmatrix} \begin{bmatrix} x_1 \\ x_2 \end{bmatrix} = \begin{bmatrix} 0 \\ 0 \end{bmatrix}$$

Thus,

$$x_1 + x_2 = 0.$$

Hence, $x_1 = -x_2$.

From normalization condition:

$$x_1^2 + x_2^2 = 1$$

or, $$2x_1^2 = 1$$

or, $$x_1^2 = \frac{1}{2}$$

or, $$x_1 = \frac{1}{\sqrt{2}}$$

$$x_2 = \frac{-1}{\sqrt{2}}$$

The required eigen vector can be written as:

$$x^{(1)} = \begin{bmatrix} x_1 \\ x_2 \end{bmatrix} = \begin{bmatrix} \frac{1}{\sqrt{2}} \\ -\frac{1}{\sqrt{2}} \end{bmatrix} = \frac{1}{\sqrt{2}} \begin{bmatrix} 1 \\ -1 \end{bmatrix}$$

For the second eigen value λ = 3.

The eigen vector $x^{(2)} = \begin{bmatrix} x_1 \\ x_2 \end{bmatrix}$

$$[A - \lambda_2 I] \begin{bmatrix} x_1 \\ x_2 \end{bmatrix} = 0$$

$$\left[\begin{pmatrix} 2 & 1 \\ 1 & 2 \end{pmatrix} - 3\begin{pmatrix} 1 & 0 \\ 0 & 1 \end{pmatrix}\right] x^{(2)} = 0$$

or, $$\left[\begin{pmatrix} 2 & 1 \\ 1 & 2 \end{pmatrix} - \begin{pmatrix} 3 & 0 \\ 0 & 3 \end{pmatrix}\right] x^{(2)} = 0$$

or, $$\begin{bmatrix} 2-3 & 1-0 \\ 1-0 & 2-3 \end{bmatrix} x^{(2)} = 0$$

or, $$\begin{bmatrix} -1 & 1 \\ 1 & -1 \end{bmatrix} x^{(2)} = 0$$

This leads to, $-x_1 + x_2 = 0$

$$x_1 - x_2 = 0$$

$$\Rightarrow x_1 = x_2.$$

Also, $x_1^2 + x_2^2 = 1$

$$2x_1^2 = 1$$

$$x_1 = \frac{1}{\sqrt{2}} = x_2$$

$$x^{(2)} = \begin{bmatrix} \frac{1}{\sqrt{2}} \\ \frac{1}{\sqrt{2}} \end{bmatrix} = \frac{1}{\sqrt{2}}\begin{bmatrix} 1 \\ 1 \end{bmatrix}$$

The second eigen vector has the form:

$$\frac{1}{\sqrt{2}}\begin{bmatrix} 1 \\ 1 \end{bmatrix}$$

6. If matrix $A = \begin{bmatrix} 1 & 2 & 3 \\ 1 & 6 & -2 \\ 3 & 4 & 01 \end{bmatrix}$, $X = \begin{bmatrix} 1 \\ 1 \\ 1 \end{bmatrix}$ Evaluate eigen value.

$$AX = \begin{bmatrix} 1 & 2 & 3 \\ 1 & 6 & -2 \\ 3 & 4 & -1 \end{bmatrix} \begin{bmatrix} 1 \\ 1 \\ 1 \end{bmatrix} = \begin{bmatrix} 1\times1+2\times1+3\times1 \\ 2\times1+6\times1-2\times1 \\ 3\times1+4\times1-1\times1 \end{bmatrix}$$

$$= \begin{bmatrix} 1+2+3 \\ 2+6-2 \\ 3+4-1 \end{bmatrix} = \begin{bmatrix} 6 \\ 6 \\ 6 \end{bmatrix} = 6\begin{bmatrix} 1 \\ 1 \\ 1 \end{bmatrix}$$

So, the vector $\begin{bmatrix} 1 \\ 1 \\ 1 \end{bmatrix}$ is the eigen vector, with eigen value 6.

$$AX = \lambda X = 6\begin{bmatrix} 1 \\ 1 \\ 1 \end{bmatrix}$$

7. Find the eigen values and eigen vectors for matrix $\begin{bmatrix} 1 & 2 \\ 2 & 1 \end{bmatrix}$

We have,

$$\det \left[\begin{pmatrix} 1 & 2 \\ 2 & 1 \end{pmatrix} - \lambda \begin{pmatrix} 1 & 0 \\ 0 & 1 \end{pmatrix}\right] = 0$$

or,
$$\left[\begin{pmatrix} 1 & 2 \\ 2 & 1 \end{pmatrix} - \begin{pmatrix} \lambda & 0 \\ 0 & \lambda \end{pmatrix}\right] = 0$$

or,
$$\begin{bmatrix} 1-\lambda & 2-0 \\ 2-0 & 1-\lambda \end{bmatrix} = 0$$

or,
$$(1-\lambda)^2 - 2 \times 2 = 0$$

$$1 - 2\lambda + \lambda^2 - 4 = 0$$

$$\lambda^2 - 2\lambda - 3 = 0$$

$$\lambda = \frac{-2 \pm \sqrt{4 - 4(-3) \times 1}}{2 \times 1}$$

$$= \frac{-2 \pm \sqrt{4 + 12}}{2}$$

$$= \frac{-2 \pm \sqrt{16}}{2} = \frac{-2 \pm 4}{2}$$

$$= -1 \pm 2 = 1 \text{ or } -3$$

$$\lambda_1 = 1 \text{ and } \lambda_2 = -3$$

We obtain eigen vectors on substituting the eigen value in the equation:

$$\begin{bmatrix} 1-\lambda_1 & 2 \\ 2 & 1-\lambda_1 \end{bmatrix} \begin{bmatrix} x_1 \\ x_2 \end{bmatrix} = \begin{bmatrix} 0 \\ 0 \end{bmatrix}$$

or,
$$(1 - \lambda_1)\, x_1 + 2x_2 = 0$$

$$2x_1 + (1 - \lambda_1)x_2 = 0$$

For, $\lambda_1 = 1$

or, $(1-1)x_1 + 2x_2 = 0$

$2x_1 + (1-1)\,x_2 = 0$

or, $0x_1 + 2x_2 = 0$

$2x_1 + 0x_2 = 0$

$\therefore$ $x_2 = 0,\ x_1 = 0$

$$x_1^2 + x_2^2 = 1 \quad (\because x_2 = 0)$$

$$x_1^2 = 1$$

$$x_1 = 1$$

$$x_2 = 0$$

The eigen vector $x^{(i)} = \begin{bmatrix} 1 \\ 0 \end{bmatrix}$

$$x^{(ii)} = \begin{bmatrix} 0 \\ 1 \end{bmatrix}$$

For $\lambda_2 = -3$

$(1+3)x_1 + 2x_2 = 0$

$4x_1 + (1+3)x_2 = 0$

or, $2x_1 + x_2 = 0$

$x_1 + x_2 = 0$

$2x_1 = -x_2$

$$x_1 = \frac{-1}{2}x_2$$

But, $x_1^2 + x_2^2 = 1,\ (2x_2)^2 + x_2^2 = 1$

$$4x_2^2 + x_2^2 = 1$$

$$5x_2^2 = 1$$

$$x_2^2 = \frac{1}{5},\ x_2 = \pm\frac{1}{\sqrt{5}}$$

$$X^{(i)} = \begin{bmatrix} \frac{2}{\sqrt{5}} \\ \frac{1}{\sqrt{5}} \end{bmatrix} = \frac{1}{\sqrt{5}} \begin{bmatrix} 2 \\ 1 \end{bmatrix}$$

Assuming other root $x_2 = -\frac{1}{\sqrt{5}}$

$$2x_1 = -x_2$$

$$x_1 = +\frac{1}{2\sqrt{5}}$$

$$\therefore \qquad X^{(ii)} = \begin{bmatrix} -\frac{1}{\sqrt{5}} \\ +\frac{1}{2\sqrt{5}} \end{bmatrix} = \frac{-1}{\sqrt{5}} \begin{bmatrix} 1 \\ -\frac{1}{2} \end{bmatrix}$$

10.12 ORTHOGONALITY CONDITION

If E_k and E_l are two allowed values for the energy the two wave functions Ψ_k and Ψ_l are given by:

$$\Psi_k = \sum_i C_{ki} \Psi_i$$

$$\Psi_l = \sum_j C_{lj} \Psi_i$$

If they are orthogonal.

This means, $\int \Psi_k \Psi_l \, d\tau = 0$

$$\int \Psi_k \Psi_l \, d\tau = \sum_{ij} C_{ki} C_{lj} \delta_{ij}$$

$$= \sum_{ij} C_{ki} C_{lj} \delta_{ij}$$

$$= \sum_m C_{km} C_{lm} 1$$

$$\text{or} \qquad \sum_m C_{km} C_{lm} = 0$$

Proof: For Kth state the secular equation is:

$$\sum H_{ki}\ C_{ki} = EC_{km}$$

m, 1, 2, ...

For ℓ^{th} state the secular equation is given by:

$$\sum_j H_{nj}\ C_{lj} = E_l\ C_{ln}$$

n = 1, 2, ...

The equation, $\sum_i H_{ki}\ C_{ki} = E_k\ C_{km}$

is multiplied by C_{lm}

$$\sum C_{lm}\ H_{mi}\ C_{ki} = E_k\ C_{lm}\ C_{km}$$

Similarly, on multiplying:

$$\sum_j H_{nj}\ C_{lj} = E_l\ C_{lm}$$

by C_{lm}

$$\sum_j C_{km}\ H_{mj}\ C_{lj} = E_l\ C_{km}\ C_{lm}$$

subtracting the two and adding all the equations in m = 1, 2, ... we get,

$$\sum_{m_1 i_{1j}} C_{lm}\ H_{mi}\ C_{ki} - \sum_{m_{1j}} C_{km}\ H_{mj}\ C_{lj}$$

$$= (E_k - E_l) \sum_m C_{km} C_{lm}$$

The two summations on the left are identical that can easily by seen.

Hence, $0 = (E_k - E_l) \sum_m C_{km}\ C_{lm}$

or $$\sum_m C_{km}\ C_{lm} = 0.$$

QUESTIONS

1. Explain: (a) Eigen value and eigen vector.
   (b) Matrix form of Schrödinger wave equation.
   (c) Matrix form of secular equation.
   (d) Effect of symmetry operator on eigen value equation involving Hamiltonian operator.

2. (a) Differentiate between arithmetic product and product of two matrices.
   (b) Multiply: $\begin{bmatrix} -1 & 3 \\ 0 & 4 \end{bmatrix}$ and $\begin{bmatrix} 1 & 0 \\ 2 & 5 \end{bmatrix}$
   (c) Comment something on matrix algebra.
   (d) Explain conformable matrices.

3. Explain:
   (a) Orthogonal matrix
   (b) Matrix transformation of linear equations.
   (c) Transpose and inverse matrices.
   (d) Symmetric and anti-symmetric matrices.

4. Evaluate λ from Ax = λx with the use of:

$$A = \begin{bmatrix} 2 & \frac{1}{2} \\ 0 & 1 \end{bmatrix}, \; X = \begin{bmatrix} x_1 \\ x_2 \end{bmatrix}$$

5. Take product of:

$$A = \begin{bmatrix} -1 & 0 \\ 0 & -1 \end{bmatrix} B = \begin{bmatrix} 1 & 0 \\ 0 & -1 \end{bmatrix}$$

   and obtain eigen value and eigen vector.

6. If, $A\begin{bmatrix} 2 & 0 \\ 0 & \frac{1}{2} \end{bmatrix}$ and $X = \begin{bmatrix} 0 \\ 1 \end{bmatrix}$ Find λ ?

7. What are the conditions for orthogonal matrix? Tell them.

8. Given (i) $A = \begin{bmatrix} 2 & 0 \\ 0 & \frac{1}{2} \end{bmatrix} X = \begin{bmatrix} 0 \\ 1 \end{bmatrix}$

   (ii) $A = \begin{bmatrix} 1 & 0 \\ 0 & 0 \end{bmatrix}$ its eigen vector takes the form $\begin{bmatrix} x \\ 0 \end{bmatrix}$

   Obtain their eigen value (λ).

GROUP THEORY AND MOLECULAR VIBRATIONS

11

11.1. INTRODUCTION

Molecular vibration is of complicated nature. We determine the total number of degrees of freedom which is equal to the co-ordinates required at all the atoms in a molecule. Each atom inside a molecule has to be specified by three co-ordinates (x, y, z) at its position. There are 3N co-ordinates for all N-atoms. This gives the total degrees of freedom, three of them belong to translational degree of freedom because in translational motion molecule as a whole is moving from one position to another through movement of its centre of mass. This is possible in three independent directions. Hence, $f_t = 3$. A molecule can orient in two different ways if it is linear or in all three ways if it is non-linear. There can be $f_r = 2$ or 3 depending upon the shape whether it is linear and non-linear. The remaining goes to viberational degree of freedom:

$$
\begin{aligned}
f_T &= f_{tr} + f_r + f_{vib}.\\
3N &= 3 + 2 \text{ or } 3 + f_{vib}.\\
f_{vib} &= 3N - 5 \text{ (linear)}\\
&= 3N - 6 \text{ (non-linear)}.
\end{aligned}
$$

Symmetry plays a dominant role in deciding the vibrational modes and their infrared and Raman activities from the very knowledge of their point group determination and character Table. Each vibration is assigned exclusively a normal co-ordinate. In this system of co-ordinates both kinetic energy and potential energy terms are expressed in diagonal form (quadratic).

11.2. DIRECT PRODUCT REPRESENTATION

We know matrices and characters are the bases of representations under a given point group of molecule. Multiplication of two or more sets of representations are possible to obtain what is known as direct product representation. Let us consider two sets of function shown as $A_1, A_2, ... A_i$ and its representation as Γ_A.

There will be another set of functions shown as $B_1, B_2, ...B_k$ whose representation is given by Γ_B.

Let R be the representative operator. Its action on these functions can be separately given as R(Ai) and R (Bk).

Where, $$R(Ai) = \sum_j a_{ji} A_j$$

$$R(Bk) = \sum_i b_{ik} B_i$$

Further we consider their product and action of operation R on such product can be given as:

$$R(Ai\ Bk) = \sum_j \sum_i a_{ji}\ b_{ik}\ A_j\ B_i$$

The product function may also form represention of the group. So that it is possible to write:

$$R(Ai\ Bk) = \sum_j \sum_i C_{ii}\ (A_j\ B_i)$$

We can derive the character as sum of diagonal elements of the matrix. Thus:

$$\chi_R\left(A.B\right) = \sum_i \sum_k C_{ik},\ _{ik}\left(A_i\ B_k\right)$$

Now suppose that i = j, k = i,

This on insertion leads to:

$$\chi_R\,(AB) = \sum_j \sum_k a_{ji}\ b_{kk}\ (A_i\ B_k)$$

$$= \sum_i a_{ii}\ A_i \sum_k b_{kk}\ B_k$$

$$= \chi_R(A).\chi_R(B)$$

For a given operation R, the direct product character is simply as the product of characters of the representation. A and B for the same operator:

$$\chi \text{ direct Product} = \chi_R(A).\chi_R(B).$$

We take up A and B as the basis of representations of a group and R as symmetry operation in a group. A set of functions as Ai. Bk is known as direct product and both Ai and Bk form basis of representation of a group is invariance of integral is indicative that it forms basis of totally symmetric representation and transition is allowed.

11.3 NORMAL CO-ORDINATES AND NORMAL VIBRATIONS

Let us introduce now normal co-ordinate and normal vibration. There are 3N-5 or 3N-6 normal modes of vibrations containing N-atoms. Each type of molecular vibration is assigned a normal co-ordinate (Q). The beauty of normal co-ordinate is that both kinetic energy and potential energy are expressed in diagonal forms and we establish a very simple relation between the two. Let q_i be the general displacement co-ordinate for its particle. Its kinetic energy is quadratic which is given as:

$$2T = \sum_{i=1}^{N} q_i^2$$

The potential energy is expressed by Tylor series:

$$V = V_0 + \sum_{i=1}^{N} \frac{\partial V}{\partial q_i} + \frac{1}{2}\left[\sum_{i=1}^{N}\sum_{j=1}^{N} \frac{\partial^2 V}{\partial q_i \partial q_j}\right] q_i\, q_j$$

Under equilibrium position $V_0 = 0$. Also its first derivative $\frac{\partial V}{\partial q_i} = 0$ at equilibrium of the potential energy. We thus left with the second derivative:

$$V = \frac{1}{2}\sum_{i=1}^{N}\sum_{j=1}^{N} \frac{\partial^2 V}{\partial q_i \partial q_i} . q_i . q_j$$

In the matrix form the potential energy term is related to:

$$2V = qFq$$
$$= qU\lambda U^{-1}q$$

where $U^{-1}q = Q$ and $q = UQ$. with Q as a normal co-ordinate such that:

$$2V = \sum_{k=1}^{3N-6} \lambda_k Q_k^2$$

Note that λ_k is frequency parameter:

$$2T = \sum_{k=1}^{3N-6} \dot{Q}_k^2$$

$\dot{Q}_k$ is the time derivative. Both T and V are invariant in normal co-ordinate system. As for example let us consider a non-degenerate case with Q_1 and Q_2 representing normal co-ordinates and normal vibrations giving:

$$2T = \dot{Q}_1^2 + \dot{Q}_2^2$$

$$2V = \lambda_1 Q_1^2 + \lambda_1 Q_2^2$$

For 3N–6 degree of freedom their would have Q_1, Q_2 .... Q_k .... Q (3N – 6) normal vibratinal frequencies and the total wave function is given by:

$$\Psi_k = \prod_{k=1}^{3N-6} \Psi_k$$

$$= \Psi_{v_1}(Q_1).\Psi_{v_2}(Q_2)\ldots\ldots \Psi_k(Q_k)\ldots\ldots\Psi_{3N-6}(Q)$$

11.4 QUANTUM MECHANICAL TREATMENT OF HARMONIC OSCILLATOR

Quantum Mechanical Treatment of Harmonic Oscillator using normal co-ordinates for 3N-6 degree of Freedom the vibrational motion is given by:

$$\sum \frac{-\hbar^2}{2mi}\left[\frac{\partial^2\Psi}{\partial x_i^2} + \frac{\partial^2\Psi}{\partial y_i^2} + \frac{\partial^2\Psi}{\partial z_i^2}\right] + V\psi = E\psi$$

We carryout a simple transformation of equation from Cartesian system of co-ordinate to normal co-ordinates in the following way:

$$H = T + V \quad 2T = \sum_k \dot{Q}_k^2$$

$$H = \tilde{T} + \tilde{V}$$

$$\tilde{T} = \frac{1}{2}\sum_k \tilde{\dot{Q}}_k^2$$

$$= \frac{1}{2}\sum_k \left(-i\hbar \frac{\partial}{\partial Q_k}\right)^2$$

$$= \frac{1}{2}\sum_k -\hbar^2 \frac{\partial^2}{\partial Q_k^2}$$

$$H = \frac{1}{2}\sum_{k=1}^{3N-6} -\hbar^2 \frac{\partial^2}{\partial Q_k^2} + \frac{1}{2}\sum_{k=1}^{3N-6} \lambda_k Q_k^2$$

The wave equation takes the form:

$$\frac{-\hbar^2}{2}\sum_k \frac{\partial^2}{\partial Q_k^2}\Psi_v + \frac{1}{2}\sum_k \lambda_k Q_k^2 \Psi_v = E_v \Psi_v$$

The equation is separated into 3N-6 equations.

Let us have Q equation one each for normal co-ordinate Q_k. The solution is:

$$\Psi_v = \psi_1(Q_1)\,\psi_2(Q_2)\ldots\ldots\ldots\psi_k(Q_k)$$

or,
$$\frac{\partial^2 \Psi_v}{\partial Q_k^2} = \Psi_1(Q_1)\,\psi_2(Q_2)\ldots\ldots\ldots\frac{\partial^2 \Psi_k(Q_k)}{\partial Q_k^2}$$

or,
$$\frac{-\hbar^2}{2}\sum_k \Psi_1(Q_1)\,\Psi_2(Q_2)\ldots\ldots\ldots\frac{\partial^2 \Psi_k(Q_k)}{\partial Q_k^2}$$

$$+\frac{1}{2}\sum_k \lambda_k Q_k^2 \Psi_v = E_v \Psi_v$$

or,
$$\frac{-\hbar^2}{2}\sum_k \frac{\Psi_1(Q_1)\,\Psi_2(Q_2)\ldots\ldots\ldots}{\Psi_1(Q_1)\,\Psi_2(Q_2)\ldots\ldots\ldots}\Psi_k(Q_k)\frac{\partial^2 \Psi_k(Q_k)}{\partial Q_k^2}$$

$$+\frac{1}{2}\sum_k \lambda_k Q_k^2 \frac{\Psi_v}{\Psi_v} = E_v \frac{\Psi_v}{\Psi_v}$$

or,
$$\frac{-\hbar^2}{2}\sum_k \frac{\partial^2 \Psi_k(Q_k)}{\Psi_k(Q_k)\,\partial Q_k^2} + \frac{1}{2}\sum_k \lambda_k Q_k^2 = E_v$$

or,
$$\frac{-\hbar^2}{2}\sum_k \frac{\partial^2 \Psi_k(Q_k)}{\partial Q_k^2} + \frac{1}{2}\sum_k \lambda_k Q_k^2 \Psi_k(Q_k)$$
$$= E_v \Psi_k(Q_k).$$

Each part of left hand side is a function of only one normal co-ordinate (Q_k) and also there is summation sign varying from K = 1 to K = 3N – 6 and there are so many independent equations and their sum is E_v a constant quantity. As such separate equation is given by:

$$\frac{-\hbar^2}{2}\frac{\partial^2 \Psi_k(Q_k)}{\partial Q_k^2} + \frac{1}{2}\lambda_k Q_k^2 \Psi_k(Q_k) = E_k \Psi_k(Q_k)$$

This equation is individually solved for Kth value from 1, 2, 3........ 3N–6. The eigen function Ψ_k (Q_k) for normal co-ordinate has the form Ψ_v (Q_k)

$$= N_{vk} H_{vk}\left(\alpha_k^{1/2} Q_k\right) e^{-1/2\alpha_k Q_k^2}$$

The Hermite polynomial of degree v_k is $Q_k = H_{vk}\left(\alpha_k^{1/2} Q_k\right)$ in which x is replaced by $\alpha_k^{1/2} Q_k$:

$$H_0(x) = 1,\ H_1(x) = 2x = 2\left(\alpha_k^{1/2} Q_k\right)$$
$$H_2(x) = 4x^2 = 4\left(\alpha_k Q_k^2\right) \text{ etc.}$$

For ground state $v_k = 0$

$$\Psi_0(Q_k) = N_0\ e^{-1/2\ \alpha_k Q_k^2}$$
$$v_k = 1,\ \Psi_1(Q_k) = N_1 Q_k\ e^{-1/2\ \alpha_k Q_k^2}$$

The total wave function for 3N–6 degree of freedom has the solution of the form:

$$\Psi_0(Q_k) = N_0\ e^{-1/2}\sum_{k=1}^{3N-6}\alpha_k Q_k^2$$

$$\Psi_1(Q_k) = N_1 Q_k\ e^{-1/2}\sum_{k=1}^{3N-6}\alpha_k Q_k^2$$

$$= \Psi_0(Q_k).Q_k$$

It has functional dependence of normal co-ordinate Q_k. Symmetry of Ψ_1 is the same as that of Q_k.

The expression for energy is $E_v(k) = \left(V_k + \frac{1}{2}\right)hv_k$ and for whole molecule there are 3N-6 vibrational modes, so E_v is obtained as their sum $E_v = \sum_k E_k$

or, $$E_v = \left(V_1 + \frac{1}{2}\right)hv_1 + \left(V_2 + \frac{1}{2}\right)hv_2 + \ldots\ldots\ldots$$

$$\ldots\ldots\ldots\ldots\ldots\left(V_{3N-6} + \frac{1}{2}\right)hv_{3N-6}$$

$$= \sum_{k=1}^{3N-6}\left(V_k + \frac{1}{2}\right)hv_k$$

The zero point energy is:

$$E_0 = E_0(1) + E_0(2)\ldots\ldots\ldots\ldots\ldots + E_0(k) + \ldots\ldots\ldots\ldots E_0(3N-6)$$

$$= \sum_{k=1}^{3N-6}\frac{1}{2}hv_k$$

The normal co-ordinate $\left(\Gamma_{Q_1}\right)$ must belong to the symmetry of the dipole moment.

11.5 SYMMETRY ASPECTS OF MOLECULAR VIBRATIONS AND CHARACTER OF Γ_{3N}

We can easily study the infrared and Raman Spectra from the knowledge of symmetry properties of translational, rotational and vibrational vectors. We need to know the characters for different operations in a point group—for all the Γ_{3N}, from which the necessary reduction is made for translational and rotational vectors which will be taken into account out of Γ_{3N} and hence $\Gamma_{3N-5 \text{ or } 6}$ may be worked out. The representation of vibrational vectors will be allowed to decompose using standard formulae by means of C.T and other procedure will be followed on the basis of selection rules. Consider the case of water molecule and position of three vectors on each atom along a set of Cartesian axis with origin at each atom. For N-atoms we generate representation which has a set of 3N basis vectors. We calculate resulting character in each operation under the given point group. The resulting characters are supposed to be derived from translation, rotation and vibration motions so as to give Γ_R or Γ_{3N}.

There are three atoms present in water and we have to consider a basis vectors:

$$x_1, y_1, z_1, x_2, y_2, z_2, x_3, y_3, z_3.$$

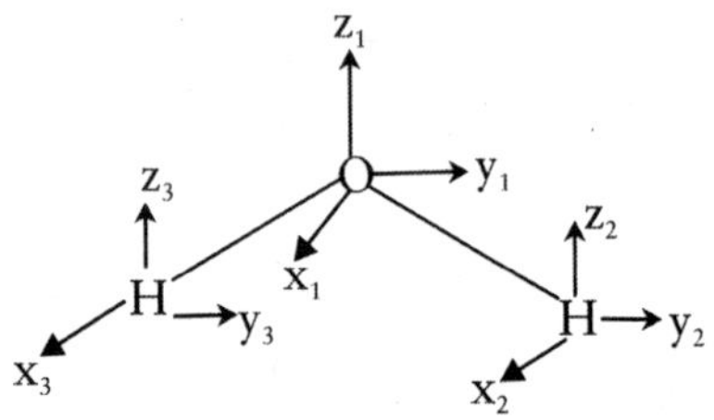

It belongs to C_{2V} point group and there are four symmetry operations:

$$E\ C_2, \sigma_{xz}, \sigma_{yz}.$$

In identity there is no change in any vector:

	x_1	y_1	z_1	x_2	y_2	z_2	x_3	y_3	z_3
x_1'	1	0	0	0	0	0	0	0	0
y_1'	0	1	0	0	0	0	0	0	0
z_1'	0	0	1	0	0	0	0	0	0
x_2'	0	0	0	1	0	0	0	0	0
y_2'	0	0	0	0	1	0	0	0	0
z_2'	0	0	0	0	0	1	0	0	0
x_3'	0	0	0	0	0	0	1	0	0
y_3'	0	0	0	0	0	0	0	1	0
z_3'	0	0	0	0	0	0	0	0	1

It has a diagonal form which has:

$$\chi(E) = 1 + 1 + 1 + 1 + 1 + 1 + 1 + 1 + 1 = 9.$$

In C_2 we have the following transformations:

$x_1' = -x_1$	$x_2' = -x_3$	$x_3' = -x_2$
$y_1' = -y_1$	$y_2' = -y_3$	$y_3' = -y_2$
$z_1' = z_1$	$z_2' = z_3$	$z_3' = z_2$

	x_1	y_1	z_1	x_2	y_2	z_2	x_3	y_3	z_3
x_1'	–1	0	0	0	0	0	0	0	0
y_1'	0	–1	0	0	0	0	0	0	0
z_1'	0	0	1	0	0	0	0	0	0
x_2'	0	0	0	0	0	0	–1	0	0
y_2'	0	0	0	0	0	0	0	–1	0
z_2'	0	0	0	0	0	0	0	0	1
x_3'	0	0	0	–1	0	0	0	0	0
y_3'	0	0	0	0	–1	0	0	0	0
z_3'	0	0	0	0	0	–1	0	0	0

There are only three non-zero elements –1, –1, 1 along the diagonal:

$$\chi(C_2) = -1 -1 + 1 = -1$$

The σ_{xz} operation will bring the following changes:

$x_1' = x_1$	$x_2' = x_3$	$x_3' = x_2$
$y_1' = -y_1$	$y_2' = -y_3$	$y_3' = -y_2$
$z_1' = z_1$	$z_2' = z_3$	$z_3' = z_2$

	x_1	y_1	z_1	x_2	y_2	z_2	x_3	y_3	z_3
x_1'	1	0	0	0	0	0	0	0	0
y_1'	0	–1	0	0	0	0	0	0	0
z_1'	0	0	1	0	0	0	0	0	0
x_2'	0	0	0	0	0	0	1	0	0
y_2'	0	0	0	0	0	0	0	–1	0
z_2'	0	0	0	0	0	0	0	0	1
x_3'	0	0	0	1	0	0	0	0	0
y_3'	0	0	0	0	–1	0	0	0	0
z_3'	0	0	0	0	0	1	0	0	0

Only three elements are along the diagonals 1, –1, 1 which gives:

$$\chi(\sigma_{xz}) = 1 + (-1) + 1 = 1$$

In reflection in σ_{yz} only x changes its sign:

$x_1' = -x_1$	$x_2' = -x_2$	$x_3' = -x_3$
$y_1' = y_1$	$y_2' = y_2$	$y_3' = y_3$
$z_1' = z_1$	$z_2' = z_3$	$z_3' = z_2$

	x_1	y_1	z_1	x_2	y_2	z_2	x_3	y_3	z_3
x_1'	–1	0	0	0	0	0	0	0	0
y_1'	0	1	0	0	0	0	0	0	0
z_1'	0	0	1	0	0	0	0	0	0
x_2'	0	0	0	–1	0	0	0	0	0
y_2'	0	0	0	0	1	0	0	0	0
z_2'	0	0	0	0	0	1	0	0	0
x_3'	0	0	0	0	0	0	–1	0	0
y_3'	0	0	0	0	0	0	0	1	0
z_3'	0	0	0	0	0	0	0	0	1

All the non zero elements lie along the diagonal:

$$\chi(\sigma_{yz}) = -1 + 1 + 1 - 1 + 1 + 1 - 1 + 1 + 1$$

$$= -3 + 6 = 3$$

$$\Gamma_R = \Gamma_{3N} = 9 \quad -1 \quad 1 \quad 3.$$

We can workout the characters for Γ_{3N} in case of NH_3, CO_3^{-2} and BF_3.

In all cases we include 12 variables with 4 atoms and 12 × 12 matrices will be constructed for each symmetry elements present in classes for C_{3v} and D_{3h} point groups.

It is a quite cumbersome method of finding out character for reducible representation of molecules. Let us consider the case of CO_3^{2-} ions. It has D_{3h} point group. The co-ordinate system is placed in the figure:

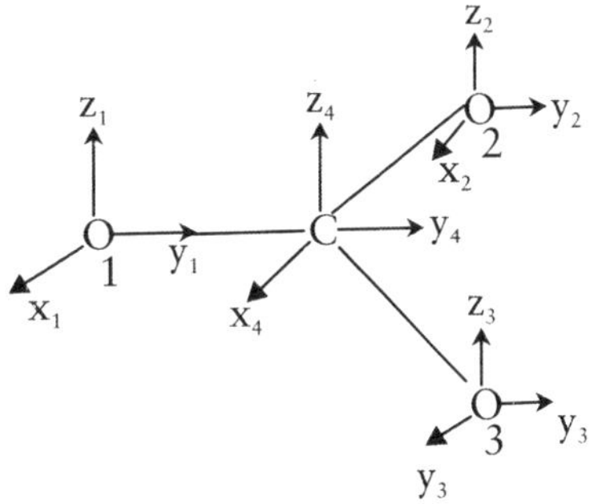

There are three oxygen atoms O_1, O_2, O_3 with their co-ordinates x_1, y_1, z_1; x_2, y_2, z_2; x_3, y_3, z_3 the carbon atom is labeled with its co-ordinates x_4, y_4, z_4.

Altogether 3 × 4 = 12 co-ordinates are needed for its specification and we deduce the 12 dimensional representation. All the vectors remain unchanged in identity (E):

	x_1	y_1	z_1	x_2	y_2	z_2	x_3	y_3	z_3	x_4	y_4	z_4
x_1'	1	0	0	0	0	0	0	0	0	0	0	0
y_1'	0	1	0	0	0	0	0	0	0	0	0	0
z_1'	0	0	1	0	0	0	0	0	0	0	0	0
x_2'	0	0	0	1	0	0	0	0	0	0	0	0
y_2'	0	0	0	0	1	0	0	0	0	0	0	0
z_2'	0	0	0	0	0	1	0	0	0	0	0	0
x_3'	0	0	0	0	0	0	1	0	0	0	0	0
y_3'	0	0	0	0	0	0	0	1	0	0	0	0
z_3'	0	0	0	0	0	0	0	0	1	0	0	0
x_4'	0	0	0	0	0	0	0	0	0	1	0	
y_4'	0	0	0	0	0	0	0	0	0	0	1	0
z_4'	0	0	0	0	0	0	0	0	0	0	0	1

This leads to $\chi(E) = \sum_{i=1}^{12} 1 = 12$.

The effect of C_3 operation is visualized on the basis of following figures:

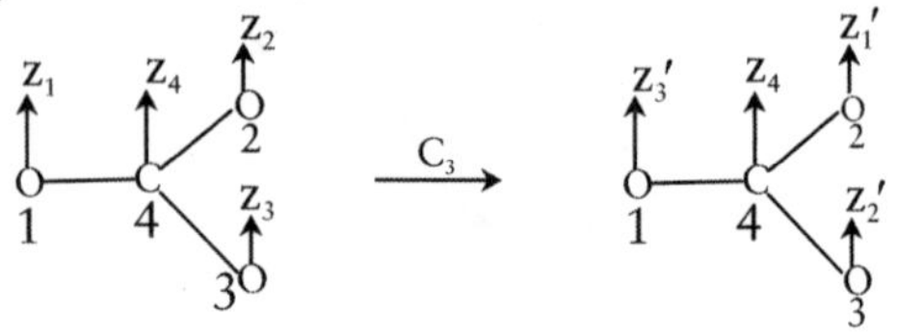

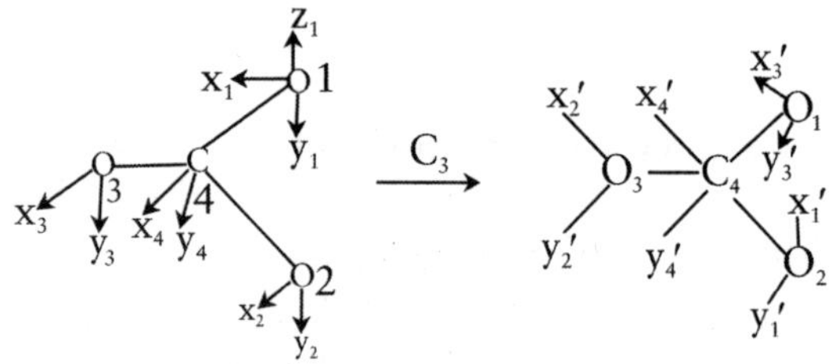

x_1' can be equal to a set of linear combination of x_2 and y_2. It so happens for y_1' which can be expressed as linear combination of x_2 and y_2 as well.

x_1' can have expression as:

$$\cos 120^\circ\, x_2 - \sin 120^\circ\, y_2$$
$$= -\cos 60^\circ x_2 - \sin 60^\circ y_2$$
$$= -½\, x_2 - \sqrt{3}/2\, y_2$$

and y_1' as,

$$\sin 120^\circ\, x_2 + \cos 120^\circ\, y_2$$
$$= \sin 60^\circ\, x_2 - \cos 60^\circ\, y_2$$
$$= \sqrt{3}/2\, x_2 - ½\, y_2$$

Similarly we have,

$$x_2' = -\frac{1}{2}x_3 - \frac{\sqrt{3}}{2}y_3$$

$$y_2' = \frac{\sqrt{3}}{2}x_3 - \frac{1}{2}y_3$$

$$x_3' = -\frac{1}{2}x_1 - \frac{\sqrt{3}}{2}y_1$$

$$y_3' = \frac{\sqrt{3}}{2}x_1 - \frac{1}{2}y_1$$

$$x_4' = -\frac{1}{2}x_4 - \frac{\sqrt{3}}{2}y_4$$

$$y_4' = \frac{\sqrt{3}}{2}x_4 - \frac{1}{2}y_4$$

and $z_1' = z_2,\ z_2' = z_3,\ z_3' = z_1,\ z_4' = z_4.$

By C_3 operation vectors associated with atom 1 come from atom 2 namely, x_1', y_1', z_1' from x_2, y_2, z_2 and so on.

Now carryout C_2 operation in which atoms 2 and 3 are shifted but atom 1 and 4 are un-affected.

On atoms 1 and 4 z-vectors are un-shifted but they transform into negatives to themselves. And y-vector to go over to their own negatives but x-vectors remain unchanged. The result is shown below:

	x_1	y_1	z_1	x_4	y_4	z_4
x_1'	1	0	0			
y_1'	0	–1	0			
z_1'	0	0	–1			
x_4'				1	0	0
y_4'				0	–1	0
z_4'				0	0	–1

The effect of σ_h operation does not shift any vector from one atom to another. It transforms x and y vectors into themselves but z-vectors into negatives. The sub-matrix will be diagonal:

$$x = 1,\ y = 1,\ z = -1.$$

$$\chi\ (\sigma_h) = 4 + 4 + -4 = 4$$

S_3 will shift all the vectors on all three oxygen atoms, and all the nine vectors may be ignored, then only the effect of S_3 on C_4 will be taken into consideration. Its effect can be taken as $S_3 = C_3.\sigma_h$ first in C_3 followed by σ_h. Its effect on x_4 and y_4 will be same as in C_3, σ_h causes to transform z_4 into $-z_4$. Hence

S_3 causes to transform the following elements appearing as diagonals: $-\frac{1}{2}-\frac{1}{2}-1=-2$.

Let us consider the operation σ_v passing through O_1 and C_4 atoms. Vectors of O_1 and C_4 are considered only those of O_2 and O_3 are shifted and ignored. It shows the vectors on O_1 such as x_1 and z_1 and those of C_4 such as x_4 and z_4 go into themselves but those of y_1 and y_4 will go into their negatives.

On reflection in σ_v be diagonal elements generated here are: 1 1 1 1 –1 –1 and its character is, 1+1+1+1–1–1 = 4 – 2 = 2

	E	$2C_3$	$3C_2$	σ_h	$2S_3$	$3\sigma_v$
Γ_{3N}	12	0	–2	4	–2	2

Use of C.T. for rotational and translational components and their irreducible representation for calculation of $\Gamma_{3N} - \Gamma_t - \Gamma_r$.

This will give $\Gamma_{vib} = \Gamma_{3N-5 \text{ or } 6}$.

Use decomposition formula for C_{2v} and D_{3h} cases (H_2O and CO_3^{2-}).

11.6 METHOD OF UN-SHIFTED VECTORS

A simplified procedure is adopted instead of first principle of looking the effect of symmetry operation, formation of bigger matrices and evaluation of their character for a given point group. The method of un-shifted vectors considers that vector associated with an atom is shifted to different positions in space by symmetry operations.

Such a vector contributes nothing to the character of the operation; $\chi(R)$. Only the vector on un-shifted atom may contribute to the character of a given symmetry operation is Γ_{3N}.

Procedure of Un-shifted Vector

1. Consider only one operation in a class for a given point group.
2. Count the number of un-shifted vectors.
3. Calculate the contribution to $\chi(R)$ for every un-shifted vector.
4. The contribution to $\chi(R)$ per un-shifted vector is equal.

5. Deduce the Γ_{3N} or Γ_R from the number of un-shifted vector/atom.

Case of Identity (E)

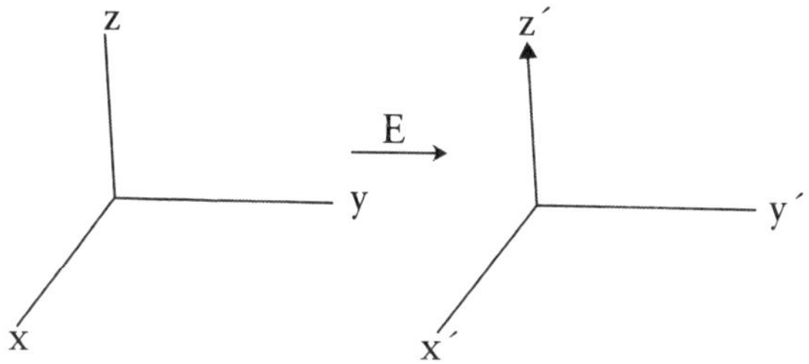

All the three vectors remain un-changed for every un-shifted atom/vector:

$$x' = x, \quad y' = y, \quad z' = z$$

$$\begin{pmatrix} x' \\ y' \\ z' \end{pmatrix} = \begin{pmatrix} 1 & 0 & 0 \\ 0 & 1 & 0 \\ 0 & 0 & 1 \end{pmatrix} \begin{pmatrix} x \\ y \\ z \end{pmatrix}$$

$$\chi = 1 + 1 + 1 = 3.$$

Therefore, χ (E) per un-shifted atom gives a contribution of +3.

Case of Inversion (i)

For each un-shifted atom we have a contribution to be determined as follows:

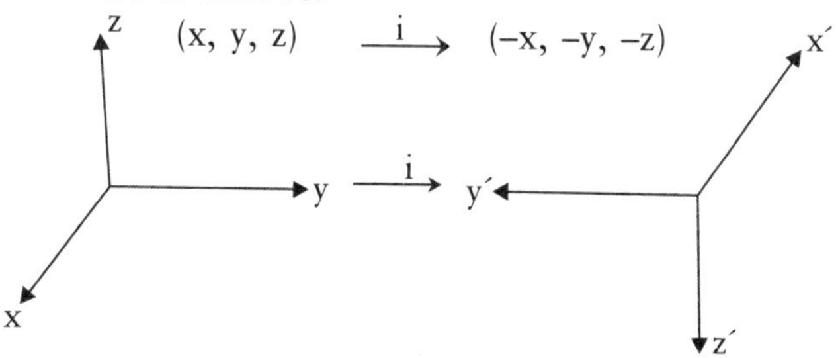

$$\begin{pmatrix} x' \\ y' \\ z' \end{pmatrix} = i \begin{pmatrix} x \\ y \\ z \end{pmatrix} = \begin{pmatrix} -x \\ -y \\ -z \end{pmatrix} = \begin{pmatrix} -1 & 0 & 0 \\ 0 & -1 & 0 \\ 0 & 0 & -1 \end{pmatrix} \begin{pmatrix} x \\ y \\ z \end{pmatrix}$$

$$\chi = -1 - 1 - 1 = -3.$$

Cases of Reflection

The affect of σ on an un-shifted atom is typical.

Consider σ_{xz}

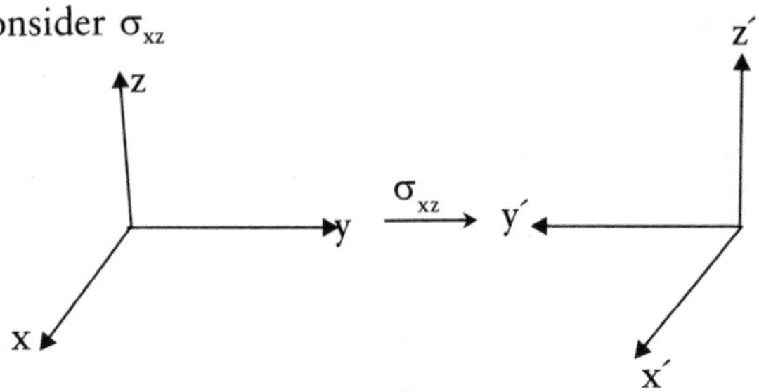

$$x' = x,\ y' = -y,\ z' = z$$

$$\begin{pmatrix} x' \\ y' \\ z' \end{pmatrix} = \sigma_{xz} \begin{pmatrix} x \\ y \\ z \end{pmatrix} = \begin{pmatrix} 1 & 0 & 0 \\ 0 & -1 & 0 \\ 0 & 0 & 1 \end{pmatrix} \begin{pmatrix} x \\ y \\ z \end{pmatrix}$$

$$\chi = 1 - 1 + 1 = 1.$$

The order of characters depends upon the relative orientation of the plane and axis. χ (σ) per un-shifted atom is +1.

Proper Rotation (C_n)

We carryout rotation usually about z-axis. For a clockwise rotation through an angle α is obtained by:

$$C_n; \begin{pmatrix} \cos\alpha & \sin\alpha & 0 \\ -\sin\alpha & \cos\alpha & 0 \\ 0 & 0 & 1 \end{pmatrix}$$

$$\chi = 1 + 2\cos\alpha$$

$C_2 \quad \chi = 1 + 2\cos 180° = 1 + 2 \times (-1) = -1$

$C_3 \quad \chi = 1 + 2\cos 120° = 1 - 2 \times ½ = 1 - 1 = 0$

$C_4 \quad \chi = 1 + 2\cos 90° = 1 + 2 \times 0 = 1$

$C_5 \quad \chi = 1 + 2\cos 72°$

$S_n = C_n\,\sigma_h$

$$= \begin{pmatrix} \cos\alpha & \sin\alpha & 0 \\ -\sin\alpha & \cos\alpha & 0 \\ 0 & 0 & 1 \end{pmatrix} \begin{pmatrix} 1 & 0 & 0 \\ 0 & 1 & 0 \\ 0 & 0 & -1 \end{pmatrix}$$

$$= \begin{pmatrix} \cos\alpha & \sin\alpha & 0 \\ -\sin\alpha & \cos\alpha & 0 \\ 0 & 0 & -1 \end{pmatrix}$$

$$\chi = 2\cos\alpha - 1$$

S_3, $\chi = 2\cos 120^\circ - 1 = 2 \times -\frac{1}{2} - 1 = -1 - 1 = -2$

$S_4, C_4 = \cos 90^\circ \qquad \chi = 2 \times \cos 90^\circ - 1$

$= 2 \times \sin 0^\circ - 1$

$= 2 \times 0 - 1 = -1$ etc.

11.7 SELECTION RULES FOR I.R. AND RAMAN ACTIVE FUNDAMENTALS

The relative population of molecules is determined by Boltzmann distribution law of energy:

$$N_i = e^{\alpha} e^{-\beta E_i}$$

$$N_j = e^{\alpha} e^{-\beta Ej}$$

$$\text{Relative population } \frac{N_i}{N_j} = e^{-\beta (E_i - E_j)} = e^{-\frac{(E_i - E_j)}{KT}}$$

$$= e^{-\Delta E_i / KT}.$$

Like other types of transition those involving vibrational states is subject to Boltzmann distribution law. According to this law ground level is highly populated at room temperature and upper levels are rarely populated. So transition occurs from the ground level to the next level subject to $\Delta v = \pm 1$ one unit change in fundamental transition. We govern the selection rule in terms of transition moment integral:

$$M = \int \Psi_i \, \mu_u \, \Psi_f \, d\tau$$

Ψ_i = Lower, it involves 1st level, which is the ground state of vibrational wave function (Ψ_0).

Ψ_f = Excited state wave function. Which involves only one unit change in vibrational quantum number, i.e. $\Psi_j = \Psi_{(Q)}$ and μ as dipole moment.

There are three components of M and μ such that:

$$M_x = \int \Psi_0 \, \mu_x \, \Psi_1 \, d\tau$$

$$M_y = \int \Psi_0 \, \mu_y \, \Psi_1 \, d\tau$$

$$M_z = \int \Psi_0 \, \mu_z \, \Psi_1 \, d\tau$$

$$\begin{pmatrix} M_x \\ M_y \\ M_z \end{pmatrix} = \begin{bmatrix} \mu_x \\ \mu_y \\ \mu_z \end{bmatrix} \times \left(\Psi_0 \times \Psi_{(Q)}\right)$$

On symmetry representations for all the three terms in the transition moment integrals we have:

$$M_x = \int \Gamma_0 \, \Gamma_1 \, \Gamma_x = \int \left(\Gamma_0 \times \Gamma_Q\right) \times \Gamma_x$$

$$M_y = \int \left(\Gamma_0 \times \Gamma_Q\right) \times \Gamma_y$$

$$M_z = \int \left(\Gamma_0 \times \Gamma_Q\right) \times \Gamma_z$$

The symmetry species of the ground state vibrational wave function is always totally symmetric, i.e. A_1, A_g, A_{1g}, etc., in normal co-ordinate system.

The excited state $\Psi_1 \ \alpha \ \Psi_0$ Q depends upon the normal co-ordinate Q only:

$$\Psi_0 = N_0 e^{-\frac{1}{2}Q^2} \equiv A_1$$

$$\Psi_1 = N_0 \Psi_0 Q$$

$$\Psi_1 \ \alpha \ Q$$

This corresponds to particular vibration of the molecule under consideration.

The dipole moment component term is related to the transnational vector x, y, z respectively.

If such term corresponds to the symmetry of the vibration the transition is allowed otherwise it is forbidden.

Symmetry species of vibrational mode corresponds to the normal co-ordinate.

There are 3 × 3 – 6 = 9 – 6 = 3 vibration modes for water.

Symmetry stretching is υ_1.

Anti-symmetry stretching is υ_2 and bending of bond angle is υ_3.

$\Gamma_r = A_1 + B_2$ are the symmetry species of these vibrational modes.

$$\Gamma_\alpha = A_1$$

From C.T. the components of dipole moment correspond to transnational vectors:

$$\Gamma_x = B_1,\ \Gamma_y = B_2,\ \Gamma_z = A_1$$

Consider A_1 vibration, $M_x = \int(\Gamma_0 \times \Gamma_Q) \times \Gamma_x$

$$= \int(A_1 \times A_1) \times B_1$$

$$= \int A_1 \times B_1 = \int B_1 \text{ forbidden.}$$

$$M_y = \int(A_1 \times A_1) \times B_2 = \int A_1 \times B_2 = \int B_2 \text{ forbidden.}$$

$$M_z = \int(A_1 \times A_1) \times A_1 = \int A_1 \text{ allowed.}$$

Case of B_2 vibration:

$$M_x = \int(A_1 \times B_2) \times B_1 = \int B_2 \times B_1 = A_2 \text{ forbidden.}$$

B_2	1	–1	–1	1	
B_1	1	–1	1	–1	
$B_2 \times B_1$ =	1×1	–1×–1	–1×1	1×–1	
	1	1	–1	–1	= A_2

$$M_y = \int(A_1 \times B_2) \times B_2$$

$$= \int B_2 \times B_2 = \int A_1 \text{ allowed.}$$

$$M_z = \int(A_1 \times B_2) \times A_1$$

$$= \int B_2 \times A_1 = \int B_2 \text{ forbidden.}$$

y component is active so allowed. The normal co-ordinate must belong to the same symmetry to the component of dipole moment then the transition is allowed.

Bending vibration is A_1 type.

The symmetry stretching vibration of A_1 type is active so does the bending mode:

$$M_z = \int (A_1 \times A_1) \times A_1 = \int A_1 \text{ allowed.}$$

Raman activity depends upon the induced dipole moment and polarizability tensor components α_{ij}.

$$\mu_{ind} = \alpha E$$

$$\begin{bmatrix} \mu_x \\ \mu_y \\ \mu_z \end{bmatrix} = \begin{bmatrix} \alpha_{xx} & \alpha_{xy} & \alpha_{xz} \\ \alpha_{yx} & \alpha_{yy} & \alpha_{yz} \\ \alpha_{zx} & \alpha_{zy} & \alpha_{zz} \end{bmatrix} \begin{bmatrix} E_x \\ E_y \\ E_z \end{bmatrix}$$

E is the electrical field of incident light.

α_{ij} a symmetric tensor for $i = j$ may be same or $i \neq j$ when they are different.

By analogy with the band will be Raman active. When,

$$M = \int \Psi_0 \ \alpha_{ij} \ \Psi_{(1)} \ d\tau$$

either $i = j$ or $i \neq j$

There are six polarizability components in transition moment integral and we need any one to be non-zero integral showing Raman activity. In order that a molecule to give rise to Raman transition the polarizability must change during transition. Consequently, Raman transition is possible during normal vibrations if the normal vibrational mode and a component of polarizability tensor belong to the same symmetry species. The transition moment integral component will be non-zero. If they belong to the binary component Cartesian co-ordinates such as, x^2, y^2, z^2, xy, xz, yz, etc.

α_{ij} has the same property as ij:

α_{xz}	x, z
α_{xy}	x, y, etc.

We have the relationships:

$$\mu_x = \alpha_{xx} E_x + \alpha_{xy} E_y + \alpha_{xz} E_z$$
$$\mu_y = \alpha_{yx} E_x + \alpha_{yy} E_y + \alpha_{yz} E_z$$
$$\mu_z = \alpha_{zx} E_x + \alpha_{zy} E_y + \alpha_{zz} E_z$$

If polarizability is a symmetric tensor:

$$\alpha_{xy} = \alpha_{yx}$$
$$\alpha_{zx} = \alpha_{xz}$$
$$\alpha_{yz} = \alpha_{zy}$$

The nine components may be reduced to only six components:

$$= \int(\Gamma_0 \times \Gamma_1) \times \Gamma_{\alpha ij} \,.$$

The direct product of ground and excited states as well as the component of polarizability may be totally symmetric only then transition will be allowed.

When the normal mode is i.r. active this vibration will also be Raman active when one component of polarizability also corresponds to the symmetry species of the vibrational mode:

$$M = \int(\Gamma_0 \times \Gamma_1) \times \Gamma_\alpha$$

In Raman spectrum there is dependence of polarizability containing binary product of quadratic terms in Cartesian co-ordinates such as:

x^2, y^2, z^2, xy, xz, yz, $x^2–y^2$ in corresponding to irreducible symmetry species belonging to the vibrational mode.

The normal co-ordinate must belong to the same representation as one of the quadratic or binary cartesian co-ordinates.

Raman activity in water:

$$\Gamma_0 = A_1, \quad \Gamma_Q = A_1 \text{ vibrational mode.}$$

$$\Gamma_{x^2}, \quad y^2, \quad z^2 = A_1$$

$$= \int A_1 \times A_1 \times A_1 = \int A_1 \text{ totally symmetic } \neq 0 \text{ allowed.}$$

Both stretching and bending vibrations are present, in Raman spectra, i.e. A_1 vibrations are Raman active.

Let us come to B_2 mode. The υ_3 band of a symmetric stretching will be examined as follows:

$$M_x = \int (A_1 \times B_2) \times \Gamma_{x^2}$$

$$= \int (A_1 \times B_2) \times B_1 = \int B_2 \times B_1 = \int A_2 \text{ forbidden.}$$

B_2	=	1	−1	−1	1
B_1	=	1	−1	1	−1
$B_2 \times B_1$	=	1	1	−1	−1 = A_2

$$M_y = \int (A_1 \times B_2) \times \Gamma_{xy}$$

$$= \int (A_1 \times B_2) \times B_2 = \int B_2 \times B_2 = \int A_1 \text{ allowed.}$$

$$M_z = \int (\Gamma_0 \times \Gamma_1) \times \Gamma_{yz}$$

$$= \int (A_1 \times B_2) \times B_2$$

$$= \int B_2 \times A_2 = \int A_1 \text{ allowed.}$$

Hence, Raman active.

B_2 vibration is Raman active because of Γ_y and Γ_z are non-zero.

It may be noted that ground state Γ_0 is totally symmetric A_1, A_g or A_{1g}. The excited state wave function corresponds to the normal co-ordinate Q, which belongs to the symmetry species of the vibration. If the symmetry species of vibrational mode also have polarizability component in C.T. The transition will be totally symmetric and Raman allowed.

11.8 OVERTONE AND COMBINATION BANDS

Besides the fundamental band with $\Delta v = \pm 1$ transitions corresponding to $\Delta v = \pm 2, \pm 3, \pm 4$ etc., are also observed in a few cases. Such transitions are known as overtones — first overtone, second overtone, third overtone respectively.

Sometimes linear combination of fundamental bands are also observed in both ways (both addition and difference), such combinations are also observed on the basis of group theory. We expand the dipole moment by Tylor series in terms of normal co-ordinates:

$$\mu = [\mu]_0 + \sum_k \left(\frac{\delta\mu}{\delta Q_k} \right)_0 Q_k + \ldots\ldots$$

Insert this expansion in transition moment integral:

$$M = \int \Psi_i \ \mu \ \Psi_f \ d\tau$$

$$= \mu_0 \int \Psi_i \ \Psi_f \ d\tau + \Sigma \left(\frac{\delta\mu}{\delta Q_k} \right)_0 \int \Psi_0 \, Q_k \ \Psi_f \ d\tau$$

The total wave function can take the form:

$$\Psi_v = N_k \ e^{-\frac{1}{2}} \sum_k \alpha Q_k^2 \prod_{k=1}^{3N-6} H_{vk} \left(\alpha k \, Q_k \right)$$

In the transition moment integral, there are two or more terms, the second term contains the factor $\left(\frac{\delta\mu}{\delta Q_k} \right)$ besides $\int \Psi_i \ Q_k \ \Psi_f \ d\tau$. This is also true for x, y, z component of dipole moment for which there can be three separate equations. The change in component of μ at equilibrium position when, $\left(\frac{\delta\mu}{\delta Q_k} \right) \neq 0$ the normal modes Q_k will be active in IR spectrum. The second term has integral for which:

$$\Psi = \sum_{k=1}^{3N-6} \Psi_k$$

Now with the explicit form of the wave function the integral can be rewritten as:

$$\int \left(\sum_{k=1}^{3N-6} \Psi_k^i \right) Q_k \left(\sum_{k=1}^{3N-6} \Psi_k^f \right) d\tau$$

$$= \int \Psi_1^i \ \Psi_1^f \ dQ \int \Psi_2^i \ \Psi_2^f \ dQ_2 \ldots\ldots\ldots \int \Psi_k^i \ Q_k \Psi_k^f \ dQ_k$$

$$\int \Psi_{k+1}^1 \ \Psi_{k+1}^f \ dQ_{k+1}$$

All the other integrals are unity except one which contains Q_k so the kth term will be of the form:

$$\left(\frac{\delta\mu}{\delta Q_k} \right) \int \Psi_k^i \ Q_k \ \Psi_k^f \ dQ_k$$

For kth vibrational mode the change in vibrational quantum number must hold $\Delta v = \pm 1$ and the integral is:

$$\left(\frac{\delta \mu}{\delta Q_k}\right)_0 \int \Psi_k^i \, Q_k \, \Psi_k^f \, dQ_k$$

For transition with $\Delta v = \pm 2, \pm 3, \pm 4$ overtone. We include the higher terms in the power series expansion of dipole moment or its components.

$$\left(\frac{\delta \mu}{\delta Q_k}\right)_0 \rangle \left(\frac{\delta^2 \mu}{\delta Q_k^2}\right)_0 \rangle\rangle \left(\frac{\delta^3 \mu}{\delta Q_k^3}\right)_0 \ldots\ldots$$

The additional lines in infrared spectra are very weak with the values $\Delta v = \pm 2, \pm 3, \pm 4, \ldots\ldots$

For overtones of vibrations in infrared spectrum the transitions are allowed when we have non-vanishing terms such as:

$$\left(\frac{\delta^2 \mu}{\delta Q_k \delta Q_l}\right)_0$$

Symmetry species is in common with $\Delta v = \pm 1, \pm 2, \pm 3, \ldots\ldots$ transitions. Symmetry species of the upper level should be same as at least one of the components of the translational vectors T_x, T_y or T_z.

Example

In case of overtone vibration band in C_{3v} point group with A_2 symmetry species. The direct product of A_2 fundamental for :

$$A_2 \times A_2 = A_1$$

So overtone of A_2 fundamental now belongs to A_1 symmetry species on taking direct product, the overtone band is allowed in infrared and Raman spectra. For non-degenerate vibrations the case of second overtone of the fundamental vibration, we consider the direct product of fundamental and first overtone.

For a doubly degenerate vibration, the relation which applies :

$$\chi_E^n(R) = \frac{1}{2}\left[\chi_E^{n-1}(R) \; \chi_E(R) + \chi_E(R^n)\right]$$

where, character of the nth overtone for symmetry operation,

$$R = \chi_E^n(R)$$

Character of the (n-1)th overtone $= \chi_E^{n-1}(R)$

Character of the fundamental for operation (R) $= \chi_E(R)$

Character of the operation R performed n times in succession $= \chi_E(R^n)$

Example

For the case of first overtone with n = 2 in case of vibrations of E symmetry species, we find out the vibrations of $\chi_E^2(R)$ and for which the equation is simplified into:

$$\chi_E^2(R) = \frac{1}{2}\left[\chi_E(R)\,\chi_E(R) + \chi_E(R^2)\right]$$

$[\chi_E(R)^2]$ represents character of the operation R performed twice in succession.

We must determine, $\chi_E(E^2)$, $\chi_E\left(C_3^2\right)$ and $\chi_E\left(\sigma_v^2\right)$.

It may be noted that:

$$\chi_E(E^2) = \chi_E(E)$$

Carrying out C_3 twice, i.e. C_3^2 is the same as, C_3^{-1}

$$\chi_E\left(C_3^2\right) = \chi_E\left(C_3^{-1}\right) = -1$$

from the C.T. of point group C_{3v}. The performance of $\sigma_v^2 = \sigma_v.\sigma_v = E$ (identity).

So, $\chi_E\left(\sigma_v^2\right) = \chi_E(E) = 2$

$\chi_E(R^n)$ upto n = 5 are given below:

	E	C_3	σ_v	
$\chi_E(R^2)$	2	−1	2	
$\chi_E(R^3)$	2	2	0	
$\chi_E(R^4)$	2	−1	2	
$\chi_E(R^5)$	2	−1	0	
$\chi_E(R)$	2	−1	0	
$\chi_E(R)$	2	−1	0	
$\chi_E(R) \times \chi_E(R)$	2 × 2	−1 × −1	0 × 0	
	4	1	0	
$\chi_E(R^2)$	2	−1	2	
$\chi_E^2(R)$	= 6	0	2	(divide by 2)
	= 3	0	1	

$$\left\{\text{Because } \chi_E^2(R) = \frac{1}{2}\left[\chi_E(R)\,\chi_E(R) + \chi_E\left(R^2\right)\right]\right\}$$

The representation of χ_E (R^2) decomposes to A_1 + E (three). As both A_1 and E are allowed in infrared so first overtone in the fundamental belonging to E representation is also allowed.

Now, the overtone (first) level of doubly degenerate vibrations having the normal mode of C_{3v} point group is doubly degenerate. They are both I.R. and Raman active transitions.

11.9 Γ_{3N} FOR WATER THROUGH THE METHOD OF UN-SHIFTED VECTOR AND ITS REDUCTION

Let us deduce the character for Γ_{3N} by the method of un-shifted atoms in H_2O

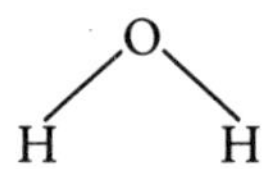

In identity all three atoms are un-shifted.

$$\chi \text{ (E) / atom} = 3$$

No. of un-shifted atoms = 3

$$\chi \text{ (E)} = 3 \times 3 = 9$$

In two fold rotation both H-atoms are shifted. Only O is invariant.

No. of un-shifted atom = 1

$$\chi (C_2) \text{ / atom} = -1$$

$$\chi (C_2) = 1 \times (-1) = -1$$

In σ_{xz} reflection only O atom is un-shifted.

$$\chi (\sigma_{xz}) \text{ / atom} = 1$$

$$\chi (\sigma_{xz}) = 1 \times 1 = 1$$

In σ_{yz} all three atoms are un-shifted.

$$\chi (\sigma_{yz}) \text{ / atom} = 1$$

$$\chi (\sigma_{xz}) = 3 \times 1 = 3$$

C_{2v}	E	C_2	σ_{xz}	σ_{yz}
Γ_{3N}	9	–1	1	3

Now irreducible representations can be deduced out of Γ_R or Γ_{3N} using reduction formula:

$$a_i = \frac{1}{h}\sum_R n_i\left(\Gamma_{3N}\right)\left(\Gamma_i\right)\left(R_i\right)$$

$$a_1 = \frac{1}{4}\left[1\times9\times1+1\times(-1)\times1+1\times1\times1+1\times1\times3\right]$$

$$= \frac{1}{4}\left[9-1+1+3\right] = \frac{1}{4}\times12 = 3$$

$$a_2 = \frac{1}{4}\left[1\times9\times1+1\times(-1)\times1+1\times(-1)\times1+1\times3\times(-1)\right]$$

$$= \frac{1}{4}\left[9-1-1-3\right] = \frac{4}{4} = 1$$

$$a_3 = \frac{1}{4}\left[1\times9\times1+1\times(-1)\times(-1)+1\times1\times1+1\times3\times-1\right]$$

$$= \frac{1}{4}\left[9+1+1-3\right] = \frac{1}{4}\times8 = 2$$

$$a_4 = \frac{1}{4}\left[1\times9\times1+1\times(-1)\times(-1)+1\times(-1)\times1+1\times3\times1\right]$$

$$= \frac{1}{4}\left[9+1-1+3\right] = \frac{12}{4} = 3$$

$$\therefore\ \Gamma_{3N} = 3A_1 + A_2 + 2B_1 + 3B_2$$

This includes translational, rotational and vibrational components. We inspect the C.T. for C_{2v} and locate the positions of T_x, T_y and T_z as well as positions of R_x, R_y and R_z and deduct them out of total or Γ_{3N}. Which may give the genuine vibrations:

C.T. (C_{2v})		
	$T_x - B_1$	$R_x - B_2$
	$T_y - B_2$	$R_y - B_1$
	$T_z - A_1$	$R_z - A_2$
	$\Gamma_{tr} = A_1 + B_1 + B_2$	$\Gamma_{rot} = A_2 + B_1 + B_2$

$\Gamma tr + rot = A_1 + A_2 + 2B_1 + 2B_2$

$\Gamma_{3N} = 3A_1 + A_2 + 2B_1 + 3B_2$

$\Gamma vib = \Gamma_{3N-6} = (3A_1+A_2+2B_1+3B_2)-(A_1+A_2+2B_1+2B_2)$

$= 2A_1 + B_2$

Knowing the symmetry species of genuine vibrational modes, it is possible to predict them whether they are I.R. active or Raman active.

11.10 SYMMETRY CLASSIFICATION OF VIBRATIONAL MODES IN WATER

We can determine the stretching of bands and deformation of bond angle through internal co-ordinates r_1, r_2 and α.

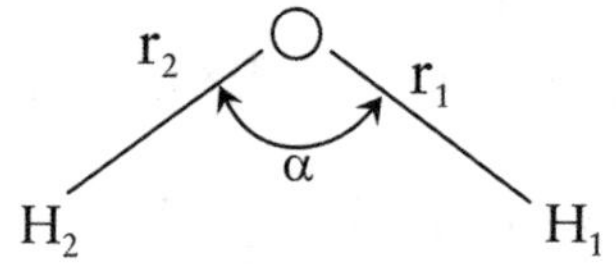

We deduce the transformation matrix in each case with r_1, r_2 and α.

In identity all the three vectors remain un-changed.

$$r_1' = r_1,\ r_2' = r_2,\ \alpha' = \alpha$$

$$\begin{bmatrix} r_1' \\ r_2' \\ \alpha_3' \end{bmatrix} = \begin{bmatrix} 1 & 0 & 0 \\ 0 & 1 & 0 \\ 0 & 0 & 1 \end{bmatrix} \begin{bmatrix} r_1 \\ r_2 \\ \alpha \end{bmatrix}$$

$$\chi\ (E) = 1 + 1 + 1 = 3$$

In C_2, where r_1 and r_2 are inter-changed but there is no change in α. $r_1' = r_2,\ r_2' = r_1,\ \alpha' = \alpha$

$$\begin{bmatrix} r_1' \\ r_2' \\ \alpha' \end{bmatrix} = \begin{bmatrix} 0 & 1 & 0 \\ 1 & 0 & 0 \\ 0 & 0 & 1 \end{bmatrix} \begin{bmatrix} r_1 \\ r_2 \\ \alpha \end{bmatrix}$$

$$\chi\ (C_2) = 1$$

In σ_{xz} plane $r_1' = r_2,\ r_2' = r_1,\ \alpha' = \alpha$

$$\sigma_{xz} \begin{bmatrix} r_1' \\ r_2' \\ \alpha' \end{bmatrix} = \begin{bmatrix} 0 & 1 & 0 \\ 1 & 0 & 0 \\ 0 & 0 & 1 \end{bmatrix} \begin{bmatrix} r_1 \\ r_2 \\ \alpha \end{bmatrix}$$

$$\chi\ (\sigma_{xz}) = 1$$

In σ_{yz} plane $r_1' = r_1$, $r_2' = r_2$, $\alpha' = \alpha$

$$\sigma_{yz}\begin{bmatrix} r_1 \\ r_2 \\ \alpha \end{bmatrix} = \begin{bmatrix} r_1' \\ r_2' \\ \alpha' \end{bmatrix} = \begin{bmatrix} 1 & 0 & 0 \\ 0 & 1 & 0 \\ 0 & 0 & 1 \end{bmatrix}\begin{bmatrix} r_1 \\ r_2 \\ \alpha \end{bmatrix}$$

$$\chi\ (\sigma_{yz}) = 1 + 1 + 1 = 3$$

Characters for stretching and bond angle deformation vectors are:

C_{2v}	E	C_2	σ_{xz}	σ_{yz}
Γ_{int}	3	1	1	3

Both r_1 and r_2 the stretching vectors are related to each other. They are interchanged in so many cases. They are related to each other and they are not independent. As such α is independent. It is unchanged throughout in all symmetry operations. Hence, 3 × 3 matrices can be block diagonalised into 2 × 2 and 1 × 1 corresponding to r_1, r_2 in the first case and α in the latter. And this is accomplishing through partitioning of matrices:

$$\begin{array}{c|cc|c} & r_1 & r_2 & \alpha \\ \hline r_1 & 1 & 0 & 0 \\ r_2 & 0 & 1 & 0 \\ \hline \alpha & 0 & 0 & 1 \end{array} \qquad \begin{array}{cc|c} r_1 & r_2 & \alpha \\ 0 & 1 & 0 \\ 1 & 0 & 0 \\ \hline 0 & 0 & 1 \end{array} \qquad \begin{array}{cc|c} & & \\ 0 & 1 & 0 \\ 1 & 0 & 0 \\ \hline 0 & 0 & 1 \end{array}$$

E $\qquad\qquad C_2 \qquad\qquad \sigma_{xz}$

$$\begin{array}{cc|c} 1 & 0 & 0 \\ 0 & 1 & 0 \\ \hline 0 & 0 & 1 \end{array}$$

σ_{yz}

	E	C_2	σ_{xz}	σ_{yz}
Γ_r	2	0	0	2
Γ_a	1	1	1	1

We apply reduction formulae to determine irreducible representations:

$$\Gamma_r = A_1 + B_2 \text{ and } \Gamma_\alpha = A_1$$

11.11 FUNDAMENTAL OVERTONE AND COMBINATION BANDS IN H_2O

Species	*Translational components*	*Polarizability*
A_1	$T_z - \mu_z$	x^2, y^2, z^2
B_1	$T_x - \mu_x$	xz
B_2	$T_y - \mu_y$	yz
A_2	——	xy

Symmetry stretching	$\upsilon_1\ (A_1)$	Q_1
Symmetry bending	$\upsilon_2\ (A_1)$	Q_2
Asymmetry stretching	$\upsilon_3\ (B_2)$	Q_3

$$\Delta v = 0 \rightarrow 1 \quad \left.\begin{matrix} 0-1 \\ 0-0 \\ 0-0 \end{matrix}\right\} \quad Q_1, A_1 \int (A_1 \times A_1) \times A_1\ (T_z) = \int A_1$$

do, Q_2, A_1 do

do Q_3, B_2 $\int (A_1 \times B_2) \times \Gamma_y$

$$= \int B_2 \times B_2$$

$$= \int A_1$$

i.r. active

Overtones $\Delta\upsilon = \pm 2, \pm 3, \ldots$ etc.

$0\ 0\ 0 \rightarrow 2\ 0\ 0\ \ A_1$

$A_1^{\ 2} = A_1 \times A_1 = A_1$

$0\ 0\ 0 \rightarrow 0\ 2\ 0$ etc, $A_1^{\ 2} = A_1 \times A_1 = A_1$

$0\ 0\ 0 \rightarrow 2\ 0\ 0$ etc. $(B_2)^2 = B_2 \times B_2 = A_1$

even, i.r. active

Combination υ_1 & υ_2, $A_1 \times A_1 = A_1$ allowed. All overtones are allowed giving the direct product $A_1^{\ 2} = A_1 \times A_1 = A_1$.

υ_3, B_2 vibration will be allowed giving the direct product for even overtones:

$$B_2^{\ 2} = B_2 \times B_2 = A_1$$

Combination band $\upsilon_1 \pm \upsilon_2 = A_1 \times A_1 = A_1$ allowed

$\upsilon_1 \pm \upsilon_3$ giving $A_1 \times B_2 = B_2$ forbidden.

11.12 NORMAL VIBRATIONS IN CASE OF AMMONIA (NH_3)

The figure shows the co-ordinate system:

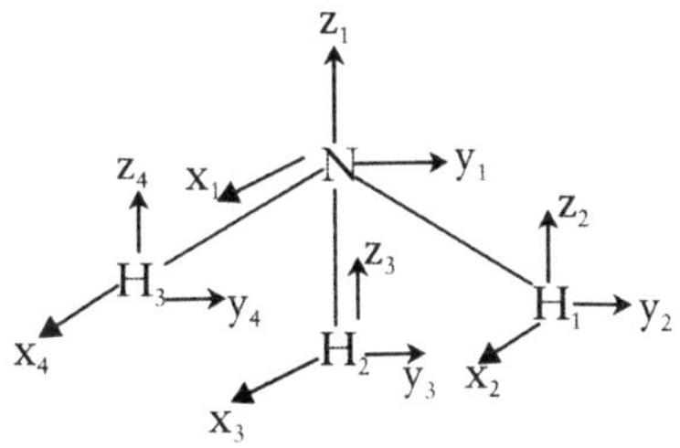

The molecule is assigned the C_{3V} point group.

It has four atoms in all and we require $4 \times 3 = 12$ co-ordinates.

They all are unmoved in identity.

Hence, χ (E) = $4 \times 3 = 12$.

In C_3 operation all the three H-atoms move but only N-atom does not shift. χ contribution per un-shifted atom is given by $2\cos\alpha + 1$

$$\chi = 2\cos\alpha + 1$$
$$= 2 \times \cos 120^\circ + 1 = 2 \times (-\tfrac{1}{2}) + 1 = -1 + 1 = 0$$
$$\chi\,(C_3) = \text{No. of UA} \times \chi\,(C_3) \text{ contribution per UA}$$
$$= 1 \times 0 = 0.$$

In σ_v two atoms lying inside the vertical plane are un-shifted, while others changed their positions. Character contribution per un-shifted atom is given by $1 + 1 - 1 = 1$.

Total χ (σ_v) = No. of U.A $\times$ character contributions per U.A.

$$= 2 \times 1 = 2$$

Hence, the character for, Γ_{3N} are 12 0 2

C.T. C_{3v}	E	$2C_3$	$3\sigma_v$		
A_1	1	1	1	z	x^2+y^2, z^2
A_2	1	1	−1	R_z	
E	2	−1	0	(x, y); (R_x, R_y)	(x^2-y^2, xy); (xz, yz).

From C.T.

$A_1 - T_z$
$E - T_x, T_y$
$A_2 - R_z$
$E - R_x, R_y$

$$\Gamma_t + \Gamma_r = \Gamma_{t,r} = A_1 + A_2 + 2E$$

Applying reduction formulae we obtain the components of Γ_{3N} as follows:

$$a_{A_1} = \frac{1}{6}[12\times1\times1+0+2\times3\times1]$$

$$= \frac{1}{6}\times18 = 3$$

$$a_{A_2} = \frac{1}{6}[12\times1\times1+0+3\times2\times-1]$$

$$= \frac{1}{6}\times[12-6] = \frac{1}{6}\times6 = 1$$

$$a_E = \frac{1}{6}[12\times2\times1+0+0]$$

$$= \frac{1}{6}\times24 = 4$$

$$\Gamma_{3N} = 3A_1 + A_2 + 4E$$
$$\Gamma t,r = \underline{A_1} + \underline{A_2} + \underline{2E}$$

$$\Gamma_{vib} = \Gamma_{3N} - \Gamma t,r = 2A_1 + 2E$$

We identify stretching and bending vectors in the following ways:

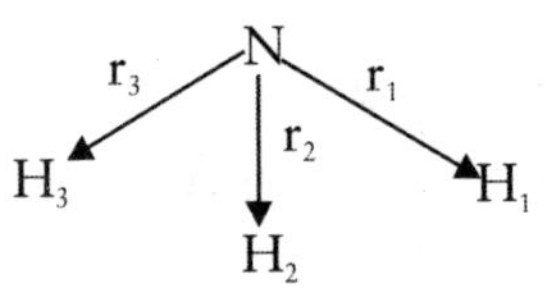

Three stretching vectors are shown by N–H bonds as r_1, r_2 and r_3. They all are un-shifted in identity:

$$r_1' = r_1,\ r_2' = r_2,\ r_3' = r_3$$

Character contribution per un-shifted vector is $\chi = 1$.

There are three such vectors, so total χ (E) = 3 × 1 = 3

All the vectors r_1, r_2 and r_3 are changing their positions in C_3.

No. of U.V = 0

Total χ (C_3) = 0 × 1 = 0.

Only two of the vectors is changing its position in σ_v.

No. of U.V = 1

χ (contribution per UV) = 1

Total χ (σ_v) = 1 × 1 = 1

χ 3 0 1

Applying the reduction formula we have:

$$a_{A_1} = \frac{1}{6}[3\times1\times1+0+3\times1\times1]$$

$$= \frac{1}{6}[3\times3] = 1$$

$$a_{A_2} = 0$$

$$a_E = \frac{1}{6}[3\times2\times1+0+0]$$

$$= \frac{1}{6}\times6 = 1$$

Γ_{str} = A_1 + E

Similarly we consider α_1, α_2, α_3 as bending vectors which are bond angles and their contribution towards character is 3, 0, 1 again.

Similarly, Γ_α = A_1 + E

Both stretching and bending vibrations involve A_1 and E type. We apply using character Table the i.r. and Raman activity of these bands. Both are i.r. and Raman active.

Overtones, A_1 band i.r. active. As such its overtones will be $\int A_1$ or $\int A_1^2 = A_1$ allowed.

For even or odd overtones E vibration is also allowed for even overtones $E^2 = E \times E = A_1 + A_2 + E$ allowed.

Combination bands:

$\upsilon_1 + \upsilon_2$ or υ_3 are allowed as the direct product $A_1 \times E = E$ and combination band will be allowed in i.r. and Raman spectra for C_{3v}.

C_{3v}	E	$2C_3$	$3\sigma_v$		
A_1	1	1	1	z	x^2+y^2, z^2
A_2	1	1	−1		
E	2	−1	0	(x, y)	$(x^2-y^2, xy), (xz, yz)$

$$\Psi_i = \Psi_0 = A_1 \text{ type} = \Gamma_0$$

$$\Psi_f = \Psi_{(1)} = \Psi_0\, Q = \Gamma_Q$$

Stretching and bending vibrations are $A_1 + E$.

A_1 Vibrations

$$M_z = \int \Gamma_0\, \Gamma_Q\, \Gamma_z$$

$$= \int (A_1 \times A_1) \times \Gamma_z = \int A_1 \times A_1 = \int A_1$$

i.r. active

The z^2 component of polarizability α_{zz} belongs to A_1. Hence this vibration is Raman active.

E Vibration

Γ_Q = E and both x and y components are present in E irreducible representations in C_{3v} having characters 2, −1, 0.

Γ_x, Γ_y have translational vectors (x, y) transforming as E. The excited state wave function corresponds to the normal co-ordinate Q in E representation ground state has A_1 representation.

$$\int \Gamma_0\, \Gamma_Q\, \Gamma_E = \int (A_1 \times E) \times E = \int E \times E$$

A_1	1	1	1
E	2	−1	0

$$A_1 \times E = 2 \times 1 \quad 1 \times -1 \quad 1 \times 0$$

$$= 2 \quad -1 \quad 0 \quad = E$$

$$E \times E = 2 \times 2 \quad -1 \times -1 \quad 0 \times 0$$

$$= 4 \quad 1 \quad 0$$

Apply formula:

$$a_{A_1} = \frac{1}{6}\left[4 \times 1 \times 1 + 2 \times 1 \times 1 + 3 \times 0 \times 1\right]$$

$$= \frac{1}{6}\left[4 + 2\right] = 1$$

$$a_{A_2} = \frac{1}{6}\left[4 \times 1 \times 1 + 2 \times 1 \times 1 + 0\right]$$

$$= \frac{6}{6} = 1$$

$$a_E = \frac{1}{6}\left[4 \times 2 \times 1 + 2 \times 1 \times -1 + 0\right]$$

$$= \frac{1}{6}\left[8 - 2\right] = \frac{6}{6} = 1$$

$$\Gamma_{E \times E} = E + A_1 + A_2$$

It consists of A_1 that renders the band i.r. active.

Because, $\int A_1 \times A_1 = \int A_1$.

We apply similar argument showing Raman activity.

11.13 NORMAL VIBRATIONS OF BF_3 MOLECULE

This molecule has got point group symbol D_{3h} (planar). The symmetry operations belong to the following classes:

E $2C_3$ $3C_2$ σ_h $2s_3$ $3\sigma_v$ h = 12

The character for Γ_{3N} is determined in each operation applying method of un-shifted atoms:

Symmetric operation	*No. of UA*	*χ per U.A.*	*χ for R.R.*
E	4	3	12
C_3	1	0	0
C_2	2	–1	–2
σ_h	4	1	+4
$S_3 = C_3\sigma_h$	1	–2	–2
σ_v	2	1	2

$S_3 = C_3\ \sigma_h$

$$= \begin{bmatrix} -1/2 & \sqrt{3}/2 & 0 \\ -\sqrt{3}/2 & -1/2 & 0 \\ 0 & 0 & 1 \end{bmatrix} \begin{bmatrix} 1 & 0 & 0 \\ 0 & 1 & 0 \\ 0 & 0 & -1 \end{bmatrix}$$

$$= \begin{bmatrix} -1/2\times1+\sqrt{3}/2\times0+0\times0 & -1/2\times0+\sqrt{3}/2\times1+0\times0 & 0+0+0 \\ -\sqrt{3}/2\times1+(-1/2)\times0+0\times0 & -\sqrt{3}/2\times0+(-1/2)\times1+0\times0 & 0\times0+0\times0+1\times0 \\ 0\times1+0\times0+1\times0 & 0\times0+0\times1+1\times0 & 0\times0+0\times0+1\times(-1) \end{bmatrix}$$

$$= \begin{bmatrix} -1/2 & \sqrt{3}/2 & 0 \\ -\sqrt{3}/2 & -1/2 & 0 \\ 0 & 0 & -1 \end{bmatrix}$$

$$\chi = -\frac{1}{2} - \frac{1}{2} - 1 = \frac{-1-1-2}{2} = \frac{-4}{2} = -2$$

D_{3h}	E	$2C_3$	$3C_2$	σ_h	$2S_3$	$3\sigma_v$
A_1'	1	1	1	1	1	1
A_2'	1	1	–1	1	1	–1
E'	2	–1	0	2	–1	0
A_1''	1	1	1	–1	–1	–1
A_2''	1	1	–1	–1	–1	1
E''	2	–1	0	–2	1	0
Γ_R	12	0	–2	4	–2	2

$$a_{A_1'} = \frac{1}{12}\left[12\times1\times1+0\times2\times1+3\times1\times-2+1\times1\times4+2\times1\times-2 +3\times1\times2\right]$$

$$= \frac{1}{12}\left[12+0-\cancel{6}+\cancel{4}-\cancel{4}+\cancel{6}\right]$$

$$= \frac{1}{12}\left[12\right]=1$$

$$a_{A_2'} = \frac{1}{12}\left[1\times1\times12+2\times1\times0+3\times-1\times-2+1\times1\times4+2\times1\times-2 +3\times-1\times2\right]$$

$$= \frac{1}{12}\left[12+0+\cancel{6}+\cancel{4}-\cancel{4}-\cancel{6}\right]$$

$$= 1$$

$$a_{E'} = \frac{1}{12}\left[1\times2\times12+2\times-1\times0+3\times0\times-2+1\times2\times4 +2\times-1\times-2+3\times0\times2\right]$$

$$= \frac{1}{12}\left[24+0+0+8+4+0\right]$$

$$= \frac{1}{12}\left[24+8+4\right]=\frac{1}{12}\times36=3$$

$$a_{A_1''} = \frac{1}{12}\left[1\times1\times12+2\times1\times0+3\times1\times-2+1\times-1\times4 +2\times-1\times-2+3\times-1\times2\right]$$

$$= \frac{1}{12}\left[\cancel{12}+0-\cancel{6}-\cancel{4}+\cancel{4}-\cancel{6}\right]$$

$$= 0$$

$$a_{A_2''} = \frac{1}{12}\left[1\times1\times12+2\times1\times0+3\times-1\times-2+1\times-1\times4+ 2\times-1\times-2+3\times1\times2\right]$$

$$= \frac{1}{12}\left[12+0+6-4+4+6\right]$$

$$= \frac{1}{12}\left[12+12\right]=\frac{24}{12}=2$$

$$a_{E''} = \frac{1}{12}\left[12\times 2\times 1+0+0-8-4\right]$$

$$= \frac{12}{12} = 1$$

$$\Gamma_{3N} = A_1' + A_2' + 3E' + 2A_2'' + E''$$

From C.T. for D_{3h}

$E' - T_x, T_y,$

$A_2'' - T_z$

$\Gamma_t = A_2'' + E'$

$A_2' - R_z$

$E'' - R_x, R_y$

$\Gamma_r = A_z' + A_z'' + E' + E''$

$$\Gamma_{3N-6} = \Gamma_{vib} = \Gamma_{3N} - \Gamma_{t+r}$$

$$= A_1' + \not{A_2'} + 3E' + 2A_2'' + \not{E''} - (\not{A_2'} + A_2'' + E' + \not{E''})$$

$$= A_1' + A_2'' + 2E'$$

We classify stretching and bending vectors as follows:

(i) Let there be r_1, r_2 and r_3 as bond stretching vectors.

(ii) α_1, α_2 and α_3 as bond deformations:

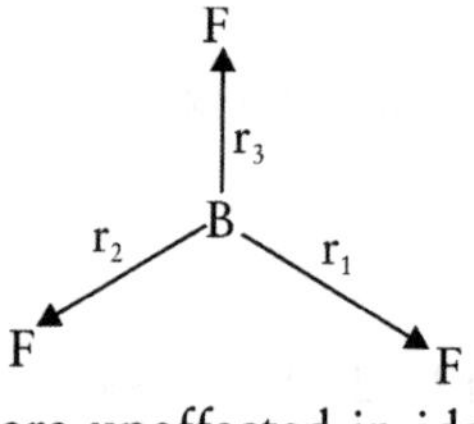

All three vectors are unaffected in identity:

$$\chi\,(E) = 3\times 1 = 3$$

In C_3 all three vectors are shifted $\chi\,(C_3) = 0$.

In C_2 only one vector un-shifted $\chi\,(C_2) = 1$.

In σ_h all the three vectors are un-shifted:

$$\chi\,(\sigma_h) = 3.$$

In $S_3 = C_3\ \sigma_h$, all are shifted:

$$\chi\ (S_3) = 0$$

In σ_v one vector is un-shifted:

$$\chi\ (\sigma_v) = 1$$

$$\Gamma_{str} = 3\quad 0\quad 1\quad 3\quad 0\quad 1$$

$$\Gamma_{str} = A_1' + E'$$

Consider bending modes with α_1, α_2 and α_3:

In E all are un-shifted $\chi = 3$

In C_3 all are shifted $\chi = 0$

In C_2 one angle is un-shifted = 1

In σ_h all are un-shifted $\chi = 3$

In S_3 all are shifted $\chi = 0$

In α_v one angle is un-shifted $\chi = 1$

$$\Gamma_\alpha = 3\quad 0\quad 1\quad 3\quad 0\quad 1 = A_1' + E'$$

A_1' occurs twice. However there is only one A_1' so the component A_1' in Γ_α is spurious. Hence, we discard it as there is only one A_1' in Γvib:

$$\Gamma_\alpha = E'$$

$$\Gamma_{str} = A_1' + E'$$

$$\Gamma_\alpha = \Gamma_{vib} - \Gamma_{str} = \cancel{A_1'} + A_2'' + 2E' - \left(\cancel{A_1'} + E'\right)$$

$$= A_2'' + E'$$

So, A_2'' is unaccounted. This may be bending vibration.

i.r. active vibrations, $A_1' + 2E' + A_2''$

Raman active, $A_1' - \alpha_{xx}, \alpha_{yy}, \alpha_{zz}$

$$E' - \alpha_{xy}$$

So, A_2'' does not appear in Raman.

11.14 I.R. AND RAMAN ACTIVITY IN BF_3

I.R. and Raman Activity of bands in BF_3 (D_{3h}) through the symmetry species is considered.

$$\Gamma_{vib} = A_1' + A_2'' + 2E'$$

The transition moment integral has three parts:

$$\Gamma = \int(\Gamma_0 \times \Gamma_Q) \times \Gamma_T$$

Γ_0 is the ground state wave function,

$= A_1'$ always totally symmetric.

For A_1' vibrational band, $\Gamma_Q = A_1'$.

Γ_T is the translational component Γ_x, Γ_y, Γ_z unfortunately A_1' symmetry species does not have any translational vector in D_{3h} point group. So A_1' fundamental band is i.r. inactive. However, there are quadratic terms such as z^2, $x^2 + y^2$, in this irreducible representation which makes the band Raman active.

D_{3h}			
A_1'		—	z^2, $x^2 + y^2$
A_2'		—	(x^2-y^2), xy
E'		(x, y)	—
A_1''		—	—
A_2''		z	—
E''		—	(xz, yz)

Let us turn towards A_2'' fundamental band:

$$M = \int(A_1' \times A_2'') \times \Gamma_T$$

A_2'' has the T_z as active component belonging to this symmetry species.

$$\therefore \quad M = \int(A_1' \times A_2'') \times A_2''$$

$$= \int A_2'' \times A_2'' = \int A_1'$$

This renders the band i.r. active.

$$A_1' \times A_2'' = 1{\times}1 \quad 1{\times}1 \quad 1{\times}{-1} \quad 1{\times}{-1} \quad 1{\times}{-1} \quad 1{\times}1$$
$$= 1 \quad 1 \quad -1 \quad -1 \quad -1 \quad 1$$
$$A_2''$$

$$A_2'' \times = A_2'' = 1{\times}1 \quad 1{\times}1 \quad -1{\times}{-1} \quad -1{\times}{-1} \quad -1{\times}{-1} \quad 1{\times}1$$
$$= 1 \quad 1 \quad 1 \quad 1 \quad 1 \quad 1$$
$$= A_1'$$

Doubly degenerate vibrations (E').

The transition moment integral would be:

$$M = \int(\Gamma_0 \times \Gamma_Q) \times \Gamma_T$$
$$= \int(A_1' \times \Gamma_Q) \times \Gamma_T$$

$$\Gamma_Q = E'$$

There corresponds $\Gamma_T = E'$ with (x, y) components:

$$= \int(A_1' \times E') \times E'$$
$$= \int E' \times E'$$

The direct product is then:

$$E' \times E' = 2 \times 2 \quad -1 \times -1 \quad 0 \times 0 \quad 2 \times 2 \quad -1 \times -1 \quad 0 \times 0$$
$$= 4 \quad 1 \quad 0 \quad 4 \quad 1 \quad 0$$

From the reduction formula we deduce the components as:

$$a_{A_1'} = \frac{1}{12}\left[4 \times 1 \times 1 + 2 \times 1 \times 1 + 0 + 1 \times 1 \times 4 + 2 \times 1 \times 1 + 0\right]$$
$$= \frac{1}{12}\left[4 + 2 + 4 + 2\right] = \frac{1}{12} \times 12 = 1$$

$$a_{A_2'} = \frac{1}{12}\left[1 \times 1 \times 4 + 2 \times 1 \times 1 + 0 + 4 \times 1 \times 1 + 2 \times 1 \times 1 + 0\right]$$
$$= \frac{12}{12} = 1$$

$$a_{E'} = \frac{1}{12}\left[4\times2\times1+2\times(-1)\times1+4\times2\times1+2\times(-1)\times1\right]$$

$$= \frac{1}{12}\left[8-2+8-2\right] = \frac{12}{12} = 1$$

$$a_{A_1''} = \frac{1}{12}\left[4\times1\times1+2\times1\times1+0+4\times(-1)\times1+2\times1\times(-1)\right]$$

$$= \frac{1}{12}\left[4+2-4-2\right] = 0$$

$$a_{A_2''} = \frac{1}{12}\left[4\times1\times1+2\times1\times1+4\times(-1)\times1+2\times1\times-1\right]$$

$$= \frac{1}{12}\left[4+2-4-2\right] = 0$$

$$a_{E''} = \frac{1}{12}\left[4\times2\times1+2\times(-1)\times1+4\times(-2)\times1+2\times(-1)\times1\right]$$

$$= 0$$

Hence, $E'\times E' = A_1' + A_2' + E'$.

It has A_1' as one of the representations, which makes the degenerate vibrations i.r. active. There correspond xy, $x^2–y^2$, polarizability portion which allow Raman activity of E' vibrations.

Conclusion

There are vibrations:

$$\Gamma vib = A_1' + A_2'' + 2E'$$

It has been shown that A_2'' and $2E'$ vibrations are i.r. active while A_1' and $2E'$ are Raman active. Hence, υ_1 band with A_1' vibration is totally symmetric but due to lack of translational component in this symmetry species makes the band i.r. inactive. Therefore, it is a forbidden band and permitted in Raman.

υ_2 with A_2'' and υ_3 and υ_4 as (E'') are also allowed in i.r. The combination bands such as, υ_1+υ_2, υ_1+υ_3 and υ_1+υ_4 are allowed in i.r. A_2'' does not appear in Raman due to lack of polarizability tensor as its component.

11.15 NORMAL VIBRATIONS OF SF_4

There are three possibilities for the molecule C_{2v}, C_{3v} and T_d point group with the structure depicted below:

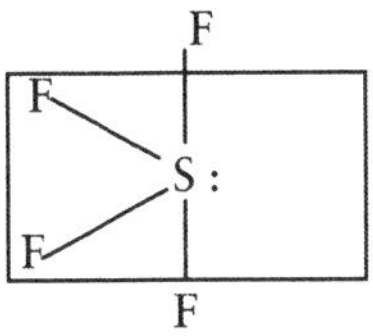

C_{2V}

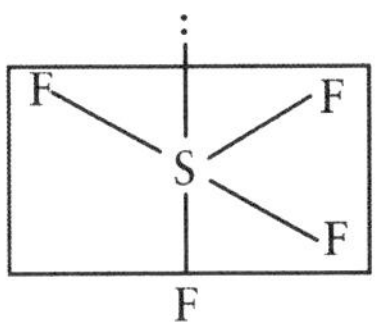

C_{3V}

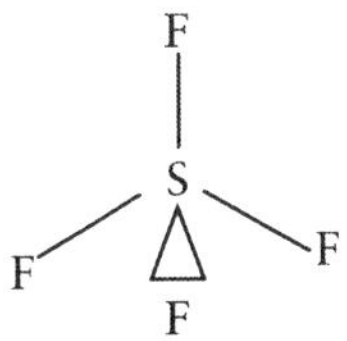

T_d

(a) For C_{2v} Point Group

We follow method of un-shifted atoms to generate reducible representation.

In identity: all the five atoms donot move each contributing 3 as such it leads to

$$\chi\ (E) = 5 \times 3 = 15.$$

In C_2, S-atom doesn't move all others are moving. Its contribution per unshifted atom is –1 giving:

$$\chi\ (C_2) = 1 \times -1 = -1$$

In σ_{xz} plane, two F-atoms and S along z axis don't move and χ per un-shifted atom is 1, which gives $\chi\ (\sigma_{xz}) = 3 \times 1 = 3$.

Reflection in σ_{yz} doesn't change the position of three atoms:

$$\chi\ (\sigma_{yz}) = 3 \times 1 = 3$$

$$\Gamma_R \qquad 15 \qquad -1 \qquad 3 \qquad 3$$

Applying reduction formula we get:

$$a_{A_1} = \frac{1}{4}\left[15 \times 1 \times 1 + 1 \times -1 \times 1 + 3 \times 1 \times 1 + 3 \times 1 \times 1\right]$$

$$= \frac{1}{4}\left[15 - 1 + 3 + 3\right] = \frac{1}{4} \times 20 = 5$$

$$a_{A_2} = \frac{1}{4}\left[15 + 1 \times -1 \times 1 + 1 \times (-1) \times 3 + 1 \times (-1) \times 3\right]$$

$$= \frac{1}{4}\left[15 - 1 - 3 - 3\right] = \frac{8}{4} = 2$$

$$a_{B_1} = \frac{1}{4}\left[15 + (-1) \times (-1) \times 1 + 1 \times (-1) \times 3 + 1 \times (-1)13\right]$$

$$= \frac{1}{4}\left[15 + 1\right] = 4$$

$$a_{B_2} = \frac{1}{4}\left[15 + (-1) \times (-1) \times 1 - \not{3} + \not{3}\right]$$

$$= \frac{1}{4}\left[15 + 1\right] = 4$$

$$\Gamma_{3N} = 5A_1 + 2A_2 + 4B_1 + 4B_2$$

Translational vectors, $T_x - B_1$, $T_y - B_2$, $T_z - A_1$

Rotational vectors, $R_x - B_1$ $R_z - B_2$

$R_y - A_z$

$$\Gamma t + r = A_1 + A_2 + 2B_1 + 2B_2$$

$$\Gamma_{3N-6} = 4A_1 + A_2 + 2B_1 + 2B_2$$

$\int \Psi_0 \ \mu \ \Psi_1 \ d\tau \neq O$ for A_1 type.

$\Psi_0 = A_1$ always.

If Γ_x, Γ_y, Γ_z should have the same symmetry as Ψ_1. As such transition is i.r. active, if the Ψ_1 excited state vibration should have same symmetry as with the dipole moment vectors. It does not have such symmetry it is inactive band.

(b) Case of T_d Symmetry of SF_4

Let us calculate the Γ_R using method of un-shifted atoms in T_d symmetry:

$$\chi\ (E) = 5 \times 3 = 15$$

Its character contribution per un-shifted atom in C_3 is:

$$\chi = 1 + 2 \cos 120°$$

$$= 1 + 2 \times -½ = 1 - 1 = 0$$

Here all are shifted except S-atom.

In σ_d two F-atoms along with S atom are un-shifted. Number of un-shifted atom = 3.

χ contribution for σ_d is 1.

$$\chi\ (\sigma_d) = 3 \times 1 = 3$$

All atoms are shifted except S in S_4. In C_2 character contribution is –1. Hence,

$$\chi = 1 \times (-1) = -1$$

$$S_4^2 = C_2 = -1$$

$$\chi\ (C_2) = -1$$

T_d	E	$8C_3$	$3C_2$	$6S_4$	$6\sigma_d$	
A_1	1	1	1	1	1	
A_2	1	1	1	–1	–1	
E	2	–1	2	0	0	
T_1	3	0	–1	1	–1	Rx, Ry, Rz
T_2	3	0	–1	–1	1	xy, xz, yz
Γ_R	15	0	–1	–1	3	

Applying reduction formula we have:

$$a_{A_1} = \frac{1}{24}[15\times1\times1+8\times1\times0+3\times1\times(-1)+6\times1\times(-1)+ 6\times1\times3]$$

$$= \frac{1}{24}[15+0-3-6+18]$$

$$= \frac{1}{24}[33-3-6] = \frac{1}{24}\times24 = 1$$

$$a_{A_2} = \frac{1}{24}[15\times1\times1+8\times1\times0+3\times(-1)\times1+6\times(-1)\times(-1) +6\times3\times-1]$$

$$= \frac{0}{24} = 0$$

$$a_E = \frac{1}{24}[15\times2\times1+8\times(-1)\times0+3\times(-1)\times2+6\times(-1)\times0 +6\times3\times0]$$

$$= \frac{1}{24}[30-6] = \frac{24}{24} = 1$$

$$a_{T_1} = \frac{1}{24}\left[15\times3\times1+8\times0\times0+3\times(-1)\times(-1)+6\times(-1)\times(-1) +6\times(-1)\times1+6\times3\times-1\right]$$

$$= \frac{1}{24}\left[45+3-6-18\right] = \frac{24}{24} = 1$$

$$a_{T_2} = \frac{1}{24}\left[15\times3\times1+8\times0\times0+3\times(-1)\times(-1)+6\times(-1)\times(-1)\right)$$

$$= \frac{1}{24}\left[45+3+6+18\right]$$

$$= \frac{72}{24} = 3$$

$\Gamma_{3N} = A_1 + E + T_1 + 3T_2$

C.T. shows that, $T_x, T_y, T_z - T_2$

$R_x, R_y, R_z - T_1$

$\Gamma t + r = T_1 + T_2$

$\Gamma vib = \Gamma_{3N-6} = A_1 + E + T_1 + 3T_2 - (T_1 + T_2)$

$= A_1 + E + 2T_2$

Two triply degenerate vibrations are infrared active, which give rise to two fundamental bands. All modes are Raman active giving rise to four fundamental bands. All are fundamentals.

(c) Case of C_{3v} Structure for SF_4

In identity all are un-shifted:

χ (E) = 5 × 3 = 15

In C_3, three are shifted and S-atom and a fluorine-atom along z-axis are un-shifted:

χ (C_3) = 2 × 0 = 0

There are three atoms one S-atom and two F-atoms, one of them on z-axis and another in a vertical plane are un-shifted χ (σ_v) = 3 × 1 = 3

	E	$2C_3$	$3\sigma_v$
Γ_{3N}	15	0	3

Irreducible components are determined to be:

$$a_{A_1} = \frac{1}{6}\left[15\times1\times1+2\times0\times1+3\times3\times1\right]$$

$$= \frac{1}{6}\left[15+9\right] = \frac{24}{6} = 4$$

$$a_{A_2} = \frac{1}{6}\left[15\times1\times1+0+3\times3\times(-1)\right]$$

$$= \frac{1}{6}\left[15-0\right] = \frac{6}{6} = 1$$

$$a_E = \frac{1}{6}\left[15\times2\times1+0+3\times3\times0\right]$$

$$= \frac{1}{6}\times30 = 5$$

$\Gamma_{3N} = 4A_1 + 5E + A_2$

C.T. shows that, $T_z - A_1$

$T_x, T_y - E$

$R_2 - A_2$

$R_x, R_y - E$

$\Gamma t{+}r = A_1 + A_2 + 2E$

$\Gamma_{3N\text{–}6} = 4A_1 + 5E + A_2 - (A_1 + A_2 + 2E)$

$= 3A_1 + 3E$

It leads to six infrared fundamental bands, three A_1 and three E and also there are six Raman fundamental bands, three A_1 and three E.

The theory in which we have 3N–6 = 3 × 5 – 6 = 9 bands corresponding to fundamental vibrations consisting of three A_1 and three E species or total of six fundamental frequencies.

The actual spectrum reveals five infrared fundamentals as well as five Raman transitions consistent with C_{2v} and C_{3v} structures and so T_d structure is discarded.

11.16 NORMAL VIBRATIONS OF TRANS 1, 2- DICHLORO-ETHYLENE AND ITS CIS FORM

(a) Case of Cis Variety

Consider the case of cis variety:

It is a case of six atoms, each atom has three co-ordinates. As such there are 6 × 3 = 18 independent motions.

$$\chi\,(E) = 6 \times 3 = 18$$

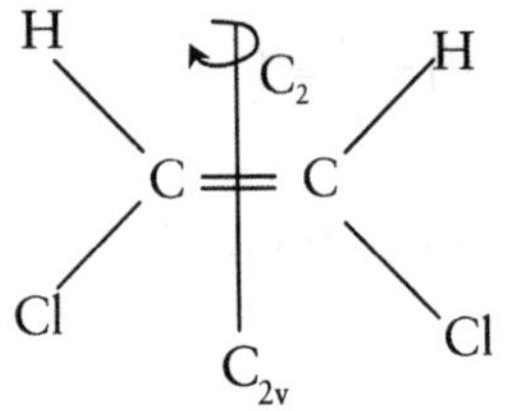

In C_2 all atoms are shifted $\chi\,(C_2) = 0$.

In σ_{xz}, all are shifted accordingly:

$$\chi\,(\sigma_{xz}) = 0$$

In σ_{yz} all are un-shifted, $\chi\,(\sigma_{yz}) = 6 \times 1 = 6$

	E	C_2	σ_{xz}	σ_{yz}
Γ_{3N}	18	0	0	6

We use decomposition formula for its reduction:

$$a_{A_1} = \frac{1}{4}\left[18\times1\times1+0+0+6\times1\times1\right]$$

$$= \frac{1}{4}\times\left[18+6\right] = \frac{24}{4} = 6$$

$$a_{A_2} = \frac{1}{4}\times\left[18+0+0-6\right] = \frac{1}{4}\times12 = 3$$

$$a_{B_1} = \frac{1}{4}\times\left[18+0+0-6\right] = \frac{12}{4} = 3$$

$$a_{B_2} = \frac{1}{4}\times\left[18+0+0+6\right] = \frac{24}{4} = 6$$

$$\Gamma_{3N} = 6A_1 + 3A_2 + 3B_1 + 6B_2$$

From C.T we have, T_z – A_1
T_x – B_1
T_y – B_z
R_x – B_z
R_y – B_1
R_z – A_2

$$\Gamma t{+}r = A_1 + A_2 + 2B_1 + 2B_2$$

$$\Gamma_{3N-6} = 6A_1 + 3A_2 + 3B_1 + 6B_2 - (A_1 + A_2 + 2B_1 + 2B_2)$$
$$= 5A_1 + 2A_2 + B_1 + 4B_2$$

Ten out of 12 are i.r. active fundamental-vibrations such as A_1, B_1 and B_2 types. These vibrations are also Raman active.

Let us consider overtones and combination bands, overtones of A_1, B_1 and B_2 are i.r. active as they have translational component along A_1, B_1 and B_2.

All such vibrations are Raman active also because they have polarizability component in each case.

(b) TRANS – 1, 2-Dichloroethylene (C_{2h})

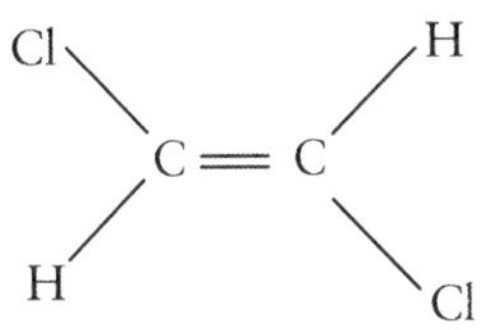

It has C_{2h} point group. There are six atoms giving the vibrational modes 3N–6 = 3 × 6 – 6 = 12.

There are twelve vibrational motions.

Let us find out the atoms which don't shift in symmetry operation.

In identity all six atoms donot shift:

$$\chi\,(E) = 6 \times 3 = 18.$$

In C_2 all atoms are displaced:

$$\chi\,(C_2) = 0 \times (-1) = 0.$$

In inversion centre all atoms are displaced:

$$\chi\,(i) = 0 \times (-3) = 0.$$

In σ_h all atoms are un-shifted:

$$\chi(\sigma_h) = 6 \times (+1) = 6$$

C_{2h}	E	C_2	i	σ_h		
Γ_{3N}	18	0	0	6		
Ag	1	1	1	1	Rz	x^2, y^2, z^2, xy
Bg	1	–1	1	–1	Rx, Ry	xz, yz
Au	1	1	–1	–1	z	
Bu	1	–1	–1	1	x, y	

Applying reduction formula:

$$a_{A_g} = \frac{1}{4}[1\times18\times1+1\times0\times1+1\times0\times1+1\times6\times1]$$

$$= \frac{1}{4}[18+6] = \frac{1}{4}\times24 = 6$$

$$a_{B_g} = \frac{1}{4}[1\times18\times1+1\times0\times-1+1\times0\times1+1\times6\times-1]$$

$$= \frac{1}{4}[18-6] = \frac{1}{4}\times12 = 3$$

$$a_{A_u} = \frac{1}{4}[1\times18\times1+1\times0\times1+1\times0\times-1+1\times6\times-1]$$

$$= \frac{1}{4}[18-6] = \frac{1}{4}\times12 = 3$$

$$a_{B_u} = \frac{1}{4}[1\times18\times1+1\times0\times-1+1\times0\times-1+1\times6\times1]$$

$$= \frac{1}{4}[18+6] = \frac{24}{4} = 6$$

$$\Gamma_{3N} = Ag + 3Bg + 3Au + 6Bu$$

From C.T. we have,

Tx, Ty – Bu

Tz – Au

Rx, Ry – Bg

Rz – Ag

$$\Gamma t{+}r = Ag + Au + 2Bg + 2Bu$$

$$\begin{aligned}\Gamma_{3N-6} &= \Gamma_{3N} - \Gamma_{t+r} \\ &= 6Ag+3Bg+3Au+6Bu-(Ag+Au+2Bg+2Bu) \\ &= 5Ag+Bg+2Au+4Bu\end{aligned}$$

Au and Bu modes of vibrations correspond to co-ordinates x, y, z and have six vibrations of such kind are i.r. active. The molecule possesses centre of symmetry, so those bands which are infrared active may not give Raman active bands.

$$M_z = \int(Ag \times Au) \times Au = \int Au \times Au = \int Ag \text{ allowed.}$$

$$M_{x\,or\,y} = \int(Ag \times Bu) \times Bu = \int Bu \times Bu = \int Ag \text{ allowed.}$$

$$Au - z,\ Bu - x,\ y$$

Thus Ag and Bg vibrations are Raman active:

$$Ag = x^2, y^2, z^2, xy$$

$$Bg = xz, yz$$

Ag vibration $M = \int(Ag \times Ag) \times Ag = \int Ag$ allowed in Raman

Bg vibration $M = \int(Ag \times Bg) \times Bg = \int Bg \times Bg$

$$= \int Ag \text{ allowed in Raman.}$$

Raman inactive vibrations may give rise to combination bands with Raman active state:

e.g. Au × Bu = Bg

$$\int Bg \times Bg = \int Ag \quad \text{active.}$$

But other combinations involving one active fundamental will not give combination band such as Ag × Bu = Bu.

The observations of these bands are difficult even of Raman fundamentals (very weak).

QUESTIONS

1. (a) How many co-ordinates are required to determine all possible motions in a polyatomic molecule?

   (b) Construct 9 × 9 matrices for determining characters for all possible molecular motions in water.

   (c) Reduce the reducible representation into irreducible components and get the components of genuine vibrational mode.

2. Classify stretching and bending mode of water constructing 3 × 3 matrices.

   Identify which are i.r. allowed and which are Raman allowed fundamental bands taking the direct product representation for transition moment with the help of character Table.

3. Give the procedure of obtaining character by method of per un-shifted vector/atom for different symmetry operations.

   Find out characters for reducible representations for CO_3^{2-} ion (D_{3h}) and decompose them into irreducible components and get the vibrational components.

4. (a) Find out the triple direct product showing i.r. and Raman activity in water and ammonia.

   (b) Identify symmetry species of stretching and bending vectors in CO_3^{2-} ion or NH_3.

5. Through method of un-shifted vectors determine the symmetry species of normal modes in NH_3 (C_{3v}), BF_3 (D_{3h}).

   Identify which vibrations are infrared active and which are Raman active?

6. (a) On the basis of symmetry arguments identify which vibrations are stretching and bending modes in BF_3 and NH_3.

   (b) Indicate which vibrations are i.r. allowed and which are Raman allowed?

7. (a) Give the three possible structures of SF_4 and assign their point group symbol.

(b) Find the irreducible representations for stretching and bending modes in C_{2v} and C_{3v} symmetry.

(c) Ascertain which point group belongs to the molecule in accordance with the infrared and Raman spectral data?

8. Taking procedure of un-shifted vector determine reducible representations for 1, 2– (Cis & trans) dichloroethylene and evaluate the different components of genuine vibrations in each case.

9. Explain any two of the following:

   (a) Direct product representations.

   (b) Normal co-ordinates and normal vibrations.

   (c) Selection rules for overtones and combination bands.

   (d) Polarizability and its importance in Raman Activity.

10. Discuss selection rules for i.r. and Raman active fundamentals. Overtones and combination bands on symmetry arguments involving transition moment integrals.

11. Discuss i.r. and Raman activity in case of overtone and combination bands in NH_3 and BF_3 and cis and trans isomers of 1, 2-dichloroethylene.

12. (a) Explain symmetry aspect of molecular vibration in terms of normal co-ordinate in CO_2.

    (b) Using normal co-ordinates solve the schrödinger wave equation for harmonic oscillator with 3N–6 vibrational degrees of freedom and give first three solutions of wave function in terms of normal coordinate.

13. (a) Explain symmetry aspects of molecular vibrations.

    (b) Construct 12 × 12 matrices for elements of each class in a CO_3^{2-} ion with D_{3h} point group and find their character.

14. (a) Applying method of un-shifted atom calculate the character for reducible representation for water and determine the symmetry species of genuine vibrational modes.

    (b) Using symmetry selection rules show the i.r. and Raman activity of υ_1 (A_1) υ_2 (A_1), υ_3 (B_2) fundamentals in water and their overtones and combination bands.

THEORY OF MOLECULAR VIBRATIONS

12

12.1 INTRODUCTION

We mainly deal here with two points in regard to molecular vibrations. Firstly, calculation of force constants, which is a part of normal vibration analysis and secondly, the assignment of infrared and Raman active fundamental bands. Molecules in diatomic case will be dealt separately from the poly-atomic systems. Motion of a body requires the position of the particles constituting such body for which we establish Newton's equation of motion. We describe at first the position of atoms inside a molecule by Cartesian system of co-ordinates and then set-up equation of motion for the system in terms of normal co-ordinates.

12.2 NEWTON'S EQUATION OF MOTION IN LANGERAGIAN FORM

Let us take up two sets of coordinates for points 1 and 2. $1(x_1, y_1, z_1)$; $2\ (x_2, y_2, z_2)$.

Its velocity is given by:

$$v = \frac{dx}{dt} = \dot{x}$$

$$\text{Acceleration,}\quad a = \frac{dx^2}{dt^2} = \ddot{x} = \frac{dv}{dt}$$

$$= \frac{d\dot{x}}{dt} = \ddot{x}$$

$$\text{Force} = \text{m.a.} = m\ddot{x}$$

This is known as Newton's equation of motion. We can resolve this equation of motion into three components. We may obtain equation of motion for a system of n point particles in terms of components of F and the co-ordinates of the ith particle (x_i, y_i, z_i) with mass m_i

$$F_{xi} = m_i \ddot{x}_i \quad ...(12.1)$$

$$F_{yi} = m_i \ddot{y}_i \quad ...(12.2)$$

$$F_{zi} = m_i \ddot{z}_i \quad ...(12.3)$$

where, F_{xi}, F_{yi} & F_{zi} are the components of the force (F) acting on the ith particle along x, y & z directions respectively:

$$K.E. = T = \frac{1}{2} \sum_{i=1}^{n} m_i \left(\dot{x}_i^2 + \dot{y}_i^2 + \dot{z}_i^2\right) \quad ...(12.4)$$

We define potential energy as another quantity in terms of position of all the particles:

$$V = V(x_1, y_1, z_1; x_2, y_2, z_2 \ldots\ldots\ldots\ldots\ldots x_i, y_i, z_i).$$

Such that,

$$Fx_i = \frac{-\partial V}{\partial x_i} \quad ...(12.5)$$

$$Fy_i = \frac{-\partial V}{\partial y_i} \quad ...(12.6)$$

$$Fz_i = \frac{-\partial V}{\partial z_i} \quad ...(12.7)$$

Equation of motion can now be written as:

$$m_i \ddot{x}_i = -\frac{\partial V}{\partial x_i}$$

$$m_i \ddot{y}_i = -\frac{\partial V}{\partial y_i}$$

$$m_i \ddot{z}_i = -\frac{\partial V}{\partial z_i}$$

$$\text{or} \quad \frac{dV}{dx_i} + m_i \ddot{x}_i = 0 \quad ...(12.8)$$

Let us come to kinetic energy term:

$$T = \frac{1}{2}\left[\sum^{n} m_i \left(\dot{x}_i^2 + \dot{y}_i^2 + \dot{z}_i^2\right)\right] \qquad ...(12.9)$$

Differentiate it with respect to $\dot{x}_i$ for the ith mass:

$$\frac{\partial T}{\partial \dot{x}_i} = \frac{1}{2} m_i \sum_{i=1}^{n}\left[\frac{\partial \dot{x}_i^2}{\partial \dot{x}_i} + \frac{\partial \dot{y}_i^2}{\partial \dot{x}_i} + \frac{\partial \dot{z}_i^2}{\partial \dot{x}_i}\right]$$

$$= \frac{1}{2} m_i \left[2\dot{x}_i + 0 + 0\right]$$

$$= \frac{1}{2} m_i \, 2\dot{x}_i = m_i \dot{x}_i \qquad ...(12.10)$$

On further differentiation with respect to time (t) we obtain time derivative:

$$\frac{d}{dt}\left(\frac{\partial T}{\partial \dot{x}_i}\right) = \frac{d}{dt}\left(m_i \ \dot{x}_i\right)$$

$$= m_i \frac{d}{dt}.\dot{x}_i$$

$$= m_i \ \ddot{x}_i \qquad ...(12.11)$$

From (12.8) and (12.11) on substitution of $m\ddot{x}_i$ leads to a new form:

$$\frac{\partial V}{\partial x_i} + \frac{d}{dt}\left(\frac{\partial T}{\partial \dot{x}_i}\right) = 0 \qquad ...(12.12)$$

This is known as Langragian equation of motion. Two more equations for the ith particle are:

$$\frac{d}{dt}\left(\frac{\partial T}{\partial \dot{y}_i}\right) + \frac{\partial V}{\partial y_i} = 0 \qquad ...(12.13)$$

and $$\frac{d}{dt}\left(\frac{\partial T}{\partial \dot{z}_i}\right) + \frac{\partial V}{\partial z_i} = 0 \qquad ...(12.14)$$

12.3 EQUATION OF MOTION IN GENERALIZED SYSTEM OF CO-ORDINATES

For every atom inside a molecule we need three co-ordinates. Hence, we select 3n co-ordinates to a system of n atoms. Let $q_1, q_2, q_3 \ldots\ldots\ldots q_{3n}$ be the generalized co-ordinates. They are related to Cartesian system of co-ordinates:

$$
\begin{aligned}
x_1 &= x_1\,(q_1, q_2, q_3 \ldots\ldots\ldots\ldots\ldots\ldots q_{3n}) \\
y_1 &= y_1\,(q_1, q_2, q_3 \ldots\ldots\ldots\ldots\ldots\ldots q_{3n}) \\
z_1 &= z_1\,(q_1, q_2, q_3 \ldots\ldots\ldots\ldots\ldots\ldots q_{3n}) \\
&\vdots \\
x_n &= x_n\,(q_1, q_2, q_3 \ldots\ldots\ldots\ldots\ldots\ldots q_{3n}) \\
y_n &= y_n\,(q_1, q_2, q_3 \ldots\ldots\ldots\ldots\ldots\ldots q_{3n}) \\
z_n &= z_n\,(q_1, q_2, q_3 \ldots\ldots\ldots\ldots\ldots\ldots q_{3n})
\end{aligned}
$$

We bring the transformation of equation of motion in generalized co-ordinates:

$$\frac{d}{dt}\left(\frac{\partial T}{\partial q_i}\right)+\frac{\partial V}{\partial q_i}=0 \qquad \ldots(12.15)$$

12.4 MASS WEIGHTED CO-ORDINATES (RELATIVE CO-ORDINATES)

Kinetic energy of a system of n particles may be expressed in terms of a suitable set of co-ordinates we select the centre of mass as the origin at equilibrium position. Let x_i, y_i, z_i as the co-ordinates of the ith particle (atom) in terms of moving system. Also, a_i, bi, c_i be the co-ordinates of the equilibrium position of the ith atom. The displacement from the equilibrium position will be measured by:

$$
\begin{aligned}
\Delta x_i &= x_i - a_i \\
\Delta y_i &= y_i - b_i \\
\Delta z_i &= z_i - c_i
\end{aligned}
$$

Where, Δx_i, Δy_i & Δz_i are the relative co-ordinates. We apply this system to vibrational problem. For first particle Δx_1, Δy_1, Δz_1.

Second particle Δx_2, Δy_2, Δz_2

Such that,

$$
\begin{aligned}
\Delta x_1 &= x_1 - a_1 \\
\Delta y_1 &= y_1 - b_1 \\
\Delta z_1 &= z_1 - c_1 \\
\Delta x_2 &= x_2 - a_2 \\
\Delta y_2 &= y_2 - b_2 \\
\Delta z_2 &= z_2 - c_2 \qquad \text{etc.}
\end{aligned}
$$

We can have also,
$$\Delta x_n = x_n - a_n$$
$$\Delta y_n = y_n - b_n$$
$$\Delta z_n = z_n - c_n$$

as the last set.

Velocity of the ith particle along three directions are:

$$\frac{d}{dt}(\Delta x_i), \frac{d}{dt}(\Delta y_i) \text{ and } \frac{d}{dt}(\Delta z_i)$$

Its expression for kinetic energy is then:

$$T = \frac{1}{2}\sum_{i=1}^{n} m_i \left(\dot{x}_i^2 + \dot{y}_i^2 + \dot{z}_i^2\right)$$

or,
$$2T = \sum_{i=1}^{n} m_i \left(\dot{x}_i^2 + \dot{y}_i^2 + \dot{z}_i^2\right)$$
$$= \sum_{i=1}^{n} m_i \left[\frac{d}{dt}(\Delta x_i)\right]^2 + \left[\frac{d}{dt}(\Delta y_i)\right]^2 + \left[\frac{d}{dt}(\Delta z_i)\right]^2$$
$$= \sum_{i=1}^{n} \left\{\left[m_i^{1/2} \frac{d}{dt}(\Delta x_i)\right]^2 + \left[m_i^{1/2} \frac{d}{dt}(\Delta y_i)\right]^2 + \left[m_i^{1/2} \frac{d}{dt}(\Delta z_i)\right]^2\right\}$$

We may consider their partial derivatives so that:

$$2T = \sum_{i=1}^{n} \left\{\left[\frac{\partial}{\partial t}\left(m_i^{1/2}\, \Delta x_i\right)\right]^2 + \left[\frac{\partial}{\partial t}\left(m_i^{1/2}\, \Delta y_i\right)\right]^2 + \left[\frac{\partial}{\partial t}\left(m_i^{1/2}\, \Delta z_i\right)\right]^2\right\} \quad ...(12.16)$$

It is convenient to replace them by a new set of co-ordinates $q_1, q_2, q_3, ...q_{3n}$ known as reduced displacement co-ordinates:

$$m_1^{1/2}\, \Delta x_1 = q_1, \quad m_1^{1/2}\, \Delta y_i = q_2 \quad m_1^{1/2}\, \Delta z_i = q_3$$

$$m_1^{1/2}\, \Delta x_2 = q_4, \quad m_2^{1/2}\, \Delta y_2 = q_5 \quad m_2^{1/2}\, \Delta z_2 = q_6 \text{ etc.}$$

So we have, $q_i = m_i^{1/2} \Delta x_i$ and we can sum over i = 1 to 3n.

$$q_i^2 = m_i (\Delta x_i)^2$$

or,
$$\frac{q_i^2}{m_i} = (\Delta x_i)^2$$

$$\therefore 2T = \sum_{i=1}^{n} \left(\frac{\partial}{\partial t} q_i\right)^2 + \left(\frac{\partial}{\partial t} q_i\right)^2 + \left(\frac{\partial}{\partial t} q_i\right)^2$$

$$= \sum_{i=1}^{n} (\dot{q}_i)^2 + (\dot{q}_i)^2 + (\dot{q}_i)^2$$

$$= \sum_{i=1}^{3n} \dot{q}_i^z \quad \text{for summing over 3n co-ordinates.} \qquad ...(12.17)$$

Now,
$$\frac{d}{dt}\left(\frac{\partial T}{\partial \dot{q}_i}\right) + \frac{\partial V}{\partial \dot{q}_i} = 0$$

$$2T = \sum_{i=1}^{3n} \dot{q}_i^2$$

$$2\left(\frac{\partial T}{\partial q_i}\right) = 2.\dot{q}_i$$

or,
$$\left(\frac{\partial T}{\partial q_i}\right) = \dot{q}_i$$

This on substitution gives:

$$\frac{d}{dt}(\dot{q}_i) + \frac{\partial V}{\partial q_i} = 0 \qquad ...(12.18)$$

Also,
$$2V = \sum_{i=1}^{n} \sum_{j=1}^{n} f_{ij}\, q_i\, q_j$$

or,
$$2\frac{\partial V}{\partial q_i} = \sum_i \sum_j f_{ij} \frac{\partial}{\partial q_i}(q_i . q_j)$$

In case, $i \neq j \quad f_{ij} = 0$.

Where, i = j, fij is for nonzero value,

i.e. $f_{ij} = f_{ji} \neq 0$.

For such case,

$$2.\frac{\partial V}{\partial q_i} = \sum_{j=1}^{n} f_{ij} \frac{\partial q_i^2}{\partial q_i}$$

$$= \sum_{j=1}^{n} f_{ij}.2q_i$$

or,
$$\frac{\partial V}{\partial q_i} = \sum_{j=1}^{n} f_{ij}\ q_j \qquad i = j$$

Hence, equation of motion is:

$$\frac{d\dot{q}_i}{dt} + \sum_{j=1}^{n} f_{ij}\ q_j = 0$$

A second order differential equation and it is very laborious to solve it for each q_i as a function of time. We get its solutions when we substitute i = j in all terms:

$$\ddot{q}_i + \sum_{j=1}^{n} f_{ij}\ q_j = 0$$

or,
$$\ddot{q}_i + f_{ij}\ q_i = 0 \qquad ...(12.19)$$

When $f_{ij} = f_{ii}$ we remove summation sign where:

$$q_i = A_i^o\ \cos\left(\sqrt{\lambda}.t + \sigma\right)$$

$$\lambda = 4\pi^2\upsilon^2$$

σ = phase angle.

12.5 NORMAL CO-ORDINATES AND NORMAL VIBRATIONS

We had two earlier relations:

$$2T = \sum_{i=1}^{3n} \dot{q}_i^2,\ 2V = \sum_{i=1}^{n}\sum_{j=1}^{n} f_{ij}\ q_i\ q_j$$

Kinetic energy is free from cross product and it is quadratic but potential energy is not quadratic.

The internal displacement co-ordinates $q_i^{'s}$ may be used to generate a new set of co-ordinates, Q_i called the normal co-ordinate of the system, so that both V and T are given in quadratic form. They are expressed by certain pure numbers, l_{ij}

$$q_1 = l_{11}\,Q_1 + l_{12}\,Q_2 + l_{13}\,Q_3$$
$$q_2 = l_{21}\,Q_1 + l_{22}\,Q_2 + l_{23}\,Q_3$$
$$q_3 = l_{31}\,Q_1 + l_{32}\,Q_3 + l_{33}\,Q_3$$

We have taken here a case of three normal modes of vibrations constituting three normal co-ordinates Q_1, Q_2 & Q_3. This is indirect way of defining the new co-ordinate system. In the matrix form we have:

$$\begin{bmatrix} q_1 \\ q_2 \\ q_3 \end{bmatrix} = \begin{bmatrix} l_{11} & l_{12} & l_{13} \\ l_{21} & l_{22} & l_{23} \\ l_{31} & l_{32} & l_{33} \end{bmatrix} \begin{bmatrix} Q_1 \\ Q_2 \\ Q_3 \end{bmatrix} \qquad \text{...(12.20)}$$

Matrix l_{ij} is a transformation matrix which affects the linear transformation of Q co-ordinates into a set of q co-ordinates, same way it has been established that the normal co-ordinates are expressed as mass weighted co-ordinates:

$$Q_1 = l_{11}\,q_1 + l_{21}\,q_2 + l_{31}\,q_3$$
$$Q_2 = l_{12}\,q_1 + l_{22}\,q_2 + l_{32}\,q_3$$
$$Q_3 = l_{13}\,q_1 + l_{23}\,q_2 + l_{33}\,q_3$$

The matrix affecting this transformation of the q co-ordinates into Q co-ordinates is:

$$\begin{bmatrix} l_{11} & l_{21} & l_{31} \\ l_{12} & l_{22} & l_{32} \\ l_{13} & l_{23} & l_{33} \end{bmatrix}$$

This brings the inverse transformation:

$$\begin{bmatrix} l_{11} & l_{12} & l_{13} \\ l_{21} & l_{22} & l_{23} \\ l_{31} & l_{32} & l_{33} \end{bmatrix} \begin{bmatrix} l_{11} & l_{21} & l_{31} \\ l_{12} & l_{22} & l_{32} \\ l_{13} & l_{23} & l_{33} \end{bmatrix}$$

$$= \begin{bmatrix} l_{11}^2 + l_{12}^2 + l_{13}^2 & l_{11}l_{21} + l_{12}l_{22} + l_{13}l_{23} & l_{11}l_{31} + l_{12}l_{32} + l_{13}l_{23} \\ l_{21}l_{11} + l_{22}l_{12} + l_{23}l_{13} & l_{21}^2 + l_{22}^2 + l_{23}^2 & l_{21}l_{31} + l_{22}l_{32} + l_{23}l_{33} \\ l_{31}l_{11} + l_{32}l_{12} + l_{33}l_{13} & l_{31}l_{21} + l_{32}l_{22} + l_{23}l_{23} & l_{31}^2 + l_{32}^2 + l_{33}^2 \end{bmatrix}$$

For a square matrix its product with its transpose is equal to identity:

$$E = \begin{bmatrix} 1 & 0 & 0 \\ 0 & 1 & 0 \\ 0 & 0 & 1 \end{bmatrix}$$

As such, $l_{11}^2 + l_{12}^2 + l_{13}^2 = 1$

$$l_{21}^2 + l_{22}^2 + l_{23}^2 = 1$$

$$l_{31}^2 + l_{32}^2 + l_{33}^2 = 1$$

Also, $l_{11}l_{21} + l_{12}l_{22} + l_{13}l_{23} = 0$

$$l_{11}l_{31} + l_{12}l_{32} + l_{13}l_{33} = 0 \quad \text{etc.}$$

L_{ij} are quantities related to amplitude of vibrations A_{ij}.

The equation of motion in terms of normal co-ordinates may be written as:

$$\frac{d}{dt}\left(\frac{\partial T}{\partial \dot{Q}_i}\right) + \left(\frac{\partial V}{\partial Q_i}\right) = 0$$

or,
$$\frac{d}{dt}\left[\frac{\partial}{\partial \dot{Q}_i}\left(\frac{1}{2}\sum_i \dot{Q}_i^2\right)\right] + \frac{\partial}{\partial Q_i}\left[\frac{1}{2}\sum \lambda_i Q_i^2\right] = 0$$

or,
$$\frac{d}{dt}\left(\frac{1}{2}.2\dot{Q}_i\right) + \frac{1}{2}2\lambda_i Q_i = 0$$

or,
$$\frac{d}{dt}\left(\dot{Q}_i\right) + \lambda_i Q_i = 0$$

or,
$$\ddot{Q}_i + \lambda_i Q_i = 0 \qquad \text{...(12.22)}$$

This is equation of motion for harmonic vibrations where i=1, 2, 3, ... 3n–6 or 3n–5. the various solutions are:

$$Q_i = A_i \cos\left(\sqrt{\lambda_i} + \phi\right)$$

$$\upsilon_i = \frac{1}{2\pi}\sqrt{\lambda_i}$$

or, $$\upsilon_i^2 = \frac{1}{4\pi^2}\lambda_i$$

$$\lambda_i = 4\pi^2 \upsilon_i^2$$

$$= 4\pi^2 c^2 \upsilon_i^2 \text{ in cm}^{-1}$$

Motion of the system along the normal co-ordinates Q_i is defined by the vibrational frequency υ_i. This is called normal vibration. We find that vibrational motion is resolved into the normal vibration. The vibrational spectrum of n-molecule will have 3N – 6 or 5 vibrational frequencies. Each observed frequency is described by its normal co-ordinate.

12.6 EXPANSION OF V AND T BY TYLOR SERIES AND THEIR MATRIX FORMS

Tylor series is a sum of powers of a number or terms. Power series of expansion of f (x) about x = 0

$$f(x) = f(0) + \frac{x}{1!}f'(0) + \frac{x^2}{2!}f''(0) + \ldots\ldots\ldots\ldots + \frac{x^n}{n!}f^n(0)$$

Consider potential energy as a function of internal co-ordinates d_1, d_2, d_3 as in case of water.

$$V = f(d)$$

$$\text{or } V = V(d_1, d_2, d_3)$$

We expand it by Tylor series as:

$$V = V_0 + \sum_{i=1}^{3} d_i \left(\frac{\partial V}{\partial d_i}\right)_0 + \frac{1}{2}\sum_{i=1}^{3} d_i^2 \left(\frac{\partial^2 V}{\partial d_i^2}\right)_0 + \sum_{\substack{i=1 \\ j=1}}^{3} d_i d_j \left(\frac{\partial^2 V}{\partial d_i \partial d_j}\right)_0$$

V_0 potential energy at equilibrium configuration, i.e. $d_1 = d_2 = d_3 = 0$. From this point we measure potential energy so it is taken to be zero. Let us come to second term, $\left(\frac{\partial V}{\partial d_1}\right)_0$, $\left(\frac{\partial V}{\partial d_2}\right)_0$, $\left(\frac{\partial V}{\partial d_3}\right)_0$. The use of zero subscripts in all three cases denotes the equilibrium configuration of the vibrating particles.

At this equilibrium configuration the value of V is minimum. Thus all the first derivatives must vanish. So,

$$\left(\frac{\partial V}{\partial d_1}\right)_0 = 0, \left(\frac{\partial V}{\partial d_2}\right)_0 = 0, \left(\frac{\partial V}{\partial d_3}\right)_0 = 0$$

We neglect the first and second terms in the Tylor series, then we have:

$$V = \frac{1}{2}\sum_{i=1}^{3} d_i^2 \left(\frac{\partial^2 V}{\partial d_i^2}\right)_0 + \sum_{i=1}^{3}\sum_{j} d_i d_j \left(\frac{\partial^2 V}{\partial d_i \partial d_j}\right)_0$$

$$= \frac{1}{2}\left[d_1^2 \left(\frac{\partial^2 V}{\partial d_1^2}\right)_0 + d_2^2 \left(\frac{\partial^2 V}{\partial d_2^2}\right)_0 + d_3^2 \left(\frac{\partial^2 V}{\partial d_3^2}\right)_0\right]$$

$$+\left[d_1 d_2 \left(\frac{\partial^2 V}{\partial d_1 \partial d_2}\right)_0 + d_2 d_3 \left(\frac{\partial^2 V}{\partial d_2 \partial d_3}\right)_0 + d_1 d_3 \left(\frac{\partial^2 V}{\partial d_1 \partial d_3}\right)_0\right]$$

or,

$$2V = d_1^2 \left(\frac{\partial^2 V}{\partial d_1^2}\right)_0 + d_2^2 \left(\frac{\partial^2 V}{\partial d_2^2}\right)_0 + d_3^2 \left(\frac{\partial^2 V}{\partial d_3^2}\right)_0$$

$$+2d_1 d_2 \left(\frac{\partial^2 V}{\partial d_1 \partial d_2}\right)_0 + 2d_2 d_3 \left(\frac{\partial^2 V}{\partial d_2 \partial d_3}\right)_0$$

$$+2d_1 d_3 \left(\frac{\partial^2 V}{\partial d_1 \partial d_3}\right)_0 \qquad \text{...(12.23)}$$

Potential energy is expressed in a quadratic form that can be expressed in matrix notation as:

$$2V = d^1 Fd$$

F is a square matrix whose elements are force constants Fij. The force constants are defined as:

$$F_{11} = \left(\frac{\partial^2 V}{\partial d_1^2}\right)_0 \qquad F_{22} = \left(\frac{\partial^2 V}{\partial d_2^2}\right)_0$$

$$F_{33} = \left(\frac{\partial^2 V}{\partial d_3^2}\right)_0 \quad \text{etc.}$$

$$2V = F_{11}\, d_1^2 + F_{22}\, d_2^2 + F_{33}\, d_3^2 + 2F_{12}\, d_1 d_2 + 2F_{23}\, d_2 d_3 + 2F_{13}\, d_1 d_3$$

F matrix is, $\begin{bmatrix} F_{11} & F_{12} & F_{13} \\ F_{21} & F_{22} & F_{23} \\ F_{31} & F_{32} & F_{33} \end{bmatrix}$ ...(12.24)

T is a function of tme derivative, i.e. velocity:

$$T = T(\dot{d}_1, \dot{d}_2, \dot{d}_3)$$

Its expansion by Tylor series gives us:

$$T = T_0 + \dot{d}_1 \left(\frac{\partial T}{\partial \dot{d}_1}\right)_0 + \dot{d}_2 \left(\frac{\partial T}{\partial \dot{d}_2}\right)_0 + \dot{d}_3 \left(\frac{\partial T}{\partial \dot{d}_3}\right)_0$$

$$+\frac{1}{2}\dot{d}_1^2 \left(\frac{\partial^2 T}{\partial \dot{d}_1^2}\right)_0 + \frac{1}{2}\dot{d}_2^2 \left(\frac{\partial^2 T}{\partial \dot{d}_2^2}\right) + \frac{1}{2}\dot{d}_3^2 \left(\frac{\partial T}{\partial \dot{d}_3^2}\right)_0$$

$$+ d_1 \dot{d}_2 \left(\frac{\partial^2 T}{\partial d_1 \partial d_2}\right)_0 + \ldots. + \qquad \text{...(12.25)}$$

At the starting point it is a constant. Its first derivative should be a minimum. Hence,

$$\left(\frac{\partial T}{\partial \dot{d}_1}\right)_0 = 0 \text{ etc.}$$

Also, $T_0 = 0$

$$T = 0 + 0 + \frac{1}{2}\dot{d}_1^2 \left(\frac{\partial^2 T}{\partial \dot{d}_1^2}\right)_0 + \frac{1}{2}\dot{d}_2^2 \left(\frac{\partial^2 T}{\partial \dot{d}_2^2}\right)_0 + \frac{1}{2}\dot{d}_3^2 \left(\frac{\partial^2 T}{\partial \dot{d}_3^2}\right)_0$$

$$+\dot{d}_1 \dot{d}_2 \left(\frac{\partial^2 T}{\partial \dot{d}_1 \partial \dot{d}_2}\right)_0 + \dot{d}_2 \dot{d}_3 \left(\frac{\partial^2 T}{\partial \dot{d}_2 \partial \dot{d}_3}\right)_0 + \dot{d}_1 \dot{d}_3 \left(\frac{\partial^2 T}{\partial \dot{d}_1 \partial \dot{d}_3}\right)_0$$

In the matrix form $2T = \dot{d}' G^{-1} \dot{d}$

$$T = \frac{1}{2} G_{11}^{-1} \dot{d}_1^2 + \frac{1}{2} G_{22}^{-1} \dot{d}_2^2 + \frac{1}{2} G_{33}^{-1} \dot{d}_3^2 + G_{12}^{-1} \dot{d}_1 \dot{d}_2$$

$$+ G_{23}^{-1} \dot{d}_2 \dot{d}_3 + G_{13}^{-1} \dot{d}_1 \dot{d}_3$$

or,

$$2T = G_{11}^{-1} \dot{d}_1^2 + G_{22}^{-1} \dot{d}_2^2 + G_{33}^{-1} \dot{d}_3^2 + 2G_{12}^{-1} \dot{d}_1 \dot{d}_2$$

$$+ 2G_{23}^{-1} \dot{d}_2 \dot{d}_3 + 2G_{13}^{-1} \dot{d}_1 \dot{d}_3$$

For non-linear triatomic system 3N–6 = 3 and so we have:

$$2\left(\frac{\partial T}{\partial \dot{d}_1}\right) = 2G_{11}^{-1}\,\dot{d}_1 + 2G_{12}^{-1}\,\dot{d}_2 + 2G_{13}^{-1}\,\dot{d}_3$$

$$\left(\frac{\partial T}{\partial \dot{d}_1}\right) = G_{11}^{-1}\,\dot{d}_1 + G_{12}^{-1}\,\dot{d}_2 + G_{13}^{-1}\,\dot{d}_3$$

$$\frac{d}{dt}\left(\frac{\partial T}{\partial \dot{d}_1}\right) = G_{11}^{-1}\,\ddot{d}_1 + G_{12}^{-1}\,\ddot{d}_2 + G_{13}^{-1}\,\ddot{d}_3$$

As, $2V = F_{11}d_1^2 + F_{22}d_2^2 + F_{33}d_3^2 + 2F_{12}d_1d_2 + 2F_{23}\,d_2d_3 + 2F_{13}d_1d_3$

or, $$2\left(\frac{\partial V}{\partial d_1}\right) = 2F_{11}d_1 + 0 + 0 + 2\,F_{12}d_2 + 0 + 2F_{13}d_3$$

$$\left(\frac{\partial V}{\partial d_1}\right) = F_{11}d_1 + F_{12}d_2 + F_{13}d_3$$

We insert the values in equation of motion which gives us:

$$\frac{d}{dt}\left(\frac{\partial T}{\partial \dot{d}_1}\right) = G_{11}^{-1}\ddot{d}_1 + G_{12}^{-1}\,\ddot{d}_2 + G_{13}^{-1}\,\ddot{d}_3 \qquad ...(12.26)$$

12.6 SOLUTION OF EQUATION OF MOTION

We seek the solution:

$$d_1 = A_1 \cos\left(\sqrt{\lambda}t + \phi\right)$$

$$d_2 = A_2 \cos\left(\sqrt{\lambda}t + \phi\right)$$

$$d_3 = A_3 \cos\left(\sqrt{\lambda}t + \phi\right)$$

ϕ be the phase angle.

υ is the normal frequency with amplitude of vibrations A_1, A_2 & A_3, then,

$$\frac{d}{dt}\,d_1 = \dot{d}_1 = -\sqrt{\lambda}\;A_1\,\sin\left(\sqrt{\lambda}t + \phi\right)$$

$$\ddot{d}_1 = -\lambda A_1 \cos\left(\sqrt{\lambda}t + \phi\right)$$

$$= -\lambda d_1$$

Similarly,

$$\ddot{d}_2 = -\lambda d_2$$

$$\ddot{d}_3 = -\lambda d_3$$

and $$\frac{d}{dt}\left(\frac{\partial T}{\partial \dot{d}_1}\right) = G_{11}^{-1}\,\ddot{d}_1 + G_{22}^{-1}\,\ddot{d}_2 + G_{33}^{-1}\,\ddot{d}_3$$

$$= G_{11}^{-1}\,(-\lambda d_1) + G_{12}^{-1}(-\lambda d_2) + G_{13}^{-1}\,(-\lambda\, d_3)$$

$$= -\lambda\left[G_{11}^{-1}\,d_1 + G_{12}^{-1}\,d_2 + G_{13}^{-1}\,d_3\right]$$

G^{-1} is reciprocal of matrix G whose elements are G_{ij}.

For d_1 case the replacement of equation of motion gives us:

$$-\lambda G_{11}^{-1}\,d_1 - \lambda G_{12}^{-1} d_2 - \lambda G_{13}^{-1} d_3 + F_{11} d_1 + F_{12} d_2 + F_{13} d_3 = 0$$

or, $$\left(F_{11} - \lambda G_{11}^{-1}\right) d_1 + \left(F_{12} - \lambda G_{12}^{-1}\right) d_2 + \left(F_{13} - \lambda G_{13}^{-1}\right) d_3 = 0$$

or, $$\left(F_{11} - \lambda G_{11}^{-1}\right) A_1 \cos\left(\sqrt{\lambda} t + \phi\right) + \left(F_{12} - \lambda G_{12}^{-1}\right) A_2 \cos\left(\sqrt{\lambda} t + \phi\right) + \left(F_{13} - \lambda G_{13}^{-1}\right) A_3 \cos\left(\sqrt{\lambda} t + \phi\right) = 0$$

or, $$\left(F_{11} - \lambda G_{11}^{-1}\right) A_1 + \left(F_{12} - \lambda G_{12}^{-1}\right) A_2 + \left(F_{13} - \lambda G_{13}^{-1}\right) A_3 = 0$$

This is amplitude equation in terms of internal co-ordinate d_1. There are two more such equations corresponding to d_2 & d_3 such as:

$$\left(F_{21} - \lambda G_{21}^{-1}\right) A_1 + \left(F_{22} - \lambda G_{22}^{-1}\right) A_2 + \left(F_{23} - \lambda G_{23}^{-1}\right) A_3 = 0$$

$$\left(F_{31} - \lambda G_{31}^{-1}\right) A_1 + \left(F_{32} - \lambda G_{32}^{-1}\right) A_2 + \left(F_{33} - \lambda G_{33}^{-1}\right) A_3 = 0$$

and for non-trivial case we have:

$$\begin{vmatrix} F_{11} - \lambda G_{11}^{-1} & F_{12} - \lambda G_{12}^{-1} & F_{13} - \lambda G_{13}^{-1} \\ F_{21} - \lambda G_{21}^{-1} & F_{22} - \lambda G_{22}^{-1} & F_{23} - \lambda G_{23}^{-1} \\ F_{31} - \lambda G_{31}^{-1} & F_{32} - \lambda G_{32}^{-1} & F_{33} - \lambda G_{33}^{-1} \end{vmatrix} = 0 \qquad \text{...(12.27)}$$

It is conveniently written in the form of F & G matrices as,

$$| F - \lambda G^{-1} | = 0$$

In the present case we have a cubic equation giving three roots of λ:

$$\lambda_i = 4\pi^2 \upsilon_i^2$$

There will be three normal vibrational frequencies of the molecule under consideration:

$$T = \dot{d}^1 G^{-1} \dot{d}$$

$$\dot{d}' = \begin{bmatrix} \dot{d}_1 & \dot{d}_2 & \dot{d}_3 \end{bmatrix}$$

$$\dot{d} = \begin{bmatrix} \dot{d}_1 \\ \dot{d}_2 \\ \dot{d}_3 \end{bmatrix} \text{ and } G^{-1} = \begin{bmatrix} G_{11}^{-1} & G_{12}^{-1} & G_{13}^{-1} \\ G_{21}^{-1} & G_{22}^{-1} & G_{23}^{-1} \\ G_{31}^{-1} & G_{32}^{-1} & G_{33}^{-1} \end{bmatrix}$$

In case of, $2V = d'Fd$

$$d' = \begin{bmatrix} d_1 & d_2 & d_3 \end{bmatrix}$$

$$d = \begin{bmatrix} d_1 \\ d_2 \\ d_3 \end{bmatrix} \;\&\; F = \begin{bmatrix} F_{11} & F_{12} & F_{13} \\ F_{21} & F_{22} & F_{23} \\ F_{31} & F_{32} & F_{33} \end{bmatrix}$$

So,

$$2V = \begin{bmatrix} d_1 \, d_2 \, d_3 \end{bmatrix} \begin{bmatrix} F_{11} & F_{12} & F_{13} \\ F_{21} & F_{22} & F_{23} \\ F_{31} & F_{32} & F_{33} \end{bmatrix} \begin{bmatrix} d_1 \\ d_2 \\ d_3 \end{bmatrix} \quad ...(12.28)$$

Similarly,

$$2T = \begin{bmatrix} \dot{d}_1 \, \dot{d}_2 \, \dot{d}_3 \end{bmatrix} \begin{bmatrix} G_{11}^{-1} & G_{12}^{-1} & G_{13}^{-1} \\ G_{21}^{-1} & G_{22}^{-1} & G_{23}^{-1} \\ G_{31}^{-1} & G_{32}^{-1} & G_{33}^{-1} \end{bmatrix} \begin{bmatrix} \dot{d}_1 \\ \dot{d}_2 \\ \dot{d}_3 \end{bmatrix} \quad ...(12.29)$$

12.7 SYMMETRY OF THE NORMAL CO-ORDINATES

Molecules are characterized by point groups. Symmetry operations are considered when atoms are at rest. The normal vibrations of a molecule may affect the symmetry and so we can apply molecular symmetry as a basis for classifying normal modes. Credit goes to Brester and later to Wigner who applied Group theory to the problems of molecular vibrations. The normal modes of vibration in water is given by:

$$\Gamma_v = 2A_1 + B_2$$

If the normal co-ordinates are known the normal modes are predicted. Symmetry representation simplifies the determination of normal co-ordinates. We can use also enternal co-ordinate for analysis.

12.8 SYMMETRY OF NORMAL VIBRATIONS

Let us consider symmetry of normal vibrations:

$$2T = \sum_i \dot{Q}_i^2$$

$$2V = \sum \lambda_i Q_i^2$$

For a case in which there is only one normal mode of vibration Q_i then $2T = \dot{Q}_i^2, 2V = \lambda Q_i^2$.

The energy is invariant by the symmetry operations (R).

Thus, $$2T = \dot{Q}_i^2 = \left(R\dot{Q}_i\right)^2$$

$$2V = \lambda_i Q_i^2 = \lambda_i (RQ_i)^2$$

In order that the two results hold.

We must have, $$(RQ_i)^2 = (Q_i)^2$$

$$RQ_i = \pm Q_i$$

Thus, the normal co-ordinate will change either into itself or its negative:

$RQ_i = + Q_i$ symmetric vibration

$RQ_i = - Q_i$ anti-symmetric vibration.

12.8.1 Consider the Case of Water Molecule

We can find out the normal modes of vibrations. Normal co-ordinates are used as basis functions. There can be three vibrational modes υ_1, υ_2 & υ_3. υ_1 is symmetric stretching, υ_2 symmetric bending and υ_3 as asymmetric stretching modes. We apply three normal co-ordinates Q_1, Q_2 and Q_3 for them respectively.

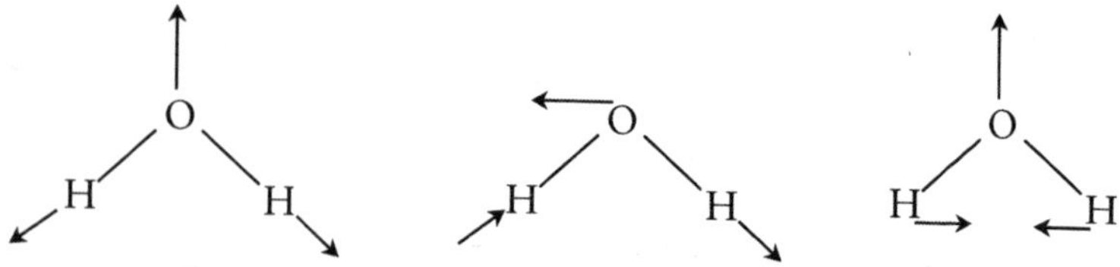

υ_1, Q_1 υ_3, Q_3 υ_2, Q_2

For C_{2v} point group we carryout the effect of E, C_2, σ_{xz} & σ_{yz} operations on these co-ordinates:

$$E\ (Q_1) = (+1)\ Q_1$$
$$E\ (Q_2) = (+1)\ Q_2$$
$$E\ (Q_3) = (+1)\ Q_3$$
$$C_2\ (Q_1) = (+1)\ Q_1$$
$$C_2\ (Q_2) = (+1)\ Q_2$$
$$C_2\ (Q_3) = (-1)\ Q_3$$
$$\sigma_{xz}\ (Q_1) = (+1)\ Q_1$$
$$\sigma_{xz}\ (Q_2) = (+1)\ Q_2$$
$$\sigma_{xz}\ (Q_3) = (-1)\ Q_3$$
$$\sigma_{xz}\ (Q_1) = (+1)\ Q_1$$
$$\sigma_{xz}\ (Q_2) = (+1)\ Q_2$$
$$\sigma_{xz}\ (Q_3) = (+1)\ Q_3$$

The transformation matrices may be shown as:

$$E\begin{bmatrix} Q_1 \\ Q_2 \\ Q_3 \end{bmatrix} = \begin{bmatrix} 1 & 0 & 0 \\ 0 & 1 & 0 \\ 0 & 0 & 1 \end{bmatrix} \begin{bmatrix} Q_1 \\ Q_2 \\ Q_3 \end{bmatrix}$$

$$C_2\begin{bmatrix} Q_1 \\ Q_2 \\ Q_3 \end{bmatrix} = \begin{bmatrix} 1 & 0 & 0 \\ 0 & 1 & 0 \\ 0 & 0 & -1 \end{bmatrix} \begin{bmatrix} Q_1 \\ Q_2 \\ Q_3 \end{bmatrix}$$

$$\sigma_{xz}\begin{bmatrix} Q_1 \\ Q_2 \\ Q_3 \end{bmatrix} = \begin{bmatrix} 1 & 0 & 0 \\ 0 & 1 & 0 \\ 0 & 0 & -1 \end{bmatrix} \begin{bmatrix} Q_1 \\ Q_2 \\ Q_3 \end{bmatrix}$$

$$\sigma_{yz}\begin{bmatrix}Q_1\\Q_2\\Q_3\end{bmatrix}=\begin{bmatrix}1&0&0\\0&1&0\\0&0&1\end{bmatrix}\begin{bmatrix}Q_1\\Q_2\\Q_3\end{bmatrix}$$

Since three modes of vibrations in water are independent to each other. We can diagonalise the matrix in each case into three 1×1 blocks:

$$E=\begin{bmatrix}1&0&0\\0&1&0\\0&0&1\end{bmatrix}\quad \chi:\ Q_1=1,\ Q_2=1,\ Q_3=1$$

$$C_2=\begin{bmatrix}1&0&0\\0&1&0\\0&0&-1\end{bmatrix}\quad Q_1=1,\ Q_2=1,\ Q_3=-1$$

$$\sigma_{xz}=\begin{bmatrix}1&0&0\\0&1&0\\0&0&-1\end{bmatrix}\quad Q_1=1,\ Q_2=1,\ Q_3=-1$$

$$\sigma_{yz}=\begin{bmatrix}1&0&0\\0&1&0\\0&0&1\end{bmatrix}\quad Q_1=1,\ Q_2=1,\ Q_3=1$$

Thus the symmetry properties of normal vibration is classified as:

	E	C_2	σ_{xz}	σ_{yz}
Q_1, Q_2	1	1	1	1
Q_3	1	−1	−1	1

Comparison of characters lead to Q_1 & Q_2 as A_1 type and Q_3 as B_2 type vibrations.

Thus, Q_1 & Q_2 are totally symmetric vibrations and Q_3 is anti-symmetric vibration.

12.9 SOLVING OF SECULAR EQUATION

$$\left|F-\lambda G^{-1'}\right|=0 \qquad \text{...(12.30)}$$

We can premultiply this equation by {G}

$$|G|\,|F-\lambda G^{-1}|=0$$

or, $$|GF-\lambda GG^{-1}|=0$$

or, $$|GF-\lambda E|=0$$

We can post-multiply by |G| so that:

$$|F-\lambda G^{-1}|\,|G|=0$$

or $$|FG-\lambda GG^{-1}|=0$$

or $$|FG-\lambda E|=0 \quad ...(12.31)$$

The sole purpose is to set up secular equation and by its solution normal frequencies can be calculated.

The projection vectors $\tilde{P}^{A_1}$ d_1, d_2 or d_3 and $\tilde{P}^{E}d_1$ d_2 or d_3 generate one vector belonging to A_1 & E symmetry species.

12.10 SYMMETRY CO-ORDINATES

From a set of normal co-ordinates we can generate new co-ordinates each of which belongs to a particular symmetry species of the given point group. Such co-ordinates are called symmetry co-ordinates, S.

Let the internal co-ordinates be denoted by row vector or, column vector $[r_1, r_2, r_3]$ or, $\begin{bmatrix} r_1 \\ r_2 \\ r_3 \end{bmatrix}$ shown by D.

Symmetry co-ordinates are, S_1, S_2 & S_3 such that, $S = [s_1, s_2, s_3]$

or, $$\begin{bmatrix} s_1 \\ s_2 \\ s_3 \end{bmatrix}$$

S is symmetry co-ordinates whereas D is internal co-ordinates. Let us suppose a matrix U which brings this transformation. For which the matrix equation may be given as:

$$S = UD.$$

12.11 MATRIX U IS DETERMINED BY PROJECTION OPERATOR METHOD

We take up the case of PCl_3 for which there are two projection operators corresponding to A_1 & E symmetry species namely $\tilde{p}^{A_1}$ & $\tilde{p}^{E}$. There are three internal co-ordinates d_1, d_2 & d_3.

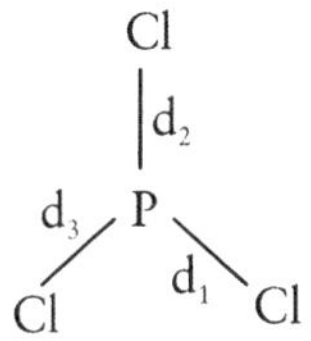

Now we evaluate projection vector for A_1

$$\tilde{P}^{A_1} d_1 \cong \sum_R \chi_R^A \tilde{R} d_1$$

$$= 1 \times 1\, \tilde{E}\, d_1 + 1 \times 1\, \tilde{C}_3\, d_1 + 1 \times 1\, \tilde{C}_3^2\, d_1 + 1 \times 1\, \tilde{\sigma}_V\, d_1 + 1 \times 1 \tilde{\sigma}_{v'}\, d_1 + 1 \times 1\, \tilde{\sigma}_{v''}\, d_1$$

$$= d_1 + d_3 + d_2 + d_1 + d_3 + d_2$$

$$= 2\ (d_1 + d_2 + d_3)$$

$$\tilde{P}_{d_1}^{E} \cong \sum_R \chi_R^E \tilde{R} d_1$$

$$= 2\tilde{E}d_1 + (-1)\tilde{C}_3\, d_1 + (-1)\, \tilde{C}_3^2\, d_1 + 0$$

$$= 2d_1 - d_3 - d_2$$

The same result would have been obtained on applying d_2 or d_3 in place of d_1.

E is two dimensional representation whereas A_1 is one dimensional representation. In case of E we got one projection vector we will search for another projection vector for E symmetry species. The vector belonging to A_1 symmetry species is to be normalized.

$$2(d_1 + d_2 + d_3)$$

$$N^2 (2^2 + 2^2 + 2^2) = 1$$

$$12N^2 = 1$$

$$N = \frac{1}{2\sqrt{3}}$$

The normalized vector is written as:

$$S^{A_1} \text{ or } S_1 = \frac{1}{\cancel{2}\sqrt{3}}\cancel{2}(d_1 + d_2 + d_3)$$

$$= \frac{1}{\sqrt{3}}(d_1 + d_2 + d_3).$$

Vectors belonging to E species may be 'a' type and 'b' type, the former is known 'a' type for E can be normalized as:

$$N^2 (2^2 + 1^2 + 1^2) = 1$$

$$6N^2 = 1$$

$$N = \frac{1}{\sqrt{6}}$$

The projection vector is:

$$S_a^E = \frac{1}{\sqrt{6}}(2d_1 - d_2 - d_3)$$

The other one is b type S_b^E.

The basis vectors d_1, d_2 & d_3 which were initially used. This is changed into a new set of basis vectors such as projection vector. The change of basis may be shown in matrix form:

$$[\text{row vector}] = [\text{row vector}]\begin{bmatrix}\text{square}\\ \text{matrix}\end{bmatrix}$$

$$\left[S^{A_1}\ S_a^E\ S_b^E\right] = [d_1\ d_2\ d_3]\begin{bmatrix}1/\sqrt{3} & 2/\sqrt{6} & b_1\\ 1/\sqrt{3} & -1/\sqrt{6} & b_2\\ 1/\sqrt{3} & -1/\sqrt{6} & b_3\end{bmatrix} \quad ...(12.32)$$

The second vector, $S_b^E = d_1b_1 + d_2b_2 + d_3b_3$. b_1, b_2 & b_3 are coefficients to be made known. The original basis and the new basis are orthogonal.

Let us come back to the original orthogonal transformation,

$$\text{viz. } \left[S^{A_1}\ S_a^E\ S_b^E\right] = [d_1\ d_2\ d_3]\begin{bmatrix}1/\sqrt{3} & 2/\sqrt{6} & b_1\\ 1/\sqrt{3} & -1/\sqrt{6} & b_2\\ 1/\sqrt{3} & -1/\sqrt{6} & b_3\end{bmatrix}$$

We deduce the following relations from the properties of orthogonal matrices:

$$b_1^2 + b_2^2 + b_3^2 = 1$$

$$\frac{1}{\sqrt{3}} b_1 + \frac{1}{\sqrt{3}} b_2 + \frac{1}{\sqrt{6}} b_3 = 0$$

$$\frac{2}{\sqrt{6}} b_1 - \frac{1}{\sqrt{6}} b_2 - \frac{1}{\sqrt{6}} b_3 = 0$$

On adding the last two:

$$\left.\begin{array}{l} \frac{1}{\sqrt{3}} b_1 + \frac{1}{\sqrt{3}} b_2 + \frac{1}{\sqrt{3}} b_3 = 0 \\ \frac{2}{\sqrt{6}} b_1 - \frac{1}{\sqrt{6}} b_2 - \frac{1}{\sqrt{6}} b_3 = 0 \end{array}\right\}$$

$$= \frac{\sqrt{2}+2}{\sqrt{6}} b_1 + \frac{\sqrt{2}-1}{\sqrt{6}} b_2 + \frac{\sqrt{2}-1}{\sqrt{6}} b_3 = 0$$

or,
$$\left(\frac{\sqrt{2}+2}{\sqrt{2}}\right)\frac{b_1}{\sqrt{3}} + \frac{\sqrt{2}-1}{\sqrt{2}}\frac{b_2}{\sqrt{3}} + \frac{\sqrt{2}-1}{\sqrt{2}}\frac{b_3}{\sqrt{3}} = 0$$

This can hold putting $b_1 = 0$, & $b_2 = -b_3$.

Hence, $b_1^2 + b_2^2 + b_3^2 = 1$

or, $0 + b_2^2 + b_2^2 = 1$

or, $b_2 = \frac{1}{\sqrt{2}}$ and $b_3 = -\frac{1}{\sqrt{2}}$

So,
$$S_b^E = b_1 d_1 + b_2 d_2 + b_3 d_3$$

$$= \frac{1}{\sqrt{2}}(d_2 - d_3).$$

The elements of square matrix are finally obtained as:

$$\begin{bmatrix} 1/\sqrt{3} & 2/\sqrt{6} & 0 \\ 1/\sqrt{3} & -1/\sqrt{6} & 1/\sqrt{2} \\ 1/\sqrt{3} & -1/\sqrt{6} & -1/\sqrt{2} \end{bmatrix} = A \qquad ...(12.33)$$

Its transpose is:

$$A^1 = \begin{bmatrix} 1/\sqrt{3} & 1/\sqrt{3} & 1/\sqrt{3} \\ 2/\sqrt{6} & -1/\sqrt{6} & -1/\sqrt{6} \\ 0 & 1/\sqrt{2} & -1/\sqrt{2} \end{bmatrix} \qquad ...(12.34)$$

The effect of change of bases upon a symmetric matrix R is obtained by similarity transformation A^{-1} RA. Since, A is orthogonal matrix. So its $A^{-1} = A'$.

Hence, $A^{-1}\,RA = A'\,RA$.

Consider C_3 operation for R. As obtained earlier the transformation matrix for C_3 with d_1, d_2 and d_3 as basis is:

$$\begin{pmatrix} 0 & 0 & 1 \\ 1 & 0 & 0 \\ 0 & 1 & 0 \end{pmatrix}$$

The new matrix for C_3 with new basis will be: $S = A'C_3A$

$$S = \begin{bmatrix} \frac{1}{\sqrt{3}} & \frac{1}{\sqrt{3}} & \frac{1}{\sqrt{3}} \\ \frac{2}{\sqrt{6}} & -\frac{1}{\sqrt{6}} & -\frac{1}{\sqrt{6}} \\ 0 & \frac{1}{\sqrt{2}} & -\frac{1}{\sqrt{2}} \end{bmatrix} \begin{bmatrix} 0 & 0 & 1 \\ 1 & 0 & 0 \\ 0 & 1 & 0 \end{bmatrix} \begin{bmatrix} \frac{1}{\sqrt{3}} & \frac{2}{\sqrt{6}} & 0 \\ \frac{1}{\sqrt{3}} & -\frac{1}{\sqrt{6}} & \frac{1}{\sqrt{2}} \\ \frac{1}{\sqrt{3}} & -\frac{1}{\sqrt{6}} & -\frac{1}{\sqrt{2}} \end{bmatrix}$$

$$= \begin{bmatrix} \frac{1}{\sqrt{3}} & \frac{1}{\sqrt{3}} & \frac{1}{\sqrt{3}} \\ \frac{2}{\sqrt{6}} & -\frac{1}{\sqrt{6}} & -\frac{1}{\sqrt{6}} \\ 0 & \frac{1}{\sqrt{2}} & -\frac{1}{\sqrt{2}} \end{bmatrix} \begin{bmatrix} \frac{1}{\sqrt{3}} & -\frac{1}{\sqrt{6}} & -\frac{1}{\sqrt{2}} \\ \frac{1}{\sqrt{3}} & \frac{2}{\sqrt{6}} & 0 \\ \frac{1}{\sqrt{3}} & -\frac{1}{\sqrt{6}} & \frac{1}{\sqrt{2}} \end{bmatrix}$$

$$= \begin{bmatrix} \frac{1}{3}+\frac{1}{3}+\frac{1}{3} & -\frac{1}{3\sqrt{2}}+\frac{2}{3\sqrt{2}}-\frac{1}{3\sqrt{2}} & -\frac{1}{\sqrt{6}}+0+\frac{1}{\sqrt{6}} \\ \frac{2}{3\sqrt{2}}-\frac{1}{3\sqrt{2}}-\frac{1}{3\sqrt{2}} & -\frac{2}{6}-\frac{2}{6}+\frac{1}{6} & -\frac{2}{2\sqrt{3}}+0-\frac{1}{2\sqrt{3}} \\ 0+\frac{1}{\sqrt{6}}-\frac{1}{\sqrt{6}} & 0+\frac{2}{2\sqrt{3}}+\frac{1}{2\sqrt{3}} & 0+0-\frac{1}{2} \end{bmatrix}$$

$$= \begin{bmatrix} 1 & 0 & 0 \\ 0 & -\frac{4}{6}+\frac{1}{6} & -\frac{3}{2\sqrt{3}} \\ 0 & \frac{3}{2\sqrt{3}} & -\frac{1}{2} \end{bmatrix}$$

$$= \begin{bmatrix} 1 & 0 & 0 \\ 0 & -\frac{3}{6} & -\frac{\sqrt{3}}{2} \\ 0 & \frac{\sqrt{3}}{2} & -\frac{1}{2} \end{bmatrix} = \begin{bmatrix} 1 & 0 & 0 \\ 0 & -\frac{1}{2} & \frac{\sqrt{3}}{2} \\ 0 & \frac{\sqrt{3}}{2} & -\frac{1}{2} \end{bmatrix} \qquad ...(12.35)$$

It is seen to have two diagonal blocks of the form 1 × 1 A (1):

$$2 \times 2 \ \ E \begin{pmatrix} -1/2 & \sqrt{3/2} \\ \sqrt{3}/2 & -1/2 \end{pmatrix}$$

The same diagonal block pattern is found for all the matrices after changing to the new bases consisting of the vectors: S^{A_1} S_a^E S_b^E

This change has obtained the desired complete reduction of the original reducible representation (3 × 3) of Γstr. The symmetry co-ordinates are related to internal co-ordinates as:

$$\begin{bmatrix} S^{A_1} & S_a^E & S_b^E \end{bmatrix} = \begin{bmatrix} r_1 & r_2 & r_3 \end{bmatrix} \begin{bmatrix} A \end{bmatrix}$$

$$= \begin{bmatrix} r_1 & r_2 & r_3 \end{bmatrix} \begin{bmatrix} \frac{1}{\sqrt{3}} & \frac{2}{\sqrt{6}} & 0 \\ \frac{1}{\sqrt{3}} & -\frac{1}{\sqrt{6}} & \frac{1}{\sqrt{2}} \\ \frac{1}{\sqrt{3}} & -\frac{1}{\sqrt{6}} & -\frac{1}{\sqrt{2}} \end{bmatrix}$$

or, $\qquad S = UD$

Conventionally set of co-ordinates are written as column matrix, so we transpose both sides of this equation which is entirely equivalent:

$$\begin{bmatrix} S^{A_1} \\ S_a^E \\ S_b^E \end{bmatrix} = \begin{bmatrix} \frac{1}{\sqrt{3}} & \frac{1}{\sqrt{3}} & \frac{1}{\sqrt{3}} \\ \frac{2}{\sqrt{6}} & -\frac{1}{\sqrt{6}} & -\frac{1}{\sqrt{6}} \\ 0 & \frac{1}{\sqrt{2}} & -\frac{1}{\sqrt{2}} \end{bmatrix} \begin{bmatrix} r_1 \\ r_2 \\ r_3 \end{bmatrix} \quad \text{...(12.36)}$$

12.13 NORMAL COORDINATE ANALYSIS OF WATER AND AMMONIA

(a) Water, H_2O

Symmetry types of Normal Modes in Water.

We generate the characters for C_{2V} (H_2O) by the method of un-shifted atoms:

C_{2v}	E	C_2	σ_{xz}	σ_{yz}
Γ_R	9	–1	1	3

Decompose it to irreducible representations:

$$\Gamma_R = 3A_1 + A_2 + 2B_1 + 3B_2$$

Determine the symmetry species of three translational components and three rotational components:

Translational Components	*Symmetry Species*
T_x	B_1
T_y	B_2
T_z	A_1
Rotational Components	
R_x	B_1
R_y	B_2
R_z	A_2

$$\Gamma_{t+r} = A_1 + A_2 + 2B_1 + 2B_2$$

$$\Gamma_{3N-6} = 2A_1 + B_2$$

Internal Co-ordinates Contributions

Use internal co-ordinates as vectors d_1 and d_2 for bond stretches from O and θ as deformation co-ordinate.

Now, use d_1, d_2 & θ as basis and obtain transformation matrices for symmetry operations E, C_2, σ_{xz} and σ_{yz}. There are two stretching and asymmetric stretching and one of bending. There can be block diagnolization of 3 × 3 matrices into 2 × 2 and 1 × 1, matrices and separate them into two sets as follows :

	E	C_2	σ_{xz}	σ_{yz}
Γ_d	2	0	0	2
Γ_θ	1	1	1	1

$\Gamma_d = A_1 + B_2$

$\Gamma_\theta = A_1$

The three normal modes are:

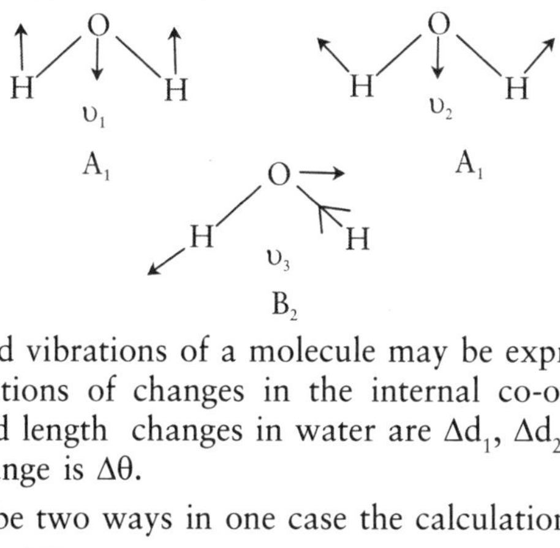

The allowed vibrations of a molecule may be expressed as linear combinations of changes in the internal co-ordinates. The set of bond length changes in water are Δd_1, Δd_2 and the bond angle change is Δθ.

There can be two ways in one case the calculation of:

$$S = UD$$

The transformation matrix U is obtained from the linear combinations:

$$S_1 = 0.\Delta d_1 + 0.\Delta d_2 + (+1)\ \Delta\theta$$

$$S_2 = \frac{1}{\sqrt{2}}\ \Delta d_1 + \frac{1}{\sqrt{2}}\Delta d_2 + (0)\ \Delta\theta$$

$$S_3 = \frac{1}{\sqrt{2}}\ \Delta d_1 + \left(-\frac{1}{\sqrt{2}}\right)\Delta d_2 + (0)\ \Delta\theta$$

This gives the transformation matrix U as

$$\begin{bmatrix} 0 & 0 & 1 \\ 1/\sqrt{2} & 1/\sqrt{2} & 0 \\ 1/\sqrt{2} & -1/\sqrt{2} & 0 \end{bmatrix}$$

$$\begin{bmatrix} S_1 \\ S_2 \\ S_3 \end{bmatrix} = \begin{bmatrix} 0 & 0 & 1 \\ 1/\sqrt{2} & 1/\sqrt{2} & 0 \\ 1/\sqrt{2} & -1/\sqrt{2} & 0 \end{bmatrix} \begin{bmatrix} \Delta d_1 \\ \Delta d_2 \\ \Delta\theta \end{bmatrix} \qquad ...(12.32)$$

$$\text{Transpose of, } U = U' = \begin{bmatrix} 0 & 1/\sqrt{2} & 1/\sqrt{2} \\ 0 & 1/\sqrt{2} & -1/\sqrt{2} \\ 1 & 0 & 0 \end{bmatrix}$$

Now, $F = Uf\,U'$

$$f\,U' = \begin{bmatrix} fd & fdd & fd\theta \\ fdd & fd & fd\theta \\ fd\theta & fd\theta & f\theta \end{bmatrix} \begin{bmatrix} 0 & 1/\sqrt{2} & 1/\sqrt{2} \\ 0 & 1/\sqrt{2} & -1/\sqrt{2} \\ 1 & 0 & 0 \end{bmatrix}$$

$$= \begin{bmatrix} fd\theta & 1/\sqrt{2}(fd + fdd) & 1/\sqrt{2}(fd - fdd) \\ fd\theta & 1/\sqrt{2}\,(fdd + fd) & 1/\sqrt{2}\,(fdd - fd) \\ f\theta & 1/\sqrt{2}\,(fd\theta + fd\theta) & 1/\sqrt{2}(fd\theta - fd\theta) \end{bmatrix}$$

$$= \begin{bmatrix} fd\theta & \frac{1}{\sqrt{2}}(fd + fdd) & \frac{1}{\sqrt{2}}(fd - fdd) \\ fd\theta & \frac{1}{\sqrt{2}}(fdd + fd) & \frac{1}{\sqrt{2}}(fdd - fd) \\ f\theta & \frac{1}{\sqrt{2}}(fd\theta + fd\theta) & 0 \end{bmatrix}$$

$$F = U f U'$$

$$= \begin{bmatrix} 0 & 0 & 1 \\ \frac{1}{\sqrt{2}} & \frac{1}{\sqrt{2}} & 0 \\ \frac{1}{\sqrt{2}} & -\frac{1}{\sqrt{2}} & 0 \end{bmatrix} \begin{bmatrix} fd\theta & \frac{1}{\sqrt{2}}(fd + fdd) & \frac{1}{\sqrt{2}}(fd - fdd) \\ fd\theta & \frac{1}{\sqrt{2}}(fd + fdd) & \frac{1}{\sqrt{2}}(fdd - fd) \\ f\theta & \sqrt{2}fd\theta & 0 \end{bmatrix}$$

$$= \begin{bmatrix} f\theta & \sqrt{2}fd\theta & 0 \\ \frac{1}{\sqrt{2}}.2fd\theta & fdd + fd & 0 \\ 0 & 0 & 1/2fd - 1/2fdd - 1/2fdd + 1/2fd \end{bmatrix} \quad ...(12.38)$$

$$\begin{array}{c} \\ A_1 \\ A_1 \\ B_2 \end{array} \begin{bmatrix} A_1 & A_1 & | & B_2 \\ f\theta & \sqrt{2}fd\theta & | & 0 \\ \sqrt{2}fd\theta & fd + fdd & | & 0 \\ \hline 0 & 0 & | & fd - fdd \end{bmatrix} \quad ...(12.39)$$

Thus, F matrix is symmetry factored into two parts a 2×2 matrix corresponding to symmetric vibrations A_1 and a 1×1 matrix corresponding to un-symmetrical vibration B_2. For A_1 type vibrations we have F matrix. Force constant is made on quantitative basis if υ's are known or υ's can be calculated from the F and G matrices.

The force constant calculation can be had from internal co-ordinates but the problem gets simplify in symmetry co-ordinates. The Wilson F and G matrices give the master equation $|FG - \lambda E| = 0$ which can be written in terms of Δd_1, Δd_2 and $\Delta\theta$ and S_1, S_2 and S_3. It would be advisable to adopt g matrix in internal co-ordinates system for kinetic energy and f matrix for potential energy in place of G and F matrices. The two capital letters will be applicable to the symmetry co-ordinate system so $|fg - \lambda E| = 0$ where E is unit matrix:

$$\lambda = 4\pi^2 C^2 \upsilon^2$$
$$= 5.8890 \times 10^{-2} \upsilon^2$$

The effect on internal co-ordinates in case of water by $C_{2\upsilon}$ symmetry operations are seen:

$E\ \Delta d_1 = \Delta d_1 \quad C_2\ \Delta d_1 = \Delta d_2 \quad \sigma_{xz}\ \Delta d_1 = \Delta d_2 \quad \sigma_{yz}\ \Delta d_1 = \Delta d_1$

$E\ \Delta d_2 = \Delta d_2 \quad C_2\ \Delta d_2 = \Delta d_1 \quad \sigma_{xz}\ \Delta d_2 = \Delta d_1 \quad \sigma_{yz}\ \Delta d_2 = \Delta d_2$

$E\ \Delta\theta = \Delta\theta \quad C_2\ \Delta\theta = \Delta\theta \quad \sigma_{xz}\ \Delta\theta = \Delta\theta \quad \sigma_{yz}\ \Delta\theta = \Delta\theta$

$C_{2\upsilon}$	E	C_2	σ_{xz}	σ_{yz}
Δd_1	Δd_1	Δd_2	Δd_2	Δd_1
Δd_2	Δd_2	Δd_1	Δd_1	Δd_2
$\Delta\theta$	$\Delta\theta$	$\Delta\theta$	$\Delta\theta$	$\Delta\theta$

Symmetry Co-ordinates of Water

We adopt projection operator technique using internal co-ordinates as basis to obtain symmetry co-ordinates as their linear combinations (SALCS):

$$\Delta d_1, \Delta d_2\ A_1 + B_2 \text{ symmetry}$$

$$\Delta\theta\ A_1$$

$$\tilde{P}^{A_1} d_1 = 1\times\tilde{E}\ \Delta d_1 + 1\times\tilde{C}_2\ \Delta d_1 + 1\times\tilde{\sigma}_{xz}\ \Delta d_1 + 1\times\tilde{\sigma}_{yz}\ \Delta d_1$$

$$= \Delta d_1 + \Delta d_2 + \Delta d_2 + \Delta d_1$$

$$= 2(\Delta d_1 + \Delta d_2)$$

$$S_1^{A_2} = S_2 = 2(\Delta d_1 + \Delta d_2)$$

We normalize it for the vectors of A_1 species:

$$N^2\left[2^2 + 2^2\right] = 1$$

$$8N^2 = 1$$

$$N = \frac{1}{2\sqrt{2}}$$

$$S_2 = \frac{1}{2\sqrt{2}}.2(\Delta d_1 + \Delta d_2)$$

$$= \frac{1}{\sqrt{2}}(\Delta d_1 + \Delta d_2)$$

Now $\Delta\theta$ is A_1 type and there is no vector to be projected otherwise:

$$P^{A_1}\,\Delta\theta = 1\times E\Delta\theta + 1\times C_2\,\Delta\theta + 1\times\sigma_{xz}\,\Delta\theta + 1\times\sigma_{yz}\,\Delta\theta$$

$$= \Delta\theta + \Delta\theta + \Delta\theta + \Delta\theta$$

$$= 4\ \Delta\theta.$$

$$N^2(4)^2 = 1$$

$$16N^2 = 1$$

$$N = \frac{1}{4}$$

$$S^{A_1} = S_1 = \frac{1}{4}.4\Delta\theta = \Delta\theta.$$

Similarly,

$$E\ (S_1) = S_1$$

$$C_2\ (S_1) = S_1$$

$$\sigma_{xz}\ (S_1) = S_1$$

$$\sigma_{yz}\ (S_1) = S_1$$

$$E\ (S_3) = S_3$$

$$C_2\ (S_3) = \frac{1}{\sqrt{2}}\,C_2\left(\Delta d_1 - \Delta d_2\right)$$

$$= \frac{1}{\sqrt{2}}\left[\Delta d_2 - \Delta d_1\right]$$

$$= -\frac{1}{\sqrt{2}}\left[\Delta d_1 - \Delta d_2\right]$$

$$= -S_3$$

$$\sigma_{xz}\ (S_3) = -S_3$$

$$\sigma_{yz}\ (S_3) = S_3$$

	C_{2v}	E	C_2	σ_{xz}	σ_{yz}
A_1	S_1	1	1	1	1
A_1	S_2	1	1	1	1
B_2	S_3	1	–1	–1	1

...(12.40)

It is possible to express potential energy in symmetry co-ordinates:

$$2V = S'FS$$

$$2V = D'fD$$

It has been provided that:

$$F = UfU'$$

where U is a matrix that transforms internal co-ordinates Δd_1, Δd_2 and $\Delta\theta$ into S. The matrix transformation in two co-ordinate system is shown as, S = UD.

There are 3 × 3 – 6 = 9 – 6 = 3 S co-ordinates and so many internal co-ordinates f and g matrices $2V = D'fD$ and there can be expansion of potential energy by means of Taylor series using internal co-ordinates. There are nine force constant terms :

$$f = \begin{matrix} \\ \Delta d_1 \\ \Delta d_2 \\ \Delta\theta \end{matrix} \begin{vmatrix} \Delta d_1 & \Delta d_2 & \Delta\theta \\ f_{11} & f_{12} & f_{13} \\ f_{21} & f_{22} & f_{23} \\ f_{31} & f_{32} & f_{33} \end{vmatrix}$$

$$= \begin{matrix} \\ \Delta d_1 \\ \Delta d_2 \\ \Delta\theta \end{matrix} \begin{vmatrix} \Delta d_1 & \Delta d_2 & \Delta\theta \\ fd_1d_1 & fd_1d_2 & fd_1\theta \\ fd_2d_1 & fd_2d_2 & fd_2\theta \\ f\theta d_1 & f\theta d_2 & f\theta\theta \end{vmatrix} \quad ...(12.41)$$

$fd_1d_1 = fd_2d_2 = fd$ stretching of 0–H bond.

$f\theta\theta = f\theta$ = bending of bondangle

$f_{12} = f_{21}$ represent interaction of

$$fd_1d_2 = fd_2d_1 = fdd$$

One bond stretching with the other. There are identical O – H bonds so the force constants are the same:

$$\text{Viz } f_{21} = f_{12} = fdd$$

Introduction of one bond angle with bond stretching involves terms like:

$$f_{13} = f_{31};\ f_{32} = f_{23}$$

They are represented by the force constant fdθ. The matrix with elements fik is symmetrical across the diagonal:

$$f = \begin{bmatrix} fd & fdd & f\theta\theta \\ fdd & fd & fd\theta \\ fd\theta & fd\theta & f\theta \end{bmatrix}$$

$$fd = fd_1d_1$$

Hence U will be orthogonal matrix with 3 × 3 – 6 = 3 rows and 3 × 3 – 6 = 3 columns in H_2O. Symmetry co-ordinates belonging to A_1 symmetry species are S_1 = Äθ:

$$S_2 = \frac{1}{\sqrt{2}}\left(\Delta d_1 + \Delta d_2\right)$$

For generating U matrix (3 × 3).

We place A_1 first and then B_2. The symmetry co-ordinate generating B_2 symmetry species is:

$$S_3 = \frac{1}{\sqrt{2}}\left(\Delta d_1 - \Delta d_2\right)$$

The elements of S and D matrices are therefore:

$$S = \begin{bmatrix} S_1 \\ S_2 \\ S_3 \end{bmatrix} \text{column matrix.}$$

$$D = \begin{bmatrix} \Delta d_1 \\ \Delta d_2 \\ \Delta\theta \end{bmatrix} \text{another column matrix.}$$

$$\begin{vmatrix} F_{11} & F_{12} \\ F_{21} & F_{22} \end{vmatrix} = \begin{bmatrix} f\theta & \sqrt{2}fd\theta \\ \sqrt{2}fd\theta & fd + fdd \end{bmatrix}$$

and for B_2 there will be f_{33} = fd – fdd.

G. Matrix.

The kinetic energy matrix is given by:

$$\frac{\partial^2 D_1}{\partial t^2} = \dot{D}_1^2 = G_{11}^{-1}$$

$$\frac{\partial^2 D_2}{\partial t^2} = \dot{D}_2^2 = G_{22}^{-1}$$

$$\frac{\partial^2 D_3}{\partial t^2} = \dot{D}_3^2 = G_{33}^{-1}$$

$$T = T\left(\dot{D}_1, \dot{D}_2, \dot{D}_3\right)$$

The internal co-ordinates are:

$$D_1 = \Delta d_1, D_2 = \Delta d_2, D_3 = \Delta\theta$$

Expanding T in Taylor series and setting first derivatives zero along with $T_0 = 0$ we get

$$2T = g_{11}^{-1}\ \dot{D}_1^2 + g_{22}^{-1}\ \dot{D}_2^2 + g_{33}^{-1}\ \dot{D}_3^2 + 2g_{12}^{-1}\ \dot{D}_1\dot{D}_2$$
$$+2g_{13}^{-1}\ \dot{D}_1\,\dot{D}_3 + 2g_{23}^{-1}\ \dot{D}_1\ \dot{D}_3$$

and we reserve capital letters G^{-1} for symmetry co-ordinates:

$$2T = \dot{D}'g^{-1}\,\dot{D}$$

where S = UD

and $\dot{S} = \frac{ds}{dt} = U\frac{dD}{dt}$

$$\dot{S} = U\dot{D}$$

g matrix for water in 3 × 3.

$$\begin{array}{c|ccc} & \Delta\dot{d}_1 & \Delta\dot{d}_2 & \Delta\dot{\theta} \\ \Delta\dot{d}_1 & g_{11} & g_{12} & g_{13} \\ \Delta\dot{d}_2 & g_{21} & g_{22} & g_{23} \\ \Delta\dot{\theta} & g_{31} & g_{32} & g_{33} \end{array} = g$$

$$g' = \begin{bmatrix} g_{11} & g_{21} & g_{31} \\ g_{12} & g_{22} & g_{32} \\ g_{13} & g_{23} & g_{33} \end{bmatrix} = g^{-1}$$

Also, $$g^{-1} = \begin{bmatrix} g_{11}^{-1} & g_{12}^{-1} & g_{13}^{-1} \\ g_{21}^{-1} & g_{22}^{-1} & g_{23}^{-1} \\ g_{31}^{-1} & g_{32}^{-1} & g_{33}^{-1} \end{bmatrix}$$

By the same analogy:

$$g_{11}^{-1} = g_d^{-1} = g_{22}^{-1}$$

$$g_{12}^{-1} = g_{dd}^{-1} = g_{21}^{-1}$$

$$g_{13}^{-1} = g_{23}^{-1} = g_{31}^{-1} = g_{32}^{-1} = g_{d\theta}^{-1}$$

$$g_{33}^{-1} = g_{\theta}^{-1}$$

Hence,

$$g = \begin{bmatrix} g_d & g_{dd} & g_{d\theta} \\ g_{dd} & g_d & g_{d\theta} \\ g_{d\theta} & g_{d\theta} & g_{\theta} \end{bmatrix} \quad ...(12.42)$$

G matrix in terms of symmetric co-ordinates:

$$\dot{S} = U\dot{D}$$

$$\dot{S} = \begin{bmatrix} \dot{S}_1 \\ \dot{S}_2 \\ \dot{S}_3 \end{bmatrix} \qquad \dot{D} = \begin{bmatrix} \Delta\dot{d}_1 \\ \Delta\dot{d}_2 \\ \Delta\dot{\theta} \end{bmatrix}$$

U matrix is already known to be:

$$\begin{bmatrix} 0 & 0 & 1 \\ \frac{1}{\sqrt{2}} & \frac{1}{\sqrt{2}} & 0 \\ \frac{1}{\sqrt{2}} & -\frac{1}{\sqrt{2}} & 0 \end{bmatrix}$$

$$\begin{bmatrix} \dot{S}_1 \\ \dot{S}_2 \\ \dot{S}_3 \end{bmatrix} = \begin{bmatrix} 0 & 0 & 1 \\ \frac{1}{\sqrt{2}} & \frac{1}{\sqrt{2}} & 0 \\ \frac{1}{\sqrt{2}} & -\frac{1}{\sqrt{2}} & 0 \end{bmatrix} \begin{bmatrix} \Delta\dot{d}_1 \\ \Delta\dot{d}_2 \\ \Delta\dot{\theta} \end{bmatrix} \quad ...(12.43)$$

We define G matrix as follows:

$$G = UgU'$$

where U is transformation matrix from internal to symmetry co-ordinates:

$$G = \begin{bmatrix} 0 & 0 & 1 \\ \frac{1}{\sqrt{2}} & \frac{1}{\sqrt{2}} & 0 \\ \frac{1}{\sqrt{2}} & -\frac{1}{\sqrt{2}} & 0 \end{bmatrix} \begin{bmatrix} gd & gdd & gd\theta \\ gdd & gd & gd\theta \\ gd\theta & gd\theta & g\theta \end{bmatrix} \begin{bmatrix} 0 & \frac{1}{\sqrt{2}} & \frac{1}{\sqrt{2}} \\ 0 & \frac{1}{\sqrt{2}} & -\frac{1}{\sqrt{2}} \\ 1 & 0 & 0 \end{bmatrix}$$

$$= \begin{bmatrix} 0 & 0 & 1 \\ \frac{1}{\sqrt{2}} & \frac{1}{\sqrt{2}} & 0 \\ \frac{1}{\sqrt{2}} & -\frac{1}{\sqrt{2}} & 0 \end{bmatrix} \begin{bmatrix} gd\theta & \frac{1}{\sqrt{2}}(gd+gdd) & \frac{1}{\sqrt{2}}(gd-gdd) \\ gd\theta & \frac{1}{\sqrt{2}}(gd+gdd) & \frac{1}{\sqrt{2}}(gdd-gd) \\ g\theta & \sqrt{2}\,gd\theta & 0 \end{bmatrix}$$

$$= \begin{bmatrix} g_\theta & \sqrt{2}gd\theta & 0 \\ \sqrt{2}gd\theta & gd+gdd & \tfrac{1}{2}(\cancel{gd}-\cancel{gdd})+\tfrac{1}{2}(\cancel{gdd}-\cancel{gd}) \\ 0 & 0 & \tfrac{1}{2}(gd-gdd-gdd+gd) \end{bmatrix}$$

$$\left[\begin{array}{cc|c} \multicolumn{2}{c|}{A_1} & B_2 \\ \hline g_\theta & \sqrt{2}gd\theta & 0 \\ \sqrt{2}gd\theta & gd+gdd & 0 \\ \hline 0 & 0 & gd-gdd \end{array}\right] \qquad \text{...(12.44)}$$

For A_1 type vibrations the G-matrix has the terms:

$$\begin{bmatrix} G_{11} & G_{12} \\ G_{21} & G_{22} \end{bmatrix} = \begin{bmatrix} g_\theta & \sqrt{2}gd\theta \\ \sqrt{2}gd\theta & gd+gdd \end{bmatrix}$$

$$G_{33} = gd - gdd$$

Elements of G matrix are solved by Wilson vector method resulting the values:

$$g_d = \mu_H + \mu_o$$
$$g_{dd} = \mu_o \cos\theta$$
$$g_{d\theta} = -(\mu_o / r)\sin\theta$$
$$g_\theta = 2\,(\mu_H + \mu_o - \mu_o \cos\theta)/r^2$$

Where, $\mu_H = \dfrac{1}{m_H}$ in amu

$$\mu_o = \frac{1}{m_O}$$

$$\theta = 104^\circ\ 31' \quad r = 0.9580\ A^\circ$$

With this the G matrix is:

$$G = \begin{bmatrix} -2.332 & -0.0893 & 0 \\ -0.0893 & 1.0390 & 0 \\ 0 & 0 & 1.0702 \end{bmatrix}$$

Hence,

$$G^{-1} = \begin{bmatrix} -2.32 & -0.0893 & 0 \\ -0.0893 & 1.0390 & 0 \\ 0 & 0 & 1.0702 \end{bmatrix}$$

Solution of secular equation:

$$\left|F - \lambda G^{-1}\right| = 0$$

or, $$\left|GF - \lambda E\right| = 0$$

For A_1 type of vibrations:

$$\left[\begin{bmatrix} G_{11} & G_{12} \\ G_{21} & G_{22} \end{bmatrix} \begin{bmatrix} F_{11} & F_{12} \\ F_{21} & F_{22} \end{bmatrix} - \begin{bmatrix} \lambda & 0 \\ 0 & \lambda \end{bmatrix}\right] = 0$$

or, $$\begin{bmatrix} G_{11}F_{11} + G_{12}F_{21} & G_{11}F_{12} + G_{12}F_{22} \\ G_{21}F_{11} + G_{22}F_{21} & G_{21}F_{12} + G_{22}F_{22} \end{bmatrix} - \begin{bmatrix} \lambda & 0 \\ 0 & \lambda \end{bmatrix} = 0$$

or, $$\begin{bmatrix} G_{11}F_{11} + G_{12}F_{21} - \lambda & G_{11}F_{12} + G_{12}F_{22} \\ G_{21}F_{11} + G_{22}F_{21} & G_{21}F_{12} + G_{22}F_{22} - \lambda \end{bmatrix} = 0$$

or, $$\left(G_{11}F_{11}+G_{12}F_{21}-\lambda\right)\left(G_{21}F_{12}+G_{32}F_{22}-\lambda\right)$$
$$-\left(G_{11}F_{12}+Q_{12}F_{22}\right)\left(G_{21}F_{11}+G_{22}F_{21}\right)=0$$

or, $$\lambda^2-\left(G_{11}F_{11}+G_{12}F_{12}+G_{12}F_{12}+G_{22}F_{23}\right)\lambda$$
$$+\left(F_{11}F_{22}-F_{12}^2\right)\left(G_{11}G_{22}-G_{12}^2\right)=0 \qquad ...(12.45)$$

This is quadratic in λ and we obtain λ values out of which υ values can be made known.

For B_2 vibrations:

$$\left[[F_{33}]\,[G_{33}]-E\lambda\right]=0$$

or, $$\left[(fd-fdd)\,(gd-gdd)-\lambda(1)\right]=0$$

Now gd – gdd = 1.0702

Hence, $$\left[(fd-fdd)1.0702-\lambda(1)\right]=0$$

or, $$1.0702\ (fd-fdd)=\lambda_3$$

$$\upsilon_3=\frac{1.0702\,(fd-fdd)}{2\pi c} \qquad ...(12.46)$$

12.13 (b) Normal Vibrational Analysis of Ammonia

There are 3N – 6 = 3 × 4 – 6 = 12 – 6 = 6 normal modes. We construct secular equation by F-G matrix method. Following the method of unshifted atoms/vectors we calculate Γ_R for NH_3:

C_{3v}	E	$2C_3$	$3\sigma_v$
Γ_R	12	0	2

$\Gamma_R = 3A_1 + A_2 + 4E$ using formula. From C.T.

$$\Gamma_t = A_1 + E$$
$$\Gamma_r = A_2 + E$$

$$\Gamma_{t+r} = A_1 + A_2 + 2E$$
$$\Gamma_{3N-6} = 3A_1 + A_2 + 4E - (A_1 + A_2 + 2E)$$
$$= 2A_1 + 2E$$

We can envoke selection rules for I.R. and Raman spectra.

Nature of Vibrations from Internal Co-ordinates

The nature of genuine vibrations ($2A_1 + 2E$) on using internal co-ordinates: d_1, d_2, d_3 & θ_1, θ_2 and θ_3.

$$\Gamma_{Str} = 3 \quad 0 \quad 1 \qquad A_1 + E$$

$$\Gamma_{\theta} = 3 \quad 0 \quad 1 \qquad A_1 + E$$

We find that both stretching and bending modes are of two types (A_1 + E):

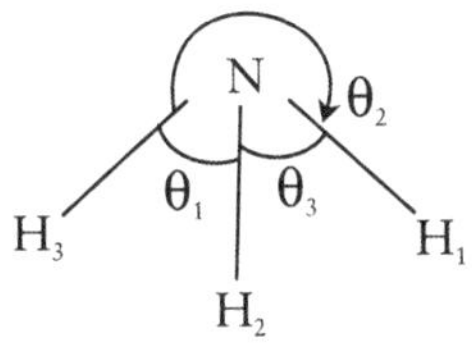

Let, $\quad H_1\hat{N}-H_2 = \theta_3 \quad H_1 - \hat{N} - H_3 = \theta_2$

$$H_2 - \hat{N} - H_3 = \theta_1$$

Changes in the internal co-ordinates are Δd_1, Δd_2, Δd_3, and $\Delta\theta_1$, $\Delta\theta_2$ and $\Delta\theta_3$ in case of normal vibrations of the molecule. For bond length changes we obtain projection vectors as follows:

$$\begin{aligned}\tilde{P}^{A_1}\ \Delta d_1 &= 1\times\tilde{E}\,\Delta d_1 + 1\times\tilde{C}_3\,\Delta d_1 + 1\times\tilde{C}_3^2\ \Delta d_1 + 1\times\tilde{\sigma}_1\ \Delta d_1 \\ &\qquad +1\times\tilde{\sigma}_2\,\Delta d_1 + 1\times\tilde{\sigma}_3\ \Delta d_1 \\ &= \Delta d_1 + \Delta d_2 + \Delta d_3 + \Delta d_1 + \Delta d_3 + \Delta d_2 \\ &= 2\left(\Delta d_1 + \Delta d_2 + \Delta d_3\right)\end{aligned}$$

Normalizing factor will be:

$$N^2\left[2^2 + 2^2 + 2^2\right] = 1$$

$$N^2 \times 12 = 1$$

$$N = \frac{1}{2\sqrt{3}}$$

$$\begin{aligned}S^{A_1} &= \frac{1}{2\sqrt{3}}\,2\left(\Delta d_1 + \Delta d_2 + \Delta d_3\right) \\ &= \frac{1}{\sqrt{3}}\left(\Delta d_1 + \Delta d_2 + \Delta d_3\right)\end{aligned}$$

$$\tilde{P}_E\ \Delta d_1 = 2\times\tilde{E}\ \Delta d_1 + (-1)\ \tilde{C}_3\ \Delta d_1 + (-1)\ \tilde{C}_3^2\ \Delta d_1 + 0$$

$$= \left[2\Delta d_1 - \Delta d_2 - \Delta d_3\right]$$

$$\therefore N^2\ [4+1+1] = 1$$

or,
$$N = \frac{1}{\sqrt{6}}$$

$$S^E = \frac{1}{\sqrt{6}}\left[2\Delta d_1 - \Delta d_2 - \Delta d_3\right]$$

Symmetry co-ordinates for A_1 & E bending vibrations are now determined:

$$P^{A_1}\ \Delta\theta_1 = 1\times E\Delta\theta_1 + 1\times C_3\ \Delta\theta_1 + 1\times C_3^2\ \Delta\theta_1 + 1\times\sigma_1\ \Delta\theta_1$$

$$+1\times\sigma_2\ \Delta\theta_1 + 1\times\sigma_3\ \Delta\theta_1$$

$$= \Delta\theta_1 + \Delta\theta_2 + \Delta\theta_3 + \Delta\theta_1 + \Delta\theta_2 + \Delta\theta_3$$

$$= 2(\Delta\theta_1 + \Delta\theta_2 + \Delta\theta_3)$$

$$N = \frac{1}{2\sqrt{3}}$$

$$\therefore S^{A_1} = \frac{1}{\sqrt{3}}(\Delta\theta_1 + \Delta\theta_2 + \Delta\theta_3)$$

$$P^E\ \Delta\theta_1 = 2\tilde{E}\ \Delta\theta_1 + (-1)\ \tilde{C}_3\ \Delta\theta_1 - 1\times\tilde{C}_3^2\ \Delta\theta_1 + 0$$

$$= 2\Delta\theta_1 - \Delta\theta_2 - \Delta\theta_3$$

$$S^E = \frac{1}{\sqrt{6}}(2\Delta\theta_1 - \Delta\theta_2 - \Delta\theta_3)$$

E type of vibrations are doubly degenerate. The expression which we had determined stands for 'a' type of E vibration, i.e.

$$S_a^E = \frac{1}{\sqrt{6}}(2\Delta\theta_1 - \Delta\theta_2 - \Delta\theta_3)$$

$$S_a^E = \frac{1}{\sqrt{6}}(2\Delta d_1 - \Delta d_2 - \Delta d_3)$$

Let us consider a second basis vector of the form $S_b^E = b_1\,\Delta d_1 + b_2\Delta d_2 + b_3\Delta d_3$ the change with basis may be given in the matrix form:

$$\left[S^{A_1}\,S_a^E\,S_b^E\right] = \left[\Delta d_1\,\Delta d_2\,\Delta d_3\right]\begin{bmatrix} 1/\sqrt{3} & 2/\sqrt{6} & b_1 \\ 1/\sqrt{3} & -1/\sqrt{6} & b_2 \\ 1/\sqrt{3} & -1/\sqrt{6} & b_3 \end{bmatrix}$$

In similar way we determine the bond deformation mode:

$$\left[S^{A_1}\,S_a^E\,S_b^E\right] = \left[\Delta\theta_1\,\Delta\theta_2\,\Delta\theta_3\right]\begin{bmatrix} 1/\sqrt{3} & 2/\sqrt{6} & b_1 \\ 1/\sqrt{3} & -1/\sqrt{6} & b_2 \\ 1/\sqrt{3} & -1/\sqrt{6} & b_3 \end{bmatrix} \quad ...(12.47)$$

Since the transformation matrix (3 × 3) is orthogonal, we may deduce the following relations from its properties:

$$b_1^2 + b_2^2 + b_3^2 = 1$$

$$\frac{1}{\sqrt{3}}b_1 + \frac{1}{\sqrt{3}}b_2 + \frac{1}{\sqrt{3}}b_3 = 0$$

$$\frac{2}{\sqrt{6}}b_1 - \frac{1}{\sqrt{6}}b_2 - \frac{1}{\sqrt{6}}b_3 = 0$$

From the last two equations there can be:

$$\frac{b_1}{\sqrt{3}}\left(\sqrt{2}+1\right) + \frac{\sqrt{2}-1}{\sqrt{6}}\left(b_2 + b_3\right) = 0$$

or, $$b_1\left(\sqrt{2}+1\right) + \frac{\sqrt{2}-1}{\sqrt{2}}\left(b_2 + b_3\right) = 0$$

or, $$b_1\left(1+\sqrt{2}\right) + \left(1 - \frac{1}{\sqrt{2}}\right)\left(b_2 + b_3\right) = 0$$

The condition holds if $b_1 = 0$.

This on substitution:

$$0.\left(\sqrt{2}+1\right) + \left(1 - \frac{1}{\sqrt{2}}\right)\left(b_2 + b_3\right) = 0$$

or, $(b_2 + b_3) = 0$ or $b_2 = -b_3$

From, $b_1^2 + b_2^2 + b_3^2 = 1$

or, $b_1^2 + 2b_2^2 = 1$

or, $0 + 2b_2^2 = 1$

$$b_2^2 = \frac{1}{2} \qquad b_2 = \frac{1}{\sqrt{2}} \qquad b_3 = -\frac{1}{\sqrt{2}}$$

$$\therefore\ S_b^E = \frac{1}{\sqrt{2}}\left(\Delta d_2 - \Delta d_3\right)$$

$$\&\ S_b^E = \frac{1}{\sqrt{2}}\left(\Delta\theta_2 - \Delta\theta_3\right).$$

Under such conditions both A_1 & E type of vibrations may have the following symmetry coordinates:

$$S_1 = \frac{1}{\sqrt{3}}\left(\Delta d_1 + \Delta d_2 + \Delta d_3\right)$$

$$S_2 = \frac{1}{\sqrt{3}}\left(\Delta\theta_1 + \Delta\theta_2 + \Delta\theta_3\right)$$

$$S_{3a} = \frac{1}{\sqrt{6}}\left(2\Delta d_1 - \Delta d_2 - \Delta d_3\right)$$

$$\Delta S_{3b} = \frac{1}{\sqrt{2}}\left(\Delta d_2 - \Delta d_3\right)$$

$$S_{4a} = \frac{1}{\sqrt{3}}\left(2\Delta\theta_1 - \Delta\theta_2 - \Delta\theta_3\right)$$

$$S_{4b} = \frac{1}{\sqrt{2}}\left(\Delta\theta_2 - \Delta\theta_3\right)$$

These symmetry co-ordinates form bases for the A_1 and E representations. (The angles have been indexed so that $\theta_i'^s$ are opposite to d_i^s. This assures that θ_i^s and changes there in $\Delta\theta_i$ are related to symmetry elements in the same way as are d_i and Δd_i). We now place the SALCs occupying corresponding positions in the expression and only then we achieve symmetry factorization otherwise we cannot. The transformation matrix will then, be S = UD.

$$S = \begin{bmatrix} S_1 \\ S_2 \\ S_{3a} \\ S_{3b} \\ S_{4a} \\ S_{4b} \end{bmatrix} \quad D = \begin{bmatrix} d_1 \\ d_2 \\ d_3 \\ \theta_1 \\ \theta_2 \\ \theta_3 \end{bmatrix} \text{ or } \begin{bmatrix} \Delta d_1 \\ \Delta d_2 \\ \Delta d_3 \\ \Delta\theta_1 \\ \Delta\theta_2 \\ \Delta\theta_3 \end{bmatrix}$$

There will be 6 × 6 transformation matrix U.

U	Δd_1	Δd_2	Δd_3	$\Delta\theta_1$	$\Delta\theta_2$	$\Delta\theta_3$
S_1	$1/\sqrt{3}$	$1/\sqrt{3}$	$1/\sqrt{3}$	0	0	0
S_2	0	0	0	$1/\sqrt{3}$	$1/\sqrt{3}$	$1/\sqrt{3}$
S_{3a}	$2/\sqrt{6}$	$-1/\sqrt{6}$	$-1/\sqrt{6}$	0	0	0
S_{3b}	0	$1/\sqrt{2}$	$-1/\sqrt{2}$	0	0	0
S_{4a}	0	0	0	$2/\sqrt{6}$	$-1/\sqrt{6}$	$-1/\sqrt{6}$
S_{4b}	0	0	0	0	$1/\sqrt{2}$	$-1/\sqrt{2}$

...(12.48)

Its transpose:

$$U' = \begin{bmatrix} 1/\sqrt{3} & 0 & 2/\sqrt{6} & 0 & 0 & 0 \\ 1/\sqrt{3} & 0 & -1/\sqrt{6} & 1/\sqrt{2} & 0 & 0 \\ 1/\sqrt{3} & 0 & -1/\sqrt{6} & -1/\sqrt{2} & 0 & 0 \\ 0 & 1/\sqrt{3} & 0 & 0 & \sqrt{2/6} & 0 \\ 0 & 1/\sqrt{3} & 0 & 0 & -1/\sqrt{6} & 1/\sqrt{2} \\ 0 & 1/\sqrt{3} & 0 & 0 & -1/\sqrt{6} & -1/\sqrt{2} \end{bmatrix}$$

The f matrix in displacement co-ordinates is:

$$\begin{array}{c} \\ \Delta d_1 \\ \Delta d_2 \\ \Delta d_3 \\ \Delta\theta_1 \\ \Delta\theta_2 \\ \Delta\theta_3 \end{array}\begin{bmatrix} \Delta d_1 & \Delta d_2 & \Delta d_3 & \Delta\theta_1 & \Delta\theta_2 & \Delta\theta_3 \\ f_{11} & f_{12} & f_{13} & f_{14} & f_{15} & f_{16} \\ f_{21} & f_{22} & f_{23} & f_{24} & f_{25} & f_{26} \\ - & - & - & - & - & - \\ - & - & - & - & - & - \\ - & - & - & - & - & - \\ f_{61} & f_{62} & f_{63} & f_{64} & f_{65} & f_{66} \end{bmatrix}$$

$$= \begin{bmatrix} fd & fdd' & fdd' & 0 & fd\theta & fd\theta \\ fdd & fd & fdd' & fd\theta & 0 & fd\theta \\ fdd & fdd' & fd & fd\theta & fd\theta & 0 \\ 0 & fd\theta & fd\theta & f\theta & 0 & 0 \\ fd\theta & 0 & fd\theta & 0 & f\theta & 0 \\ fd\theta & fd\theta & 0 & 0 & 0 & f\theta \end{bmatrix} \quad ...(12.49)$$

The interaction between stretching a bond and deforming an angle to which the bond does not belong and also the interaction between two angle deformation respectively have been omitted. There are two sets of doubly degenerate vibrations, altogether there are only four fundamental frequencies. It would not be possible to solve for all six force constants by using the data for only a single isotopic species so two terms are also ignored. In the valency force field we have quadratic force field and it is directly related to bond length extensions and bond angle increases in the internal coordinates.

All three bonds as well as three bond angles are symmetrically equivalent. There are only six distinct f matrix elements to occupy 21 places out of 6 × 6 = 36. The stretching of bonds will have force constants term across the diagonal:

$$f_{11} = f_{22} = f_{33} = fd. \text{ (say)}$$

The force constants for increase in bond angle fθ will occupy the remaining diagonal positions, $f_{44} = f_{55} = f_{66} = f_\theta$.

The interaction force constants appear as off diagonal elements they represent contribution to potential energy arising from products of two internal co-ordinates:

$$fdd' = f_{12} = f_{23} = f_{13}$$

$$f\theta\theta' = f_{45} = f_{46} = f_{56}$$

The terms of the type, $fd\theta = f_{16} = f_{15} = f_{24} = f_{26} = f_{34} = f_{35}$

Then we have:

$$fd\theta' = f_{14} = f_{25} = f_{36} = 0$$

Now fU′ is taken which is then premultiplied by U, viz. UfU′.

This gives, $F = UfU'$

We finally write down the F matrix in the block structure. There is one A_1 block and two E blocks:

$$F = \left|\begin{array}{c|c|c} \begin{array}{c} A_1 \text{ modes} \\ fd + fdd' \; 2fd\theta \end{array} & \begin{array}{c} \text{a component} \\ \text{of E mode} \\ 0 \end{array} & \begin{array}{c} \text{b component of} \\ \text{E mode} \end{array} \\ \hline 0 & \begin{array}{c} fd - fdd' - fd\theta \\ - fd\theta \; f\theta \end{array} & \\ \hline & & \begin{array}{c} fd - fdd' - fd\theta \\ - fd\theta \; f\theta \end{array} \end{array}\right.$$

It has block structure. Both a and b component of 2 × 2 matrices are identical. Consider G matrix. There are six co-ordinates in ammonia and there are 6 × 6 = 36 elements of the g matrix:

$$\begin{array}{c} g \\ \Delta d_1 \\ \Delta d_2 \\ \Delta d_3 \\ \Delta\theta_1 \\ \Delta\theta_2 \\ \Delta\theta_3 \end{array} \begin{bmatrix} \Delta d_1 & \Delta d_2 & \Delta d_3 & \Delta\theta_1 & \Delta\theta_2 & \Delta\theta_3 \\ g^2_{dd} & g'_{dd'} & g'_{dd'} & g'_{d\theta^{(2)}} & g^2_{\ d\theta} & g^2_{d\theta} \\ & g^2_{\ dd} & g'_{dd'} & g^2_{\ d\theta} & g'_{d\theta^{(2)}} & g^2_{\ d\theta} \\ & & g^2dd & g^2d\theta & gd\theta^2 & g'd'\theta^{(2)} \\ & & & g^3_{\ \theta\theta} & g^2_{\ \theta\theta'^{(1)}} & g^2_{\ d\theta'^{(1)}} \\ & & & & g^3_{\ \theta\theta} & g_{\theta\theta'^{(1)}} \\ & & & & & g^3_{\ \theta\theta} \end{bmatrix}$$

There were three classes of g matrix elements g_{dd}, $g_{\theta\theta}$ & $g_{d\theta}$. We use double scripts to specify the kinds of internal co-ordinates involved. This will give off diagonal elements similar, showing only other side of the off diagonal elements one has the matrix as above. We have utilized earlier the values of U and U'. Similarly on this basis we obtain $G = UgU'$. Similarly G matrix is symmetry factored into 2 × 2 block for A_1 and two identical 2 × 2 blocks corresponding to E:

A_1		E_a		E_b	
$g_{dd} + 2g'_{dd'}$	$g'_{d\theta(2)} + g^2{}_{d\theta}$	0	0	0	0
$g'_{d\theta(2)} + g^2{}_{d\theta}$	$g^3{}_{\theta\theta} + 2g^2{}_{\theta\theta(1)}$	0	0	0	0
0	0	$g^2{}_{dd} - g'_{dd'}$	$g'_{d\theta(2)} - 2g^2{}_{d\theta}$	0	0
0	0	$g'_{d\theta(2)} - 2g^2{}_{d\theta}$	$g^3{}_{\theta\theta} - 2g^2{}_{\theta\theta(1)}$	0	0
0	0	0	0	$g^2{}_{dd} - g'_{dd'}$	$g'_{d\theta(2)} - 2g^2{}_{\theta\theta}$
0	0	0	0	$g'_{d\theta(2)} - 2g^2{}_{d\theta}$	$g^3{}_{\theta\theta} - 2g^2{}_{\theta\theta(1)}$

Both F and G matrices are similarly factorized, and so their product is obtained for each block separately. There will be three separate secular equations for A_1, E & E block. The two blocks are of same elements, so we consider only one of them. The secular equation brought from A_1 is:

$$\begin{bmatrix} fd + 2fdd' & 2fd\theta \\ 2fd\theta & f\theta \end{bmatrix}\begin{bmatrix} g^2{}_{dd} + 2g'_{dd'} & g'_{d\theta(2)} + 2g^2{}_{d\theta} \\ g'_{d\theta(2)} + 2g^2{}_{d\theta} & g^3{}_{\theta\theta} + 2g^2{}_{\theta\theta(1)} \end{bmatrix} - \lambda\begin{bmatrix} 1 & 0 \\ 0 & 1 \end{bmatrix} = 0$$

We can apply the same designations of g matrix elements as were done for f matrix. However, due to symmetry of the molecule many of the g elements are equivalent. The equivalent elements are listed in the following way:

$$g_{dd} = g_d = g^2{}_{dd}$$

$$g_{dd'} = g'_{dd'}$$

$$g_{d\theta_1} = g_{d\theta_2} = g_{d\theta_3} = g'_{d\theta(1)}$$

$$g_{d_1d_2} = g'_{dd} \text{ etc.}$$

$$g_{\theta_1\theta_1} = g_{\theta_2\theta_2} = g_{\theta_3\theta_3} = g^3{}_{\theta\theta}$$

$$g_{\theta_1\theta_2} = g_{\theta_2\theta_3} = g_{\theta_1\theta_3} = g^2{}_{\theta\theta}$$

The equivalent g elements are listed and given a common symbol. The g matrix is also symmetric about the diagonal. By the same procedure G matrices for the A_1 & E. Vibrations may be determined from the matrix multiplication. The U and U′ matrices are the same as used for the F matrix.

Use of Symmetry Co-ordinates

The F matrix will be determined for each vibrational species which for NH_3 are A_1 and E. For A_1 vibration only A_1 symmetry co-ordinates are used for the U matrix while calculating F matrix.

For A_1 type there were two symmetry co-ordinates S_1 & S_2.

$$S_1 = \frac{1}{\sqrt{3}}\left(\Delta d_1 + \Delta d_2 + \Delta d_3\right)$$

$$S_2 = \frac{1}{\sqrt{3}}\left(\Delta\theta_1 + \Delta\theta_2 + \Delta\theta_3\right)$$

Our U matrix was:

$$U = \begin{bmatrix} 1/\sqrt{3} & 1/\sqrt{3} & 1/\sqrt{3} & 0 & 0 & 0 \\ 0 & 0 & 0 & 1/\sqrt{3} & 1/\sqrt{3} & 1/\sqrt{3} \end{bmatrix}$$

On exchanging rows and columns we have:

$$U' = \begin{bmatrix} 1/\sqrt{3} & 0 \\ 1/\sqrt{3} & 0 \\ 1/\sqrt{3} & 0 \\ 0 & 1/\sqrt{3} \\ 0 & 1/\sqrt{3} \\ 0 & 1/\sqrt{3} \end{bmatrix}$$

The complete f matrix is used for fU'.

$$
fU' = \underset{6\times 6}{\begin{bmatrix} fd & fdd' & fdd' & 0 & fd\theta & fd\theta \\ fdd' & fd & fdd' & fd\theta & 0 & fd\theta \\ fdd' & fdd' & fd & fd\theta & fd\theta & 0 \\ 0 & fd\theta & fd\theta & f\theta & 0 & 0 \\ fd\theta & 0 & fd\theta & 0 & f\theta & 0 \\ fd\theta & fd\theta & 0 & 0 & 0 & f\theta \end{bmatrix}} \underset{6\times 2}{\begin{bmatrix} 1/\sqrt{3} & 0 \\ 1/\sqrt{3} & 0 \\ 1/\sqrt{3} & 0 \\ 0 & 1/\sqrt{3} \\ 0 & 1/\sqrt{3} \\ 0 & 1/\sqrt{3} \end{bmatrix}}
$$

$$
= \underset{6\times 2}{\begin{bmatrix} 1/\sqrt{3}(fd + fdd' + fdd') & 1/\sqrt{3}(fd\theta + fd\theta) \\ 1/\sqrt{3}(fdd' + fd + fdd') & 1/\sqrt{3}(fd\theta + fd\theta) \\ 1/\sqrt{3}(fdd' + fdd' + fd) & 2/\sqrt{3}\, fd\theta \\ 2/\sqrt{3}\, fd\theta & 1/\sqrt{3}\, f\theta \\ 2/\sqrt{3}\, fd\theta & 1/\sqrt{3}\, f\theta \\ 2/\sqrt{3}\, fd\theta & 1/\sqrt{3}\, f\theta \end{bmatrix}}
$$

$$
= \begin{bmatrix} 1/\sqrt{3}(fd + 2fdd') & 2/\sqrt{3}\, fd\theta \\ 1/\sqrt{3}(2fdd' + fd) & 2/\sqrt{3}\, fd\theta \\ 1/\sqrt{3}(2fdd' + fd) & 2/\sqrt{3}\, fd\theta \\ 2/\sqrt{3}\, fd\theta & 1/\sqrt{3}\, f\theta \\ 2/\sqrt{3}\, fd\theta & 1/\sqrt{3}\, f\theta \\ 2/\sqrt{3}\, fd\theta & 1/\sqrt{3}\, f\theta \end{bmatrix}
$$

This in turn is multiplied by U.

$$
\underset{2\times 6}{\begin{bmatrix} 1/\sqrt{3} & 1/\sqrt{3} & 1/\sqrt{3} & 0 & 0 & 0 \\ 0 & 0 & 0 & 1/\sqrt{3} & 1/\sqrt{3} & 1/\sqrt{3} \end{bmatrix}} \underset{6\times 2}{\begin{bmatrix} 1/\sqrt{3}(2fdd' + fd) & 2/\sqrt{3}\, fd\theta \\ 1/\sqrt{3}(2fdd' + fd) & 2/\sqrt{3}\, fd\theta \\ 1/\sqrt{3}(2fdd' + fd) & 2/\sqrt{3}\, fd\theta \\ 2/\sqrt{3}\, fd\theta & 1/\sqrt{3}\, f\theta \\ 2/\sqrt{3}\, fd\theta & 1/\sqrt{3}\, f\theta \\ 2/\sqrt{3}\, fd\theta & 1/\sqrt{3}\, f\theta \end{bmatrix}}
$$

$$= \begin{bmatrix} 1/3\left(2\text{fdd}' + \text{fd}\right) \times 3 & 2/3\left(\text{fd}\theta\right) \times 3 \\ 2/3\left(\text{fd}\theta\right) \times 3 & 1/3\left(\text{f}\theta\right) \times 3 \end{bmatrix}_{2\times 2}$$

$$= \begin{bmatrix} 2\,\text{fdd}' + \text{fd} & 2\text{fd}\theta \\ 2\text{fd}\theta & \text{f}\theta \end{bmatrix} = \text{F matrix} = \text{UfU}' \text{ for } A_1 .$$

Similarly, we use (S_{3a} and S_{4a}) or (S_{3b} and S_{4b}) for generating F matrix belonging to E vibrations (both yield identical results). U matrix for S_{3a} and S_{4a} corresponding to E symmetry species is:

$$\begin{bmatrix} 2/\sqrt{6} & -1/\sqrt{6} & -1/\sqrt{6} & 0 & 0 & 0 \\ 0 & 0 & 0 & 2/\sqrt{6} & -1/\sqrt{6} & -1/\sqrt{6} \end{bmatrix}$$

Similarly, $\text{U}' = \begin{bmatrix} 2/\sqrt{6} & 0 \\ -1/\sqrt{6} & 0 \\ -1/\sqrt{6} & 0 \\ 0 & 2/\sqrt{6} \\ 0 & -1/\sqrt{6} \\ 0 & -1/\sqrt{6} \end{bmatrix}$

So,

$$\text{fU}' = \begin{bmatrix} \text{fd} & \text{fdd}' & \text{fdd}' & 0 & \text{fd}\theta & \text{fd}\theta \\ \text{fdd}' & \text{fd} & \text{fdd}' & \text{fd}\theta & 0 & \text{fd}\theta \\ \text{fdd}' & \text{fdd}' & \text{fd} & \text{fd}\theta & \text{fd}\theta & 0 \\ 0 & \text{fd}\theta & \text{fd}\theta & \text{f}\theta & 0 & 0 \\ \text{fd}\theta & 0 & \text{fd}\theta & 0 & \text{f}\theta & 0 \\ \text{fd}\theta & \text{fd}\theta & 0 & 0 & 0 & \text{f}\theta \end{bmatrix}_{6\times 6} \cdot \begin{bmatrix} 2/\sqrt{6} & 0 \\ -1/\sqrt{6} & 0 \\ -1/\sqrt{6} & 0 \\ 0 & 2/\sqrt{6} \\ 0 & -1/\sqrt{3} \\ 0 & -1/\sqrt{3} \end{bmatrix}_{6\times 2}$$

$$= \begin{bmatrix} 2/\sqrt{6}\,(fd - fdd' & -2/\sqrt{6}fd\theta \\ 1/\sqrt{6}\left(fdd' - fd - fdd'\right) & 1/\sqrt{6}\,fd\theta \\ 1/\sqrt{6}\left(fdd' - fd\right) & 1/\sqrt{6}\,fd\theta \\ -2/\sqrt{6}\;fd\theta & 2/\sqrt{6}\;f\theta \\ 1/\sqrt{6}\;fd\theta & -1/\sqrt{6}\,f\theta \\ 1/\sqrt{6}\,fd\theta & -1/\sqrt{6}\,f\theta \end{bmatrix}$$

$$6 \times 2$$

Now, we take up $F = UfU'$ for E vibrations:

$$= \begin{bmatrix} 2/\sqrt{6} & -1/\sqrt{6} & -1/\sqrt{6} & 0 & 0 & 0 \\ 0 & 0 & 0 & 2/\sqrt{6} & -1/\sqrt{6} & -1/\sqrt{6} \end{bmatrix} \begin{bmatrix} 2/\sqrt{6}\left(fd - fdd'\right) & -1/\sqrt{6}fd\theta \\ 1/\sqrt{6}\left(fdd' - fd\right) & 1/\sqrt{6}\,fd\theta \\ 1/\sqrt{6}\left(fdd' - fd\right) & 1/\sqrt{6}\,fd\theta \\ -2/\sqrt{6}\,fd\theta & 2/\sqrt{6}f\theta \\ 1/\sqrt{6}\,fd\theta & -1/\sqrt{6}\,f\theta \\ 1/\sqrt{6}\,fd\theta & -fd\theta \end{bmatrix}$$

$$= \begin{bmatrix} 4/6\left(fd - fdd'\right) - 1/6\,\left(fdd' - fd\right) - \frac{1}{6}\left(fdd' - fd\right) & -fd\theta \\ -fd\theta & f\theta \end{bmatrix}$$

$$= \begin{bmatrix} \frac{1}{6}\left[4fd + 2fd\right] - \frac{1}{6}\,6fdd' & -fd\theta \\ -fd\theta & f\theta \end{bmatrix}$$

$$= \begin{bmatrix} fd - fdd' & -fd\theta \\ -fd\theta & f\theta \end{bmatrix}$$

Solved Examples

1. Express the equation in quadratic form in the matrix form:

$$5x_1^2 + 6x_1x_2 + 2x_2^2$$

is in a quadratic form. It can be written in a matrix form using row and column.

Such as,

$$\begin{bmatrix} x_1 \, x_2 \end{bmatrix} \begin{bmatrix} 5 & 3 \\ 3 & 2 \end{bmatrix} \begin{bmatrix} x_1 \\ x_2 \end{bmatrix}$$

There is a 2×2 matrix in the middle. The off diagonal elements are so chosen that the sum is fixed. The other matrix will also serve. $\begin{bmatrix} 5 & 4 \\ 2 & 2 \end{bmatrix} \begin{bmatrix} 5 & 0 \\ 6 & 2 \end{bmatrix}$ But only $\begin{bmatrix} 5 & 3 \\ 3 & 2 \end{bmatrix}$ is a symmetric matrix.

Potential energy is always expressed by symmetric matrix whose elements are force constants.

2. Discuss normal vibrations of CO_2.

The numbers of internal motion of a linear molecule is given by 3n-5 Q co-ordinates. The forms of normal modes of vibrations of AB_2 linear are shown below:

(a) Q_1

(b) Q_4

(c) Q_2

(d) Q_3

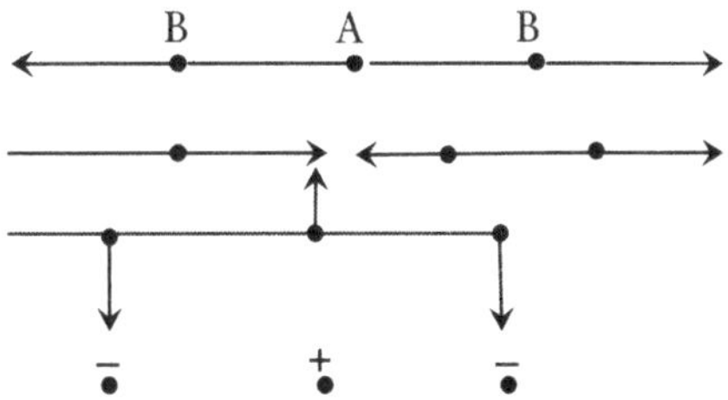

Four normal co-ordinates are assigned from Q_1, Q_2, Q_3 & Q_4 for these motions:

(a) Involves motion of three atoms in the same plane. It occurs in the plane of the paper. (c) and (d) are similar except that it takes place in a plane at right angles to the plane of paper. They form a degenerate pair.

3. Outline procedure of writing out the character Table for CO_2 ($D_{\alpha h}$) and evaluate characters for stretching and bending vectors for this point group for such a molecule.

There are two possible cases of linear system Cαv and Dαh and both cases designations are the same as in electronic states of diatomic molecules, if character is 1 for symmetric with the plane of symmetry through molecular axis it is given Σ^+.

If character is –1 for anti-symmetric with the plane of symmetry through the molecular axis it is assigned the designation Σ^-.

For degenerate vibrations Π, Δ, Φ will be given with the increasing order of degeneracy in case of CO_2 for which the point group is Dαh. It includes operations such as E, Cϕ, $C_{-\phi}$. It has clockwise and counter clockwise rotations by an arbitrary angle ϕ about the Cα axis, we write in character Table as 2 Cϕ. The improper rotations are Sϕ and $S_{-\phi}$ = 2Sϕ. There are other operations such as ασv i $2S_\phi$ ..... αC_2

Dαh	E	2Cϕ.......ασv		i	$2S_\phi$.......αC_2		
Σ_g^+	1	1	1	1	1	1	
Σ_u^+	1	1	1	–1	–1	–1	z
Σ_g^-	1	1	–1	1	1	–1	Rz
Σ_u^-	1	1	–1	–1	–1	1	
Π_g^-	2	2cosϕ	0	1	–2cosϕ	0	R_x, R_y
Π_u^-	2	2cosϕ	0	–2	.2cosϕ	0	x, y

There are two stretching vectors r_1 & r_2. Both r_1 & r_2 are un-shifted $O \overset{r_1}{\_\_} C \overset{r_2}{\_\_} O \rightarrow$ z-axis and θ is the angle deformation which is also un-shifted and their characters are 2 and 2 respectively for identity.

Any rotation about the molecular axis (z) makes them un-shifted so the character of Cϕ =2. Since σv contains the principal axis hence reflection is ασv leads to no change in r_1 & r_2.

Hence, $\chi = 2$

i leads to $r_1 \rightarrow r_2$ and $r_2 \rightarrow r_1$ both are shifted. Hence, there is no un-shifted vector $\chi = 0$.

$$S\phi = C\phi.\sigma h$$

σh is the plant ⊥r to the molecular axis. Both are shifted.

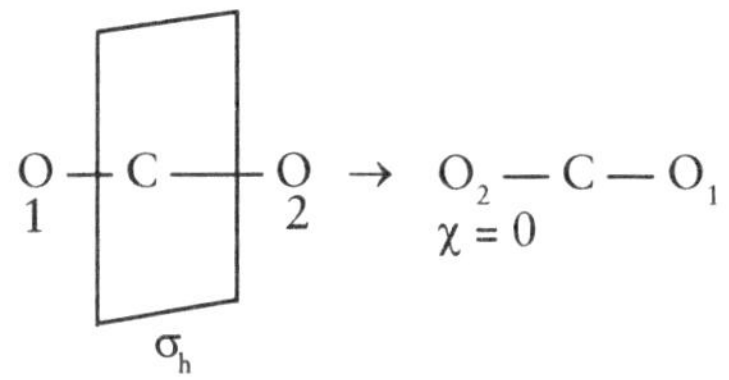

Hence, for Sϕ, χ = 0

C_2 exchanges the vectors. So χ = 0.

χ (r)	2	2	2	0	0	0
χ (θ)	2	2cosϕ	0	–1	2cosϕ	0

Γr is the sum of the character of the species. Σ_g^+ & Σ_u^+

$$\Gamma_r = \Sigma_g^+ + \Sigma_u^+$$

Now consider the bending modes. There are two modes at mutually perpendicular directions and we have two angular deformation co-ordinates x & y, other is z-axis which is the principal axis. These transform in exactly the same way as the components of translation x & y.

χ(E) = 2, there is no effect.

For z we have, i (x) = (–1) x

i (y)= (–1) y so χ = –2.

They can interchange in other operations:

$$C\phi \begin{pmatrix} \cos\phi & \sin\phi \\ -\sin\phi & \cos\phi \end{pmatrix} \begin{pmatrix} x \\ y \end{pmatrix} = \begin{pmatrix} x' \\ y' \end{pmatrix}$$

$$\chi = \cos\phi + \cos\phi = 2\cos\phi$$

The σv contains the principal axis so both of them are shifted in σv.

In C_2 operation both x & y are changed. Its χ = 0. In Sϕ = Cϕ.σ_h where, $\sigma_h = \sigma_{xy}$. There is no effect $x_1 = x$, $y_1 = y$.

$$\sigma_h : \begin{pmatrix} 1 & 0 \\ 0 & 1 \end{pmatrix}$$

$$C\phi : \begin{pmatrix} \cos\phi & \sin\phi \\ -\sin\phi & \cos\phi \end{pmatrix}$$

$$Sd : \begin{pmatrix} \cos\phi & \sin\phi \\ -\sin\phi & \cos\phi \end{pmatrix} \begin{pmatrix} 1 & 0 \\ 0 & 1 \end{pmatrix}$$

$$= \begin{pmatrix} \cos\phi & \sin\phi \\ -\sin\phi & \cos\phi \end{pmatrix}$$

$$\chi\ (S\phi) = 2\cos\phi$$

Obviously it involves the irreducible representation: Πu for CO_2.

$$\Gamma\ (v) = \Pi_u$$

$$\Gamma_v = \Gamma_{(r)} + \Gamma_{(\theta)}$$

$$= \Sigma_g^+ + \Sigma_u^+ + \Pi_u$$

There are three modes of vibrations, stretching modes are $\Sigma_g^+ + \Sigma_u^+$ the third one is doubly degenerate as χ (E) = 2 i.e. Π_u is a pure angular deformation υ_1 is Σ_g^+. υ_3 is Σ_u^+ and υ_2 is Π_u.

4. Expand the potential and kinetic energies in more appropriate form in case of water:

$$2V = D'fD.$$

$$D' = [\Delta d_1\ \Delta d_2\ \Delta\theta]$$

$$D = \begin{bmatrix} \Delta d_1 \\ \Delta d_2 \\ \Delta\theta \end{bmatrix}$$

$$f = \begin{bmatrix} fd & fdd & fd\theta \\ fdd & fd & fd\theta \\ fd\theta & fd\theta & f\theta \end{bmatrix}$$

$$D'fD = [\Delta d_1\ \Delta d_2\ \Delta\theta] \begin{bmatrix} fd & fdd & fd\theta \\ fdd & fd & fd\theta \\ fd\theta & fd\theta & f\theta \end{bmatrix} \begin{bmatrix} \Delta d_1 \\ \Delta d_2 \\ \Delta\theta \end{bmatrix}$$

$$= \begin{bmatrix} \Delta d_1 & \Delta d_2 & \Delta\theta \end{bmatrix} \begin{bmatrix} fd.\Delta d_1 + fdd\Delta d_2 + fd\theta\Delta\theta \\ fdd\Delta d_1 + fd\Delta d_2 + fd\theta\Delta\theta \\ fd\theta\Delta d_1 + fd\theta\Delta d_2 + f\theta\Delta\theta \end{bmatrix}$$

$$= fd(\Delta d_1)^2 + fdd(\Delta d_1)(\Delta d_2) + fd\theta(\Delta d_1)(\Delta\theta) + fdd(\Delta d_1)$$
$$(\Delta d_2) + fd(\Delta d_2)^2 + fd\theta(\Delta\theta)(\Delta d_2) + fd\theta(\Delta d_1)(\Delta\theta) +$$
$$fd\theta(\Delta d_2)(\Delta d_2)(\Delta\theta) + f\theta(\Delta\theta)^2$$

$$= fd(\Delta d_1)^2 + fd(\Delta d_2)^2 + f\theta(\Delta\theta) + 2fdd(\Delta d_1)(\Delta d_2)$$
$$+2fd\theta(\Delta d_1)(\Delta\theta) + 2fd\theta(\Delta d_2)(\Delta\theta)$$

$$2T = g_{11}^{-1}\left(\Delta\dot{d}_1\right)^2 + (g_{22}^{-1})(\Delta\dot{d}_2)^2 + (g_{33}^{-1})(\Delta\dot{d}_1)$$
$$\left(\Delta\dot{d}_2\right) + 2g^{-1}\left(\Delta\dot{d}_1\right)\left(\Delta\dot{\theta}\right) + 2g_{23}^{-1}\left(\Delta\dot{d}_2\right)\left(\Delta\theta\right)^{13}$$

5. Give the expressions for 2T & 2V in symmetry co-ordinates (matrix form).

S is used to denote symmetry co-ordinates:

$$2T = \dot{D}'G^{-1}\dot{D} \qquad \dot{D} = \frac{\partial D}{\partial t}$$

Also we had:

$$2T = \dot{S}'G^{-1}\dot{S} \qquad \dot{S} = \frac{\partial S}{\partial t}$$

$$2V = D'FD$$

$$2V = S'FS$$

The transformation is carried out by:

$$S = UD \quad \text{and} \quad \dot{S} = U\dot{D}$$

$$S' = U'D' \qquad \dot{S}' = U'\dot{D}'$$

$$2T = \dot{S}'G^{-1}\dot{S}$$
$$= U'\dot{D}'G^{-1}\,U\dot{D}$$
$$= U'\dot{D}'G^{-1}\,U\dot{D}$$
$$= U^{-1}\,\dot{D}'G^{-1}\,\dot{D}U$$
$$= U^{-1}\,U\dot{D}'G^{-1}\,\dot{D}$$
$$= \dot{D}'G^{-1}\,\dot{D} \;\left(\text{Since } U^{-1}\,U = E\right)$$

Hence G^{-1} in one set = $U'G^{-1}U$ of another set.

6. How do we use secular equation

$$\left[GF = E\lambda\right] = 0\ ?$$

From the knowledge of G and F matrices in symmetry co-ordinates there can be secular equation:

$$|FG - \lambda E| = 0\ ,$$

and the roots are the same without taking the symmetry co-ordinates which was done earlier. Each G & F matrix has the same block and they are so multiplied that each block is separately zero.

G^{-1}	S^{A_1}	S^E_a	S^E_b	
S^{A_1}	1×1	A_1 block		
S^E_a		2×2		E block
S^E_b				

F	S^{A_1}	S^E_a	S^E_b	
S^{A_1}	1×1	A_1		
S^E_a		2×2		E
S^E_b				

S^{A_1} gives 1×1 block in each like $\underset{1\times 1}{\left[G^{-1}_{11}\right]}$ & $\underset{1\times 1}{\left[F_{11}\right]}$

Hence, secular equation takes the form:

$$\left[F_{11} - \lambda G^{-1}_{11}\right] = 0$$

Also, S^E_a. & S^E_b is 2×2

Viz. $\begin{bmatrix} G^{-1}_{22} & G^{-1}_{23} \\ G^{-1}_{32} & G^{-1}_{33} \end{bmatrix} \quad \begin{bmatrix} F_{22} & F_{23} \\ F_{32} & F_{33} \end{bmatrix}$

Such that we get secular equation of the form:

$$\left[\begin{bmatrix} F_{22} & F_{23} \\ F_{32} & F_{33} \end{bmatrix} - \lambda \begin{bmatrix} G_{22}^{-1} & G_{23}^{-1} \\ G_{32}^{-1} & G_{33}^{-1} \end{bmatrix}\right] = 0$$

or, $$\left[GF - \lambda E\right] = 0$$

or, $$\left[\begin{bmatrix} G_{22} & G_{23} \\ G_{32} & G_{33} \end{bmatrix} \begin{bmatrix} F_{22} & F_{23} \\ F_{32} & F_{33} \end{bmatrix} - \lambda \begin{bmatrix} 1 & 0 \\ 0 & 1 \end{bmatrix}\right] = 0\,.$$

QUESTIONS

1. Discuss equation of motion is Langragian form in terms of Cartesian co-ordinates.
2. Express kinetic energy and potential energy in Cartesian co-ordinates and generalized system of co-ordinates.
3. What do you understand from mass weighted co-ordinates? Convert the equation of motion in reduced displacement co-ordinates.
4. (a) Explain normal co-ordinates and normal vibrations.

   (b) Deduce the equation of motion in terms of normal co-ordinates and outline a procedure of finding its solutions.
5. Give expansion of kinetic energy and potential energy by means of Taylor series and write down finally the expressions for T & V.

   Define elements of force constants and F matrix.
6. Establish first order time derivatives for T and first order derivative with displacement co-ordinate of V and find the possible solutions of equation of motion.

   Given d_1, d_2, d_3, as displacement co-ordinates and the solution will be of possible form as $d = A\cos\left(\sqrt{\lambda}\ t + \phi\right)$ with ϕ as phase angle and υ as normal frequency of vibration.
7. Express V & T in matrix form for a case of three displacement co-ordinates d_1, d_2 & d_3.

   What do you mean by symmetry of the normal coordinates? Visualize the effect of symmetry operation over the normal co-ordinates on potential and kinetic energy expressions in general.
8. Give a brief account of normal vibrations of water molecule looking into the effect of symmetry operations. Show the transformation matrices and their symmetry classification formed on the basis of normal co-ordinates classify on the basis of symmetry the normal vibration of water.

9. Comment on secular equation:

   (a) $|FG - \lambda E| = 0$.

   (b) Define symmetry co-ordinates. Give the matrix equation between S and D co-ordinates using transformation matrix U taking a suitable example find the matrix U by projection operator and classify the vibrations.

10. (a) Discuss symmetry generating characters for reducible and irreducible representations of water and from it deduct the symmetry species of translational and rotational components to obtain normal vibrational modes.

    (b) Taking d_1, d_2 & θ as basis for bond stretch and bond deformation co-ordinates find the internal co-ordinate contributions.

    (c) If allowed vibrations are taken by changes in bond length and bond angle and factorize the F matrix.

11. Classify the vectors of changes in internal co-ordinates for vibration in water based on symmetry and obtain symmetry co-ordinates out of V by a suitable method. If fd, fθ & fdd be the force constant components of stretching and bending.

12. Carryout normal co-ordinate analysis in case of ammonia using generalized co-ordinates, normal co-ordinates as well as symmetry co-ordinates. Evaluate their force constants.

13. Give an account of the following:

    (a) Newtons equation of motions in different co-ordinate systems.

    (b) Normal co-ordinate and normal vibrations.

    (c) Symmetry co-ordinates.

    (d) Wilson secular equation $[GF - \lambda E] = 0$.

    (e) Orthogonal transformation.

    (f) Symmetric matrix in case of algebraic expression giving suitable example.